MARGUERITE ABOUET     CLÉMENT OUBRERIE

# AYA

## LOVE IN YOP CITY

DRAWN & QUARTERLY
MONTREAL

# The characters

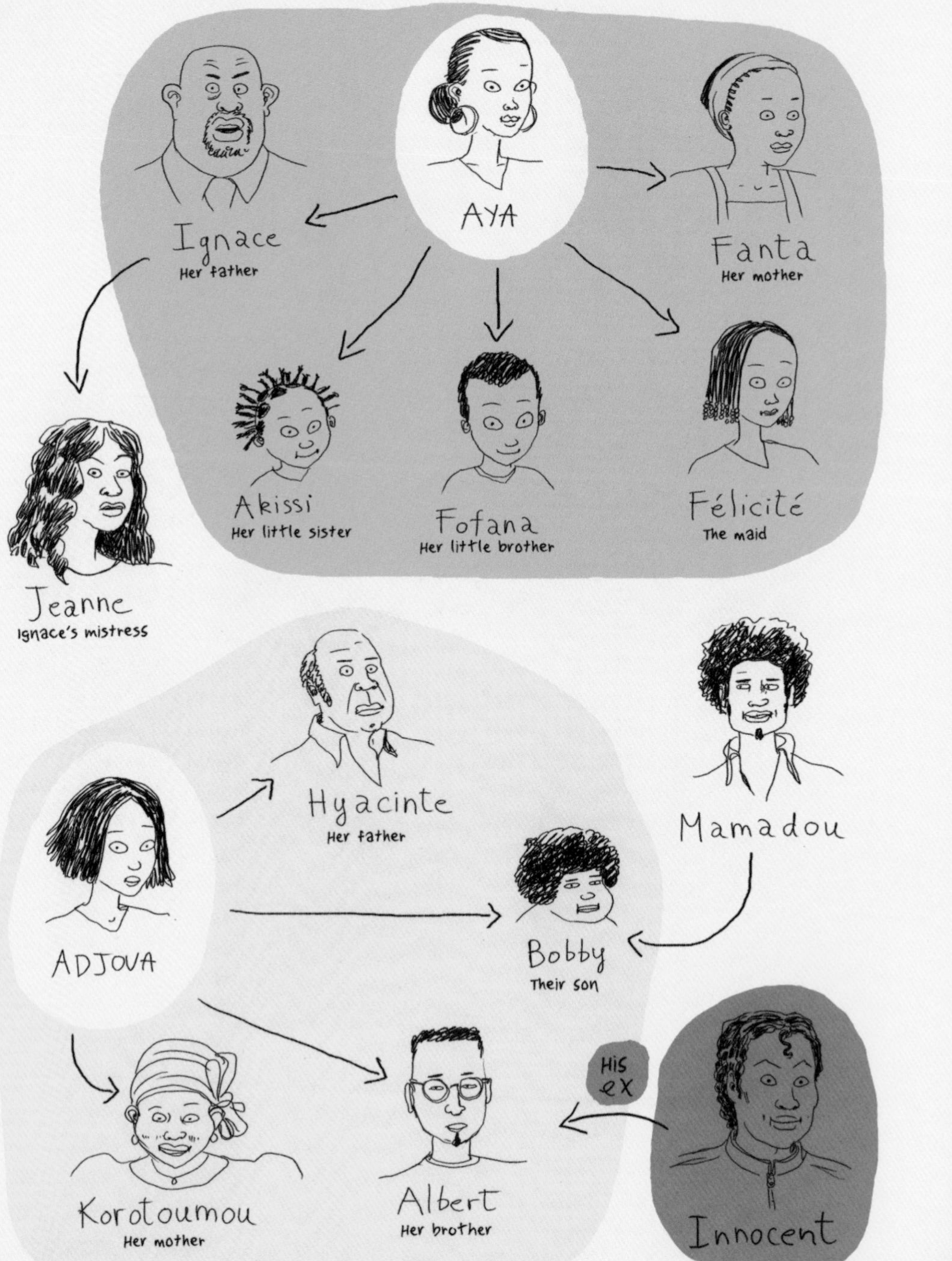
AYA
Ignace
Her father
Fanta
Her mother
Akissi
Her little sister
Fofana
Her little brother
Félicité
The maid
Jeanne
Ignace's mistress
Hyacinte
Her father
Mamadou
ADJOVA
Bobby
Their son
His ex
Korotoumou
Her mother
Albert
Her brother
Innocent

AFRICA
IVORY
COAST

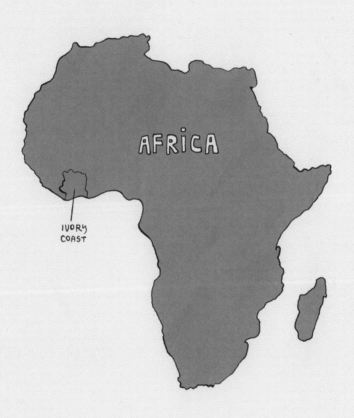

Translation by Helge Dascher. Translation assistance by Dag Dascher, with thanks to Herman Koutouan for sharing his knowledge of Ivorian culture.

Thank you Antoine Delesvaux, Agathe Faucompré, Nina and Patricia N'Gbandjui, Olivier Vitrat, Ernest Odje, Nicolas Merki, Patrick Chapatte, Reynold Leclercq, Mendozza, Christian Ronget, Guillaume Boilève, 1 Jour 2 Mai, and Beybson for their beautiful color photos, without forgetting the participation of the Grezaud family.

And, lastly, our gratitude to Hyppolite B. for the music!

Originally published in French by Gallimard Jeunesse as part of the Joann Sfar edited Bayou collection.

Published in the USA by Drawn & Quarterly, a client publisher of Farrar, Straus & Giroux. Orders: 888.330.8477
Published in Canada by Drawn & Quarterly, a client publisher of Raincoast Books. Orders: 800.663.5714
Published in the United Kingdom by Drawn & Quarterly, a client publisher of Publishers Group UK. Orders: info@pguk.co.uk
drawnandquarterly.com

First paperback edition: January 2013.
Second printing: February 2015.
ISBN 978-1-77046-092-8.
Printed in Singapore.
10 9 8 7 6 5 4 3 2

Liberté • Égalité • Fraternité
RÉPUBLIQUE FRANÇAISE

This work, published as part of grant programs for publication (Acquisition of Rights and Translation), received support from the French Ministry of Foreign and European Affairs and from the Institut français. Cet ouvrage, publié dans le cadre du Programme d'Aide à la Publication (Cession de droits et traduction), a bénéficié du soutien du Ministère des Affaires étrangères et européennes et de l'Institut français.

Drawn & Quarterly acknowledges the financial contribution of the Government of Canada through the Canada Book Fund for our publishing activities and for support of this edition.

Library and Archives Canada Cataloguing in Publication
Abouet, Marguerite, 1971–
        Aya : love in Yop City / Marguerite Abouet & Clément Oubrerie.
ISBN 978-1-77046-092-8
        1. Teenage girls--Côte d'Ivoire--Comic books, strips, etc.  2. Côte d'Ivoire--Comic books, strips, etc.  3. Graphic novels.  I. Oubrerie, Clément  II. Title.
PN6790.I93A26413 2012          741.5'96668          C2012-902519-4

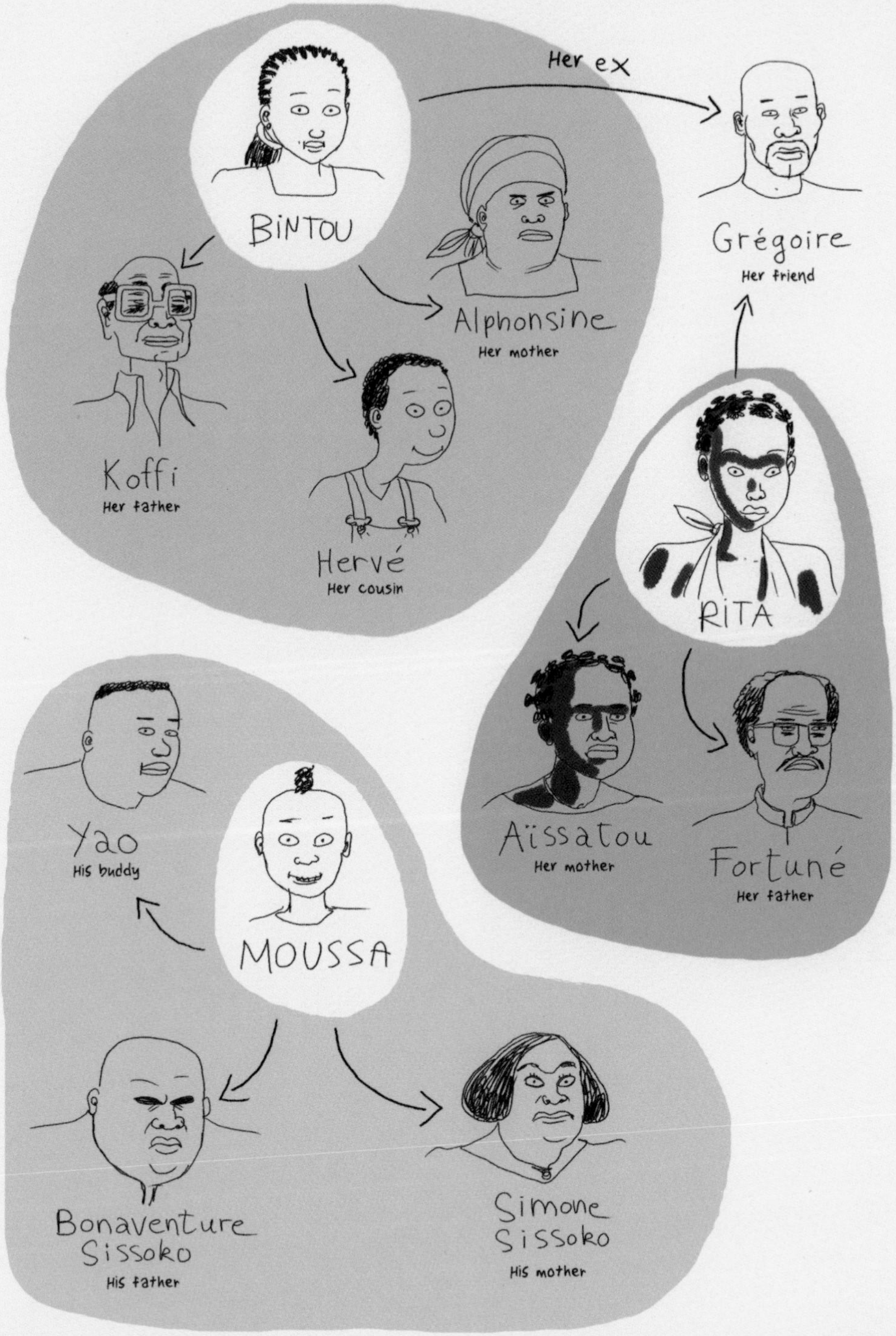
BINTOU
Her ex
Grégoire
Her friend
Alphonsine
Her mother
Koffi
Her father
Hervé
Her cousin
RITA
Aïssatou
Her mother
Fortuné
Her father
Yao
His buddy
MOUSSA
Bonaventure
Sissoko
His father
Simone
Sissoko
His mother

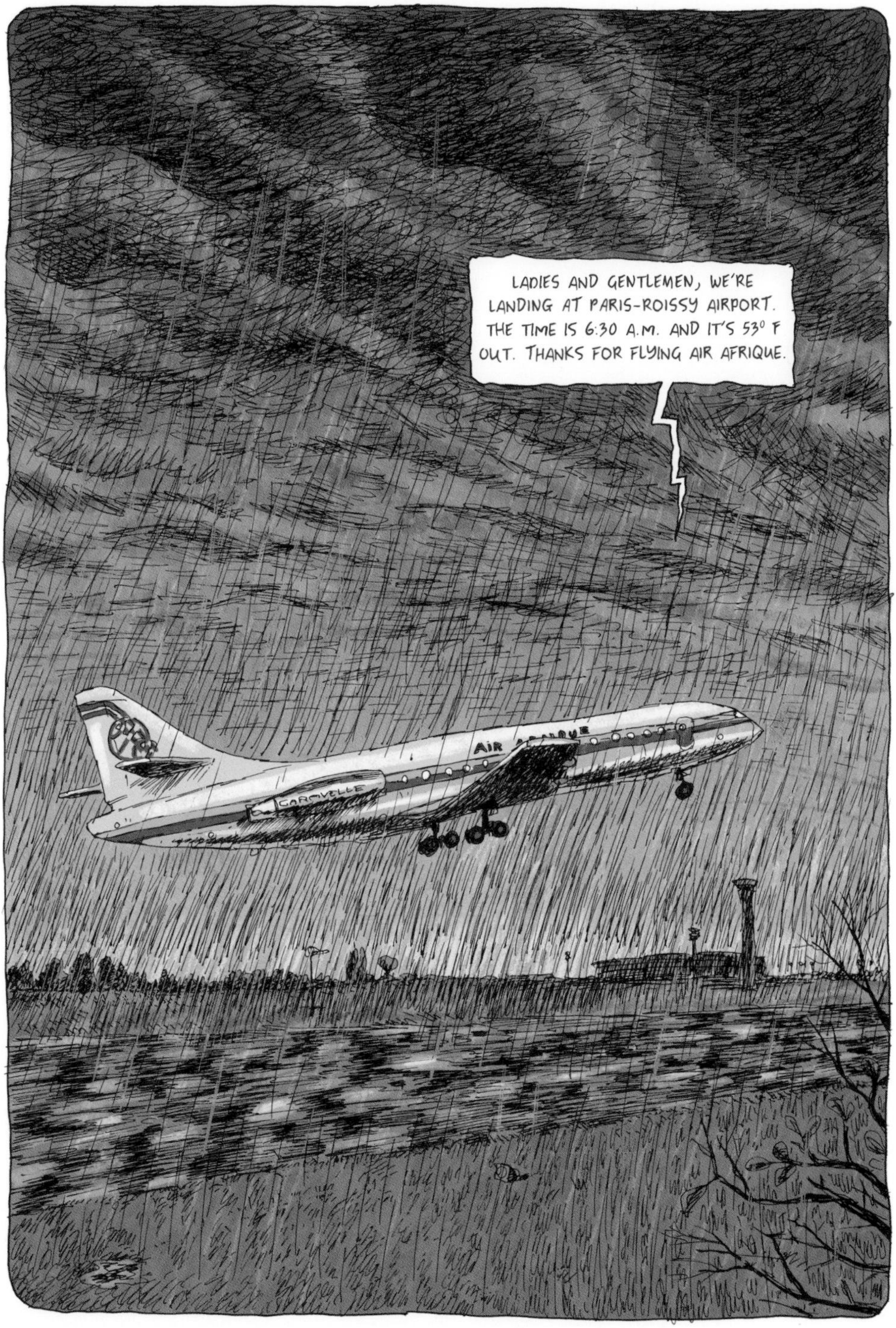
LADIES AND GENTLEMEN, WE'RE LANDING AT PARIS-ROISSY AIRPORT. THE TIME IS 6:30 A.M. AND IT'S 53° F OUT. THANKS FOR FLYING AIR AFRIQUE.
AIR
CARAVELLE

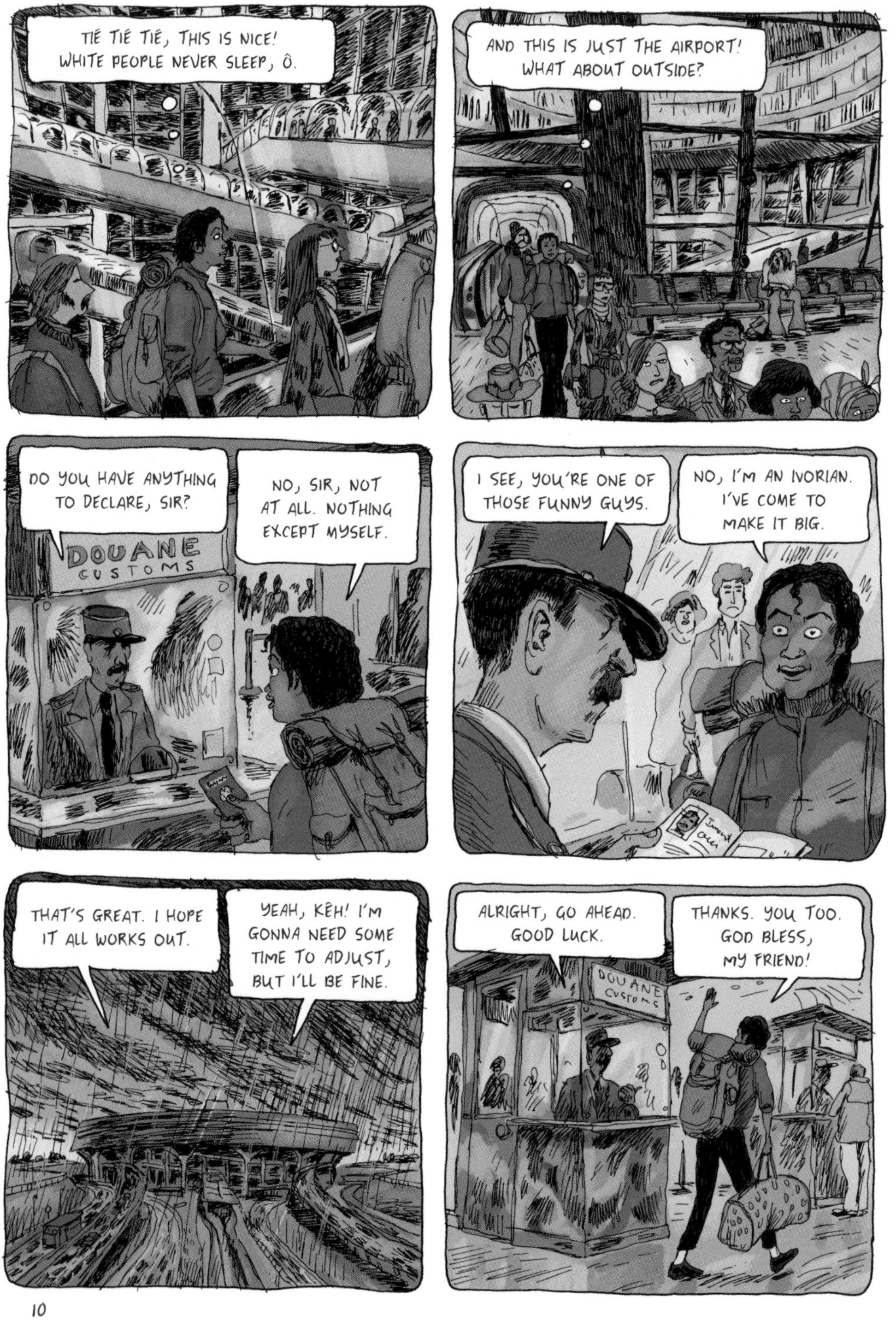
TIÉ TIÉ TIÉ, THIS IS NICE! WHITE PEOPLE NEVER SLEEP, Ô.
AND THIS IS JUST THE AIRPORT! WHAT ABOUT OUTSIDE?
DO YOU HAVE ANYTHING TO DECLARE, SIR?
DOUANE CUSTOMS
NO, SIR, NOT AT ALL. NOTHING EXCEPT MYSELF.
I SEE, YOU'RE ONE OF THOSE FUNNY GUYS.
NO, I'M AN IVORIAN. I'VE COME TO MAKE IT BIG.
THAT'S GREAT. I HOPE IT ALL WORKS OUT.
YEAH, KÊH! I'M GONNA NEED SOME TIME TO ADJUST, BUT I'LL BE FINE.
ALRIGHT, GO AHEAD. GOOD LUCK.
DOUANE CUSTOMS
THANKS. YOU TOO. GOD BLESS, MY FRIEND!

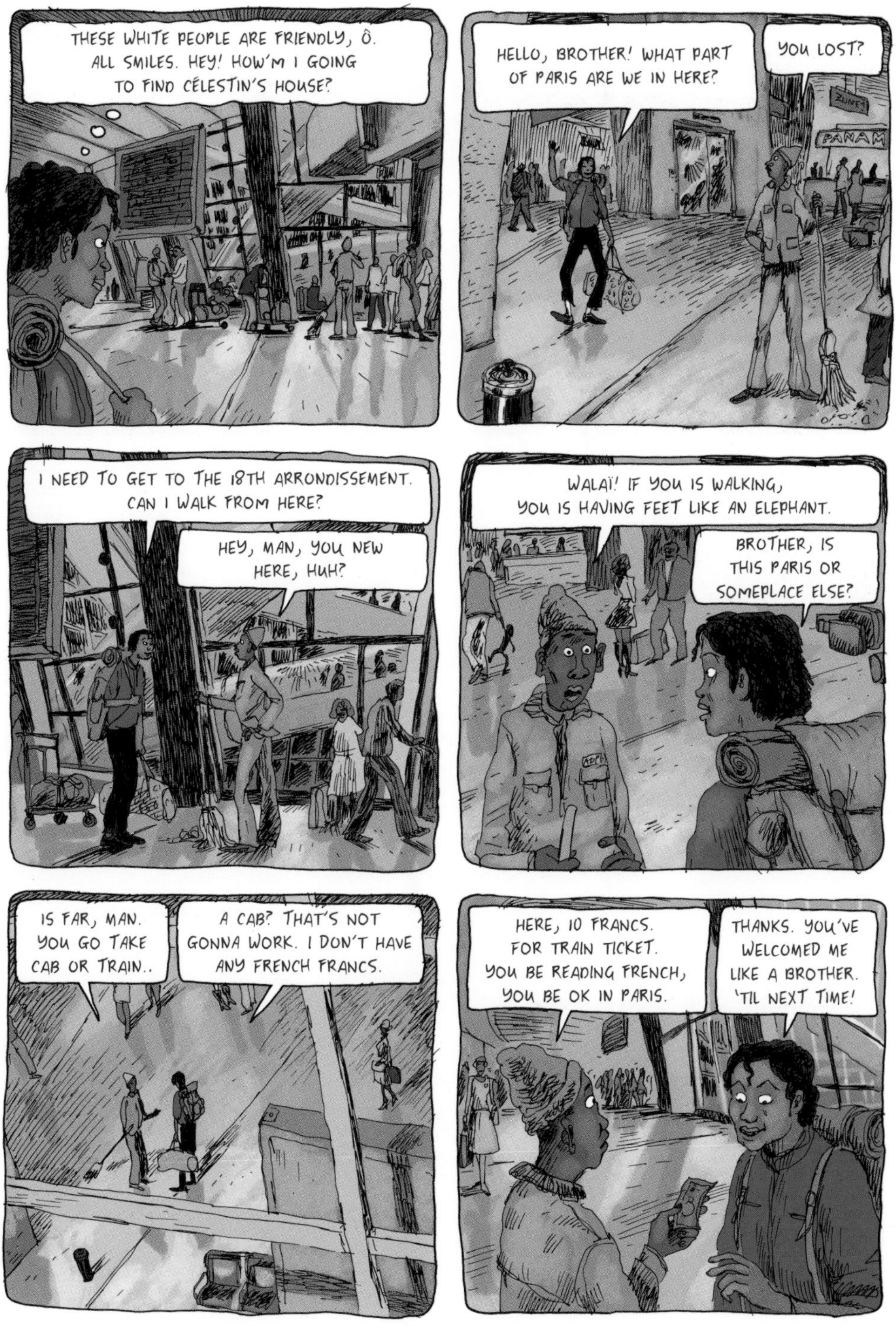
THESE WHITE PEOPLE ARE FRIENDLY, Ô. ALL SMILES. HEY! HOW'M I GOING TO FIND CÉLESTIN'S HOUSE?
HELLO, BROTHER! WHAT PART OF PARIS ARE WE IN HERE?
YOU LOST?
PANAM
I NEED TO GET TO THE 18TH ARRONDISSEMENT. CAN I WALK FROM HERE?
HEY, MAN, YOU NEW HERE, HUH?
WALAÏ! IF YOU IS WALKING, YOU IS HAVING FEET LIKE AN ELEPHANT.
BROTHER, IS THIS PARIS OR SOMEPLACE ELSE?
IS FAR, MAN. YOU GO TAKE CAB OR TRAIN..
A CAB? THAT'S NOT GONNA WORK. I DON'T HAVE ANY FRENCH FRANCS.
HERE, 10 FRANCS. FOR TRAIN TICKET. YOU BE READING FRENCH, YOU BE OK IN PARIS.
THANKS. YOU'VE WELCOMED ME LIKE A BROTHER. 'TIL NEXT TIME!

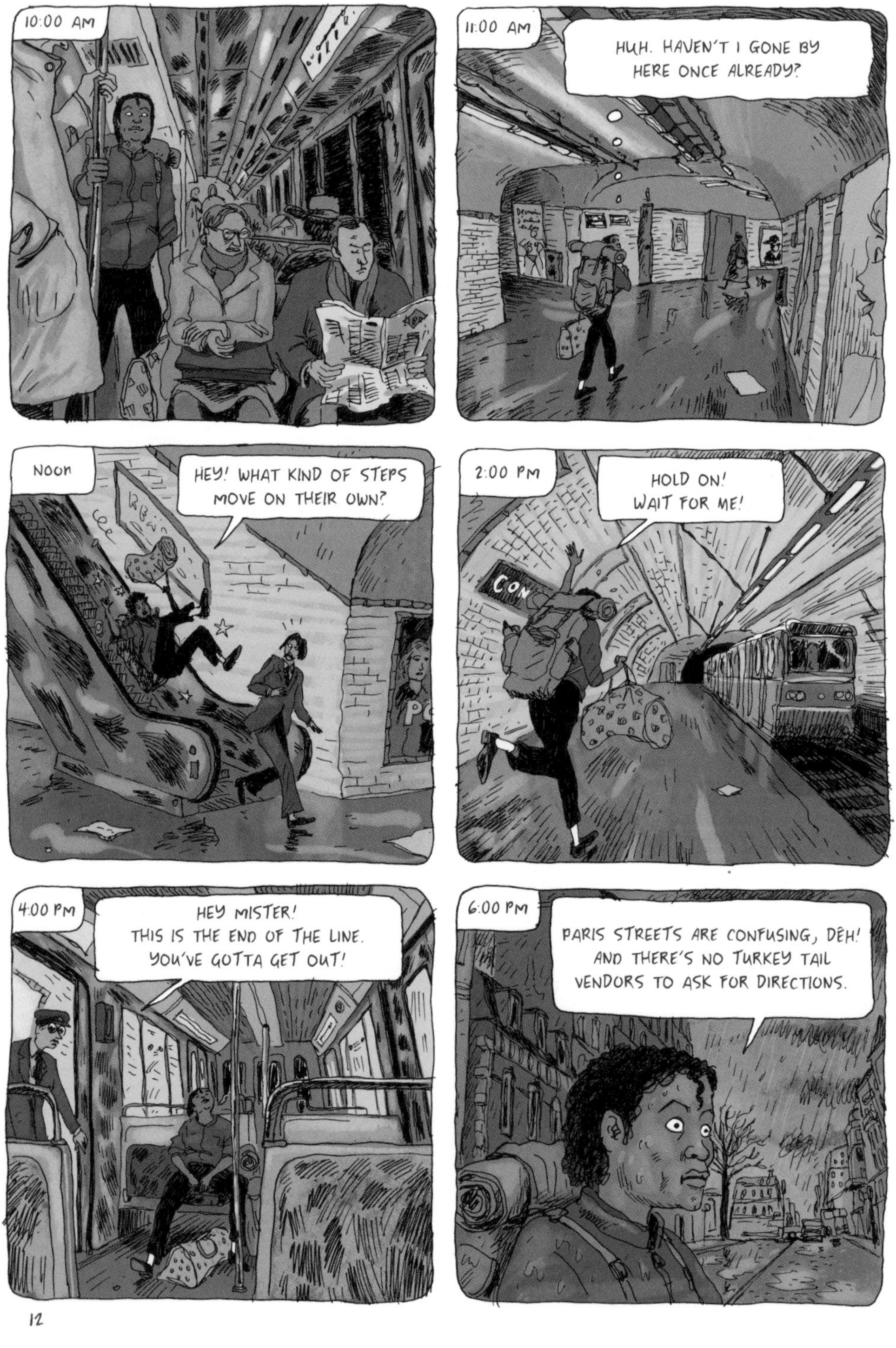
10:00 AM
11:00 AM
HUH. HAVEN'T I GONE BY HERE ONCE ALREADY?
Noon
HEY! WHAT KIND OF STEPS MOVE ON THEIR OWN?
2:00 PM
HOLD ON! WAIT FOR ME!
CON
4:00 PM
HEY MISTER! THIS IS THE END OF THE LINE. YOU'VE GOTTA GET OUT!
6:00 PM
PARIS STREETS ARE CONFUSING, DÊH! AND THERE'S NO TURKEY TAIL VENDORS TO ASK FOR DIRECTIONS.

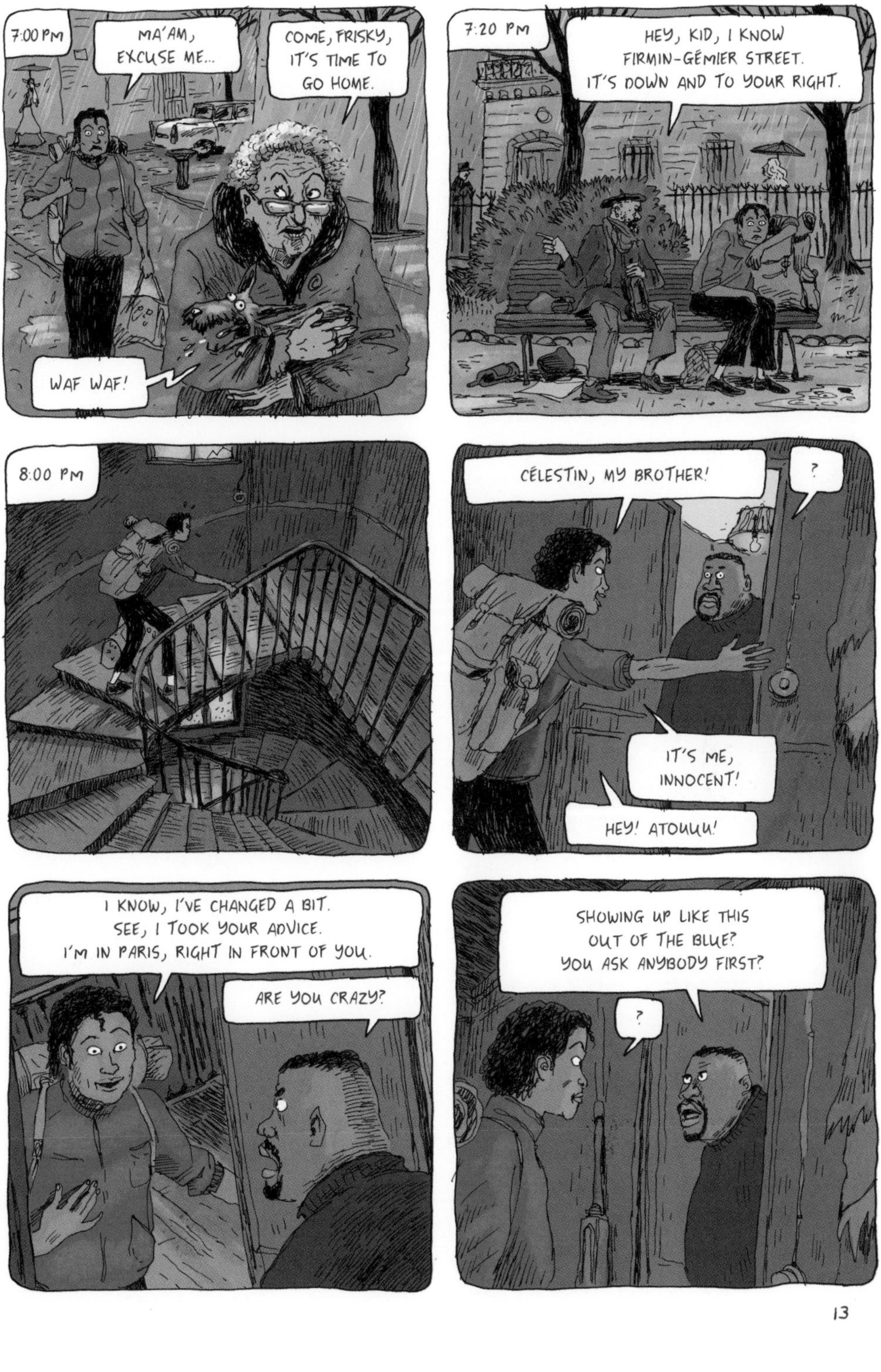
7:00 PM
MA'AM, EXCUSE ME...
COME, FRISKY, IT'S TIME TO GO HOME.
WAF WAF!
7:20 PM
HEY, KID, I KNOW FIRMIN-GÉMIER STREET. IT'S DOWN AND TO YOUR RIGHT.
8:00 PM
CÉLESTIN, MY BROTHER!
?
IT'S ME, INNOCENT!
HEY! ATOUUU!
I KNOW, I'VE CHANGED A BIT. SEE, I TOOK YOUR ADVICE. I'M IN PARIS, RIGHT IN FRONT OF YOU.
ARE YOU CRAZY?
SHOWING UP LIKE THIS OUT OF THE BLUE? YOU ASK ANYBODY FIRST?
?

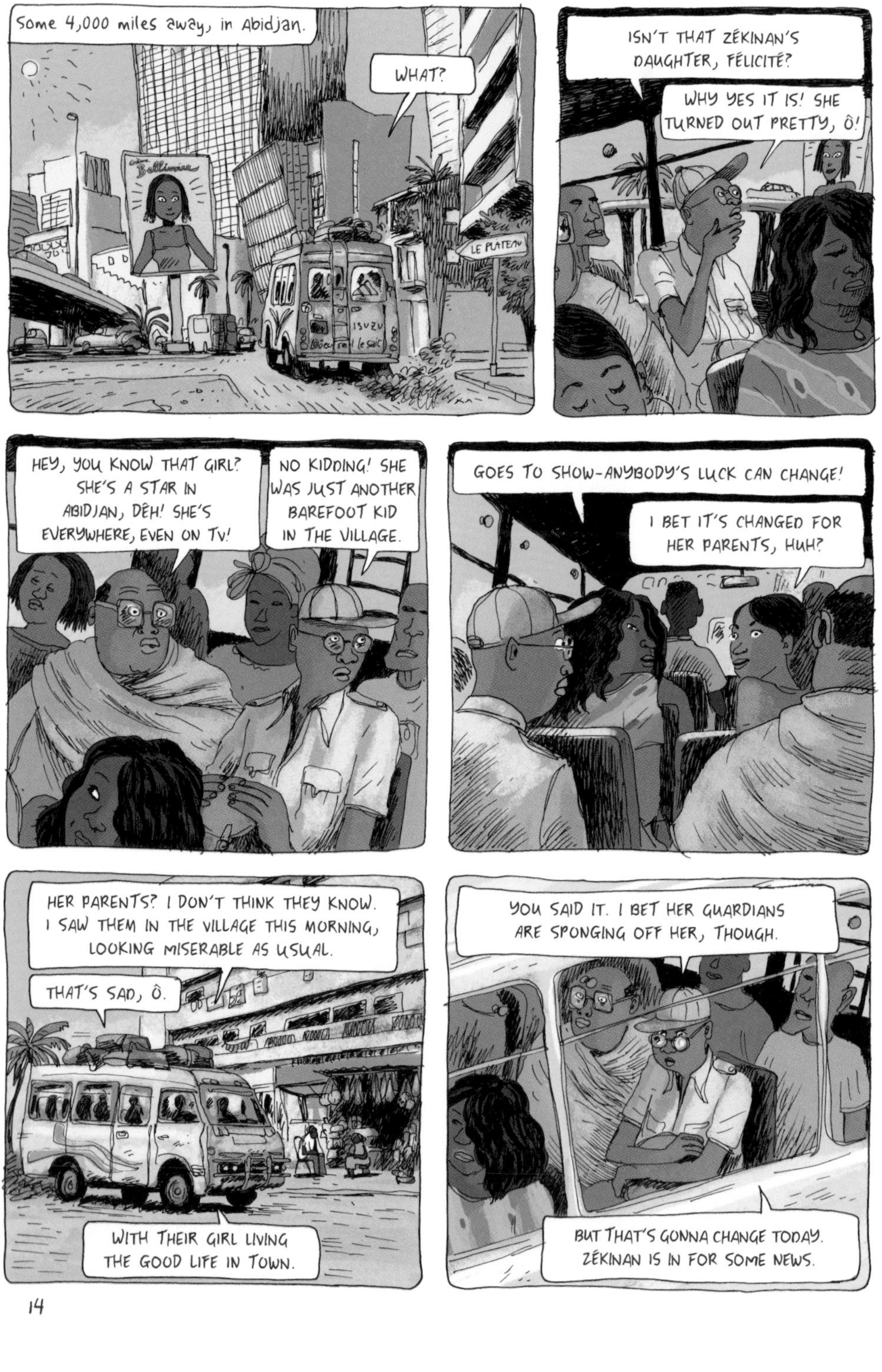

Some 4,000 miles away, in Abidjan.
WHAT?
LE PLATEAU
ISUZU
ISN'T THAT ZÉKINAN'S DAUGHTER, FÉLICITÉ?
WHY YES IT IS! SHE TURNED OUT PRETTY, Ô!
HEY, YOU KNOW THAT GIRL? SHE'S A STAR IN ABIDJAN, DÊH! SHE'S EVERYWHERE, EVEN ON TV!
NO KIDDING! SHE WAS JUST ANOTHER BAREFOOT KID IN THE VILLAGE.
GOES TO SHOW—ANYBODY'S LUCK CAN CHANGE!
I BET IT'S CHANGED FOR HER PARENTS, HUH?
HER PARENTS? I DON'T THINK THEY KNOW. I SAW THEM IN THE VILLAGE THIS MORNING, LOOKING MISERABLE AS USUAL.
THAT'S SAD, Ô.
WITH THEIR GIRL LIVING THE GOOD LIFE IN TOWN.
YOU SAID IT. I BET HER GUARDIANS ARE SPONGING OFF HER, THOUGH.
BUT THAT'S GONNA CHANGE TODAY. ZÉKINAN IS IN FOR SOME NEWS.

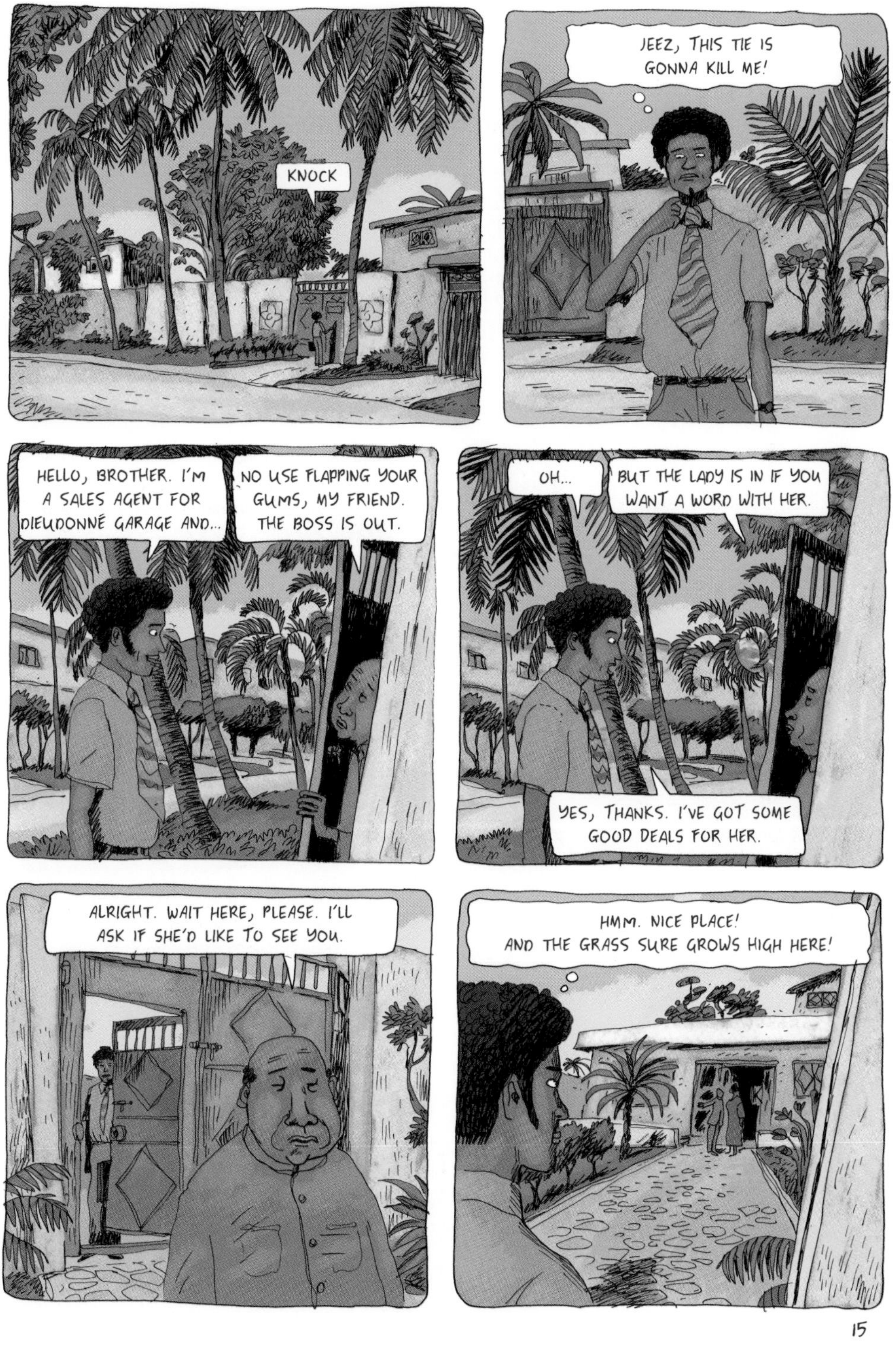
KNOCK
JEEZ, THIS TIE IS GONNA KILL ME!
HELLO, BROTHER. I'M A SALES AGENT FOR DIEUDONNÉ GARAGE AND...
NO USE FLAPPING YOUR GUMS, MY FRIEND. THE BOSS IS OUT.
OH...
BUT THE LADY IS IN IF YOU WANT A WORD WITH HER.
YES, THANKS. I'VE GOT SOME GOOD DEALS FOR HER.
ALRIGHT. WAIT HERE, PLEASE. I'LL ASK IF SHE'D LIKE TO SEE YOU.
HMM. NICE PLACE! AND THE GRASS SURE GROWS HIGH HERE!

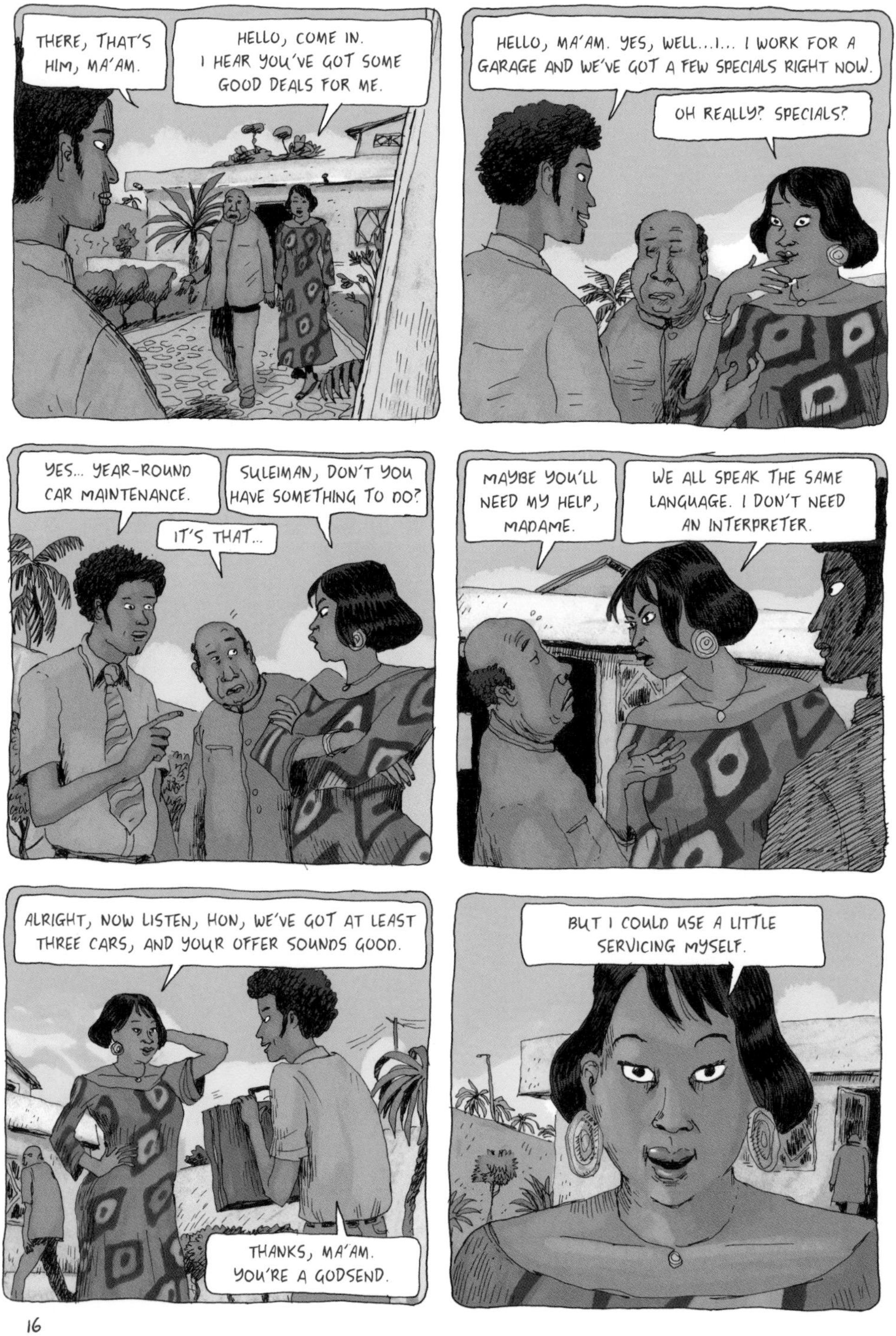
THERE, THAT'S HIM, MA'AM.
HELLO, COME IN. I HEAR YOU'VE GOT SOME GOOD DEALS FOR ME.
HELLO, MA'AM. YES, WELL...I... I WORK FOR A GARAGE AND WE'VE GOT A FEW SPECIALS RIGHT NOW.
OH REALLY? SPECIALS?
YES... YEAR-ROUND CAR MAINTENANCE.
IT'S THAT...
SULEIMAN, DON'T YOU HAVE SOMETHING TO DO?
MAYBE YOU'LL NEED MY HELP, MADAME.
WE ALL SPEAK THE SAME LANGUAGE. I DON'T NEED AN INTERPRETER.
ALRIGHT, NOW LISTEN, HON, WE'VE GOT AT LEAST THREE CARS, AND YOUR OFFER SOUNDS GOOD.
THANKS, MA'AM. YOU'RE A GODSEND.
BUT I COULD USE A LITTLE SERVICING MYSELF.

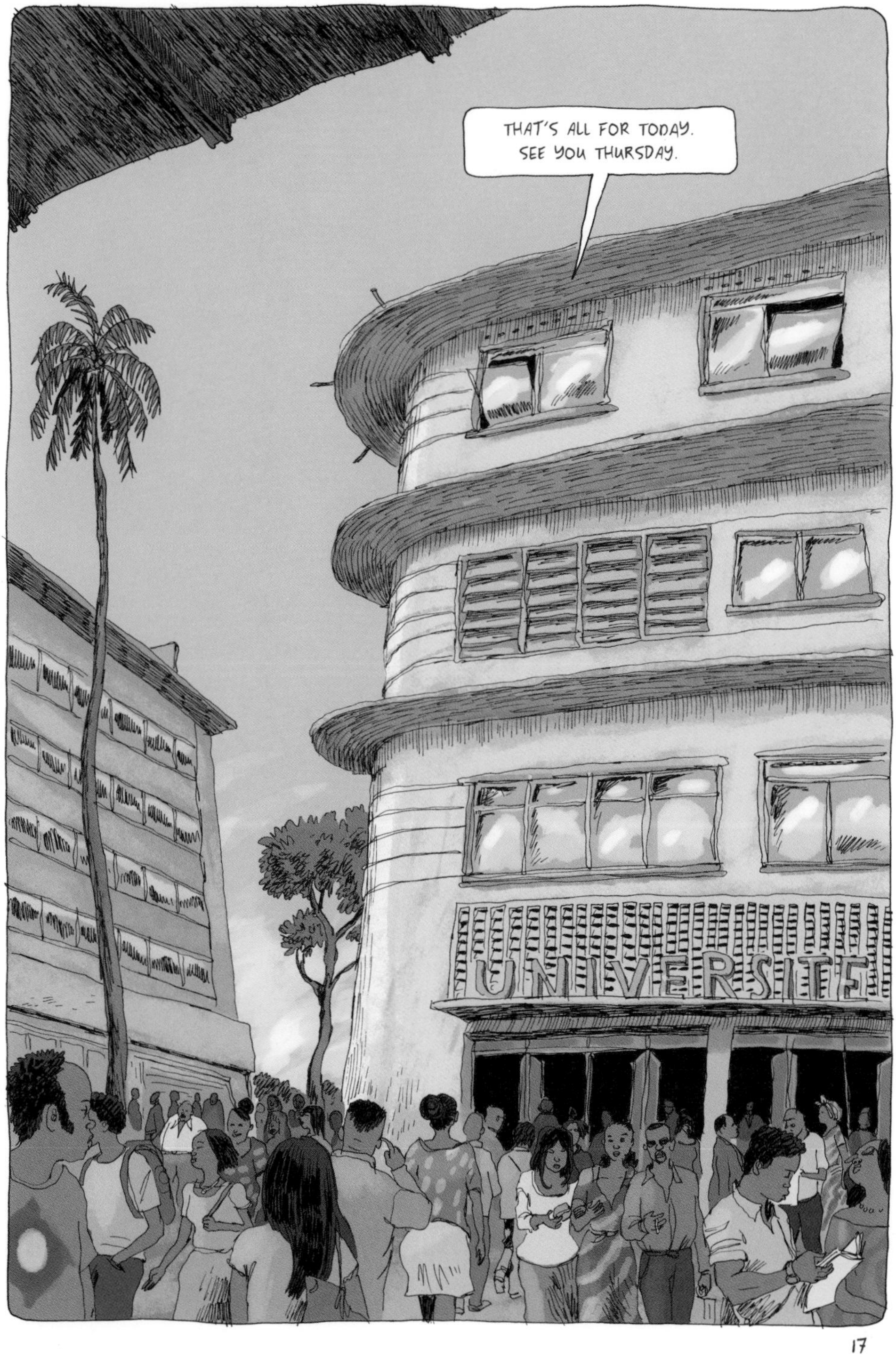
THAT'S ALL FOR TODAY. SEE YOU THURSDAY.
UNIVERSITE

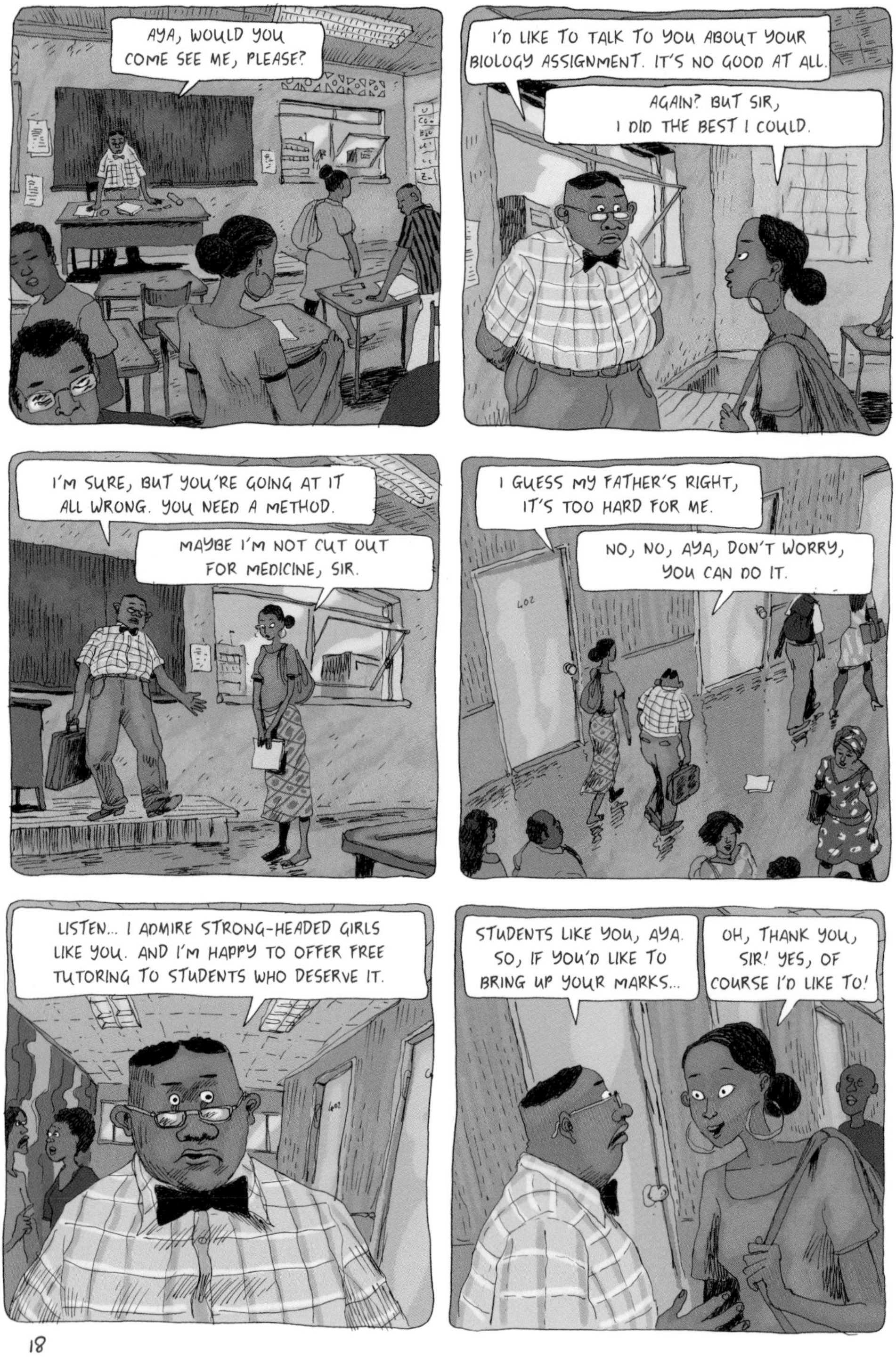
AYA, WOULD YOU COME SEE ME, PLEASE?
I'D LIKE TO TALK TO YOU ABOUT YOUR BIOLOGY ASSIGNMENT. IT'S NO GOOD AT ALL.
AGAIN? BUT SIR, I DID THE BEST I COULD.
I'M SURE, BUT YOU'RE GOING AT IT ALL WRONG. YOU NEED A METHOD.
MAYBE I'M NOT CUT OUT FOR MEDICINE, SIR.
I GUESS MY FATHER'S RIGHT, IT'S TOO HARD FOR ME.
NO, NO, AYA, DON'T WORRY, YOU CAN DO IT.
LISTEN... I ADMIRE STRONG-HEADED GIRLS LIKE YOU. AND I'M HAPPY TO OFFER FREE TUTORING TO STUDENTS WHO DESERVE IT.
STUDENTS LIKE YOU, AYA. SO, IF YOU'D LIKE TO BRING UP YOUR MARKS...
OH, THANK YOU, SIR! YES, OF COURSE I'D LIKE TO!

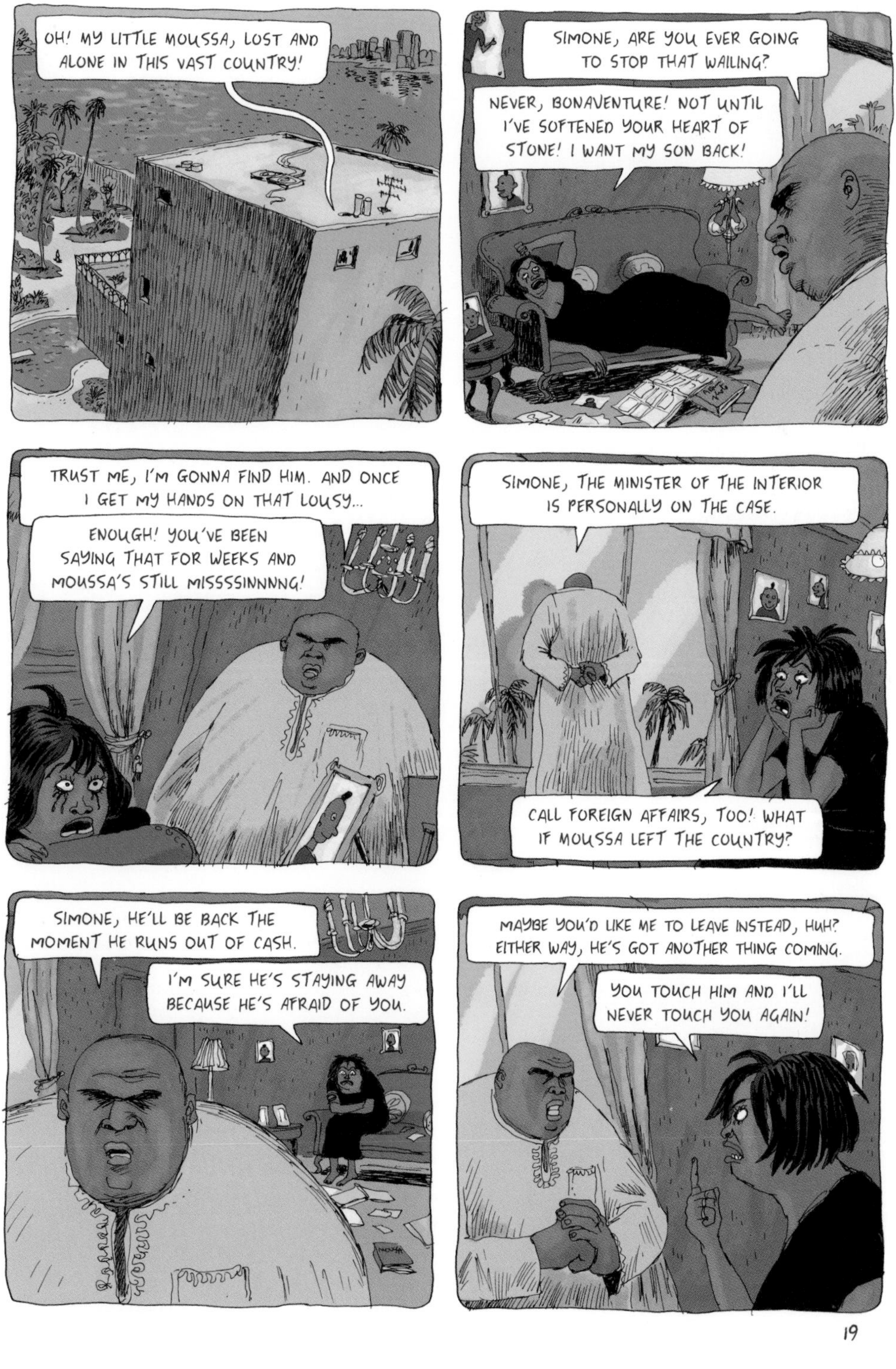
OH! MY LITTLE MOUSSA, LOST AND ALONE IN THIS VAST COUNTRY!
SIMONE, ARE YOU EVER GOING TO STOP THAT WAILING?
NEVER, BONAVENTURE! NOT UNTIL I'VE SOFTENED YOUR HEART OF STONE! I WANT MY SON BACK!
TRUST ME, I'M GONNA FIND HIM. AND ONCE I GET MY HANDS ON THAT LOUSY...
ENOUGH! YOU'VE BEEN SAYING THAT FOR WEEKS AND MOUSSA'S STILL MISSSSINNNNG!
SIMONE, THE MINISTER OF THE INTERIOR IS PERSONALLY ON THE CASE.
CALL FOREIGN AFFAIRS, TOO! WHAT IF MOUSSA LEFT THE COUNTRY?
SIMONE, HE'LL BE BACK THE MOMENT HE RUNS OUT OF CASH.
I'M SURE HE'S STAYING AWAY BECAUSE HE'S AFRAID OF YOU.
MAYBE YOU'D LIKE ME TO LEAVE INSTEAD, HUH? EITHER WAY, HE'S GOT ANOTHER THING COMING.
YOU TOUCH HIM AND I'LL NEVER TOUCH YOU AGAIN!

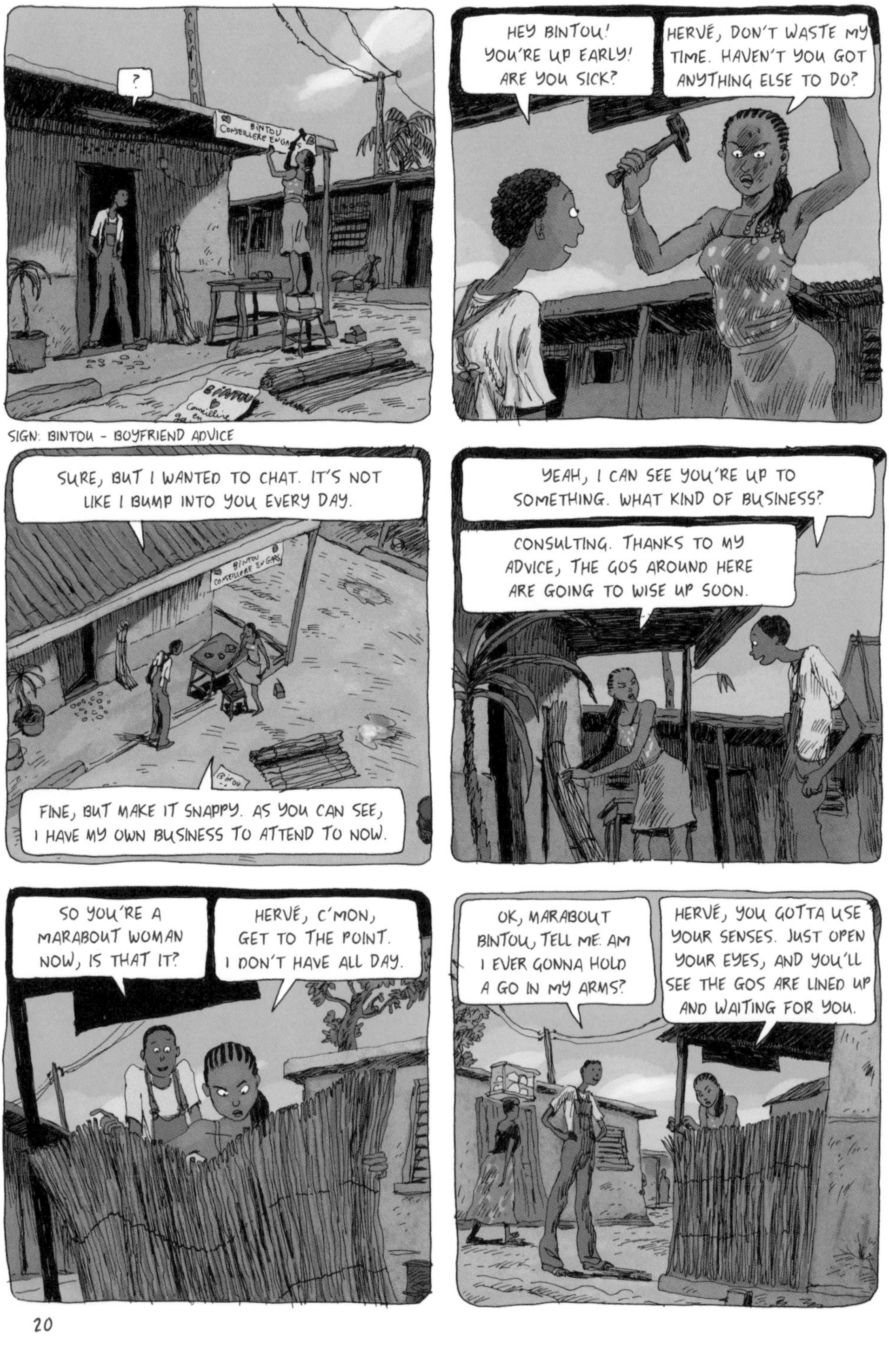
?
BINTOU CONSEILLERE EN GARS
SIGN: BINTOU - BOYFRIEND ADVICE
HEY BINTOU! YOU'RE UP EARLY! ARE YOU SICK?
HERVÉ, DON'T WASTE MY TIME. HAVEN'T YOU GOT ANYTHING ELSE TO DO?
SURE, BUT I WANTED TO CHAT. IT'S NOT LIKE I BUMP INTO YOU EVERY DAY.
FINE, BUT MAKE IT SNAPPY. AS YOU CAN SEE, I HAVE MY OWN BUSINESS TO ATTEND TO NOW.
YEAH, I CAN SEE YOU'RE UP TO SOMETHING. WHAT KIND OF BUSINESS?
CONSULTING. THANKS TO MY ADVICE, THE GOS AROUND HERE ARE GOING TO WISE UP SOON.
SO YOU'RE A MARABOUT WOMAN NOW, IS THAT IT?
HERVÉ, C'MON, GET TO THE POINT. I DON'T HAVE ALL DAY.
OK, MARABOUT BINTOU, TELL ME. AM I EVER GONNA HOLD A GO IN MY ARMS?
HERVÉ, YOU GOTTA USE YOUR SENSES. JUST OPEN YOUR EYES, AND YOU'LL SEE THE GOS ARE LINED UP AND WAITING FOR YOU.

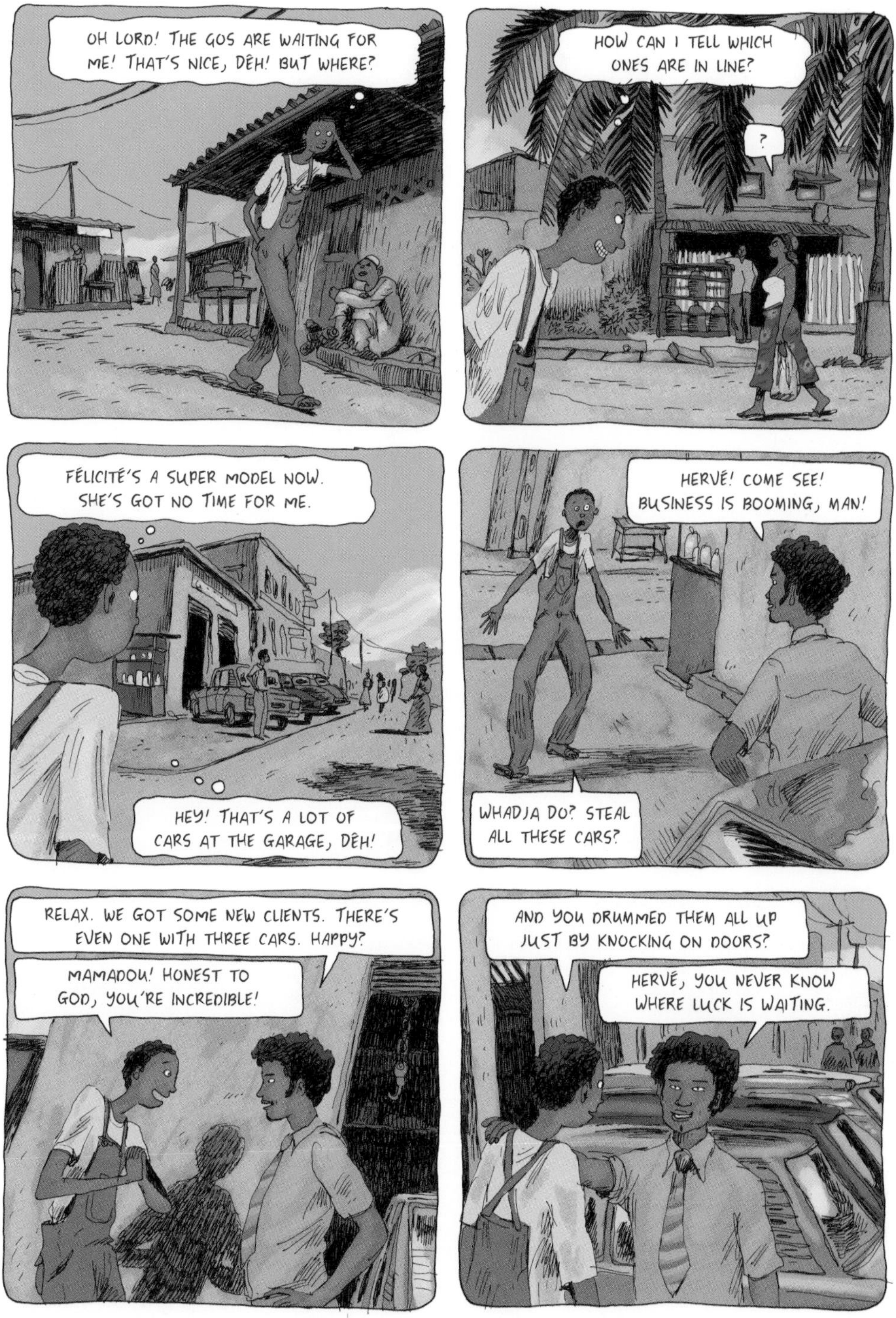
OH LORD! THE GOS ARE WAITING FOR ME! THAT'S NICE, DÊH! BUT WHERE?
HOW CAN I TELL WHICH ONES ARE IN LINE?
?
FÉLICITÉ'S A SUPER MODEL NOW. SHE'S GOT NO TIME FOR ME.
HEY! THAT'S A LOT OF CARS AT THE GARAGE, DÊH!
HERVÉ! COME SEE! BUSINESS IS BOOMING, MAN!
WHADJA DO? STEAL ALL THESE CARS?
RELAX. WE GOT SOME NEW CLIENTS. THERE'S EVEN ONE WITH THREE CARS. HAPPY?
MAMADOU! HONEST TO GOD, YOU'RE INCREDIBLE!
AND YOU DRUMMED THEM ALL UP JUST BY KNOCKING ON DOORS?
HERVÉ, YOU NEVER KNOW WHERE LUCK IS WAITING.

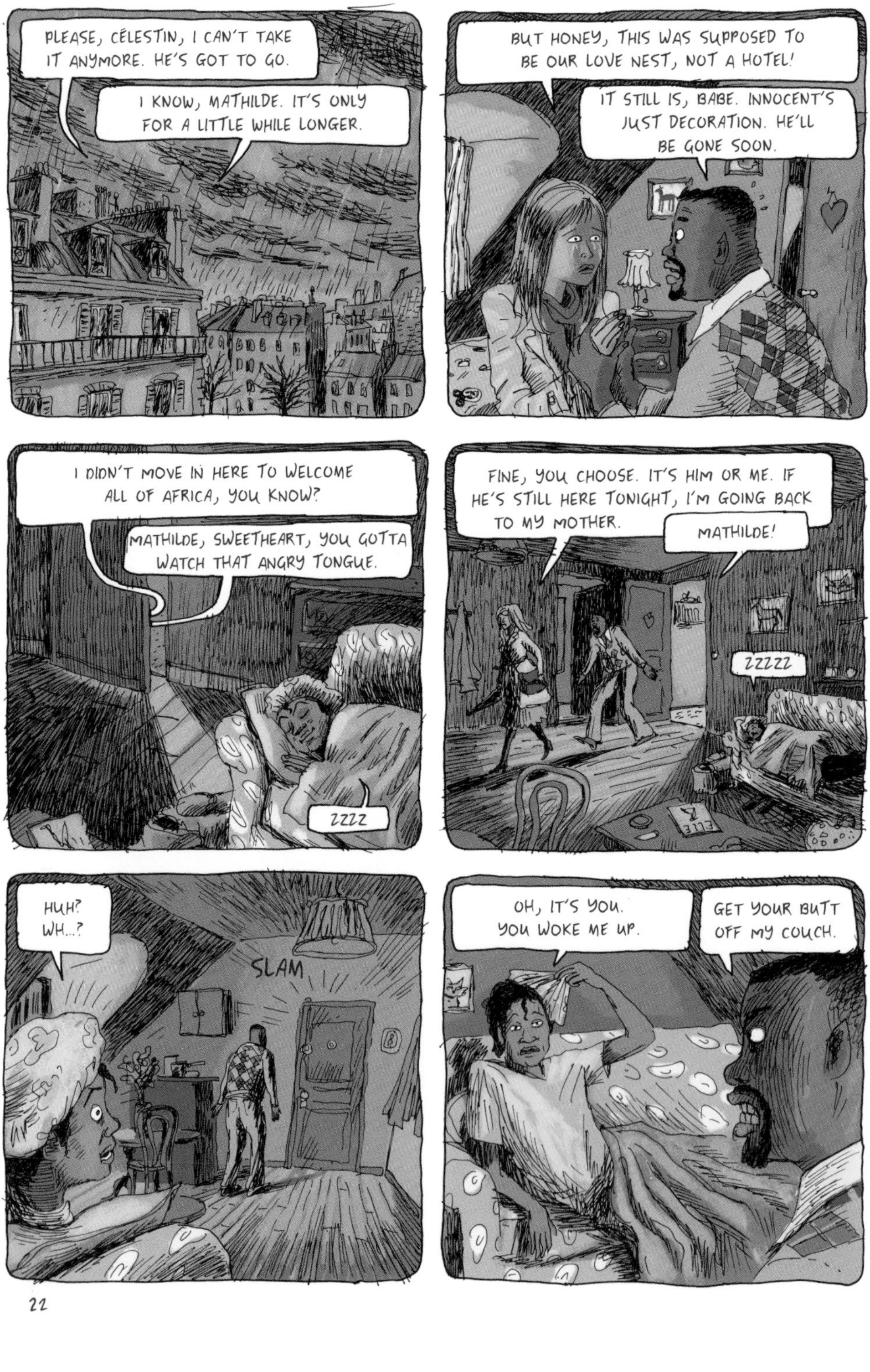
PLEASE, CÉLESTIN, I CAN'T TAKE IT ANYMORE. HE'S GOT TO GO.
I KNOW, MATHILDE. IT'S ONLY FOR A LITTLE WHILE LONGER.
BUT HONEY, THIS WAS SUPPOSED TO BE OUR LOVE NEST, NOT A HOTEL!
IT STILL IS, BABE. INNOCENT'S JUST DECORATION. HE'LL BE GONE SOON.
I DIDN'T MOVE IN HERE TO WELCOME ALL OF AFRICA, YOU KNOW?
MATHILDE, SWEETHEART, YOU GOTTA WATCH THAT ANGRY TONGUE.
ZZZZ
FINE, YOU CHOOSE. IT'S HIM OR ME. IF HE'S STILL HERE TONIGHT, I'M GOING BACK TO MY MOTHER.
MATHILDE!
ZZZZZ
HUH? WH...?
SLAM
OH, IT'S YOU. YOU WOKE ME UP.
GET YOUR BUTT OFF MY COUCH.

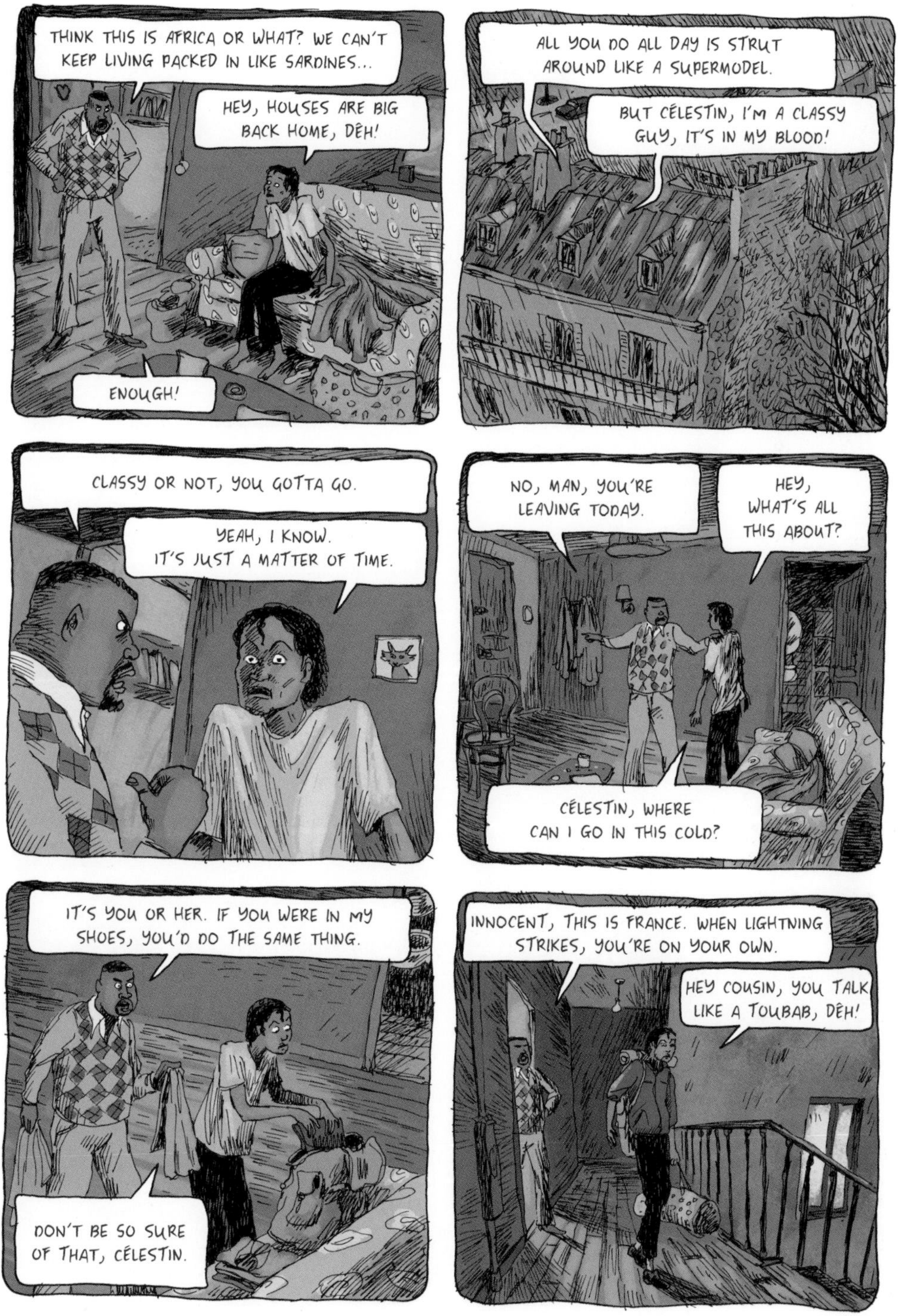
THINK THIS IS AFRICA OR WHAT? WE CAN'T KEEP LIVING PACKED IN LIKE SARDINES...
HEY, HOUSES ARE BIG BACK HOME, DÊH!
ENOUGH!
ALL YOU DO ALL DAY IS STRUT AROUND LIKE A SUPERMODEL.
BUT CÉLESTIN, I'M A CLASSY GUY, IT'S IN MY BLOOD!
CLASSY OR NOT, YOU GOTTA GO.
YEAH, I KNOW. IT'S JUST A MATTER OF TIME.
NO, MAN, YOU'RE LEAVING TODAY.
HEY, WHAT'S ALL THIS ABOUT?
CÉLESTIN, WHERE CAN I GO IN THIS COLD?
IT'S YOU OR HER. IF YOU WERE IN MY SHOES, YOU'D DO THE SAME THING.
DON'T BE SO SURE OF THAT, CÉLESTIN.
INNOCENT, THIS IS FRANCE. WHEN LIGHTNING STRIKES, YOU'RE ON YOUR OWN.
HEY COUSIN, YOU TALK LIKE A TOUBAB, DÊH!

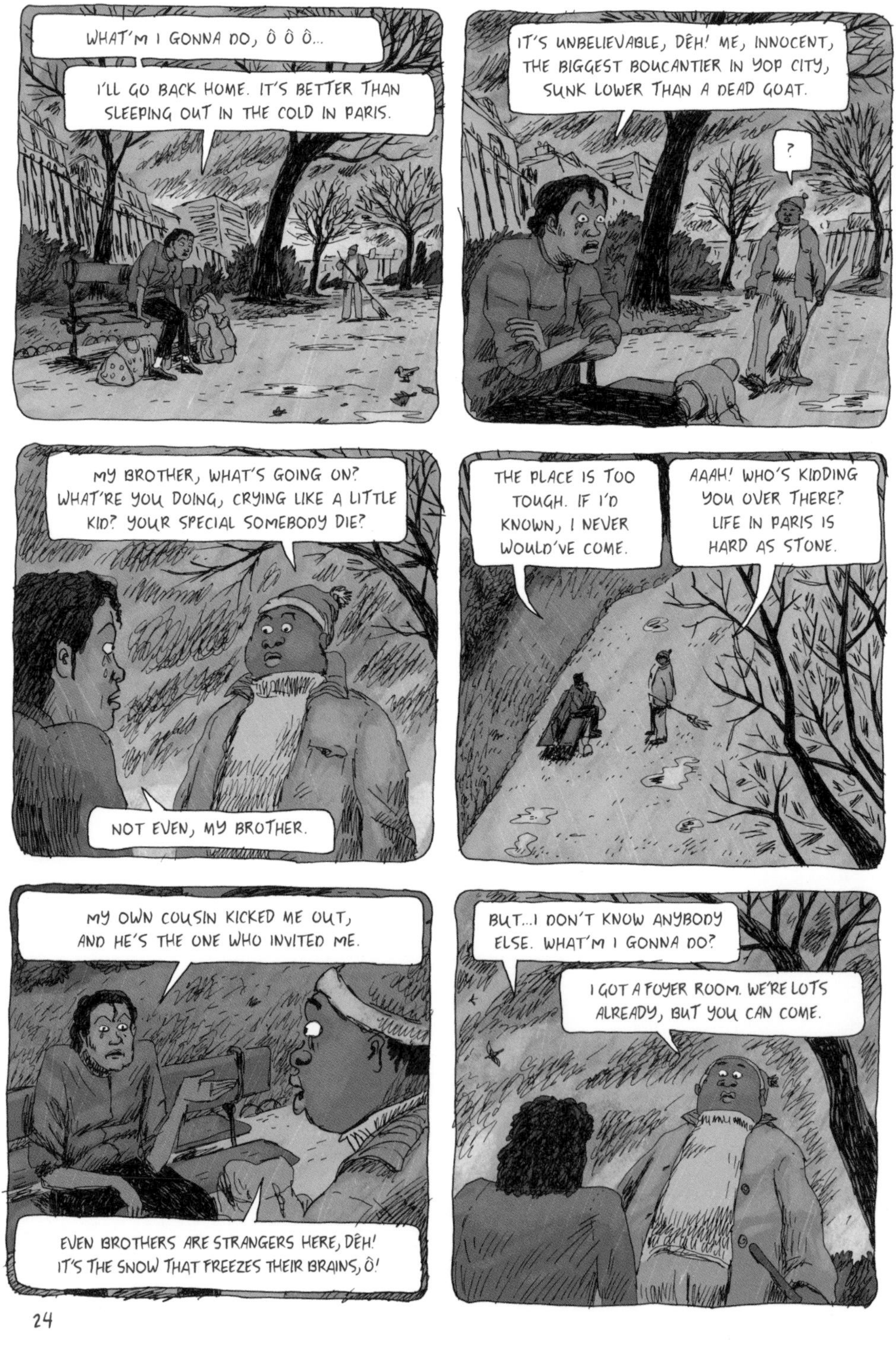
WHAT'M I GONNA DO, Ô Ô Ô...
I'LL GO BACK HOME. IT'S BETTER THAN SLEEPING OUT IN THE COLD IN PARIS.
IT'S UNBELIEVABLE, DÊH! ME, INNOCENT, THE BIGGEST BOUCANTIER IN YOP CITY, SUNK LOWER THAN A DEAD GOAT.
?
MY BROTHER, WHAT'S GOING ON? WHAT'RE YOU DOING, CRYING LIKE A LITTLE KID? YOUR SPECIAL SOMEBODY DIE?
NOT EVEN, MY BROTHER.
THE PLACE IS TOO TOUGH. IF I'D KNOWN, I NEVER WOULD'VE COME.
AAAH! WHO'S KIDDING YOU OVER THERE? LIFE IN PARIS IS HARD AS STONE.
MY OWN COUSIN KICKED ME OUT, AND HE'S THE ONE WHO INVITED ME.
EVEN BROTHERS ARE STRANGERS HERE, DÊH! IT'S THE SNOW THAT FREEZES THEIR BRAINS, Ô!
BUT...I DON'T KNOW ANYBODY ELSE. WHAT'M I GONNA DO?
I GOT A FOYER ROOM. WE'RE LOTS ALREADY, BUT YOU CAN COME.

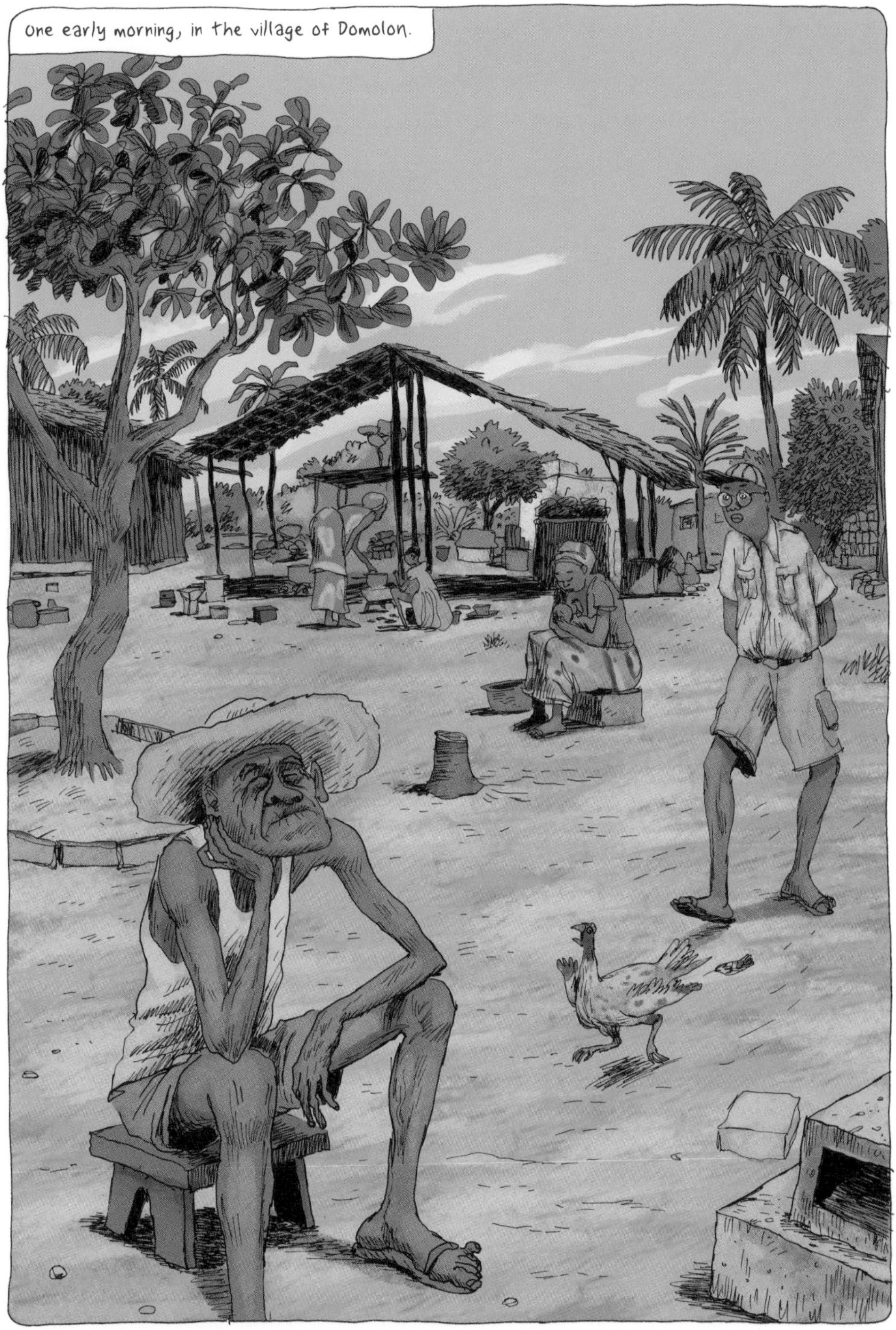
One early morning, in the village of Domolon.

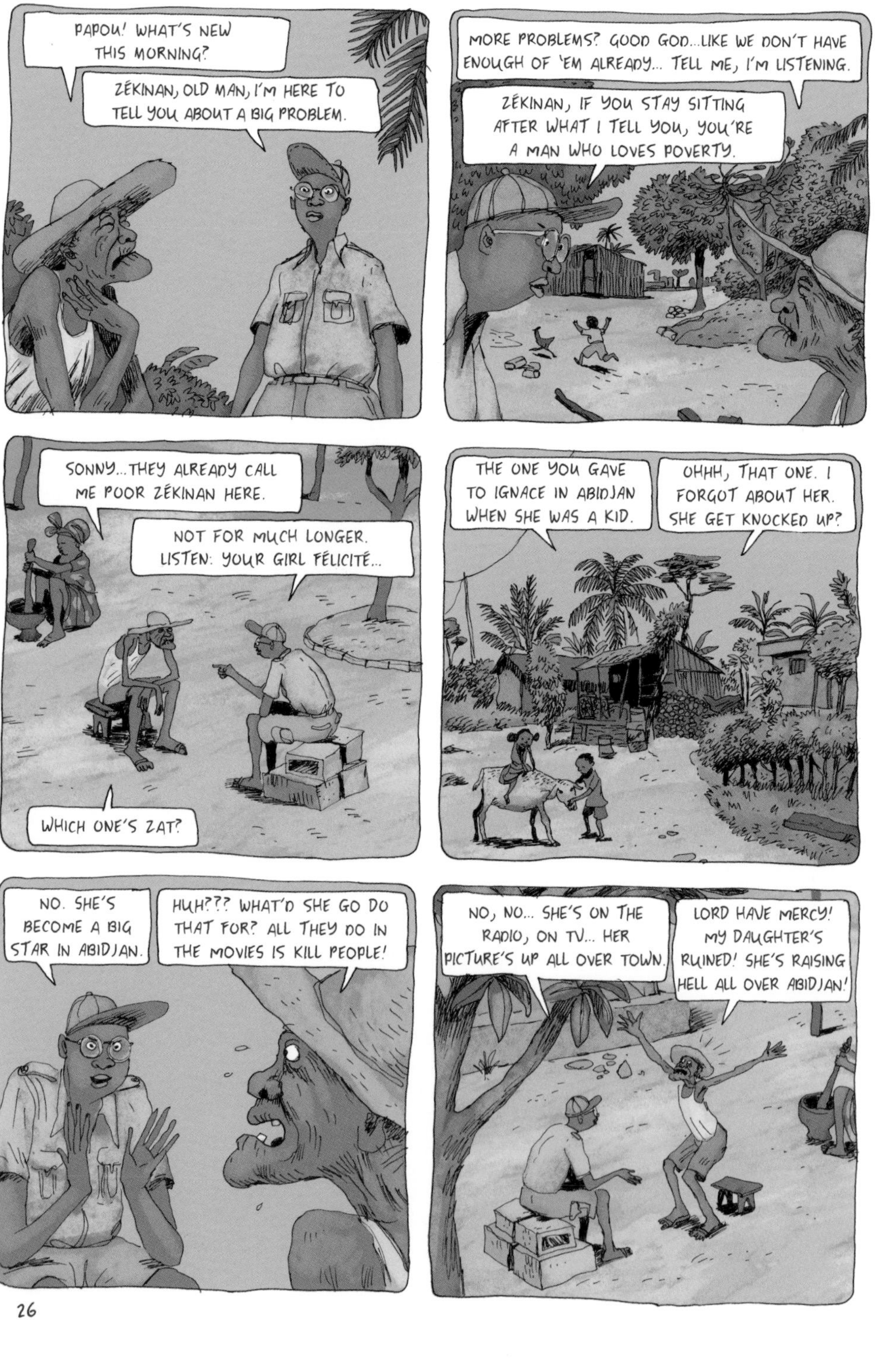
PAPOU! WHAT'S NEW THIS MORNING?
ZÉKINAN, OLD MAN, I'M HERE TO TELL YOU ABOUT A BIG PROBLEM.
MORE PROBLEMS? GOOD GOD...LIKE WE DON'T HAVE ENOUGH OF 'EM ALREADY... TELL ME, I'M LISTENING.
ZÉKINAN, IF YOU STAY SITTING AFTER WHAT I TELL YOU, YOU'RE A MAN WHO LOVES POVERTY.
SONNY...THEY ALREADY CALL ME POOR ZÉKINAN HERE.
NOT FOR MUCH LONGER. LISTEN: YOUR GIRL FÉLICITÉ...
WHICH ONE'S ZAT?
THE ONE YOU GAVE TO IGNACE IN ABIDJAN WHEN SHE WAS A KID.
OHHH, THAT ONE. I FORGOT ABOUT HER. SHE GET KNOCKED UP?
NO. SHE'S BECOME A BIG STAR IN ABIDJAN.
HUH??? WHAT'D SHE GO DO THAT FOR? ALL THEY DO IN THE MOVIES IS KILL PEOPLE!
NO, NO... SHE'S ON THE RADIO, ON TV... HER PICTURE'S UP ALL OVER TOWN.
LORD HAVE MERCY! MY DAUGHTER'S RUINED! SHE'S RAISING HELL ALL OVER ABIDJAN!

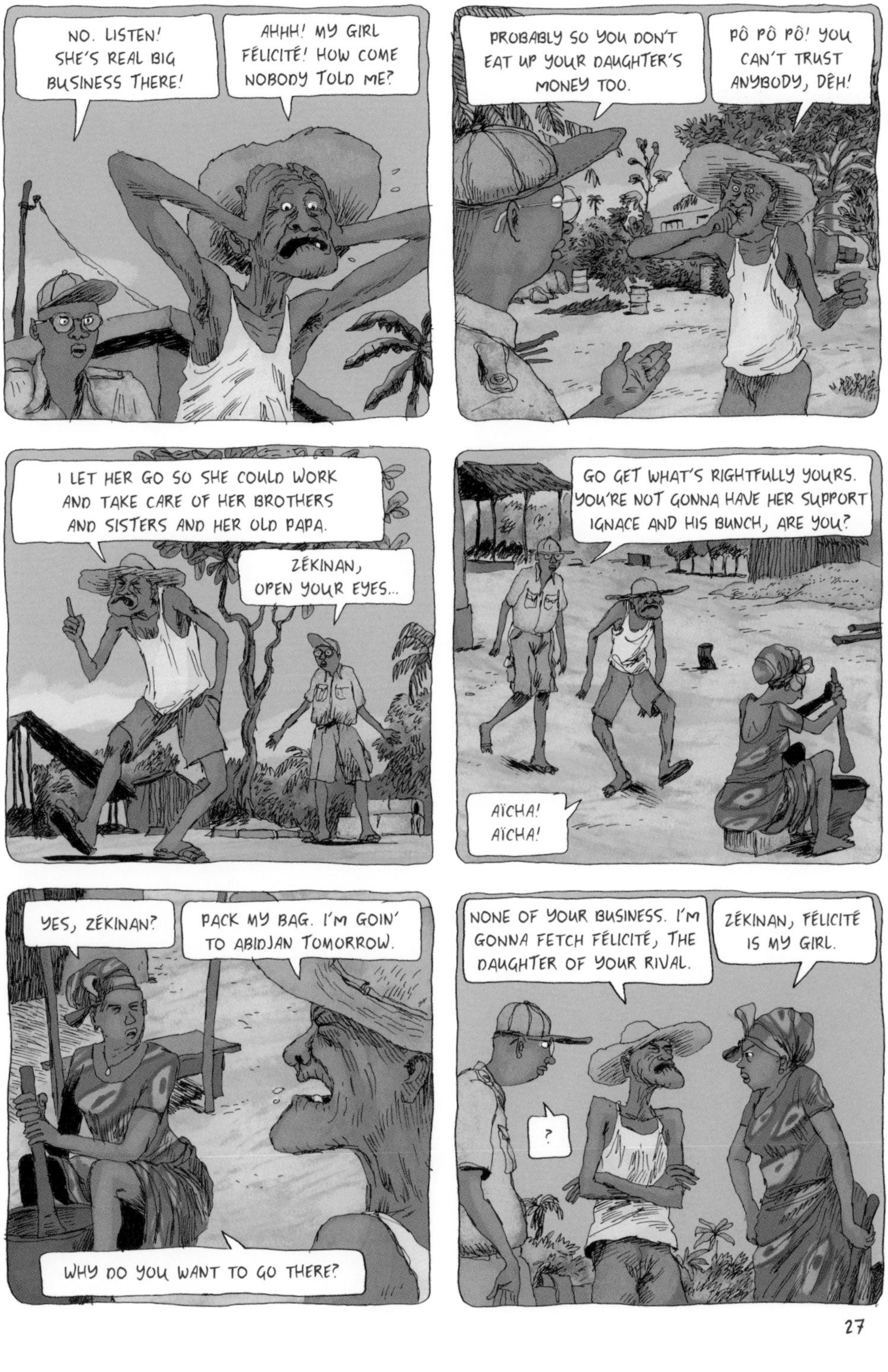
NO. LISTEN! SHE'S REAL BIG BUSINESS THERE!
AHHH! MY GIRL FÉLICITÉ! HOW COME NOBODY TOLD ME?
PROBABLY SO YOU DON'T EAT UP YOUR DAUGHTER'S MONEY TOO.
PÔ PÔ PÔ! YOU CAN'T TRUST ANYBODY, DÊH!
I LET HER GO SO SHE COULD WORK AND TAKE CARE OF HER BROTHERS AND SISTERS AND HER OLD PAPA.
ZÉKINAN, OPEN YOUR EYES...
GO GET WHAT'S RIGHTFULLY YOURS. YOU'RE NOT GONNA HAVE HER SUPPORT IGNACE AND HIS BUNCH, ARE YOU?
AÏCHA! AÏCHA!
YES, ZÉKINAN?
PACK MY BAG. I'M GOIN' TO ABIDJAN TOMORROW.
WHY DO YOU WANT TO GO THERE?
NONE OF YOUR BUSINESS. I'M GONNA FETCH FÉLICITÉ, THE DAUGHTER OF YOUR RIVAL.
ZÉKINAN, FÉLICITÉ IS MY GIRL.
?

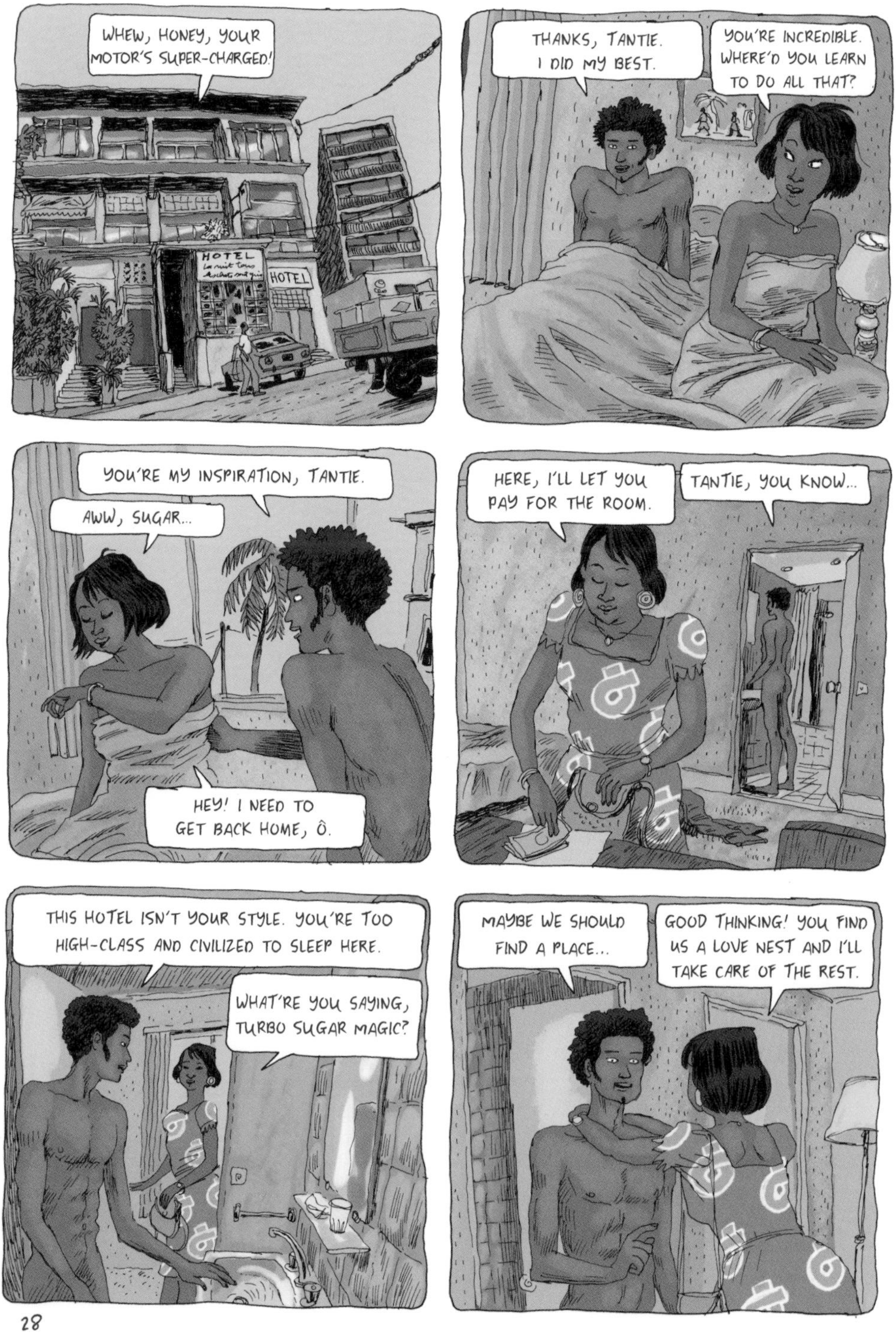
WHEW, HONEY, YOUR MOTOR'S SUPER-CHARGED!
HOTEL
HOTEL
THANKS, TANTIE. I DID MY BEST.
YOU'RE INCREDIBLE. WHERE'D YOU LEARN TO DO ALL THAT?
YOU'RE MY INSPIRATION, TANTIE.
AWW, SUGAR...
HEY! I NEED TO GET BACK HOME, Ô.
HERE, I'LL LET YOU PAY FOR THE ROOM.
TANTIE, YOU KNOW...
THIS HOTEL ISN'T YOUR STYLE. YOU'RE TOO HIGH-CLASS AND CIVILIZED TO SLEEP HERE.
WHAT'RE YOU SAYING, TURBO SUGAR MAGIC?
MAYBE WE SHOULD FIND A PLACE...
GOOD THINKING! YOU FIND US A LOVE NEST AND I'LL TAKE CARE OF THE REST.

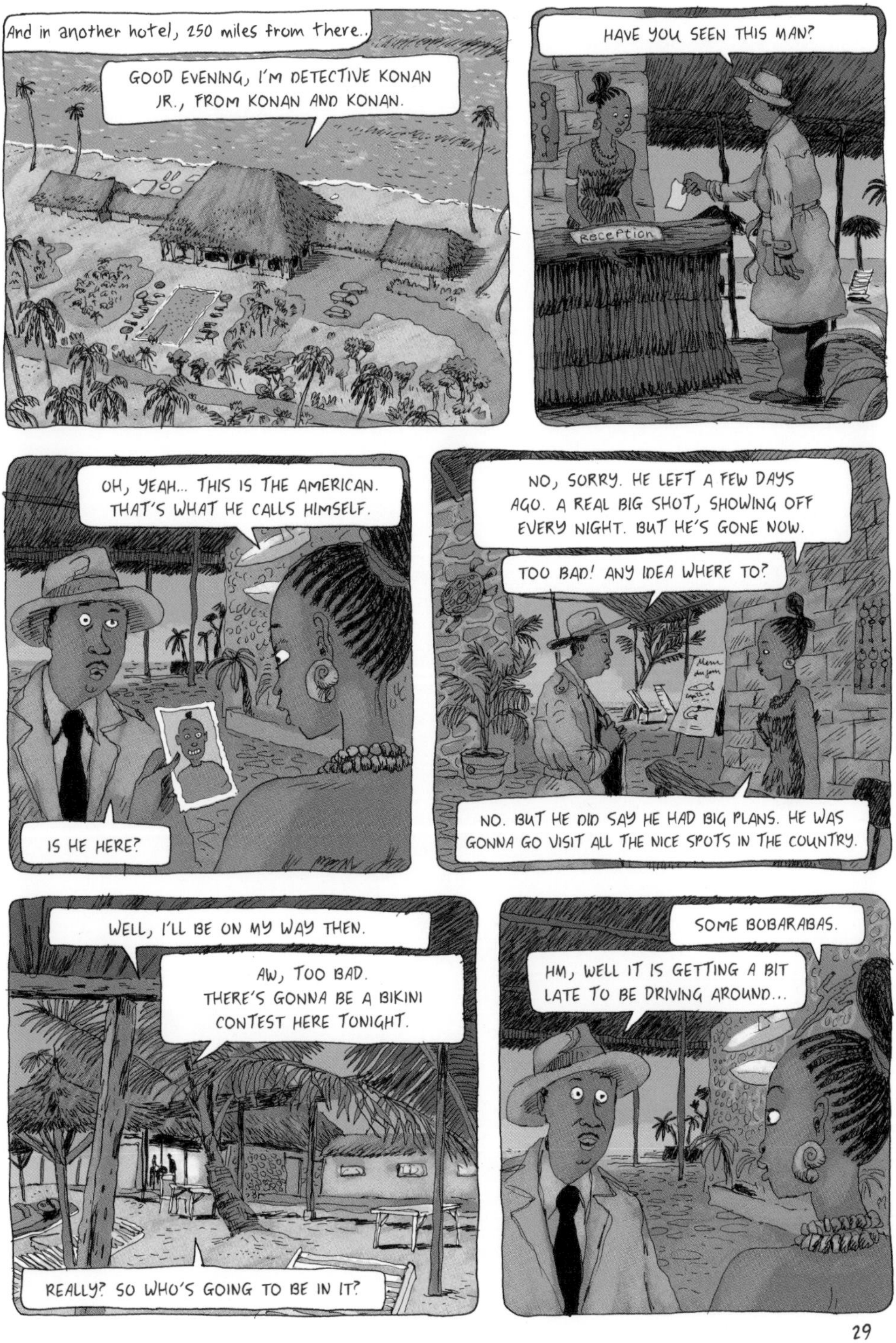
And in another hotel, 250 miles from there..
GOOD EVENING, I'M DETECTIVE KONAN JR., FROM KONAN AND KONAN.
HAVE YOU SEEN THIS MAN?
Reception
OH, YEAH... THIS IS THE AMERICAN. THAT'S WHAT HE CALLS HIMSELF.
IS HE HERE?
NO, SORRY. HE LEFT A FEW DAYS AGO. A REAL BIG SHOT, SHOWING OFF EVERY NIGHT. BUT HE'S GONE NOW.
TOO BAD! ANY IDEA WHERE TO?
NO. BUT HE DID SAY HE HAD BIG PLANS. HE WAS GONNA GO VISIT ALL THE NICE SPOTS IN THE COUNTRY.
WELL, I'LL BE ON MY WAY THEN.
AW, TOO BAD. THERE'S GONNA BE A BIKINI CONTEST HERE TONIGHT.
REALLY? SO WHO'S GOING TO BE IN IT?
SOME BOBARABAS.
HM, WELL IT IS GETTING A BIT LATE TO BE DRIVING AROUND...

SO, MICHELINE, WHAT CAN I DO FOR YOU?

BINTOU Conseillère en gars

WELL, IT'S LIKE THIS: I'VE BEEN GOING OUT WITH ÉMILE FOR SIX MONTHS. AT FIRST I WASN'T READY FOR SOMETHING SERIOUS, BUT THEN MY SISTERS ENCOURAGED ME AND I WENT ALONG WITH IT...

At the start, my guy was sweet, attentive... It was love with a capital L.

Émile, my love

Baby, I'm gonna take you to Mono Gaga next weekend!

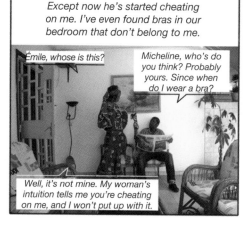

Except now he's started cheating on me. I've even found bras in our bedroom that don't belong to me.

Émile, whose is this?

Micheline, who's do you think? Probably yours. Since when do I wear a bra?

Well, it's not mine. My woman's intuition tells me you're cheating on me, and I won't put up with it.

Friends told me to drop it, and I did, since I had no other proof. But now my baby's changed. He's drifting away from me, and nothing I do to win him back is working.

I'm going out. Don't wait with supper.

But...I've made your favorite dish!

I love him, but I'm losing him. I don't know what to do anymore.

Boo hoo hoo

I WANT TO MAKE THINGS THE WAY THEY USED TO BE, BUT I DON'T KNOW HOW. HELP ME, BINTOU.

MY DEAR, I'M SORRY...

PEOPLE SAY THAT WHEN YOU'RE MARRIED, SOMETIMES YOU NEED TO LOOK THE OTHER WAY, BUT THAT'S NOT HOW IT IS. HE NEEDS TO CLEAN UP HIS ACT AND SHOW SOME RESPECT. HE CAN'T BE DRAGGING HIS MISCHIEF INTO YOUR BEDROOM.

If I was you, here's what I'd do.

What the hell is this?

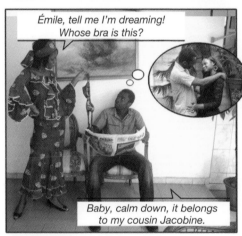

Émile, tell me I'm dreaming! Whose bra is this?

Baby, calm down, it belongs to my cousin Jacobine.

Your cousin? You kidding me? I give you everything, and all I ever get from you is lies.

How dare you slap me! Look out, or I'm gonna smack you, too.

Fine! If that's how it is, I'm gonna kill myself, and you'll have my death on your conscience!

Hey! What're you doing? Stop!

BUT BINTOU... WHAT IF HE COULDN'T CARE LESS AND DOESN'T HOLD ME BACK?

SISTER, LISTEN TO ME. IF YOU PLAY CRAZY, YOU'LL SCARE THE DAYLIGHTS OUT OF HIM AND HE WON'T DARE LEAVE YOU. THAT'LL BE 1,000 FRANCS.

31

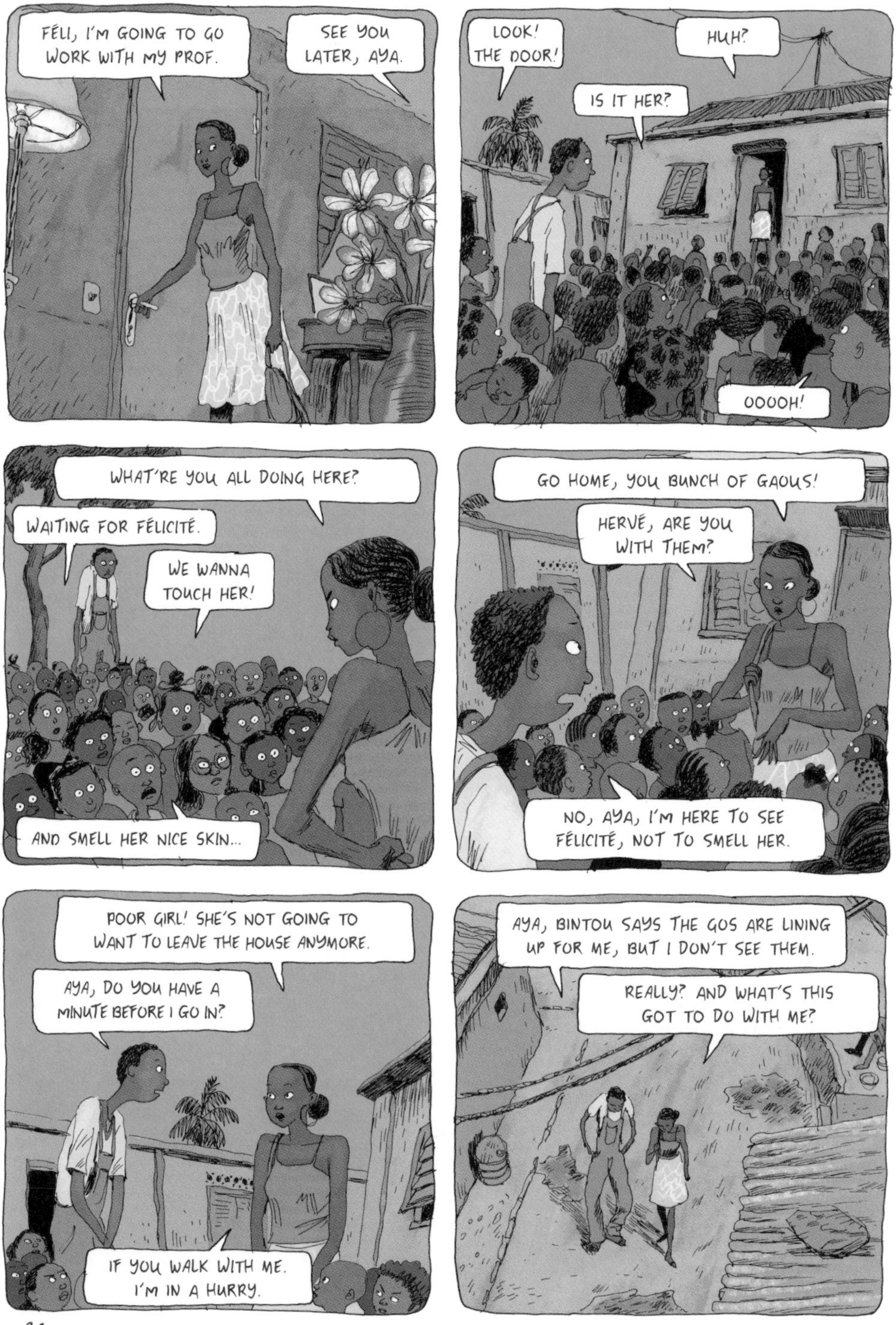
FÉLI, I'M GOING TO GO WORK WITH MY PROF.
SEE YOU LATER, AYA.
LOOK! THE DOOR!
HUH?
IS IT HER?
OOOOH!
WHAT'RE YOU ALL DOING HERE?
WAITING FOR FÉLICITÉ.
WE WANNA TOUCH HER!
AND SMELL HER NICE SKIN...
GO HOME, YOU BUNCH OF GAOUS!
HERVÉ, ARE YOU WITH THEM?
NO, AYA, I'M HERE TO SEE FÉLICITÉ, NOT TO SMELL HER.
POOR GIRL! SHE'S NOT GOING TO WANT TO LEAVE THE HOUSE ANYMORE.
AYA, DO YOU HAVE A MINUTE BEFORE I GO IN?
IF YOU WALK WITH ME. I'M IN A HURRY.
AYA, BINTOU SAYS THE GOS ARE LINING UP FOR ME, BUT I DON'T SEE THEM.
REALLY? AND WHAT'S THIS GOT TO DO WITH ME?

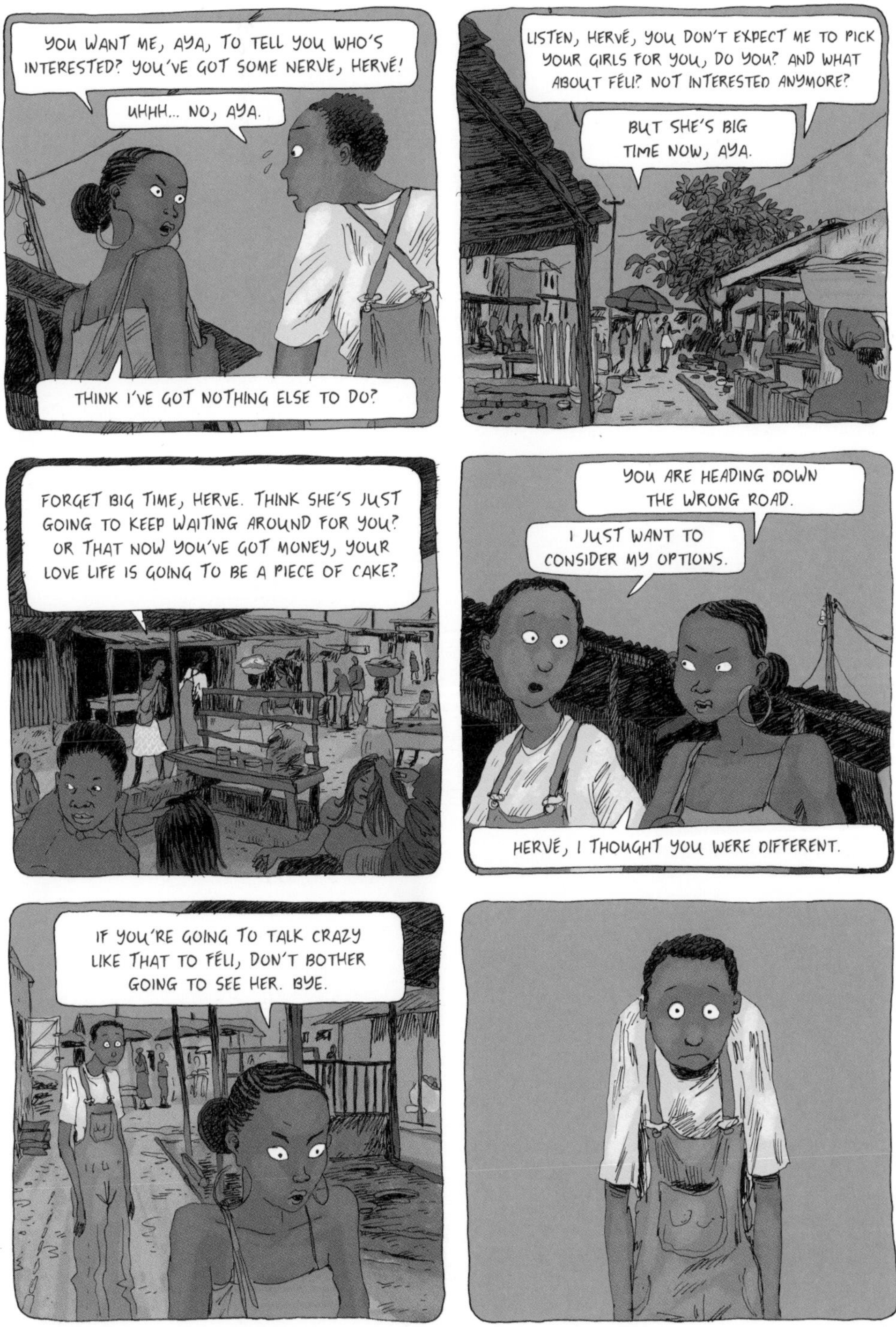
YOU WANT ME, AYA, TO TELL YOU WHO'S INTERESTED? YOU'VE GOT SOME NERVE, HERVÉ!
UHHH... NO, AYA.
THINK I'VE GOT NOTHING ELSE TO DO?
LISTEN, HERVÉ, YOU DON'T EXPECT ME TO PICK YOUR GIRLS FOR YOU, DO YOU? AND WHAT ABOUT FÉLI? NOT INTERESTED ANYMORE?
BUT SHE'S BIG TIME NOW, AYA.
FORGET BIG TIME, HERVE. THINK SHE'S JUST GOING TO KEEP WAITING AROUND FOR YOU? OR THAT NOW YOU'VE GOT MONEY, YOUR LOVE LIFE IS GOING TO BE A PIECE OF CAKE?
I JUST WANT TO CONSIDER MY OPTIONS.
YOU ARE HEADING DOWN THE WRONG ROAD.
HERVÉ, I THOUGHT YOU WERE DIFFERENT.
IF YOU'RE GOING TO TALK CRAZY LIKE THAT TO FÉLI, DON'T BOTHER GOING TO SEE HER. BYE.

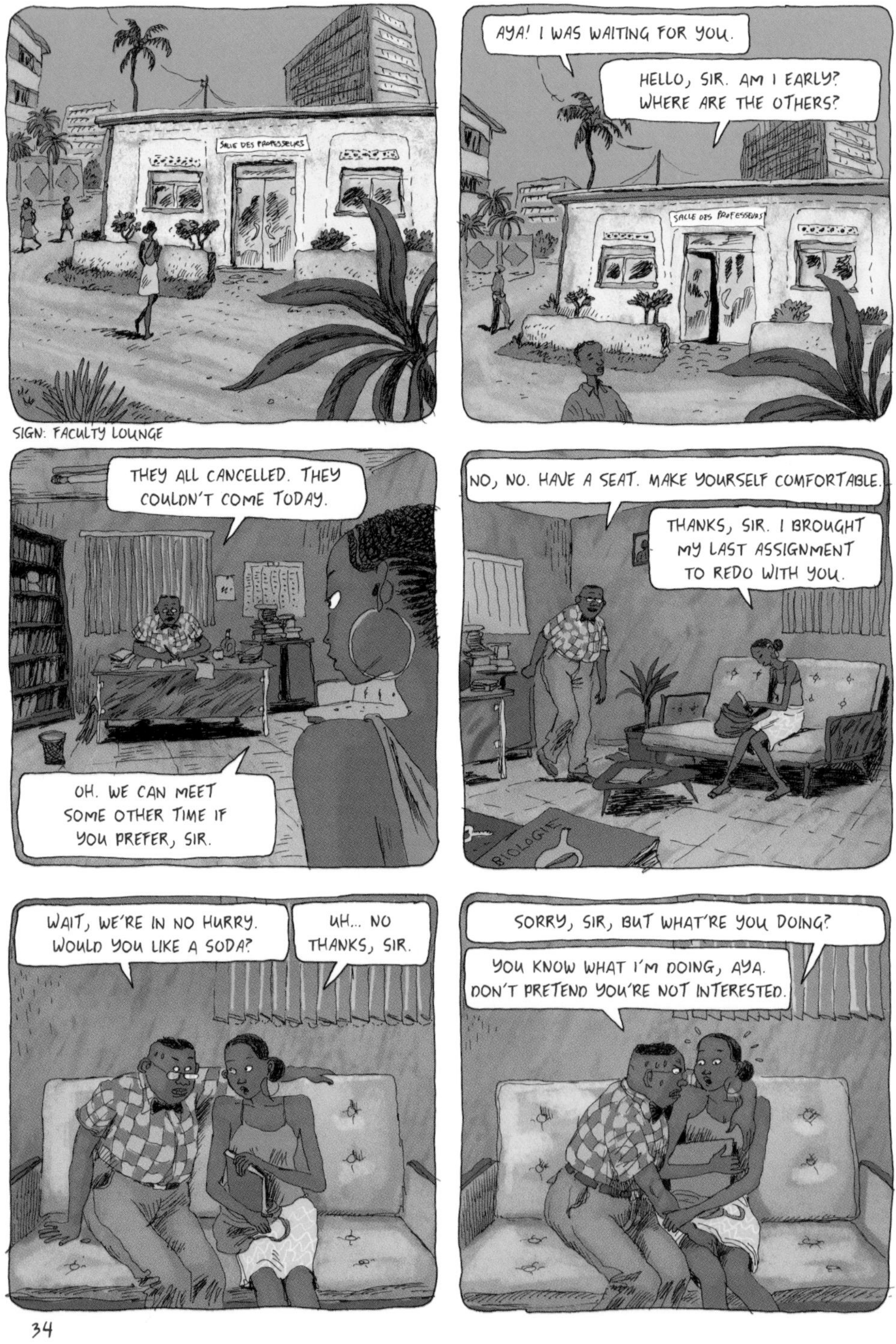
SALLE DES PROFESSEURS
SIGN: FACULTY LOUNGE
AYA! I WAS WAITING FOR YOU.
HELLO, SIR. AM I EARLY? WHERE ARE THE OTHERS?
THEY ALL CANCELLED. THEY COULDN'T COME TODAY.
OH. WE CAN MEET SOME OTHER TIME IF YOU PREFER, SIR.
NO, NO. HAVE A SEAT. MAKE YOURSELF COMFORTABLE.
THANKS, SIR. I BROUGHT MY LAST ASSIGNMENT TO REDO WITH YOU.
BIOLOGIE
WAIT, WE'RE IN NO HURRY. WOULD YOU LIKE A SODA?
UH... NO THANKS, SIR.
SORRY, SIR, BUT WHAT'RE YOU DOING?
YOU KNOW WHAT I'M DOING, AYA. DON'T PRETEND YOU'RE NOT INTERESTED.

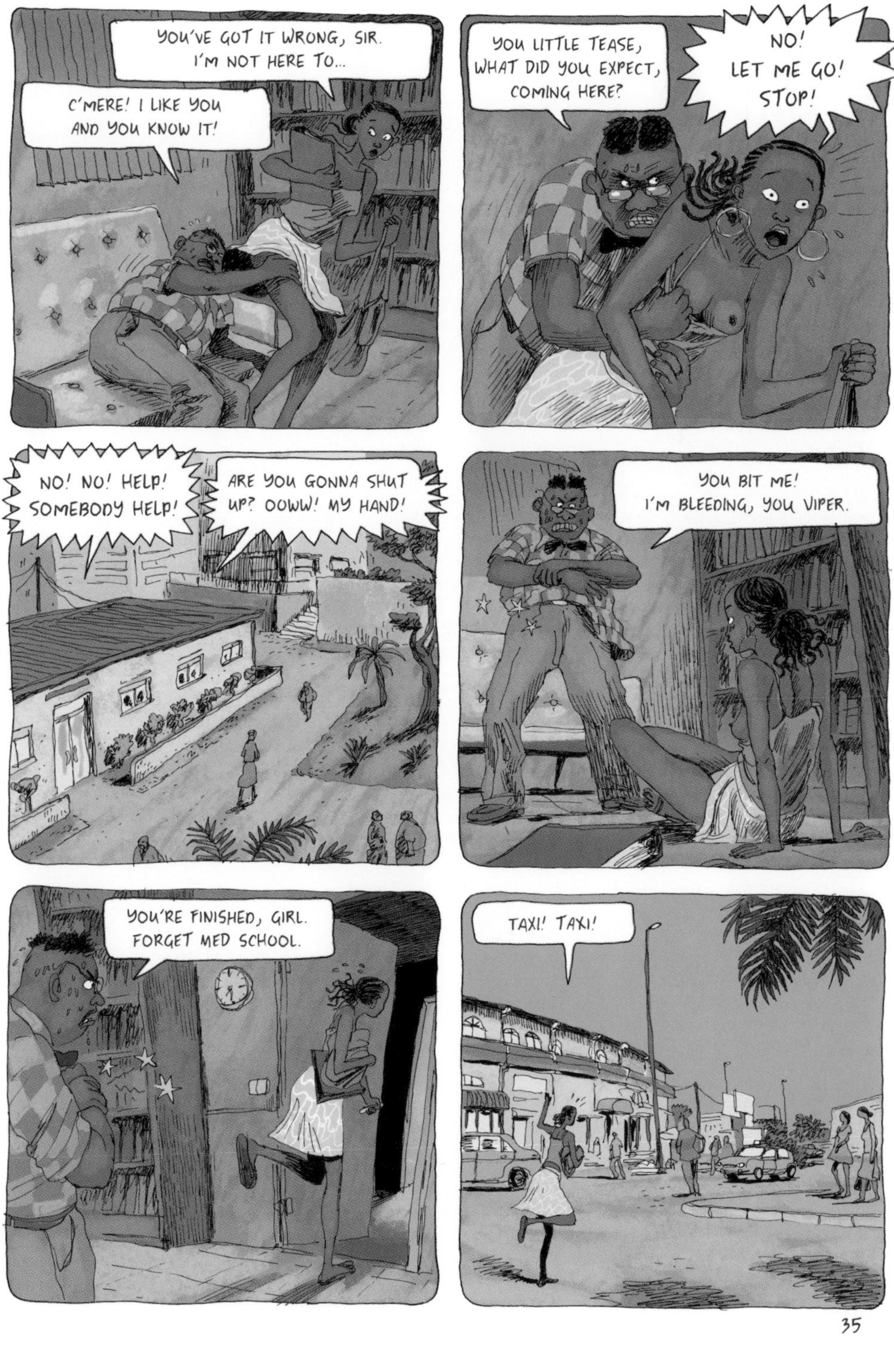
YOU'VE GOT IT WRONG, SIR.
I'M NOT HERE TO...
C'MERE! I LIKE YOU
AND YOU KNOW IT!
YOU LITTLE TEASE,
WHAT DID YOU EXPECT,
COMING HERE?
NO!
LET ME GO!
STOP!
NO! NO! HELP!
SOMEBODY HELP!
ARE YOU GONNA SHUT
UP? OOWW! MY HAND!
YOU BIT ME!
I'M BLEEDING, YOU VIPER.
YOU'RE FINISHED, GIRL.
FORGET MED SCHOOL.
TAXI! TAXI!

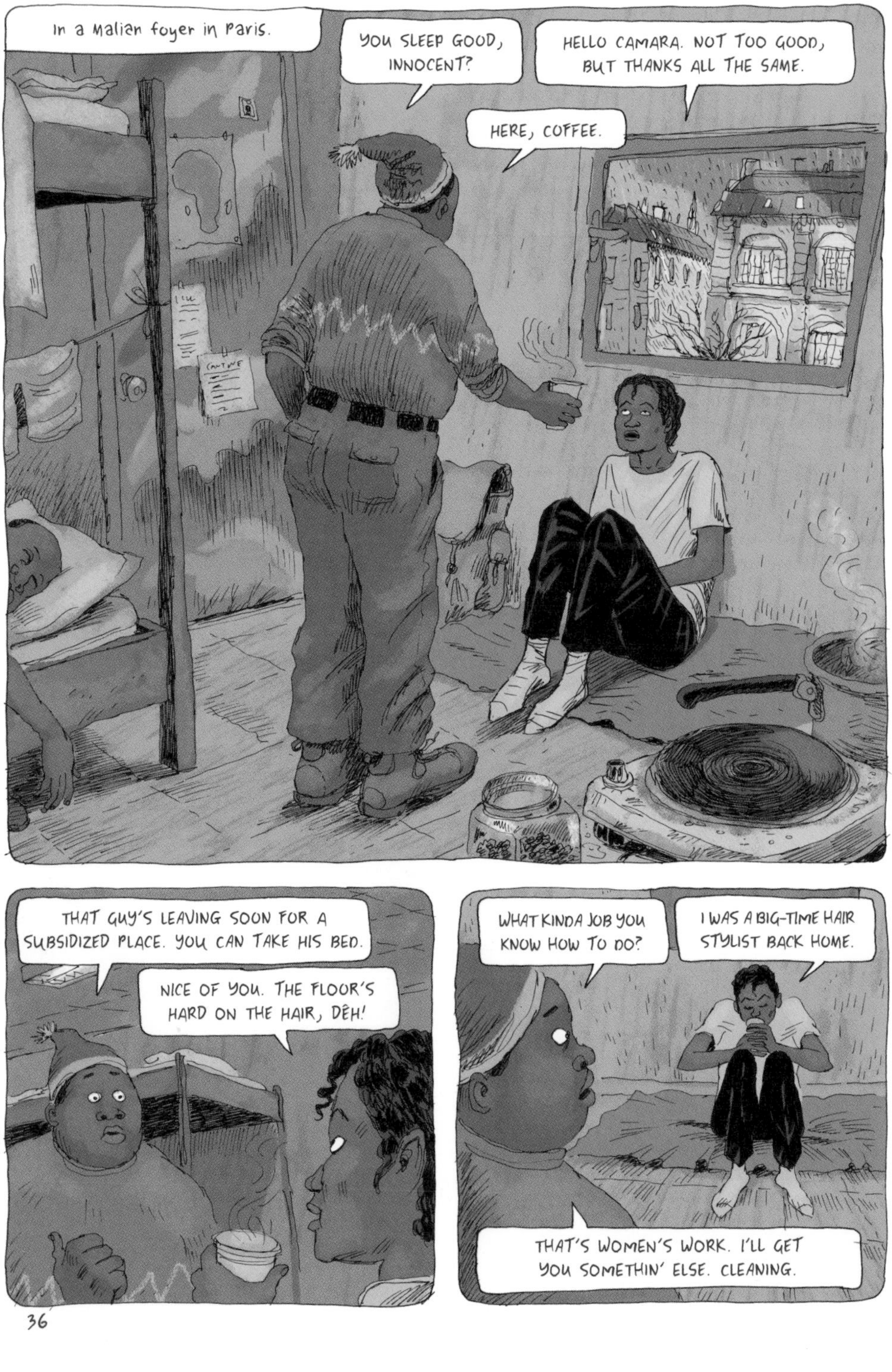

In a Malian foyer in Paris.
YOU SLEEP GOOD, INNOCENT?
HELLO CAMARA. NOT TOO GOOD, BUT THANKS ALL THE SAME.
HERE, COFFEE.
THAT GUY'S LEAVING SOON FOR A SUBSIDIZED PLACE. YOU CAN TAKE HIS BED.
NICE OF YOU. THE FLOOR'S HARD ON THE HAIR, DÊH!
WHAT KINDA JOB YOU KNOW HOW TO DO?
I WAS A BIG-TIME HAIR STYLIST BACK HOME.
THAT'S WOMEN'S WORK. I'LL GET YOU SOMETHIN' ELSE. CLEANING.

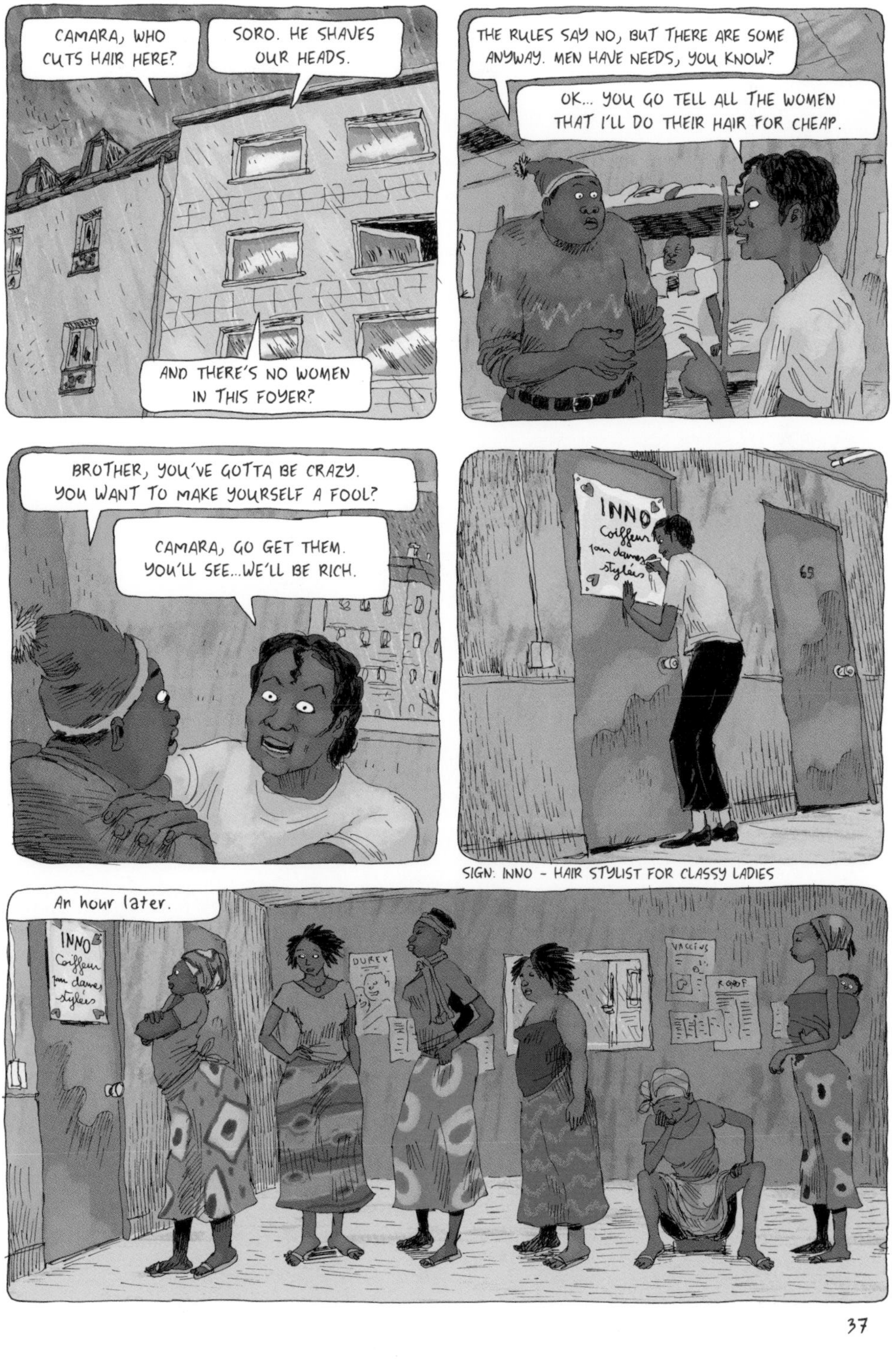
CAMARA, WHO CUTS HAIR HERE?
SORO. HE SHAVES OUR HEADS.
AND THERE'S NO WOMEN IN THIS FOYER?
THE RULES SAY NO, BUT THERE ARE SOME ANYWAY. MEN HAVE NEEDS, YOU KNOW?
OK... YOU GO TELL ALL THE WOMEN THAT I'LL DO THEIR HAIR FOR CHEAP.
BROTHER, YOU'VE GOTTA BE CRAZY. YOU WANT TO MAKE YOURSELF A FOOL?
CAMARA, GO GET THEM. YOU'LL SEE...WE'LL BE RICH.
INNO
Coiffeur pour dames stylées
SIGN: INNO - HAIR STYLIST FOR CLASSY LADIES
An hour later.

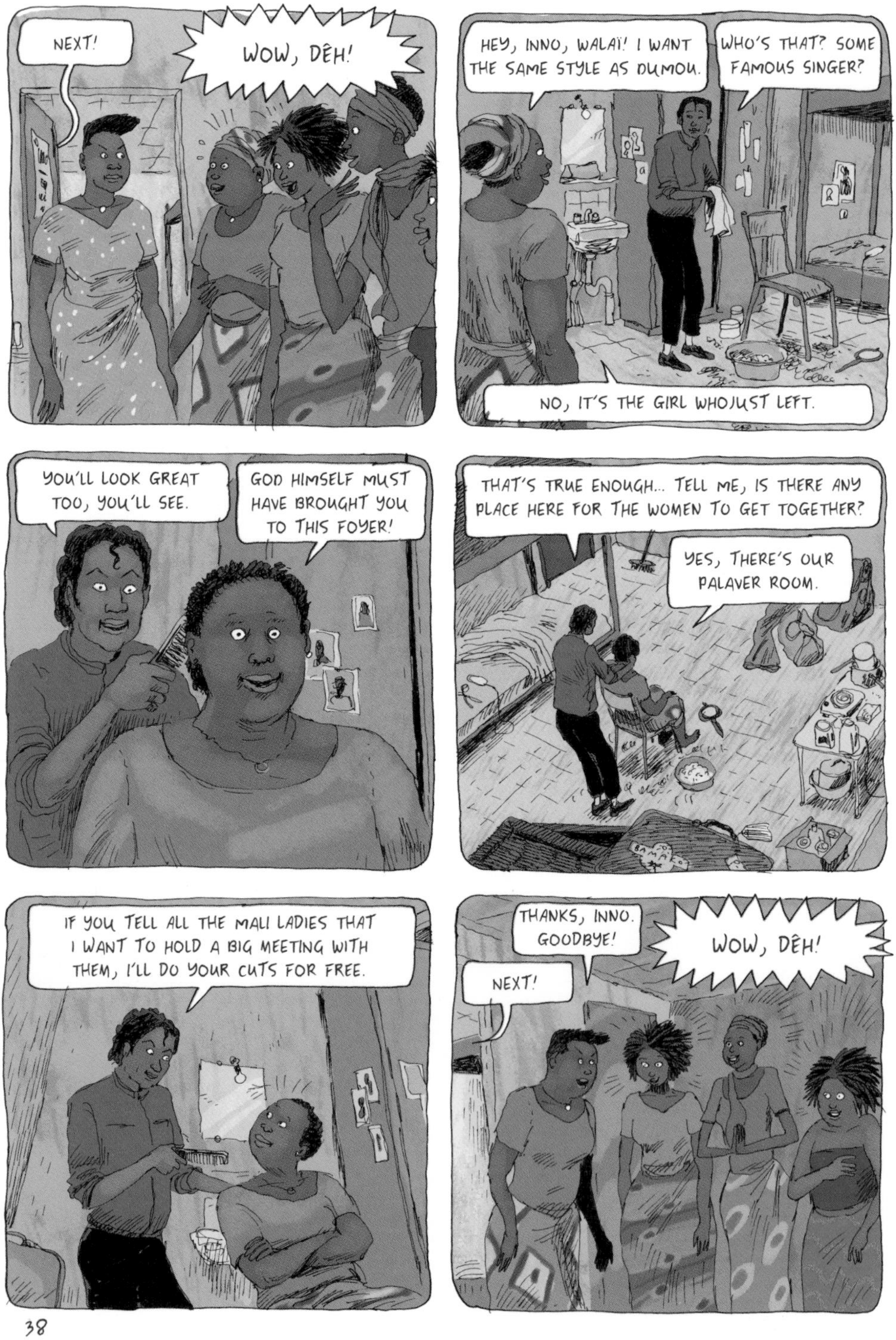
NEXT!
WOW, DÊH!
HEY, INNO, WALAÏ! I WANT THE SAME STYLE AS DUMOU.
WHO'S THAT? SOME FAMOUS SINGER?
NO, IT'S THE GIRL WHOJUST LEFT.
YOU'LL LOOK GREAT TOO, YOU'LL SEE.
GOD HIMSELF MUST HAVE BROUGHT YOU TO THIS FOYER!
THAT'S TRUE ENOUGH... TELL ME, IS THERE ANY PLACE HERE FOR THE WOMEN TO GET TOGETHER?
YES, THERE'S OUR PALAVER ROOM.
BAMAKO
IF YOU TELL ALL THE MALI LADIES THAT I WANT TO HOLD A BIG MEETING WITH THEM, I'LL DO YOUR CUTS FOR FREE.
THANKS, INNO. GOODBYE!
WOW, DÊH!
NEXT!

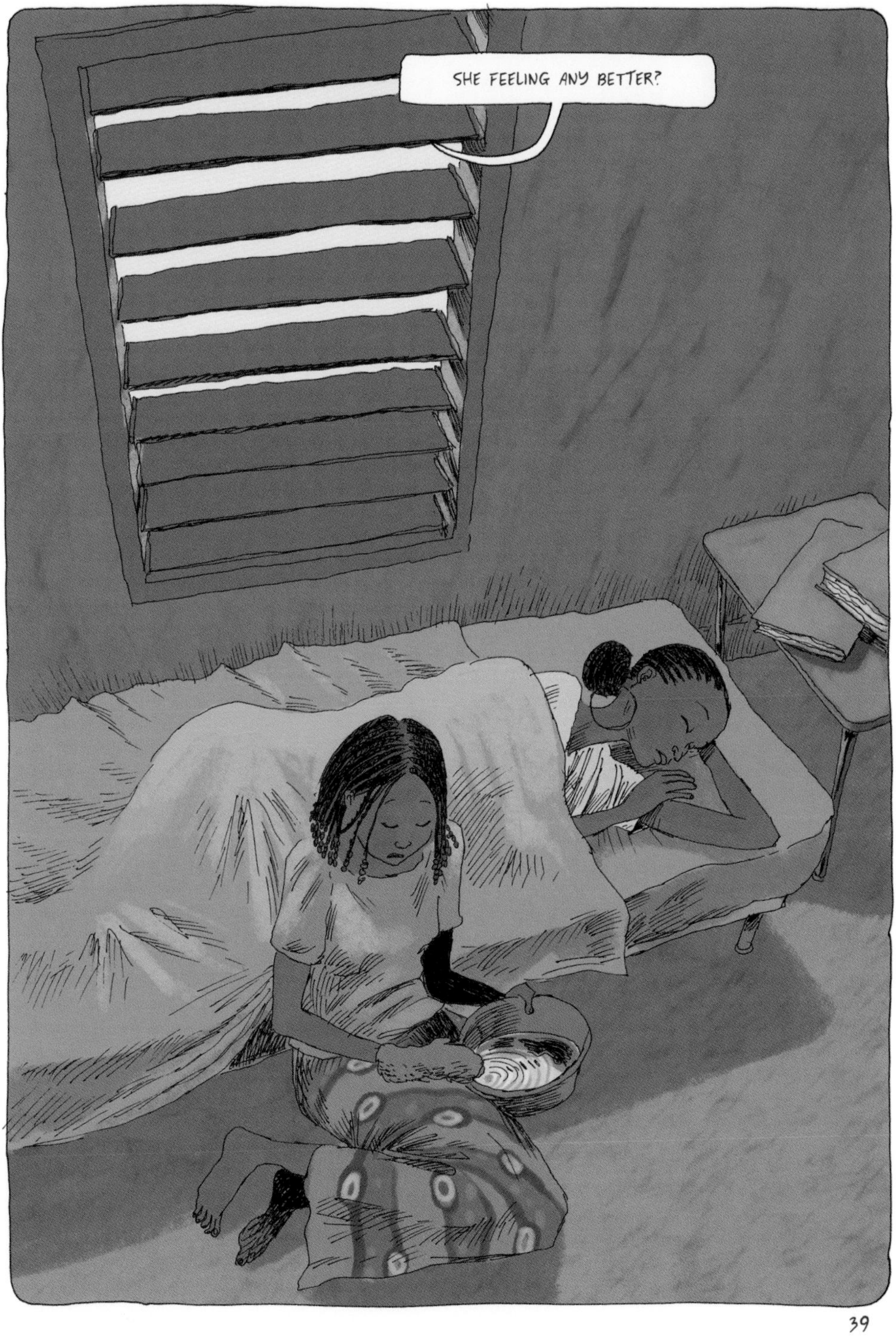
SHE FEELING ANY BETTER?

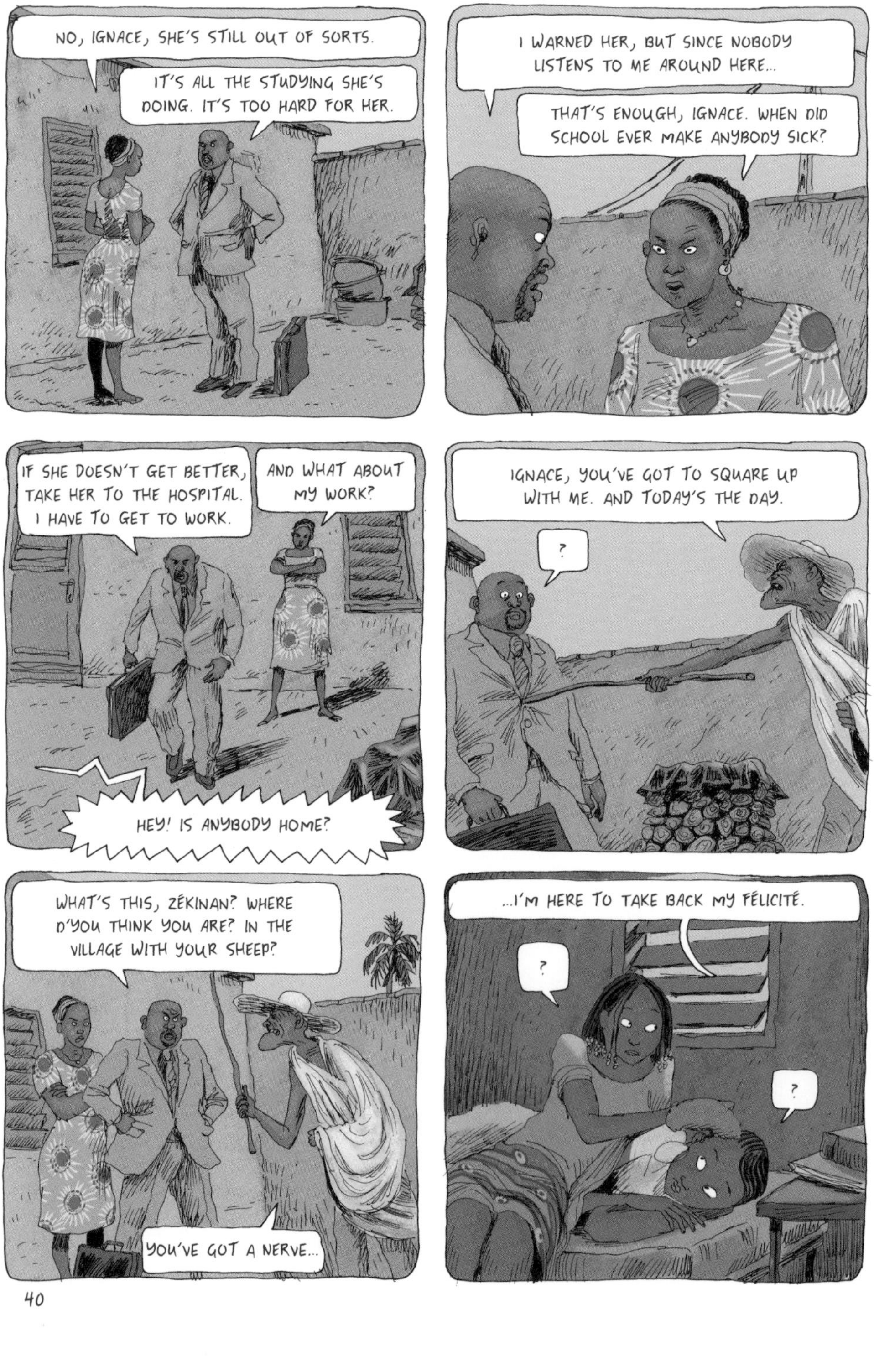

NO, IGNACE, SHE'S STILL OUT OF SORTS.
IT'S ALL THE STUDYING SHE'S DOING. IT'S TOO HARD FOR HER.
I WARNED HER, BUT SINCE NOBODY LISTENS TO ME AROUND HERE...
THAT'S ENOUGH, IGNACE. WHEN DID SCHOOL EVER MAKE ANYBODY SICK?
IF SHE DOESN'T GET BETTER, TAKE HER TO THE HOSPITAL. I HAVE TO GET TO WORK.
AND WHAT ABOUT MY WORK?
HEY! IS ANYBODY HOME?
IGNACE, YOU'VE GOT TO SQUARE UP WITH ME. AND TODAY'S THE DAY.
?
WHAT'S THIS, ZÉKINAN? WHERE D'YOU THINK YOU ARE? IN THE VILLAGE WITH YOUR SHEEP?
YOU'VE GOT A NERVE...
...I'M HERE TO TAKE BACK MY FÉLICITÉ.
?
?

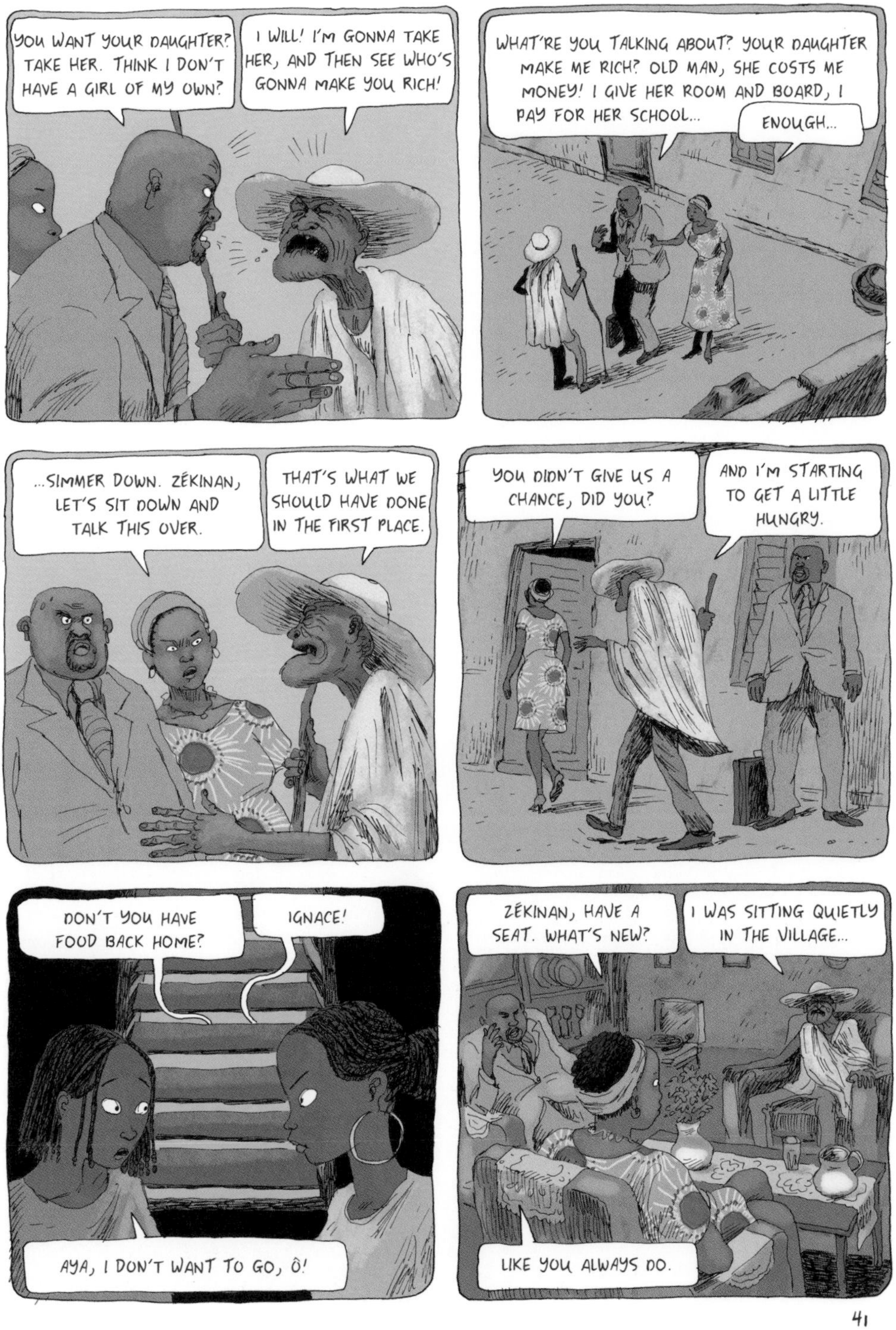
YOU WANT YOUR DAUGHTER? TAKE HER. THINK I DON'T HAVE A GIRL OF MY OWN?
I WILL! I'M GONNA TAKE HER, AND THEN SEE WHO'S GONNA MAKE YOU RICH!
WHAT'RE YOU TALKING ABOUT? YOUR DAUGHTER MAKE ME RICH? OLD MAN, SHE COSTS ME MONEY! I GIVE HER ROOM AND BOARD, I PAY FOR HER SCHOOL...
ENOUGH...
...SIMMER DOWN. ZÉKINAN, LET'S SIT DOWN AND TALK THIS OVER.
THAT'S WHAT WE SHOULD HAVE DONE IN THE FIRST PLACE.
YOU DIDN'T GIVE US A CHANCE, DID YOU?
AND I'M STARTING TO GET A LITTLE HUNGRY.
DON'T YOU HAVE FOOD BACK HOME?
IGNACE!
AYA, I DON'T WANT TO GO, Ô!
ZÉKINAN, HAVE A SEAT. WHAT'S NEW?
I WAS SITTING QUIETLY IN THE VILLAGE...
LIKE YOU ALWAYS DO.

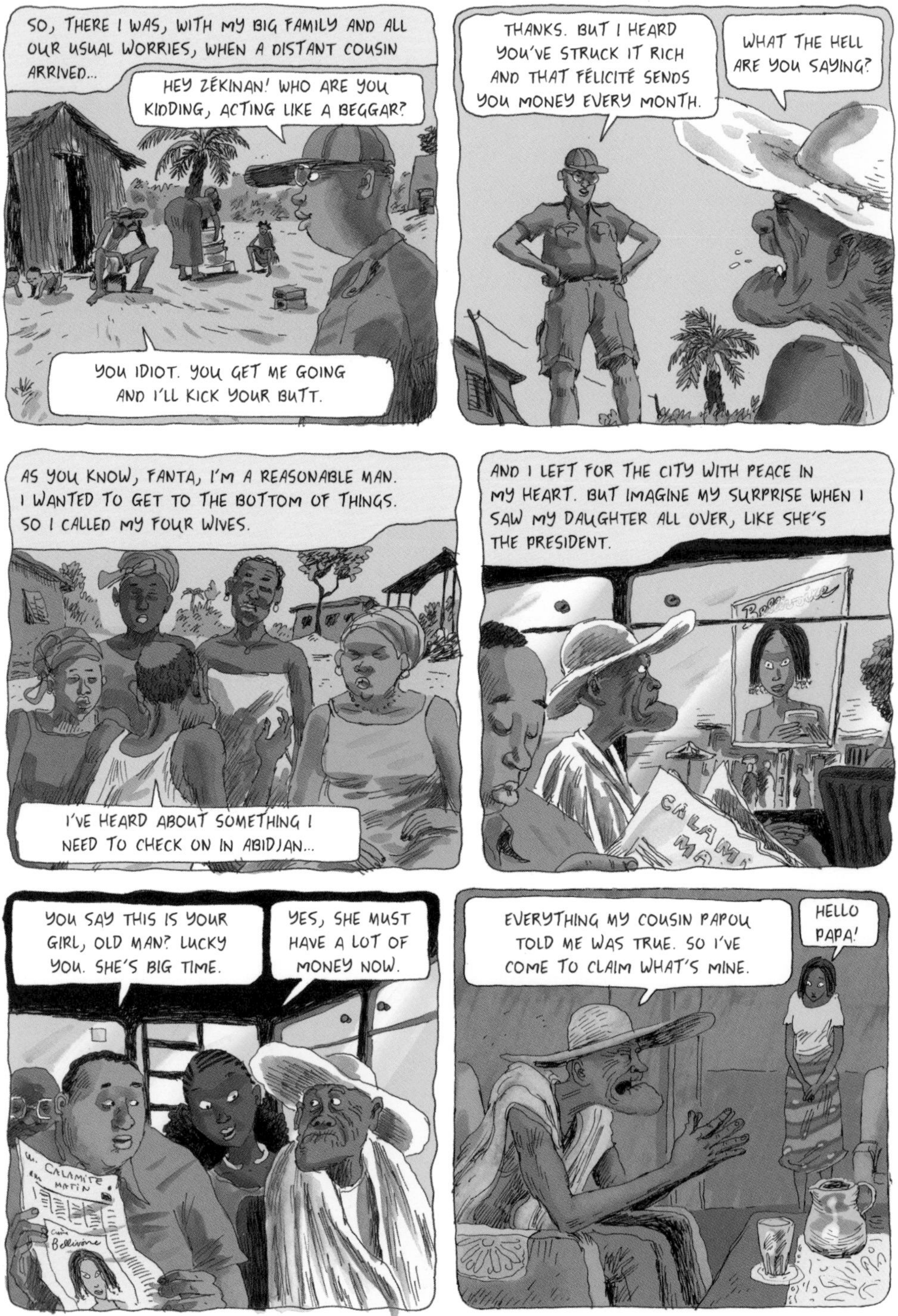
SO, THERE I WAS, WITH MY BIG FAMILY AND ALL OUR USUAL WORRIES, WHEN A DISTANT COUSIN ARRIVED...
HEY ZÉKINAN! WHO ARE YOU KIDDING, ACTING LIKE A BEGGAR?
YOU IDIOT. YOU GET ME GOING AND I'LL KICK YOUR BUTT.
THANKS. BUT I HEARD YOU'VE STRUCK IT RICH AND THAT FÉLICITÉ SENDS YOU MONEY EVERY MONTH.
WHAT THE HELL ARE YOU SAYING?
AS YOU KNOW, FANTA, I'M A REASONABLE MAN. I WANTED TO GET TO THE BOTTOM OF THINGS. SO I CALLED MY FOUR WIVES.
I'VE HEARD ABOUT SOMETHING I NEED TO CHECK ON IN ABIDJAN...
AND I LEFT FOR THE CITY WITH PEACE IN MY HEART. BUT IMAGINE MY SURPRISE WHEN I SAW MY DAUGHTER ALL OVER, LIKE SHE'S THE PRESIDENT.
YOU SAY THIS IS YOUR GIRL, OLD MAN? LUCKY YOU. SHE'S BIG TIME.
YES, SHE MUST HAVE A LOT OF MONEY NOW.
CALAMITÉ MATIN
EVERYTHING MY COUSIN PAPOU TOLD ME WAS TRUE. SO I'VE COME TO CLAIM WHAT'S MINE.
HELLO PAPA!

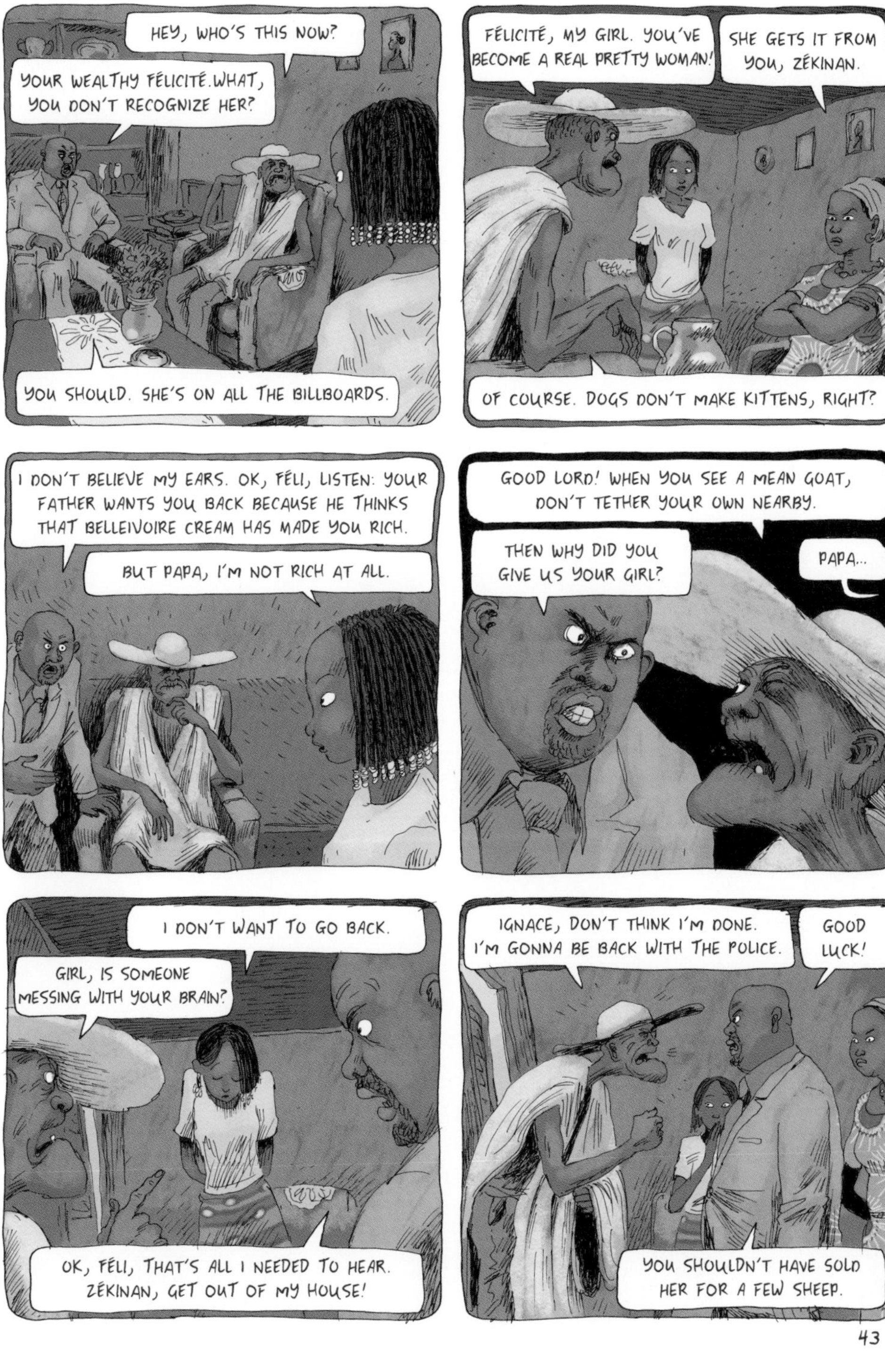
HEY, WHO'S THIS NOW?
YOUR WEALTHY FÉLICITÉ.WHAT, YOU DON'T RECOGNIZE HER?
YOU SHOULD. SHE'S ON ALL THE BILLBOARDS.
FÉLICITÉ, MY GIRL. YOU'VE BECOME A REAL PRETTY WOMAN!
SHE GETS IT FROM YOU, ZÉKINAN.
OF COURSE. DOGS DON'T MAKE KITTENS, RIGHT?
I DON'T BELIEVE MY EARS. OK, FÉLI, LISTEN: YOUR FATHER WANTS YOU BACK BECAUSE HE THINKS THAT BELLEIVOIRE CREAM HAS MADE YOU RICH.
BUT PAPA, I'M NOT RICH AT ALL.
GOOD LORD! WHEN YOU SEE A MEAN GOAT, DON'T TETHER YOUR OWN NEARBY.
THEN WHY DID YOU GIVE US YOUR GIRL?
PAPA...
I DON'T WANT TO GO BACK.
GIRL, IS SOMEONE MESSING WITH YOUR BRAIN?
OK, FÉLI, THAT'S ALL I NEEDED TO HEAR. ZÉKINAN, GET OUT OF MY HOUSE!
IGNACE, DON'T THINK I'M DONE. I'M GONNA BE BACK WITH THE POLICE.
GOOD LUCK!
YOU SHOULDN'T HAVE SOLD HER FOR A FEW SHEEP.

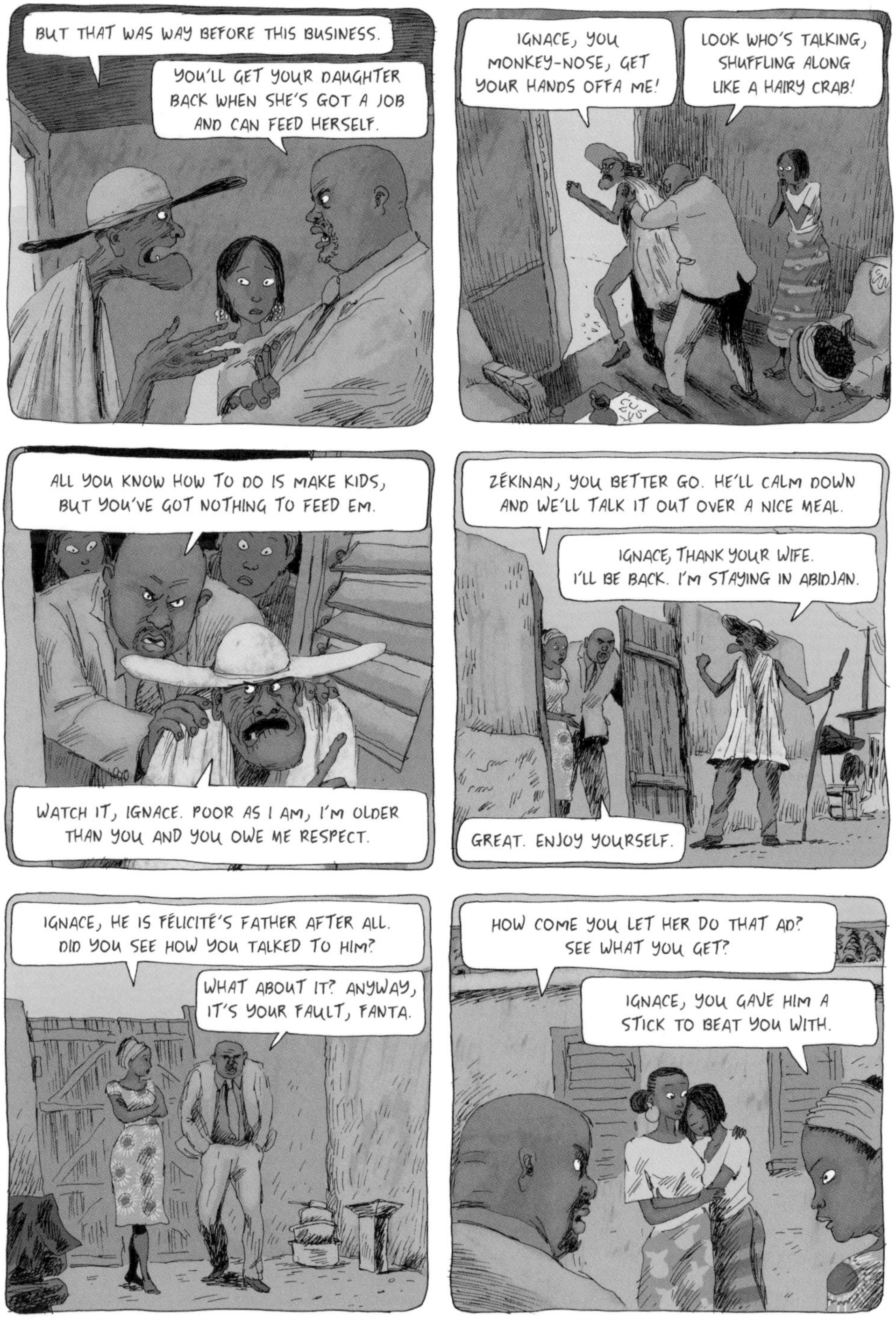
BUT THAT WAS WAY BEFORE THIS BUSINESS.
YOU'LL GET YOUR DAUGHTER BACK WHEN SHE'S GOT A JOB AND CAN FEED HERSELF.
IGNACE, YOU MONKEY-NOSE, GET YOUR HANDS OFFA ME!
LOOK WHO'S TALKING, SHUFFLING ALONG LIKE A HAIRY CRAB!
ALL YOU KNOW HOW TO DO IS MAKE KIDS, BUT YOU'VE GOT NOTHING TO FEED EM.
WATCH IT, IGNACE. POOR AS I AM, I'M OLDER THAN YOU AND YOU OWE ME RESPECT.
ZÉKINAN, YOU BETTER GO. HE'LL CALM DOWN AND WE'LL TALK IT OUT OVER A NICE MEAL.
IGNACE, THANK YOUR WIFE. I'LL BE BACK. I'M STAYING IN ABIDJAN.
GREAT. ENJOY YOURSELF.
IGNACE, HE IS FÉLICITÉ'S FATHER AFTER ALL. DID YOU SEE HOW YOU TALKED TO HIM?
WHAT ABOUT IT? ANYWAY, IT'S YOUR FAULT, FANTA.
HOW COME YOU LET HER DO THAT AD? SEE WHAT YOU GET?
IGNACE, YOU GAVE HIM A STICK TO BEAT YOU WITH.

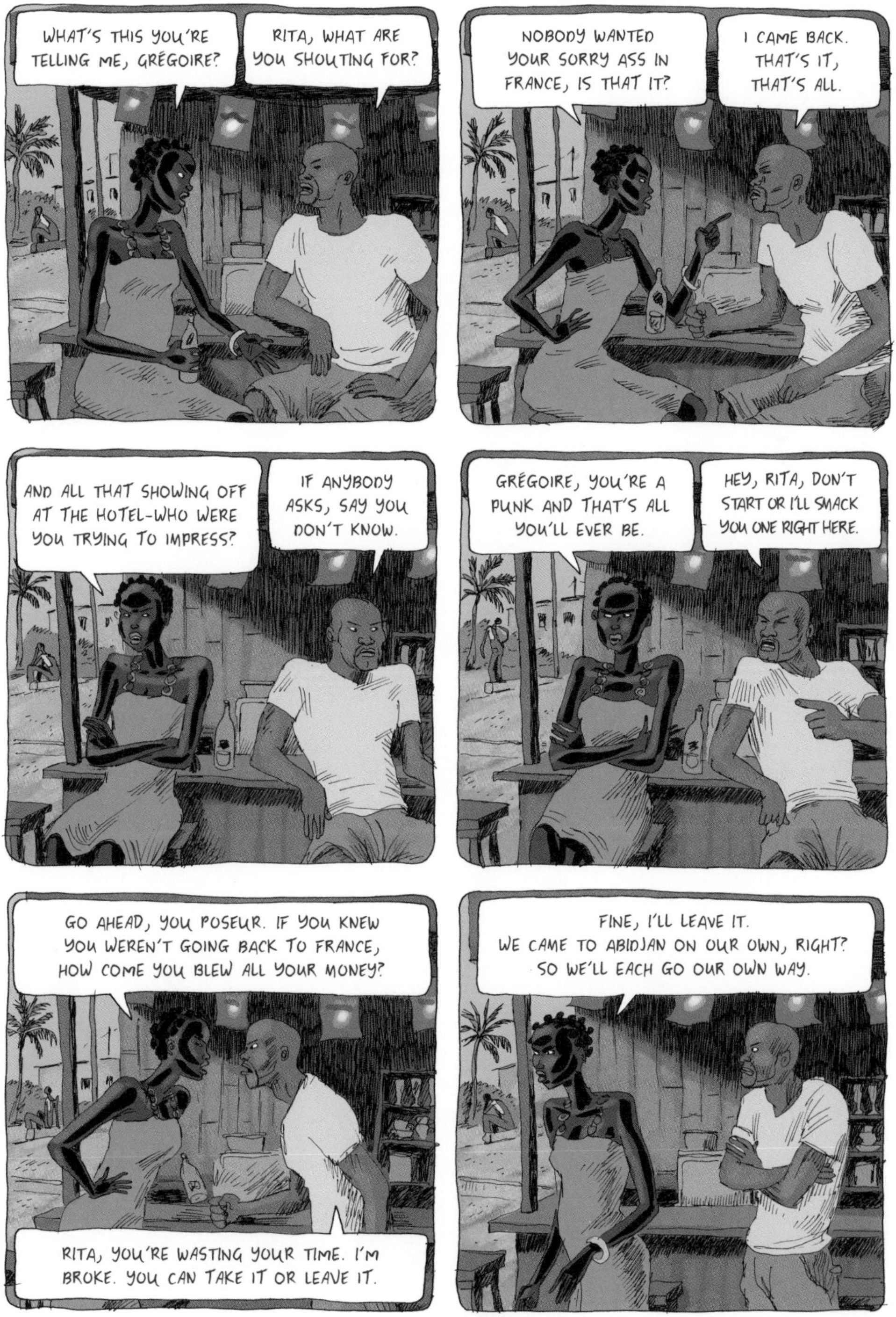
WHAT'S THIS YOU'RE TELLING ME, GRÉGOIRE?
RITA, WHAT ARE YOU SHOUTING FOR?
NOBODY WANTED YOUR SORRY ASS IN FRANCE, IS THAT IT?
I CAME BACK. THAT'S IT, THAT'S ALL.
AND ALL THAT SHOWING OFF AT THE HOTEL-WHO WERE YOU TRYING TO IMPRESS?
IF ANYBODY ASKS, SAY YOU DON'T KNOW.
GRÉGOIRE, YOU'RE A PUNK AND THAT'S ALL YOU'LL EVER BE.
HEY, RITA, DON'T START OR I'LL SMACK YOU ONE RIGHT HERE.
GO AHEAD, YOU POSEUR. IF YOU KNEW YOU WEREN'T GOING BACK TO FRANCE, HOW COME YOU BLEW ALL YOUR MONEY?
RITA, YOU'RE WASTING YOUR TIME. I'M BROKE. YOU CAN TAKE IT OR LEAVE IT.
FINE, I'LL LEAVE IT. WE CAME TO ABIDJAN ON OUR OWN, RIGHT? SO WE'LL EACH GO OUR OWN WAY.

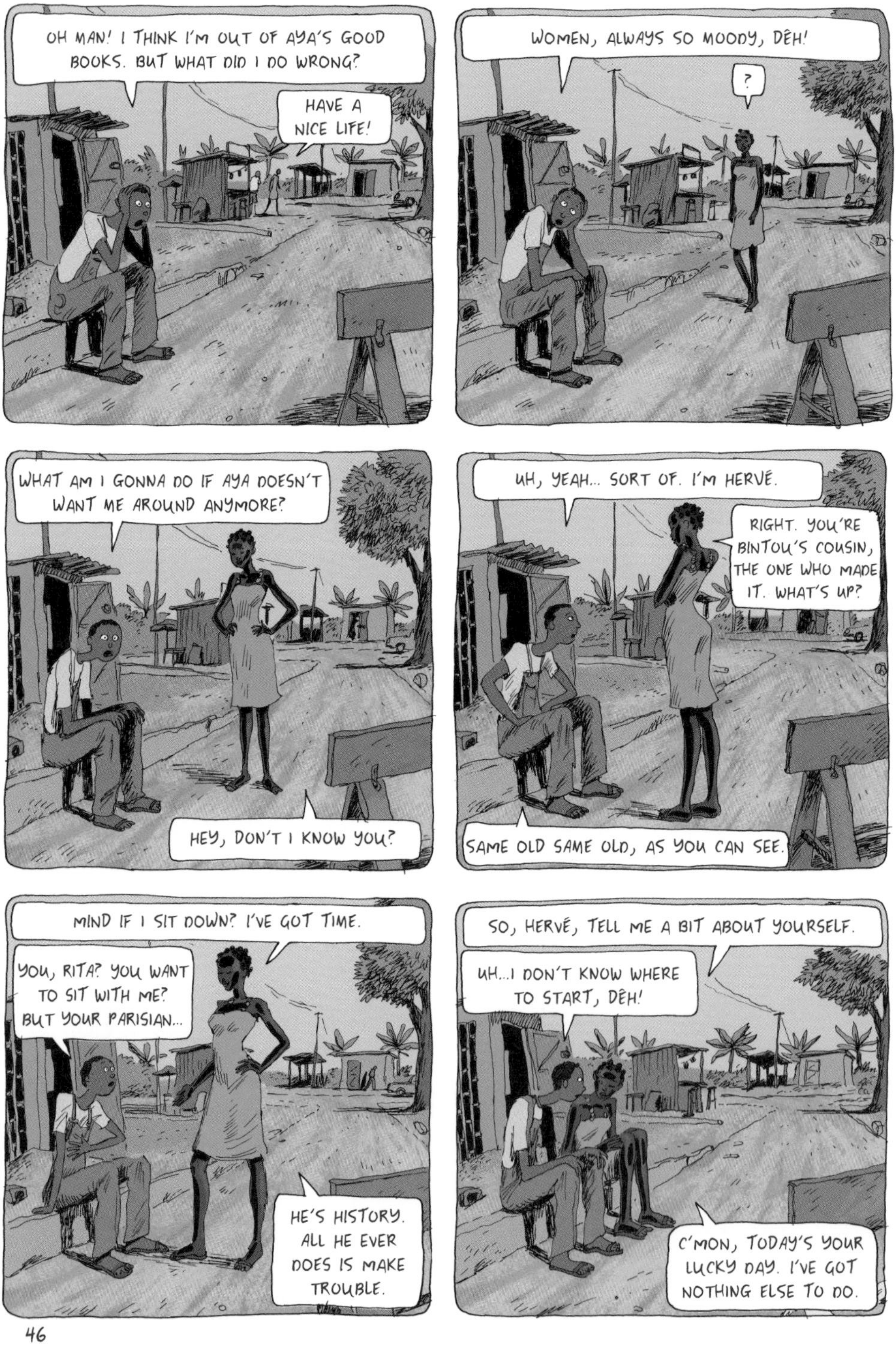
OH MAN! I THINK I'M OUT OF AYA'S GOOD BOOKS. BUT WHAT DID I DO WRONG?
HAVE A NICE LIFE!
WOMEN, ALWAYS SO MOODY, DÊH!
?
WHAT AM I GONNA DO IF AYA DOESN'T WANT ME AROUND ANYMORE?
HEY, DON'T I KNOW YOU?
UH, YEAH... SORT OF. I'M HERVÉ.
RIGHT. YOU'RE BINTOU'S COUSIN, THE ONE WHO MADE IT. WHAT'S UP?
SAME OLD SAME OLD, AS YOU CAN SEE.
MIND IF I SIT DOWN? I'VE GOT TIME.
YOU, RITA? YOU WANT TO SIT WITH ME? BUT YOUR PARISIAN...
HE'S HISTORY. ALL HE EVER DOES IS MAKE TROUBLE.
SO, HERVÉ, TELL ME A BIT ABOUT YOURSELF.
UH...I DON'T KNOW WHERE TO START, DÊH!
C'MON, TODAY'S YOUR LUCKY DAY. I'VE GOT NOTHING ELSE TO DO.

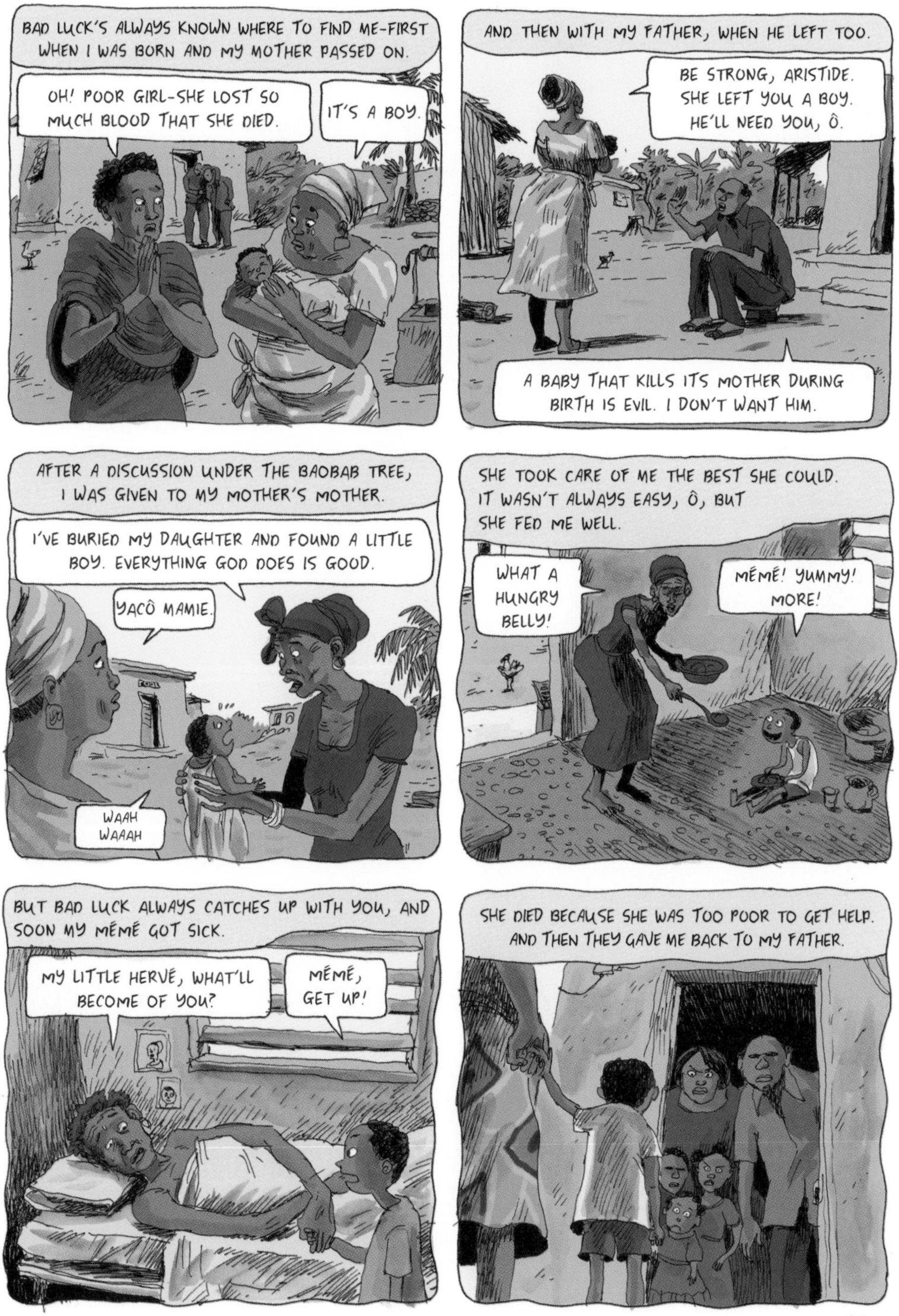
BAD LUCK'S ALWAYS KNOWN WHERE TO FIND ME-FIRST WHEN I WAS BORN AND MY MOTHER PASSED ON.
OH! POOR GIRL-SHE LOST SO MUCH BLOOD THAT SHE DIED.
IT'S A BOY.
AND THEN WITH MY FATHER, WHEN HE LEFT TOO.
BE STRONG, ARISTIDE. SHE LEFT YOU A BOY. HE'LL NEED YOU, Ô.
A BABY THAT KILLS ITS MOTHER DURING BIRTH IS EVIL. I DON'T WANT HIM.
AFTER A DISCUSSION UNDER THE BAOBAB TREE, I WAS GIVEN TO MY MOTHER'S MOTHER.
I'VE BURIED MY DAUGHTER AND FOUND A LITTLE BOY. EVERYTHING GOD DOES IS GOOD.
YACÔ MAMIE.
WAAH WAAAH
SHE TOOK CARE OF ME THE BEST SHE COULD. IT WASN'T ALWAYS EASY, Ô, BUT SHE FED ME WELL.
WHAT A HUNGRY BELLY!
MÉMÉ! YUMMY! MORE!
BUT BAD LUCK ALWAYS CATCHES UP WITH YOU, AND SOON MY MÉMÉ GOT SICK.
MY LITTLE HERVÉ, WHAT'LL BECOME OF YOU?
MÉMÉ, GET UP!
SHE DIED BECAUSE SHE WAS TOO POOR TO GET HELP. AND THEN THEY GAVE ME BACK TO MY FATHER.

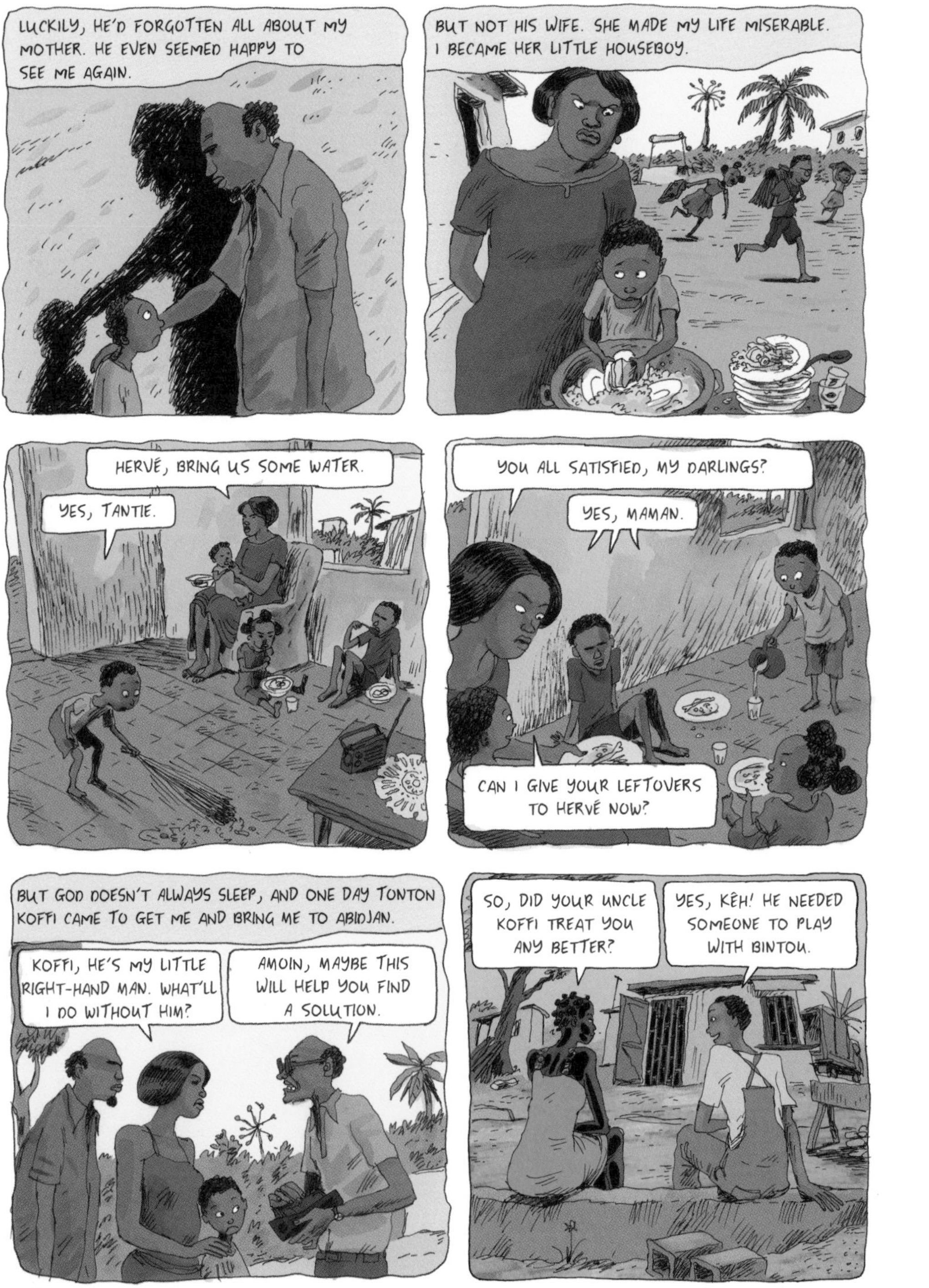
LUCKILY, HE'D FORGOTTEN ALL ABOUT MY MOTHER. HE EVEN SEEMED HAPPY TO SEE ME AGAIN.
BUT NOT HIS WIFE. SHE MADE MY LIFE MISERABLE. I BECAME HER LITTLE HOUSEBOY.
HERVÉ, BRING US SOME WATER.
YES, TANTIE.
YOU ALL SATISFIED, MY DARLINGS?
YES, MAMAN.
CAN I GIVE YOUR LEFTOVERS TO HERVÉ NOW?
BUT GOD DOESN'T ALWAYS SLEEP, AND ONE DAY TONTON KOFFI CAME TO GET ME AND BRING ME TO ABIDJAN.
KOFFI, HE'S MY LITTLE RIGHT-HAND MAN. WHAT'LL I DO WITHOUT HIM?
AMOIN, MAYBE THIS WILL HELP YOU FIND A SOLUTION.
SO, DID YOUR UNCLE KOFFI TREAT YOU ANY BETTER?
YES, KÊH! HE NEEDED SOMEONE TO PLAY WITH BINTOU.

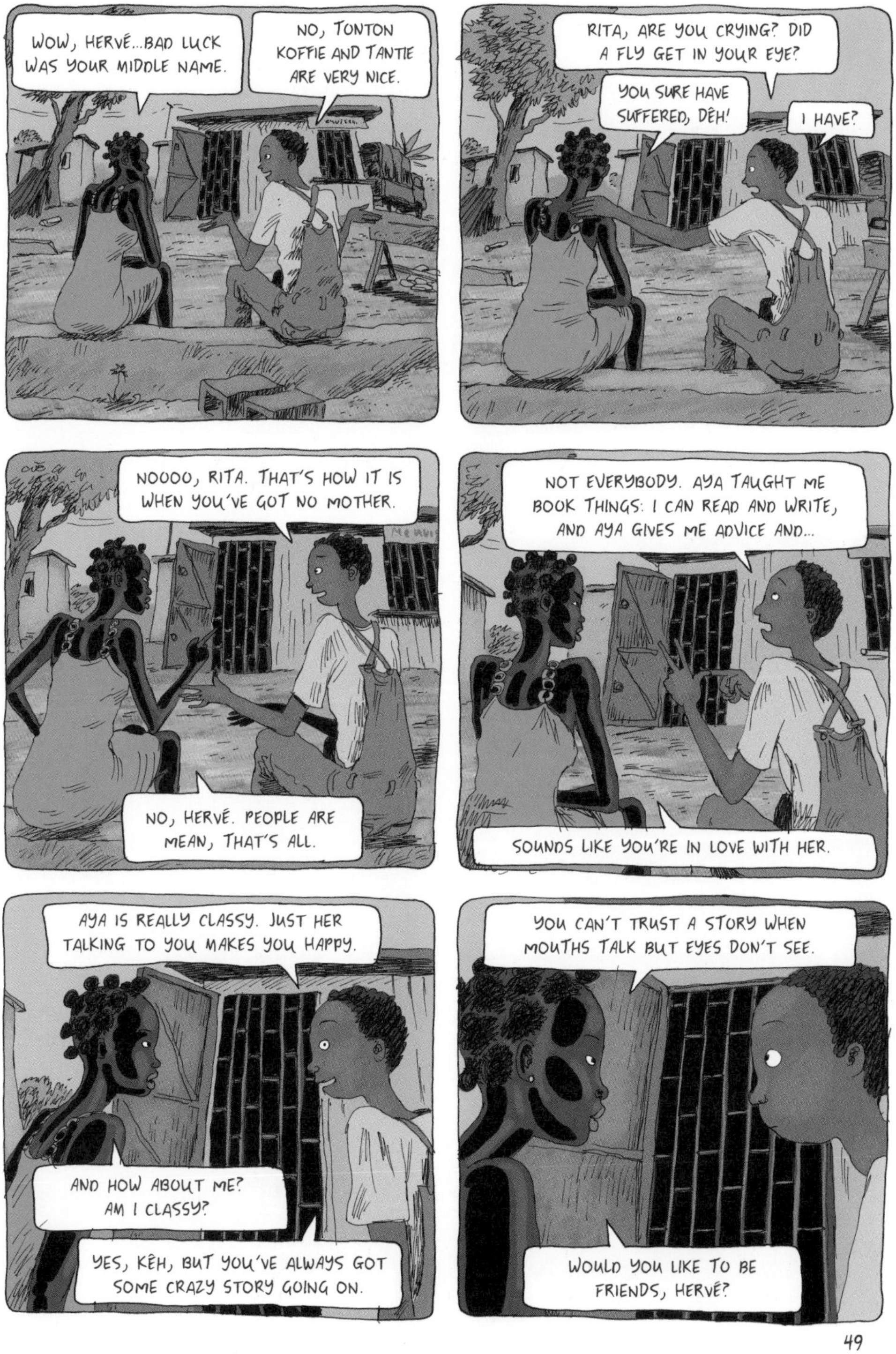
WOW, HERVÉ...BAD LUCK WAS YOUR MIDDLE NAME.
NO, TONTON KOFFIE AND TANTIE ARE VERY NICE.
RITA, ARE YOU CRYING? DID A FLY GET IN YOUR EYE?
YOU SURE HAVE SUFFERED, DÊH!
I HAVE?
NOOOO, RITA. THAT'S HOW IT IS WHEN YOU'VE GOT NO MOTHER.
NO, HERVÉ. PEOPLE ARE MEAN, THAT'S ALL.
NOT EVERYBODY. AYA TAUGHT ME BOOK THINGS: I CAN READ AND WRITE, AND AYA GIVES ME ADVICE AND...
SOUNDS LIKE YOU'RE IN LOVE WITH HER.
AYA IS REALLY CLASSY. JUST HER TALKING TO YOU MAKES YOU HAPPY.
AND HOW ABOUT ME? AM I CLASSY?
YES, KÊH, BUT YOU'VE ALWAYS GOT SOME CRAZY STORY GOING ON.
YOU CAN'T TRUST A STORY WHEN MOUTHS TALK BUT EYES DON'T SEE.
WOULD YOU LIKE TO BE FRIENDS, HERVÉ?

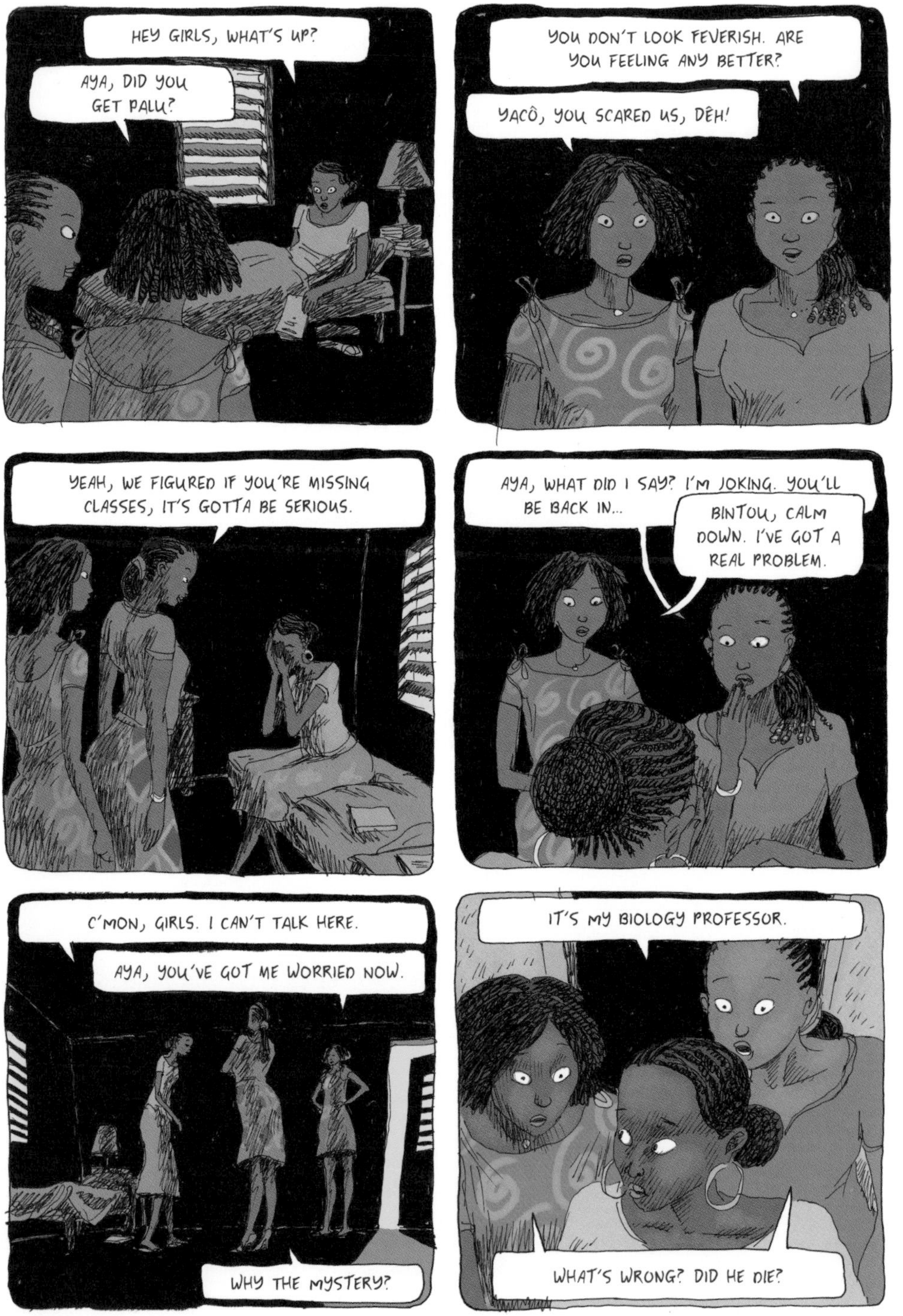
HEY GIRLS, WHAT'S UP?
AYA, DID YOU GET PALU?
YOU DON'T LOOK FEVERISH. ARE YOU FEELING ANY BETTER?
YACÔ, YOU SCARED US, DÊH!
YEAH, WE FIGURED IF YOU'RE MISSING CLASSES, IT'S GOTTA BE SERIOUS.
AYA, WHAT DID I SAY? I'M JOKING. YOU'LL BE BACK IN...
BINTOU, CALM DOWN. I'VE GOT A REAL PROBLEM.
C'MON, GIRLS. I CAN'T TALK HERE.
AYA, YOU'VE GOT ME WORRIED NOW.
WHY THE MYSTERY?
IT'S MY BIOLOGY PROFESSOR.
WHAT'S WRONG? DID HE DIE?

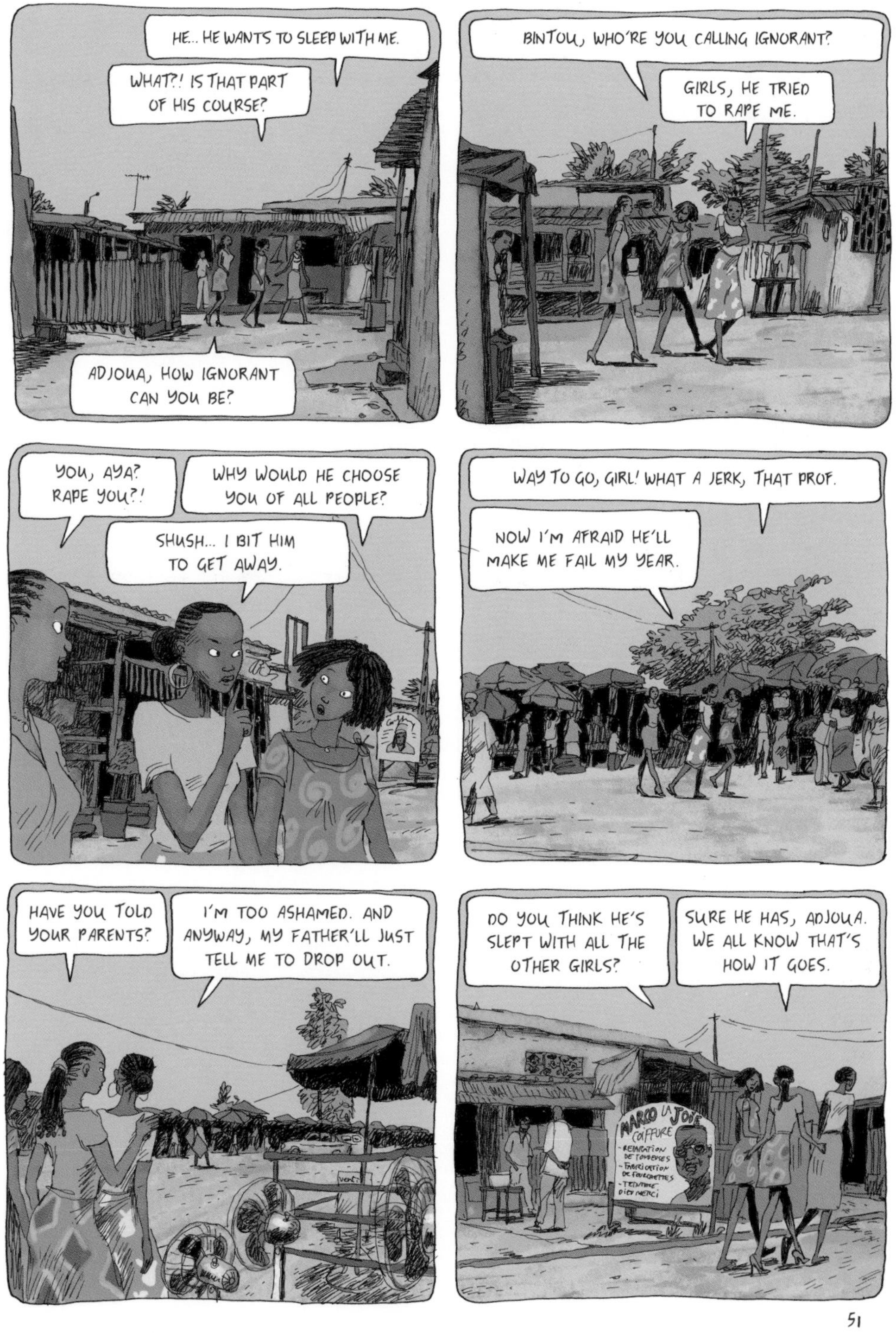
HE... HE WANTS TO SLEEP WITH ME.
WHAT?! IS THAT PART OF HIS COURSE?
ADJOUA, HOW IGNORANT CAN YOU BE?
BINTOU, WHO'RE YOU CALLING IGNORANT?
GIRLS, HE TRIED TO RAPE ME.
YOU, AYA? RAPE YOU?!
WHY WOULD HE CHOOSE YOU OF ALL PEOPLE?
SHUSH... I BIT HIM TO GET AWAY.
WAY TO GO, GIRL! WHAT A JERK, THAT PROF.
NOW I'M AFRAID HE'LL MAKE ME FAIL MY YEAR.
HAVE YOU TOLD YOUR PARENTS?
I'M TOO ASHAMED. AND ANYWAY, MY FATHER'LL JUST TELL ME TO DROP OUT.
DO YOU THINK HE'S SLEPT WITH ALL THE OTHER GIRLS?
SURE HE HAS, ADJOUA. WE ALL KNOW THAT'S HOW IT GOES.
MARCO LA JOIE
COIFFURE

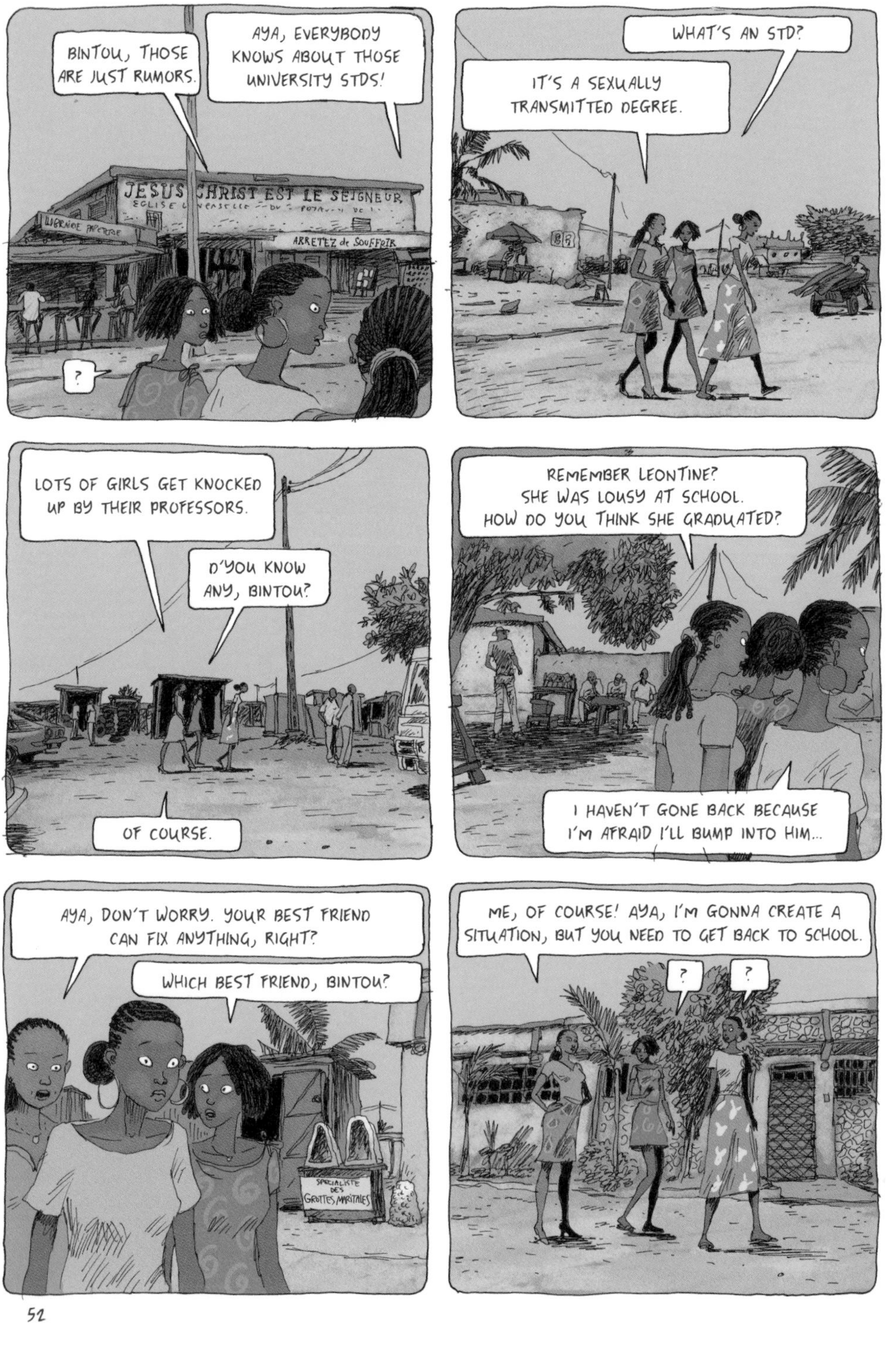
BINTOU, THOSE ARE JUST RUMORS.
AYA, EVERYBODY KNOWS ABOUT THOSE UNIVERSITY STDS!
JESUS CHRIST EST LE SEIGNEUR
ARRETEZ de SOUFFRIR
?
WHAT'S AN STD?
IT'S A SEXUALLY TRANSMITTED DEGREE.
LOTS OF GIRLS GET KNOCKED UP BY THEIR PROFESSORS.
D'YOU KNOW ANY, BINTOU?
OF COURSE.
REMEMBER LEONTINE? SHE WAS LOUSY AT SCHOOL. HOW DO YOU THINK SHE GRADUATED?
I HAVEN'T GONE BACK BECAUSE I'M AFRAID I'LL BUMP INTO HIM...
AYA, DON'T WORRY. YOUR BEST FRIEND CAN FIX ANYTHING, RIGHT?
WHICH BEST FRIEND, BINTOU?
SPECIALISTE DES GROTTES MARITALES
ME, OF COURSE! AYA, I'M GONNA CREATE A SITUATION, BUT YOU NEED TO GET BACK TO SCHOOL.
?
?

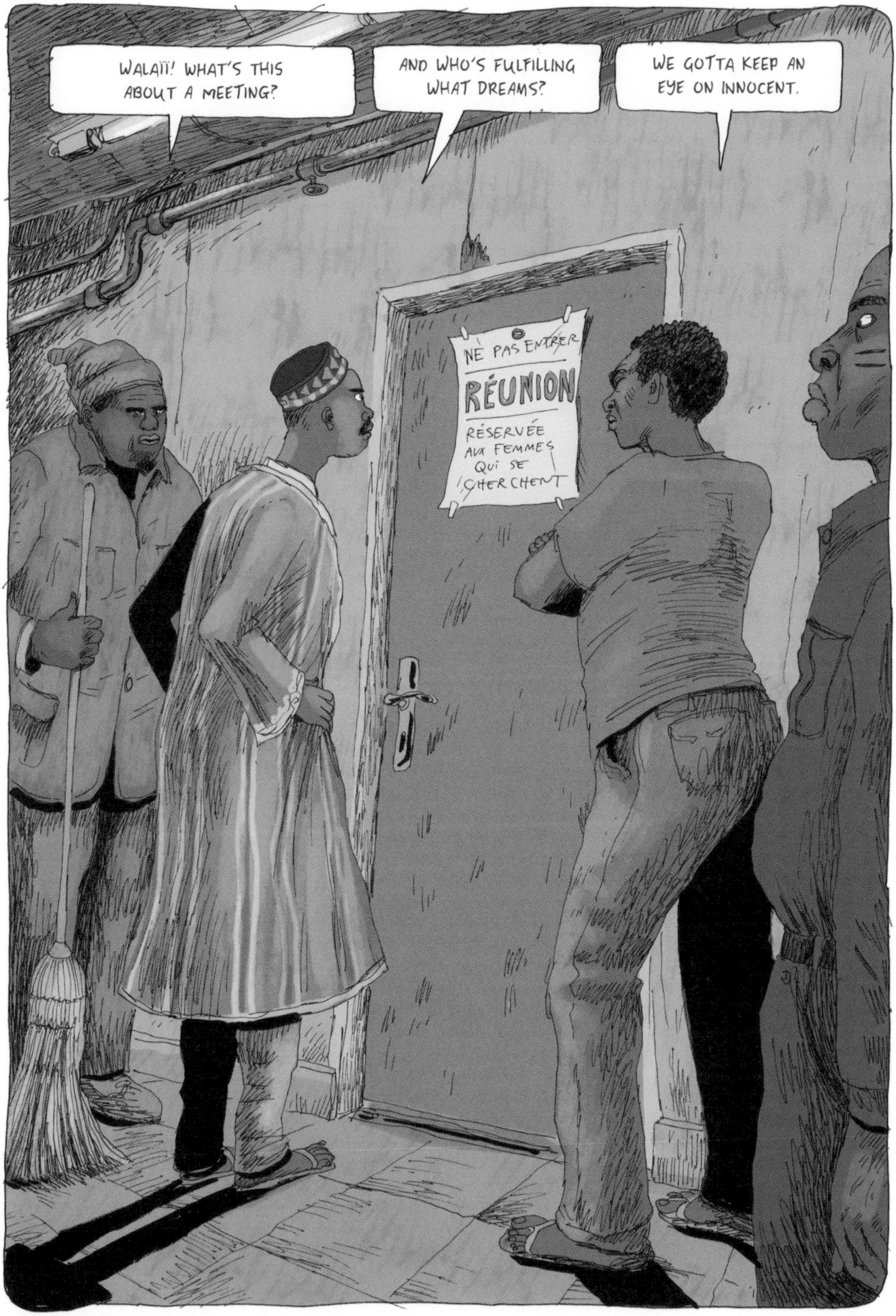
WALAÏÏ! WHAT'S THIS ABOUT A MEETING?
AND WHO'S FULFILLING WHAT DREAMS?
WE GOTTA KEEP AN EYE ON INNOCENT.
NE PAS ENTRER
RÉUNION
RÉSERVÉE AUX FEMMES QUI SE CHERCHENT
SIGN: DO NOT ENTER - MEETING - RESERVED FOR WOMEN WHO WANT TO GET AHEAD

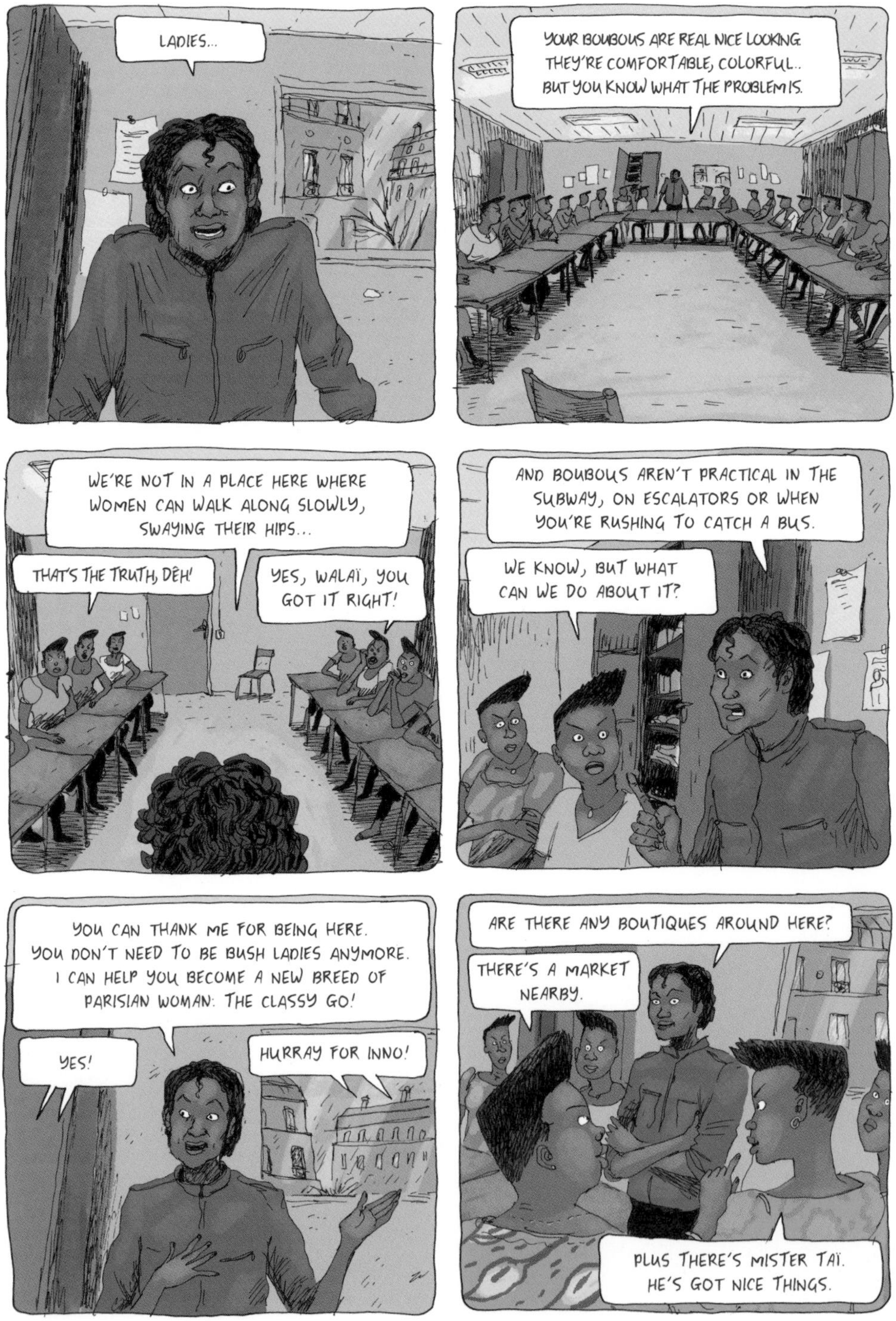
LADIES...
YOUR BOUBOUS ARE REAL NICE LOOKING. THEY'RE COMFORTABLE, COLORFUL.. BUT YOU KNOW WHAT THE PROBLEM IS.
WE'RE NOT IN A PLACE HERE WHERE WOMEN CAN WALK ALONG SLOWLY, SWAYING THEIR HIPS...
THAT'S THE TRUTH, DÊH!
YES, WALAÏ, YOU GOT IT RIGHT!
AND BOUBOUS AREN'T PRACTICAL IN THE SUBWAY, ON ESCALATORS OR WHEN YOU'RE RUSHING TO CATCH A BUS.
WE KNOW, BUT WHAT CAN WE DO ABOUT IT?
YOU CAN THANK ME FOR BEING HERE. YOU DON'T NEED TO BE BUSH LADIES ANYMORE. I CAN HELP YOU BECOME A NEW BREED OF PARISIAN WOMAN: THE CLASSY GO!
YES!
HURRAY FOR INNO!
ARE THERE ANY BOUTIQUES AROUND HERE?
THERE'S A MARKET NEARBY.
PLUS THERE'S MISTER TAÏ. HE'S GOT NICE THINGS.

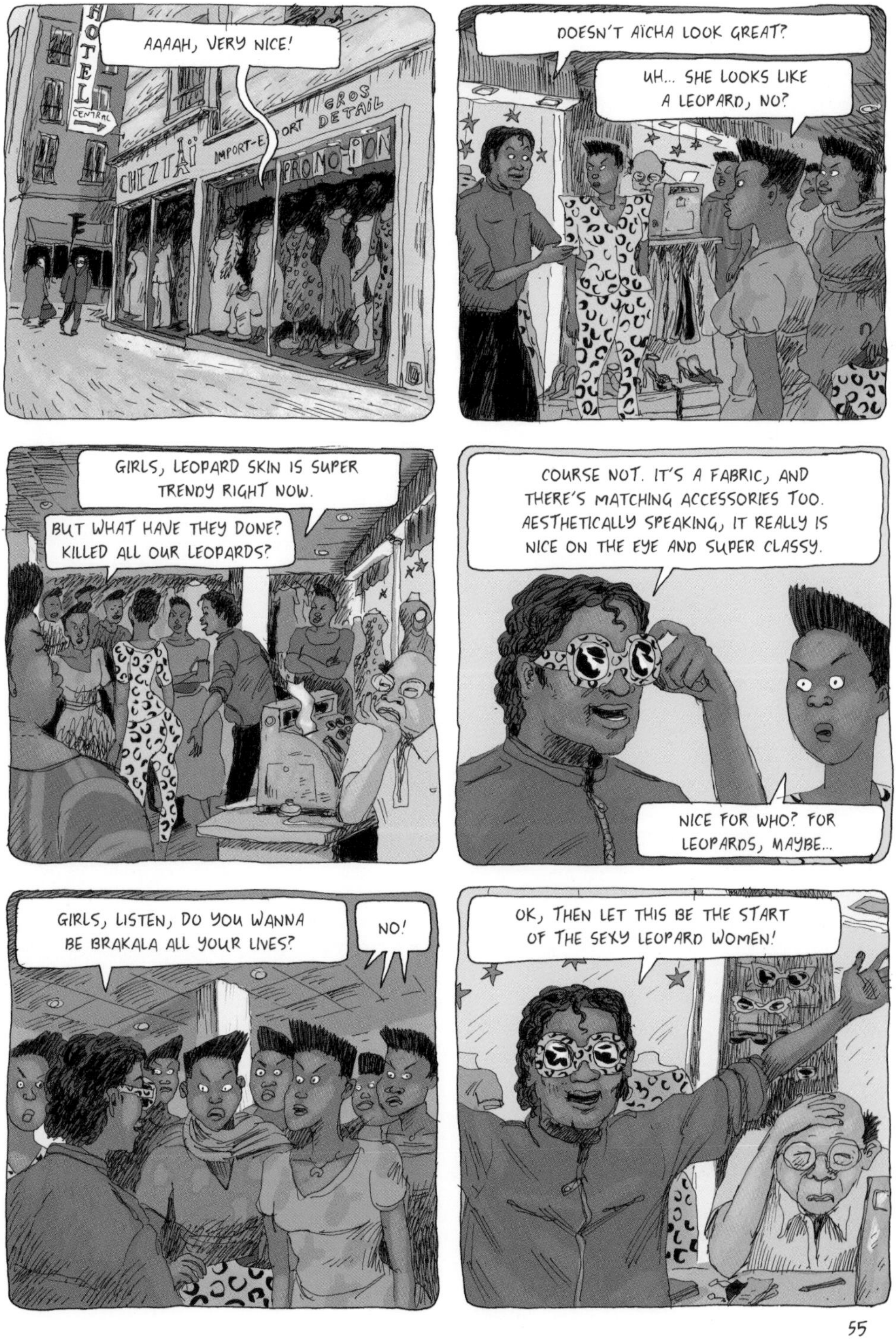
HOTEL
CENTRAL
CHEZ TAÏ
IMPORT-EXPORT
GROS DETAIL
PROMOTION
AAAAH, VERY NICE!
DOESN'T AÏCHA LOOK GREAT?
UH... SHE LOOKS LIKE A LEOPARD, NO?
GIRLS, LEOPARD SKIN IS SUPER TRENDY RIGHT NOW.
BUT WHAT HAVE THEY DONE? KILLED ALL OUR LEOPARDS?
COURSE NOT. IT'S A FABRIC, AND THERE'S MATCHING ACCESSORIES TOO. AESTHETICALLY SPEAKING, IT REALLY IS NICE ON THE EYE AND SUPER CLASSY.
NICE FOR WHO? FOR LEOPARDS, MAYBE...
GIRLS, LISTEN, DO YOU WANNA BE BRAKALA ALL YOUR LIVES?
NO!
OK, THEN LET THIS BE THE START OF THE SEXY LEOPARD WOMEN!

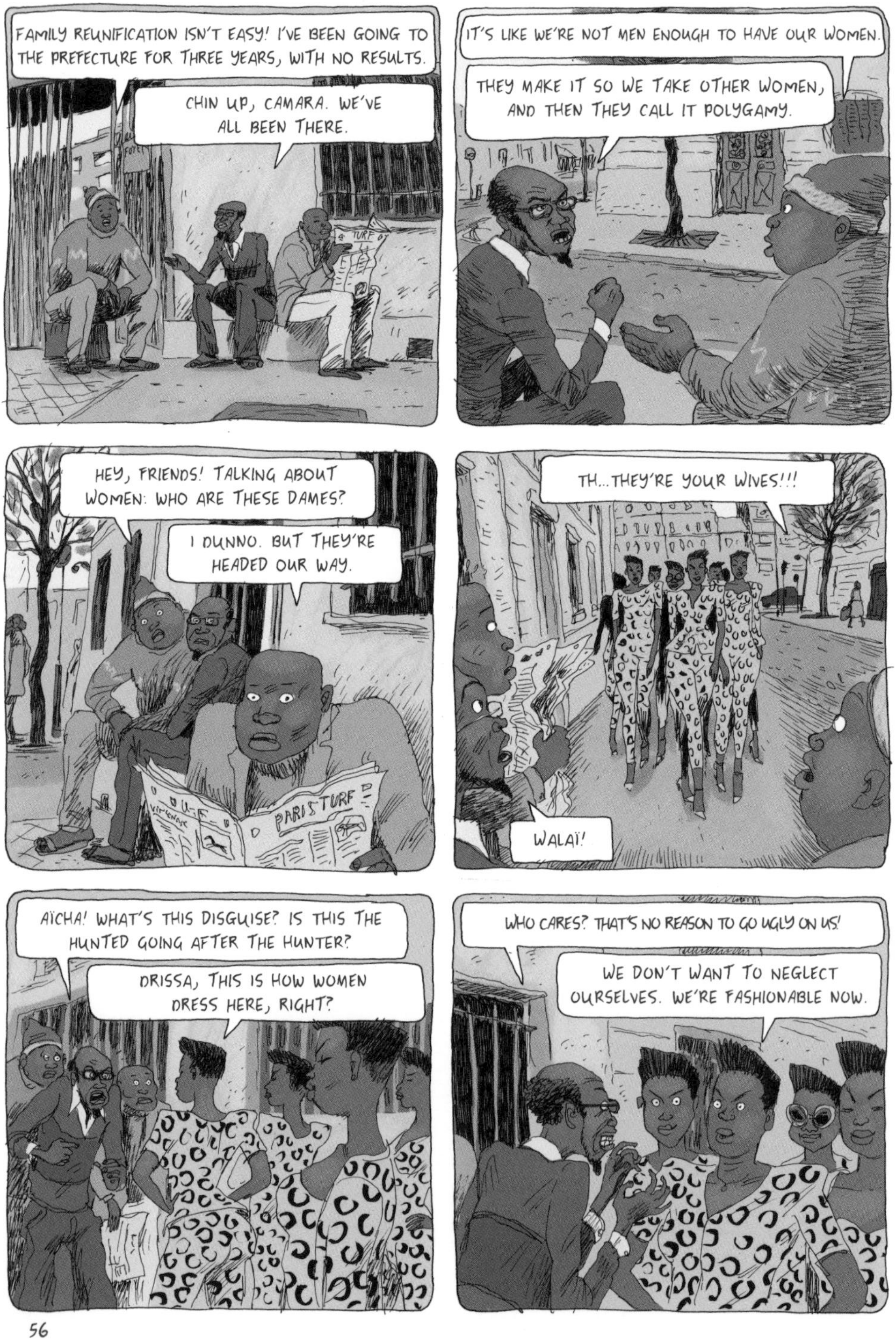
FAMILY REUNIFICATION ISN'T EASY! I'VE BEEN GOING TO THE PREFECTURE FOR THREE YEARS, WITH NO RESULTS.
CHIN UP, CAMARA. WE'VE ALL BEEN THERE.
IT'S LIKE WE'RE NOT MEN ENOUGH TO HAVE OUR WOMEN.
THEY MAKE IT SO WE TAKE OTHER WOMEN, AND THEN THEY CALL IT POLYGAMY.
HEY, FRIENDS! TALKING ABOUT WOMEN: WHO ARE THESE DAMES?
I DUNNO. BUT THEY'RE HEADED OUR WAY.
PARIS TURF
TH... THEY'RE YOUR WIVES!!!
WALAÏ!
AÏCHA! WHAT'S THIS DISGUISE? IS THIS THE HUNTED GOING AFTER THE HUNTER?
DRISSA, THIS IS HOW WOMEN DRESS HERE, RIGHT?
WHO CARES? THAT'S NO REASON TO GO UGLY ON US!
WE DON'T WANT TO NEGLECT OURSELVES. WE'RE FASHIONABLE NOW.

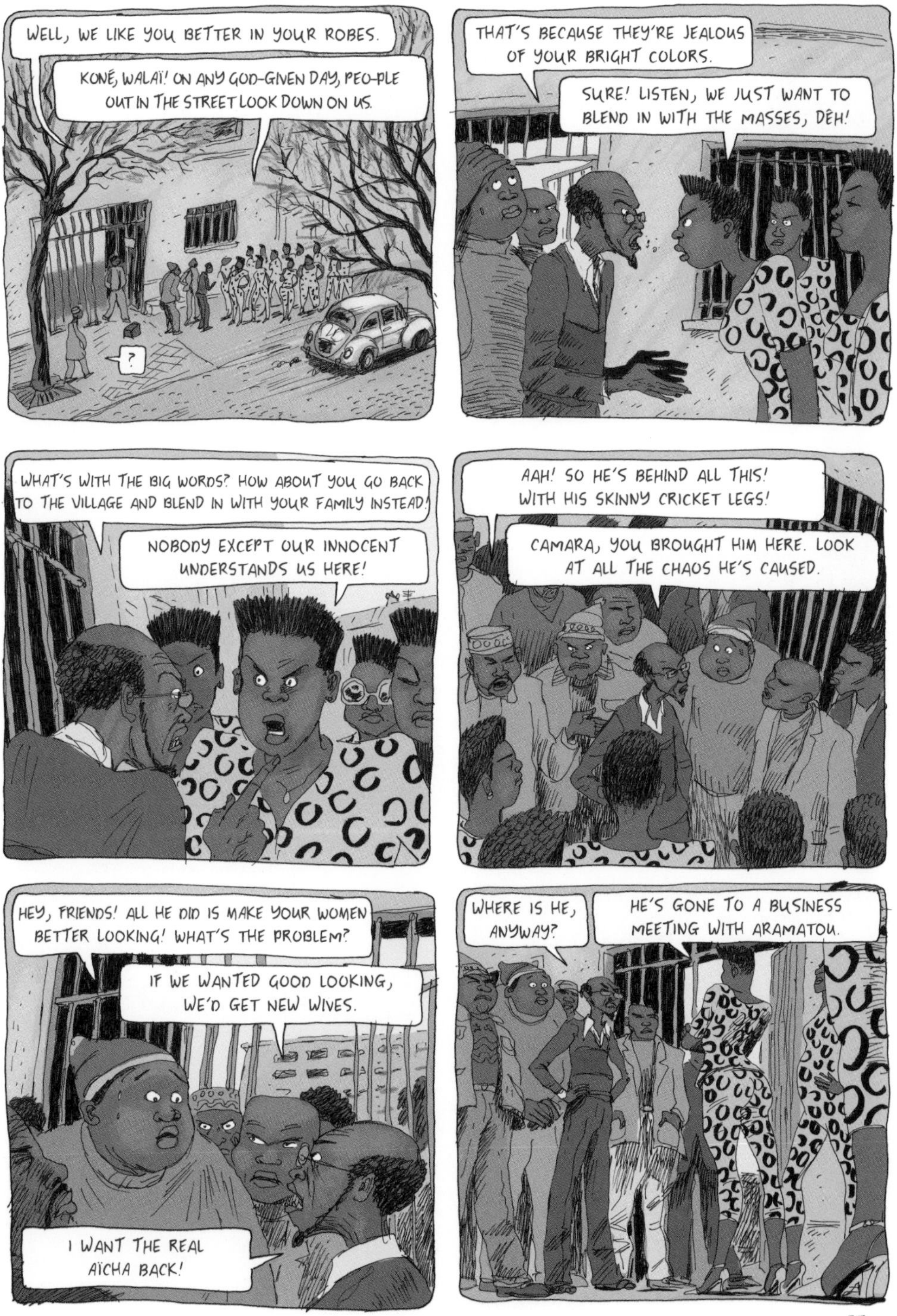

WELL, WE LIKE YOU BETTER IN YOUR ROBES.
KONÉ, WALAÏ! ON ANY GOD-GIVEN DAY, PEO-PLE OUT IN THE STREET LOOK DOWN ON US.
?
THAT'S BECAUSE THEY'RE JEALOUS OF YOUR BRIGHT COLORS.
SURE! LISTEN, WE JUST WANT TO BLEND IN WITH THE MASSES, DÊH!
WHAT'S WITH THE BIG WORDS? HOW ABOUT YOU GO BACK TO THE VILLAGE AND BLEND IN WITH YOUR FAMILY INSTEAD!
NOBODY EXCEPT OUR INNOCENT UNDERSTANDS US HERE!
AAH! SO HE'S BEHIND ALL THIS! WITH HIS SKINNY CRICKET LEGS!
CAMARA, YOU BROUGHT HIM HERE. LOOK AT ALL THE CHAOS HE'S CAUSED.
HEY, FRIENDS! ALL HE DID IS MAKE YOUR WOMEN BETTER LOOKING! WHAT'S THE PROBLEM?
IF WE WANTED GOOD LOOKING, WE'D GET NEW WIVES.
I WANT THE REAL AÏCHA BACK!
WHERE IS HE, ANYWAY?
HE'S GONE TO A BUSINESS MEETING WITH ARAMATOU.

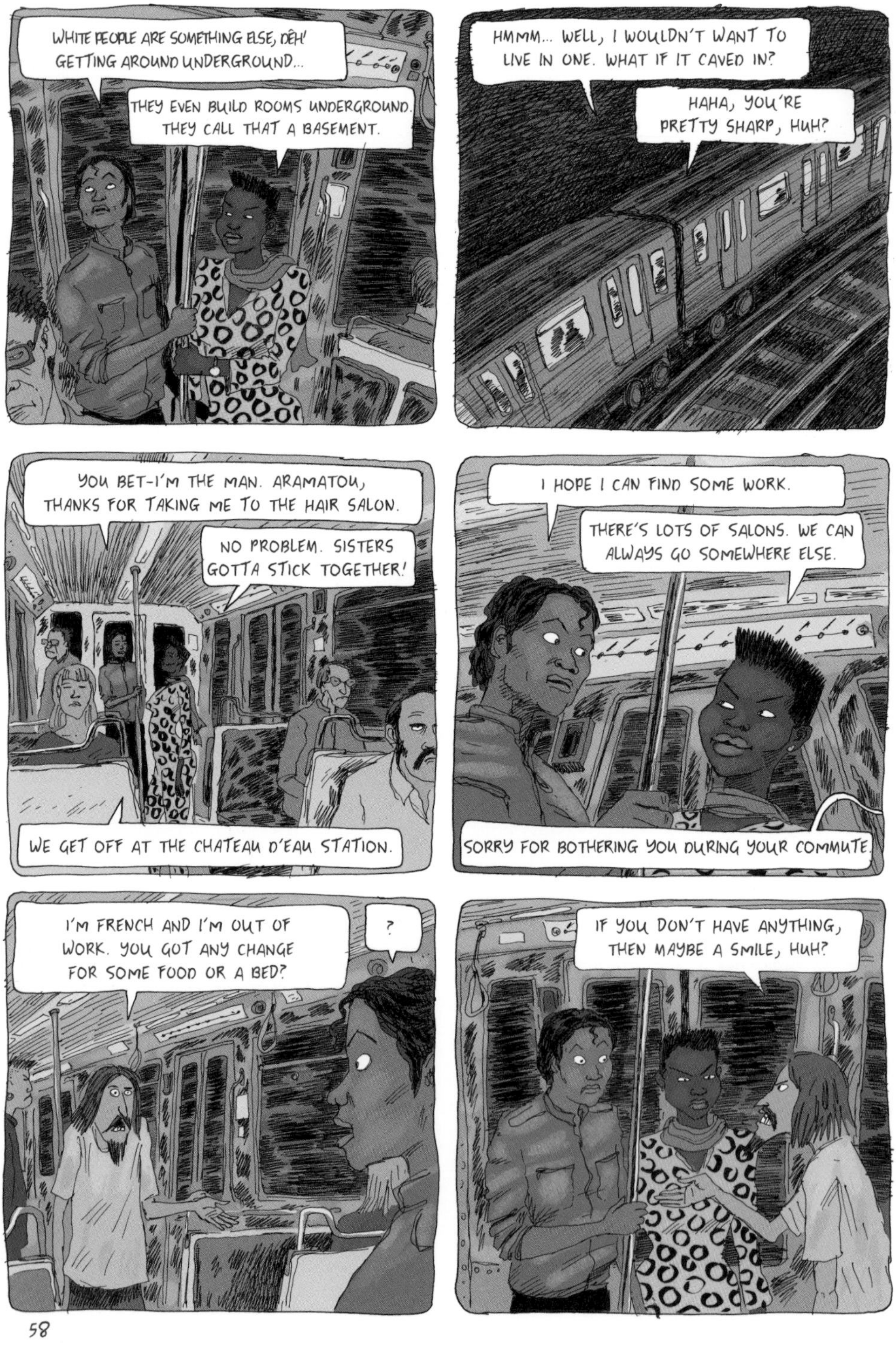
WHITE PEOPLE ARE SOMETHING ELSE, DÊH! GETTING AROUND UNDERGROUND...
THEY EVEN BUILD ROOMS UNDERGROUND. THEY CALL THAT A BASEMENT.
HMMM... WELL, I WOULDN'T WANT TO LIVE IN ONE. WHAT IF IT CAVED IN?
HAHA, YOU'RE PRETTY SHARP, HUH?
YOU BET-I'M THE MAN. ARAMATOU, THANKS FOR TAKING ME TO THE HAIR SALON.
NO PROBLEM. SISTERS GOTTA STICK TOGETHER!
WE GET OFF AT THE CHATEAU D'EAU STATION.
I HOPE I CAN FIND SOME WORK.
THERE'S LOTS OF SALONS. WE CAN ALWAYS GO SOMEWHERE ELSE.
SORRY FOR BOTHERING YOU DURING YOUR COMMUTE.
I'M FRENCH AND I'M OUT OF WORK. YOU GOT ANY CHANGE FOR SOME FOOD OR A BED?
?
IF YOU DON'T HAVE ANYTHING, THEN MAYBE A SMILE, HUH?

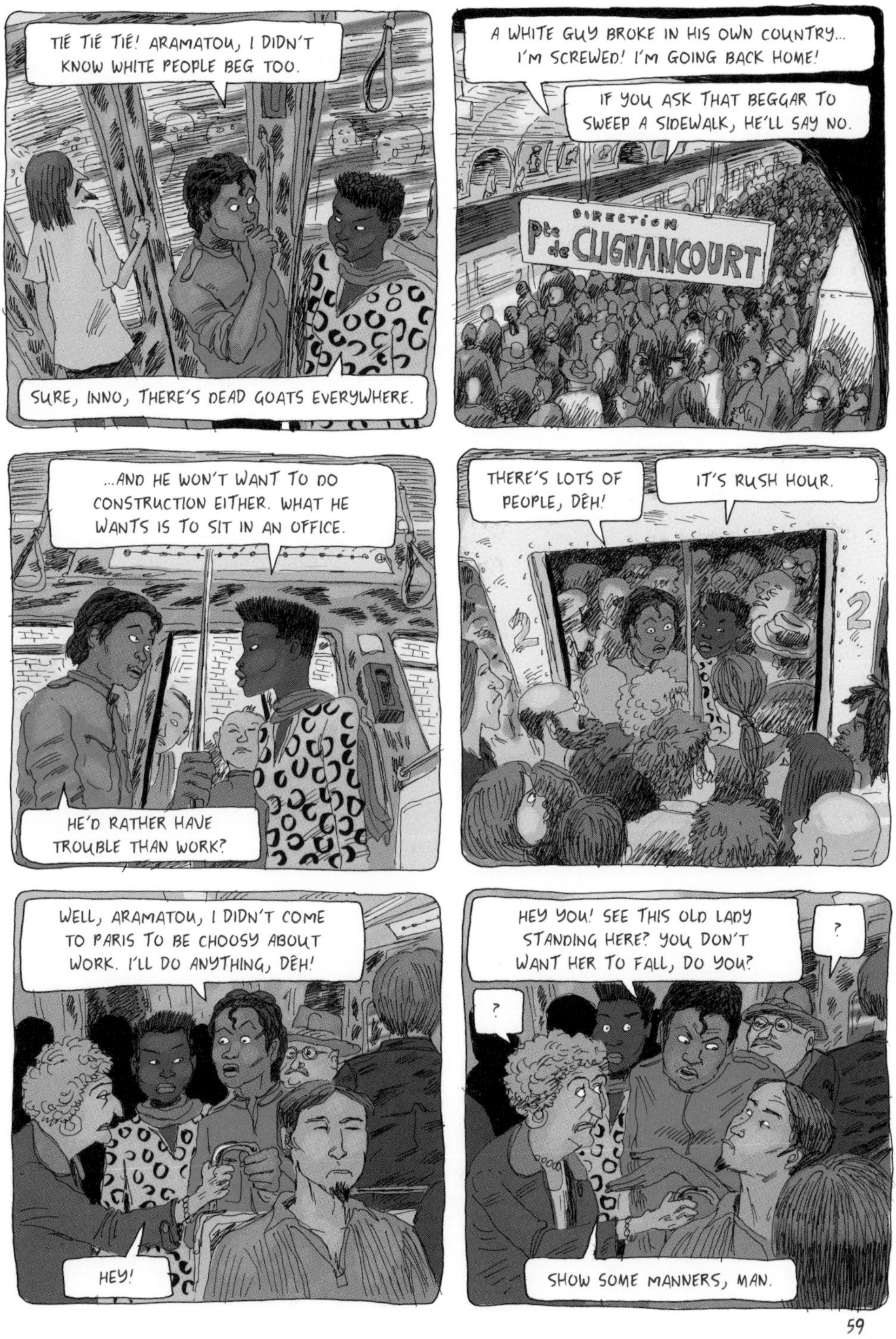

TIÉ TIÉ TIÉ! ARAMATOU, I DIDN'T KNOW WHITE PEOPLE BEG TOO.
SURE, INNO, THERE'S DEAD GOATS EVERYWHERE.
A WHITE GUY BROKE IN HIS OWN COUNTRY... I'M SCREWED! I'M GOING BACK HOME!
IF YOU ASK THAT BEGGAR TO SWEEP A SIDEWALK, HE'LL SAY NO.
DIRECTION Pte de CLIGNANCOURT
...AND HE WON'T WANT TO DO CONSTRUCTION EITHER. WHAT HE WANTS IS TO SIT IN AN OFFICE.
HE'D RATHER HAVE TROUBLE THAN WORK?
THERE'S LOTS OF PEOPLE, DÊH!
IT'S RUSH HOUR.
WELL, ARAMATOU, I DIDN'T COME TO PARIS TO BE CHOOSY ABOUT WORK. I'LL DO ANYTHING, DÊH!
HEY!
HEY YOU! SEE THIS OLD LADY STANDING HERE? YOU DON'T WANT HER TO FALL, DO YOU?
?
?
SHOW SOME MANNERS, MAN.

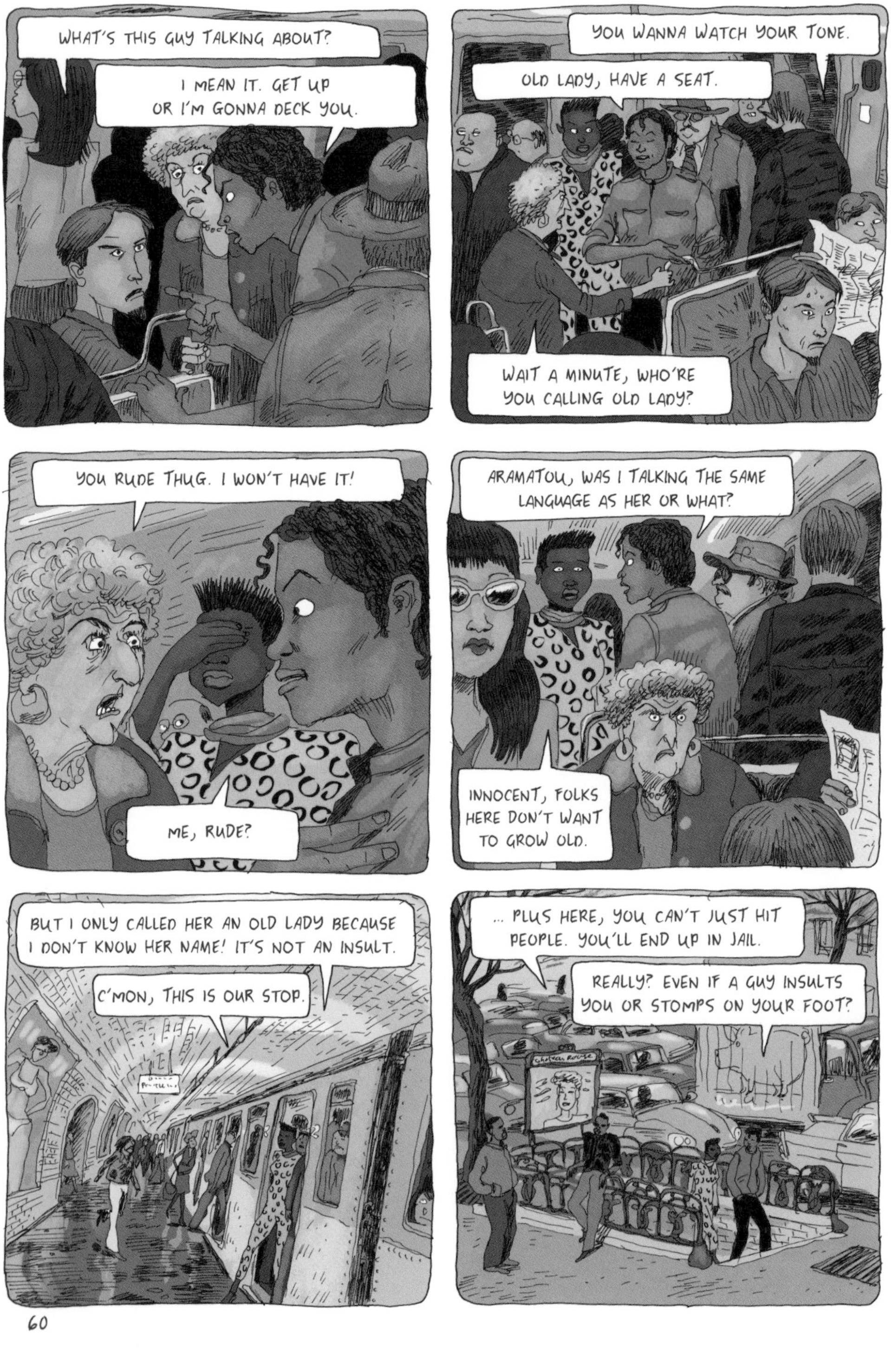
WHAT'S THIS GUY TALKING ABOUT?
I MEAN IT. GET UP OR I'M GONNA DECK YOU.
YOU WANNA WATCH YOUR TONE.
OLD LADY, HAVE A SEAT.
WAIT A MINUTE, WHO'RE YOU CALLING OLD LADY?
YOU RUDE THUG. I WON'T HAVE IT!
ME, RUDE?
ARAMATOU, WAS I TALKING THE SAME LANGUAGE AS HER OR WHAT?
INNOCENT, FOLKS HERE DON'T WANT TO GROW OLD.
BUT I ONLY CALLED HER AN OLD LADY BECAUSE I DON'T KNOW HER NAME! IT'S NOT AN INSULT.
C'MON, THIS IS OUR STOP.
... PLUS HERE, YOU CAN'T JUST HIT PEOPLE. YOU'LL END UP IN JAIL.
REALLY? EVEN IF A GUY INSULTS YOU OR STOMPS ON YOUR FOOT?

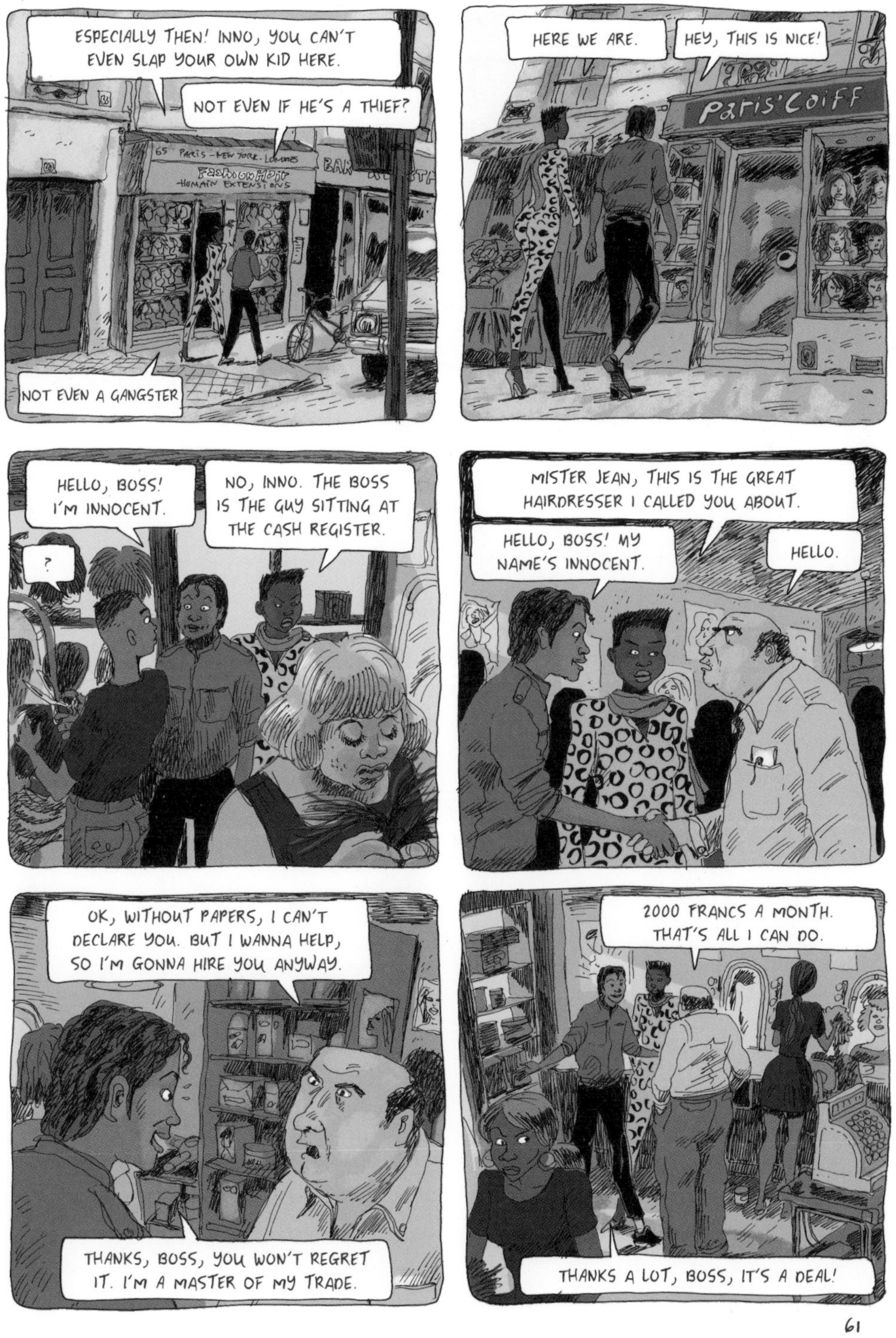

ESPECIALLY THEN! INNO, YOU CAN'T EVEN SLAP YOUR OWN KID HERE.
NOT EVEN IF HE'S A THIEF?
NOT EVEN A GANGSTER
HERE WE ARE.
HEY, THIS IS NICE!
Paris'Coiff
HELLO, BOSS! I'M INNOCENT.
NO, INNO. THE BOSS IS THE GUY SITTING AT THE CASH REGISTER.
?
MISTER JEAN, THIS IS THE GREAT HAIRDRESSER I CALLED YOU ABOUT.
HELLO, BOSS! MY NAME'S INNOCENT.
HELLO.
OK, WITHOUT PAPERS, I CAN'T DECLARE YOU. BUT I WANNA HELP, SO I'M GONNA HIRE YOU ANYWAY.
THANKS, BOSS, YOU WON'T REGRET IT. I'M A MASTER OF MY TRADE.
2000 FRANCS A MONTH. THAT'S ALL I CAN DO.
THANKS A LOT, BOSS, IT'S A DEAL!

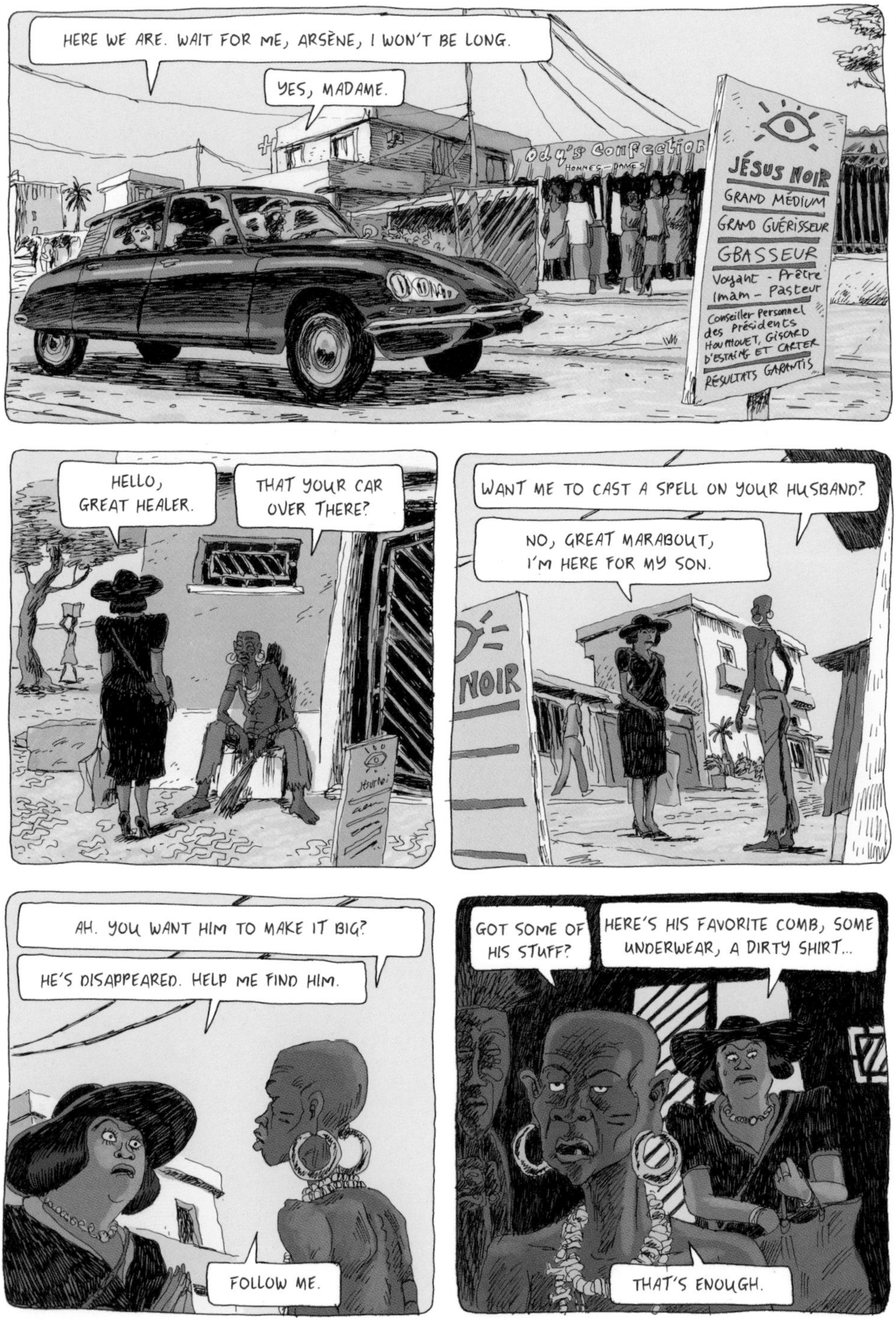
HERE WE ARE. WAIT FOR ME, ARSÈNE, I WON'T BE LONG.
YES, MADAME.
Ody's Confection
HOMMES — DAMES
JÉSUS NOIR
GRAND MÉDIUM
GRAND GUÉRISSEUR
GBASSEUR
Voyant - Prêtre
Imam - Pasteur
Conseiller Personnel des Présidents Houphouet, Giscard d'Estaing et Carter
Résultats Garantis
HELLO, GREAT HEALER.
THAT YOUR CAR OVER THERE?
WANT ME TO CAST A SPELL ON YOUR HUSBAND?
NO, GREAT MARABOUT, I'M HERE FOR MY SON.
AH. YOU WANT HIM TO MAKE IT BIG?
HE'S DISAPPEARED. HELP ME FIND HIM.
FOLLOW ME.
GOT SOME OF HIS STUFF?
HERE'S HIS FAVORITE COMB, SOME UNDERWEAR, A DIRTY SHIRT...
THAT'S ENOUGH.

 SIGN (TOP PANEL): BLACK JESUS - GREAT PSYCHIC - LEGENDARY HEALER - WITCH DOCTOR - FORTUNE TELLER - PRIEST - IMAM - PASTOR - PERSONAL ADVISOR TO PRESIDENTS HOUFFLOUET, GISCARD D'ESTAING, AND CARTER - GUARANTEED RESULTS

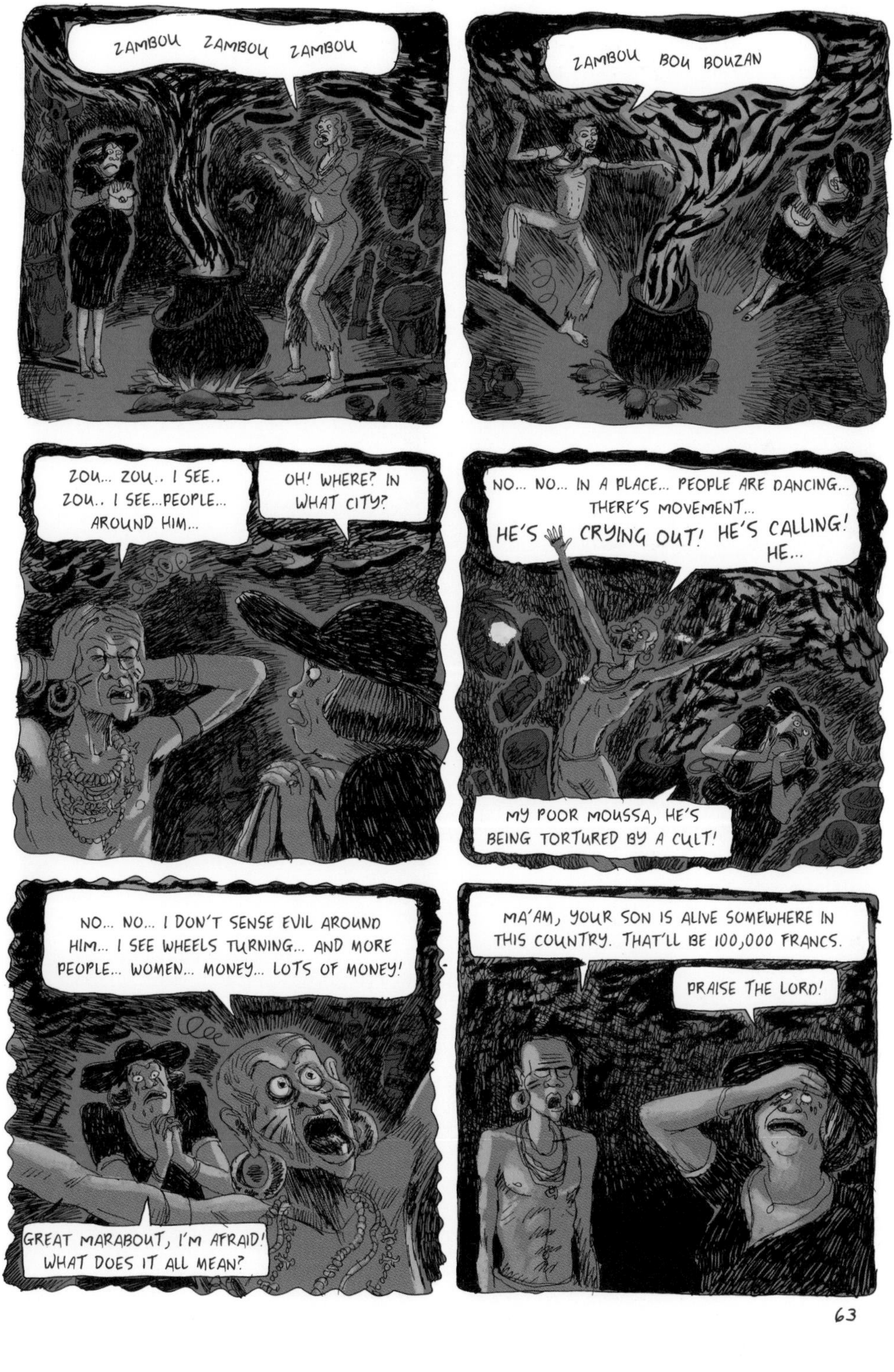
ZAMBOU ZAMBOU ZAMBOU
ZAMBOU BOU BOUZAN
ZOU... ZOU.. I SEE.. ZOU.. I SEE...PEOPLE... AROUND HIM...
OH! WHERE? IN WHAT CITY?
NO... NO... IN A PLACE... PEOPLE ARE DANCING... THERE'S MOVEMENT... HE'S CRYING OUT! HE'S CALLING! HE...
MY POOR MOUSSA, HE'S BEING TORTURED BY A CULT!
NO... NO... I DON'T SENSE EVIL AROUND HIM... I SEE WHEELS TURNING... AND MORE PEOPLE... WOMEN... MONEY... LOTS OF MONEY!
GREAT MARABOUT, I'M AFRAID! WHAT DOES IT ALL MEAN?
MA'AM, YOUR SON IS ALIVE SOMEWHERE IN THIS COUNTRY. THAT'LL BE 100,000 FRANCS.
PRAISE THE LORD!

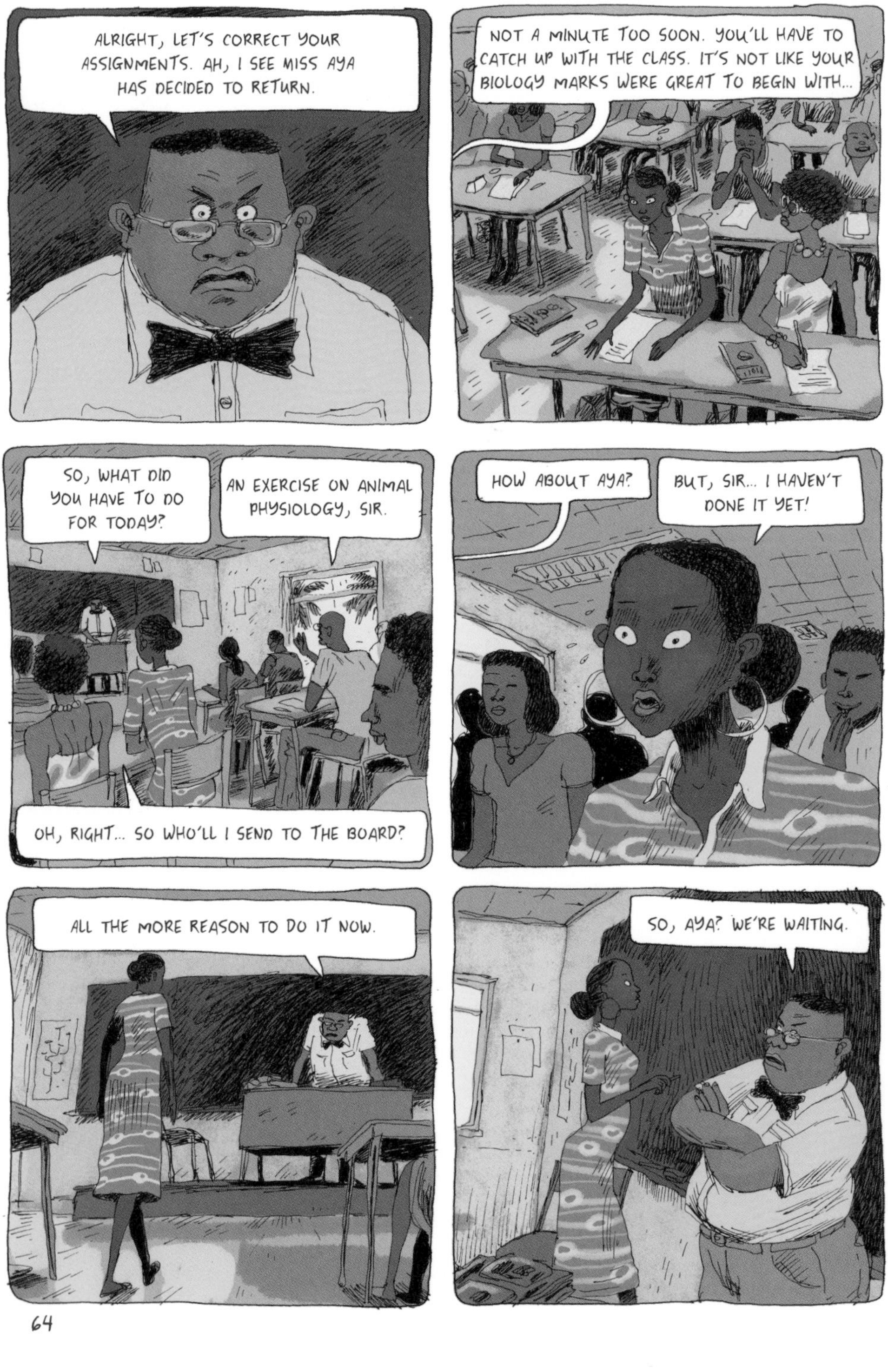
ALRIGHT, LET'S CORRECT YOUR ASSIGNMENTS. AH, I SEE MISS AYA HAS DECIDED TO RETURN.
NOT A MINUTE TOO SOON. YOU'LL HAVE TO CATCH UP WITH THE CLASS. IT'S NOT LIKE YOUR BIOLOGY MARKS WERE GREAT TO BEGIN WITH...
SO, WHAT DID YOU HAVE TO DO FOR TODAY?
AN EXERCISE ON ANIMAL PHYSIOLOGY, SIR.
OH, RIGHT... SO WHO'LL I SEND TO THE BOARD?
HOW ABOUT AYA?
BUT, SIR... I HAVEN'T DONE IT YET!
ALL THE MORE REASON TO DO IT NOW.
SO, AYA? WE'RE WAITING.

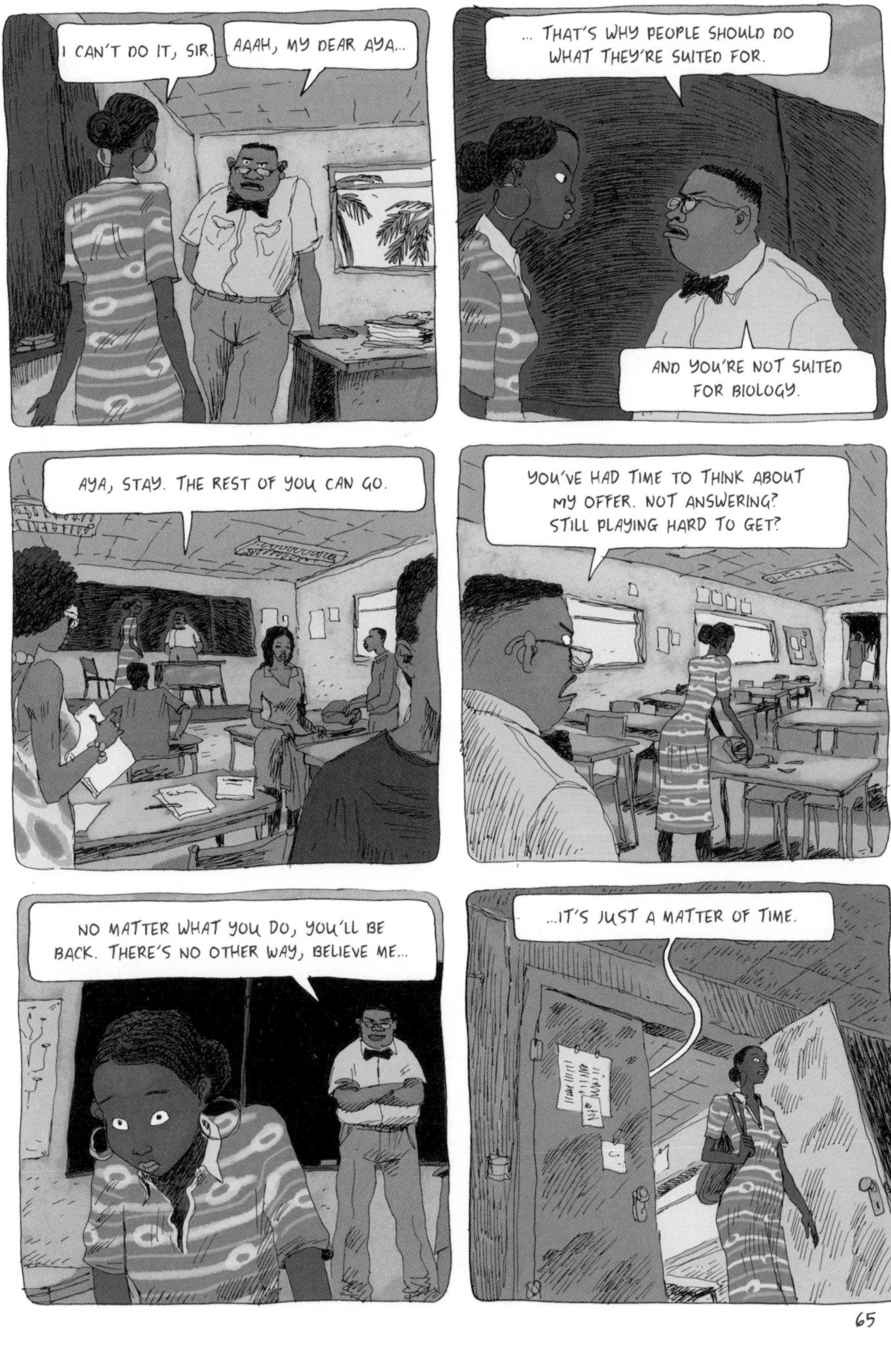
I CAN'T DO IT, SIR.
AAAH, MY DEAR AYA...
... THAT'S WHY PEOPLE SHOULD DO WHAT THEY'RE SUITED FOR.
AND YOU'RE NOT SUITED FOR BIOLOGY.
AYA, STAY. THE REST OF YOU CAN GO.
YOU'VE HAD TIME TO THINK ABOUT MY OFFER. NOT ANSWERING? STILL PLAYING HARD TO GET?
NO MATTER WHAT YOU DO, YOU'LL BE BACK. THERE'S NO OTHER WAY, BELIEVE ME...
...IT'S JUST A MATTER OF TIME.

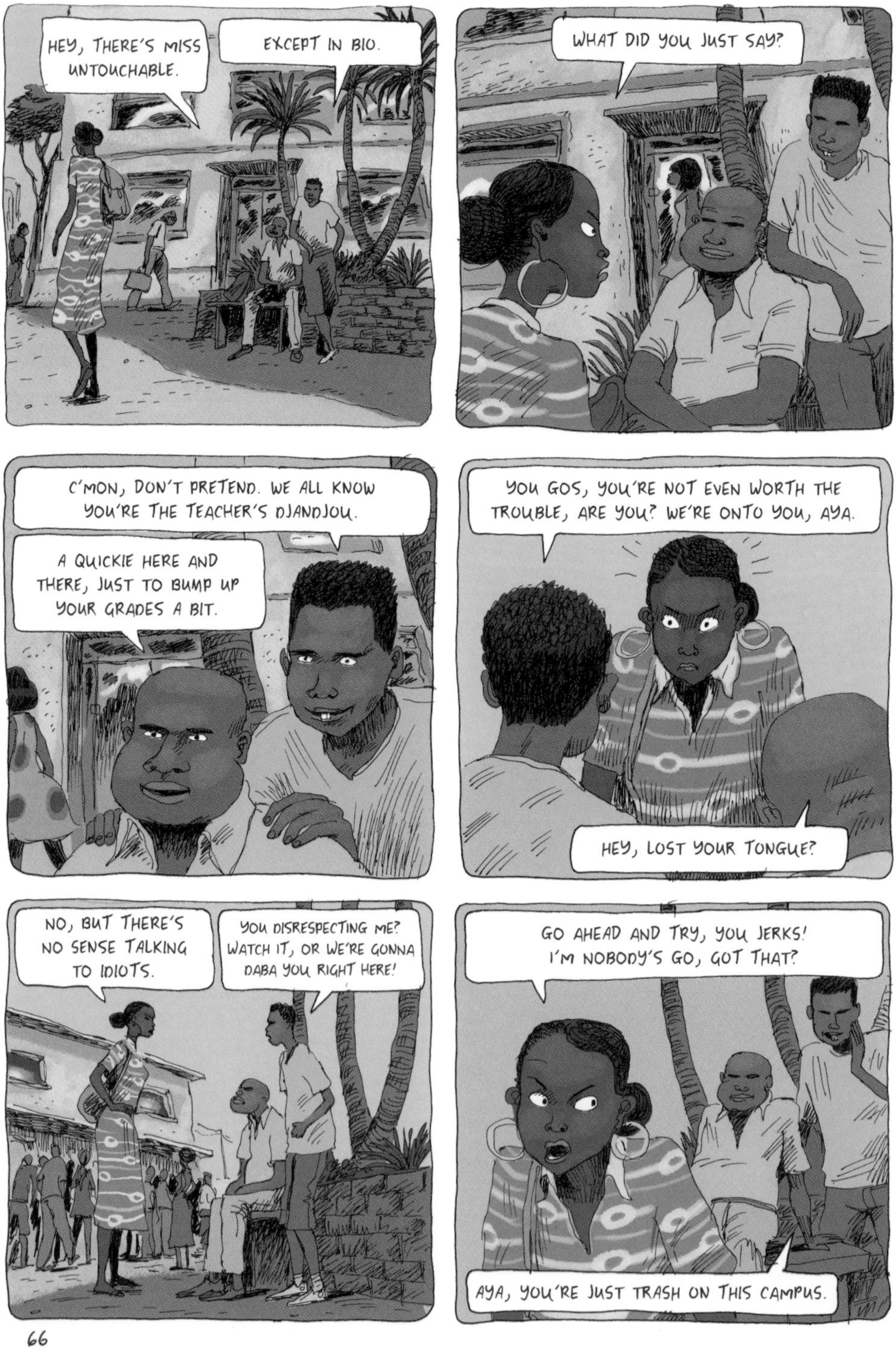
HEY, THERE'S MISS UNTOUCHABLE.
EXCEPT IN BIO.
WHAT DID YOU JUST SAY?
C'MON, DON'T PRETEND. WE ALL KNOW YOU'RE THE TEACHER'S DJANDJOU.
A QUICKIE HERE AND THERE, JUST TO BUMP UP YOUR GRADES A BIT.
YOU GOS, YOU'RE NOT EVEN WORTH THE TROUBLE, ARE YOU? WE'RE ONTO YOU, AYA.
HEY, LOST YOUR TONGUE?
NO, BUT THERE'S NO SENSE TALKING TO IDIOTS.
YOU DISRESPECTING ME? WATCH IT, OR WE'RE GONNA DABA YOU RIGHT HERE!
GO AHEAD AND TRY, YOU JERKS! I'M NOBODY'S GO, GOT THAT?
AYA, YOU'RE JUST TRASH ON THIS CAMPUS.

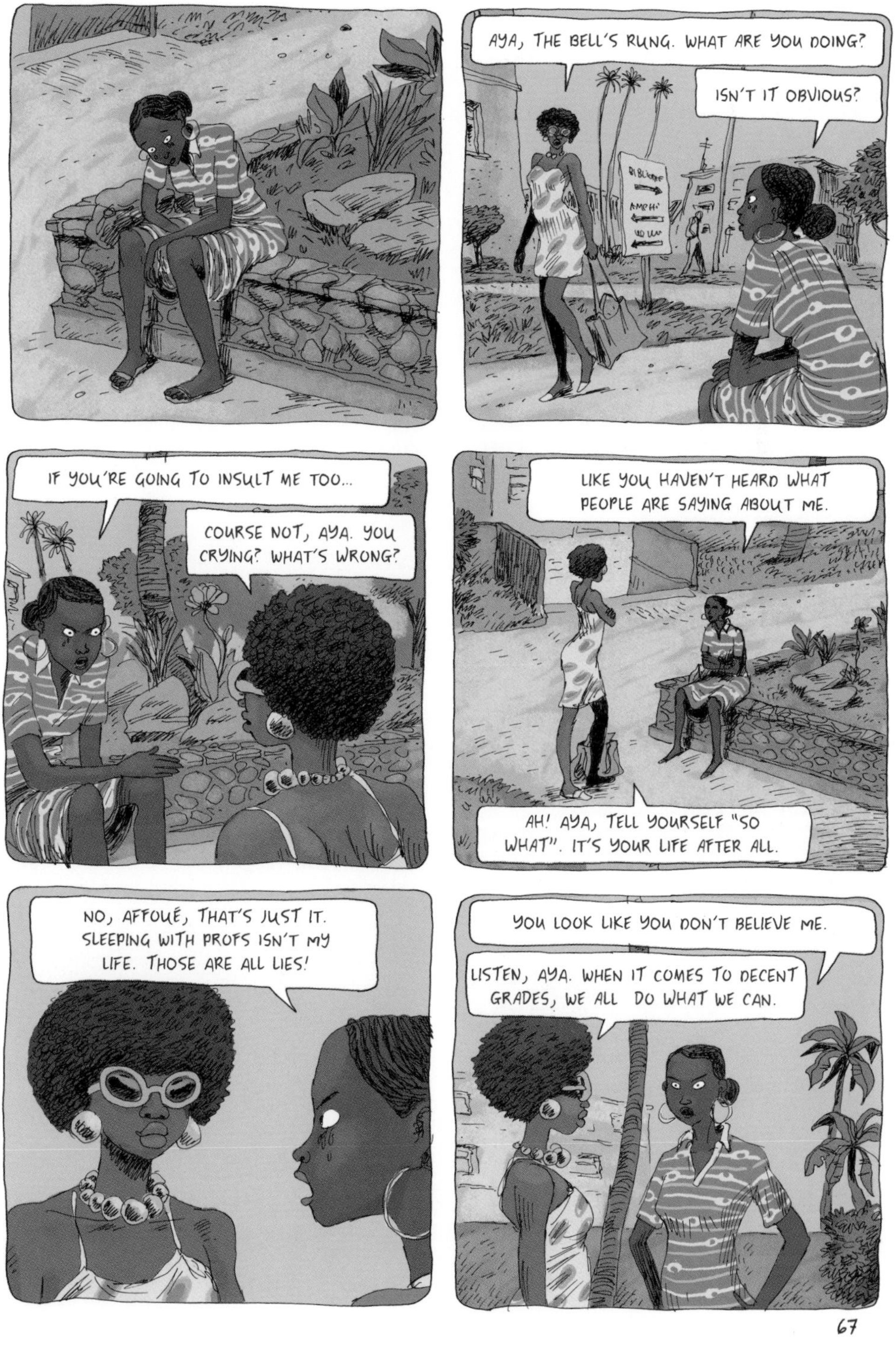
AYA, THE BELL'S RUNG. WHAT ARE YOU DOING?
ISN'T IT OBVIOUS?
IF YOU'RE GOING TO INSULT ME TOO...
COURSE NOT, AYA. YOU CRYING? WHAT'S WRONG?
LIKE YOU HAVEN'T HEARD WHAT PEOPLE ARE SAYING ABOUT ME.
AH! AYA, TELL YOURSELF "SO WHAT". IT'S YOUR LIFE AFTER ALL.
NO, AFFOUÉ, THAT'S JUST IT. SLEEPING WITH PROFS ISN'T MY LIFE. THOSE ARE ALL LIES!
YOU LOOK LIKE YOU DON'T BELIEVE ME.
LISTEN, AYA. WHEN IT COMES TO DECENT GRADES, WE ALL DO WHAT WE CAN.

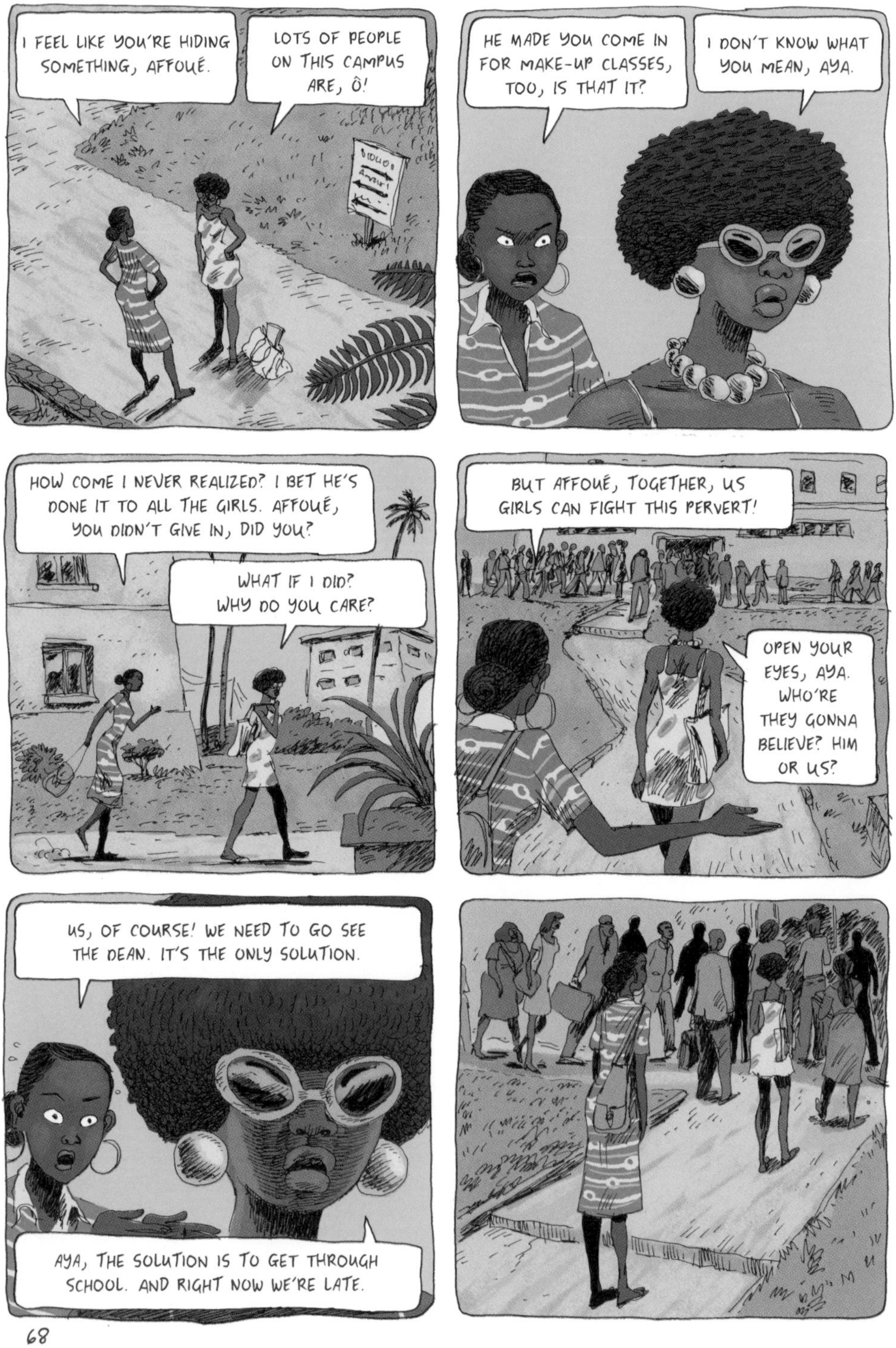
I FEEL LIKE YOU'RE HIDING SOMETHING, AFFOUÉ.
LOTS OF PEOPLE ON THIS CAMPUS ARE, Ô!
HE MADE YOU COME IN FOR MAKE-UP CLASSES, TOO, IS THAT IT?
I DON'T KNOW WHAT YOU MEAN, AYA.
HOW COME I NEVER REALIZED? I BET HE'S DONE IT TO ALL THE GIRLS. AFFOUÉ, YOU DIDN'T GIVE IN, DID YOU?
WHAT IF I DID? WHY DO YOU CARE?
BUT AFFOUÉ, TOGETHER, US GIRLS CAN FIGHT THIS PERVERT!
OPEN YOUR EYES, AYA. WHO'RE THEY GONNA BELIEVE? HIM OR US?
US, OF COURSE! WE NEED TO GO SEE THE DEAN. IT'S THE ONLY SOLUTION.
AYA, THE SOLUTION IS TO GET THROUGH SCHOOL. AND RIGHT NOW WE'RE LATE.

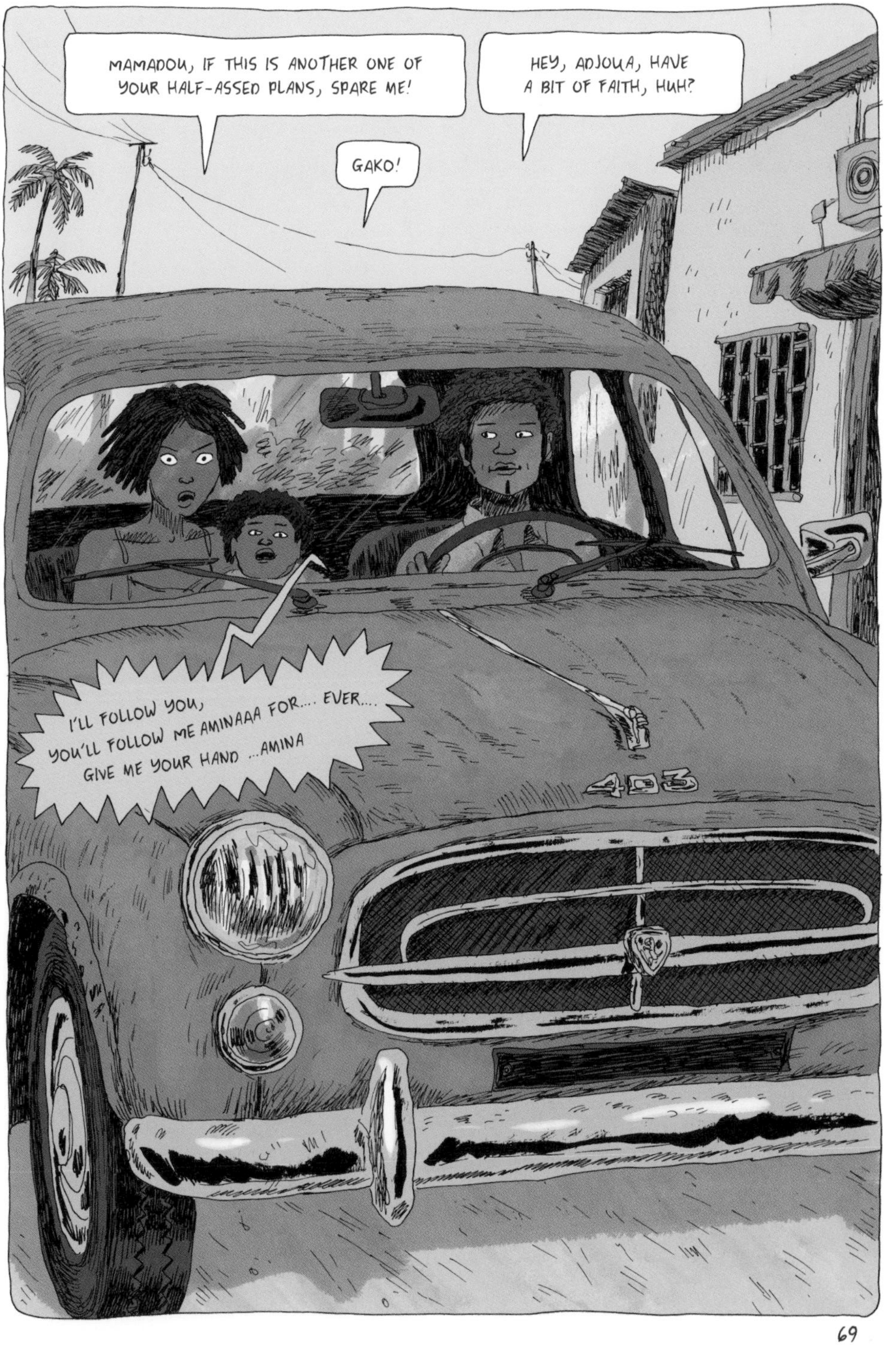
MAMADOU, IF THIS IS ANOTHER ONE OF YOUR HALF-ASSED PLANS, SPARE ME!
GAKO!
HEY, ADJOUA, HAVE A BIT OF FAITH, HUH?
I'LL FOLLOW YOU, YOU'LL FOLLOW ME AMINAAA FOR.... EVER.... GIVE ME YOUR HAND ...AMINA
403

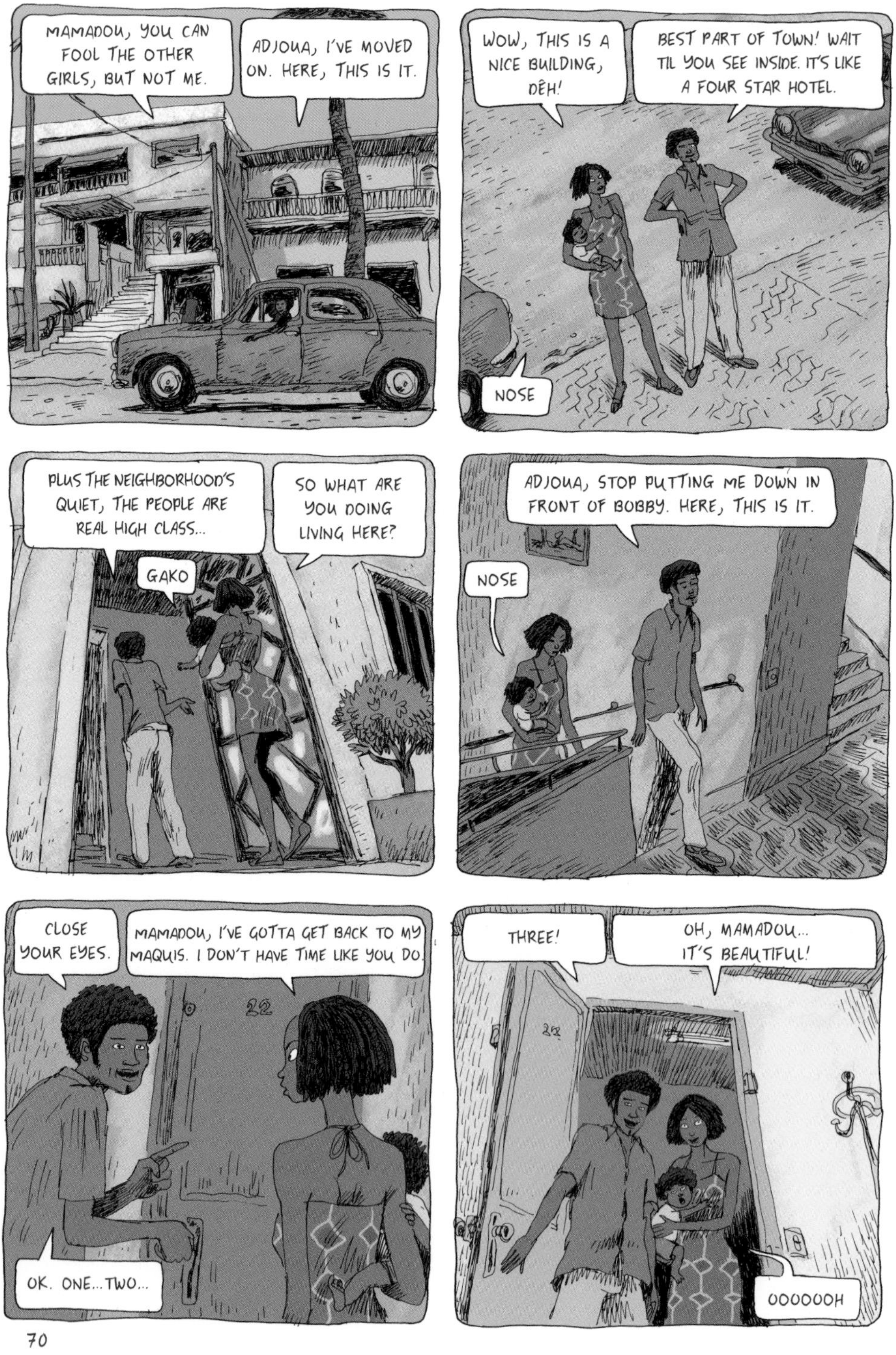
MAMADOU, YOU CAN FOOL THE OTHER GIRLS, BUT NOT ME.
ADJOUA, I'VE MOVED ON. HERE, THIS IS IT.
WOW, THIS IS A NICE BUILDING, DÊH!
BEST PART OF TOWN! WAIT TIL YOU SEE INSIDE. IT'S LIKE A FOUR STAR HOTEL.
NOSE
PLUS THE NEIGHBORHOOD'S QUIET, THE PEOPLE ARE REAL HIGH CLASS...
SO WHAT ARE YOU DOING LIVING HERE?
GAKO
ADJOUA, STOP PUTTING ME DOWN IN FRONT OF BOBBY. HERE, THIS IS IT.
NOSE
CLOSE YOUR EYES.
MAMADOU, I'VE GOTTA GET BACK TO MY MAQUIS. I DON'T HAVE TIME LIKE YOU DO.
OK. ONE...TWO...
THREE!
OH, MAMADOU... IT'S BEAUTIFUL!
OOOOOOH

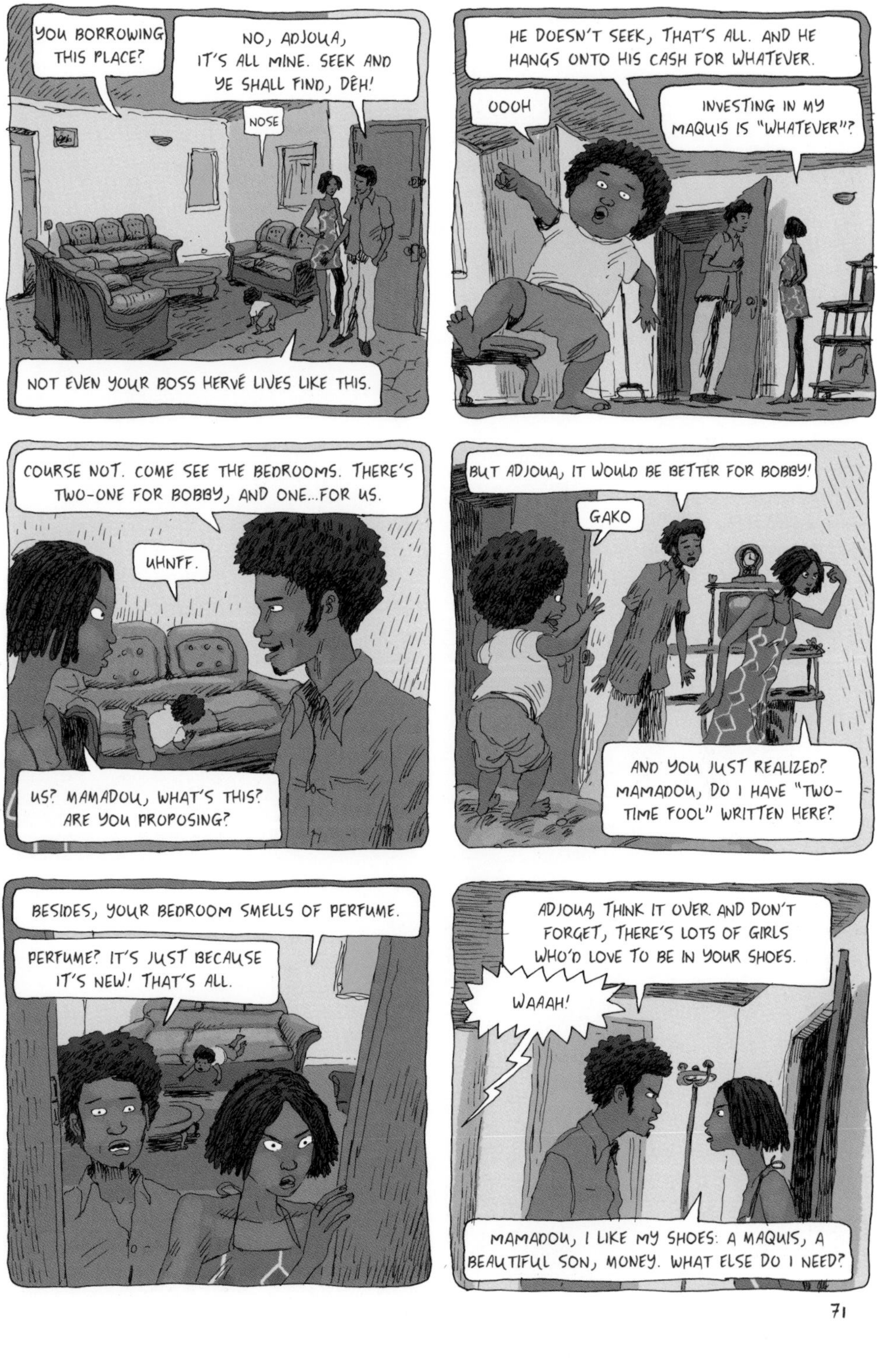
YOU BORROWING THIS PLACE?
NO, ADJOUA, IT'S ALL MINE. SEEK AND YE SHALL FIND, DÊH!
NOSE
NOT EVEN YOUR BOSS HERVÉ LIVES LIKE THIS.
HE DOESN'T SEEK, THAT'S ALL. AND HE HANGS ONTO HIS CASH FOR WHATEVER.
OOOH
INVESTING IN MY MAQUIS IS "WHATEVER"?
COURSE NOT. COME SEE THE BEDROOMS. THERE'S TWO-ONE FOR BOBBY, AND ONE...FOR US.
UHNFF.
US? MAMADOU, WHAT'S THIS? ARE YOU PROPOSING?
BUT ADJOUA, IT WOULD BE BETTER FOR BOBBY!
GAKO
AND YOU JUST REALIZED? MAMADOU, DO I HAVE "TWO-TIME FOOL" WRITTEN HERE?
BESIDES, YOUR BEDROOM SMELLS OF PERFUME.
PERFUME? IT'S JUST BECAUSE IT'S NEW! THAT'S ALL.
ADJOUA, THINK IT OVER. AND DON'T FORGET, THERE'S LOTS OF GIRLS WHO'D LOVE TO BE IN YOUR SHOES.
WAAAH!
MAMADOU, I LIKE MY SHOES: A MAQUIS, A BEAUTIFUL SON, MONEY. WHAT ELSE DO I NEED?

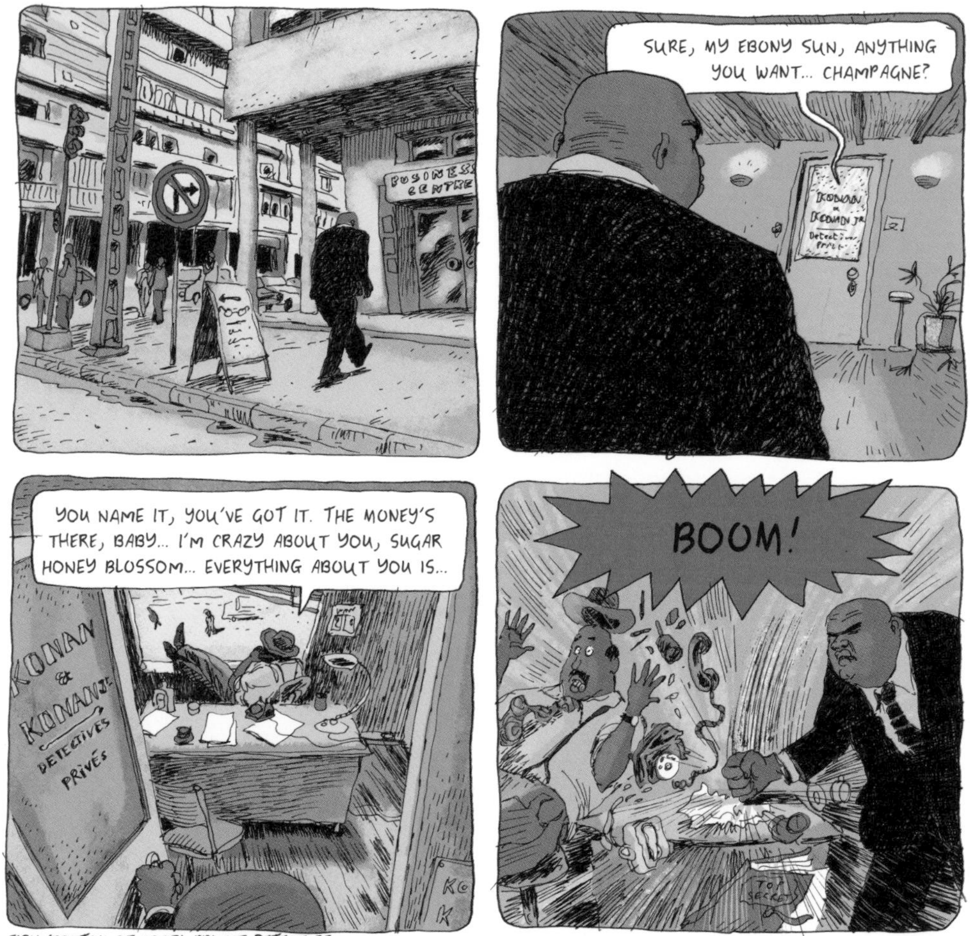
BUSINESS CENTRE
SURE, MY EBONY SUN, ANYTHING YOU WANT... CHAMPAGNE?
YOU NAME IT, YOU'VE GOT IT. THE MONEY'S THERE, BABY... I'M CRAZY ABOUT YOU, SUGAR HONEY BLOSSOM... EVERYTHING ABOUT YOU IS...
KONAN & KONAN JR. DETECTIVES PRIVÉS
BOOM!
TOP SECRET

SIGN (BOTTOM OF DOOR): PRIVATE DETECTIVES

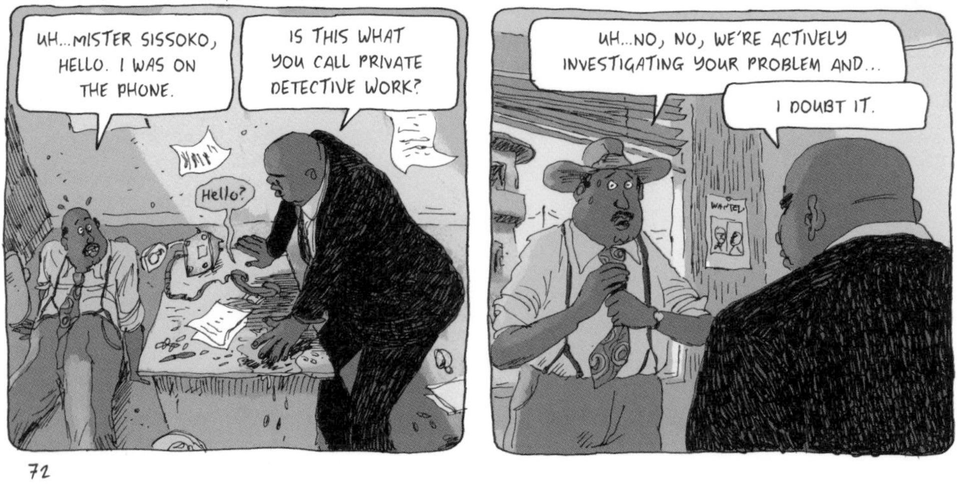
UH...MISTER SISSOKO, HELLO. I WAS ON THE PHONE.
IS THIS WHAT YOU CALL PRIVATE DETECTIVE WORK?
Hello?
UH...NO, NO, WE'RE ACTIVELY INVESTIGATING YOUR PROBLEM AND...
I DOUBT IT.
WANTED

MISTER SISSOKO, I SWEAR, ALL MY MEN ARE OUT LOOKING FOR YOUR SON.
KONAN, DON'T COUNT ON OTHERS AND YOU WON'T BE DISAPPOINTED.
I PUT MY BEST MEN ON THE CASE!
REALLY? BEST AT WHAT? I WANT RESULTS THIS WEEK.
BUT MISTER SISSOKO, HE KEEPS MOVING AROUND.
SO? WHAT AM I PAYING YOU FOR? WANT HIM TO SEND YOU HIS RETURN ADDRESS?
DON'T WORRY, MR. SISSOKO. I'LL HANDLE THIS MYSELF.
EXCELLENT. THE EBONY SUN'S A STAR BEST ADMIRED FROM FAR, KONAN.
TH... THAT WAS MY WIFE.
SURE IT WAS! REMEMBER, KONAN: BEFORE THE WEEKEND!
KONAN & KONAN Jr.
DÉTECTIVES PRIVÉS

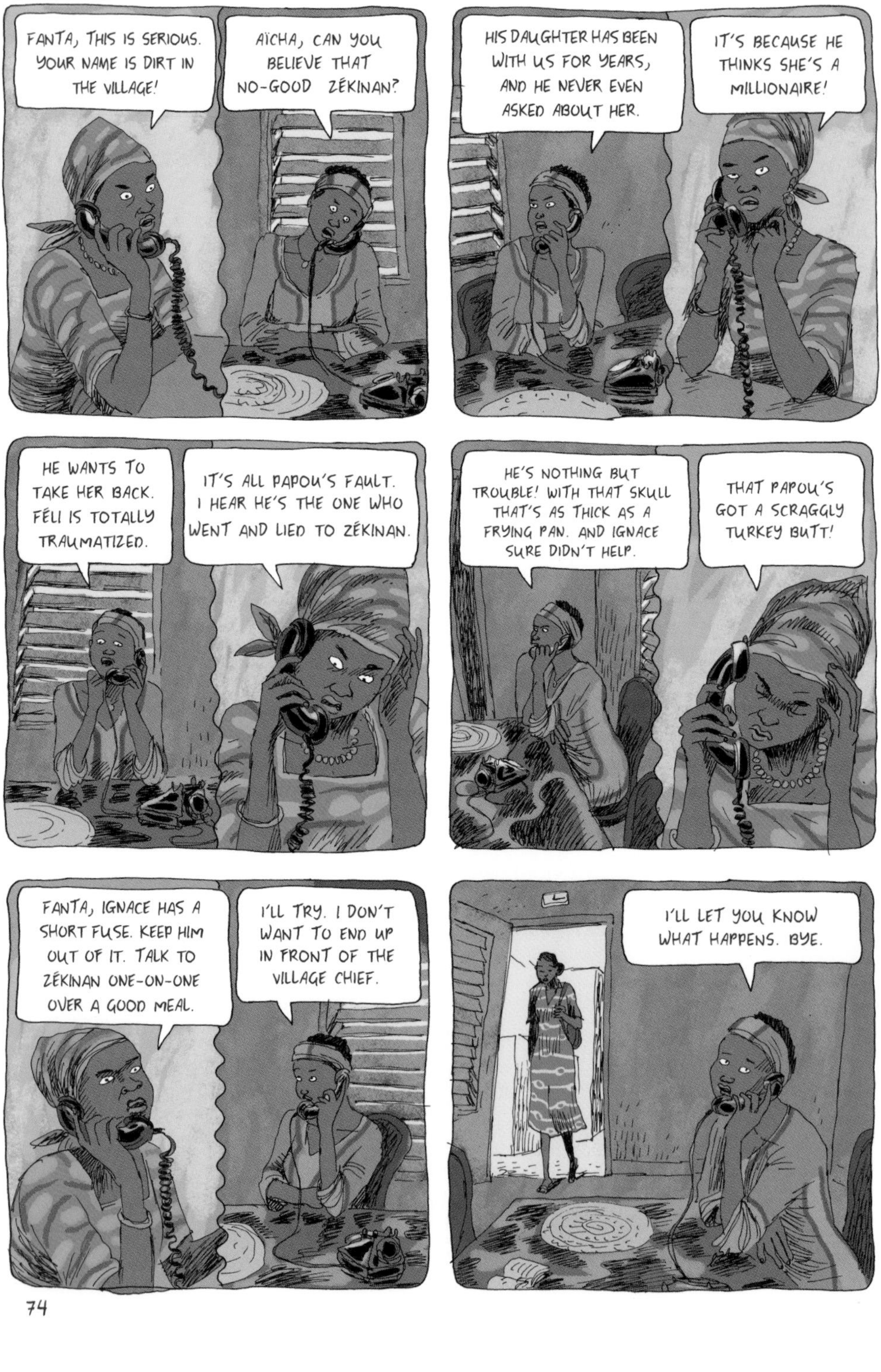
FANTA, THIS IS SERIOUS. YOUR NAME IS DIRT IN THE VILLAGE!
AÏCHA, CAN YOU BELIEVE THAT NO-GOOD ZÉKINAN?
HIS DAUGHTER HAS BEEN WITH US FOR YEARS, AND HE NEVER EVEN ASKED ABOUT HER.
IT'S BECAUSE HE THINKS SHE'S A MILLIONAIRE!
HE WANTS TO TAKE HER BACK. FÉLI IS TOTALLY TRAUMATIZED.
IT'S ALL PAPOU'S FAULT. I HEAR HE'S THE ONE WHO WENT AND LIED TO ZÉKINAN.
HE'S NOTHING BUT TROUBLE! WITH THAT SKULL THAT'S AS THICK AS A FRYING PAN. AND IGNACE SURE DIDN'T HELP.
THAT PAPOU'S GOT A SCRAGGLY TURKEY BUTT!
FANTA, IGNACE HAS A SHORT FUSE. KEEP HIM OUT OF IT. TALK TO ZÉKINAN ONE-ON-ONE OVER A GOOD MEAL.
I'LL TRY. I DON'T WANT TO END UP IN FRONT OF THE VILLAGE CHIEF.
I'LL LET YOU KNOW WHAT HAPPENS. BYE.

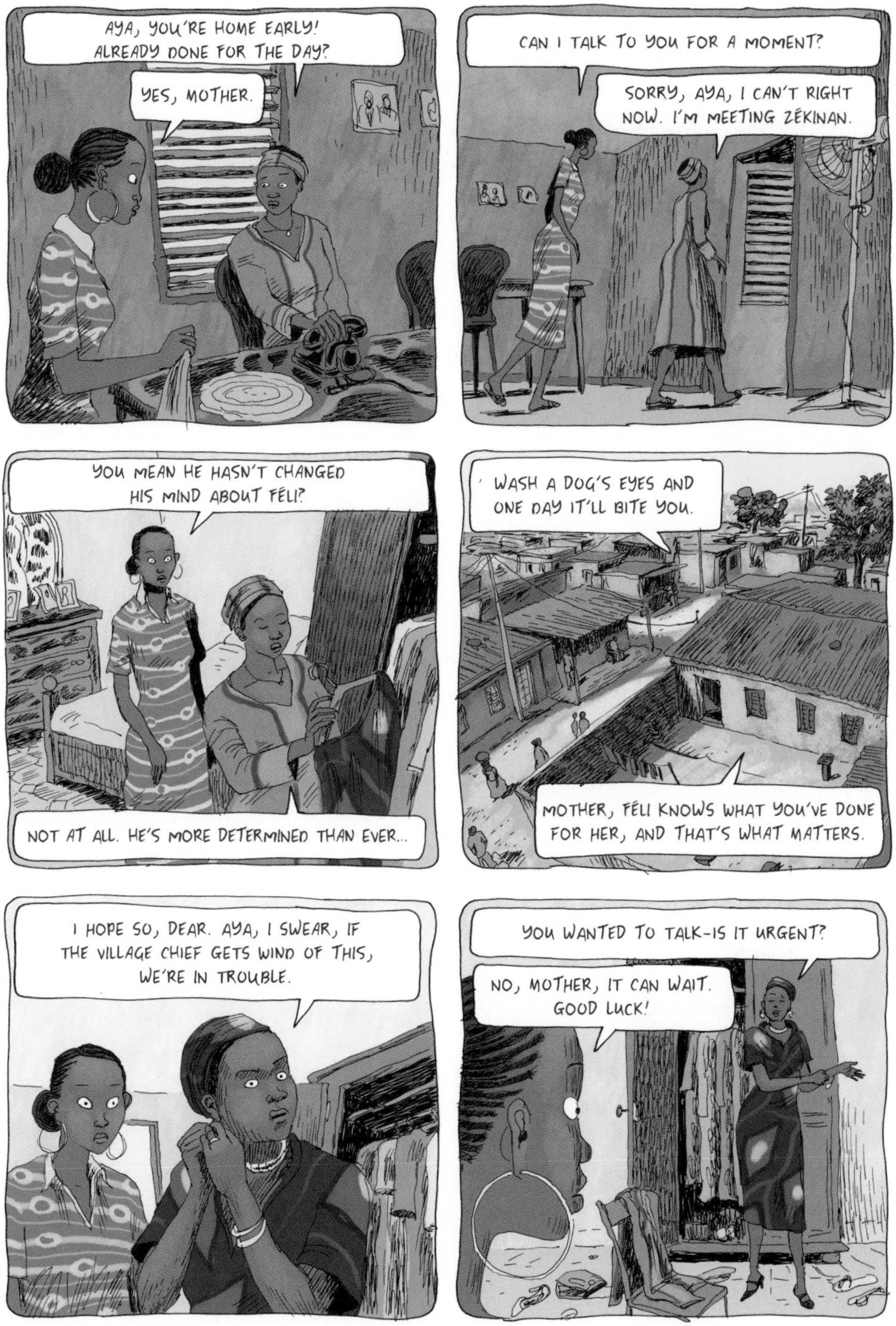
AYA, YOU'RE HOME EARLY! ALREADY DONE FOR THE DAY?
YES, MOTHER.
CAN I TALK TO YOU FOR A MOMENT?
SORRY, AYA, I CAN'T RIGHT NOW. I'M MEETING ZÉKINAN.
YOU MEAN HE HASN'T CHANGED HIS MIND ABOUT FÉLI?
NOT AT ALL. HE'S MORE DETERMINED THAN EVER...
WASH A DOG'S EYES AND ONE DAY IT'LL BITE YOU.
MOTHER, FÉLI KNOWS WHAT YOU'VE DONE FOR HER, AND THAT'S WHAT MATTERS.
I HOPE SO, DEAR. AYA, I SWEAR, IF THE VILLAGE CHIEF GETS WIND OF THIS, WE'RE IN TROUBLE.
YOU WANTED TO TALK-IS IT URGENT?
NO, MOTHER, IT CAN WAIT. GOOD LUCK!

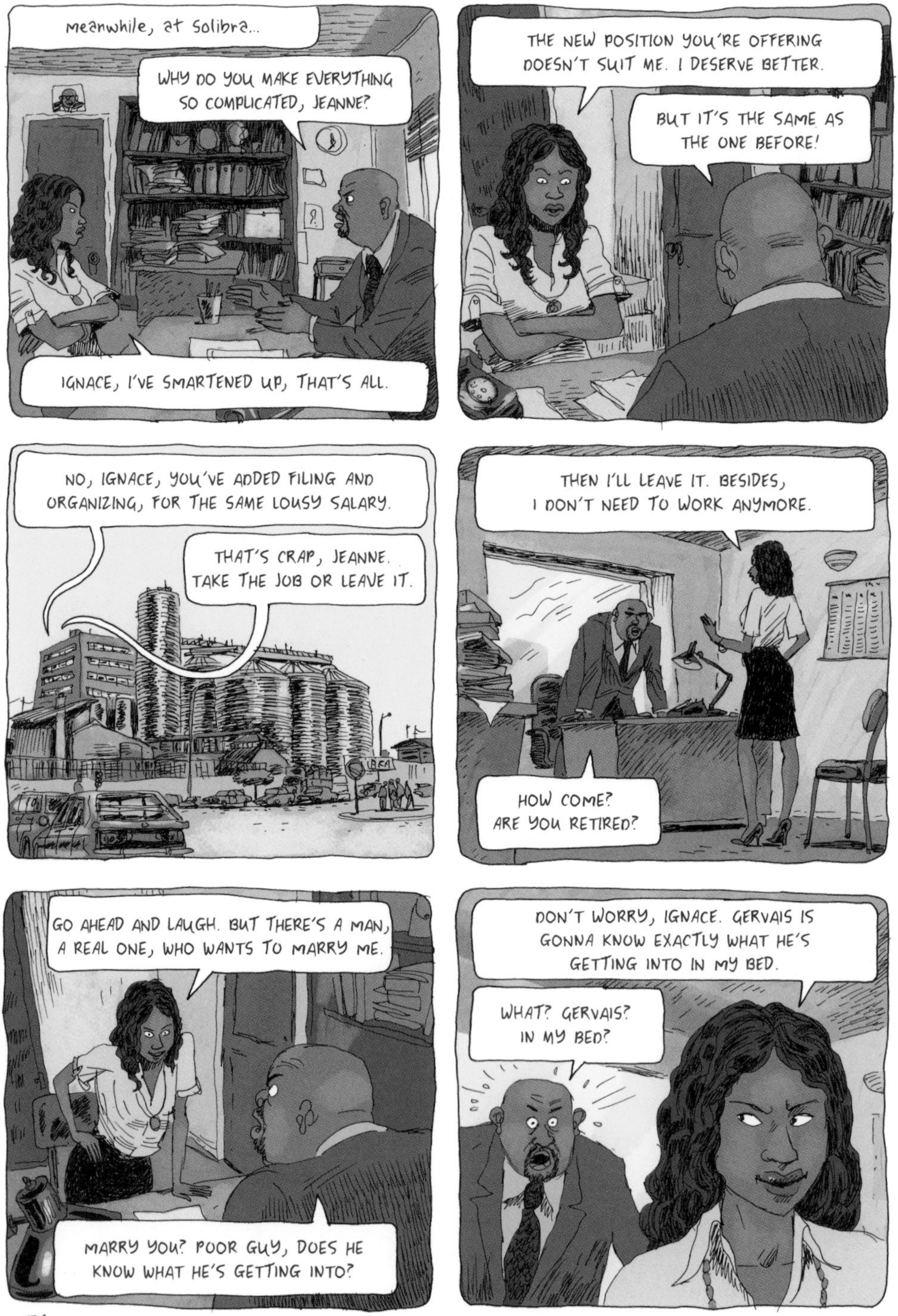
Meanwhile, at Solibra...
WHY DO YOU MAKE EVERYTHING SO COMPLICATED, JEANNE?
IGNACE, I'VE SMARTENED UP, THAT'S ALL.
THE NEW POSITION YOU'RE OFFERING DOESN'T SUIT ME. I DESERVE BETTER.
BUT IT'S THE SAME AS THE ONE BEFORE!
NO, IGNACE, YOU'VE ADDED FILING AND ORGANIZING, FOR THE SAME LOUSY SALARY.
THAT'S CRAP, JEANNE. TAKE THE JOB OR LEAVE IT.
THEN I'LL LEAVE IT. BESIDES, I DON'T NEED TO WORK ANYMORE.
HOW COME? ARE YOU RETIRED?
GO AHEAD AND LAUGH. BUT THERE'S A MAN, A REAL ONE, WHO WANTS TO MARRY ME.
MARRY YOU? POOR GUY, DOES HE KNOW WHAT HE'S GETTING INTO?
DON'T WORRY, IGNACE. GERVAIS IS GONNA KNOW EXACTLY WHAT HE'S GETTING INTO IN MY BED.
WHAT? GERVAIS? IN MY BED?

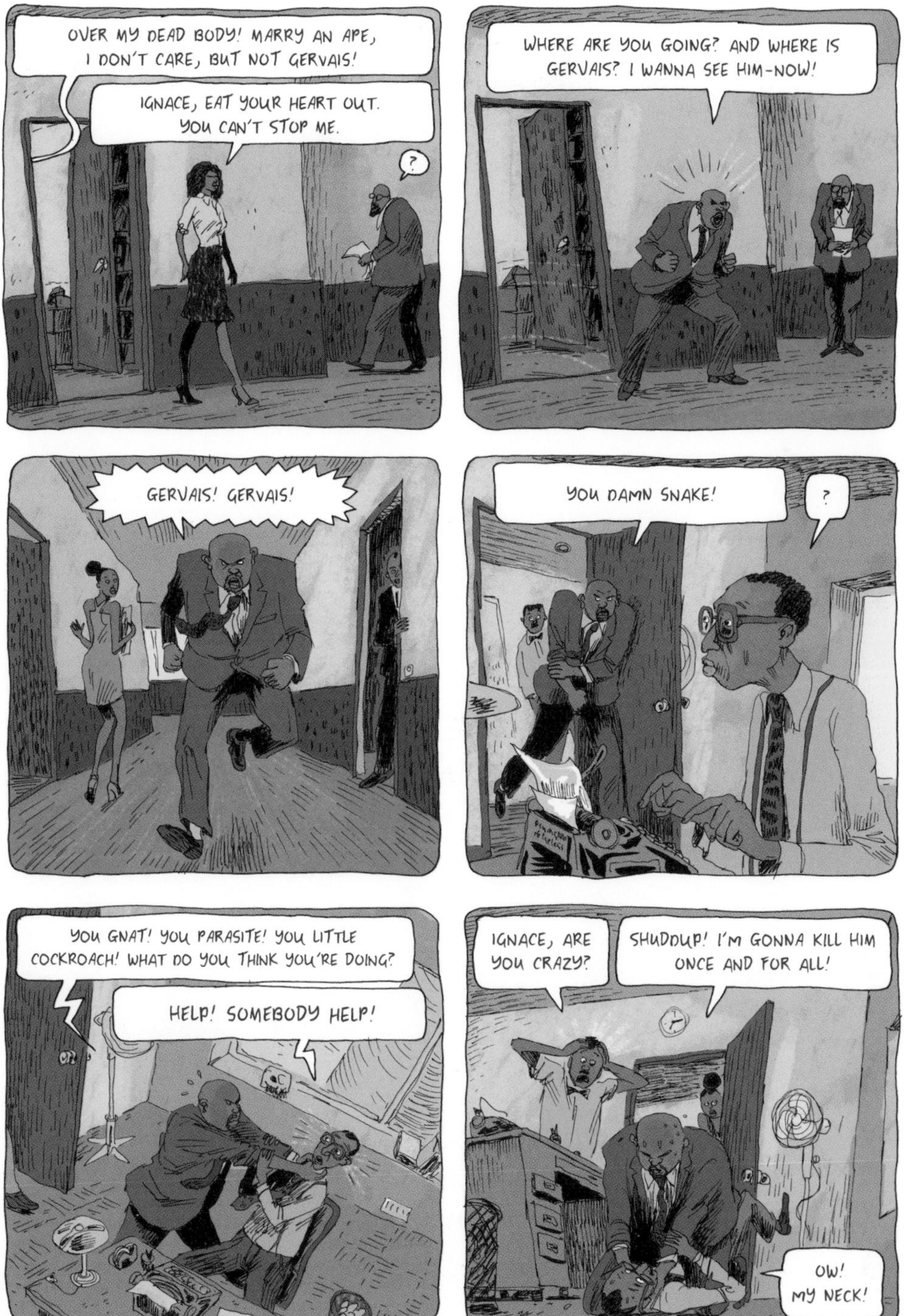
OVER MY DEAD BODY! MARRY AN APE, I DON'T CARE, BUT NOT GERVAIS!
IGNACE, EAT YOUR HEART OUT. YOU CAN'T STOP ME.
?
WHERE ARE YOU GOING? AND WHERE IS GERVAIS? I WANNA SEE HIM-NOW!
GERVAIS! GERVAIS!
YOU DAMN SNAKE!
?
YOU GNAT! YOU PARASITE! YOU LITTLE COCKROACH! WHAT DO YOU THINK YOU'RE DOING?
HELP! SOMEBODY HELP!
IGNACE, ARE YOU CRAZY?
SHUDDUP! I'M GONNA KILL HIM ONCE AND FOR ALL!
OW! MY NECK!

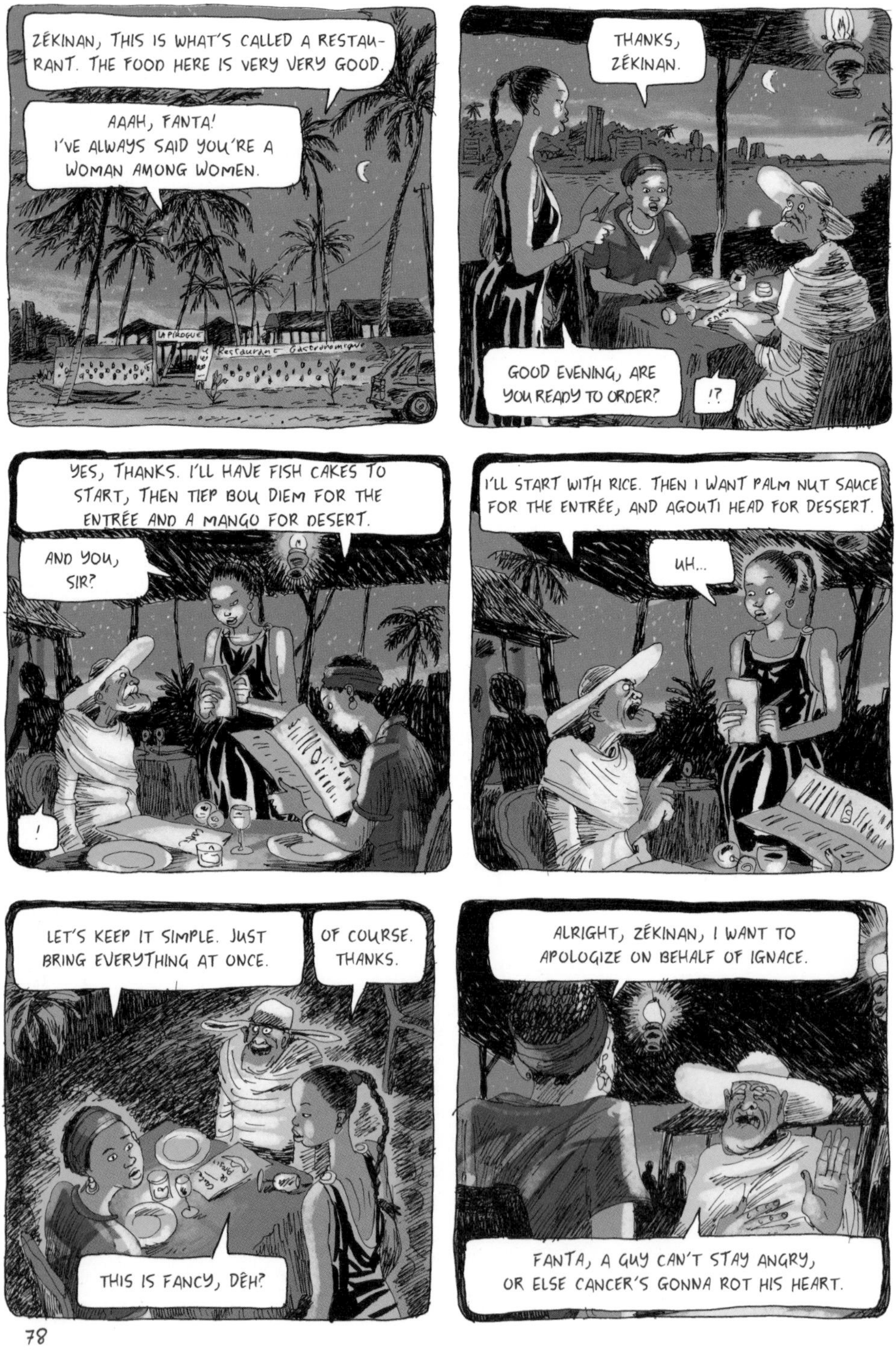
ZÉKINAN, THIS IS WHAT'S CALLED A RESTAU-RANT. THE FOOD HERE IS VERY VERY GOOD.
AAAH, FANTA! I'VE ALWAYS SAID YOU'RE A WOMAN AMONG WOMEN.
LA PIROGUE
Restaurant Gastronomique
THANKS, ZÉKINAN.
GOOD EVENING, ARE YOU READY TO ORDER?
!?
YES, THANKS. I'LL HAVE FISH CAKES TO START, THEN TIEP BOU DIEM FOR THE ENTRÉE AND A MANGO FOR DESERT.
AND YOU, SIR?
!
I'LL START WITH RICE. THEN I WANT PALM NUT SAUCE FOR THE ENTRÉE, AND AGOUTI HEAD FOR DESSERT.
UH...
LET'S KEEP IT SIMPLE. JUST BRING EVERYTHING AT ONCE.
OF COURSE. THANKS.
THIS IS FANCY, DÊH?
ALRIGHT, ZÉKINAN, I WANT TO APOLOGIZE ON BEHALF OF IGNACE.
FANTA, A GUY CAN'T STAY ANGRY, OR ELSE CANCER'S GONNA ROT HIS HEART.

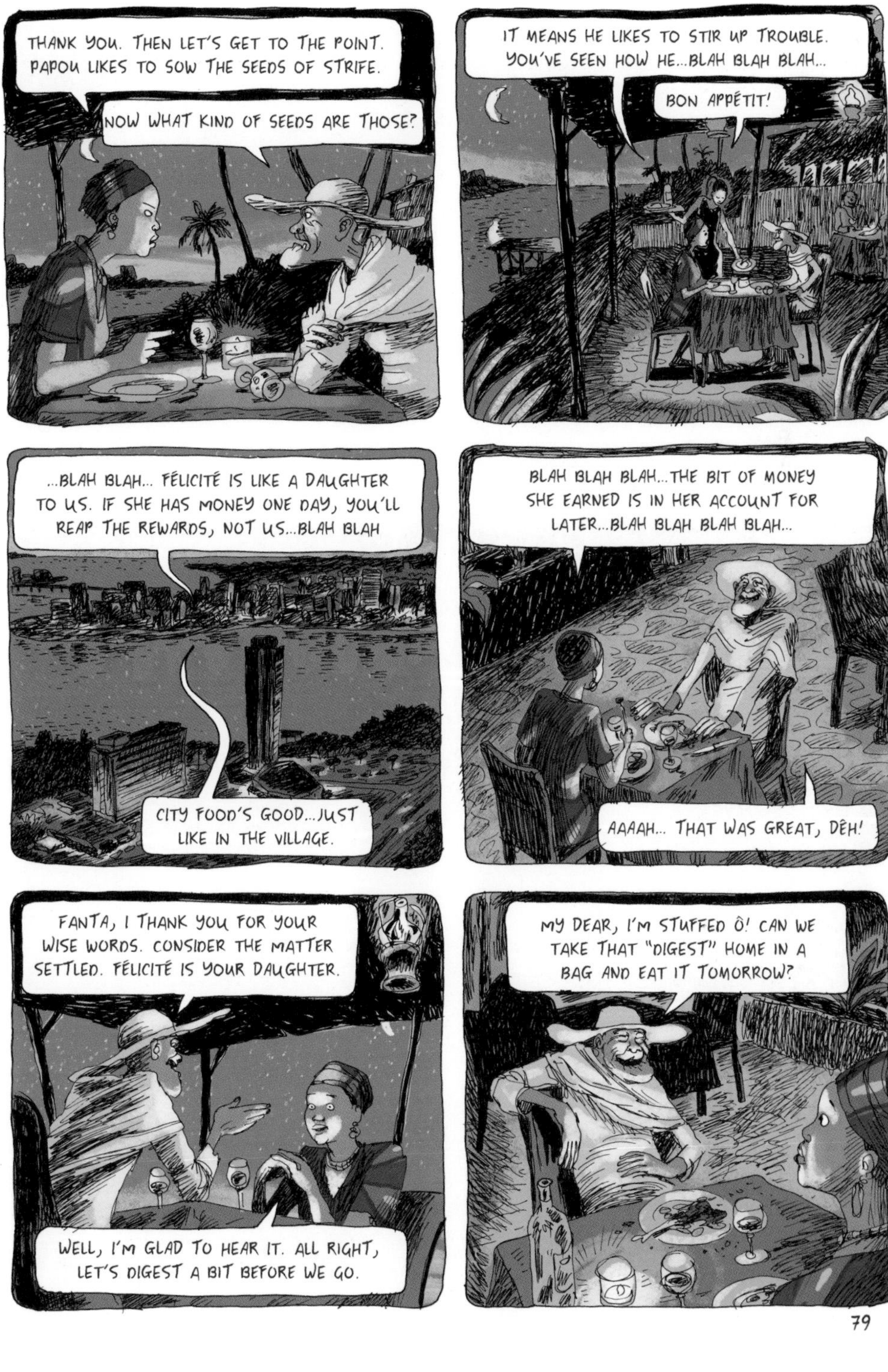
THANK YOU. THEN LET'S GET TO THE POINT. PAPOU LIKES TO SOW THE SEEDS OF STRIFE.
NOW WHAT KIND OF SEEDS ARE THOSE?
IT MEANS HE LIKES TO STIR UP TROUBLE. YOU'VE SEEN HOW HE...BLAH BLAH BLAH...
BON APPÉTIT!
...BLAH BLAH... FÉLICITÉ IS LIKE A DAUGHTER TO US. IF SHE HAS MONEY ONE DAY, YOU'LL REAP THE REWARDS, NOT US...BLAH BLAH
CITY FOOD'S GOOD...JUST LIKE IN THE VILLAGE.
BLAH BLAH BLAH...THE BIT OF MONEY SHE EARNED IS IN HER ACCOUNT FOR LATER...BLAH BLAH BLAH BLAH...
AAAAH... THAT WAS GREAT, DÊH!
FANTA, I THANK YOU FOR YOUR WISE WORDS. CONSIDER THE MATTER SETTLED. FÉLICITÉ IS YOUR DAUGHTER.
WELL, I'M GLAD TO HEAR IT. ALL RIGHT, LET'S DIGEST A BIT BEFORE WE GO.
MY DEAR, I'M STUFFED Ô! CAN WE TAKE THAT "DIGEST" HOME IN A BAG AND EAT IT TOMORROW?

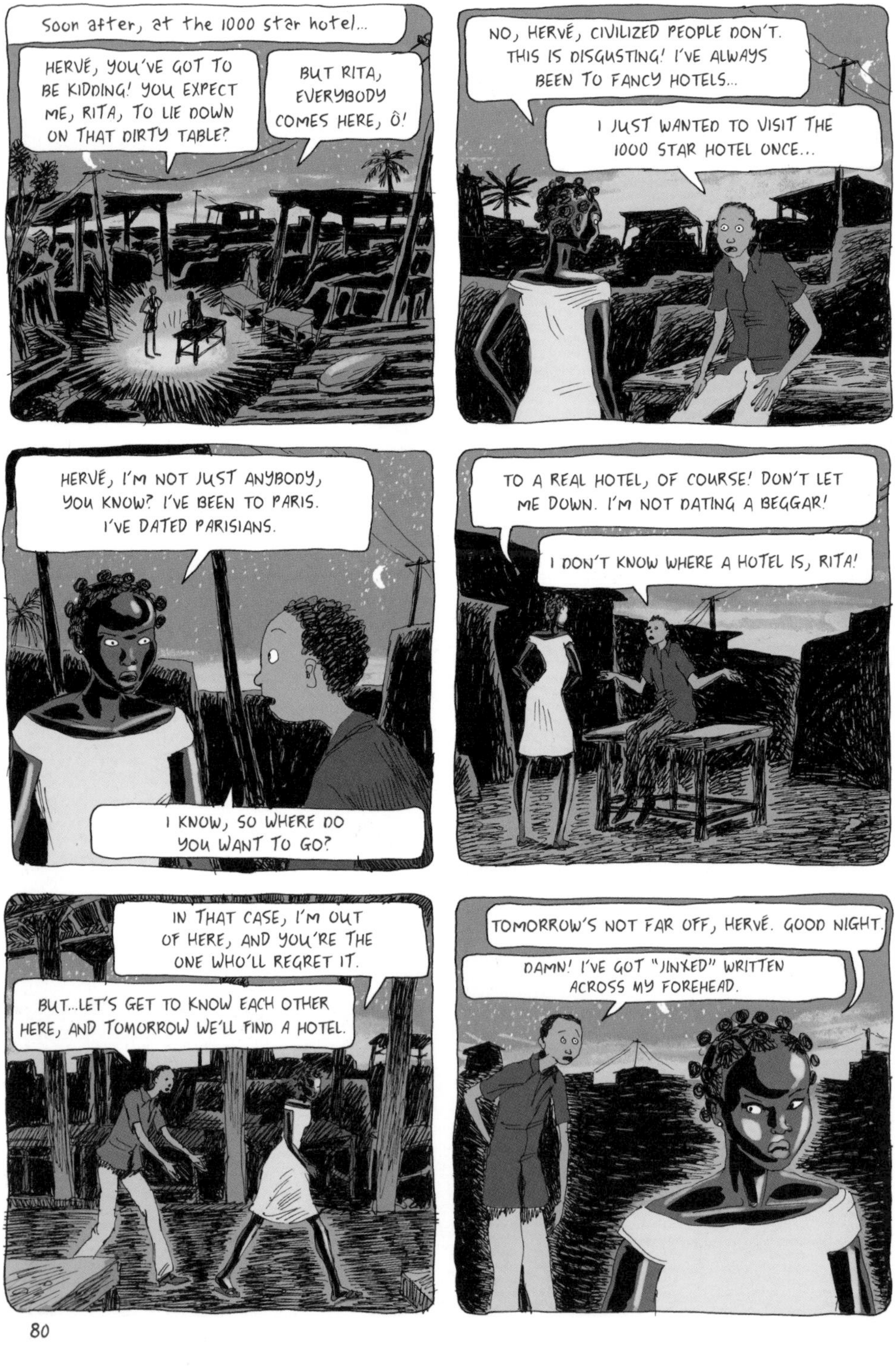
Soon after, at the 1000 star hotel...
HERVÉ, YOU'VE GOT TO BE KIDDING! YOU EXPECT ME, RITA, TO LIE DOWN ON THAT DIRTY TABLE?
BUT RITA, EVERYBODY COMES HERE, Ô!
NO, HERVÉ, CIVILIZED PEOPLE DON'T. THIS IS DISGUSTING! I'VE ALWAYS BEEN TO FANCY HOTELS...
I JUST WANTED TO VISIT THE 1000 STAR HOTEL ONCE...
HERVÉ, I'M NOT JUST ANYBODY, YOU KNOW? I'VE BEEN TO PARIS. I'VE DATED PARISIANS.
I KNOW, SO WHERE DO YOU WANT TO GO?
TO A REAL HOTEL, OF COURSE! DON'T LET ME DOWN. I'M NOT DATING A BEGGAR!
I DON'T KNOW WHERE A HOTEL IS, RITA!
IN THAT CASE, I'M OUT OF HERE, AND YOU'RE THE ONE WHO'LL REGRET IT.
BUT...LET'S GET TO KNOW EACH OTHER HERE, AND TOMORROW WE'LL FIND A HOTEL.
TOMORROW'S NOT FAR OFF, HERVÉ. GOOD NIGHT.
DAMN! I'VE GOT "JINXED" WRITTEN ACROSS MY FOREHEAD.

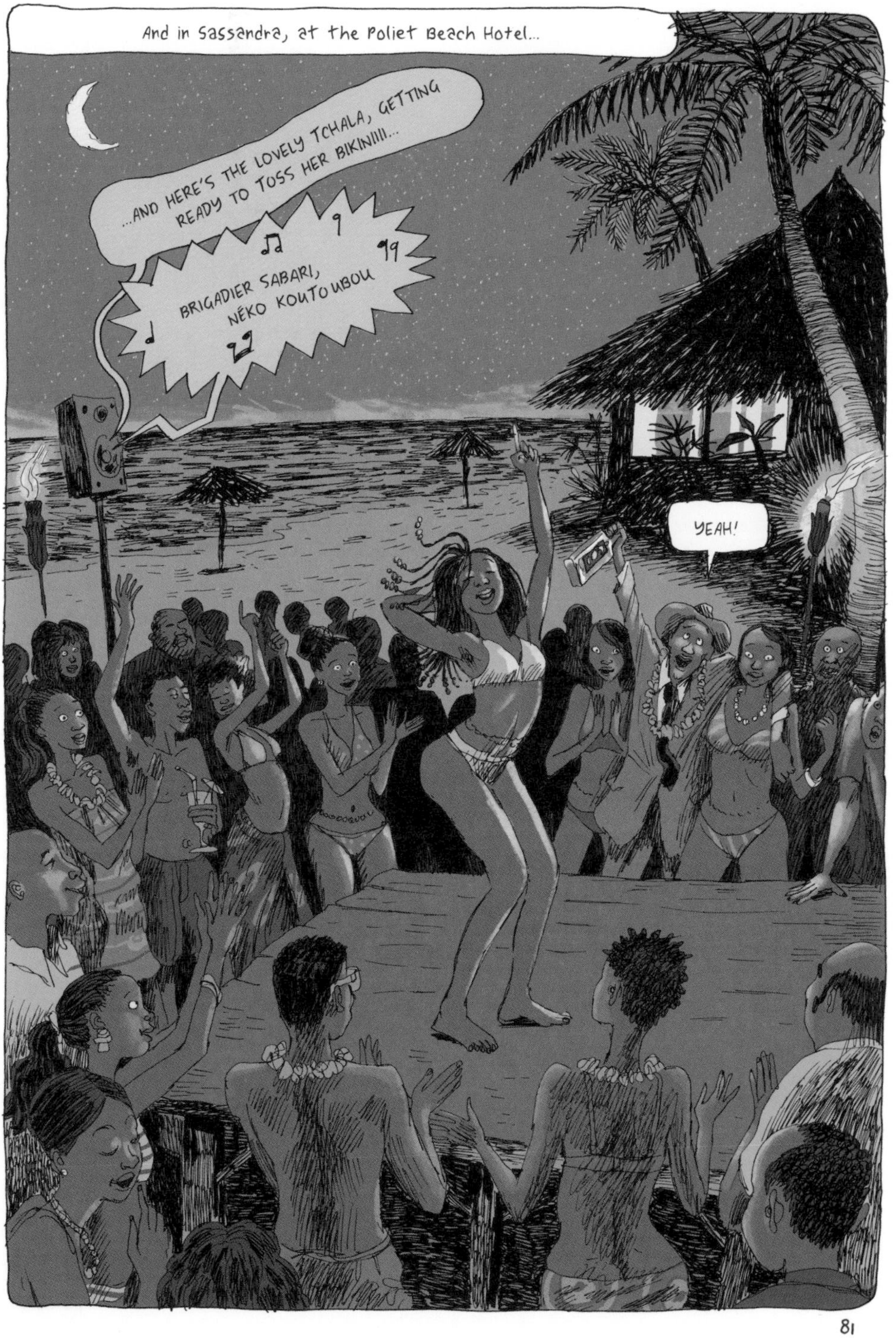
And in Sassandra, at the Poliet Beach Hotel...
...AND HERE'S THE LOVELY TCHALA, GETTING READY TO TOSS HER BIKINIIII...
BRIGADIER SABARI, NÉKO KOUTOUBOU
YEAH!

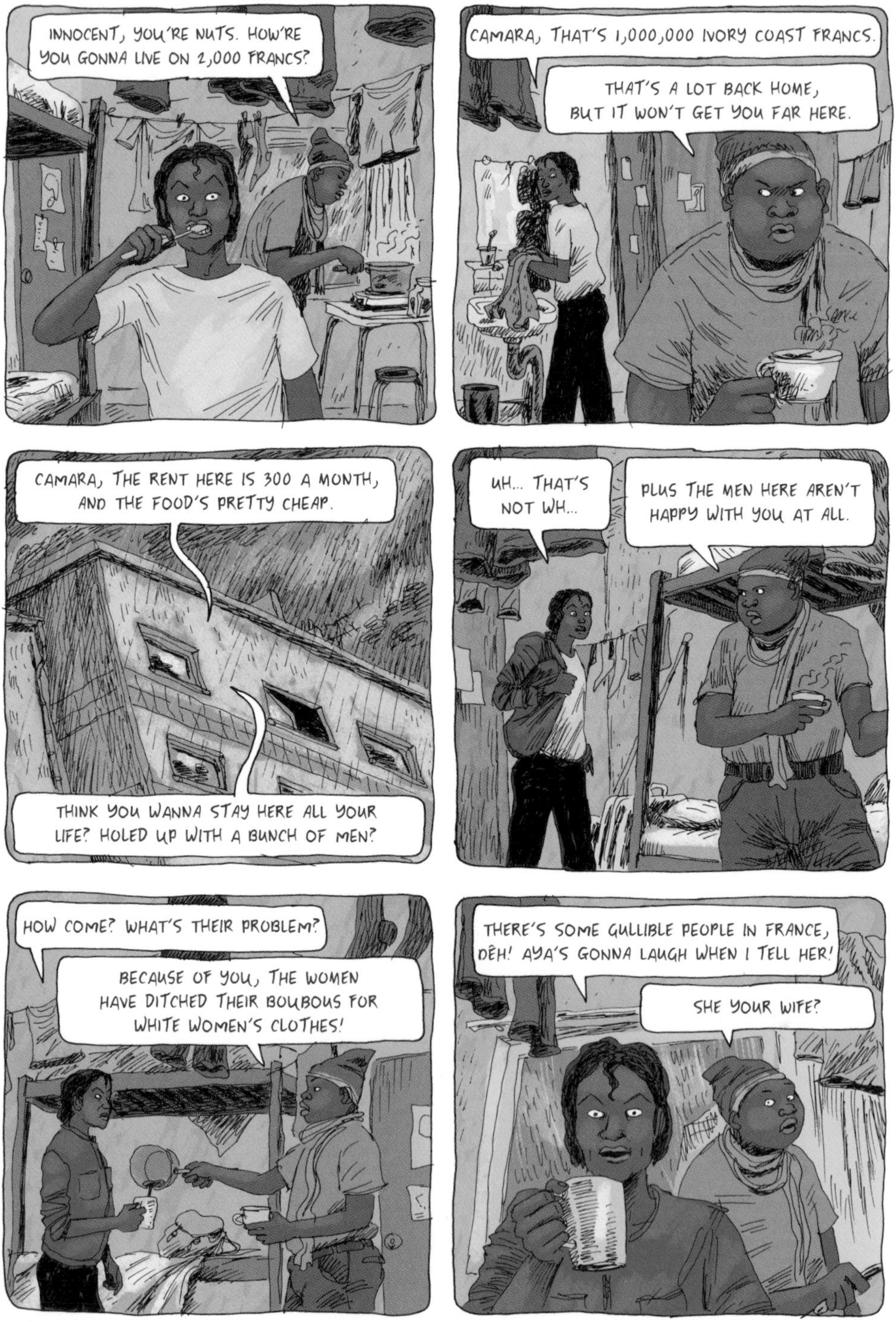
INNOCENT, YOU'RE NUTS. HOW'RE YOU GONNA LIVE ON 2,000 FRANCS?
CAMARA, THAT'S 1,000,000 IVORY COAST FRANCS.
THAT'S A LOT BACK HOME, BUT IT WON'T GET YOU FAR HERE.
CAMARA, THE RENT HERE IS 300 A MONTH, AND THE FOOD'S PRETTY CHEAP.
THINK YOU WANNA STAY HERE ALL YOUR LIFE? HOLED UP WITH A BUNCH OF MEN?
UH... THAT'S NOT WH...
PLUS THE MEN HERE AREN'T HAPPY WITH YOU AT ALL.
HOW COME? WHAT'S THEIR PROBLEM?
BECAUSE OF YOU, THE WOMEN HAVE DITCHED THEIR BOUBOUS FOR WHITE WOMEN'S CLOTHES!
THERE'S SOME GULLIBLE PEOPLE IN FRANCE, DÊH! AYA'S GONNA LAUGH WHEN I TELL HER!
SHE YOUR WIFE?

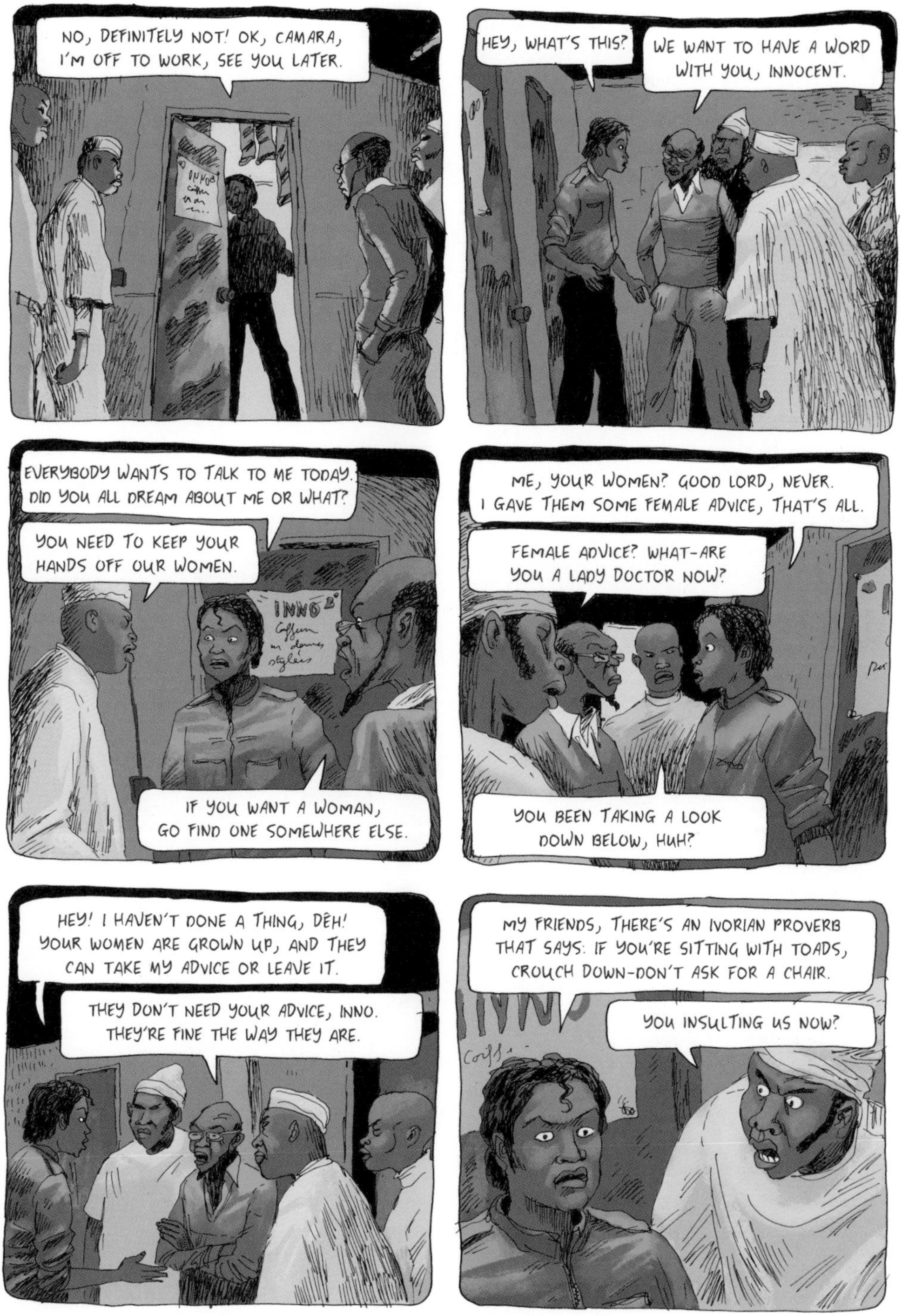
NO, DEFINITELY NOT! OK, CAMARA, I'M OFF TO WORK, SEE YOU LATER.
HEY, WHAT'S THIS?
WE WANT TO HAVE A WORD WITH YOU, INNOCENT.
EVERYBODY WANTS TO TALK TO ME TODAY. DID YOU ALL DREAM ABOUT ME OR WHAT?
YOU NEED TO KEEP YOUR HANDS OFF OUR WOMEN.
IF YOU WANT A WOMAN, GO FIND ONE SOMEWHERE ELSE.
ME, YOUR WOMEN? GOOD LORD, NEVER. I GAVE THEM SOME FEMALE ADVICE, THAT'S ALL.
FEMALE ADVICE? WHAT-ARE YOU A LADY DOCTOR NOW?
YOU BEEN TAKING A LOOK DOWN BELOW, HUH?
HEY! I HAVEN'T DONE A THING, DÊH! YOUR WOMEN ARE GROWN UP, AND THEY CAN TAKE MY ADVICE OR LEAVE IT.
THEY DON'T NEED YOUR ADVICE, INNO. THEY'RE FINE THE WAY THEY ARE.
MY FRIENDS, THERE'S AN IVORIAN PROVERB THAT SAYS: IF YOU'RE SITTING WITH TOADS, CROUCH DOWN-DON'T ASK FOR A CHAIR.
YOU INSULTING US NOW?

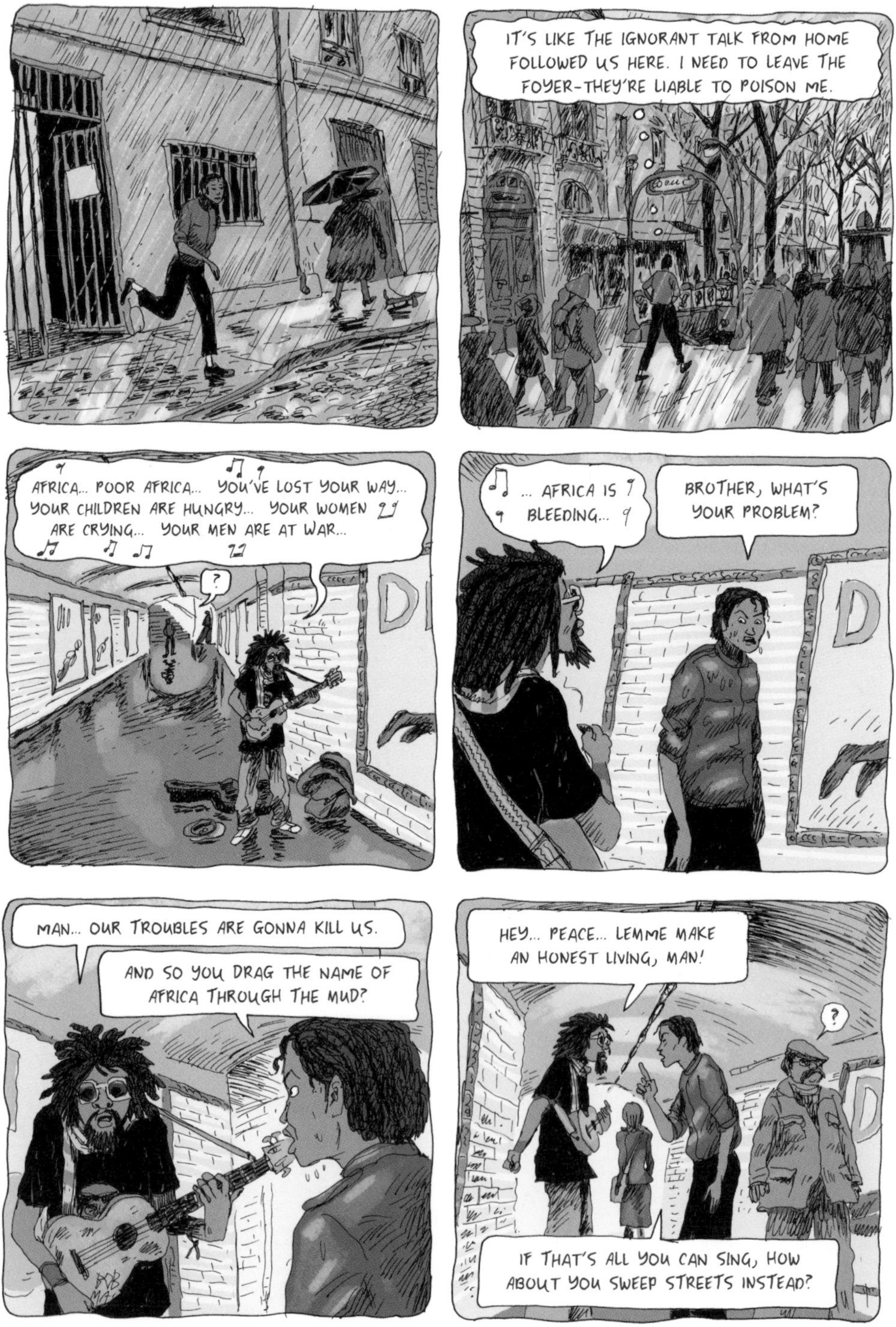

IT'S LIKE THE IGNORANT TALK FROM HOME FOLLOWED US HERE. I NEED TO LEAVE THE FOYER–THEY'RE LIABLE TO POISON ME.
AFRICA... POOR AFRICA... YOU'VE LOST YOUR WAY... YOUR CHILDREN ARE HUNGRY... YOUR WOMEN ARE CRYING... YOUR MEN ARE AT WAR...
?
... AFRICA IS BLEEDING...
BROTHER, WHAT'S YOUR PROBLEM?
MAN... OUR TROUBLES ARE GONNA KILL US.
AND SO YOU DRAG THE NAME OF AFRICA THROUGH THE MUD?
HEY... PEACE... LEMME MAKE AN HONEST LIVING, MAN!
?
IF THAT'S ALL YOU CAN SING, HOW ABOUT YOU SWEEP STREETS INSTEAD?

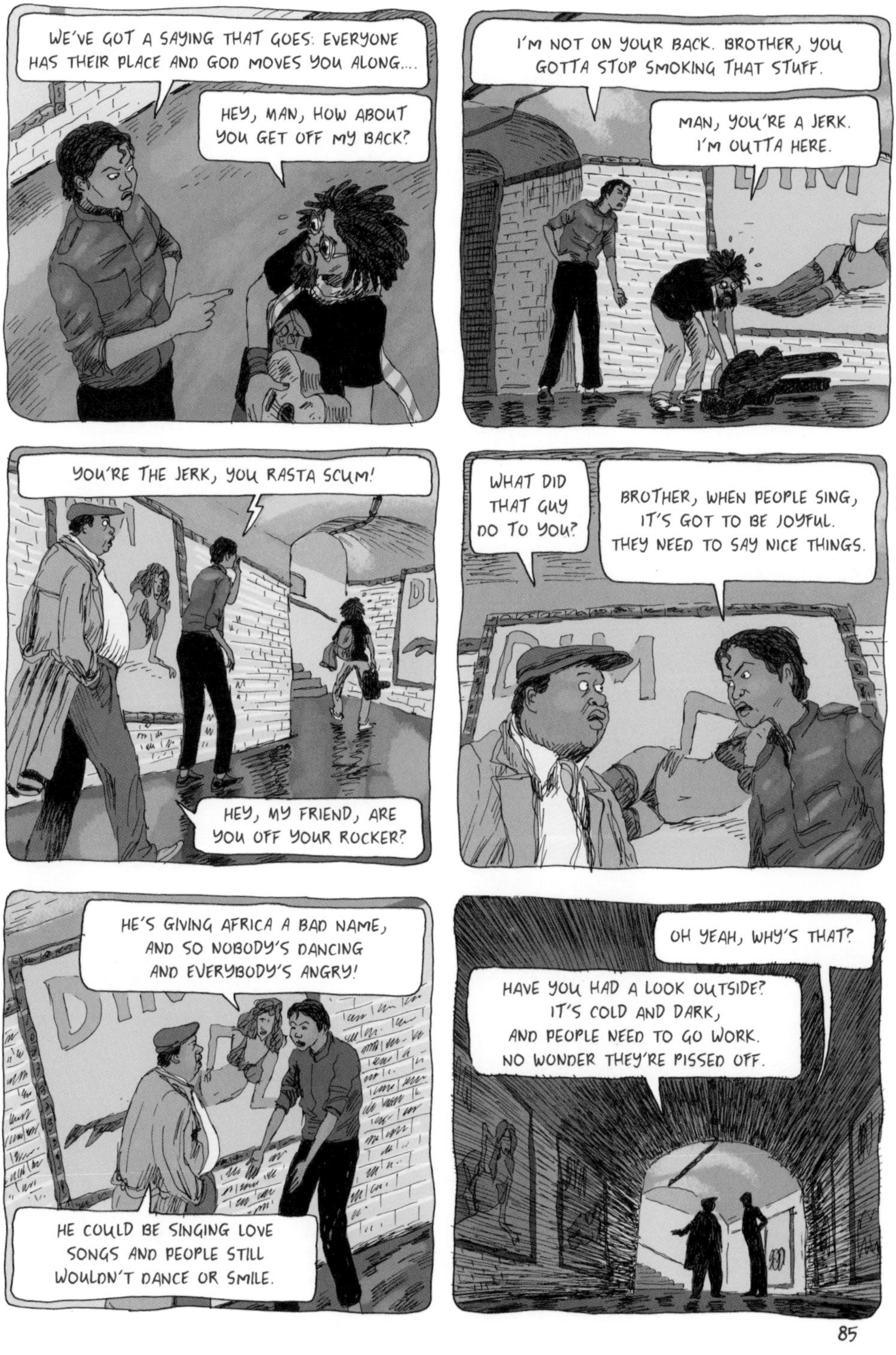

WE'VE GOT A SAYING THAT GOES: EVERYONE HAS THEIR PLACE AND GOD MOVES YOU ALONG....
HEY, MAN, HOW ABOUT YOU GET OFF MY BACK?
I'M NOT ON YOUR BACK. BROTHER, YOU GOTTA STOP SMOKING THAT STUFF.
MAN, YOU'RE A JERK. I'M OUTTA HERE.
YOU'RE THE JERK, YOU RASTA SCUM!
HEY, MY FRIEND, ARE YOU OFF YOUR ROCKER?
WHAT DID THAT GUY DO TO YOU?
BROTHER, WHEN PEOPLE SING, IT'S GOT TO BE JOYFUL. THEY NEED TO SAY NICE THINGS.
HE'S GIVING AFRICA A BAD NAME, AND SO NOBODY'S DANCING AND EVERYBODY'S ANGRY!
HE COULD BE SINGING LOVE SONGS AND PEOPLE STILL WOULDN'T DANCE OR SMILE.
OH YEAH, WHY'S THAT?
HAVE YOU HAD A LOOK OUTSIDE? IT'S COLD AND DARK, AND PEOPLE NEED TO GO WORK. NO WONDER THEY'RE PISSED OFF.

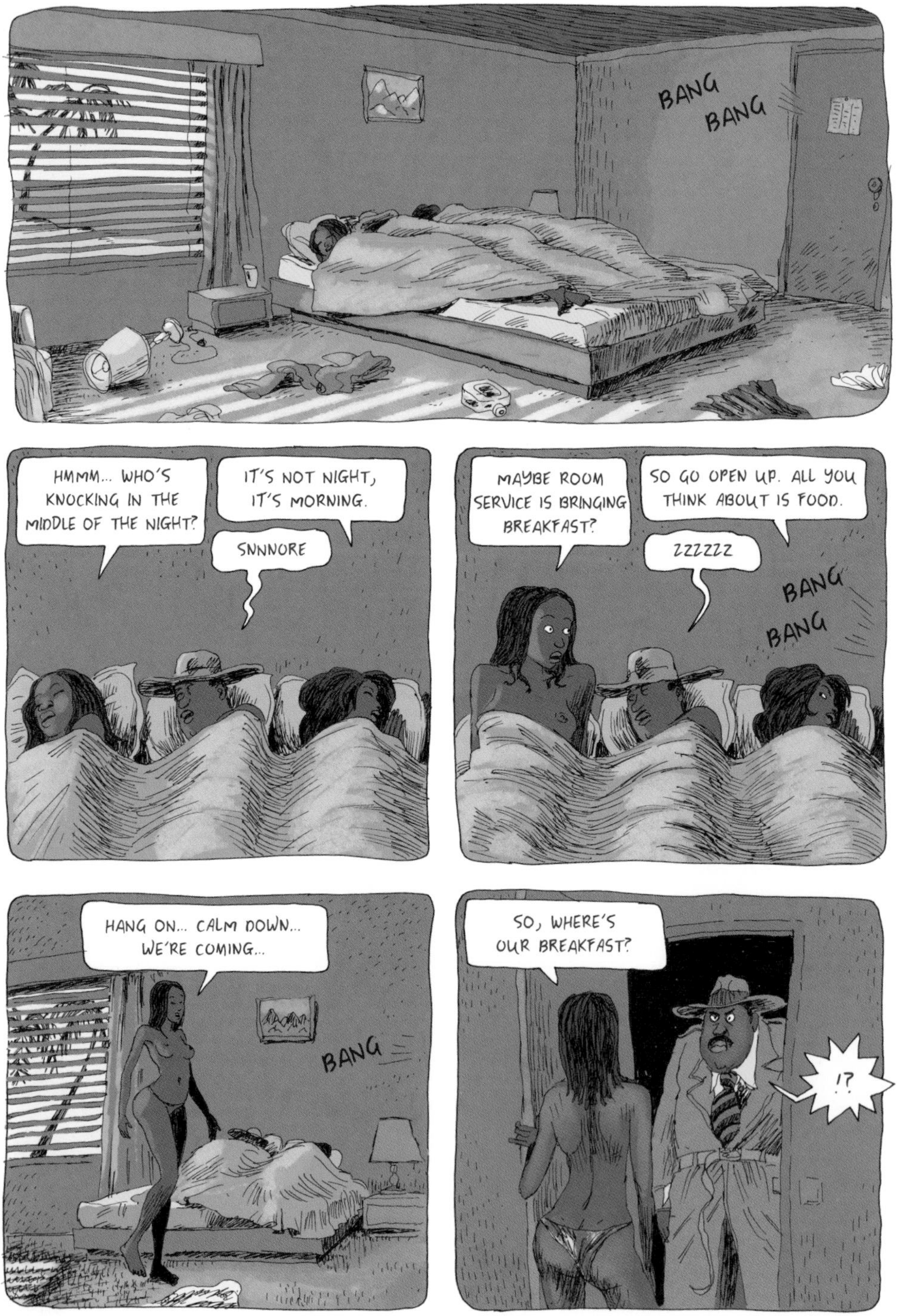
BANG
BANG
HMMM... WHO'S KNOCKING IN THE MIDDLE OF THE NIGHT?
IT'S NOT NIGHT, IT'S MORNING.
SNNNORE
MAYBE ROOM SERVICE IS BRINGING BREAKFAST?
SO GO OPEN UP. ALL YOU THINK ABOUT IS FOOD.
ZZZZZZ
BANG
BANG
HANG ON... CALM DOWN... WE'RE COMING...
BANG
SO, WHERE'S OUR BREAKFAST?
!?

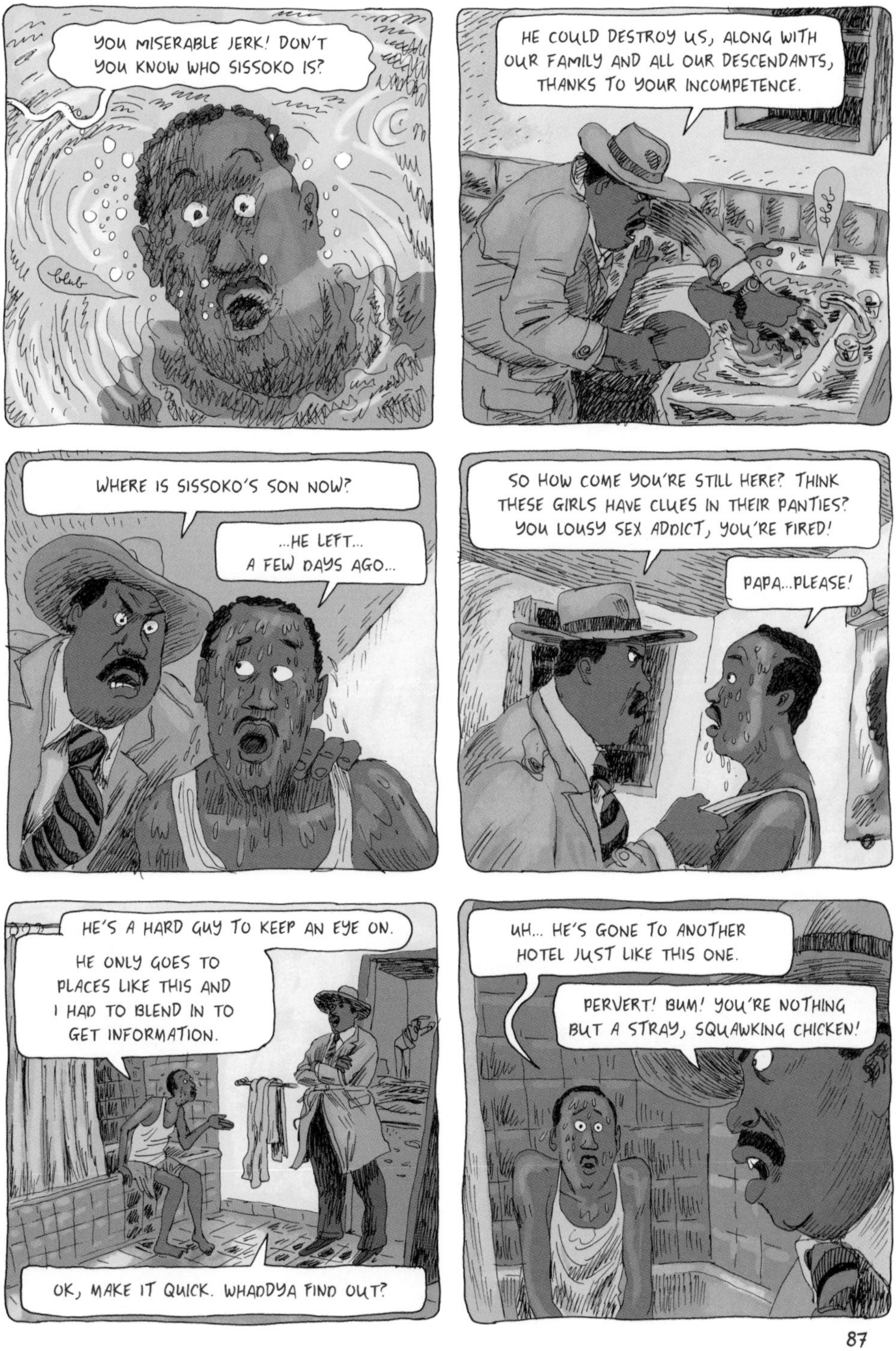
YOU MISERABLE JERK! DON'T YOU KNOW WHO SISSOKO IS?
blub
HE COULD DESTROY US, ALONG WITH OUR FAMILY AND ALL OUR DESCENDANTS, THANKS TO YOUR INCOMPETENCE.
WHERE IS SISSOKO'S SON NOW?
...HE LEFT... A FEW DAYS AGO...
SO HOW COME YOU'RE STILL HERE? THINK THESE GIRLS HAVE CLUES IN THEIR PANTIES? YOU LOUSY SEX ADDICT, YOU'RE FIRED!
PAPA...PLEASE!
HE'S A HARD GUY TO KEEP AN EYE ON.
HE ONLY GOES TO PLACES LIKE THIS AND I HAD TO BLEND IN TO GET INFORMATION.
OK, MAKE IT QUICK. WHADDYA FIND OUT?
UH... HE'S GONE TO ANOTHER HOTEL JUST LIKE THIS ONE.
PERVERT! BUM! YOU'RE NOTHING BUT A STRAY, SQUAWKING CHICKEN!

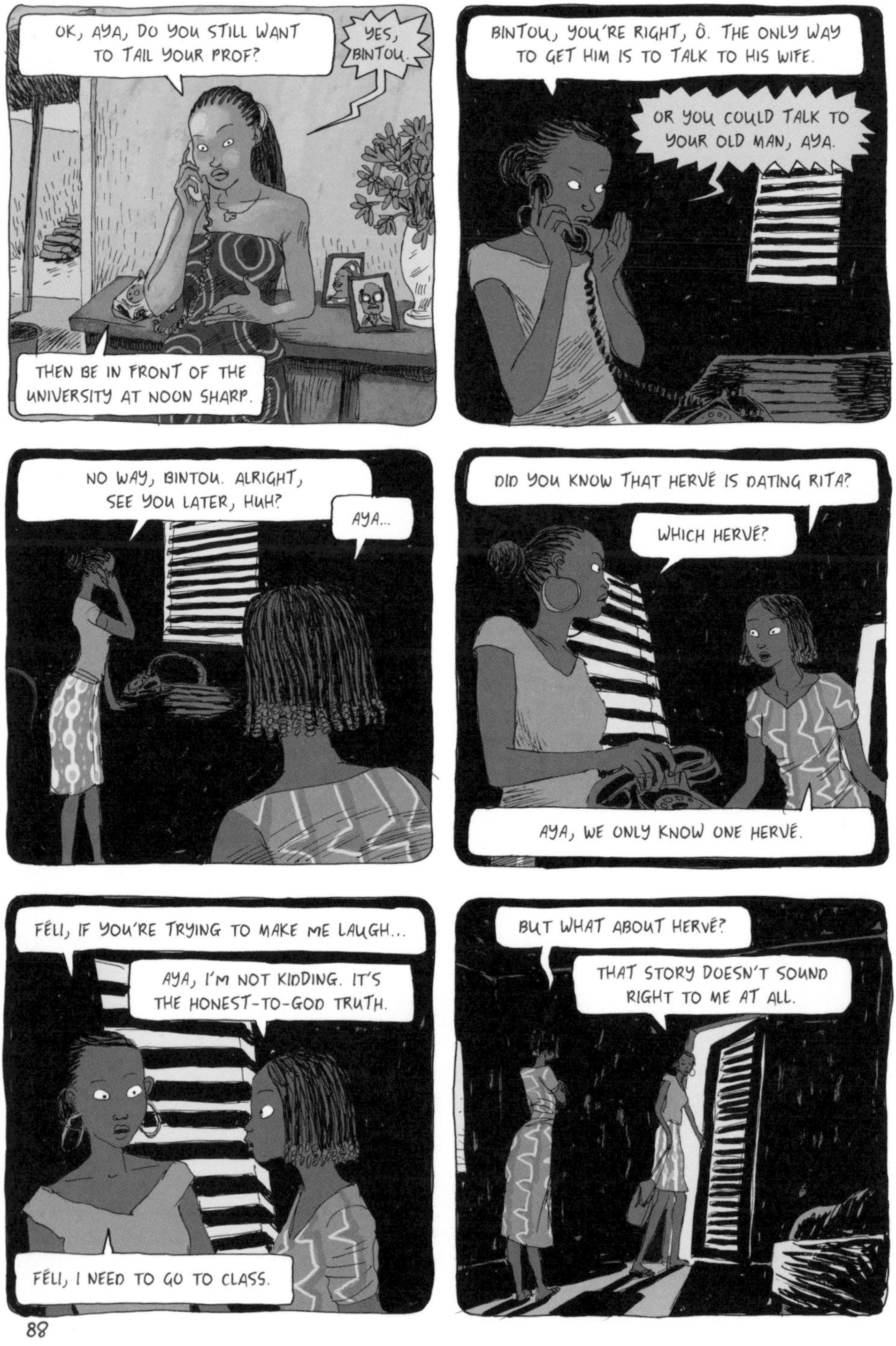
OK, AYA, DO YOU STILL WANT TO TAIL YOUR PROF?
YES, BINTOU.
THEN BE IN FRONT OF THE UNIVERSITY AT NOON SHARP.
BINTOU, YOU'RE RIGHT, Ô. THE ONLY WAY TO GET HIM IS TO TALK TO HIS WIFE.
OR YOU COULD TALK TO YOUR OLD MAN, AYA.
NO WAY, BINTOU. ALRIGHT, SEE YOU LATER, HUH?
AYA...
DID YOU KNOW THAT HERVÉ IS DATING RITA?
WHICH HERVÉ?
AYA, WE ONLY KNOW ONE HERVÉ.
FÉLI, IF YOU'RE TRYING TO MAKE ME LAUGH...
AYA, I'M NOT KIDDING. IT'S THE HONEST-TO-GOD TRUTH.
FÉLI, I NEED TO GO TO CLASS.
BUT WHAT ABOUT HERVÉ?
THAT STORY DOESN'T SOUND RIGHT TO ME AT ALL.

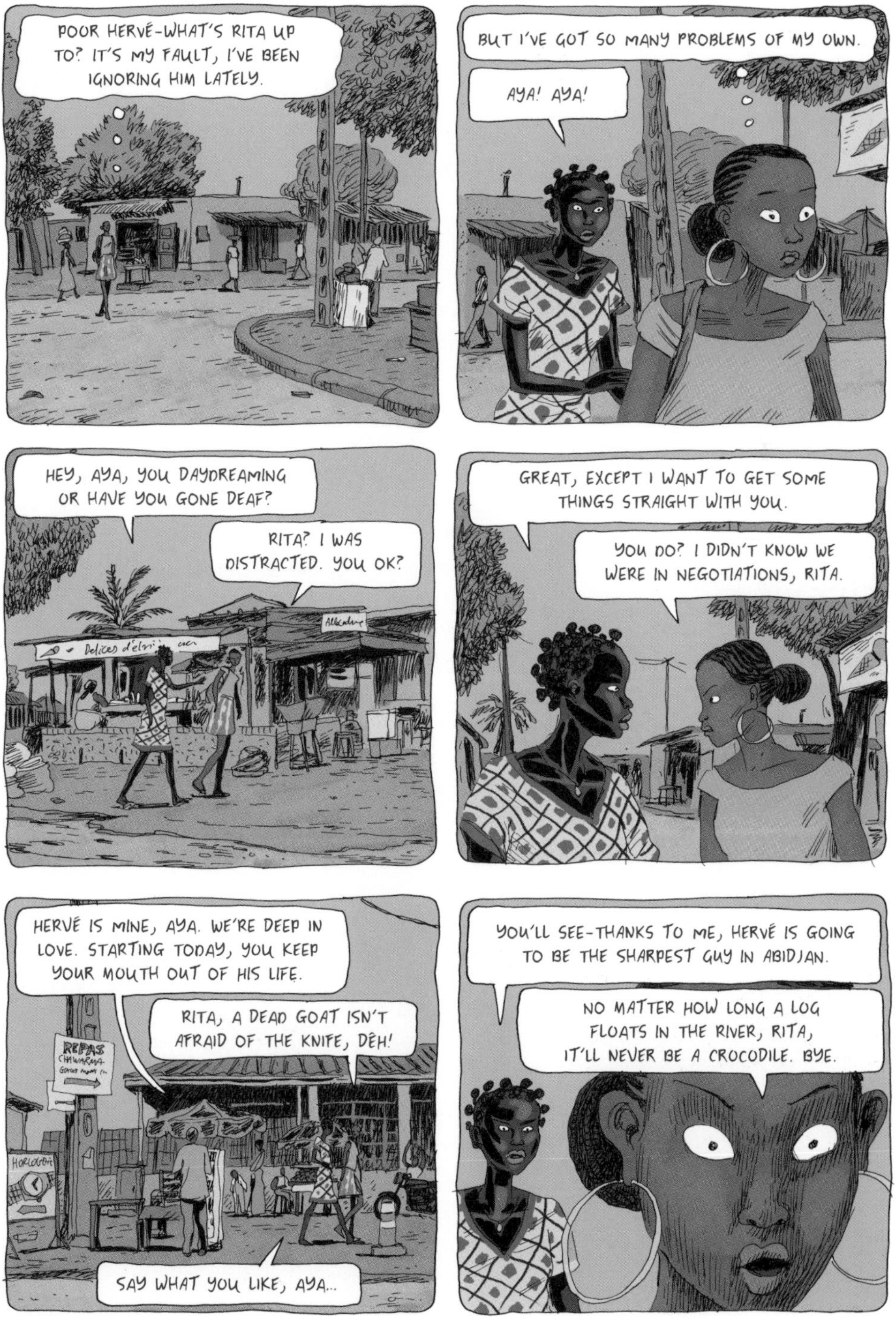
POOR HERVÉ-WHAT'S RITA UP TO? IT'S MY FAULT, I'VE BEEN IGNORING HIM LATELY.
BUT I'VE GOT SO MANY PROBLEMS OF MY OWN.
AYA! AYA!
HEY, AYA, YOU DAYDREAMING OR HAVE YOU GONE DEAF?
RITA? I WAS DISTRACTED. YOU OK?
GREAT, EXCEPT I WANT TO GET SOME THINGS STRAIGHT WITH YOU.
YOU DO? I DIDN'T KNOW WE WERE IN NEGOTIATIONS, RITA.
HERVÉ IS MINE, AYA. WE'RE DEEP IN LOVE. STARTING TODAY, YOU KEEP YOUR MOUTH OUT OF HIS LIFE.
RITA, A DEAD GOAT ISN'T AFRAID OF THE KNIFE, DÊH!
REPAS
CHAWARMA
SAY WHAT YOU LIKE, AYA...
YOU'LL SEE-THANKS TO ME, HERVÉ IS GOING TO BE THE SHARPEST GUY IN ABIDJAN.
NO MATTER HOW LONG A LOG FLOATS IN THE RIVER, RITA, IT'LL NEVER BE A CROCODILE. BYE.

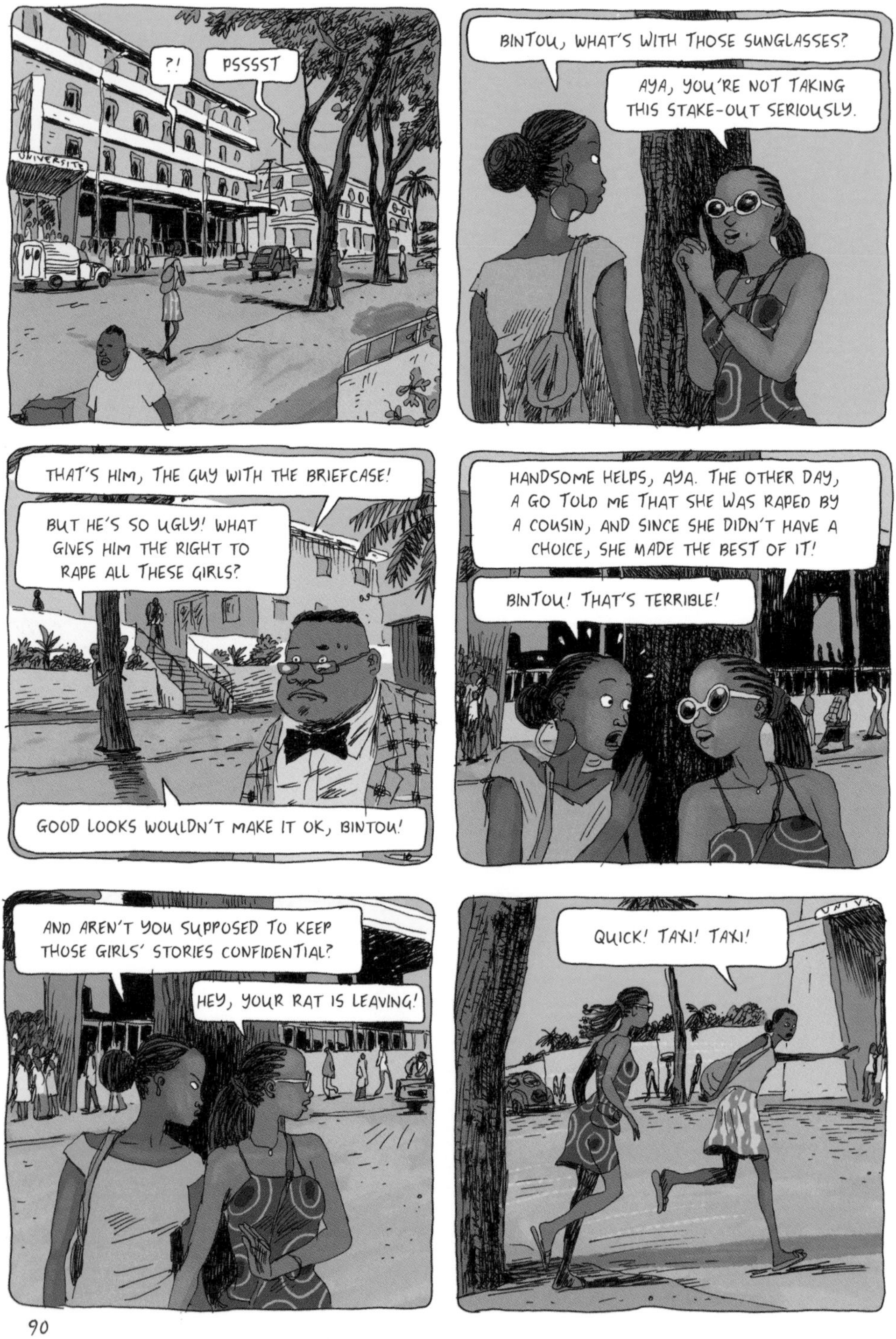
?!
PSSSST
BINTOU, WHAT'S WITH THOSE SUNGLASSES?
AYA, YOU'RE NOT TAKING THIS STAKE-OUT SERIOUSLY.
THAT'S HIM, THE GUY WITH THE BRIEFCASE!
BUT HE'S SO UGLY! WHAT GIVES HIM THE RIGHT TO RAPE ALL THESE GIRLS?
GOOD LOOKS WOULDN'T MAKE IT OK, BINTOU!
HANDSOME HELPS, AYA. THE OTHER DAY, A GO TOLD ME THAT SHE WAS RAPED BY A COUSIN, AND SINCE SHE DIDN'T HAVE A CHOICE, SHE MADE THE BEST OF IT!
BINTOU! THAT'S TERRIBLE!
AND AREN'T YOU SUPPOSED TO KEEP THOSE GIRLS' STORIES CONFIDENTIAL?
HEY, YOUR RAT IS LEAVING!
QUICK! TAXI! TAXI!

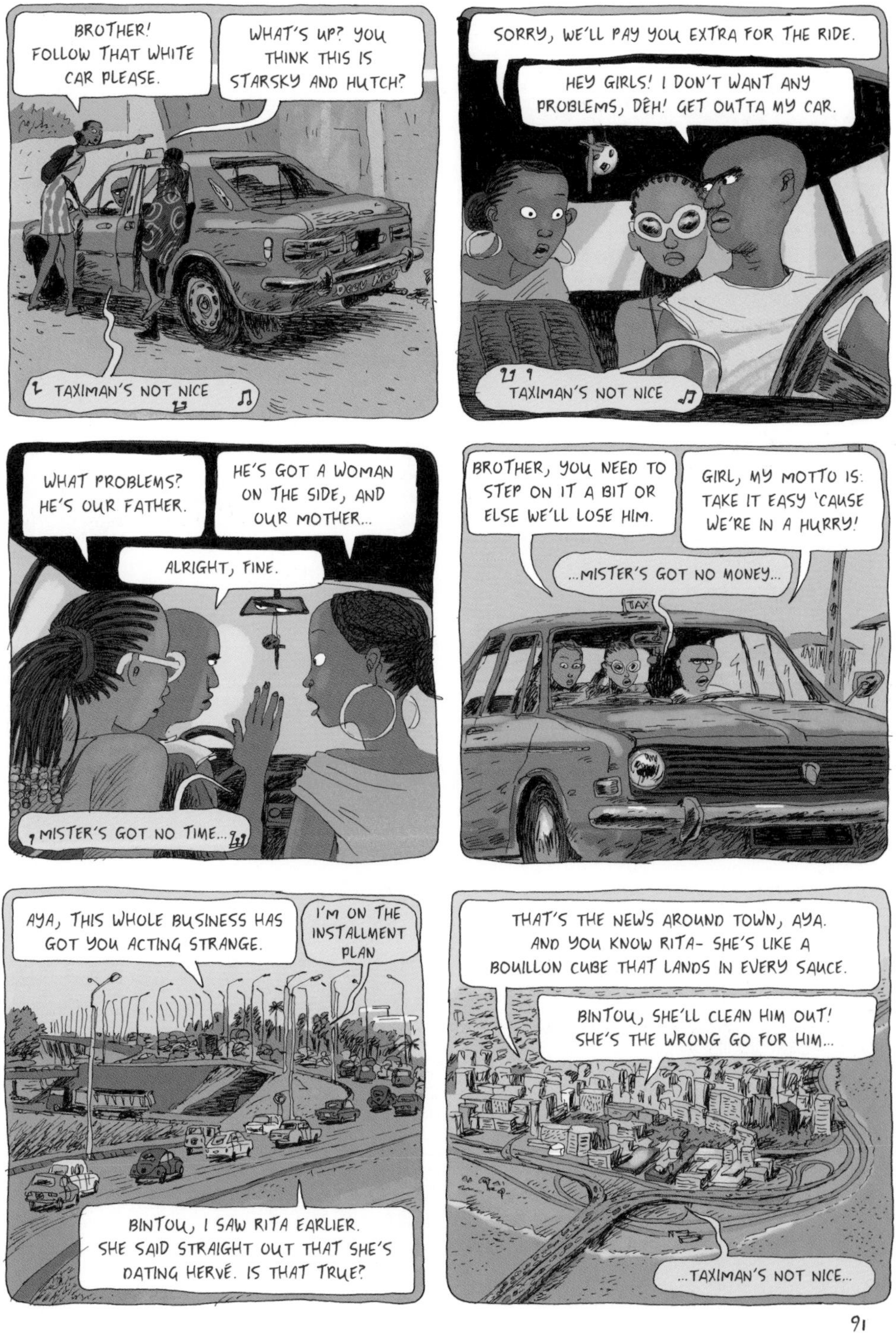
BROTHER! FOLLOW THAT WHITE CAR PLEASE.
WHAT'S UP? YOU THINK THIS IS STARSKY AND HUTCH?
TAXIMAN'S NOT NICE
SORRY, WE'LL PAY YOU EXTRA FOR THE RIDE.
HEY GIRLS! I DON'T WANT ANY PROBLEMS, DÊH! GET OUTTA MY CAR.
TAXIMAN'S NOT NICE
WHAT PROBLEMS? HE'S OUR FATHER.
HE'S GOT A WOMAN ON THE SIDE, AND OUR MOTHER...
ALRIGHT, FINE.
MISTER'S GOT NO TIME...
BROTHER, YOU NEED TO STEP ON IT A BIT OR ELSE WE'LL LOSE HIM.
GIRL, MY MOTTO IS: TAKE IT EASY 'CAUSE WE'RE IN A HURRY!
...MISTER'S GOT NO MONEY...
AYA, THIS WHOLE BUSINESS HAS GOT YOU ACTING STRANGE.
I'M ON THE INSTALLMENT PLAN
BINTOU, I SAW RITA EARLIER. SHE SAID STRAIGHT OUT THAT SHE'S DATING HERVÉ. IS THAT TRUE?
THAT'S THE NEWS AROUND TOWN, AYA. AND YOU KNOW RITA- SHE'S LIKE A BOUILLON CUBE THAT LANDS IN EVERY SAUCE.
BINTOU, SHE'LL CLEAN HIM OUT! SHE'S THE WRONG GO FOR HIM...
...TAXIMAN'S NOT NICE...

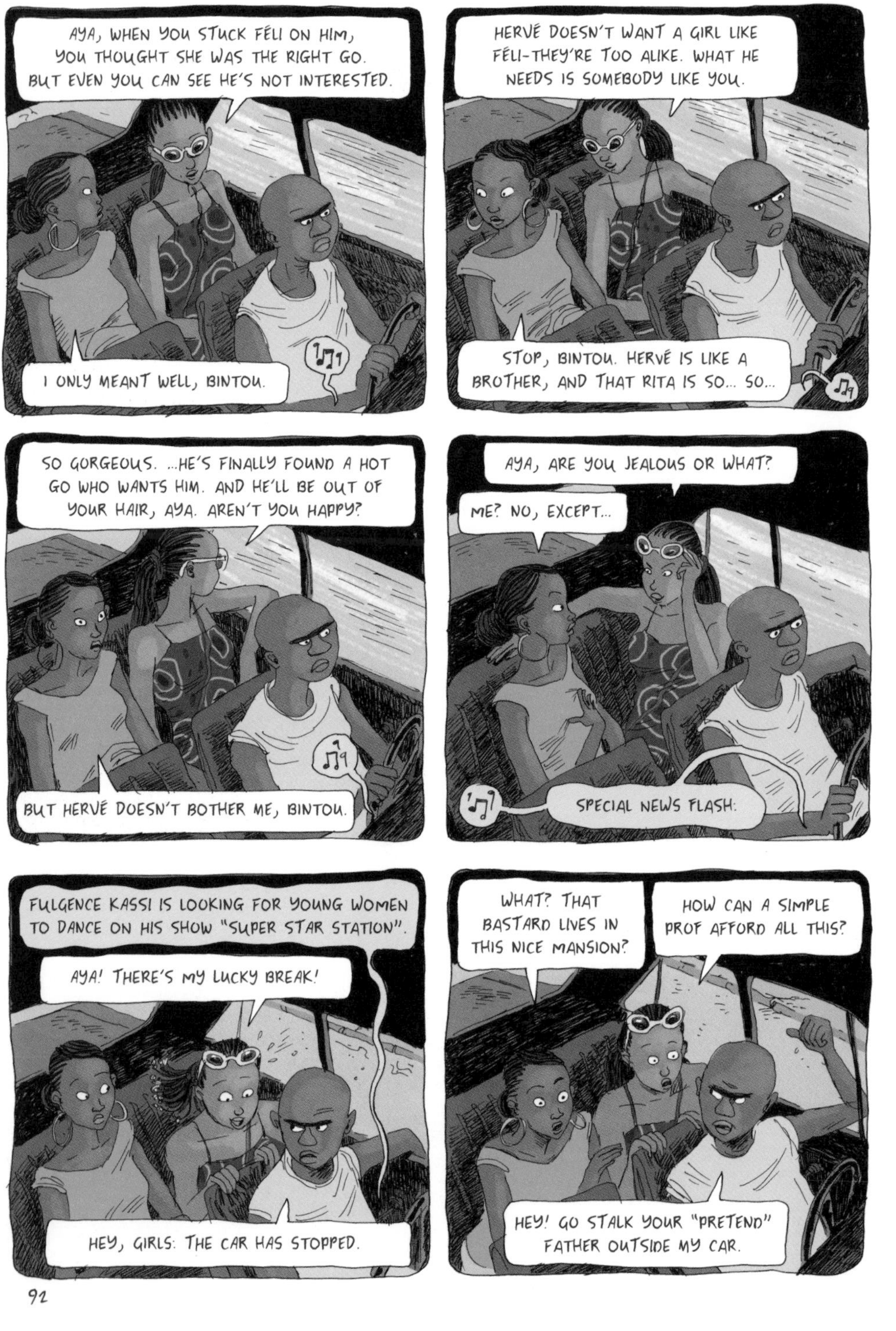
AYA, WHEN YOU STUCK FÉLI ON HIM, YOU THOUGHT SHE WAS THE RIGHT GO. BUT EVEN YOU CAN SEE HE'S NOT INTERESTED.
I ONLY MEANT WELL, BINTOU.
HERVÉ DOESN'T WANT A GIRL LIKE FÉLI-THEY'RE TOO ALIKE. WHAT HE NEEDS IS SOMEBODY LIKE YOU.
STOP, BINTOU. HERVÉ IS LIKE A BROTHER, AND THAT RITA IS SO... SO...
SO GORGEOUS. ...HE'S FINALLY FOUND A HOT GO WHO WANTS HIM. AND HE'LL BE OUT OF YOUR HAIR, AYA. AREN'T YOU HAPPY?
BUT HERVÉ DOESN'T BOTHER ME, BINTOU.
AYA, ARE YOU JEALOUS OR WHAT?
ME? NO, EXCEPT...
SPECIAL NEWS FLASH:
FULGENCE KASSI IS LOOKING FOR YOUNG WOMEN TO DANCE ON HIS SHOW "SUPER STAR STATION".
AYA! THERE'S MY LUCKY BREAK!
HEY, GIRLS: THE CAR HAS STOPPED.
WHAT? THAT BASTARD LIVES IN THIS NICE MANSION?
HOW CAN A SIMPLE PROF AFFORD ALL THIS?
HEY! GO STALK YOUR "PRETEND" FATHER OUTSIDE MY CAR.

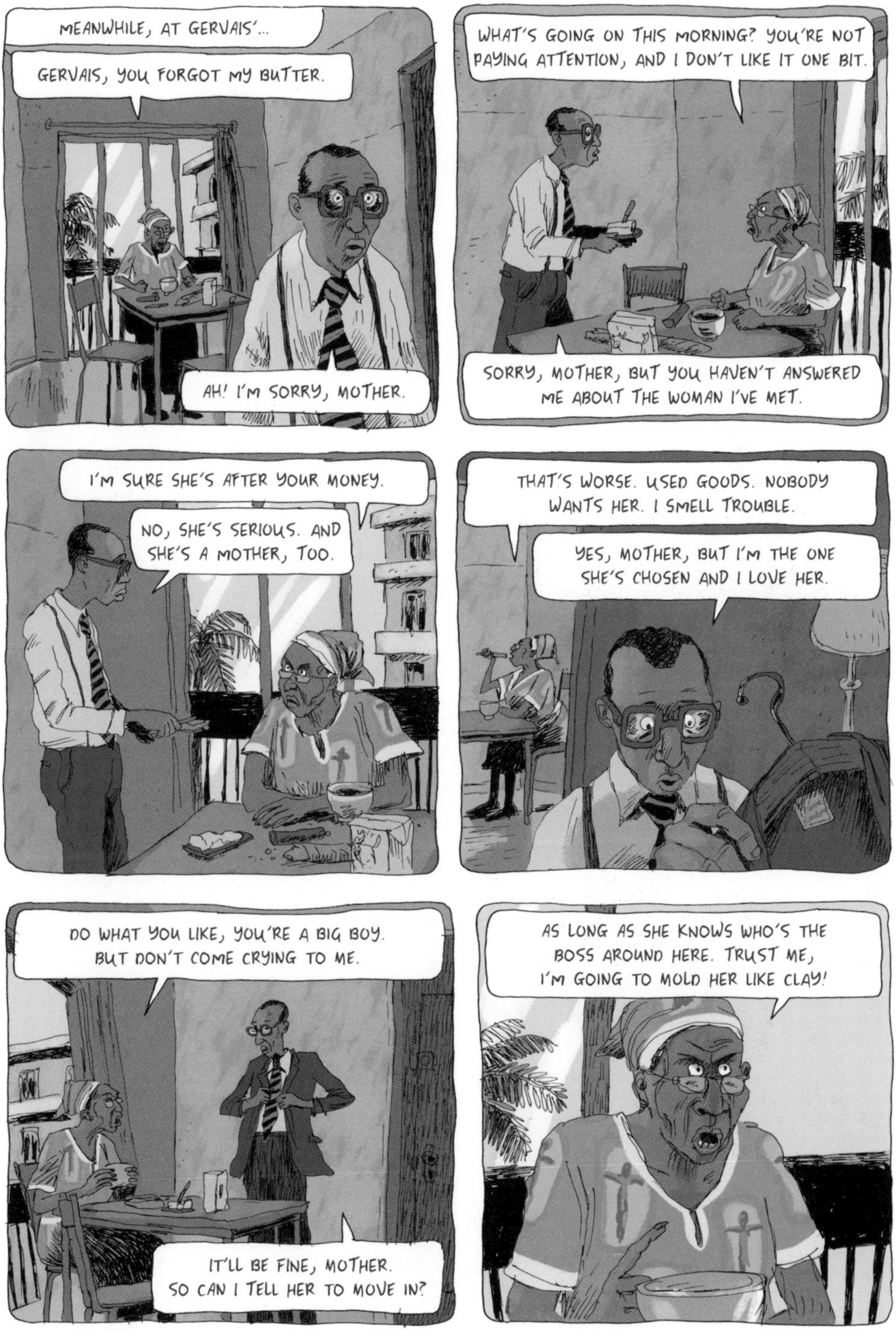
MEANWHILE, AT GERVAIS'...
GERVAIS, YOU FORGOT MY BUTTER.
AH! I'M SORRY, MOTHER.
WHAT'S GOING ON THIS MORNING? YOU'RE NOT PAYING ATTENTION, AND I DON'T LIKE IT ONE BIT.
SORRY, MOTHER, BUT YOU HAVEN'T ANSWERED ME ABOUT THE WOMAN I'VE MET.
I'M SURE SHE'S AFTER YOUR MONEY.
NO, SHE'S SERIOUS. AND SHE'S A MOTHER, TOO.
THAT'S WORSE. USED GOODS. NOBODY WANTS HER. I SMELL TROUBLE.
YES, MOTHER, BUT I'M THE ONE SHE'S CHOSEN AND I LOVE HER.
DO WHAT YOU LIKE, YOU'RE A BIG BOY. BUT DON'T COME CRYING TO ME.
IT'LL BE FINE, MOTHER. SO CAN I TELL HER TO MOVE IN?
AS LONG AS SHE KNOWS WHO'S THE BOSS AROUND HERE. TRUST ME, I'M GOING TO MOLD HER LIKE CLAY!

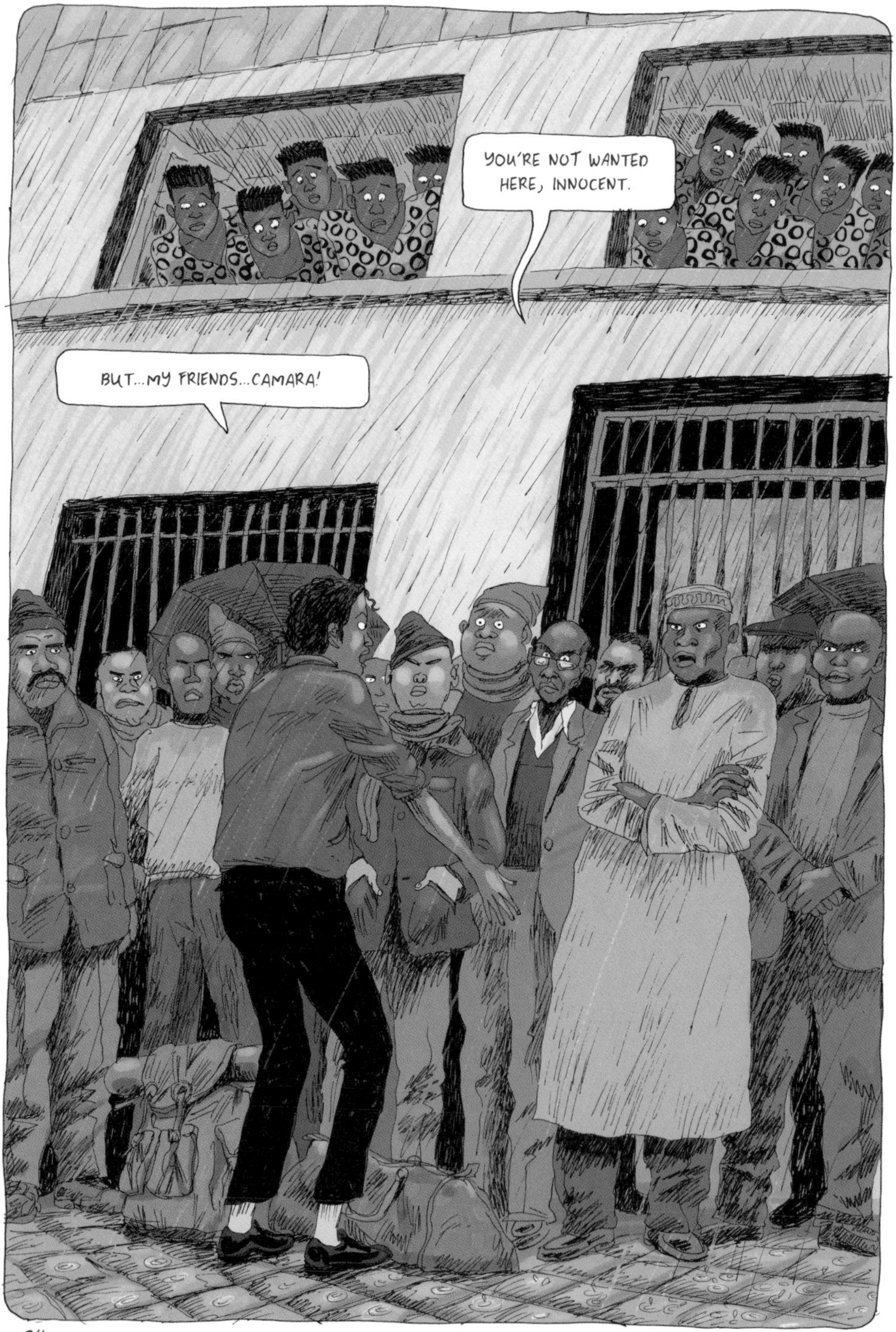
YOU'RE NOT WANTED HERE, INNOCENT.
BUT...MY FRIENDS...CAMARA!

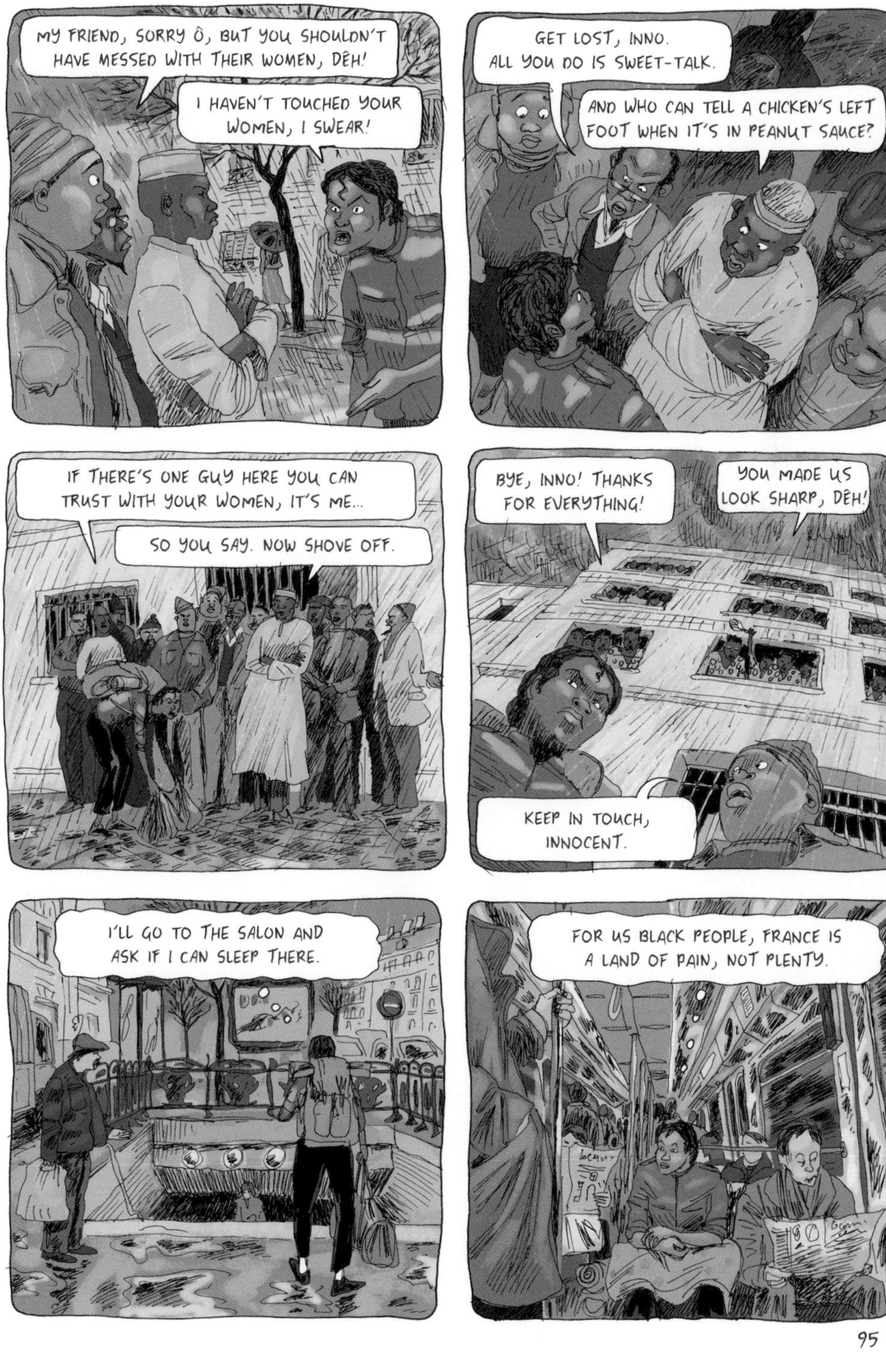
MY FRIEND, SORRY Ô, BUT YOU SHOULDN'T HAVE MESSED WITH THEIR WOMEN, DÊH!
I HAVEN'T TOUCHED YOUR WOMEN, I SWEAR!
GET LOST, INNO. ALL YOU DO IS SWEET-TALK.
AND WHO CAN TELL A CHICKEN'S LEFT FOOT WHEN IT'S IN PEANUT SAUCE?
IF THERE'S ONE GUY HERE YOU CAN TRUST WITH YOUR WOMEN, IT'S ME...
SO YOU SAY. NOW SHOVE OFF.
BYE, INNO! THANKS FOR EVERYTHING!
YOU MADE US LOOK SHARP, DÊH!
KEEP IN TOUCH, INNOCENT.
I'LL GO TO THE SALON AND ASK IF I CAN SLEEP THERE.
FOR US BLACK PEOPLE, FRANCE IS A LAND OF PAIN, NOT PLENTY.

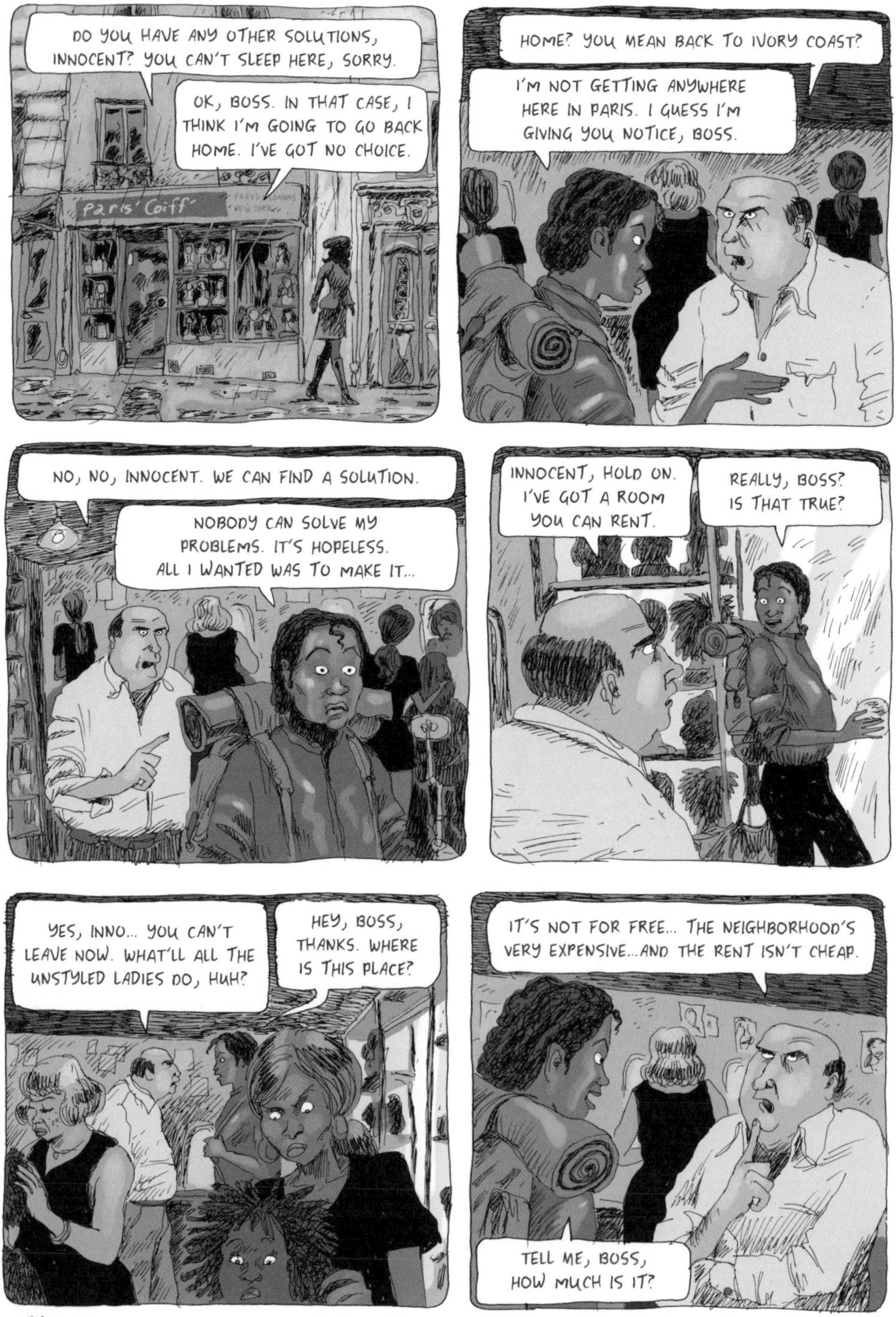
DO YOU HAVE ANY OTHER SOLUTIONS, INNOCENT? YOU CAN'T SLEEP HERE, SORRY.
OK, BOSS. IN THAT CASE, I THINK I'M GOING TO GO BACK HOME. I'VE GOT NO CHOICE.
Paris' Coiff'
HOME? YOU MEAN BACK TO IVORY COAST?
I'M NOT GETTING ANYWHERE HERE IN PARIS. I GUESS I'M GIVING YOU NOTICE, BOSS.
NO, NO, INNOCENT. WE CAN FIND A SOLUTION.
NOBODY CAN SOLVE MY PROBLEMS. IT'S HOPELESS. ALL I WANTED WAS TO MAKE IT...
INNOCENT, HOLD ON. I'VE GOT A ROOM YOU CAN RENT.
REALLY, BOSS? IS THAT TRUE?
YES, INNO... YOU CAN'T LEAVE NOW. WHAT'LL ALL THE UNSTYLED LADIES DO, HUH?
HEY, BOSS, THANKS. WHERE IS THIS PLACE?
IT'S NOT FOR FREE... THE NEIGHBORHOOD'S VERY EXPENSIVE...AND THE RENT ISN'T CHEAP.
TELL ME, BOSS, HOW MUCH IS IT?

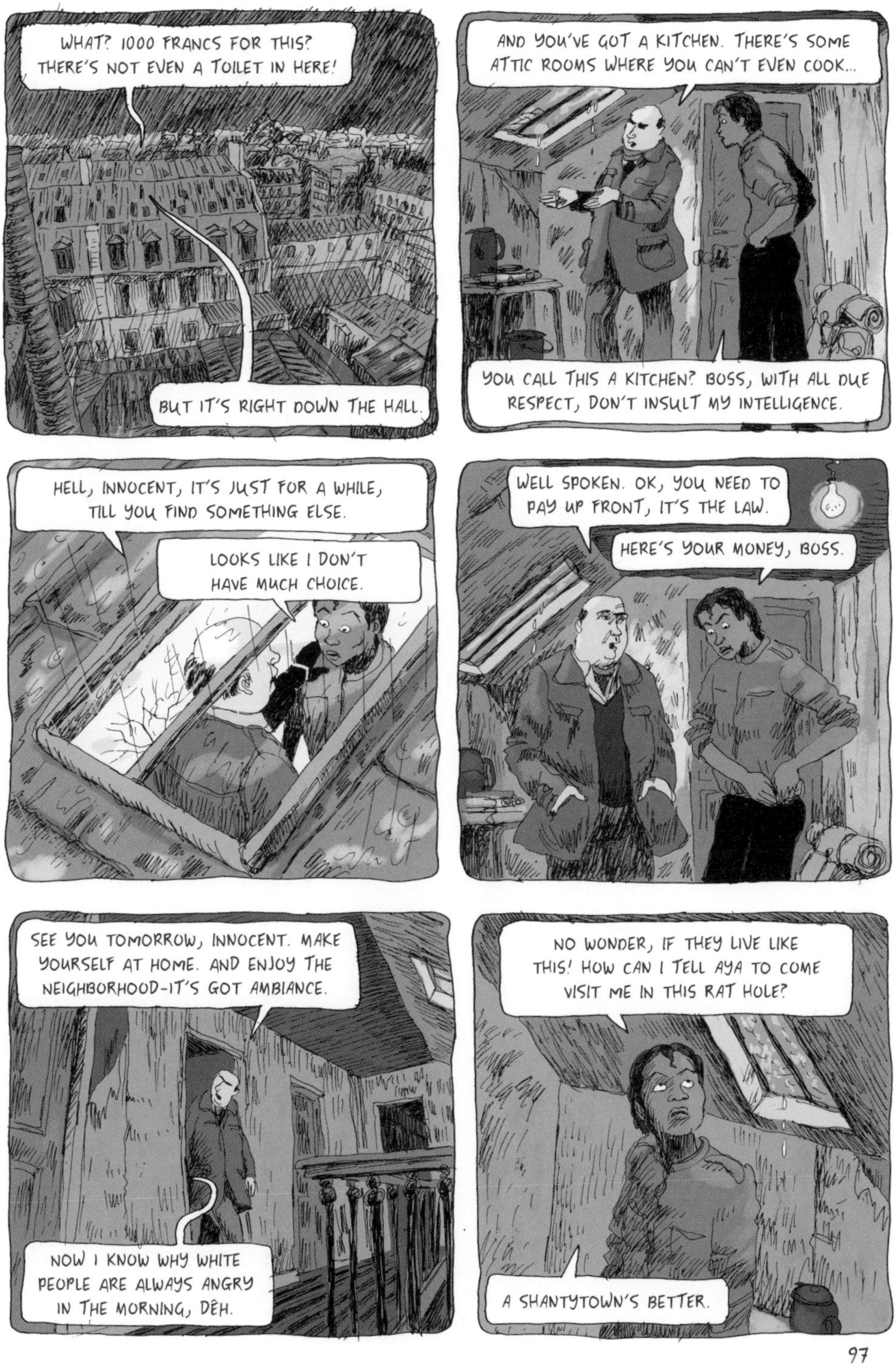
WHAT? 1000 FRANCS FOR THIS? THERE'S NOT EVEN A TOILET IN HERE!
BUT IT'S RIGHT DOWN THE HALL.
AND YOU'VE GOT A KITCHEN. THERE'S SOME ATTIC ROOMS WHERE YOU CAN'T EVEN COOK...
YOU CALL THIS A KITCHEN? BOSS, WITH ALL DUE RESPECT, DON'T INSULT MY INTELLIGENCE.
HELL, INNOCENT, IT'S JUST FOR A WHILE, TILL YOU FIND SOMETHING ELSE.
LOOKS LIKE I DON'T HAVE MUCH CHOICE.
WELL SPOKEN. OK, YOU NEED TO PAY UP FRONT, IT'S THE LAW.
HERE'S YOUR MONEY, BOSS.
SEE YOU TOMORROW, INNOCENT. MAKE YOURSELF AT HOME. AND ENJOY THE NEIGHBORHOOD-IT'S GOT AMBIANCE.
NOW I KNOW WHY WHITE PEOPLE ARE ALWAYS ANGRY IN THE MORNING, DÊH.
NO WONDER, IF THEY LIVE LIKE THIS! HOW CAN I TELL AYA TO COME VISIT ME IN THIS RAT HOLE?
A SHANTYTOWN'S BETTER.

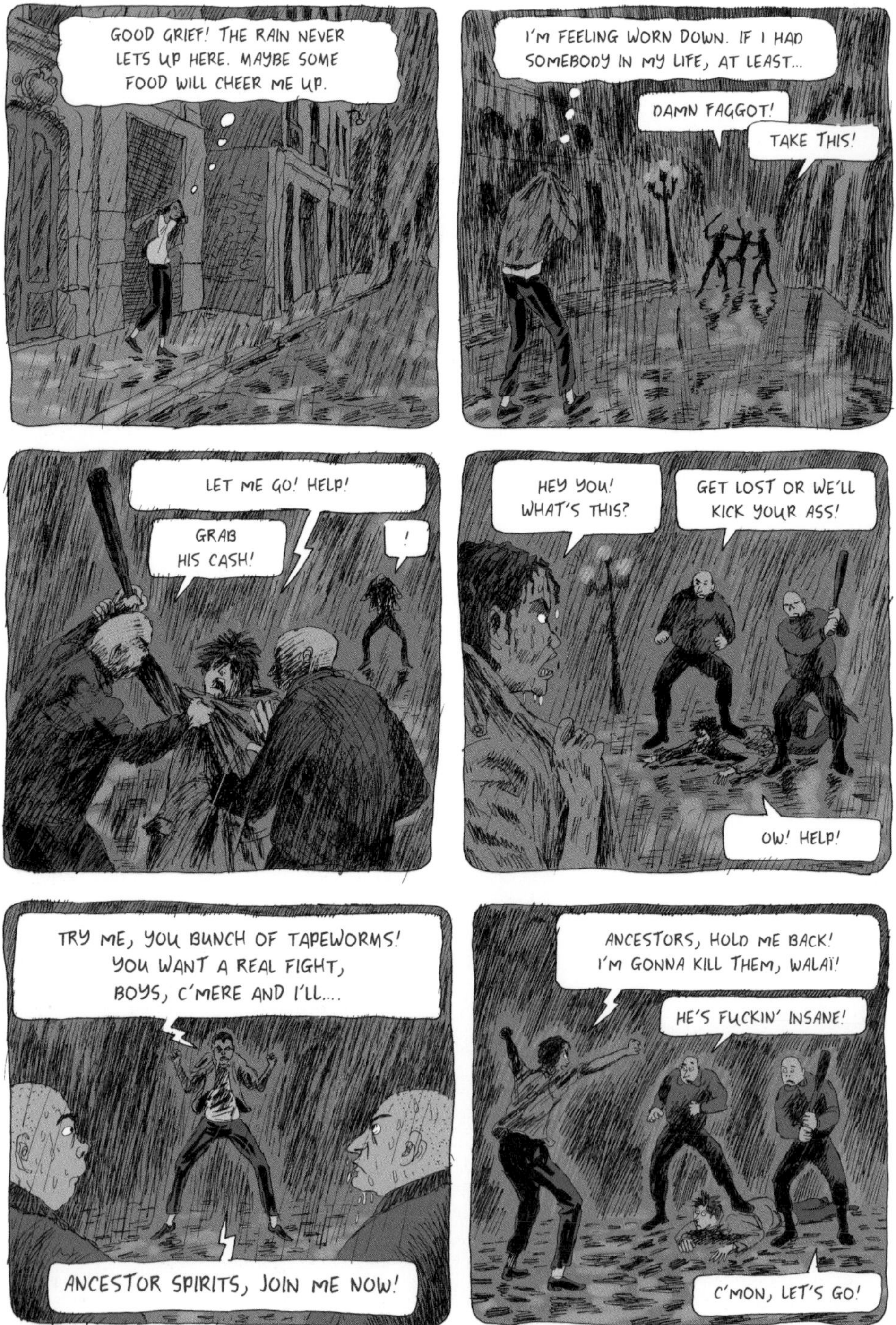
GOOD GRIEF! THE RAIN NEVER LETS UP HERE. MAYBE SOME FOOD WILL CHEER ME UP.
I'M FEELING WORN DOWN. IF I HAD SOMEBODY IN MY LIFE, AT LEAST...
DAMN FAGGOT!
TAKE THIS!
LET ME GO! HELP!
GRAB HIS CASH!
!
HEY YOU! WHAT'S THIS?
GET LOST OR WE'LL KICK YOUR ASS!
OW! HELP!
TRY ME, YOU BUNCH OF TAPEWORMS! YOU WANT A REAL FIGHT, BOYS, C'MERE AND I'LL....
ANCESTOR SPIRITS, JOIN ME NOW!
ANCESTORS, HOLD ME BACK! I'M GONNA KILL THEM, WALAÏ!
HE'S FUCKIN' INSANE!
C'MON, LET'S GO!

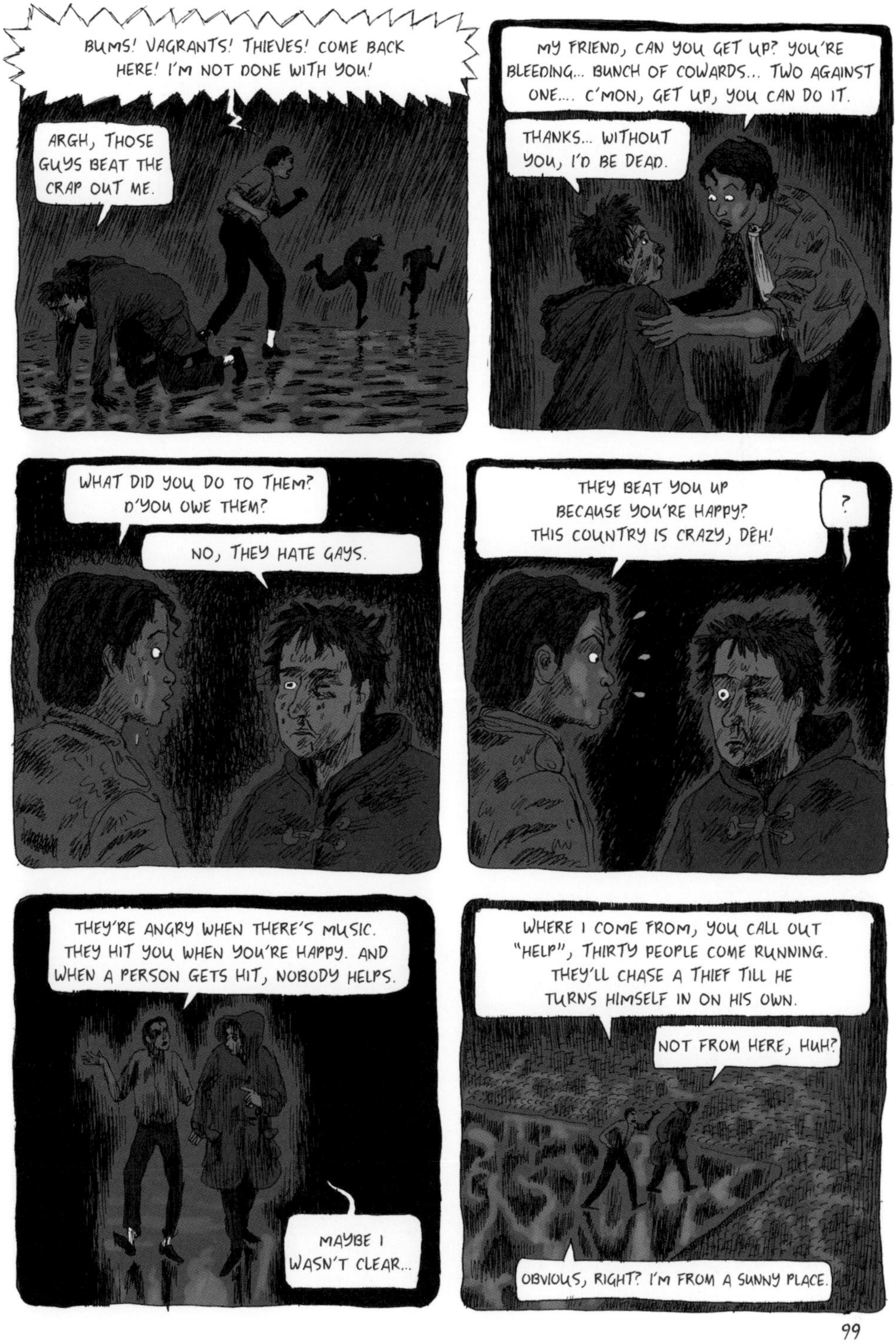
BUMS! VAGRANTS! THIEVES! COME BACK HERE! I'M NOT DONE WITH YOU!
ARGH, THOSE GUYS BEAT THE CRAP OUT ME.
MY FRIEND, CAN YOU GET UP? YOU'RE BLEEDING... BUNCH OF COWARDS... TWO AGAINST ONE.... C'MON, GET UP, YOU CAN DO IT.
THANKS... WITHOUT YOU, I'D BE DEAD.
WHAT DID YOU DO TO THEM? D'YOU OWE THEM?
NO, THEY HATE GAYS.
THEY BEAT YOU UP BECAUSE YOU'RE HAPPY? THIS COUNTRY IS CRAZY, DÊH!
?
THEY'RE ANGRY WHEN THERE'S MUSIC. THEY HIT YOU WHEN YOU'RE HAPPY. AND WHEN A PERSON GETS HIT, NOBODY HELPS.
MAYBE I WASN'T CLEAR...
WHERE I COME FROM, YOU CALL OUT "HELP", THIRTY PEOPLE COME RUNNING. THEY'LL CHASE A THIEF TILL HE TURNS HIMSELF IN ON HIS OWN.
NOT FROM HERE, HUH?
OBVIOUS, RIGHT? I'M FROM A SUNNY PLACE.

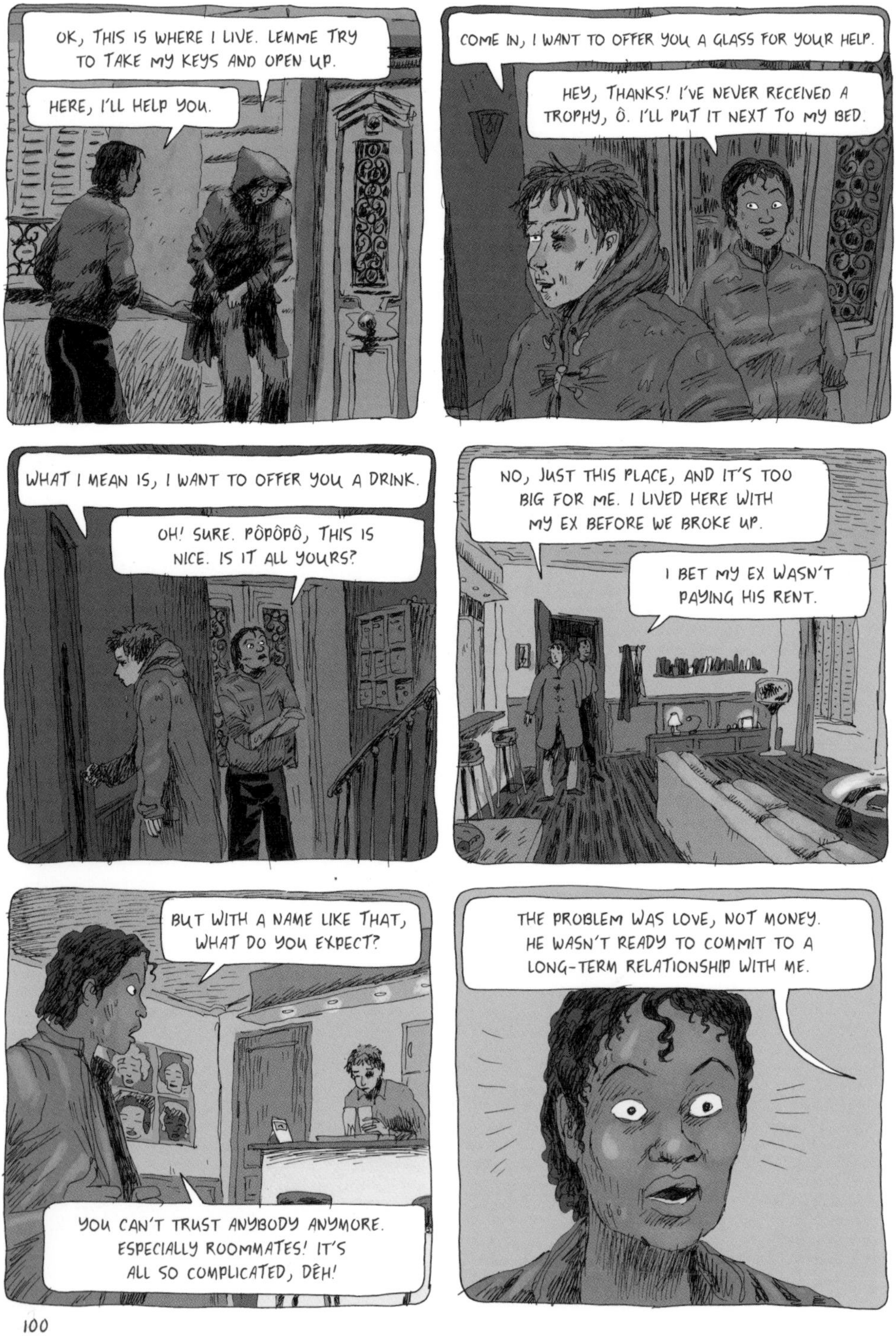
OK, THIS IS WHERE I LIVE. LEMME TRY TO TAKE MY KEYS AND OPEN UP.
HERE, I'LL HELP YOU.
COME IN, I WANT TO OFFER YOU A GLASS FOR YOUR HELP.
HEY, THANKS! I'VE NEVER RECEIVED A TROPHY, Ô. I'LL PUT IT NEXT TO MY BED.
WHAT I MEAN IS, I WANT TO OFFER YOU A DRINK.
OH! SURE. PÔPÔPÔ, THIS IS NICE. IS IT ALL YOURS?
NO, JUST THIS PLACE, AND IT'S TOO BIG FOR ME. I LIVED HERE WITH MY EX BEFORE WE BROKE UP.
I BET MY EX WASN'T PAYING HIS RENT.
BUT WITH A NAME LIKE THAT, WHAT DO YOU EXPECT?
YOU CAN'T TRUST ANYBODY ANYMORE. ESPECIALLY ROOMMATES! IT'S ALL SO COMPLICATED, DÊH!
THE PROBLEM WAS LOVE, NOT MONEY. HE WASN'T READY TO COMMIT TO A LONG-TERM RELATIONSHIP WITH ME.

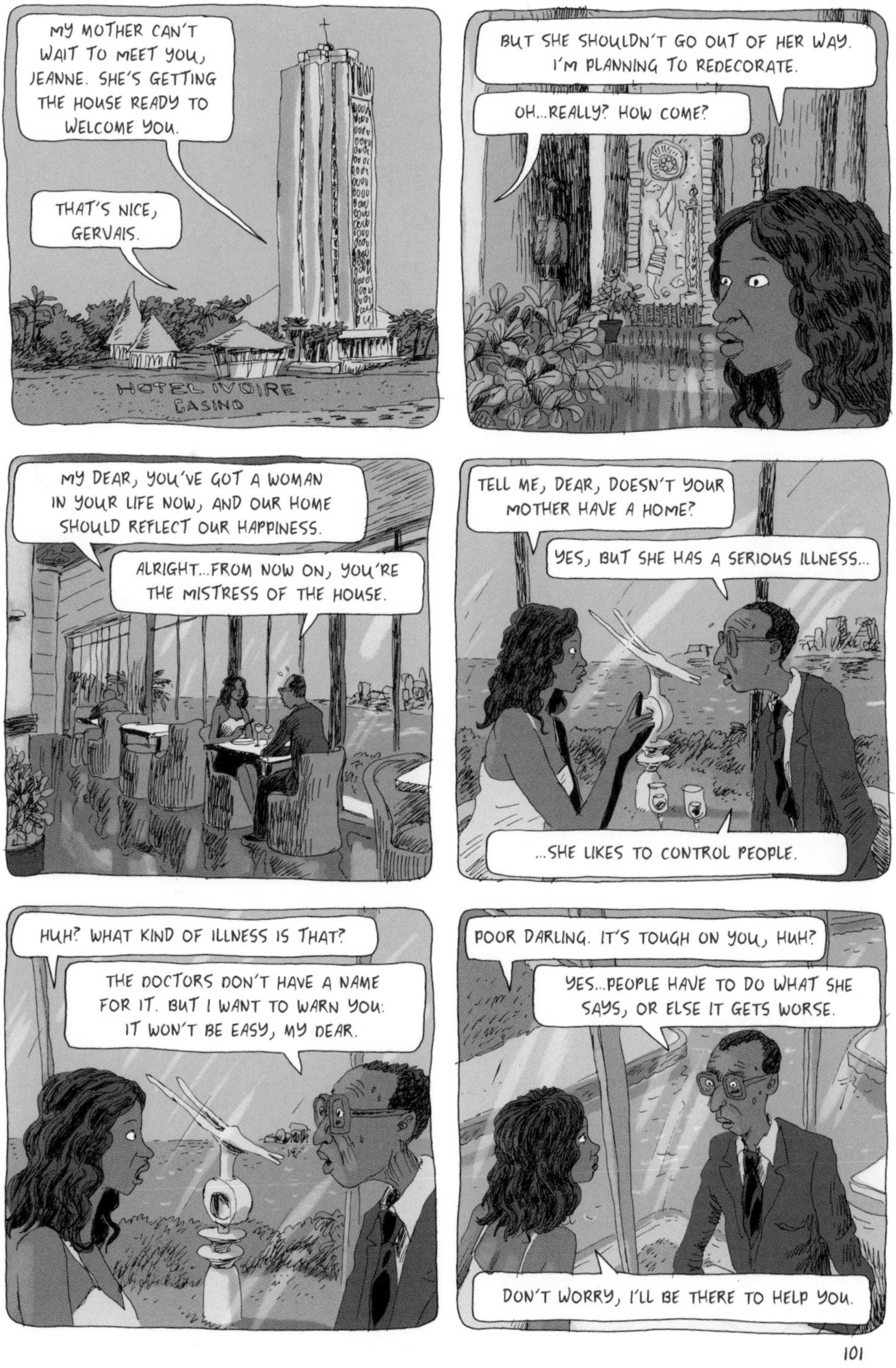
MY MOTHER CAN'T WAIT TO MEET YOU, JEANNE. SHE'S GETTING THE HOUSE READY TO WELCOME YOU.
THAT'S NICE, GERVAIS.
HOTEL IVOIRE
CASINO
BUT SHE SHOULDN'T GO OUT OF HER WAY. I'M PLANNING TO REDECORATE.
OH...REALLY? HOW COME?
MY DEAR, YOU'VE GOT A WOMAN IN YOUR LIFE NOW, AND OUR HOME SHOULD REFLECT OUR HAPPINESS.
ALRIGHT...FROM NOW ON, YOU'RE THE MISTRESS OF THE HOUSE.
TELL ME, DEAR, DOESN'T YOUR MOTHER HAVE A HOME?
YES, BUT SHE HAS A SERIOUS ILLNESS...
...SHE LIKES TO CONTROL PEOPLE.
HUH? WHAT KIND OF ILLNESS IS THAT?
THE DOCTORS DON'T HAVE A NAME FOR IT. BUT I WANT TO WARN YOU: IT WON'T BE EASY, MY DEAR.
POOR DARLING. IT'S TOUGH ON YOU, HUH?
YES...PEOPLE HAVE TO DO WHAT SHE SAYS, OR ELSE IT GETS WORSE.
DON'T WORRY, I'LL BE THERE TO HELP YOU.

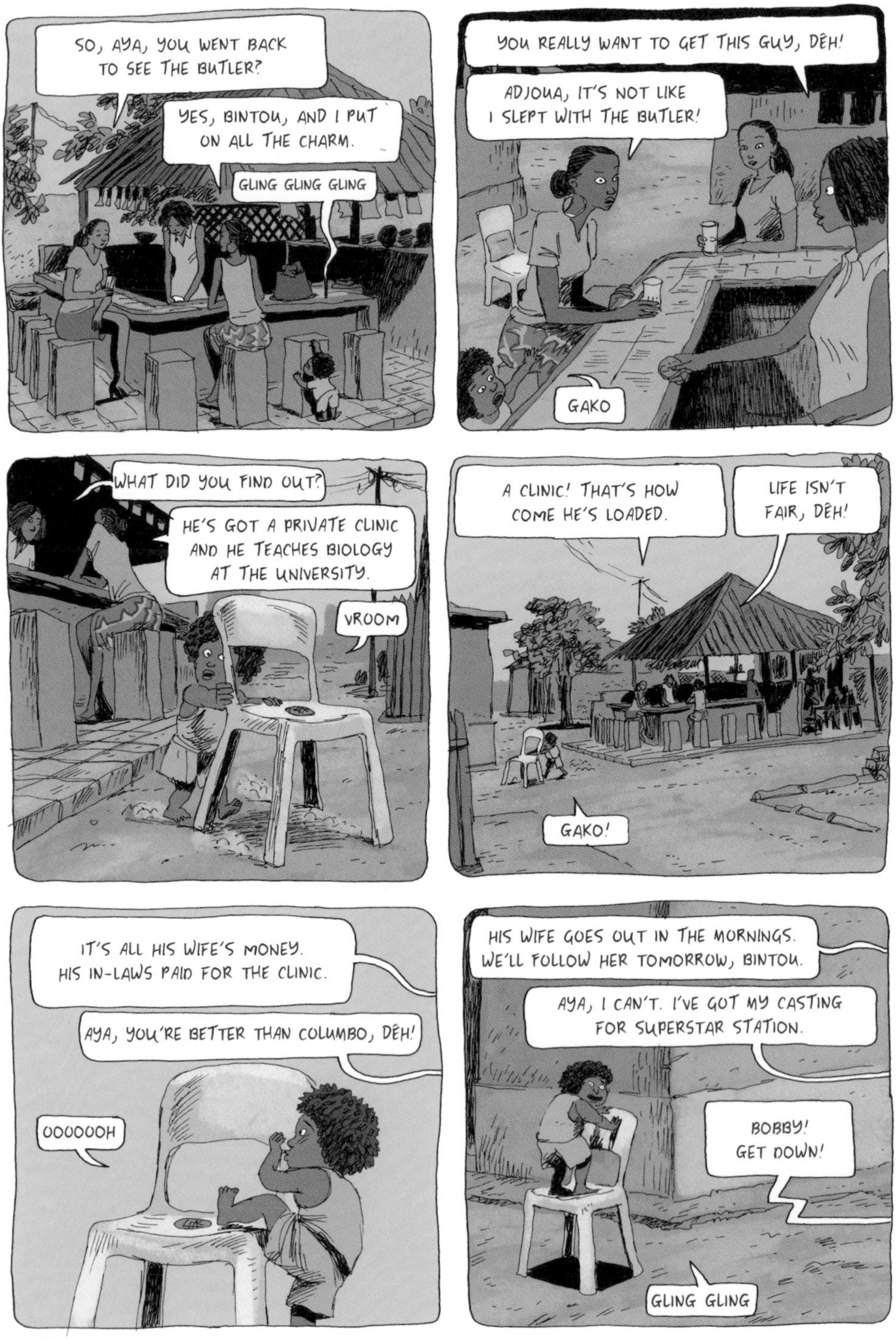
SO, AYA, YOU WENT BACK TO SEE THE BUTLER?
YES, BINTOU, AND I PUT ON ALL THE CHARM.
GLING GLING GLING
YOU REALLY WANT TO GET THIS GUY, DÊH!
ADJOUA, IT'S NOT LIKE I SLEPT WITH THE BUTLER!
GAKO
WHAT DID YOU FIND OUT?
HE'S GOT A PRIVATE CLINIC AND HE TEACHES BIOLOGY AT THE UNIVERSITY.
VROOM
A CLINIC! THAT'S HOW COME HE'S LOADED.
LIFE ISN'T FAIR, DÊH!
GAKO!
IT'S ALL HIS WIFE'S MONEY. HIS IN-LAWS PAID FOR THE CLINIC.
AYA, YOU'RE BETTER THAN COLUMBO, DÊH!
OOOOOOH
HIS WIFE GOES OUT IN THE MORNINGS. WE'LL FOLLOW HER TOMORROW, BINTOU.
AYA, I CAN'T. I'VE GOT MY CASTING FOR SUPERSTAR STATION.
BOBBY! GET DOWN!
GLING GLING

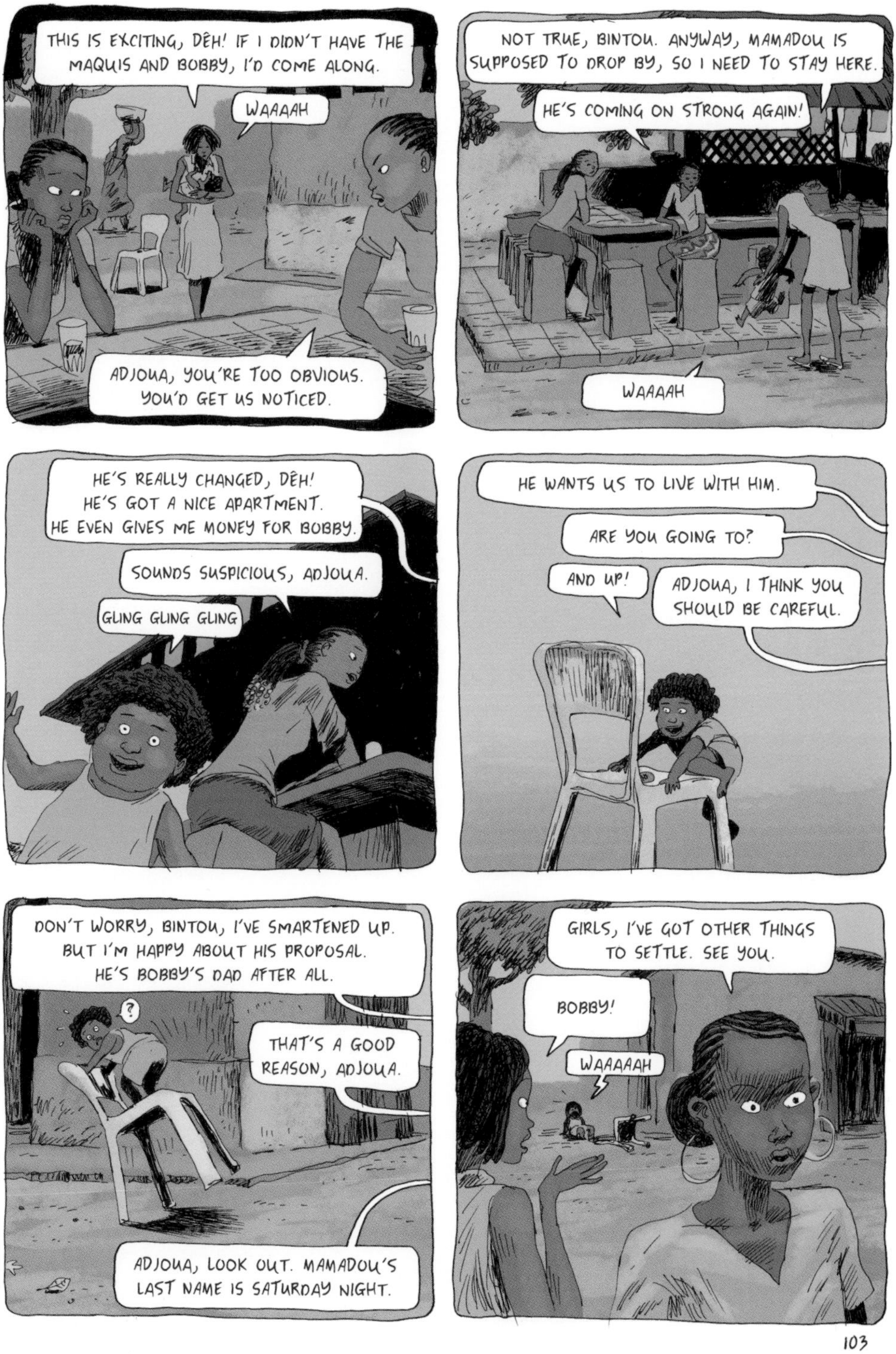
THIS IS EXCITING, DÊH! IF I DIDN'T HAVE THE MAQUIS AND BOBBY, I'D COME ALONG.
WAAAAH
ADJOUA, YOU'RE TOO OBVIOUS. YOU'D GET US NOTICED.
NOT TRUE, BINTOU. ANYWAY, MAMADOU IS SUPPOSED TO DROP BY, SO I NEED TO STAY HERE.
HE'S COMING ON STRONG AGAIN!
WAAAAH
HE'S REALLY CHANGED, DÊH! HE'S GOT A NICE APARTMENT. HE EVEN GIVES ME MONEY FOR BOBBY.
SOUNDS SUSPICIOUS, ADJOUA.
GLING GLING GLING
HE WANTS US TO LIVE WITH HIM.
ARE YOU GOING TO?
AND UP!
ADJOUA, I THINK YOU SHOULD BE CAREFUL.
DON'T WORRY, BINTOU, I'VE SMARTENED UP. BUT I'M HAPPY ABOUT HIS PROPOSAL. HE'S BOBBY'S DAD AFTER ALL.
?
THAT'S A GOOD REASON, ADJOUA.
ADJOUA, LOOK OUT. MAMADOU'S LAST NAME IS SATURDAY NIGHT.
GIRLS, I'VE GOT OTHER THINGS TO SETTLE. SEE YOU.
BOBBY!
WAAAAAH

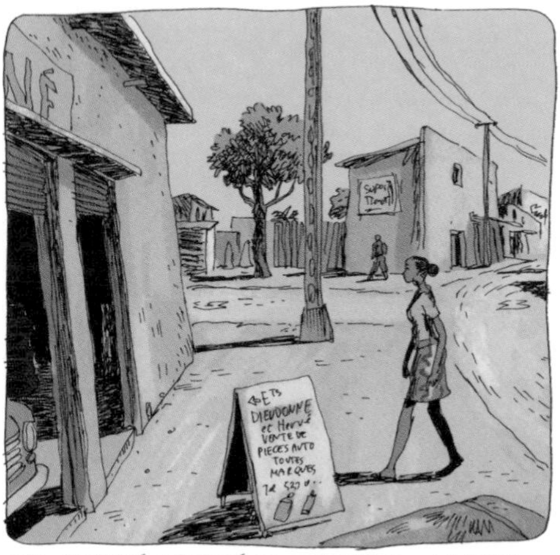

SIGN: DIEUDONNÉ AND HERVÉ CO. - CAR PARTS - ALL MAKES

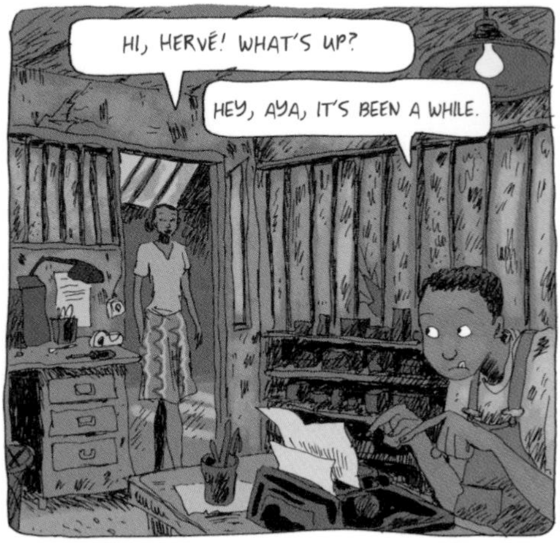

HI, HERVÉ! WHAT'S UP?
HEY, AYA, IT'S BEEN A WHILE.


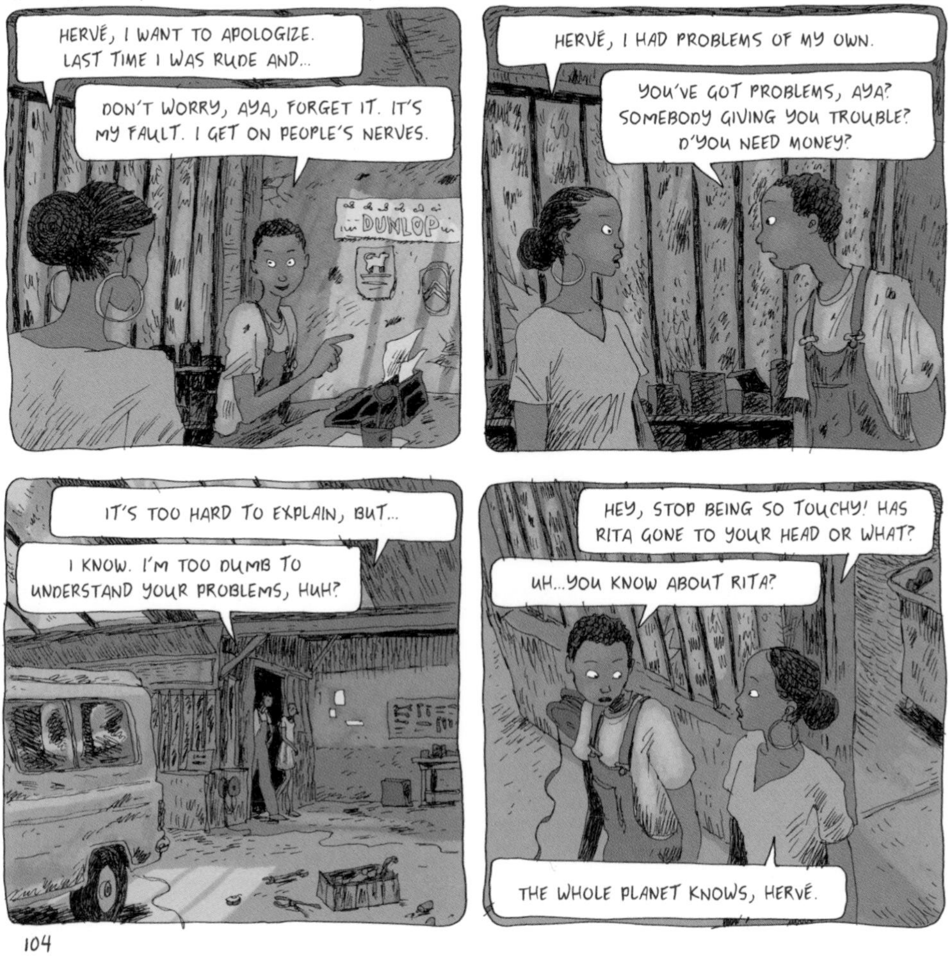

HERVÉ, I WANT TO APOLOGIZE. LAST TIME I WAS RUDE AND...
DON'T WORRY, AYA, FORGET IT. IT'S MY FAULT. I GET ON PEOPLE'S NERVES.
DUNLOP
HERVÉ, I HAD PROBLEMS OF MY OWN.
YOU'VE GOT PROBLEMS, AYA? SOMEBODY GIVING YOU TROUBLE? D'YOU NEED MONEY?
IT'S TOO HARD TO EXPLAIN, BUT...
I KNOW. I'M TOO DUMB TO UNDERSTAND YOUR PROBLEMS, HUH?
HEY, STOP BEING SO TOUCHY! HAS RITA GONE TO YOUR HEAD OR WHAT?
UH...YOU KNOW ABOUT RITA?
THE WHOLE PLANET KNOWS, HERVÉ.

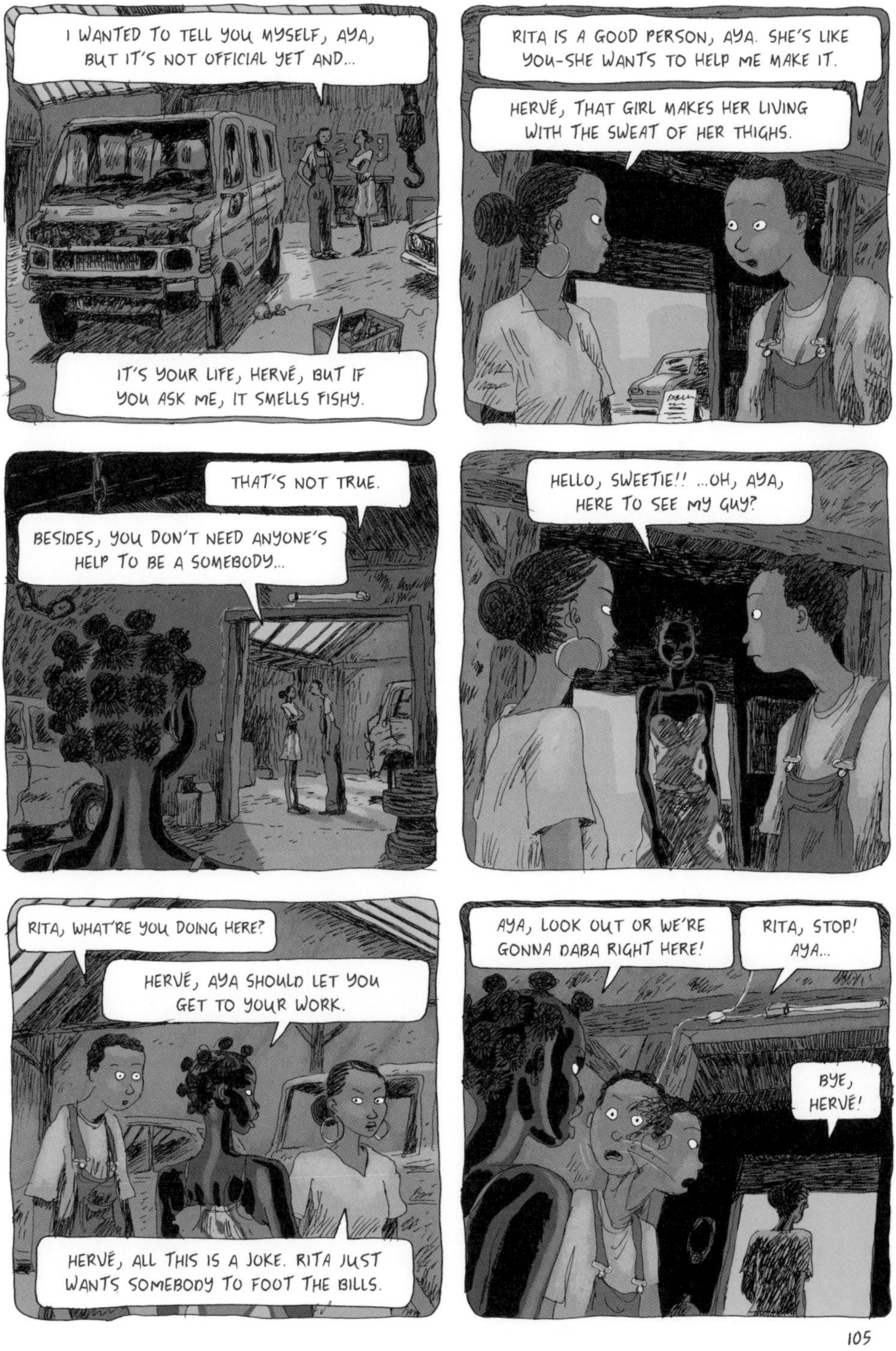
I WANTED TO TELL YOU MYSELF, AYA, BUT IT'S NOT OFFICIAL YET AND...
IT'S YOUR LIFE, HERVÉ, BUT IF YOU ASK ME, IT SMELLS FISHY.
RITA IS A GOOD PERSON, AYA. SHE'S LIKE YOU-SHE WANTS TO HELP ME MAKE IT.
HERVÉ, THAT GIRL MAKES HER LIVING WITH THE SWEAT OF HER THIGHS.
THAT'S NOT TRUE.
BESIDES, YOU DON'T NEED ANYONE'S HELP TO BE A SOMEBODY...
HELLO, SWEETIE!! ...OH, AYA, HERE TO SEE MY GUY?
RITA, WHAT'RE YOU DOING HERE?
HERVÉ, AYA SHOULD LET YOU GET TO YOUR WORK.
HERVÉ, ALL THIS IS A JOKE. RITA JUST WANTS SOMEBODY TO FOOT THE BILLS.
AYA, LOOK OUT OR WE'RE GONNA DABA RIGHT HERE!
RITA, STOP! AYA...
BYE, HERVÉ!

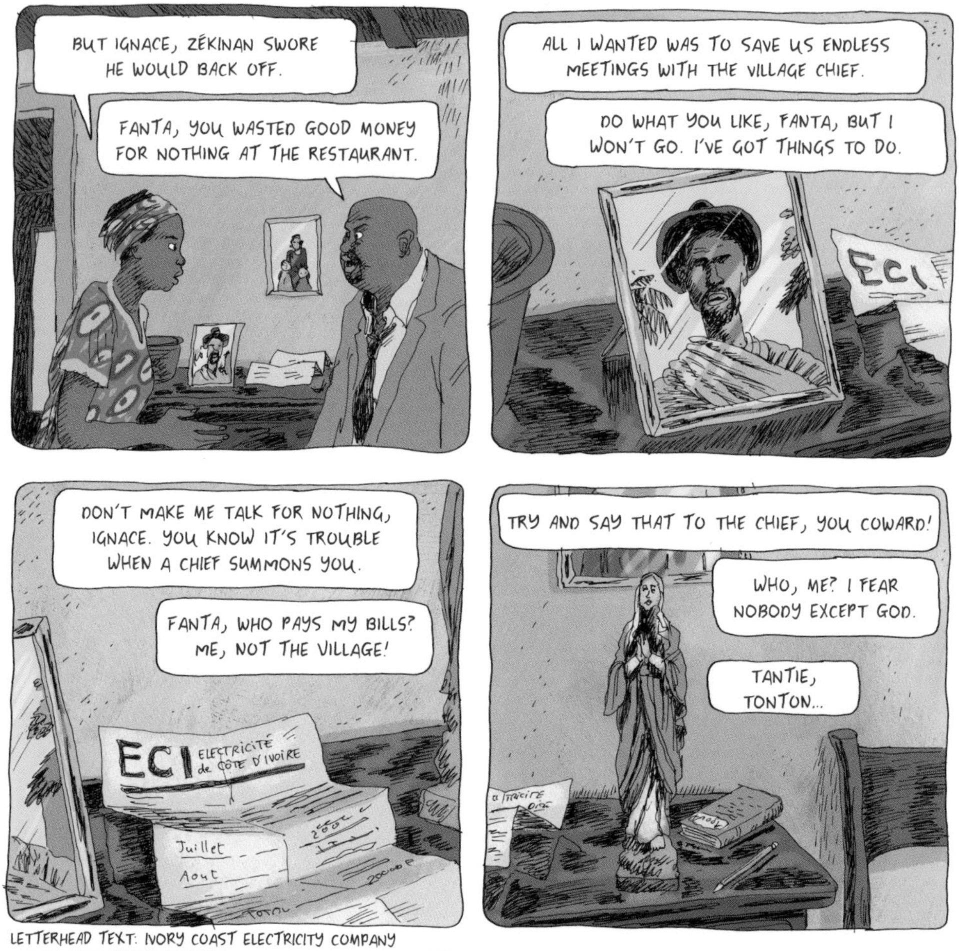
BUT IGNACE, ZÉKINAN SWORE HE WOULD BACK OFF.
FANTA, YOU WASTED GOOD MONEY FOR NOTHING AT THE RESTAURANT.
ALL I WANTED WAS TO SAVE US ENDLESS MEETINGS WITH THE VILLAGE CHIEF.
DO WHAT YOU LIKE, FANTA, BUT I WON'T GO. I'VE GOT THINGS TO DO.
ECI
DON'T MAKE ME TALK FOR NOTHING, IGNACE. YOU KNOW IT'S TROUBLE WHEN A CHIEF SUMMONS YOU.
FANTA, WHO PAYS MY BILLS? ME, NOT THE VILLAGE!
ECI ELECTRICITÉ de CÔTE D'IVOIRE
Juillet
Aout
TRY AND SAY THAT TO THE CHIEF, YOU COWARD!
WHO, ME? I FEAR NOBODY EXCEPT GOD.
TANTIE, TONTON...

LETTERHEAD TEXT: IVORY COAST ELECTRICITY COMPANY

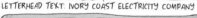

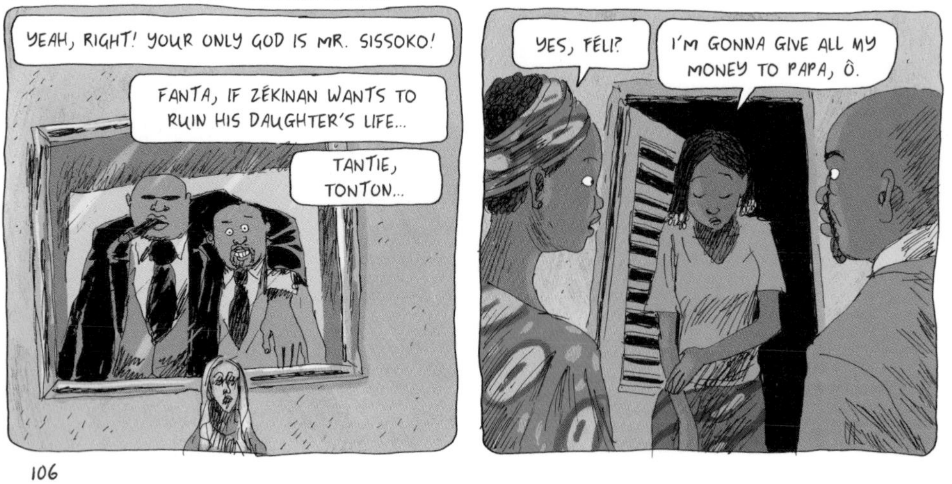
YEAH, RIGHT! YOUR ONLY GOD IS MR. SISSOKO!
FANTA, IF ZÉKINAN WANTS TO RUIN HIS DAUGHTER'S LIFE...
TANTIE, TONTON...
YES, FÉLI?
I'M GONNA GIVE ALL MY MONEY TO PAPA, Ô.

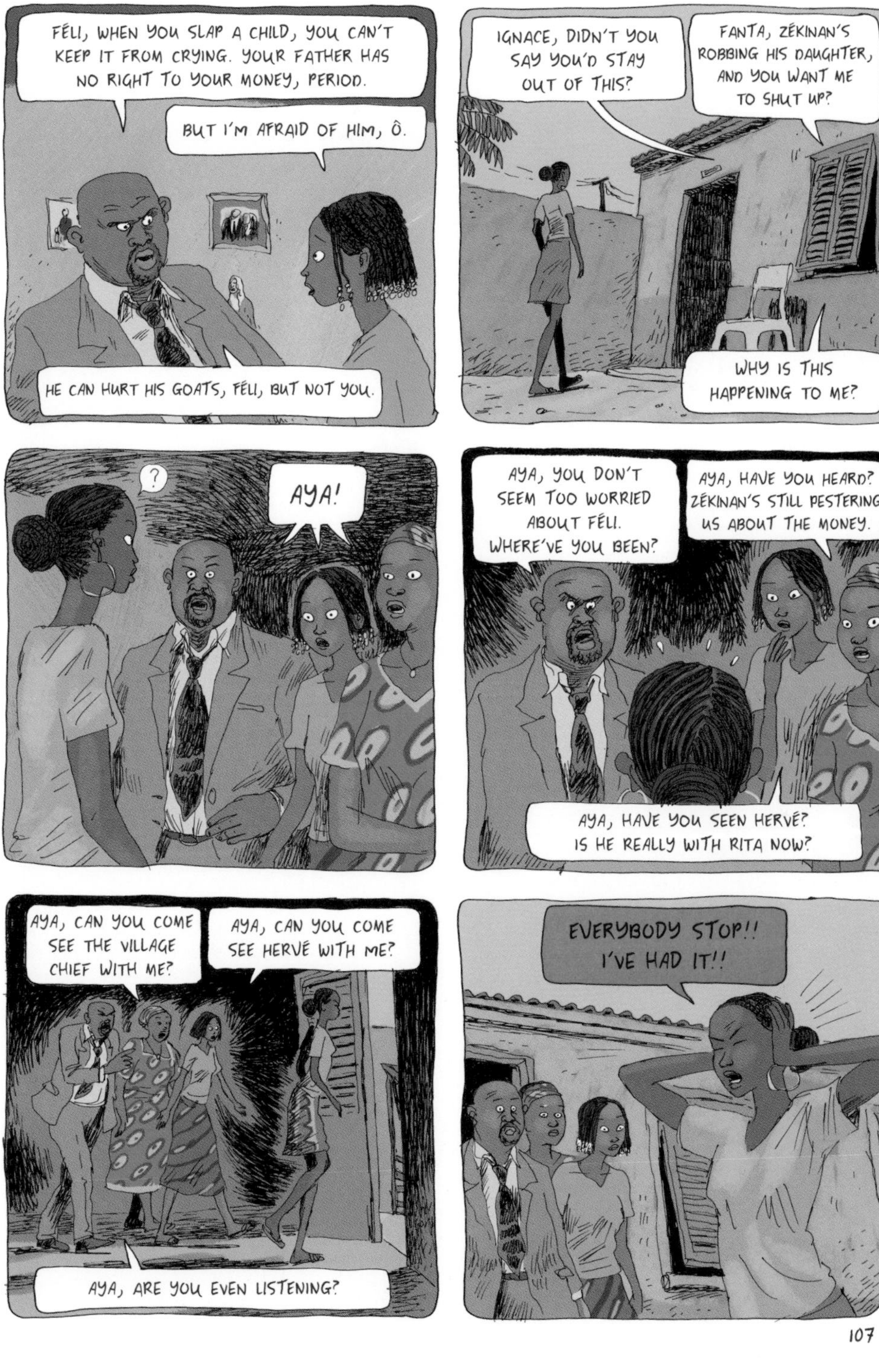
FÉLI, WHEN YOU SLAP A CHILD, YOU CAN'T KEEP IT FROM CRYING. YOUR FATHER HAS NO RIGHT TO YOUR MONEY, PERIOD.
BUT I'M AFRAID OF HIM, Ô.
HE CAN HURT HIS GOATS, FÉLI, BUT NOT YOU.
IGNACE, DIDN'T YOU SAY YOU'D STAY OUT OF THIS?
FANTA, ZÉKINAN'S ROBBING HIS DAUGHTER, AND YOU WANT ME TO SHUT UP?
WHY IS THIS HAPPENING TO ME?
?
AYA!
AYA, YOU DON'T SEEM TOO WORRIED ABOUT FÉLI. WHERE'VE YOU BEEN?
AYA, HAVE YOU HEARD? ZÉKINAN'S STILL PESTERING US ABOUT THE MONEY.
AYA, HAVE YOU SEEN HERVÉ? IS HE REALLY WITH RITA NOW?
AYA, CAN YOU COME SEE THE VILLAGE CHIEF WITH ME?
AYA, CAN YOU COME SEE HERVÉ WITH ME?
AYA, ARE YOU EVEN LISTENING?
EVERYBODY STOP!! I'VE HAD IT!!

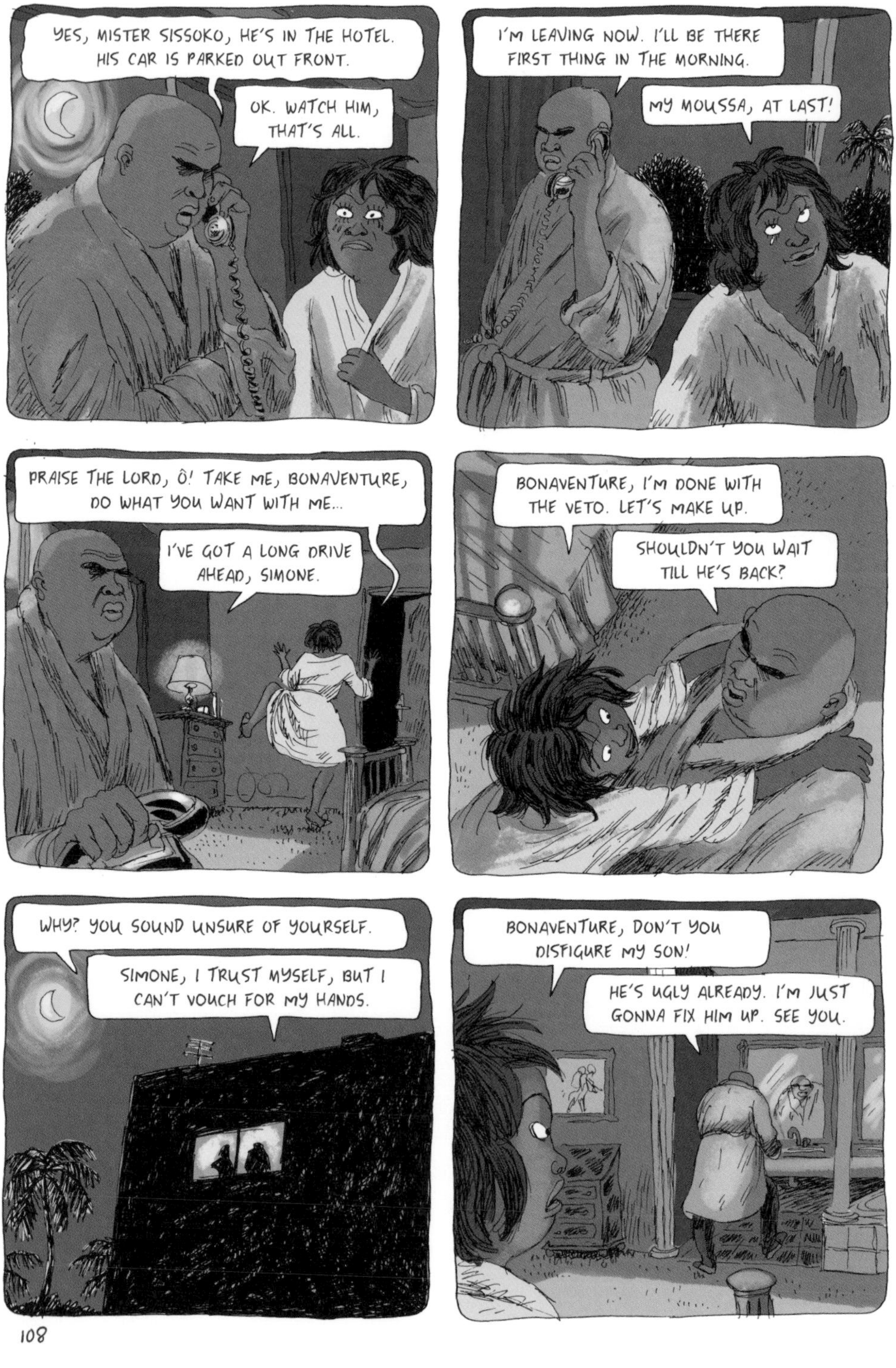
YES, MISTER SISSOKO, HE'S IN THE HOTEL. HIS CAR IS PARKED OUT FRONT.
OK. WATCH HIM, THAT'S ALL.
I'M LEAVING NOW. I'LL BE THERE FIRST THING IN THE MORNING.
MY MOUSSA, AT LAST!
PRAISE THE LORD, Ô! TAKE ME, BONAVENTURE, DO WHAT YOU WANT WITH ME...
I'VE GOT A LONG DRIVE AHEAD, SIMONE.
BONAVENTURE, I'M DONE WITH THE VETO. LET'S MAKE UP.
SHOULDN'T YOU WAIT TILL HE'S BACK?
WHY? YOU SOUND UNSURE OF YOURSELF.
SIMONE, I TRUST MYSELF, BUT I CAN'T VOUCH FOR MY HANDS.
BONAVENTURE, DON'T YOU DISFIGURE MY SON!
HE'S UGLY ALREADY. I'M JUST GONNA FIX HIM UP. SEE YOU.

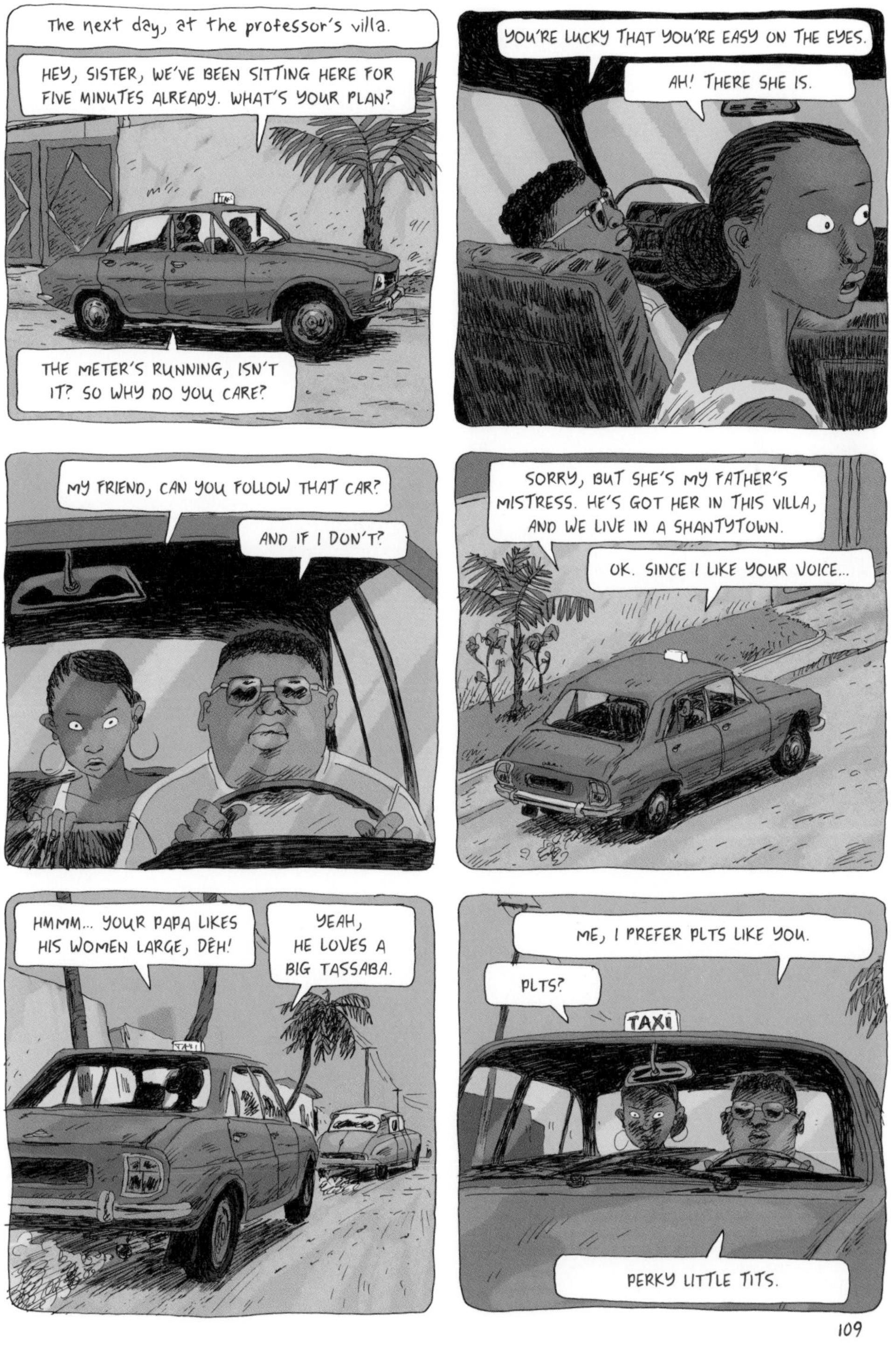
The next day, at the professor's villa.
HEY, SISTER, WE'VE BEEN SITTING HERE FOR FIVE MINUTES ALREADY. WHAT'S YOUR PLAN?
THE METER'S RUNNING, ISN'T IT? SO WHY DO YOU CARE?
YOU'RE LUCKY THAT YOU'RE EASY ON THE EYES.
AH! THERE SHE IS.
MY FRIEND, CAN YOU FOLLOW THAT CAR?
AND IF I DON'T?
SORRY, BUT SHE'S MY FATHER'S MISTRESS. HE'S GOT HER IN THIS VILLA, AND WE LIVE IN A SHANTYTOWN.
OK. SINCE I LIKE YOUR VOICE...
HMMM... YOUR PAPA LIKES HIS WOMEN LARGE, DÊH!
YEAH, HE LOVES A BIG TASSABA.
ME, I PREFER PLTS LIKE YOU.
PLTS?
TAXI
PERKY LITTLE TITS.

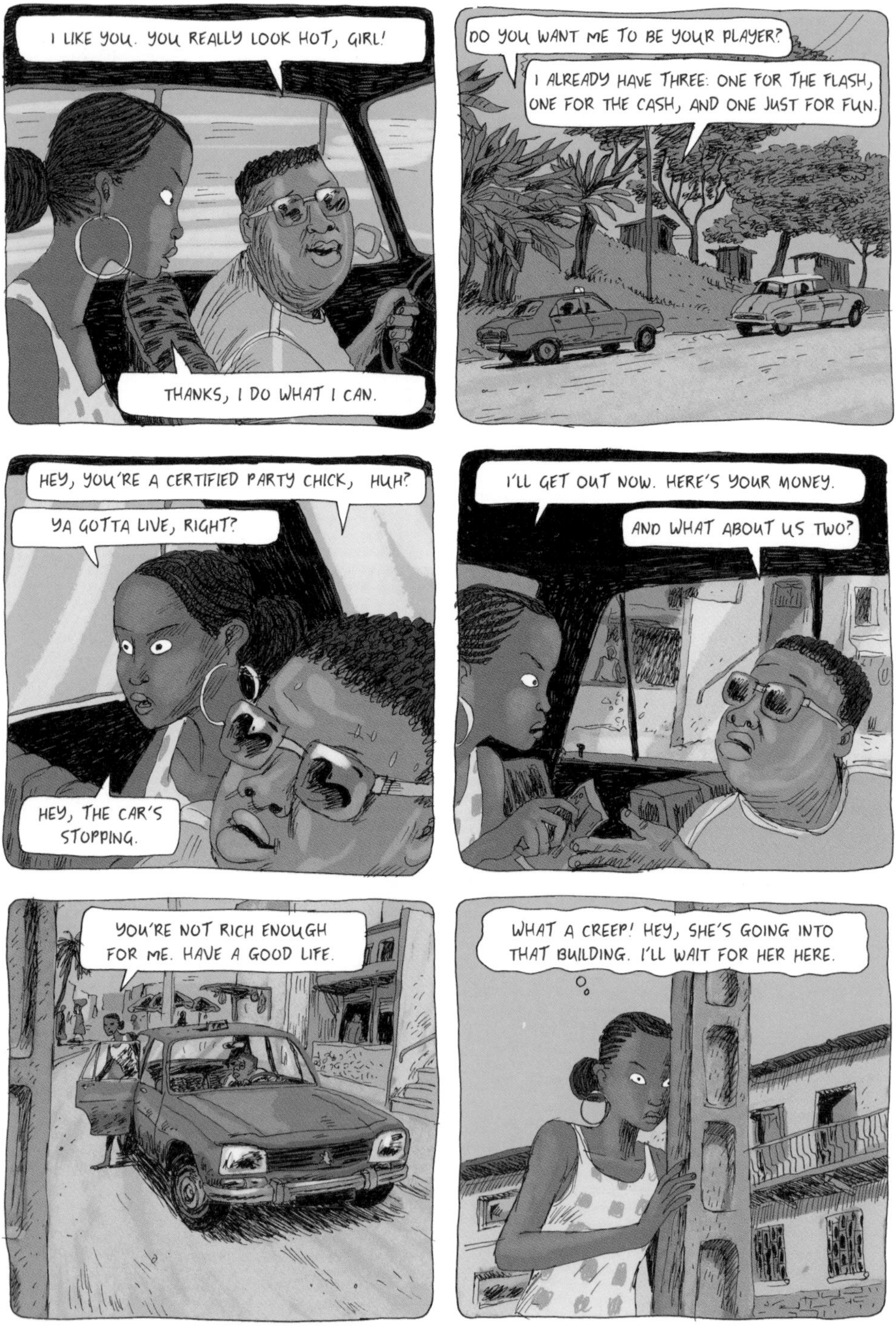
I LIKE YOU. YOU REALLY LOOK HOT, GIRL!
THANKS, I DO WHAT I CAN.
DO YOU WANT ME TO BE YOUR PLAYER?
I ALREADY HAVE THREE: ONE FOR THE FLASH, ONE FOR THE CASH, AND ONE JUST FOR FUN.
HEY, YOU'RE A CERTIFIED PARTY CHICK, HUH?
YA GOTTA LIVE, RIGHT?
HEY, THE CAR'S STOPPING.
I'LL GET OUT NOW. HERE'S YOUR MONEY.
AND WHAT ABOUT US TWO?
YOU'RE NOT RICH ENOUGH FOR ME. HAVE A GOOD LIFE.
WHAT A CREEP! HEY, SHE'S GOING INTO THAT BUILDING. I'LL WAIT FOR HER HERE.

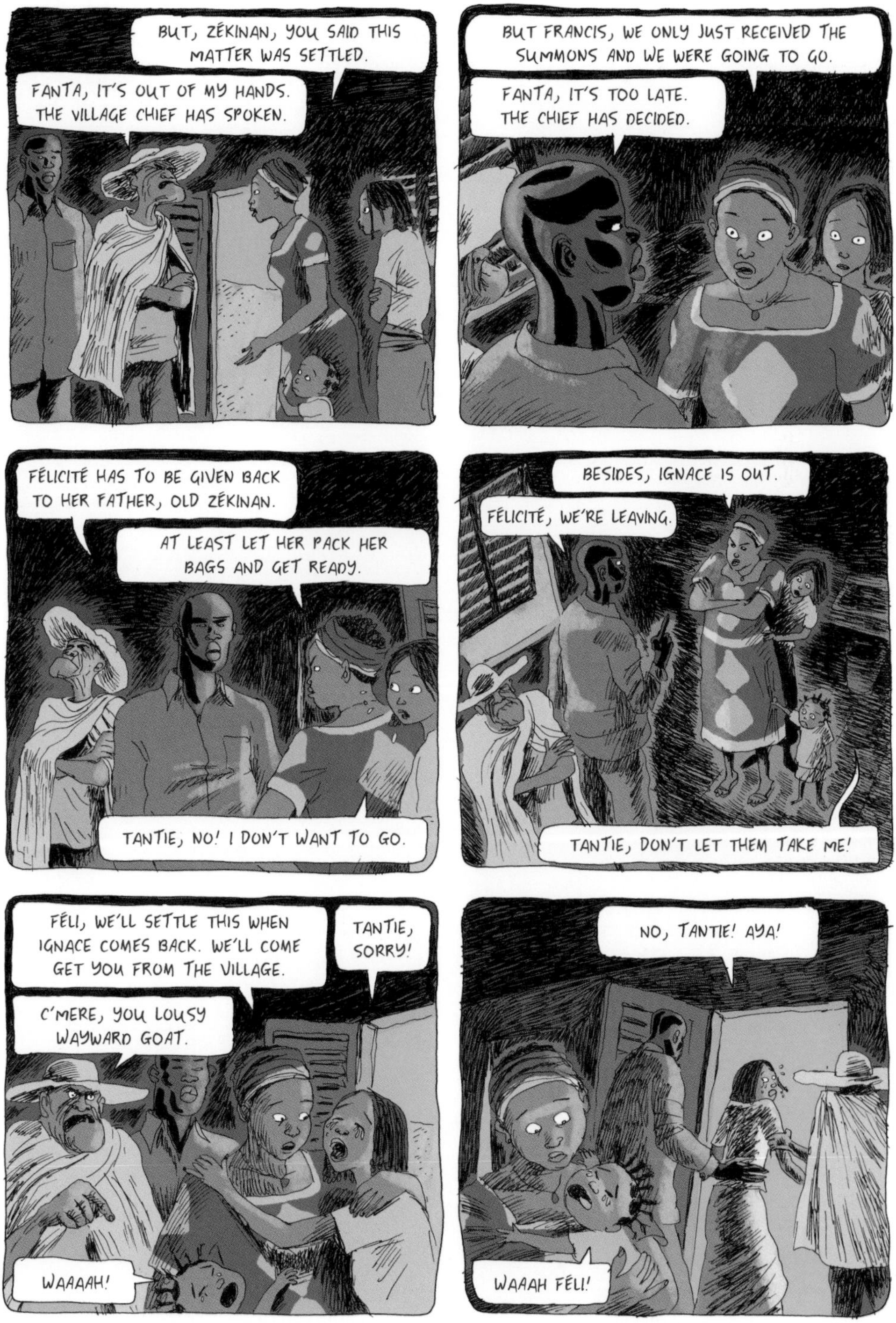
BUT, ZÉKINAN, YOU SAID THIS MATTER WAS SETTLED.
FANTA, IT'S OUT OF MY HANDS. THE VILLAGE CHIEF HAS SPOKEN.
BUT FRANCIS, WE ONLY JUST RECEIVED THE SUMMONS AND WE WERE GOING TO GO.
FANTA, IT'S TOO LATE. THE CHIEF HAS DECIDED.
FÉLICITÉ HAS TO BE GIVEN BACK TO HER FATHER, OLD ZÉKINAN.
AT LEAST LET HER PACK HER BAGS AND GET READY.
TANTIE, NO! I DON'T WANT TO GO.
BESIDES, IGNACE IS OUT.
FÉLICITÉ, WE'RE LEAVING.
TANTIE, DON'T LET THEM TAKE ME!
FÉLI, WE'LL SETTLE THIS WHEN IGNACE COMES BACK. WE'LL COME GET YOU FROM THE VILLAGE.
TANTIE, SORRY!
C'MERE, YOU LOUSY WAYWARD GOAT.
WAAAAH!
NO, TANTIE! AYA!
WAAAH FÉLI!

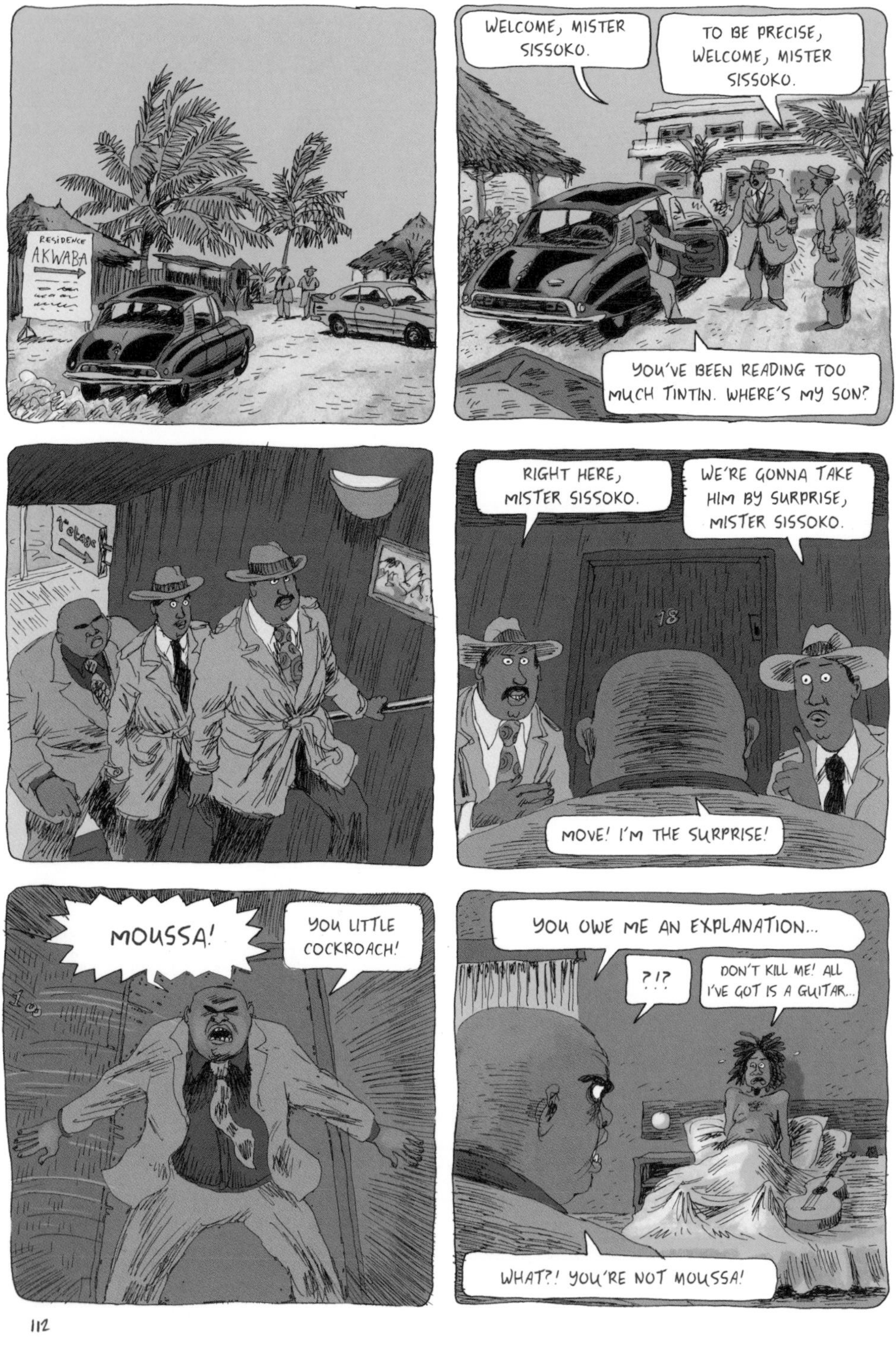
RESIDENCE AKWABA
WELCOME, MISTER SISSOKO.
TO BE PRECISE, WELCOME, MISTER SISSOKO.
YOU'VE BEEN READING TOO MUCH TINTIN. WHERE'S MY SON?
RIGHT HERE, MISTER SISSOKO.
WE'RE GONNA TAKE HIM BY SURPRISE, MISTER SISSOKO.
18
MOVE! I'M THE SURPRISE!
MOUSSA!
YOU LITTLE COCKROACH!
YOU OWE ME AN EXPLANATION...
?!?
DON'T KILL ME! ALL I'VE GOT IS A GUITAR...
WHAT?! YOU'RE NOT MOUSSA!

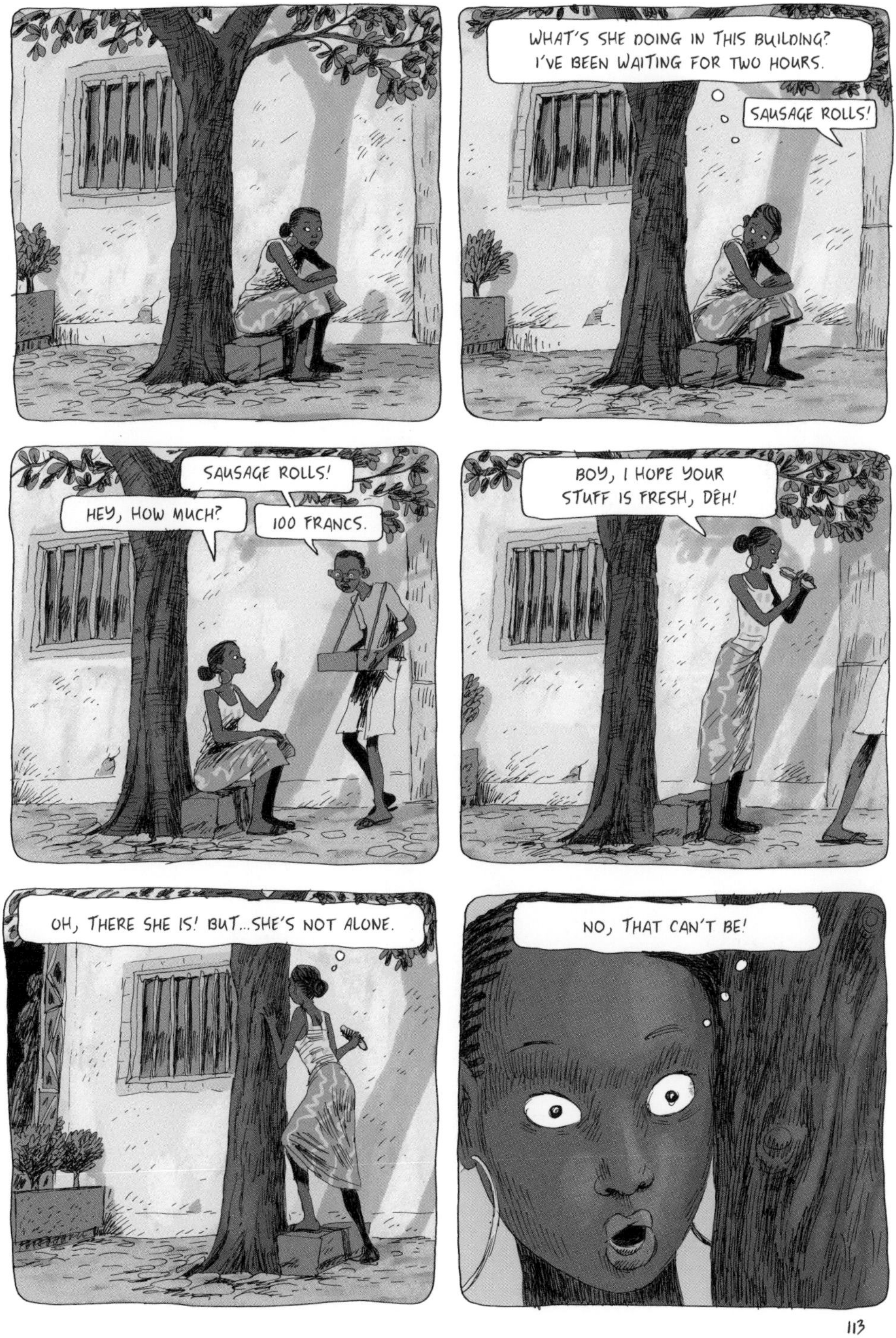
WHAT'S SHE DOING IN THIS BUILDING? I'VE BEEN WAITING FOR TWO HOURS.
SAUSAGE ROLLS!
SAUSAGE ROLLS!
HEY, HOW MUCH?
100 FRANCS.
BOY, I HOPE YOUR STUFF IS FRESH, DÊH!
OH, THERE SHE IS! BUT...SHE'S NOT ALONE.
NO, THAT CAN'T BE!

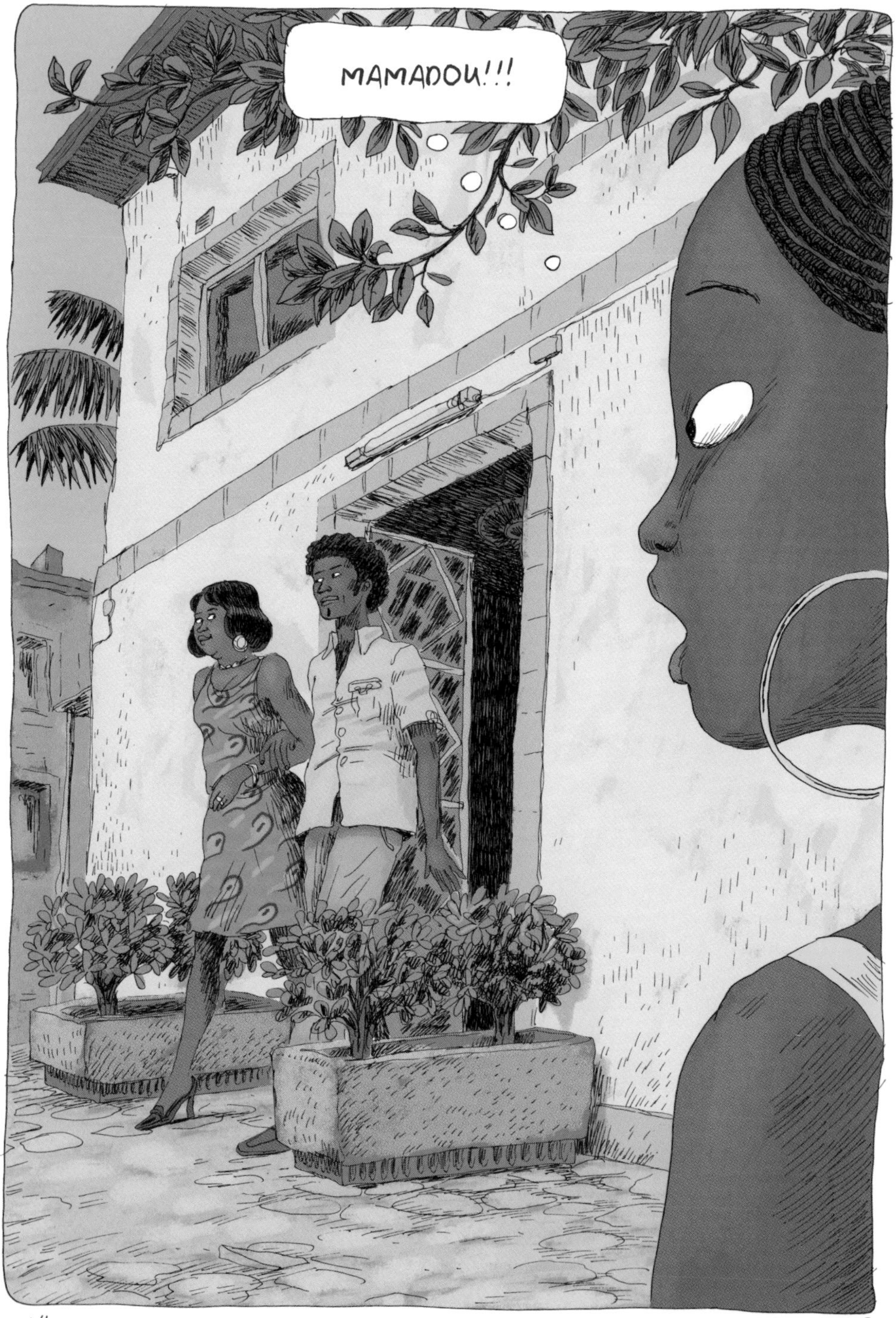
MAMADOU!!!



PARIS, SEPTEMBER 22, 2008

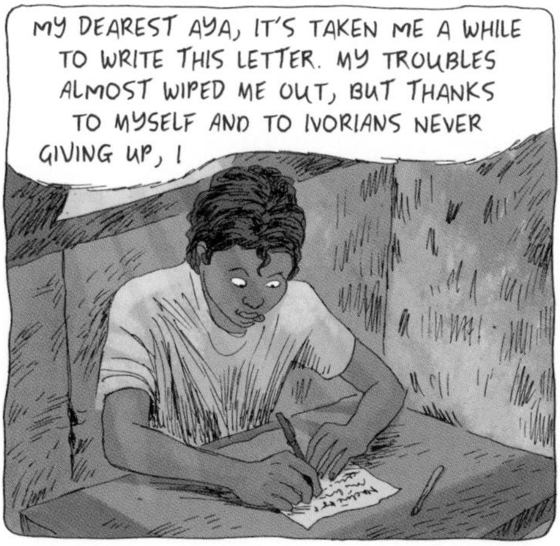
MY DEAREST AYA, IT'S TAKEN ME A WHILE TO WRITE THIS LETTER. MY TROUBLES ALMOST WIPED ME OUT, BUT THANKS TO MYSELF AND TO IVORIANS NEVER GIVING UP, I

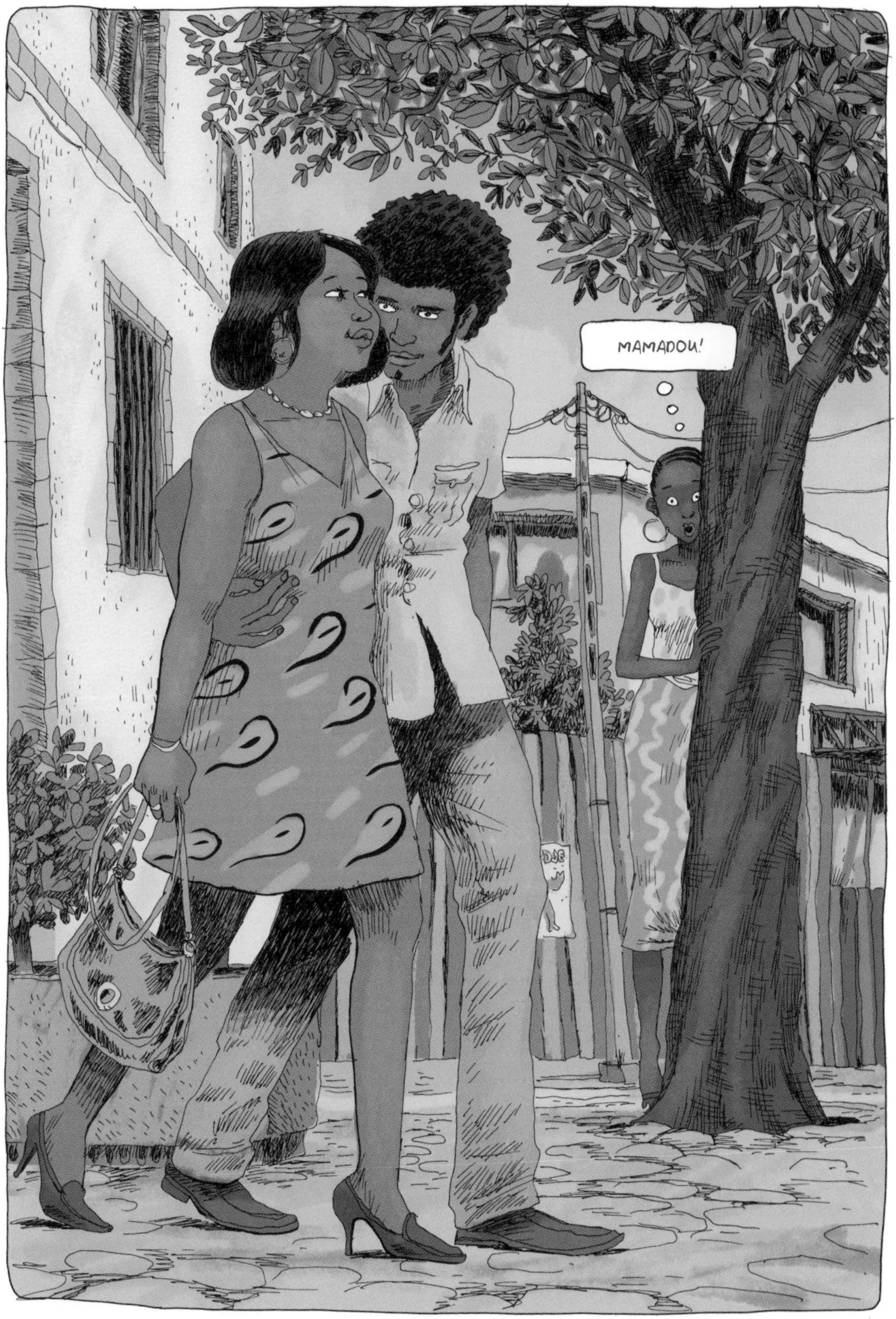
MAMADOU!

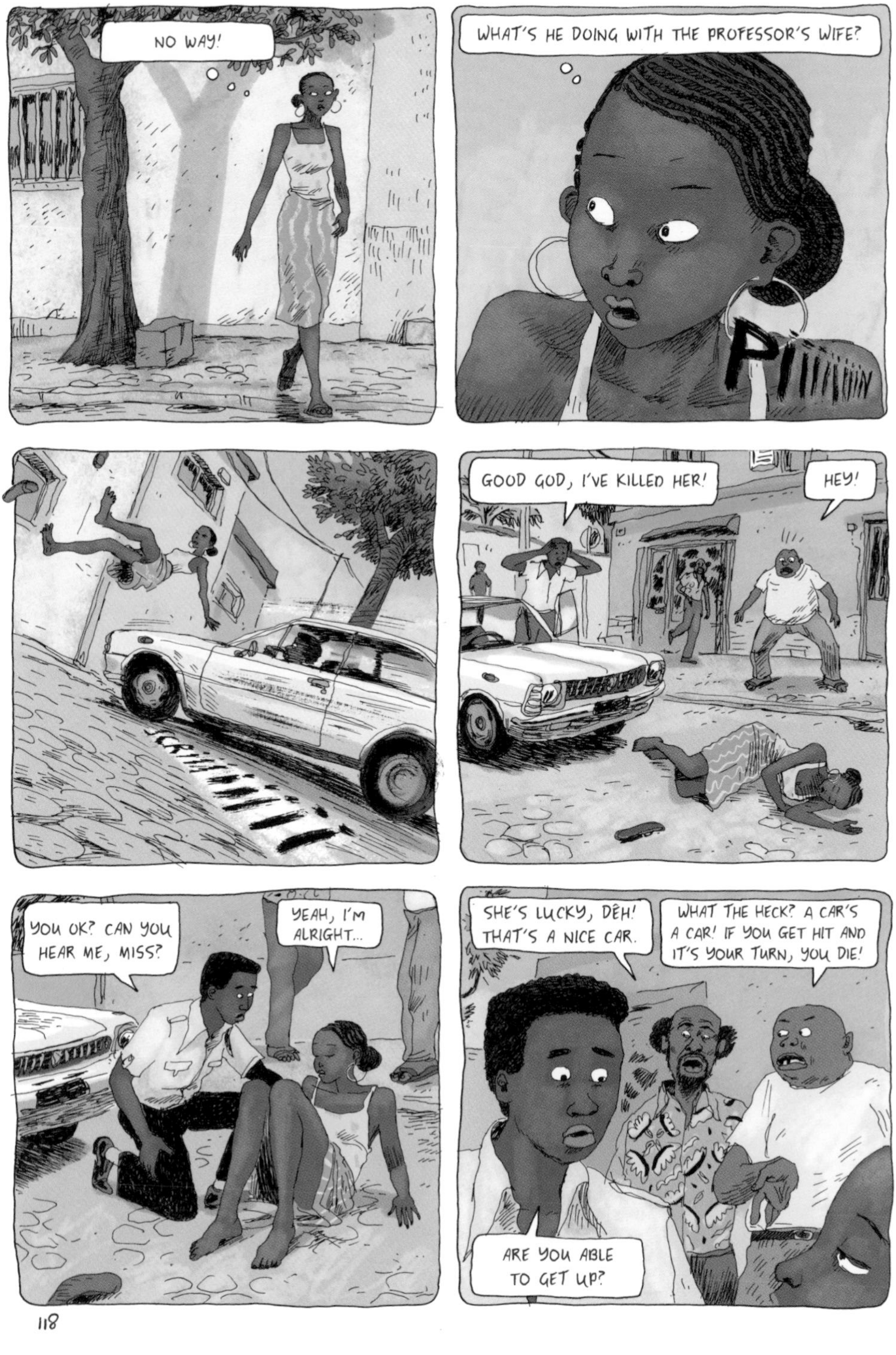
NO WAY!
WHAT'S HE DOING WITH THE PROFESSOR'S WIFE?
PI
SCRIIII
GOOD GOD, I'VE KILLED HER!
HEY!
YOU OK? CAN YOU HEAR ME, MISS?
YEAH, I'M ALRIGHT...
SHE'S LUCKY, DÊH! THAT'S A NICE CAR.
WHAT THE HECK? A CAR'S A CAR! IF YOU GET HIT AND IT'S YOUR TURN, YOU DIE!
ARE YOU ABLE TO GET UP?

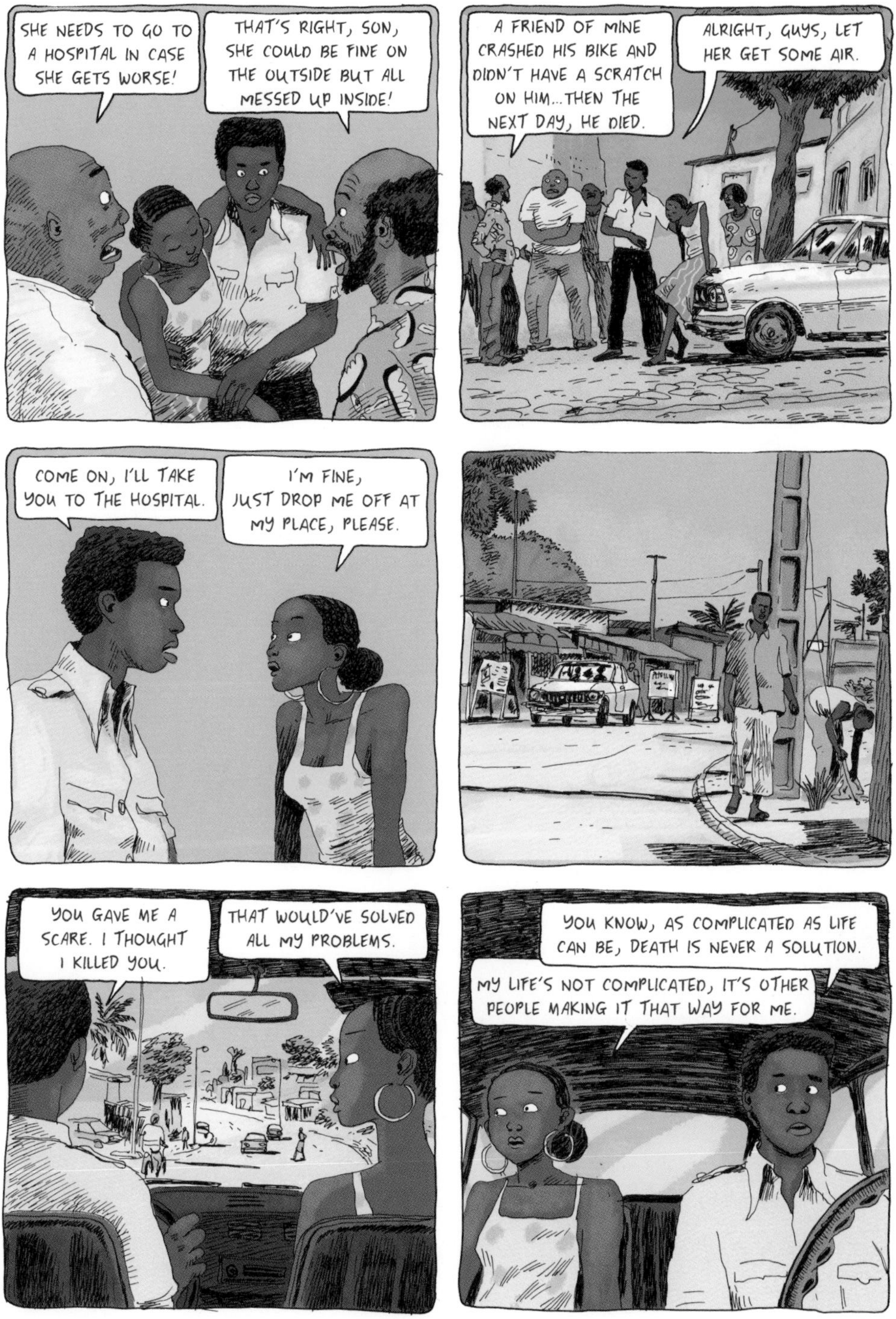
SHE NEEDS TO GO TO A HOSPITAL IN CASE SHE GETS WORSE!
THAT'S RIGHT, SON, SHE COULD BE FINE ON THE OUTSIDE BUT ALL MESSED UP INSIDE!
A FRIEND OF MINE CRASHED HIS BIKE AND DIDN'T HAVE A SCRATCH ON HIM...THEN THE NEXT DAY, HE DIED.
ALRIGHT, GUYS, LET HER GET SOME AIR.
COME ON, I'LL TAKE YOU TO THE HOSPITAL.
I'M FINE, JUST DROP ME OFF AT MY PLACE, PLEASE.
YOU GAVE ME A SCARE. I THOUGHT I KILLED YOU.
THAT WOULD'VE SOLVED ALL MY PROBLEMS.
YOU KNOW, AS COMPLICATED AS LIFE CAN BE, DEATH IS NEVER A SOLUTION.
MY LIFE'S NOT COMPLICATED, IT'S OTHER PEOPLE MAKING IT THAT WAY FOR ME.

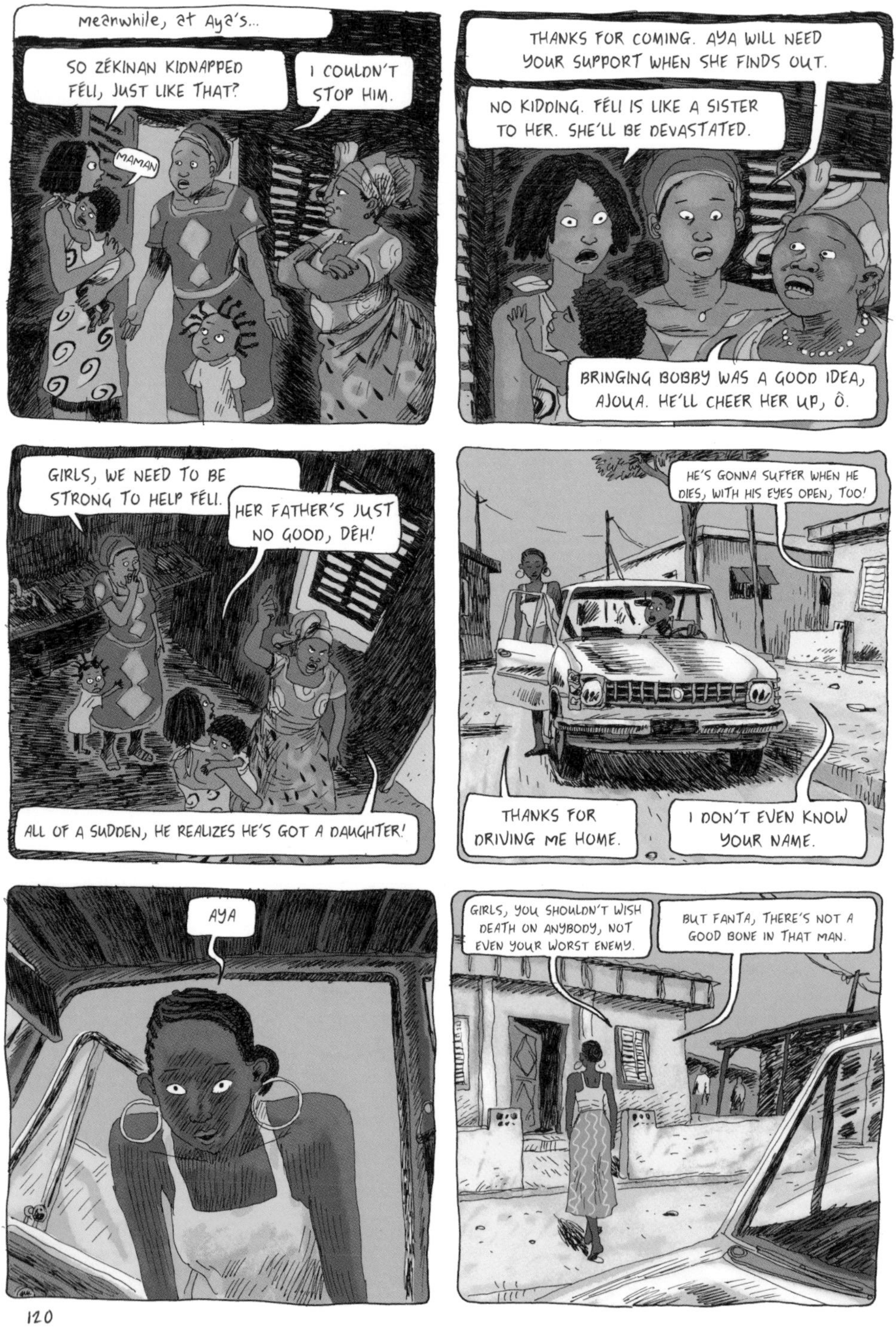
Meanwhile, at Aya's...
SO ZÉKINAN KIDNAPPED FÉLI, JUST LIKE THAT?
I COULDN'T STOP HIM.
MAMAN
THANKS FOR COMING. AYA WILL NEED YOUR SUPPORT WHEN SHE FINDS OUT.
NO KIDDING. FÉLI IS LIKE A SISTER TO HER. SHE'LL BE DEVASTATED.
BRINGING BOBBY WAS A GOOD IDEA, AJOUA. HE'LL CHEER HER UP, Ô.
GIRLS, WE NEED TO BE STRONG TO HELP FÉLI.
HER FATHER'S JUST NO GOOD, DÊH!
ALL OF A SUDDEN, HE REALIZES HE'S GOT A DAUGHTER!
HE'S GONNA SUFFER WHEN HE DIES, WITH HIS EYES OPEN, TOO!
THANKS FOR DRIVING ME HOME.
I DON'T EVEN KNOW YOUR NAME.
AYA
GIRLS, YOU SHOULDN'T WISH DEATH ON ANYBODY, NOT EVEN YOUR WORST ENEMY.
BUT FANTA, THERE'S NOT A GOOD BONE IN THAT MAN.

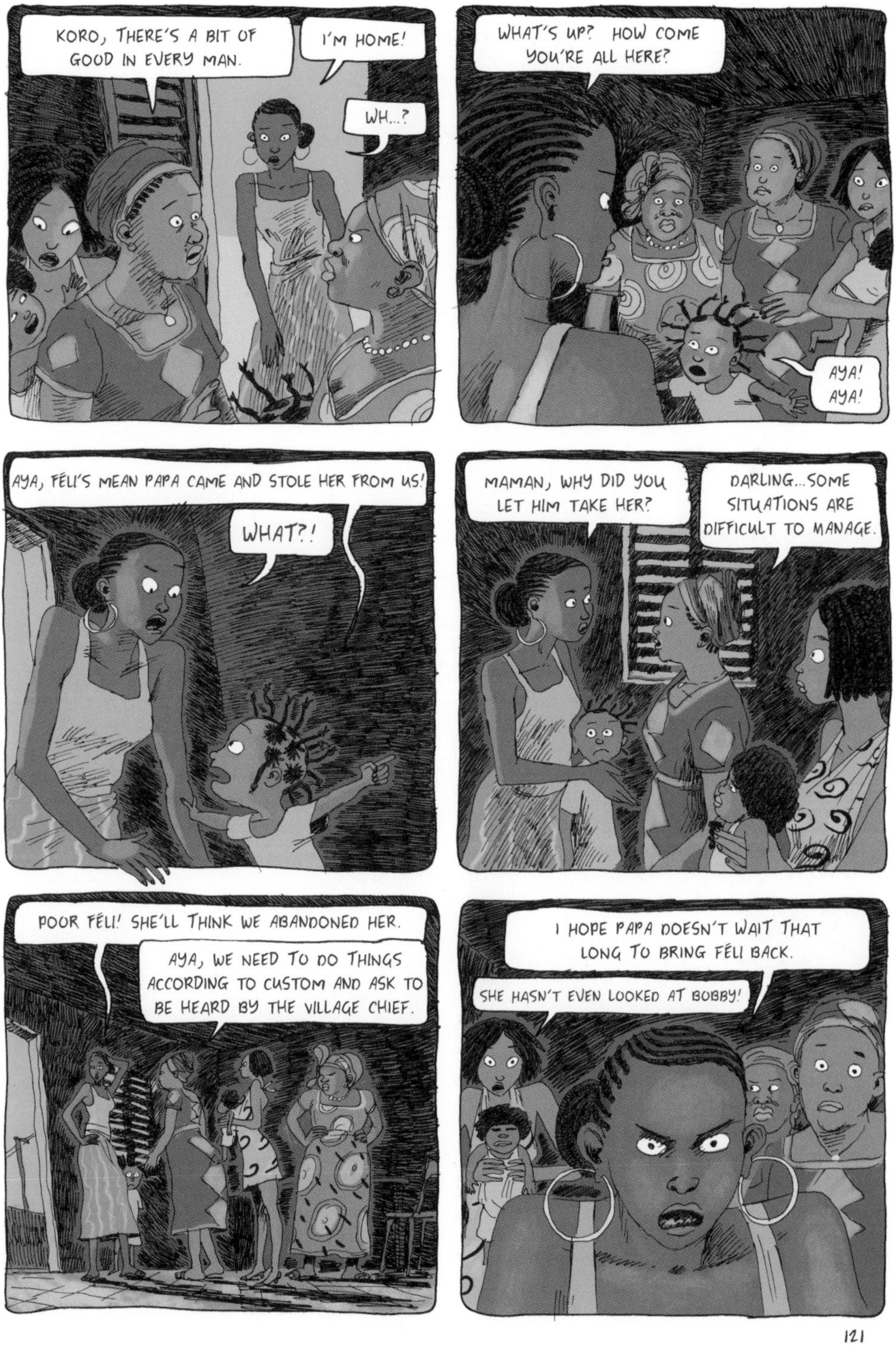
KORO, THERE'S A BIT OF GOOD IN EVERY MAN.
I'M HOME!
WH...?
WHAT'S UP? HOW COME YOU'RE ALL HERE?
AYA! AYA!
AYA, FÉLI'S MEAN PAPA CAME AND STOLE HER FROM US!
WHAT?!
MAMAN, WHY DID YOU LET HIM TAKE HER?
DARLING...SOME SITUATIONS ARE DIFFICULT TO MANAGE.
POOR FÉLI! SHE'LL THINK WE ABANDONED HER.
AYA, WE NEED TO DO THINGS ACCORDING TO CUSTOM AND ASK TO BE HEARD BY THE VILLAGE CHIEF.
I HOPE PAPA DOESN'T WAIT THAT LONG TO BRING FÉLI BACK.
SHE HASN'T EVEN LOOKED AT BOBBY!

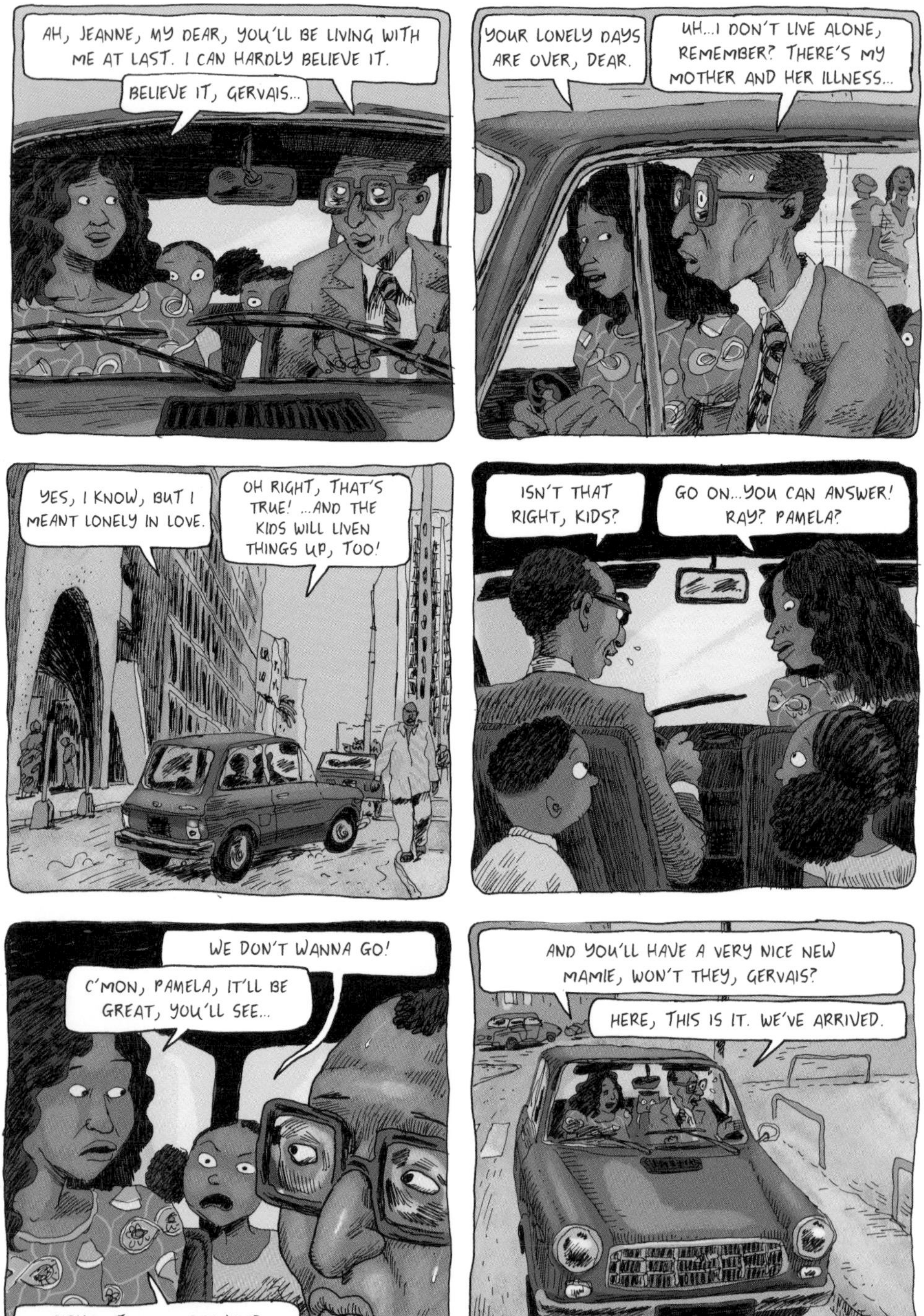
AH, JEANNE, MY DEAR, YOU'LL BE LIVING WITH ME AT LAST. I CAN HARDLY BELIEVE IT.
BELIEVE IT, GERVAIS...
YOUR LONELY DAYS ARE OVER, DEAR.
UH...I DON'T LIVE ALONE, REMEMBER? THERE'S MY MOTHER AND HER ILLNESS...
YES, I KNOW, BUT I MEANT LONELY IN LOVE.
OH RIGHT, THAT'S TRUE! ...AND THE KIDS WILL LIVEN THINGS UP, TOO!
ISN'T THAT RIGHT, KIDS?
GO ON...YOU CAN ANSWER! RAY? PAMELA?
WE DON'T WANNA GO!
C'MON, PAMELA, IT'LL BE GREAT, YOU'LL SEE...
RIGHT, TONTON GERVAIS?
AND YOU'LL HAVE A VERY NICE NEW MAMIE, WON'T THEY, GERVAIS?
HERE, THIS IS IT. WE'VE ARRIVED.

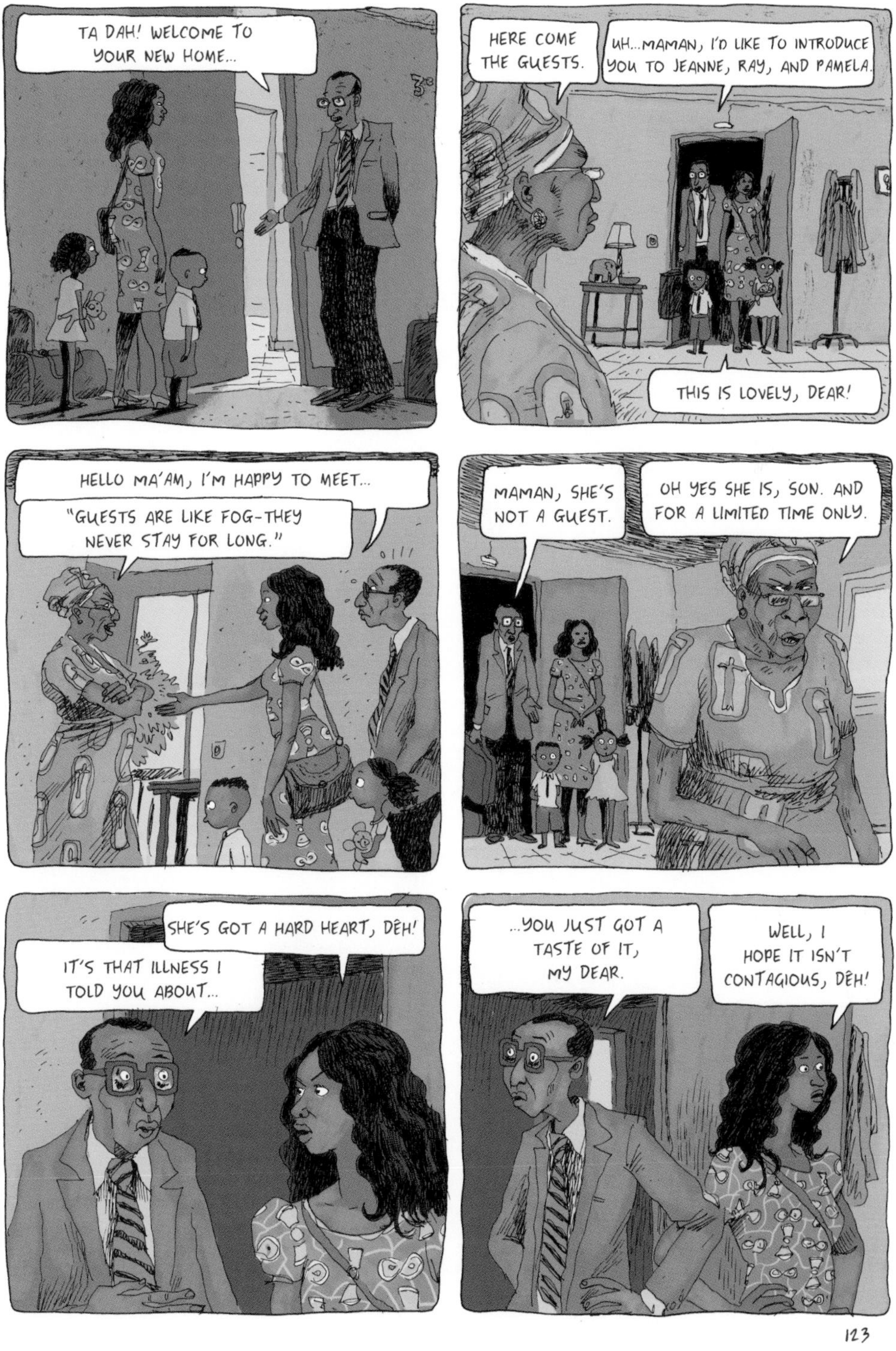
TA DAH! WELCOME TO YOUR NEW HOME...
HERE COME THE GUESTS.
UH...MAMAN, I'D LIKE TO INTRODUCE YOU TO JEANNE, RAY, AND PAMELA.
THIS IS LOVELY, DEAR!
HELLO MA'AM, I'M HAPPY TO MEET...
"GUESTS ARE LIKE FOG-THEY NEVER STAY FOR LONG."
MAMAN, SHE'S NOT A GUEST.
OH YES SHE IS, SON. AND FOR A LIMITED TIME ONLY.
SHE'S GOT A HARD HEART, DÊH!
IT'S THAT ILLNESS I TOLD YOU ABOUT...
...YOU JUST GOT A TASTE OF IT, MY DEAR.
WELL, I HOPE IT ISN'T CONTAGIOUS, DÊH!

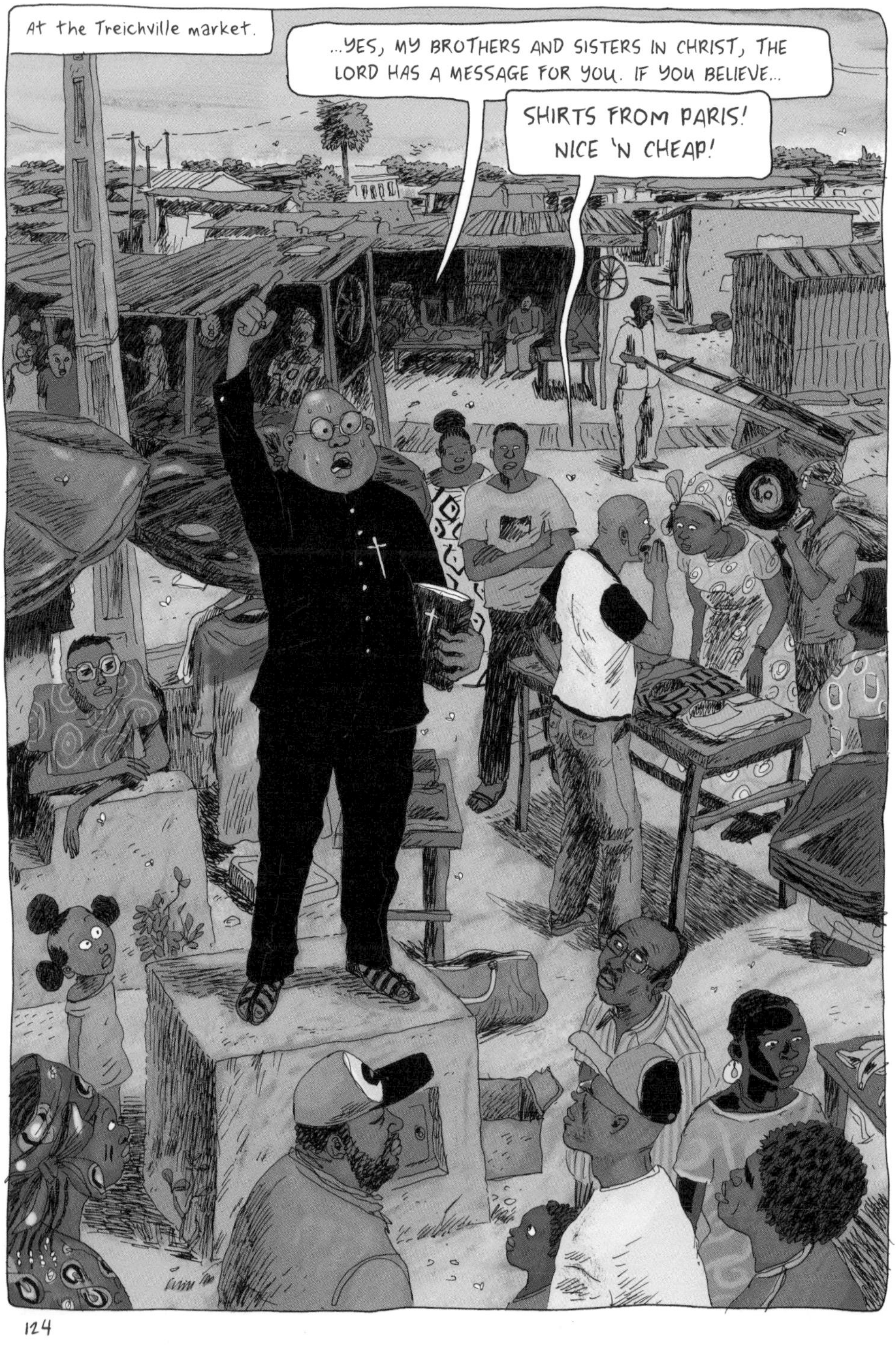
At the Treichville market.
...YES, MY BROTHERS AND SISTERS IN CHRIST, THE LORD HAS A MESSAGE FOR YOU. IF YOU BELIEVE...
SHIRTS FROM PARIS! NICE 'N CHEAP!

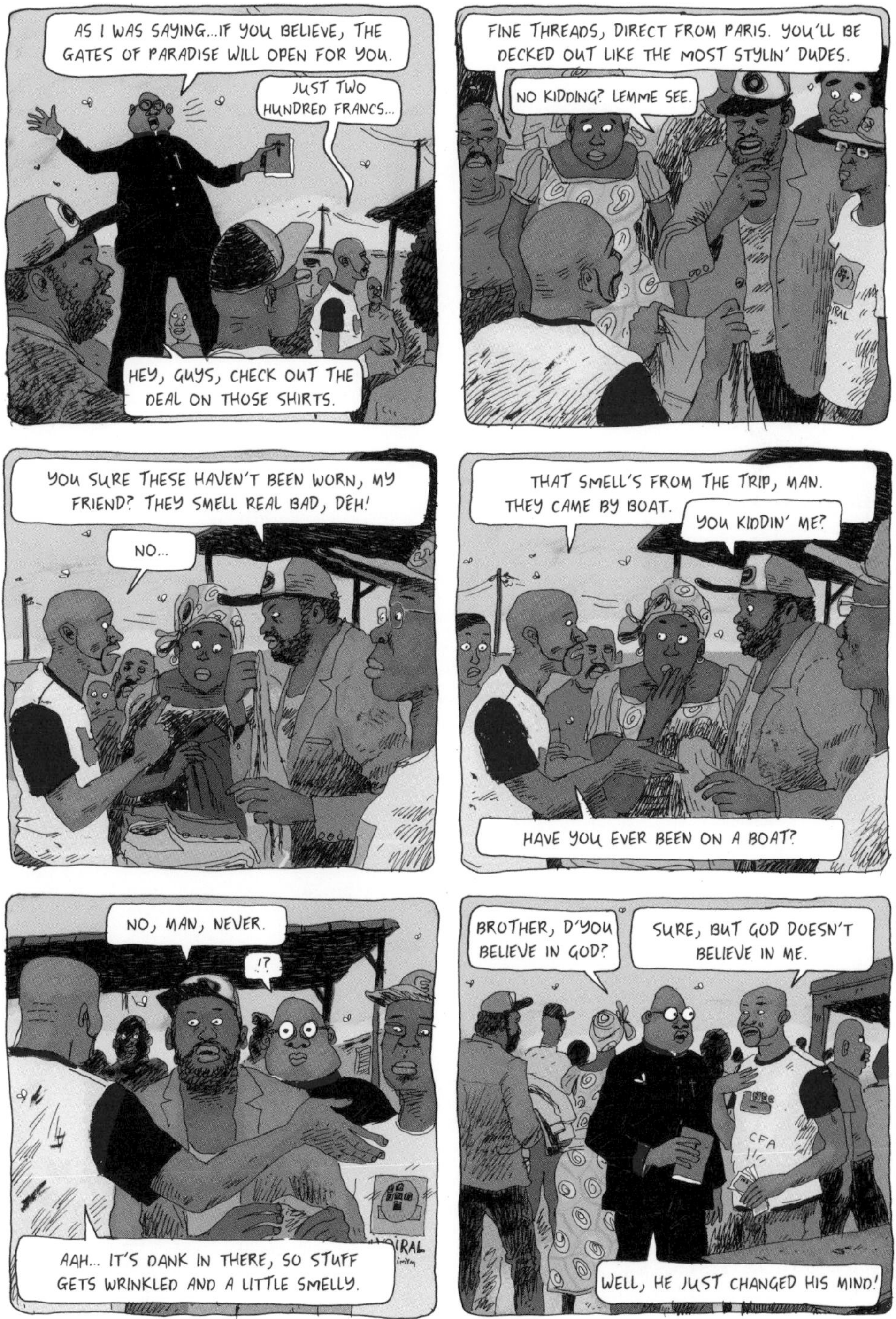
AS I WAS SAYING...IF YOU BELIEVE, THE GATES OF PARADISE WILL OPEN FOR YOU.
JUST TWO HUNDRED FRANCS...
HEY, GUYS, CHECK OUT THE DEAL ON THOSE SHIRTS.
FINE THREADS, DIRECT FROM PARIS. YOU'LL BE DECKED OUT LIKE THE MOST STYLIN' DUDES.
NO KIDDING? LEMME SEE.
YOU SURE THESE HAVEN'T BEEN WORN, MY FRIEND? THEY SMELL REAL BAD, DÊH!
NO...
THAT SMELL'S FROM THE TRIP, MAN. THEY CAME BY BOAT.
YOU KIDDIN' ME?
HAVE YOU EVER BEEN ON A BOAT?
NO, MAN, NEVER.
!?
AAH... IT'S DANK IN THERE, SO STUFF GETS WRINKLED AND A LITTLE SMELLY.
BROTHER, D'YOU BELIEVE IN GOD?
SURE, BUT GOD DOESN'T BELIEVE IN ME.
CFA
WELL, HE JUST CHANGED HIS MIND!

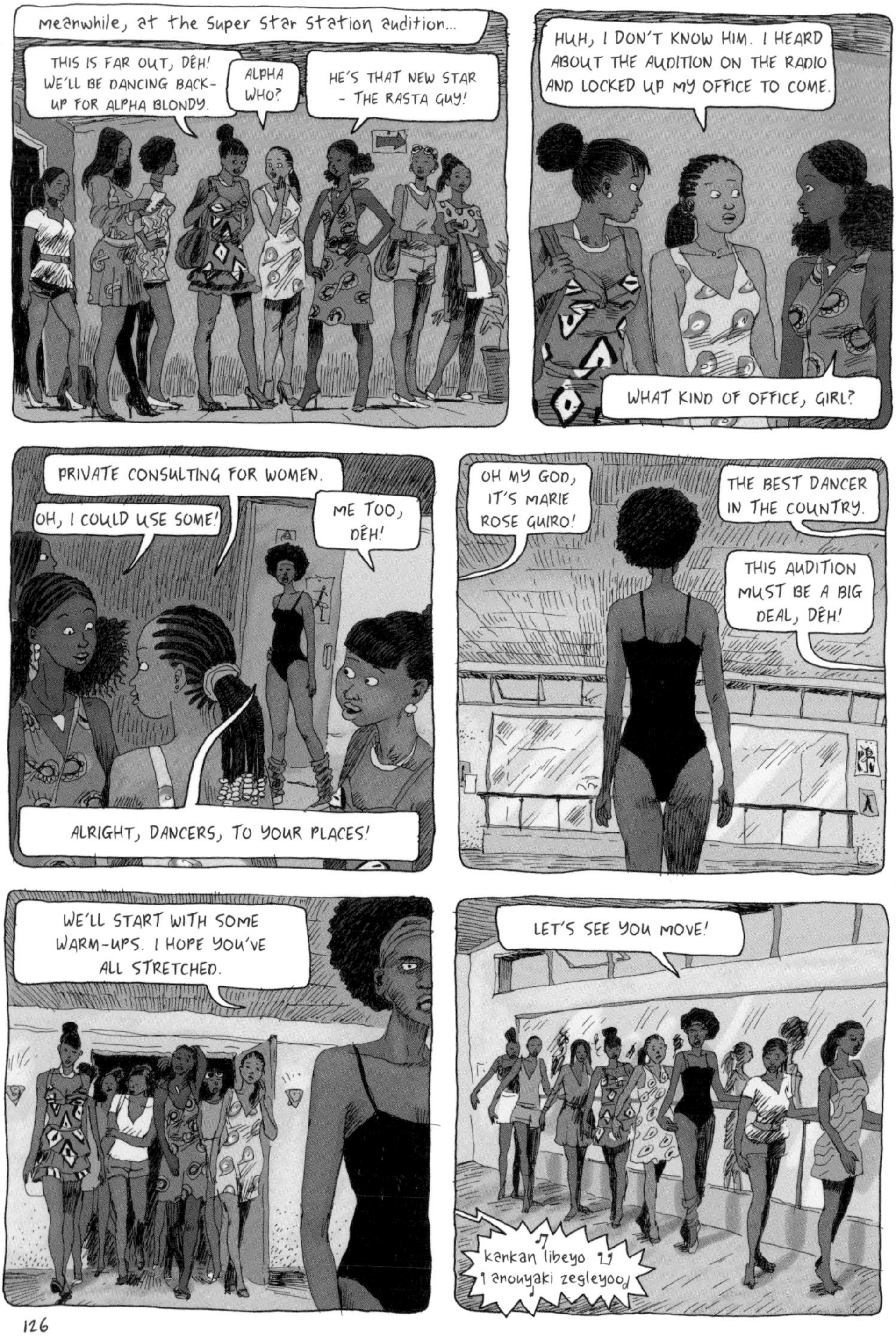
Meanwhile, at the Super Star Station audition...
THIS IS FAR OUT, DÊH! WE'LL BE DANCING BACK-UP FOR ALPHA BLONDY.
ALPHA WHO?
HE'S THAT NEW STAR - THE RASTA GUY!
HUH, I DON'T KNOW HIM. I HEARD ABOUT THE AUDITION ON THE RADIO AND LOCKED UP MY OFFICE TO COME.
WHAT KIND OF OFFICE, GIRL?
PRIVATE CONSULTING FOR WOMEN.
OH, I COULD USE SOME!
ME TOO, DÊH!
ALRIGHT, DANCERS, TO YOUR PLACES!
OH MY GOD, IT'S MARIE ROSE GUIRO!
THE BEST DANCER IN THE COUNTRY.
THIS AUDITION MUST BE A BIG DEAL, DÊH!
WE'LL START WITH SOME WARM-UPS. I HOPE YOU'VE ALL STRETCHED.
LET'S SEE YOU MOVE!
kankan libeyo
anouyaki zegleyoo

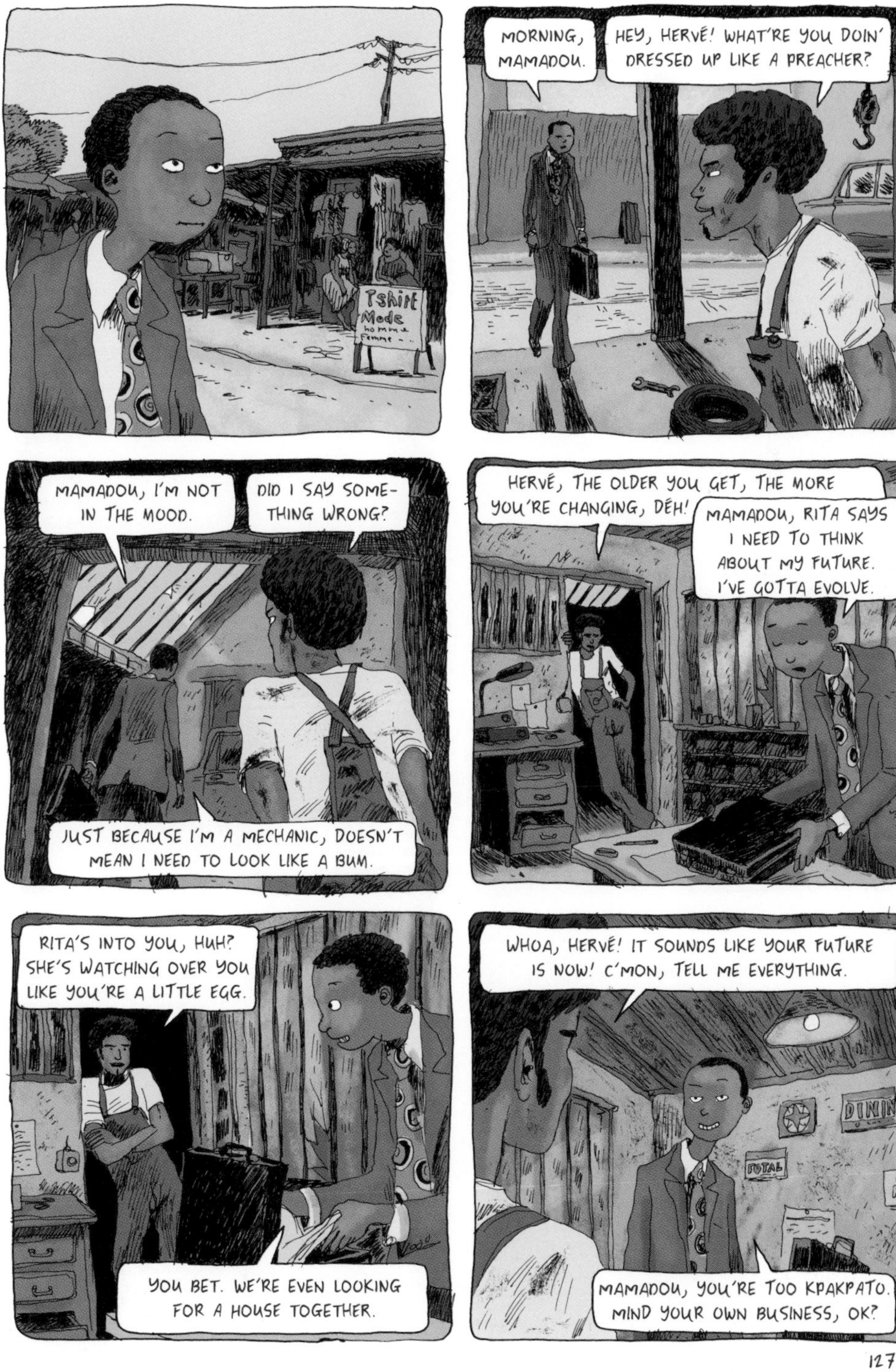
Tshirt
Mode
homme
Femme
MORNING, MAMADOU.
HEY, HERVÉ! WHAT'RE YOU DOIN' DRESSED UP LIKE A PREACHER?
MAMADOU, I'M NOT IN THE MOOD.
DID I SAY SOMETHING WRONG?
JUST BECAUSE I'M A MECHANIC, DOESN'T MEAN I NEED TO LOOK LIKE A BUM.
HERVÉ, THE OLDER YOU GET, THE MORE YOU'RE CHANGING, DÉH!
MAMADOU, RITA SAYS I NEED TO THINK ABOUT MY FUTURE. I'VE GOTTA EVOLVE.
RITA'S INTO YOU, HUH? SHE'S WATCHING OVER YOU LIKE YOU'RE A LITTLE EGG.
YOU BET. WE'RE EVEN LOOKING FOR A HOUSE TOGETHER.
WHOA, HERVÉ! IT SOUNDS LIKE YOUR FUTURE IS NOW! C'MON, TELL ME EVERYTHING.
TOTAL
MAMADOU, YOU'RE TOO KPAKPATO. MIND YOUR OWN BUSINESS, OK?

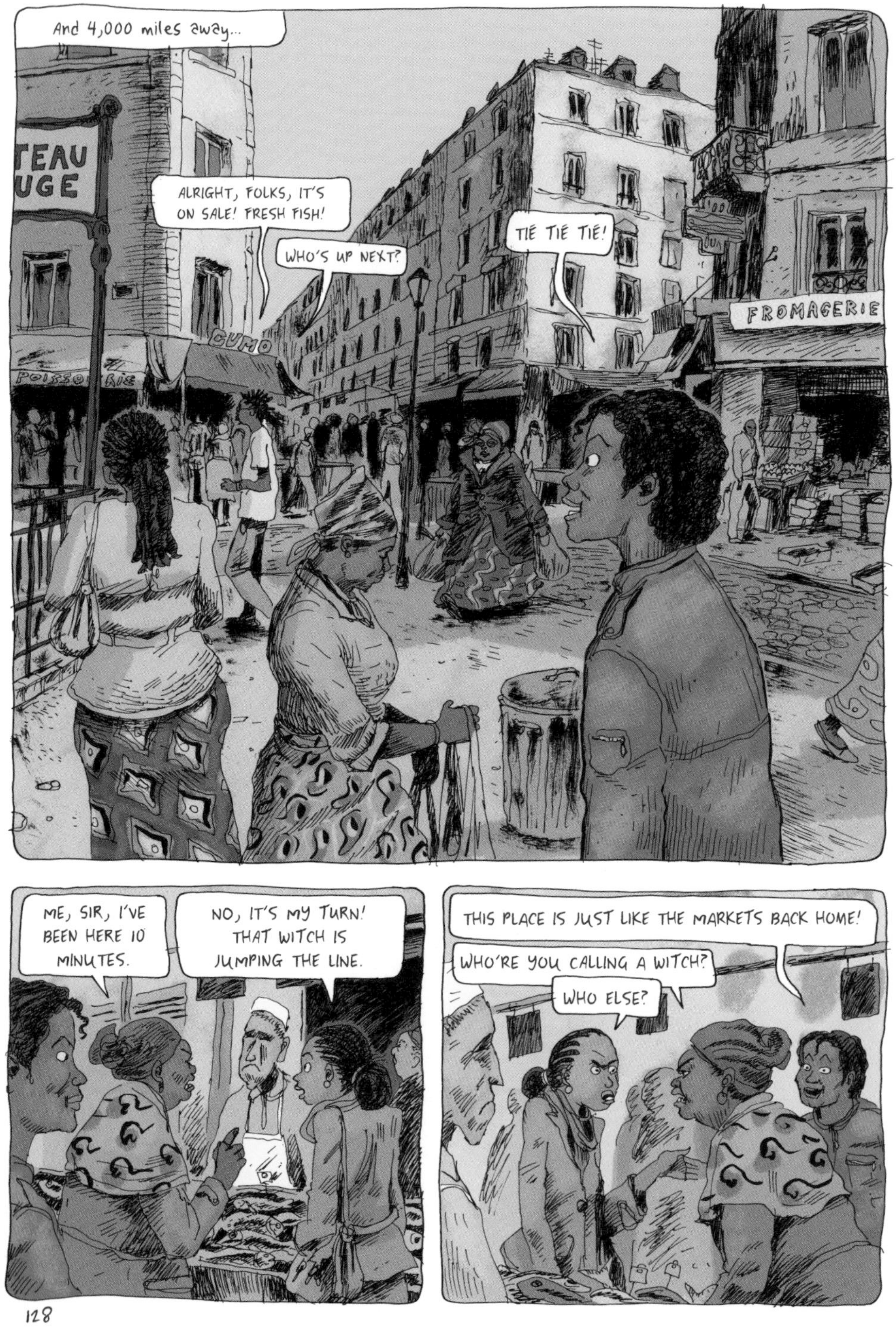
And 4,000 miles away...
ALRIGHT, FOLKS, IT'S ON SALE! FRESH FISH!
WHO'S UP NEXT?
TIÉ TIÉ TIÉ!
FROMAGERIE
ME, SIR, I'VE BEEN HERE 10 MINUTES.
NO, IT'S MY TURN! THAT WITCH IS JUMPING THE LINE.
THIS PLACE IS JUST LIKE THE MARKETS BACK HOME!
WHO'RE YOU CALLING A WITCH?
WHO ELSE?

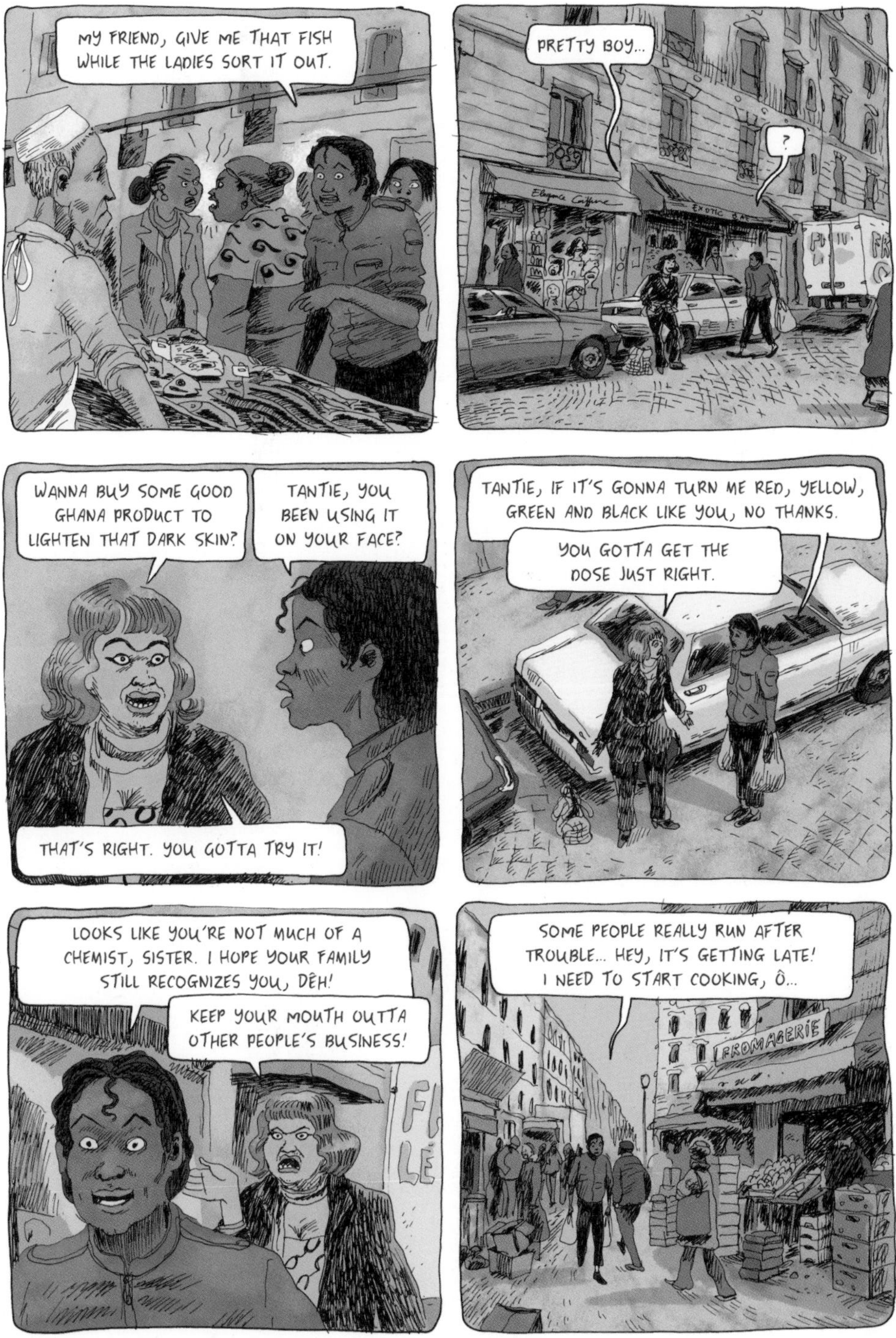
MY FRIEND, GIVE ME THAT FISH WHILE THE LADIES SORT IT OUT.
PRETTY BOY...
?
WANNA BUY SOME GOOD GHANA PRODUCT TO LIGHTEN THAT DARK SKIN?
TANTIE, YOU BEEN USING IT ON YOUR FACE?
THAT'S RIGHT. YOU GOTTA TRY IT!
TANTIE, IF IT'S GONNA TURN ME RED, YELLOW, GREEN AND BLACK LIKE YOU, NO THANKS.
YOU GOTTA GET THE DOSE JUST RIGHT.
LOOKS LIKE YOU'RE NOT MUCH OF A CHEMIST, SISTER. I HOPE YOUR FAMILY STILL RECOGNIZES YOU, DÊH!
KEEP YOUR MOUTH OUTTA OTHER PEOPLE'S BUSINESS!
SOME PEOPLE REALLY RUN AFTER TROUBLE... HEY, IT'S GETTING LATE! I NEED TO START COOKING, Ô...
FROMAGERIE

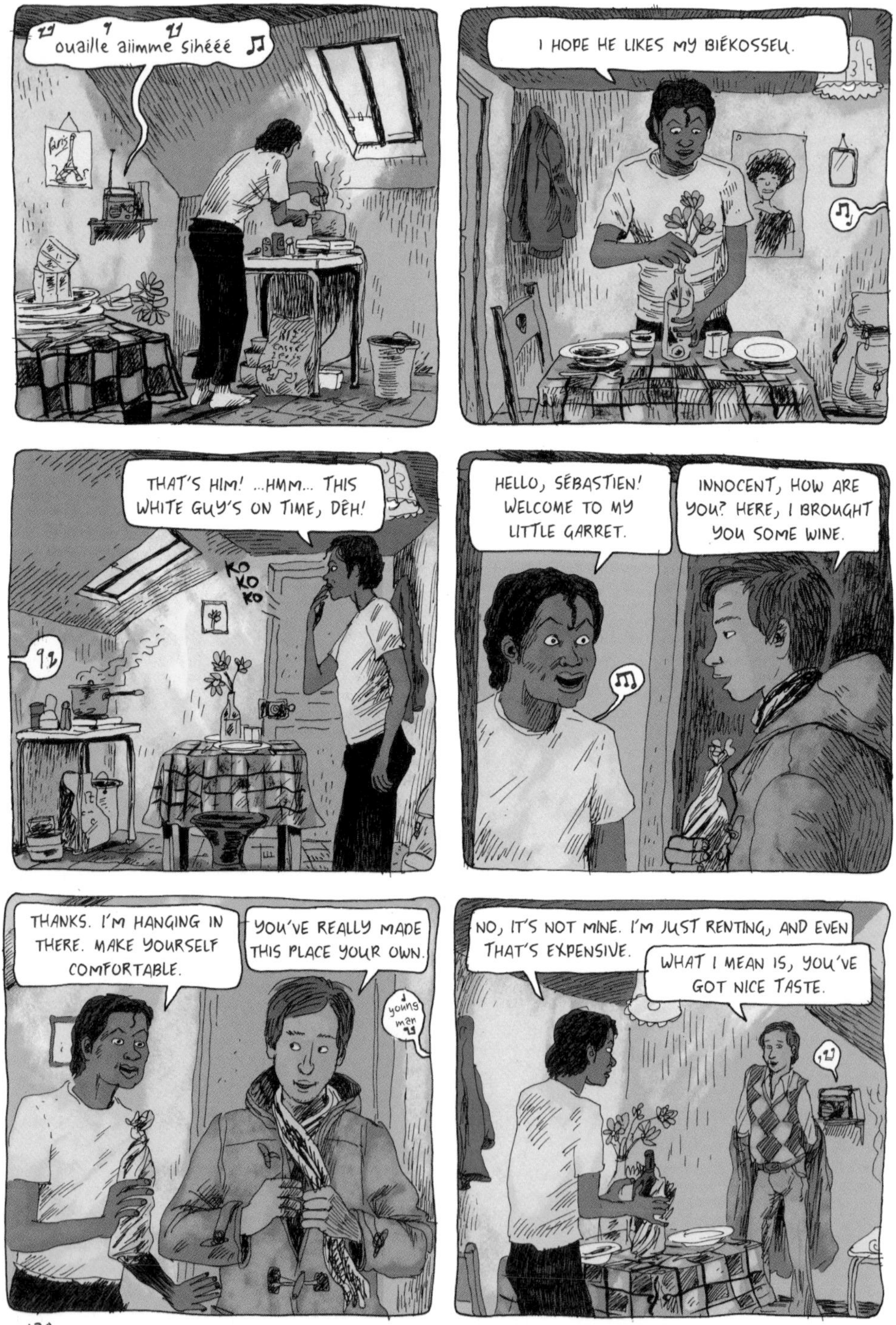
ouaille aiimme sihééé
I HOPE HE LIKES MY BIÉKOSSEU.
THAT'S HIM! ...HMM... THIS WHITE GUY'S ON TIME, DÊH!
KO KO KO
HELLO, SÉBASTIEN! WELCOME TO MY LITTLE GARRET.
INNOCENT, HOW ARE YOU? HERE, I BROUGHT YOU SOME WINE.
THANKS. I'M HANGING IN THERE. MAKE YOURSELF COMFORTABLE.
YOU'VE REALLY MADE THIS PLACE YOUR OWN.
young man
NO, IT'S NOT MINE. I'M JUST RENTING, AND EVEN THAT'S EXPENSIVE.
WHAT I MEAN IS, YOU'VE GOT NICE TASTE.

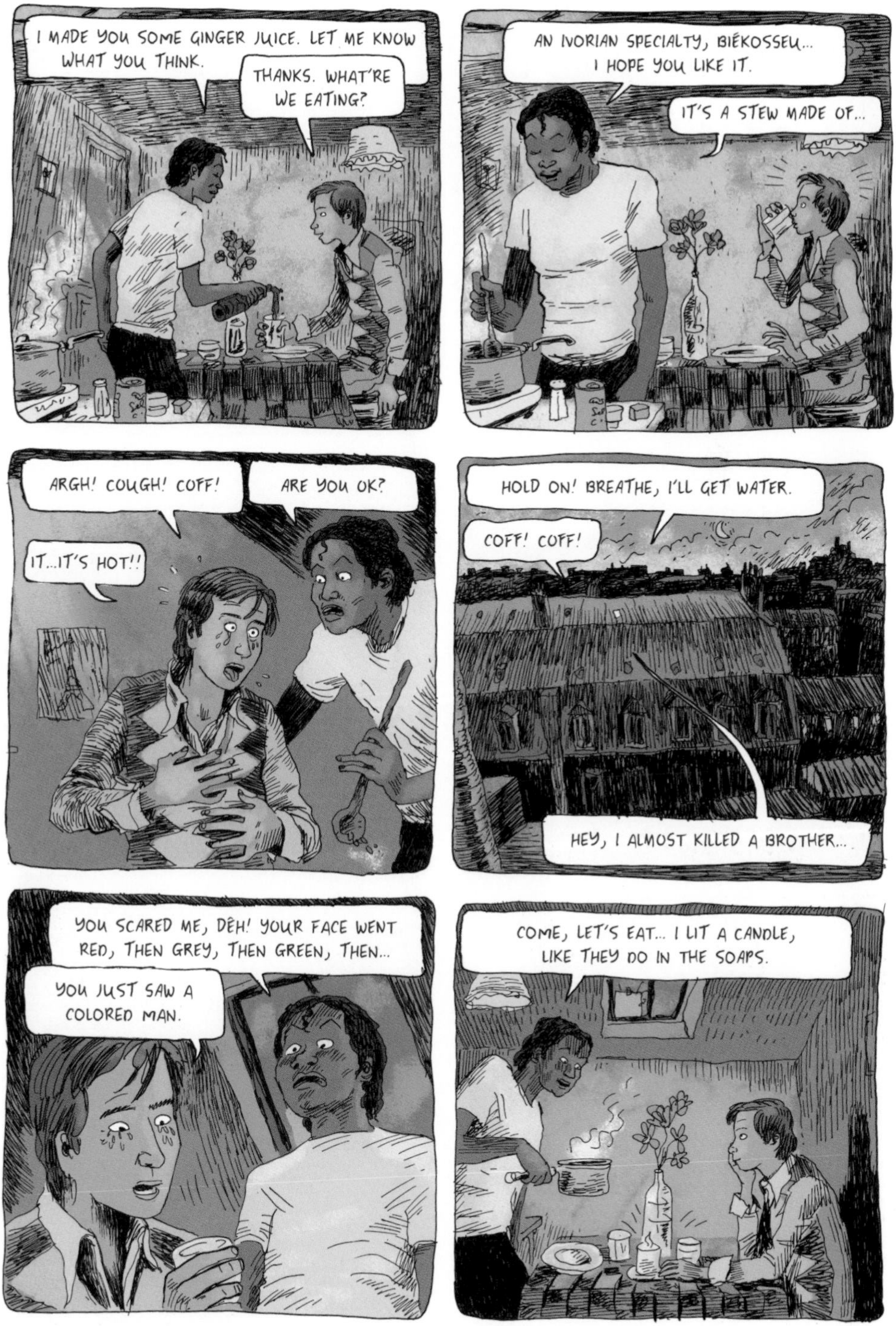
I MADE YOU SOME GINGER JUICE. LET ME KNOW WHAT YOU THINK.
THANKS. WHAT'RE WE EATING?
AN IVORIAN SPECIALTY, BIÉKOSSEU... I HOPE YOU LIKE IT.
IT'S A STEW MADE OF...
ARGH! COUGH! COFF!
ARE YOU OK?
IT...IT'S HOT!!
HOLD ON! BREATHE, I'LL GET WATER.
COFF! COFF!
HEY, I ALMOST KILLED A BROTHER...
YOU SCARED ME, DÊH! YOUR FACE WENT RED, THEN GREY, THEN GREEN, THEN...
YOU JUST SAW A COLORED MAN.
COME, LET'S EAT... I LIT A CANDLE, LIKE THEY DO IN THE SOAPS.

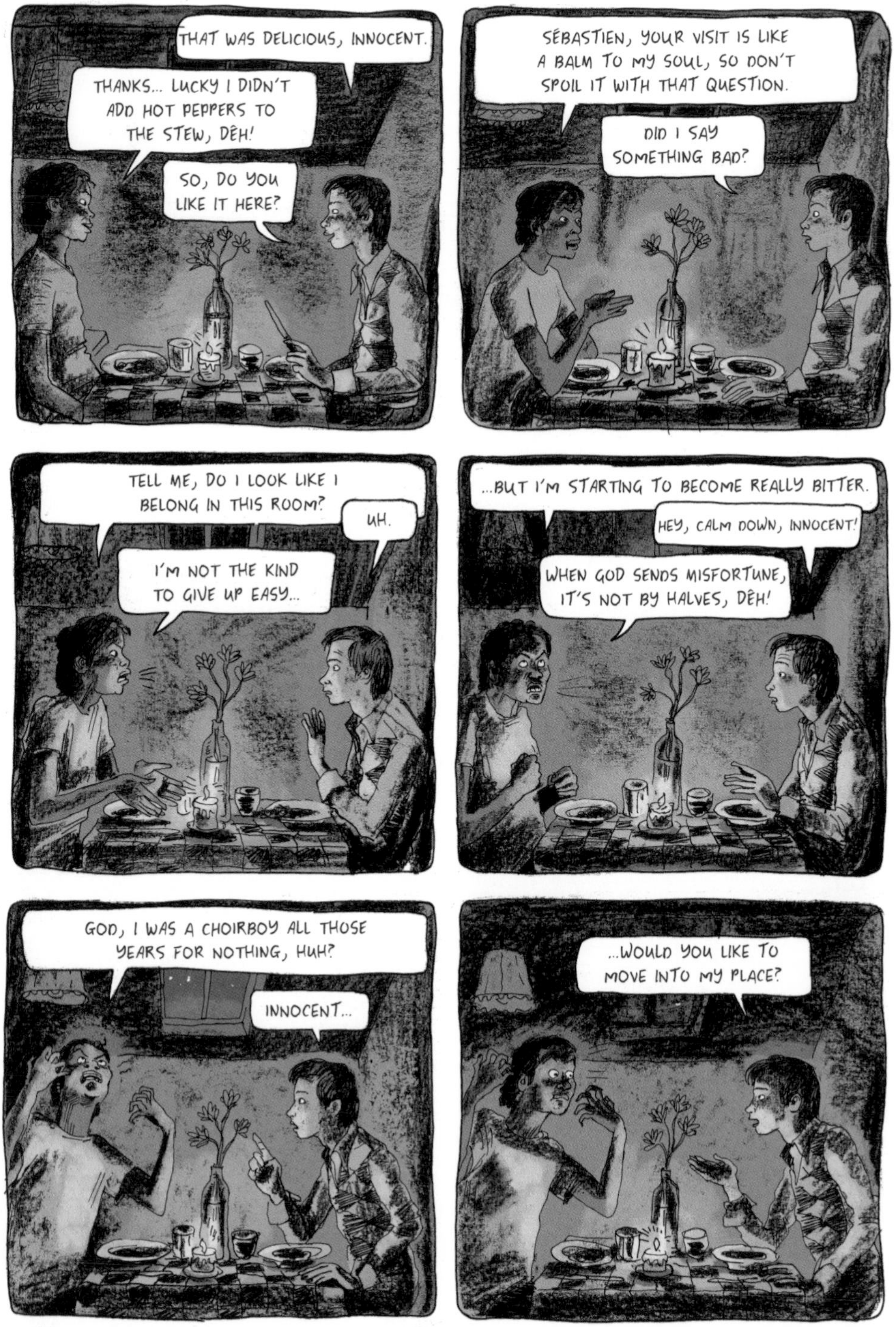
THAT WAS DELICIOUS, INNOCENT.
THANKS... LUCKY I DIDN'T ADD HOT PEPPERS TO THE STEW, DÊH!
SO, DO YOU LIKE IT HERE?
SÉBASTIEN, YOUR VISIT IS LIKE A BALM TO MY SOUL, SO DON'T SPOIL IT WITH THAT QUESTION.
DID I SAY SOMETHING BAD?
TELL ME, DO I LOOK LIKE I BELONG IN THIS ROOM?
UH.
I'M NOT THE KIND TO GIVE UP EASY...
...BUT I'M STARTING TO BECOME REALLY BITTER.
HEY, CALM DOWN, INNOCENT!
WHEN GOD SENDS MISFORTUNE, IT'S NOT BY HALVES, DÊH!
GOD, I WAS A CHOIRBOY ALL THOSE YEARS FOR NOTHING, HUH?
INNOCENT...
...WOULD YOU LIKE TO MOVE INTO MY PLACE?

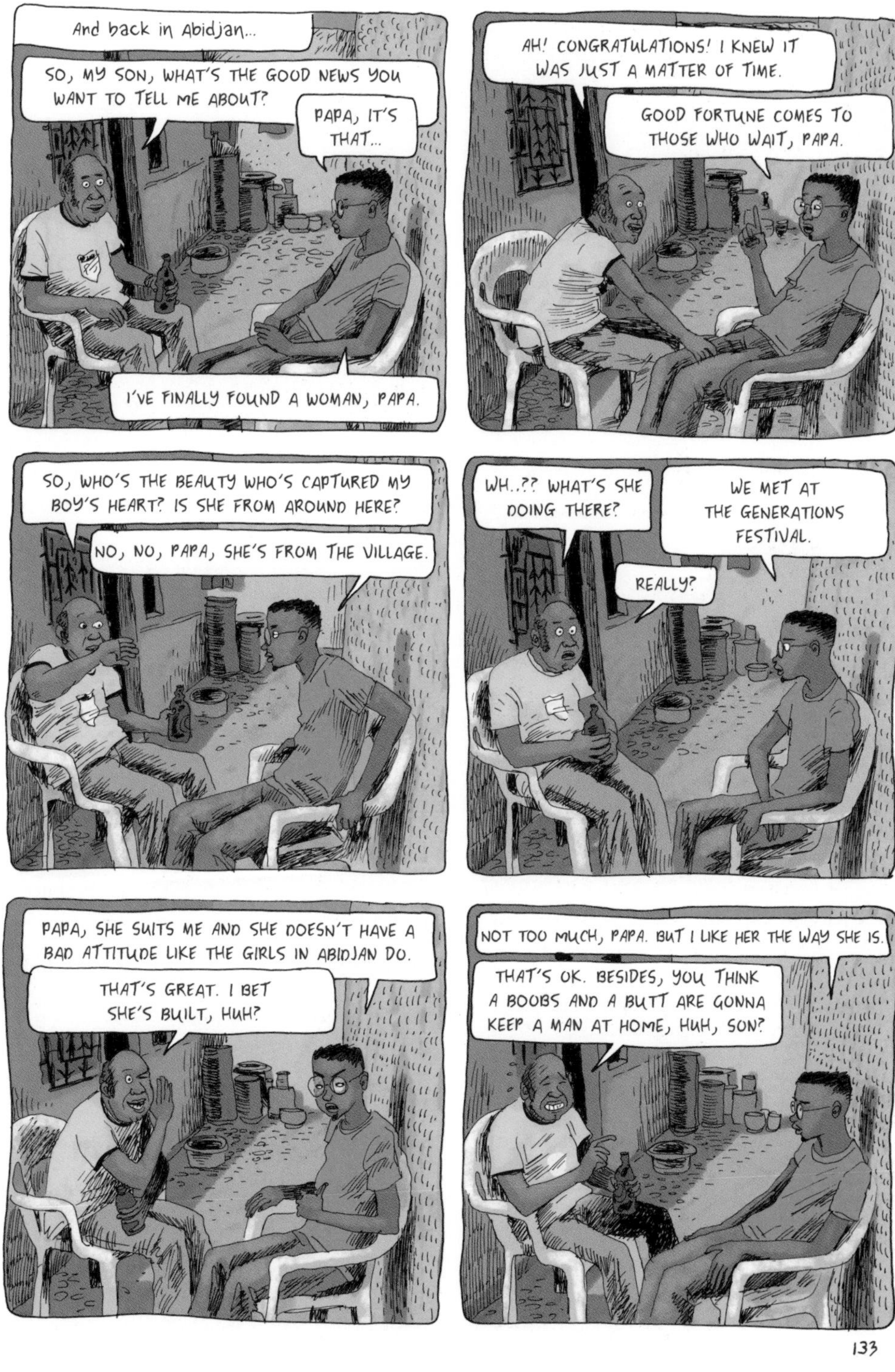
And back in Abidjan...
SO, MY SON, WHAT'S THE GOOD NEWS YOU WANT TO TELL ME ABOUT?
PAPA, IT'S THAT...
I'VE FINALLY FOUND A WOMAN, PAPA.
AH! CONGRATULATIONS! I KNEW IT WAS JUST A MATTER OF TIME.
GOOD FORTUNE COMES TO THOSE WHO WAIT, PAPA.
SO, WHO'S THE BEAUTY WHO'S CAPTURED MY BOY'S HEART? IS SHE FROM AROUND HERE?
NO, NO, PAPA, SHE'S FROM THE VILLAGE.
WH..?? WHAT'S SHE DOING THERE?
WE MET AT THE GENERATIONS FESTIVAL.
REALLY?
PAPA, SHE SUITS ME AND SHE DOESN'T HAVE A BAD ATTITUDE LIKE THE GIRLS IN ABIDJAN DO.
THAT'S GREAT. I BET SHE'S BUILT, HUH?
NOT TOO MUCH, PAPA. BUT I LIKE HER THE WAY SHE IS.
THAT'S OK. BESIDES, YOU THINK A BOOBS AND A BUTT ARE GONNA KEEP A MAN AT HOME, HUH, SON?

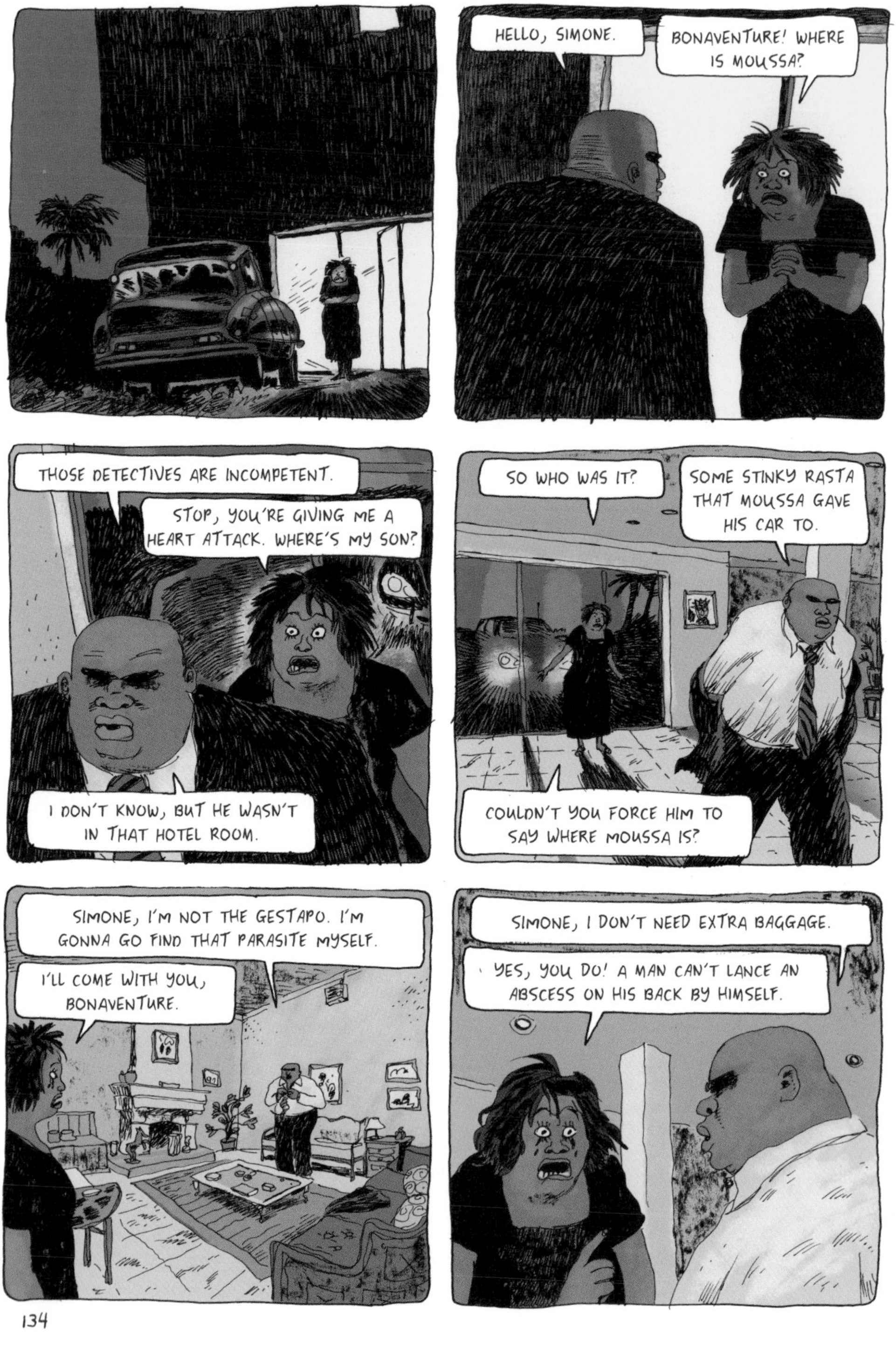
HELLO, SIMONE.
BONAVENTURE! WHERE IS MOUSSA?
THOSE DETECTIVES ARE INCOMPETENT.
STOP, YOU'RE GIVING ME A HEART ATTACK. WHERE'S MY SON?
I DON'T KNOW, BUT HE WASN'T IN THAT HOTEL ROOM.
SO WHO WAS IT?
SOME STINKY RASTA THAT MOUSSA GAVE HIS CAR TO.
COULDN'T YOU FORCE HIM TO SAY WHERE MOUSSA IS?
SIMONE, I'M NOT THE GESTAPO. I'M GONNA GO FIND THAT PARASITE MYSELF.
I'LL COME WITH YOU, BONAVENTURE.
SIMONE, I DON'T NEED EXTRA BAGGAGE.
YES, YOU DO! A MAN CAN'T LANCE AN ABSCESS ON HIS BACK BY HIMSELF.

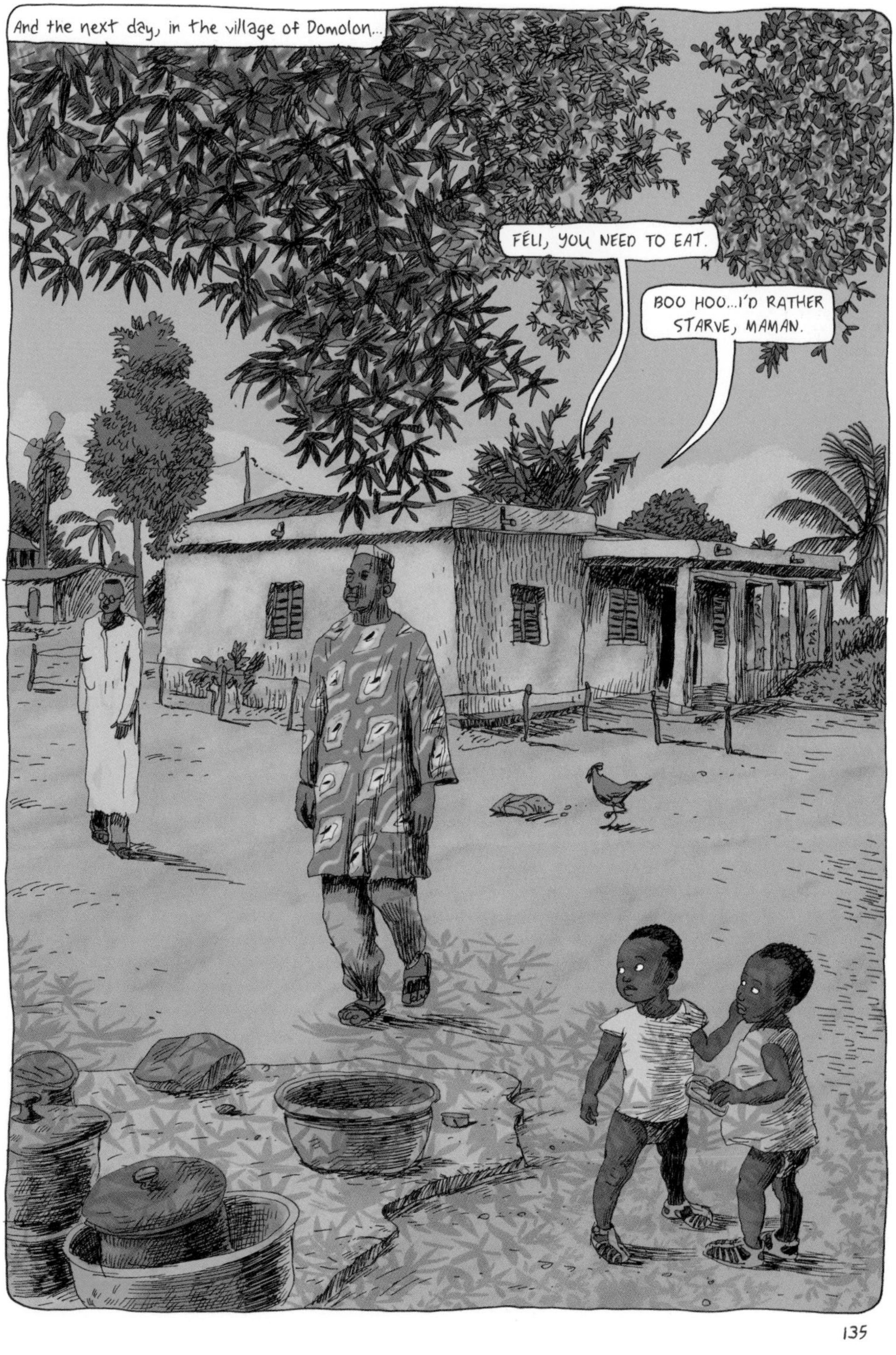
And the next day, in the village of Domolon...
FÉLI, YOU NEED TO EAT.
BOO HOO...I'D RATHER STARVE, MAMAN.

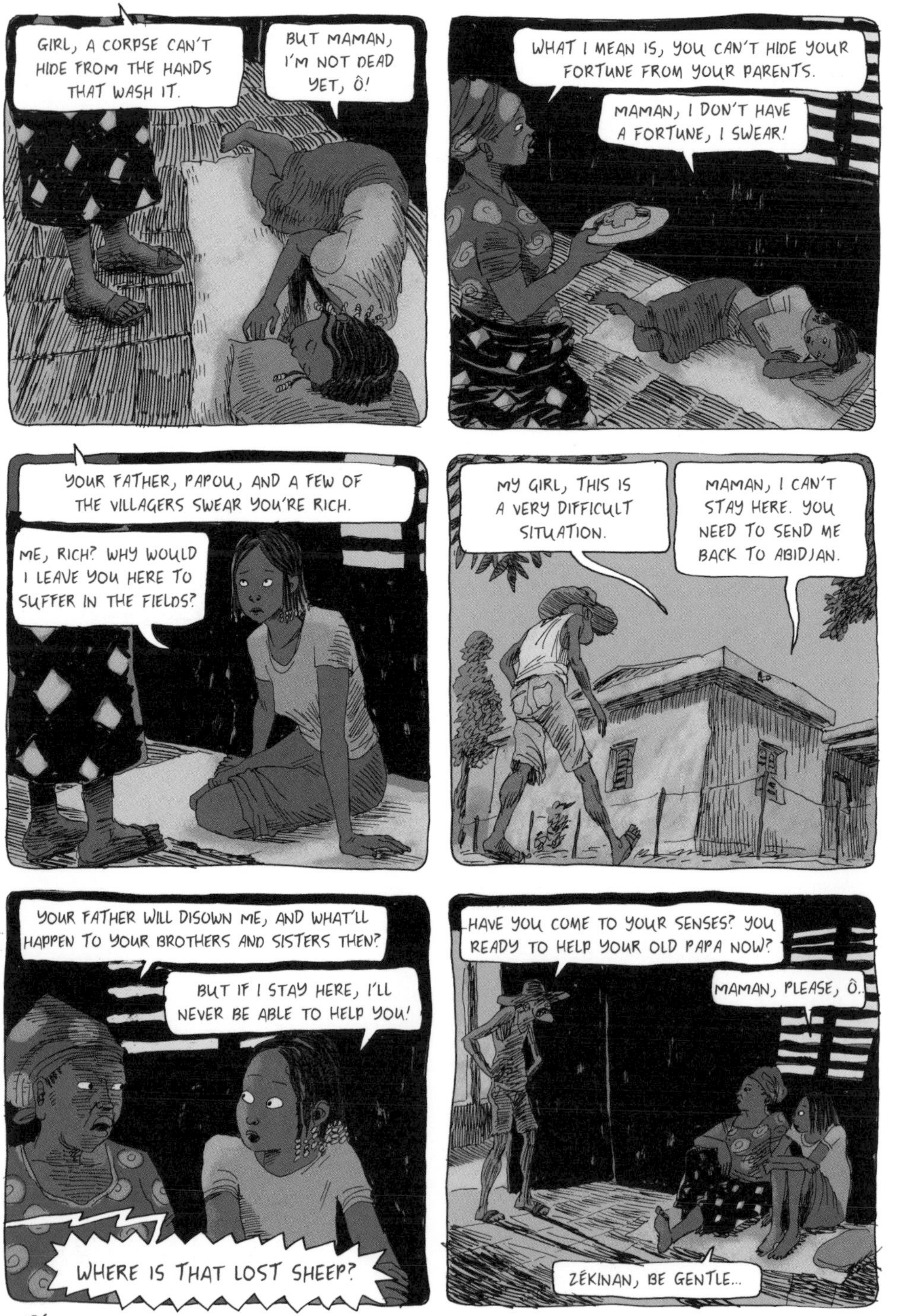
GIRL, A CORPSE CAN'T HIDE FROM THE HANDS THAT WASH IT.
BUT MAMAN, I'M NOT DEAD YET, Ô!
WHAT I MEAN IS, YOU CAN'T HIDE YOUR FORTUNE FROM YOUR PARENTS.
MAMAN, I DON'T HAVE A FORTUNE, I SWEAR!
YOUR FATHER, PAPOU, AND A FEW OF THE VILLAGERS SWEAR YOU'RE RICH.
ME, RICH? WHY WOULD I LEAVE YOU HERE TO SUFFER IN THE FIELDS?
MY GIRL, THIS IS A VERY DIFFICULT SITUATION.
MAMAN, I CAN'T STAY HERE. YOU NEED TO SEND ME BACK TO ABIDJAN.
YOUR FATHER WILL DISOWN ME, AND WHAT'LL HAPPEN TO YOUR BROTHERS AND SISTERS THEN?
BUT IF I STAY HERE, I'LL NEVER BE ABLE TO HELP YOU!
WHERE IS THAT LOST SHEEP?
HAVE YOU COME TO YOUR SENSES? YOU READY TO HELP YOUR OLD PAPA NOW?
MAMAN, PLEASE, Ô...
ZÉKINAN, BE GENTLE...

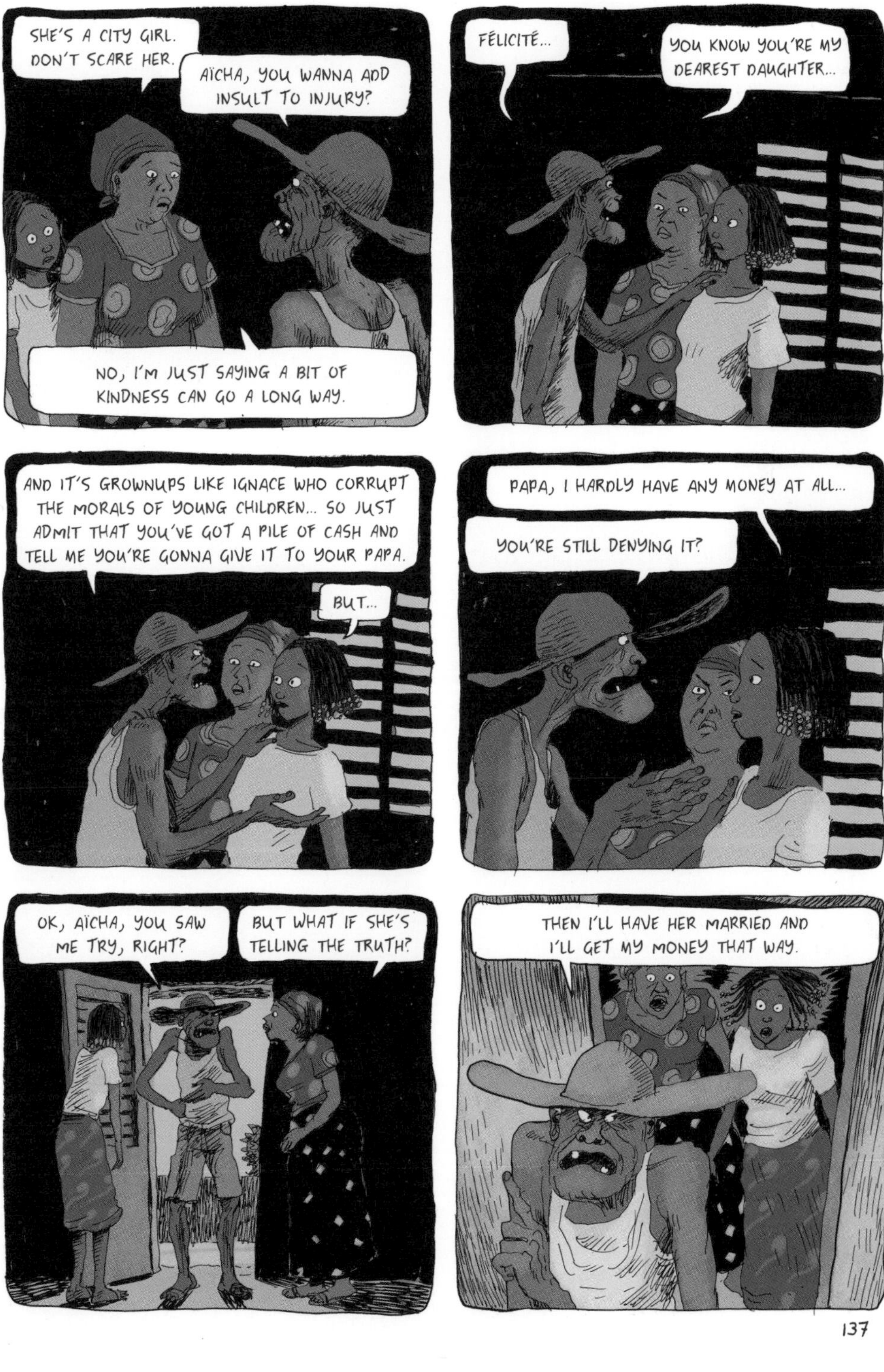
SHE'S A CITY GIRL. DON'T SCARE HER.
AÏCHA, YOU WANNA ADD INSULT TO INJURY?
NO, I'M JUST SAYING A BIT OF KINDNESS CAN GO A LONG WAY.
FÉLICITÉ...
YOU KNOW YOU'RE MY DEAREST DAUGHTER...
AND IT'S GROWNUPS LIKE IGNACE WHO CORRUPT THE MORALS OF YOUNG CHILDREN... SO JUST ADMIT THAT YOU'VE GOT A PILE OF CASH AND TELL ME YOU'RE GONNA GIVE IT TO YOUR PAPA.
BUT...
PAPA, I HARDLY HAVE ANY MONEY AT ALL...
YOU'RE STILL DENYING IT?
OK, AÏCHA, YOU SAW ME TRY, RIGHT?
BUT WHAT IF SHE'S TELLING THE TRUTH?
THEN I'LL HAVE HER MARRIED AND I'LL GET MY MONEY THAT WAY.

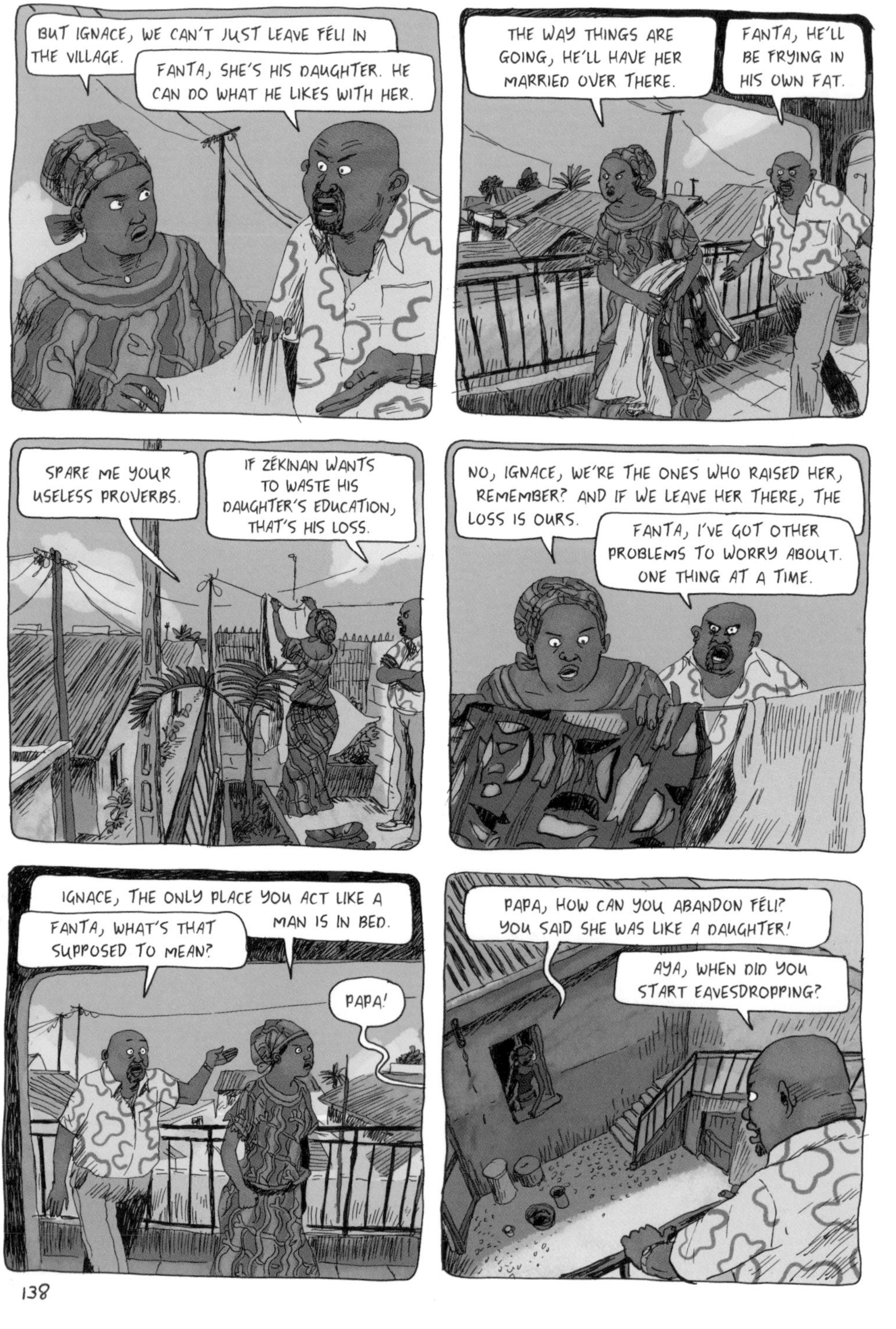
BUT IGNACE, WE CAN'T JUST LEAVE FÉLI IN THE VILLAGE.
FANTA, SHE'S HIS DAUGHTER. HE CAN DO WHAT HE LIKES WITH HER.
THE WAY THINGS ARE GOING, HE'LL HAVE HER MARRIED OVER THERE.
FANTA, HE'LL BE FRYING IN HIS OWN FAT.
SPARE ME YOUR USELESS PROVERBS.
IF ZÉKINAN WANTS TO WASTE HIS DAUGHTER'S EDUCATION, THAT'S HIS LOSS.
NO, IGNACE, WE'RE THE ONES WHO RAISED HER, REMEMBER? AND IF WE LEAVE HER THERE, THE LOSS IS OURS.
FANTA, I'VE GOT OTHER PROBLEMS TO WORRY ABOUT. ONE THING AT A TIME.
IGNACE, THE ONLY PLACE YOU ACT LIKE A MAN IS IN BED.
FANTA, WHAT'S THAT SUPPOSED TO MEAN?
PAPA!
PAPA, HOW CAN YOU ABANDON FÉLI? YOU SAID SHE WAS LIKE A DAUGHTER!
AYA, WHEN DID YOU START EAVESDROPPING?

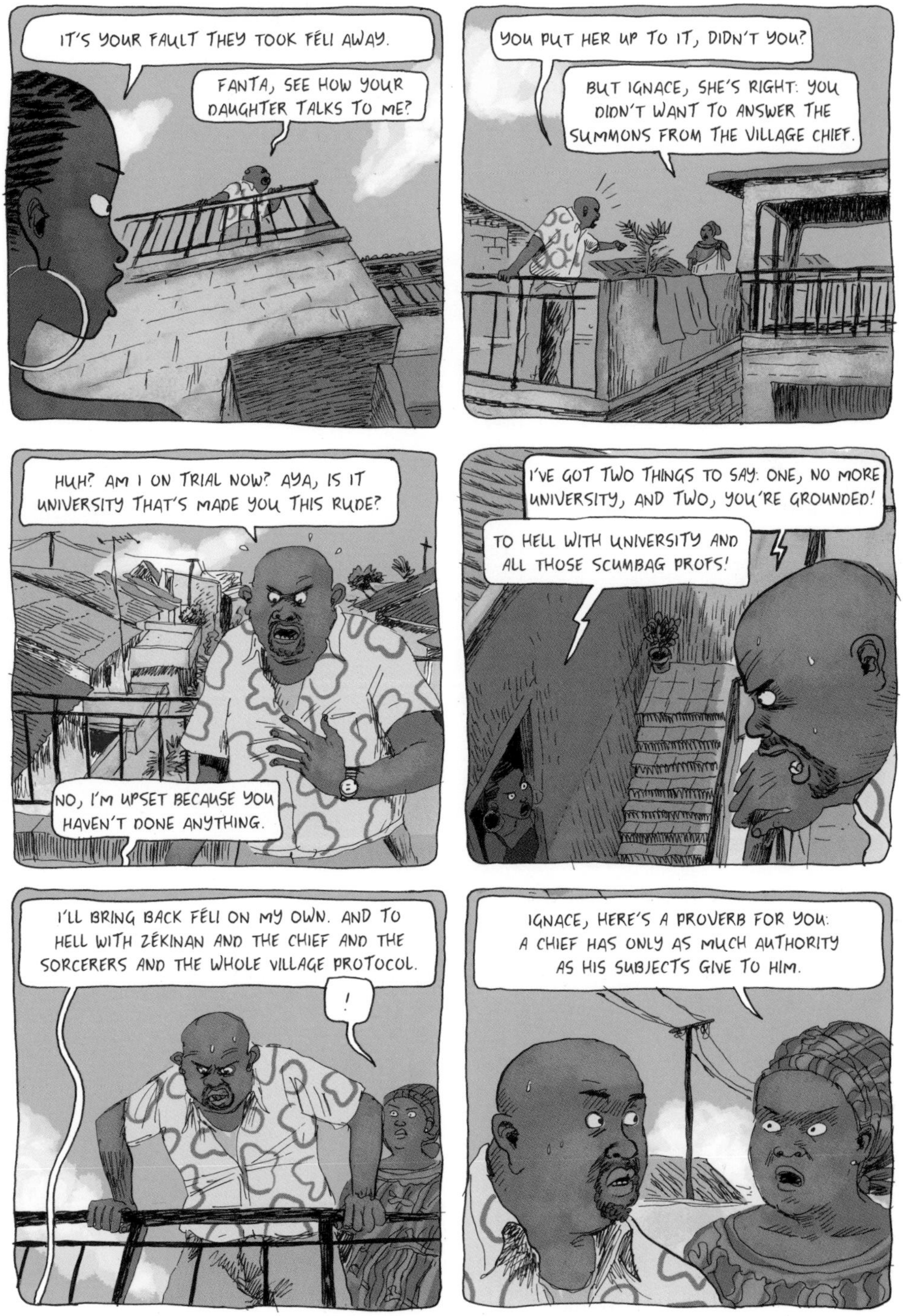
IT'S YOUR FAULT THEY TOOK FÉLI AWAY.
FANTA, SEE HOW YOUR DAUGHTER TALKS TO ME?
YOU PUT HER UP TO IT, DIDN'T YOU?
BUT IGNACE, SHE'S RIGHT: YOU DIDN'T WANT TO ANSWER THE SUMMONS FROM THE VILLAGE CHIEF.
HUH? AM I ON TRIAL NOW? AYA, IS IT UNIVERSITY THAT'S MADE YOU THIS RUDE?
NO, I'M UPSET BECAUSE YOU HAVEN'T DONE ANYTHING.
I'VE GOT TWO THINGS TO SAY: ONE, NO MORE UNIVERSITY, AND TWO, YOU'RE GROUNDED!
TO HELL WITH UNIVERSITY AND ALL THOSE SCUMBAG PROFS!
I'LL BRING BACK FÉLI ON MY OWN. AND TO HELL WITH ZÉKINAN AND THE CHIEF AND THE SORCERERS AND THE WHOLE VILLAGE PROTOCOL.
!
IGNACE, HERE'S A PROVERB FOR YOU: A CHIEF HAS ONLY AS MUCH AUTHORITY AS HIS SUBJECTS GIVE TO HIM.

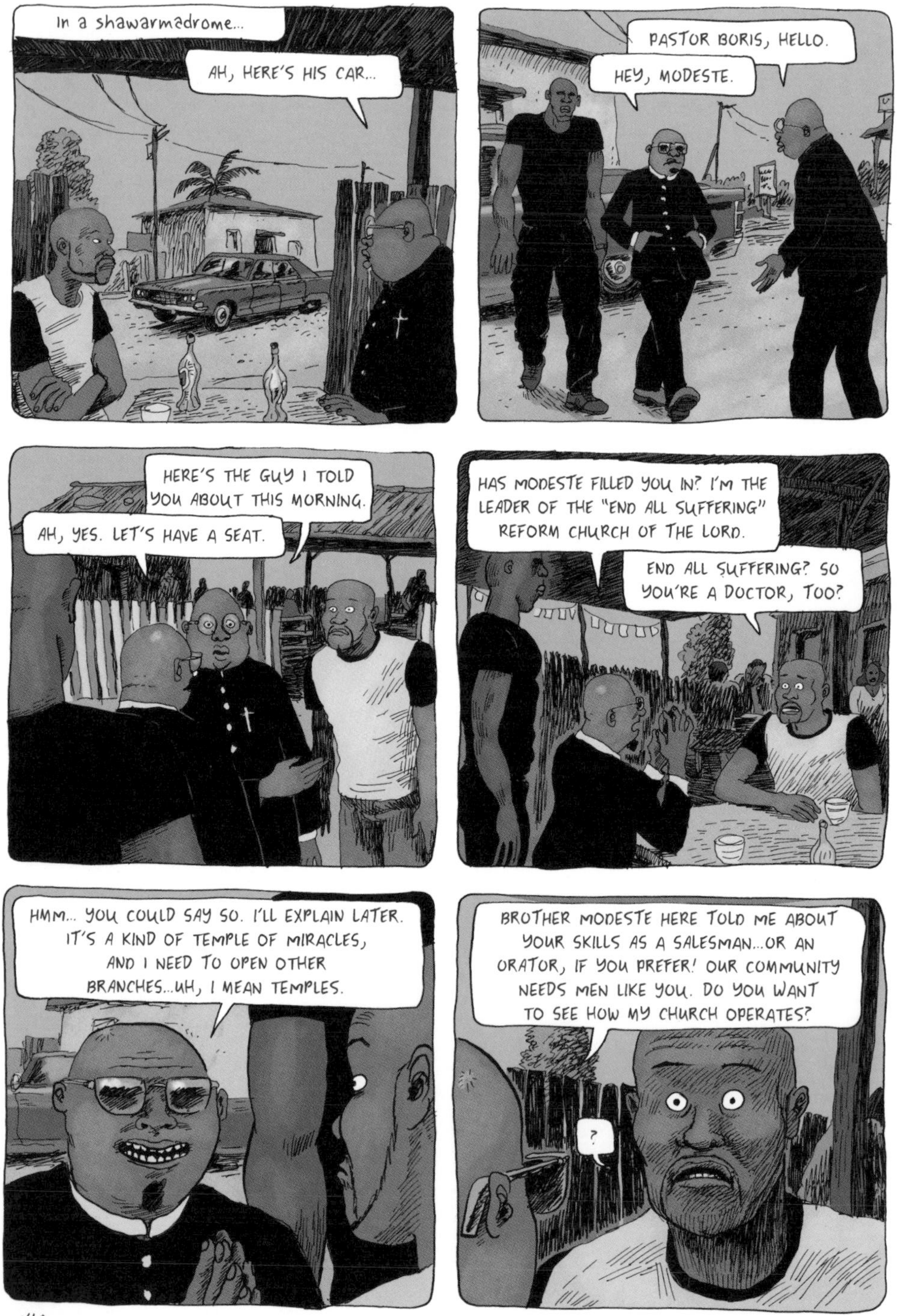
In a shawarmadrome...
AH, HERE'S HIS CAR...
PASTOR BORIS, HELLO.
HEY, MODESTE.
HERE'S THE GUY I TOLD YOU ABOUT THIS MORNING.
AH, YES. LET'S HAVE A SEAT.
HAS MODESTE FILLED YOU IN? I'M THE LEADER OF THE "END ALL SUFFERING" REFORM CHURCH OF THE LORD.
END ALL SUFFERING? SO YOU'RE A DOCTOR, TOO?
HMM... YOU COULD SAY SO. I'LL EXPLAIN LATER. IT'S A KIND OF TEMPLE OF MIRACLES, AND I NEED TO OPEN OTHER BRANCHES...UH, I MEAN TEMPLES.
BROTHER MODESTE HERE TOLD ME ABOUT YOUR SKILLS AS A SALESMAN...OR AN ORATOR, IF YOU PREFER! OUR COMMUNITY NEEDS MEN LIKE YOU. DO YOU WANT TO SEE HOW MY CHURCH OPERATES?
?

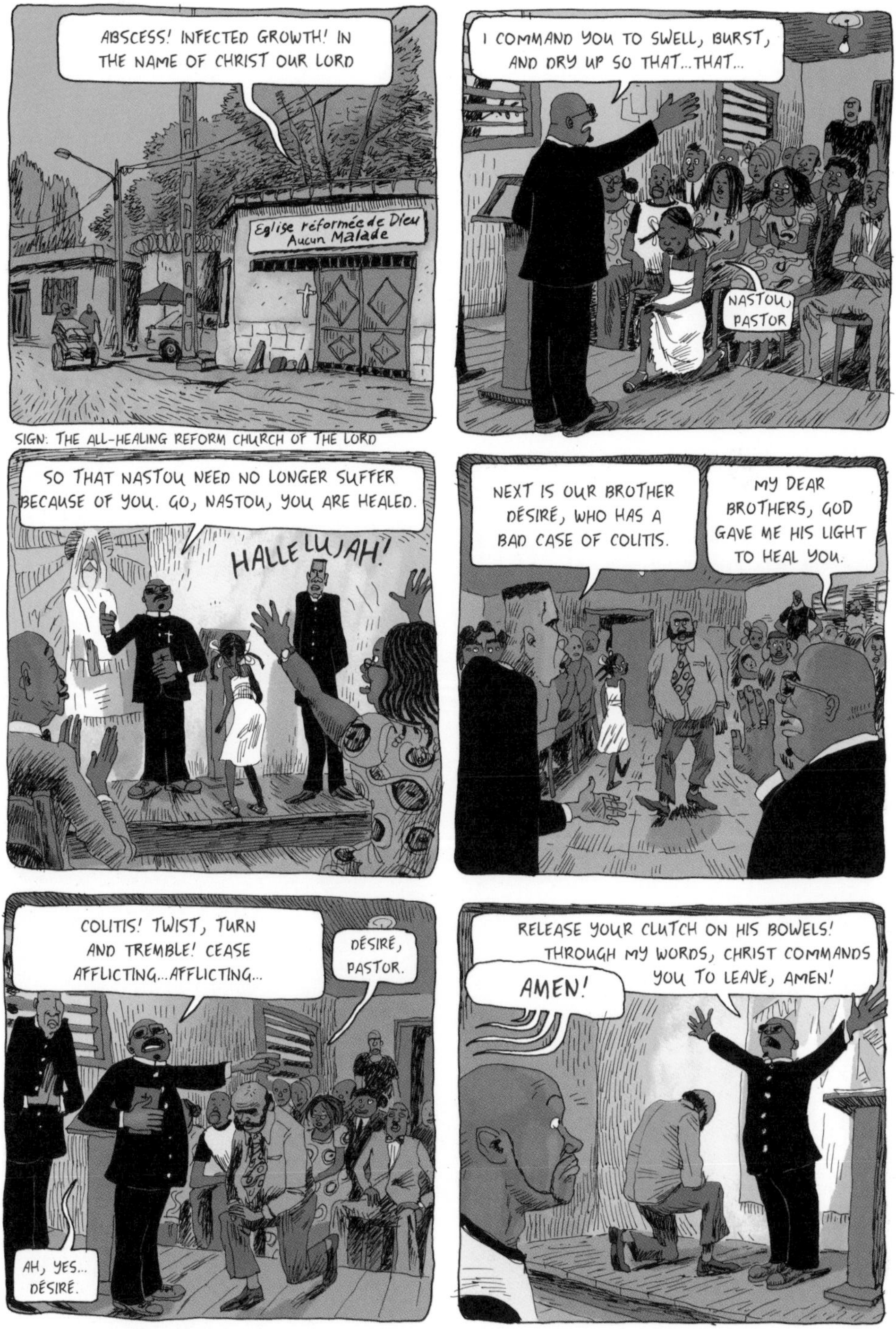
ABSCESS! INFECTED GROWTH! IN THE NAME OF CHRIST OUR LORD
Eglise réformée de Dieu Aucun Malade
SIGN: THE ALL-HEALING REFORM CHURCH OF THE LORD
I COMMAND YOU TO SWELL, BURST, AND DRY UP SO THAT...THAT...
NASTOU, PASTOR
SO THAT NASTOU NEED NO LONGER SUFFER BECAUSE OF YOU. GO, NASTOU, YOU ARE HEALED.
HALLELUJAH!
NEXT IS OUR BROTHER DÉSIRÉ, WHO HAS A BAD CASE OF COLITIS.
MY DEAR BROTHERS, GOD GAVE ME HIS LIGHT TO HEAL YOU.
COLITIS! TWIST, TURN AND TREMBLE! CEASE AFFLICTING...AFFLICTING...
DÉSIRÉ, PASTOR.
AH, YES... DÉSIRÉ.
RELEASE YOUR CLUTCH ON HIS BOWELS! THROUGH MY WORDS, CHRIST COMMANDS YOU TO LEAVE, AMEN!
AMEN!

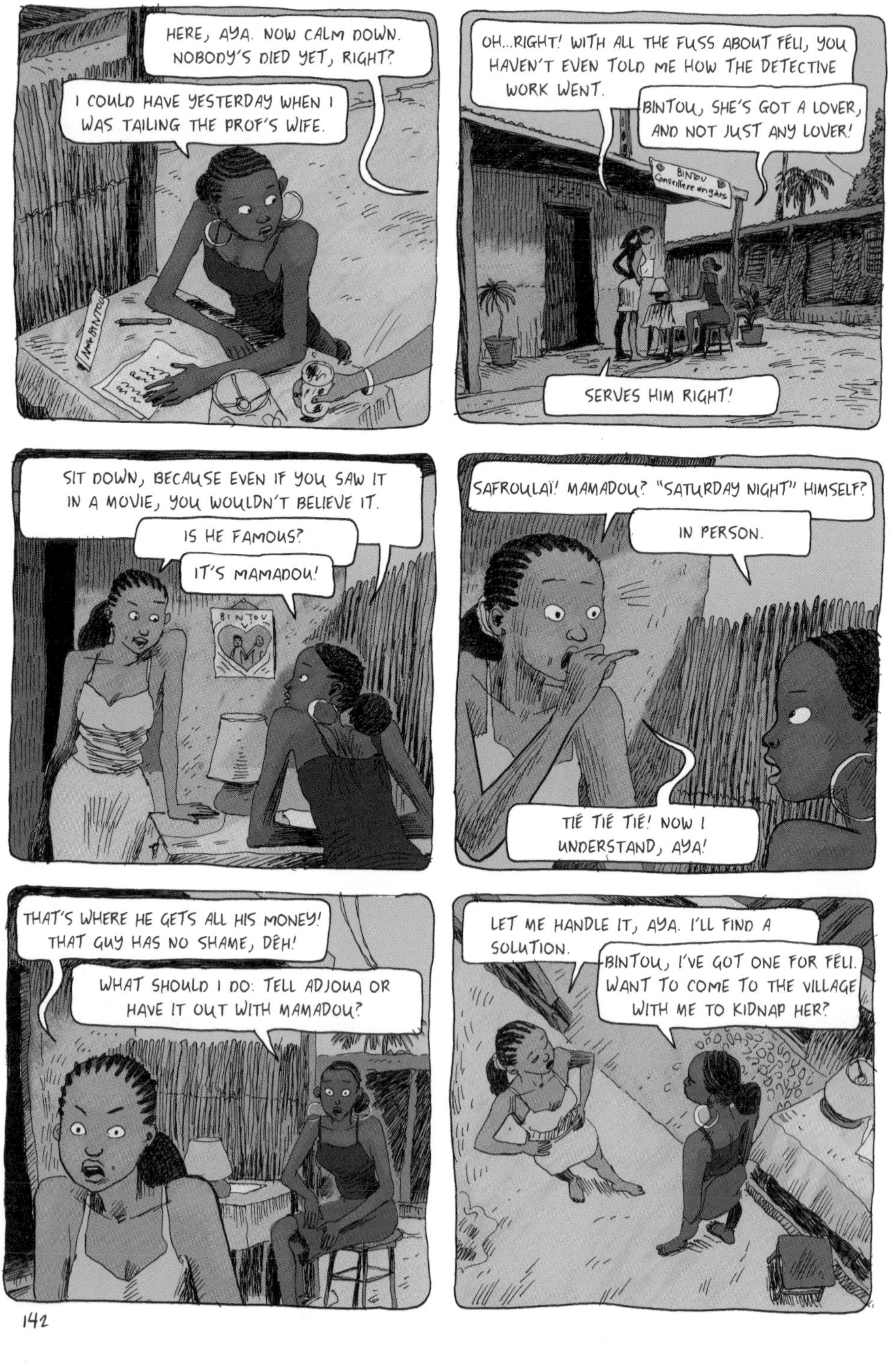
HERE, AYA. NOW CALM DOWN. NOBODY'S DIED YET, RIGHT?
I COULD HAVE YESTERDAY WHEN I WAS TAILING THE PROF'S WIFE.
OH...RIGHT! WITH ALL THE FUSS ABOUT FÉLI, YOU HAVEN'T EVEN TOLD ME HOW THE DETECTIVE WORK WENT.
BINTOU, SHE'S GOT A LOVER, AND NOT JUST ANY LOVER!
SERVES HIM RIGHT!
SIT DOWN, BECAUSE EVEN IF YOU SAW IT IN A MOVIE, YOU WOULDN'T BELIEVE IT.
IS HE FAMOUS?
IT'S MAMADOU!
SAFROULAÏ! MAMADOU? "SATURDAY NIGHT" HIMSELF?
IN PERSON.
TIÉ TIÉ TIÉ! NOW I UNDERSTAND, AYA!
THAT'S WHERE HE GETS ALL HIS MONEY! THAT GUY HAS NO SHAME, DÊH!
WHAT SHOULD I DO: TELL ADJOUA OR HAVE IT OUT WITH MAMADOU?
LET ME HANDLE IT, AYA. I'LL FIND A SOLUTION.
BINTOU, I'VE GOT ONE FOR FÉLI. WANT TO COME TO THE VILLAGE WITH ME TO KIDNAP HER?

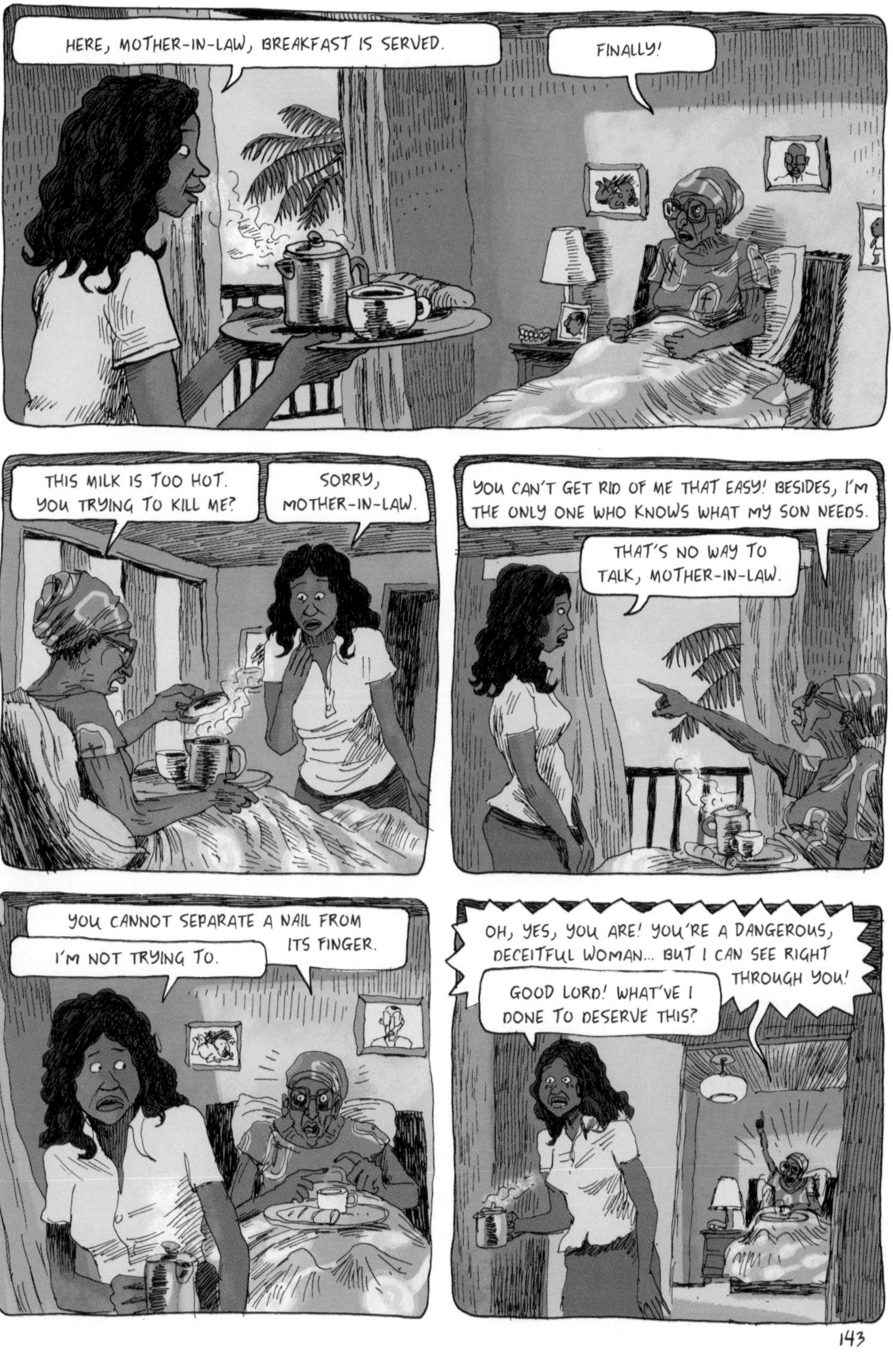
HERE, MOTHER-IN-LAW, BREAKFAST IS SERVED.
FINALLY!
THIS MILK IS TOO HOT. YOU TRYING TO KILL ME?
SORRY, MOTHER-IN-LAW.
YOU CAN'T GET RID OF ME THAT EASY! BESIDES, I'M THE ONLY ONE WHO KNOWS WHAT MY SON NEEDS.
THAT'S NO WAY TO TALK, MOTHER-IN-LAW.
YOU CANNOT SEPARATE A NAIL FROM ITS FINGER.
I'M NOT TRYING TO.
OH, YES, YOU ARE! YOU'RE A DANGEROUS, DECEITFUL WOMAN... BUT I CAN SEE RIGHT THROUGH YOU!
GOOD LORD! WHAT'VE I DONE TO DESERVE THIS?

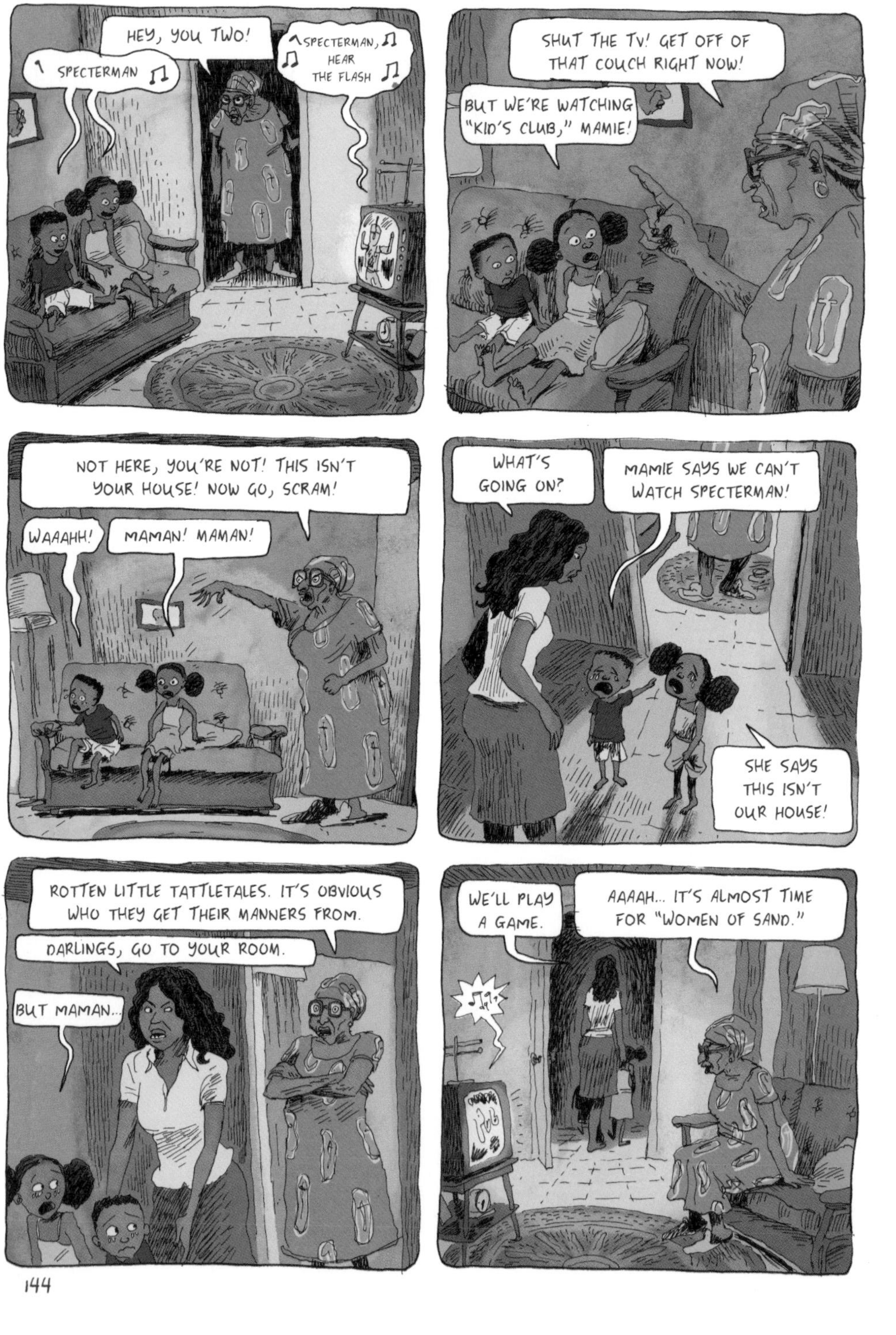
SPECTERMAN
HEY, YOU TWO!
SPECTERMAN, HEAR THE FLASH
SHUT THE TV! GET OFF OF THAT COUCH RIGHT NOW!
BUT WE'RE WATCHING "KID'S CLUB," MAMIE!
NOT HERE, YOU'RE NOT! THIS ISN'T YOUR HOUSE! NOW GO, SCRAM!
WAAAHH!
MAMAN! MAMAN!
WHAT'S GOING ON?
MAMIE SAYS WE CAN'T WATCH SPECTERMAN!
SHE SAYS THIS ISN'T OUR HOUSE!
ROTTEN LITTLE TATTLETALES. IT'S OBVIOUS WHO THEY GET THEIR MANNERS FROM.
DARLINGS, GO TO YOUR ROOM.
BUT MAMAN...
WE'LL PLAY A GAME.
AAAAH... IT'S ALMOST TIME FOR "WOMEN OF SAND."

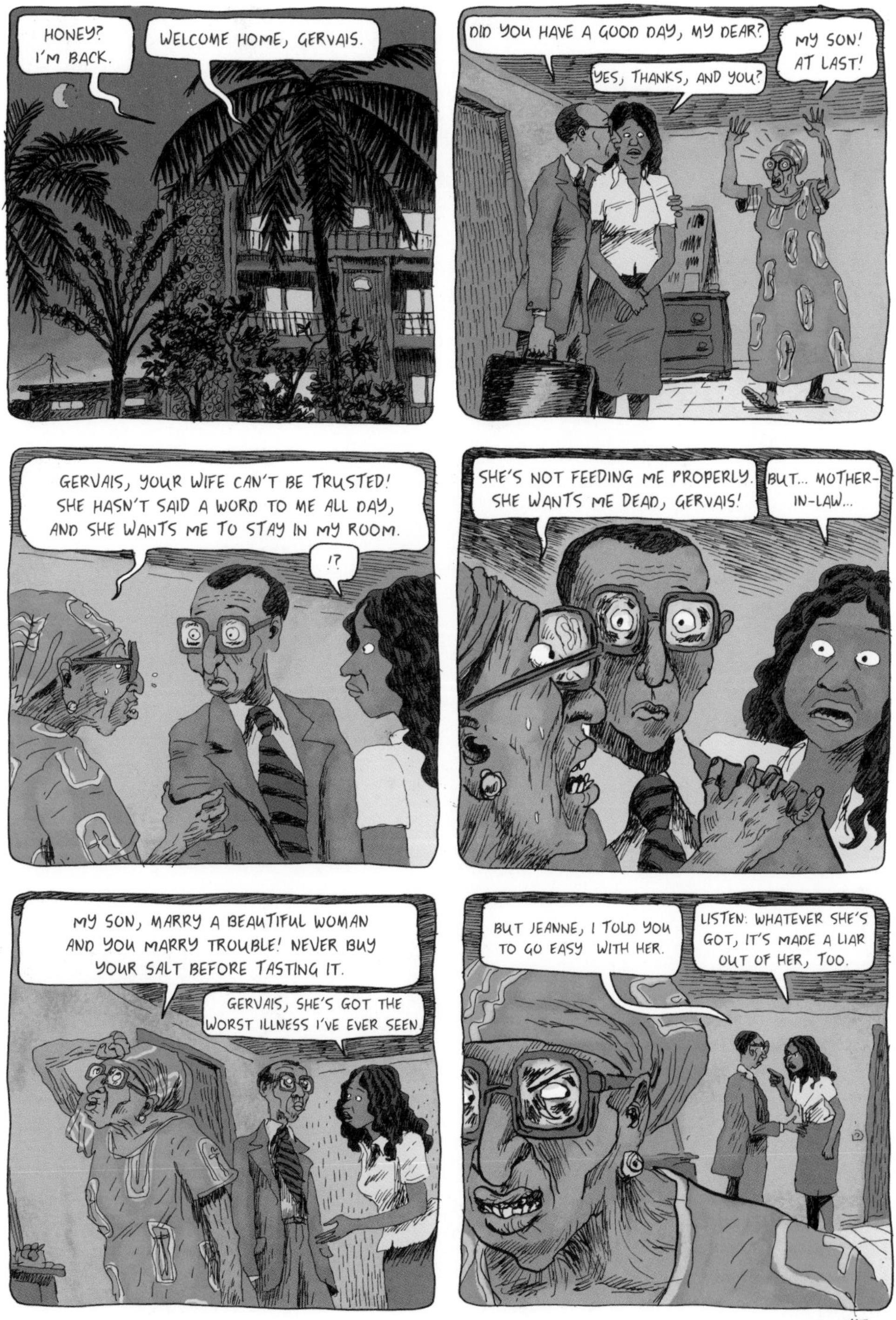
HONEY? I'M BACK.
WELCOME HOME, GERVAIS.
DID YOU HAVE A GOOD DAY, MY DEAR?
YES, THANKS, AND YOU?
MY SON! AT LAST!
GERVAIS, YOUR WIFE CAN'T BE TRUSTED! SHE HASN'T SAID A WORD TO ME ALL DAY, AND SHE WANTS ME TO STAY IN MY ROOM.
!?
SHE'S NOT FEEDING ME PROPERLY. SHE WANTS ME DEAD, GERVAIS!
BUT... MOTHER-IN-LAW...
MY SON, MARRY A BEAUTIFUL WOMAN AND YOU MARRY TROUBLE! NEVER BUY YOUR SALT BEFORE TASTING IT.
GERVAIS, SHE'S GOT THE WORST ILLNESS I'VE EVER SEEN.
BUT JEANNE, I TOLD YOU TO GO EASY WITH HER.
LISTEN: WHATEVER SHE'S GOT, IT'S MADE A LIAR OUT OF HER, TOO.

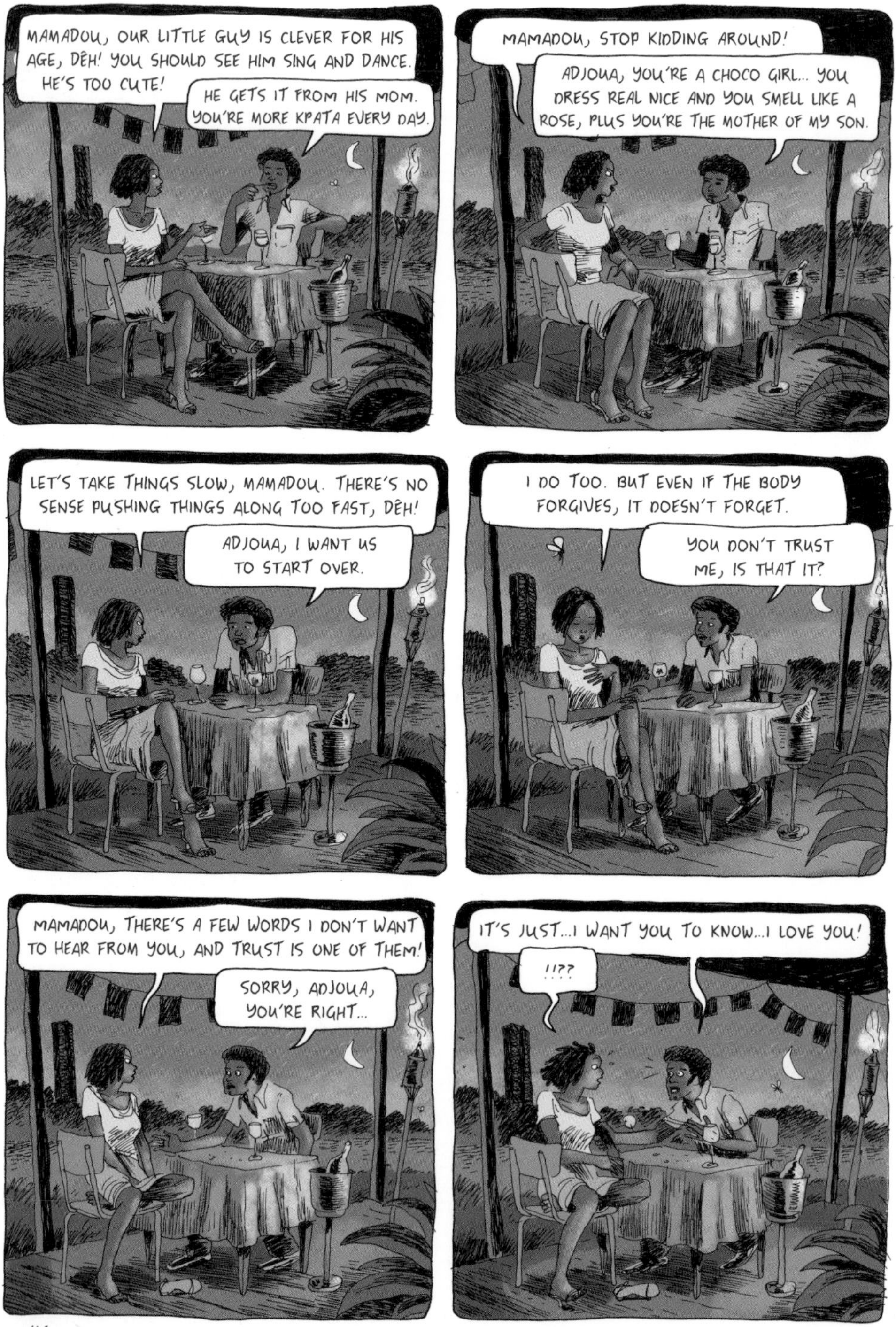
MAMADOU, OUR LITTLE GUY IS CLEVER FOR HIS AGE, DÊH! YOU SHOULD SEE HIM SING AND DANCE. HE'S TOO CUTE!
HE GETS IT FROM HIS MOM. YOU'RE MORE KPATA EVERY DAY.
MAMADOU, STOP KIDDING AROUND!
ADJOUA, YOU'RE A CHOCO GIRL... YOU DRESS REAL NICE AND YOU SMELL LIKE A ROSE, PLUS YOU'RE THE MOTHER OF MY SON.
LET'S TAKE THINGS SLOW, MAMADOU. THERE'S NO SENSE PUSHING THINGS ALONG TOO FAST, DÊH!
ADJOUA, I WANT US TO START OVER.
I DO TOO. BUT EVEN IF THE BODY FORGIVES, IT DOESN'T FORGET.
YOU DON'T TRUST ME, IS THAT IT?
MAMADOU, THERE'S A FEW WORDS I DON'T WANT TO HEAR FROM YOU, AND TRUST IS ONE OF THEM!
SORRY, ADJOUA, YOU'RE RIGHT...
IT'S JUST...I WANT YOU TO KNOW...I LOVE YOU!
!!??

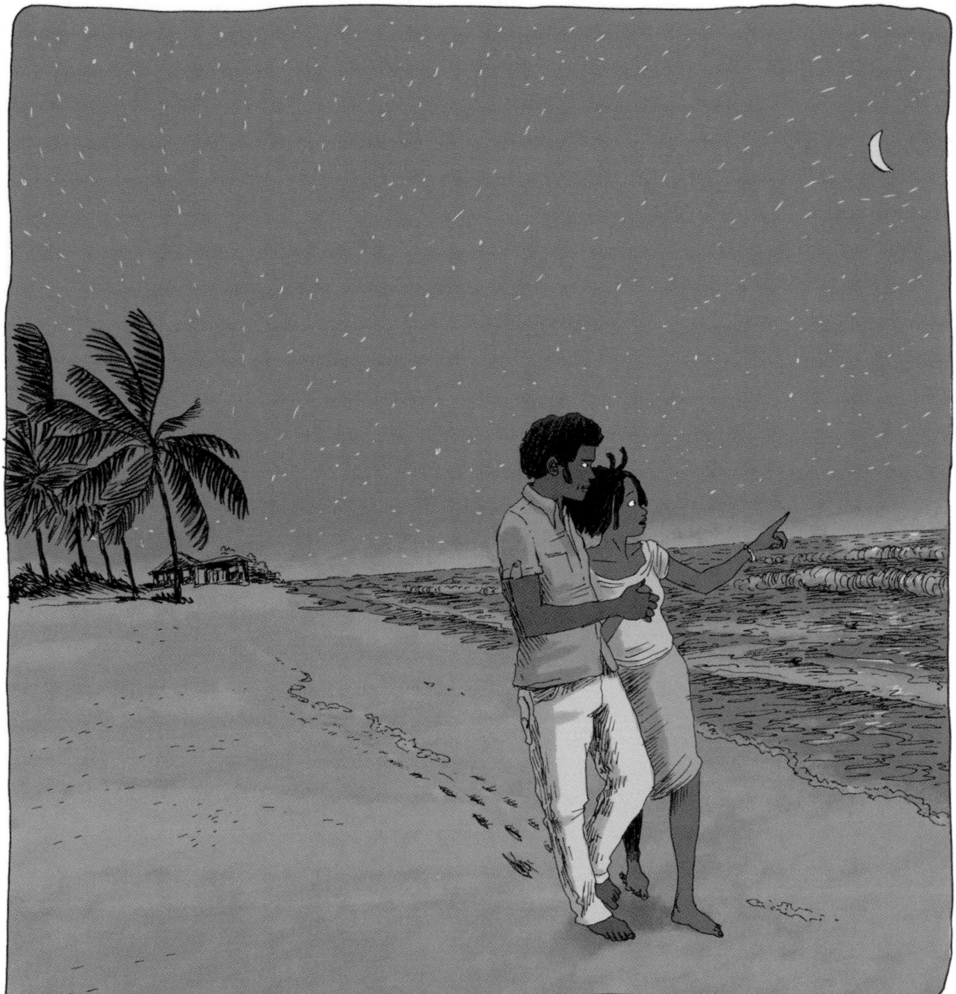

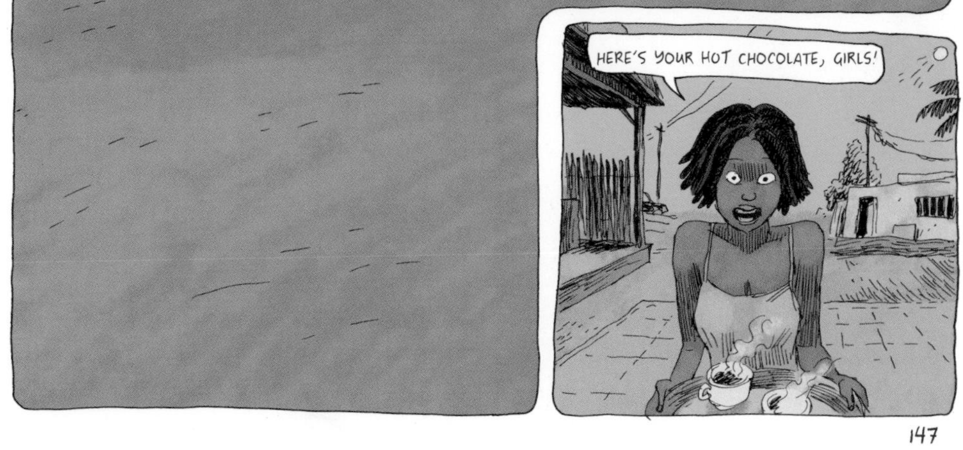
HERE'S YOUR HOT CHOCOLATE, GIRLS!

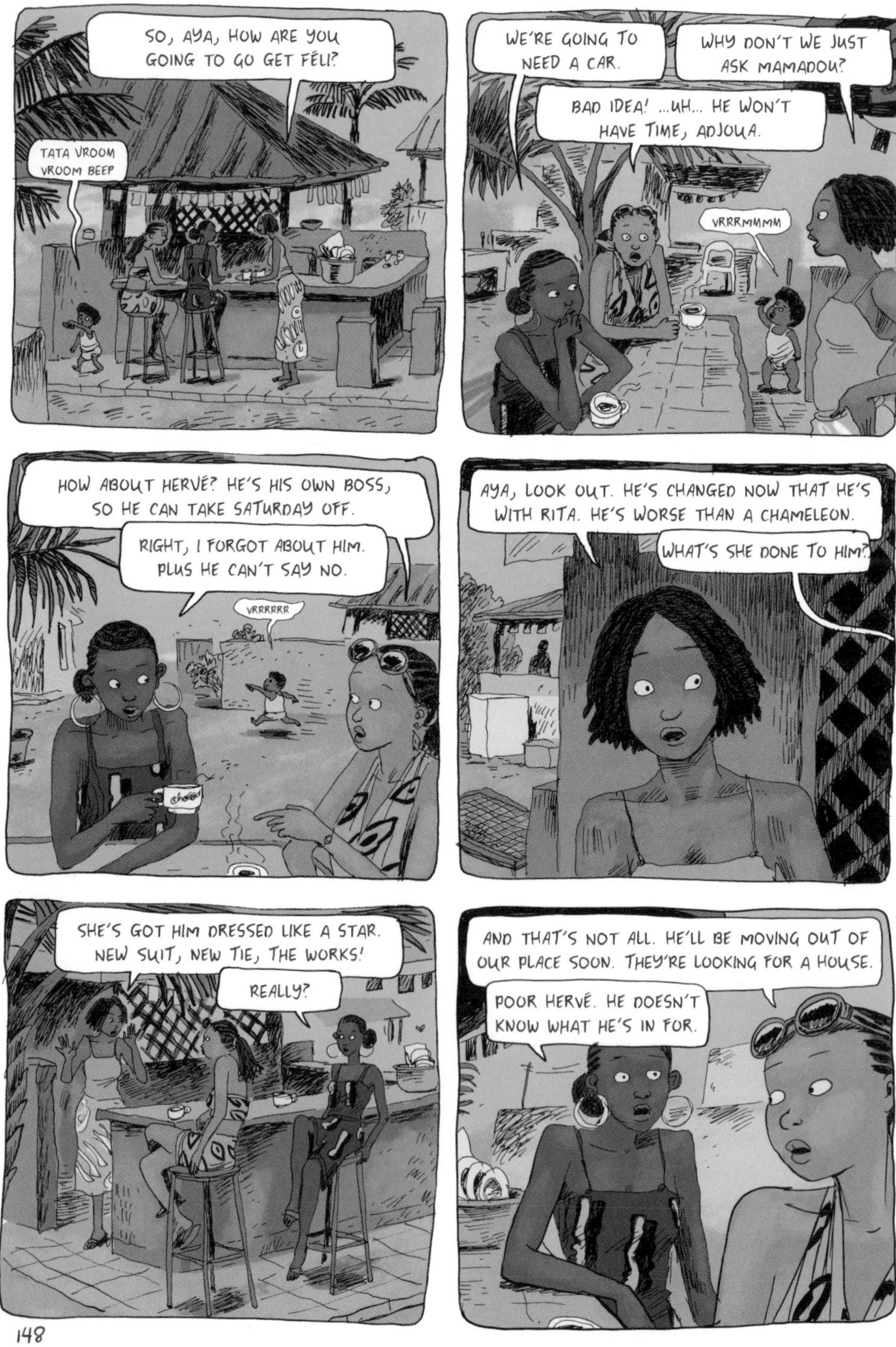
SO, AYA, HOW ARE YOU GOING TO GO GET FÉLI?
TATA VROOM VROOM BEEP
WE'RE GOING TO NEED A CAR.
WHY DON'T WE JUST ASK MAMADOU?
BAD IDEA! ...UH... HE WON'T HAVE TIME, ADJOUA.
VRRRMMMM
HOW ABOUT HERVÉ? HE'S HIS OWN BOSS, SO HE CAN TAKE SATURDAY OFF.
RIGHT, I FORGOT ABOUT HIM. PLUS HE CAN'T SAY NO.
VRRRRRR
AYA, LOOK OUT. HE'S CHANGED NOW THAT HE'S WITH RITA. HE'S WORSE THAN A CHAMELEON.
WHAT'S SHE DONE TO HIM?
SHE'S GOT HIM DRESSED LIKE A STAR. NEW SUIT, NEW TIE, THE WORKS!
REALLY?
AND THAT'S NOT ALL. HE'LL BE MOVING OUT OF OUR PLACE SOON. THEY'RE LOOKING FOR A HOUSE.
POOR HERVÉ. HE DOESN'T KNOW WHAT HE'S IN FOR.

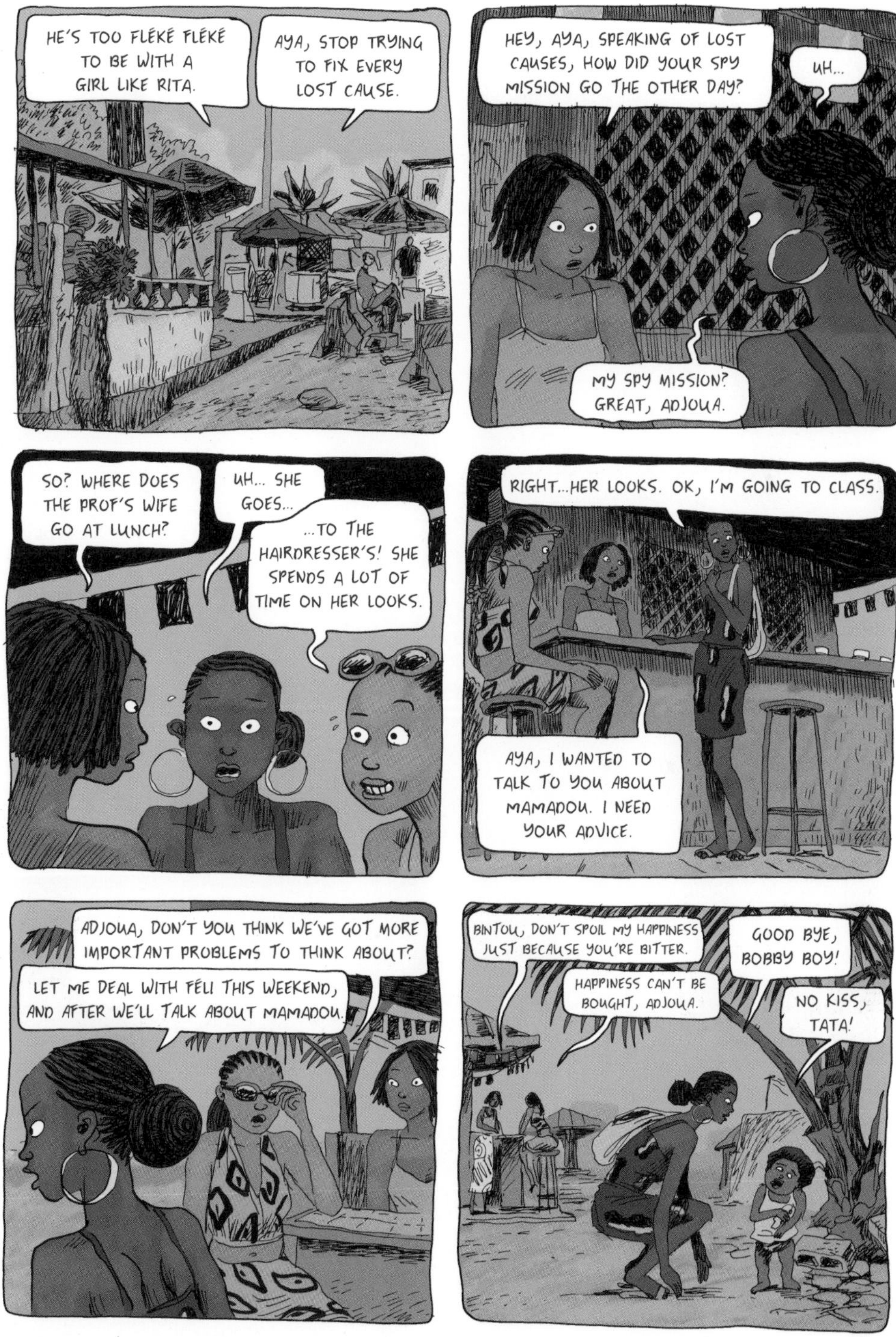
HE'S TOO FLÉKÉ FLÉKÉ TO BE WITH A GIRL LIKE RITA.
AYA, STOP TRYING TO FIX EVERY LOST CAUSE.
HEY, AYA, SPEAKING OF LOST CAUSES, HOW DID YOUR SPY MISSION GO THE OTHER DAY?
UH...
MY SPY MISSION? GREAT, ADJOUA.
SO? WHERE DOES THE PROF'S WIFE GO AT LUNCH?
UH... SHE GOES...
...TO THE HAIRDRESSER'S! SHE SPENDS A LOT OF TIME ON HER LOOKS.
RIGHT...HER LOOKS. OK, I'M GOING TO CLASS.
AYA, I WANTED TO TALK TO YOU ABOUT MAMADOU. I NEED YOUR ADVICE.
ADJOUA, DON'T YOU THINK WE'VE GOT MORE IMPORTANT PROBLEMS TO THINK ABOUT?
LET ME DEAL WITH FÉLI THIS WEEKEND, AND AFTER WE'LL TALK ABOUT MAMADOU.
BINTOU, DON'T SPOIL MY HAPPINESS JUST BECAUSE YOU'RE BITTER.
HAPPINESS CAN'T BE BOUGHT, ADJOUA.
GOOD BYE, BOBBY BOY!
NO KISS, TATA!

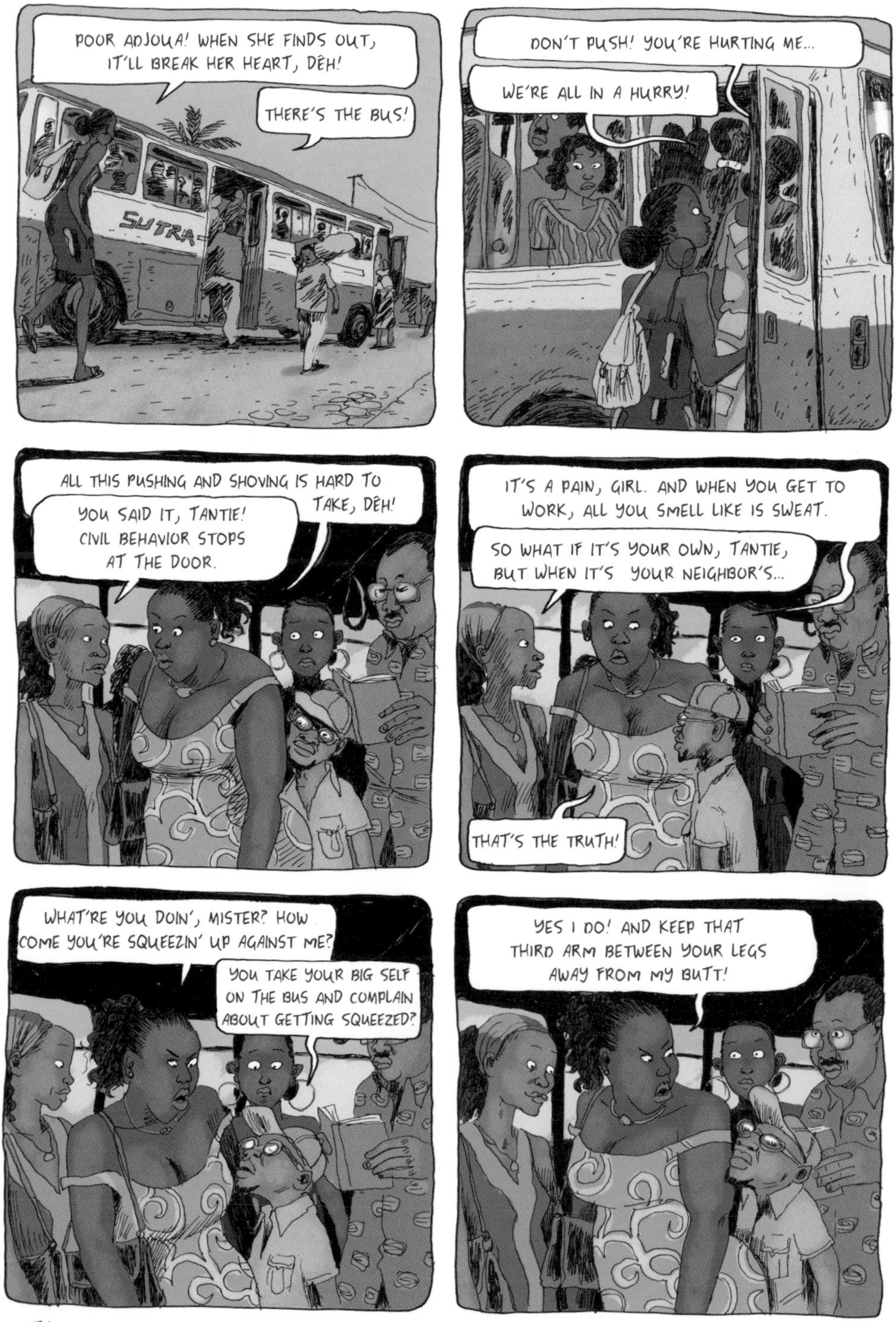
POOR ADJOUA! WHEN SHE FINDS OUT, IT'LL BREAK HER HEART, DÊH!
THERE'S THE BUS!
SUTRA
DON'T PUSH! YOU'RE HURTING ME...
WE'RE ALL IN A HURRY!
ALL THIS PUSHING AND SHOVING IS HARD TO TAKE, DÊH!
YOU SAID IT, TANTIE! CIVIL BEHAVIOR STOPS AT THE DOOR.
IT'S A PAIN, GIRL. AND WHEN YOU GET TO WORK, ALL YOU SMELL LIKE IS SWEAT.
SO WHAT IF IT'S YOUR OWN, TANTIE, BUT WHEN IT'S YOUR NEIGHBOR'S...
THAT'S THE TRUTH!
WHAT'RE YOU DOIN', MISTER? HOW COME YOU'RE SQUEEZIN' UP AGAINST ME?
YOU TAKE YOUR BIG SELF ON THE BUS AND COMPLAIN ABOUT GETTING SQUEEZED?
YES I DO! AND KEEP THAT THIRD ARM BETWEEN YOUR LEGS AWAY FROM MY BUTT!

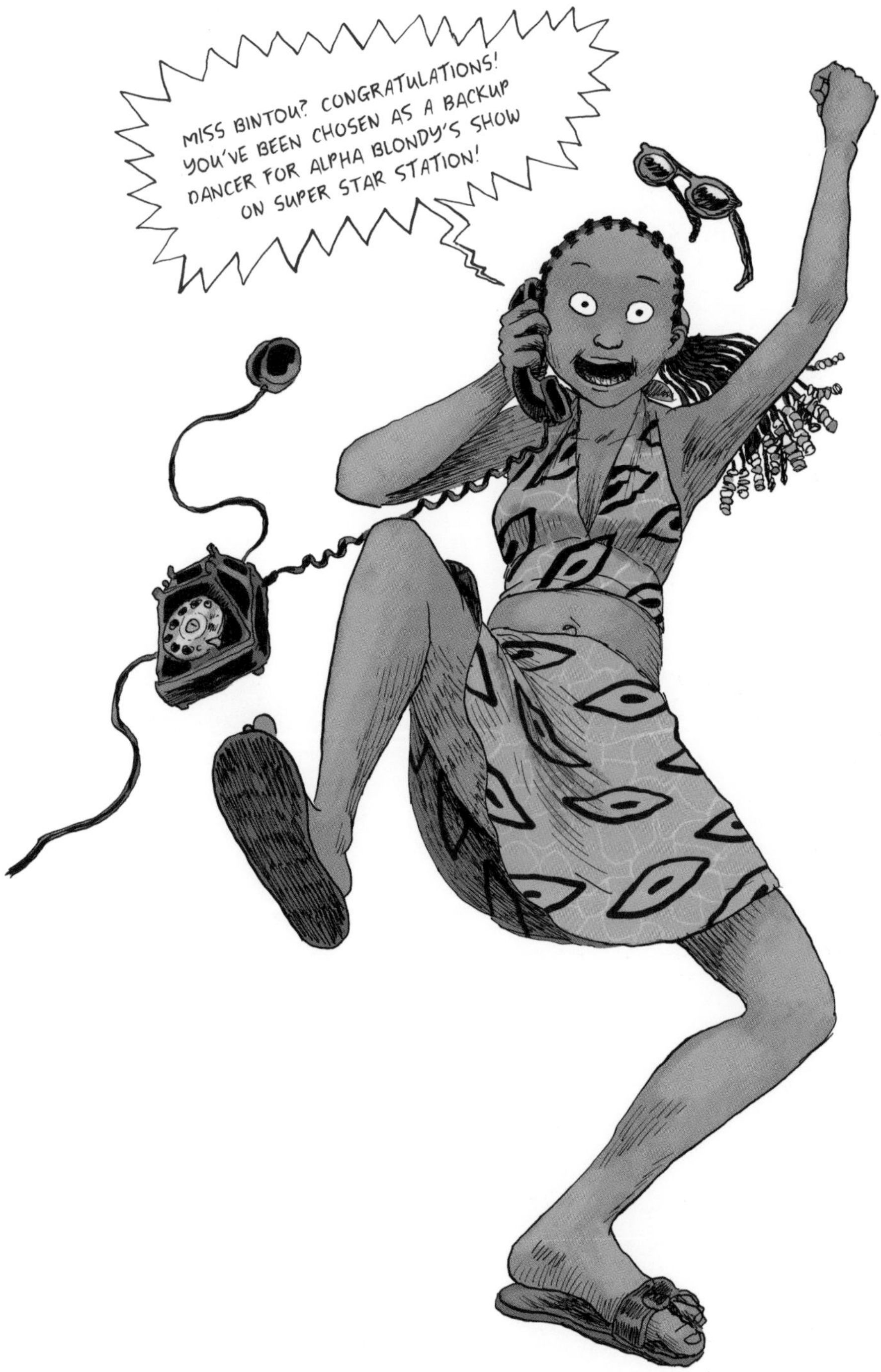
MISS BINTOU? CONGRATULATIONS! YOU'VE BEEN CHOSEN AS A BACKUP DANCER FOR ALPHA BLONDY'S SHOW ON SUPER STAR STATION!

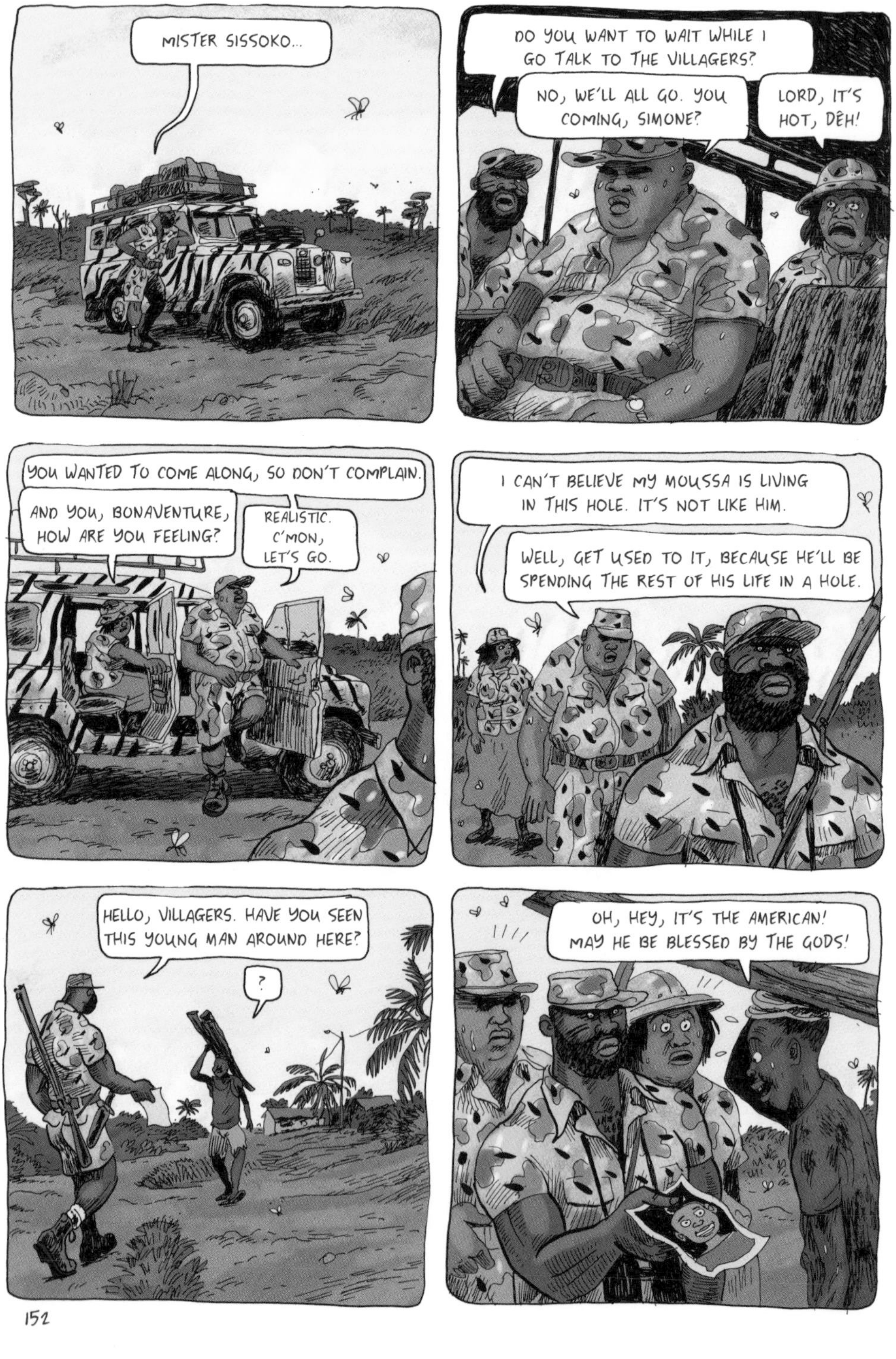
MISTER SISSOKO...
DO YOU WANT TO WAIT WHILE I GO TALK TO THE VILLAGERS?
NO, WE'LL ALL GO. YOU COMING, SIMONE?
LORD, IT'S HOT, DÊH!
YOU WANTED TO COME ALONG, SO DON'T COMPLAIN.
AND YOU, BONAVENTURE, HOW ARE YOU FEELING?
REALISTIC. C'MON, LET'S GO.
I CAN'T BELIEVE MY MOUSSA IS LIVING IN THIS HOLE. IT'S NOT LIKE HIM.
WELL, GET USED TO IT, BECAUSE HE'LL BE SPENDING THE REST OF HIS LIFE IN A HOLE.
HELLO, VILLAGERS. HAVE YOU SEEN THIS YOUNG MAN AROUND HERE?
?
OH, HEY, IT'S THE AMERICAN! MAY HE BE BLESSED BY THE GODS!

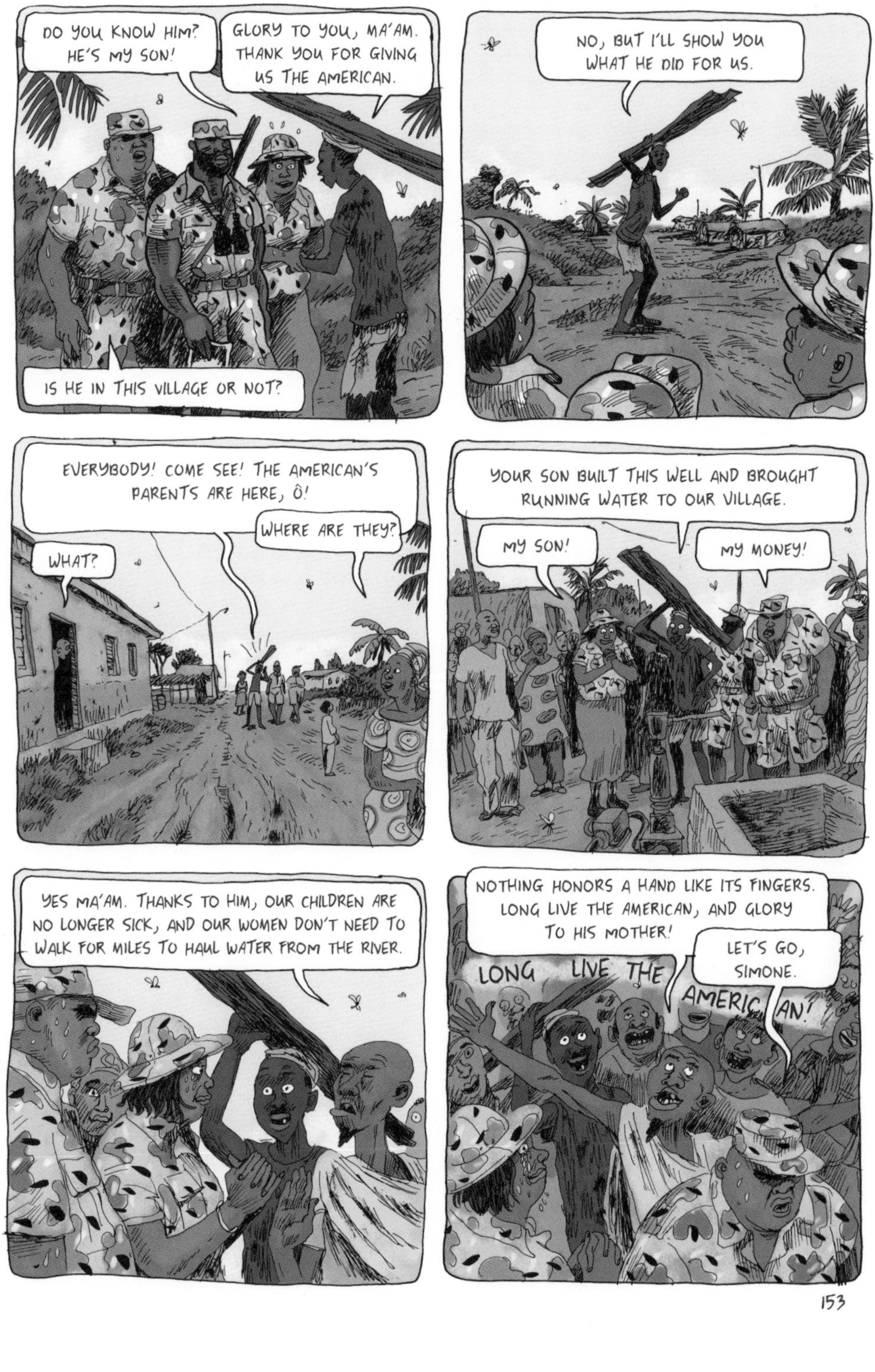
DO YOU KNOW HIM? HE'S MY SON!
GLORY TO YOU, MA'AM. THANK YOU FOR GIVING US THE AMERICAN.
IS HE IN THIS VILLAGE OR NOT?
NO, BUT I'LL SHOW YOU WHAT HE DID FOR US.
EVERYBODY! COME SEE! THE AMERICAN'S PARENTS ARE HERE, Ô!
WHAT?
WHERE ARE THEY?
YOUR SON BUILT THIS WELL AND BROUGHT RUNNING WATER TO OUR VILLAGE.
MY SON!
MY MONEY!
YES MA'AM. THANKS TO HIM, OUR CHILDREN ARE NO LONGER SICK, AND OUR WOMEN DON'T NEED TO WALK FOR MILES TO HAUL WATER FROM THE RIVER.
NOTHING HONORS A HAND LIKE ITS FINGERS. LONG LIVE THE AMERICAN, AND GLORY TO HIS MOTHER!
LONG LIVE THE AMERICAN!
LET'S GO, SIMONE.

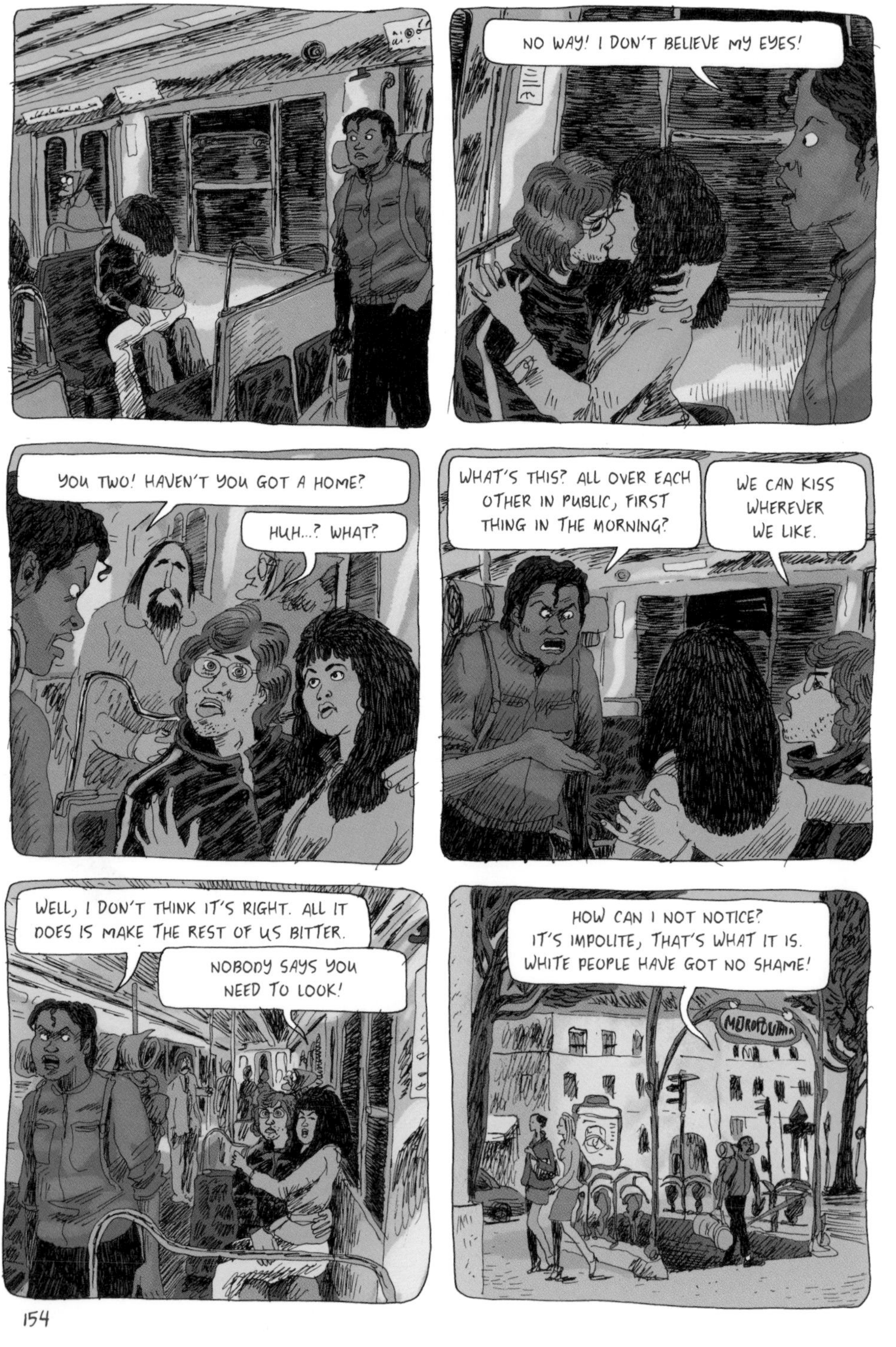
NO WAY! I DON'T BELIEVE MY EYES!
YOU TWO! HAVEN'T YOU GOT A HOME?
HUH...? WHAT?
WHAT'S THIS? ALL OVER EACH OTHER IN PUBLIC, FIRST THING IN THE MORNING?
WE CAN KISS WHEREVER WE LIKE.
WELL, I DON'T THINK IT'S RIGHT. ALL IT DOES IS MAKE THE REST OF US BITTER.
NOBODY SAYS YOU NEED TO LOOK!
HOW CAN I NOT NOTICE? IT'S IMPOLITE, THAT'S WHAT IT IS. WHITE PEOPLE HAVE GOT NO SHAME!

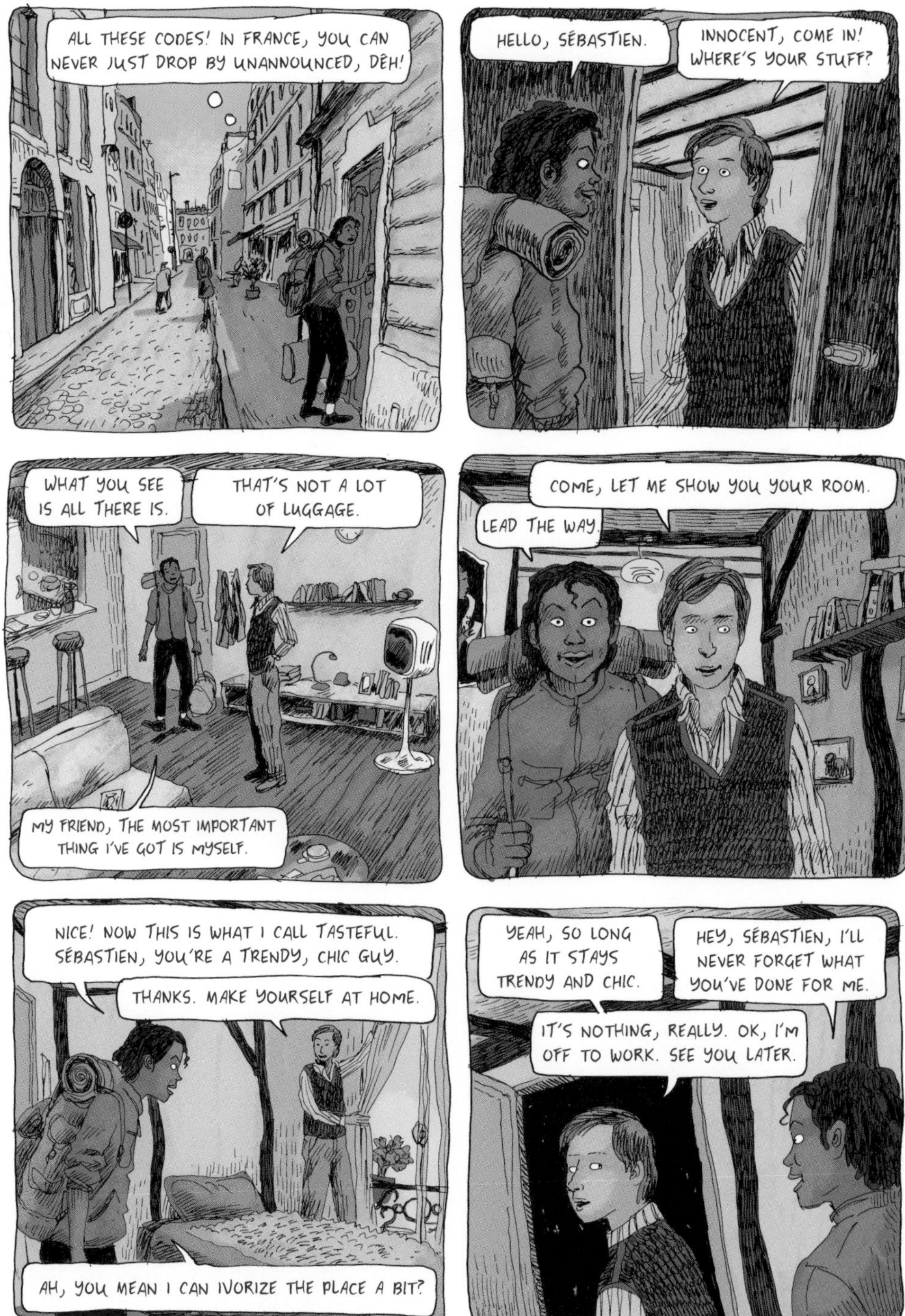
ALL THESE CODES! IN FRANCE, YOU CAN NEVER JUST DROP BY UNANNOUNCED, DÊH!
HELLO, SÉBASTIEN.
INNOCENT, COME IN! WHERE'S YOUR STUFF?
WHAT YOU SEE IS ALL THERE IS.
THAT'S NOT A LOT OF LUGGAGE.
MY FRIEND, THE MOST IMPORTANT THING I'VE GOT IS MYSELF.
COME, LET ME SHOW YOU YOUR ROOM.
LEAD THE WAY.
NICE! NOW THIS IS WHAT I CALL TASTEFUL. SÉBASTIEN, YOU'RE A TRENDY, CHIC GUY.
THANKS. MAKE YOURSELF AT HOME.
AH, YOU MEAN I CAN IVORIZE THE PLACE A BIT?
YEAH, SO LONG AS IT STAYS TRENDY AND CHIC.
HEY, SÉBASTIEN, I'LL NEVER FORGET WHAT YOU'VE DONE FOR ME.
IT'S NOTHING, REALLY. OK, I'M OFF TO WORK. SEE YOU LATER.

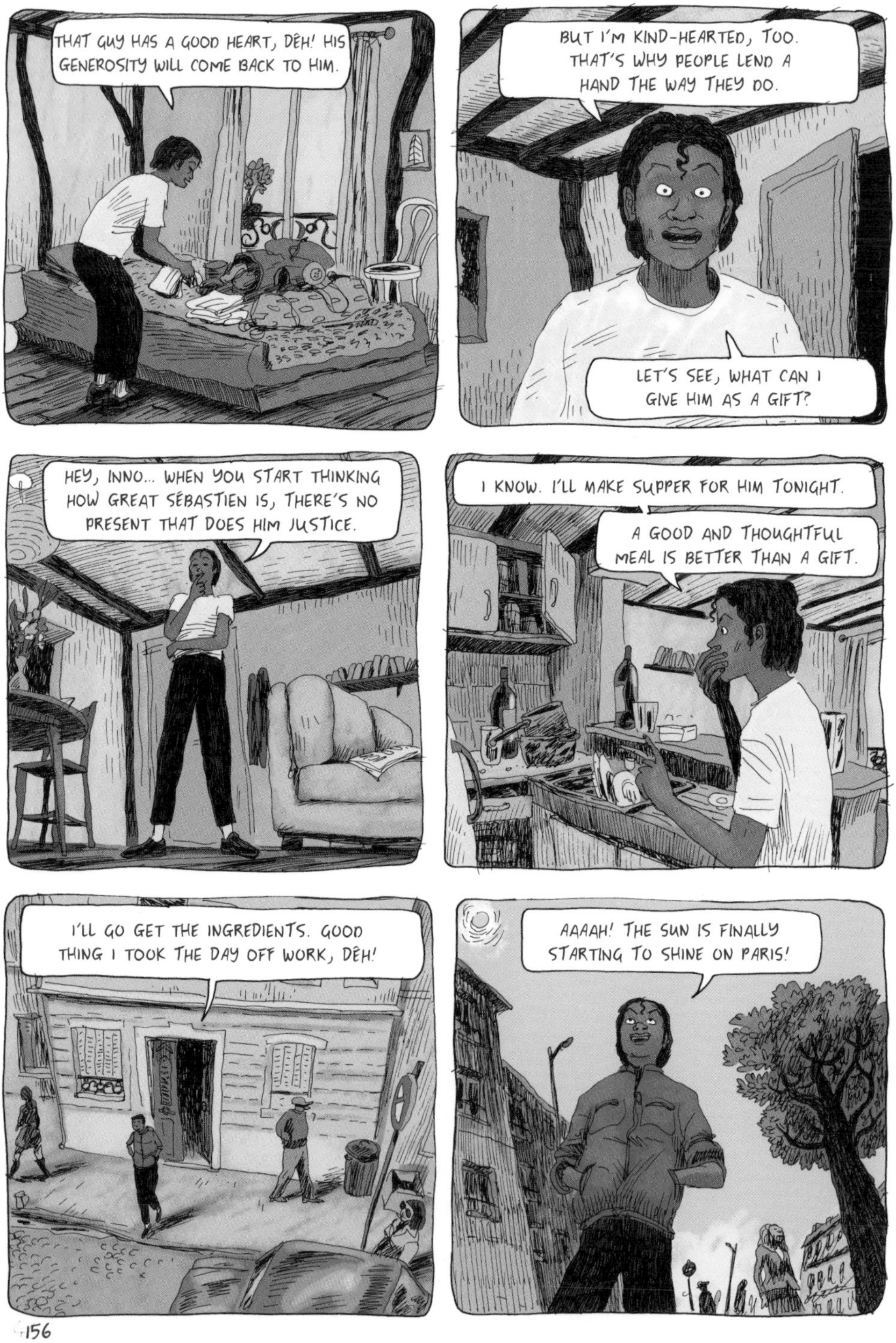
THAT GUY HAS A GOOD HEART, DÊH! HIS GENEROSITY WILL COME BACK TO HIM.
BUT I'M KIND-HEARTED, TOO. THAT'S WHY PEOPLE LEND A HAND THE WAY THEY DO.
LET'S SEE, WHAT CAN I GIVE HIM AS A GIFT?
HEY, INNO... WHEN YOU START THINKING HOW GREAT SÉBASTIEN IS, THERE'S NO PRESENT THAT DOES HIM JUSTICE.
I KNOW. I'LL MAKE SUPPER FOR HIM TONIGHT.
A GOOD AND THOUGHTFUL MEAL IS BETTER THAN A GIFT.
I'LL GO GET THE INGREDIENTS. GOOD THING I TOOK THE DAY OFF WORK, DÊH!
AAAAH! THE SUN IS FINALLY STARTING TO SHINE ON PARIS!

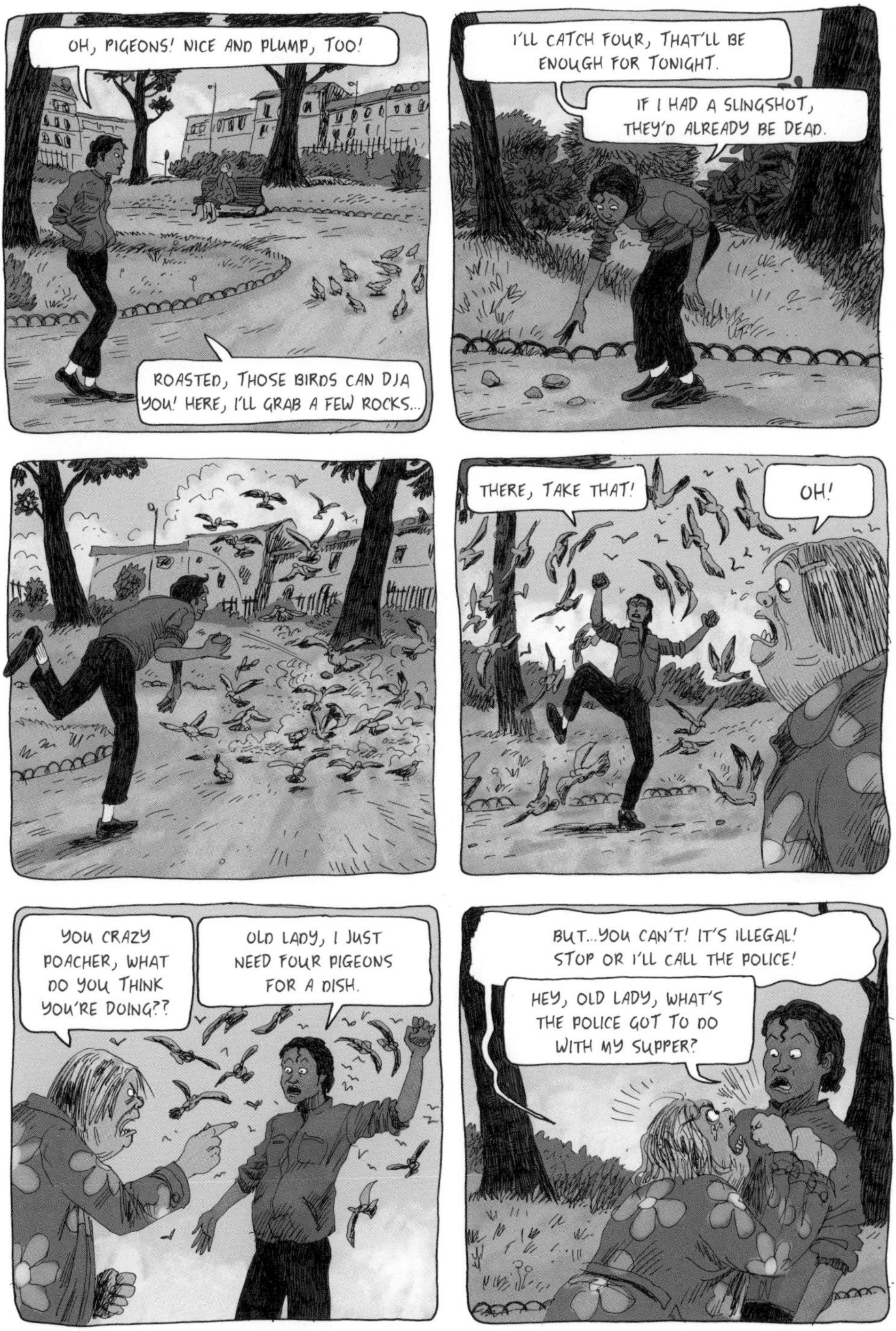

OH, PIGEONS! NICE AND PLUMP, TOO!
ROASTED, THOSE BIRDS CAN DJA YOU! HERE, I'LL GRAB A FEW ROCKS...
I'LL CATCH FOUR, THAT'LL BE ENOUGH FOR TONIGHT.
IF I HAD A SLINGSHOT, THEY'D ALREADY BE DEAD.
THERE, TAKE THAT!
OH!
YOU CRAZY POACHER, WHAT DO YOU THINK YOU'RE DOING??
OLD LADY, I JUST NEED FOUR PIGEONS FOR A DISH.
BUT...YOU CAN'T! IT'S ILLEGAL! STOP OR I'LL CALL THE POLICE!
HEY, OLD LADY, WHAT'S THE POLICE GOT TO DO WITH MY SUPPER?

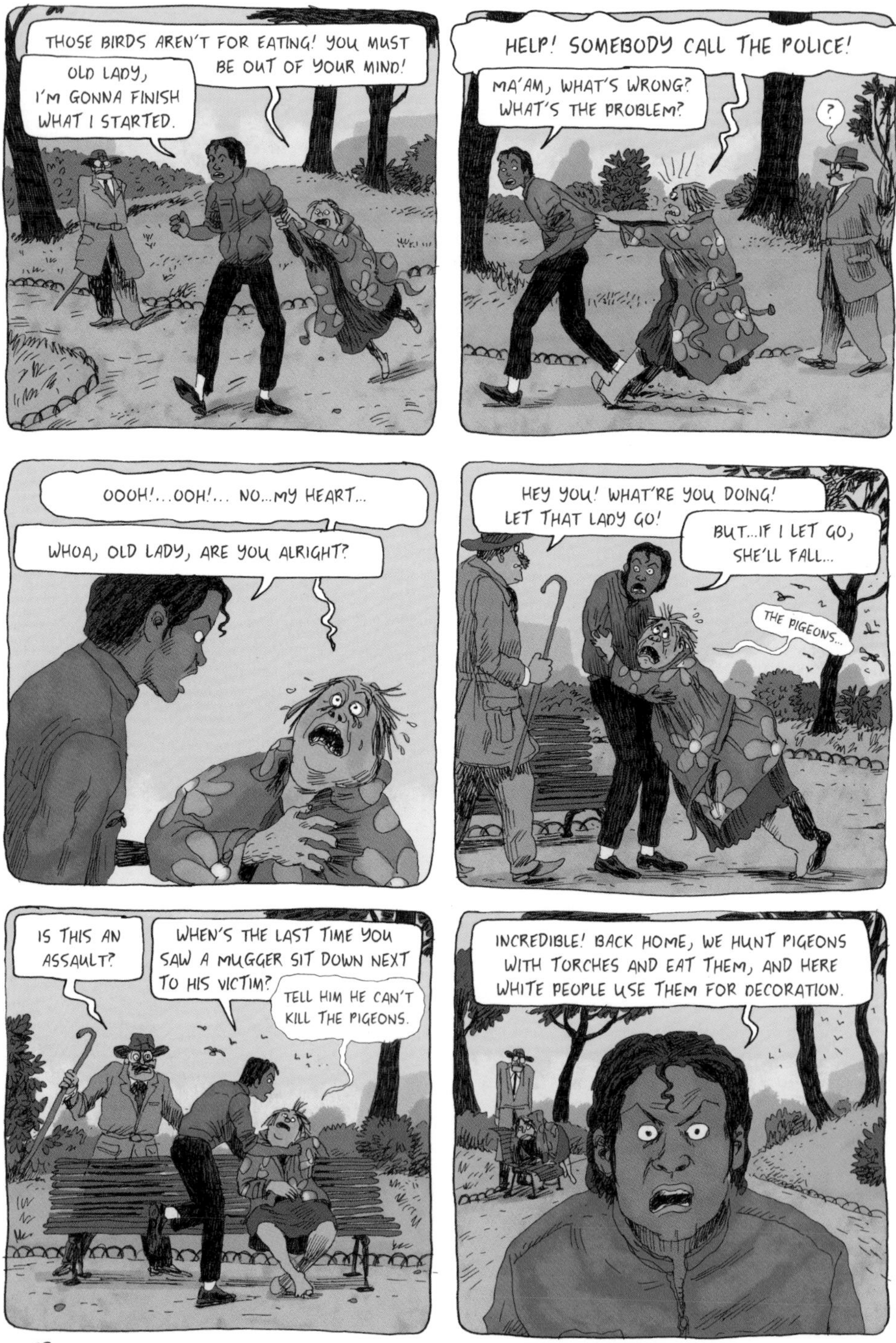

THOSE BIRDS AREN'T FOR EATING! YOU MUST BE OUT OF YOUR MIND!
OLD LADY, I'M GONNA FINISH WHAT I STARTED.
HELP! SOMEBODY CALL THE POLICE!
MA'AM, WHAT'S WRONG? WHAT'S THE PROBLEM?
?
OOOH!...OOH!... NO...MY HEART...
WHOA, OLD LADY, ARE YOU ALRIGHT?
HEY YOU! WHAT'RE YOU DOING! LET THAT LADY GO!
BUT...IF I LET GO, SHE'LL FALL...
THE PIGEONS...
IS THIS AN ASSAULT?
WHEN'S THE LAST TIME YOU SAW A MUGGER SIT DOWN NEXT TO HIS VICTIM?
TELL HIM HE CAN'T KILL THE PIGEONS.
INCREDIBLE! BACK HOME, WE HUNT PIGEONS WITH TORCHES AND EAT THEM, AND HERE WHITE PEOPLE USE THEM FOR DECORATION.

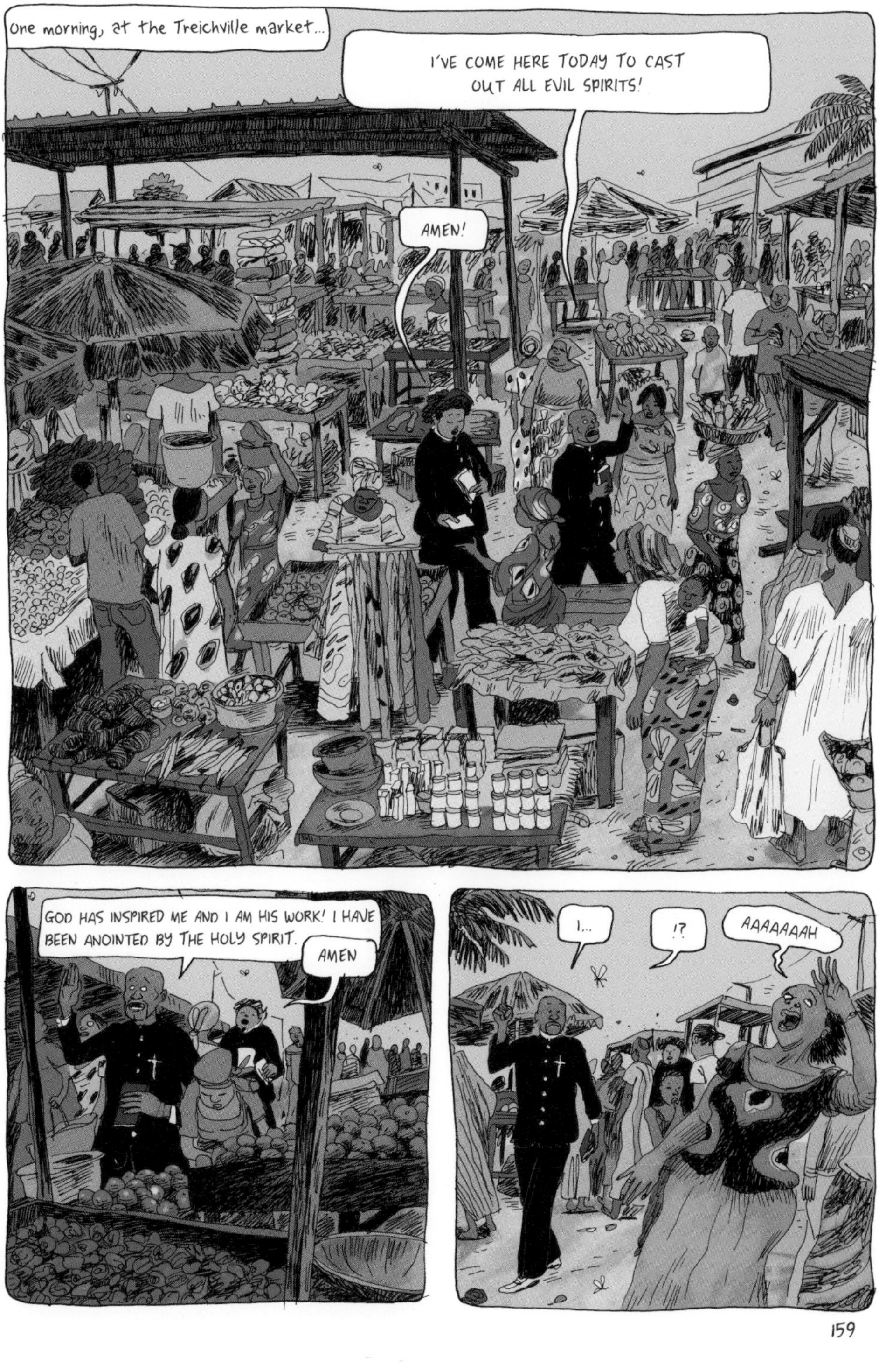
One morning, at the Treichville market...
I'VE COME HERE TODAY TO CAST OUT ALL EVIL SPIRITS!
AMEN!
GOD HAS INSPIRED ME AND I AM HIS WORK! I HAVE BEEN ANOINTED BY THE HOLY SPIRIT.
AMEN
I...
!?
AAAAAAAH

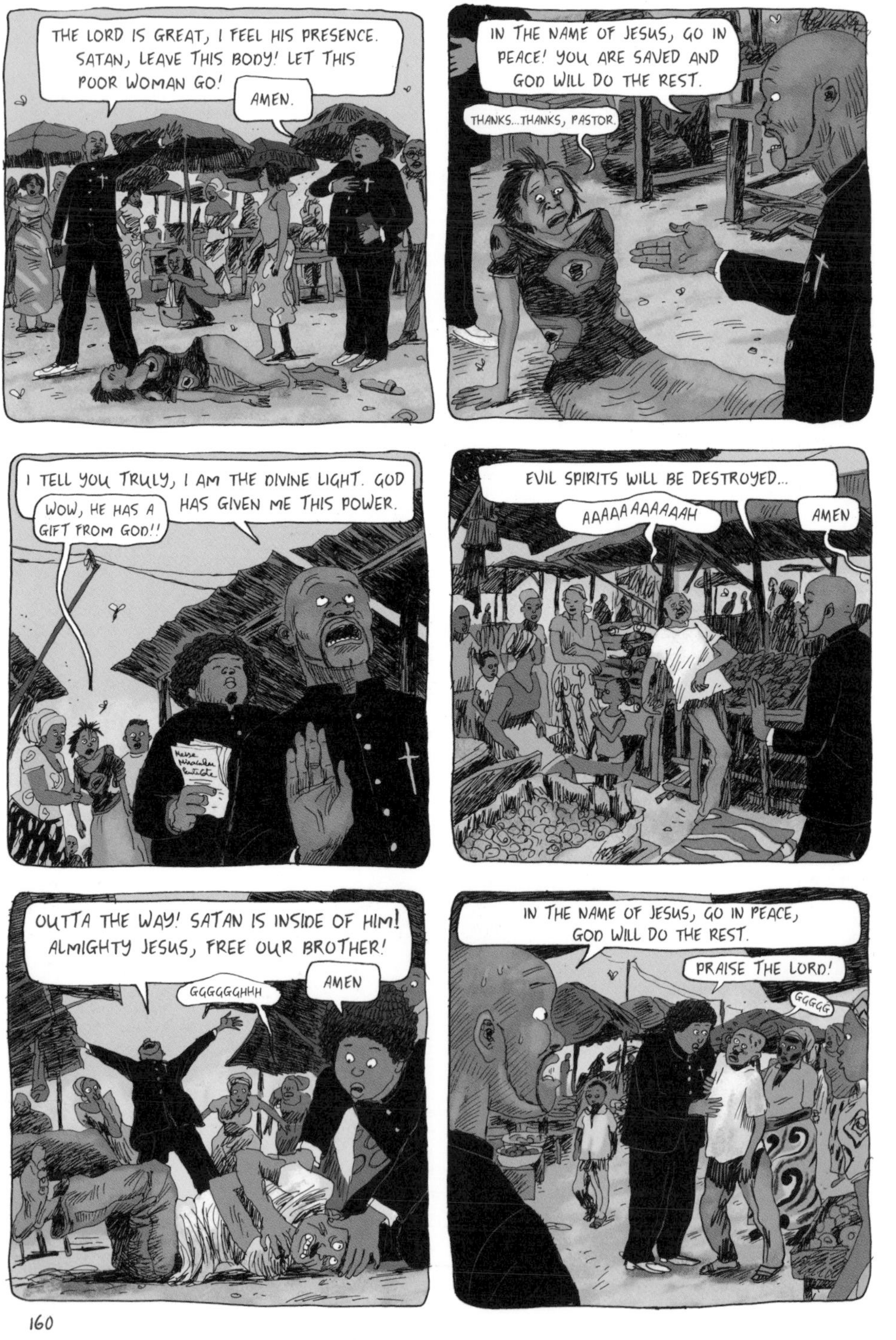
THE LORD IS GREAT, I FEEL HIS PRESENCE. SATAN, LEAVE THIS BODY! LET THIS POOR WOMAN GO!
AMEN.
IN THE NAME OF JESUS, GO IN PEACE! YOU ARE SAVED AND GOD WILL DO THE REST.
THANKS...THANKS, PASTOR.
I TELL YOU TRULY, I AM THE DIVINE LIGHT. GOD HAS GIVEN ME THIS POWER.
WOW, HE HAS A GIFT FROM GOD!!
EVIL SPIRITS WILL BE DESTROYED...
AAAAAAAAAAAH
AMEN
OUTTA THE WAY! SATAN IS INSIDE OF HIM! ALMIGHTY JESUS, FREE OUR BROTHER!
GGGGGGHHH
AMEN
IN THE NAME OF JESUS, GO IN PEACE, GOD WILL DO THE REST.
PRAISE THE LORD!
GGGGG

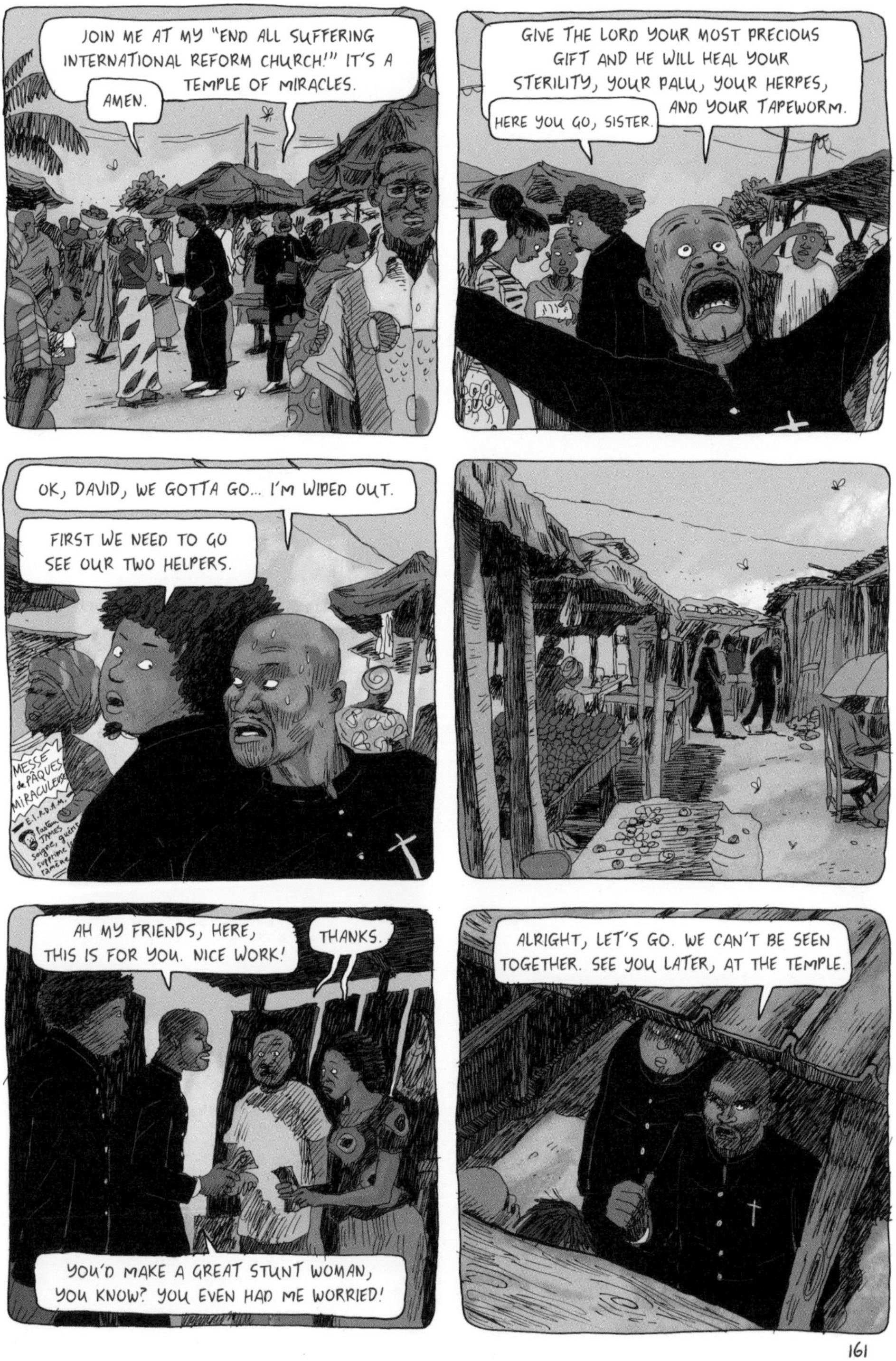
JOIN ME AT MY "END ALL SUFFERING INTERNATIONAL REFORM CHURCH!" IT'S A TEMPLE OF MIRACLES.
AMEN.
GIVE THE LORD YOUR MOST PRECIOUS GIFT AND HE WILL HEAL YOUR STERILITY, YOUR PALU, YOUR HERPES, AND YOUR TAPEWORM.
HERE YOU GO, SISTER.
OK, DAVID, WE GOTTA GO... I'M WIPED OUT.
FIRST WE NEED TO GO SEE OUR TWO HELPERS.
MESSE
de PÂQUES
AH MY FRIENDS, HERE, THIS IS FOR YOU. NICE WORK!
THANKS.
YOU'D MAKE A GREAT STUNT WOMAN, YOU KNOW? YOU EVEN HAD ME WORRIED!
ALRIGHT, LET'S GO. WE CAN'T BE SEEN TOGETHER. SEE YOU LATER, AT THE TEMPLE.

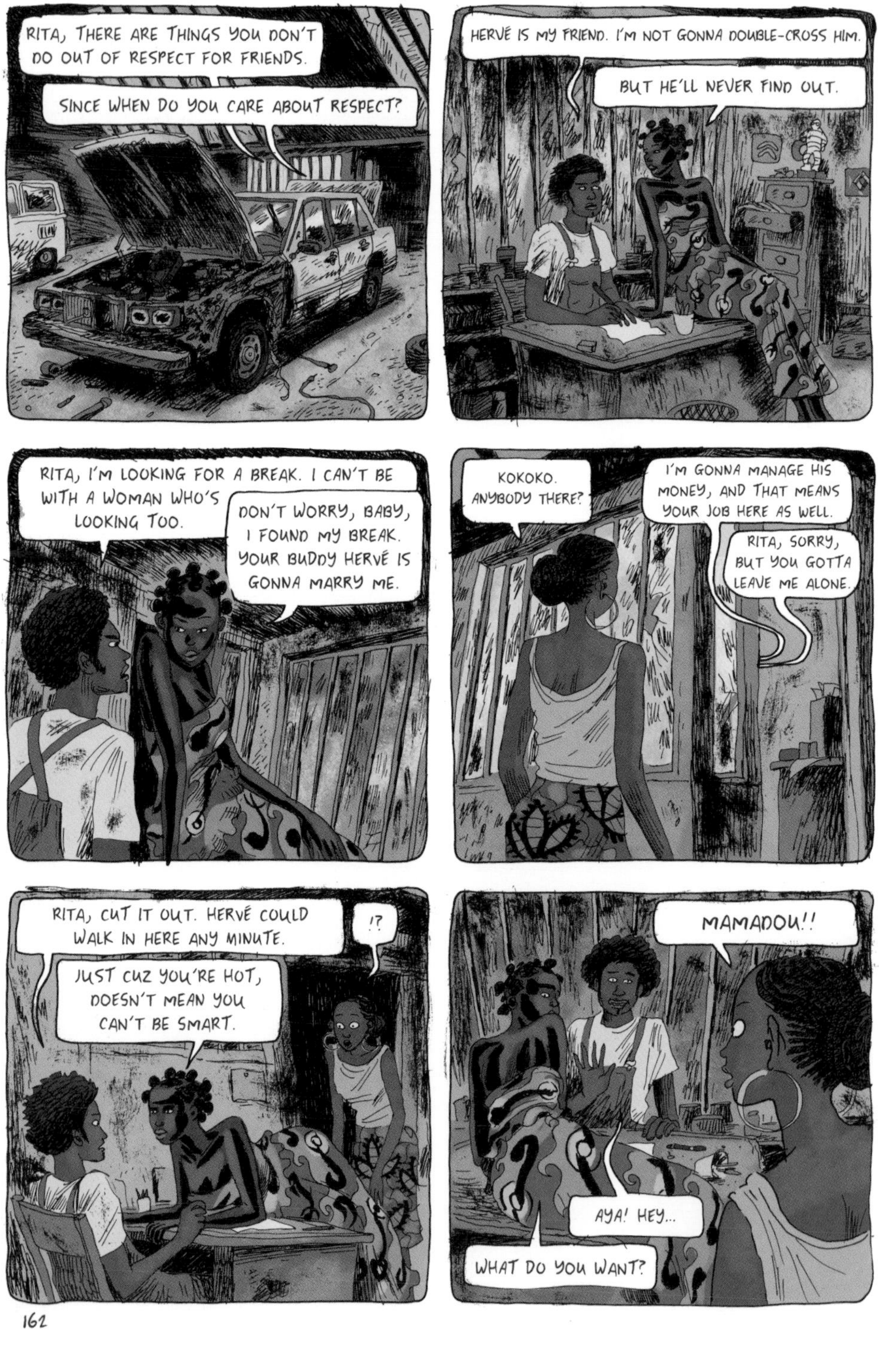
RITA, THERE ARE THINGS YOU DON'T DO OUT OF RESPECT FOR FRIENDS.
SINCE WHEN DO YOU CARE ABOUT RESPECT?
HERVÉ IS MY FRIEND. I'M NOT GONNA DOUBLE-CROSS HIM.
BUT HE'LL NEVER FIND OUT.
RITA, I'M LOOKING FOR A BREAK. I CAN'T BE WITH A WOMAN WHO'S LOOKING TOO.
DON'T WORRY, BABY, I FOUND MY BREAK. YOUR BUDDY HERVÉ IS GONNA MARRY ME.
KOKOKO. ANYBODY THERE?
I'M GONNA MANAGE HIS MONEY, AND THAT MEANS YOUR JOB HERE AS WELL.
RITA, SORRY, BUT YOU GOTTA LEAVE ME ALONE.
RITA, CUT IT OUT. HERVÉ COULD WALK IN HERE ANY MINUTE.
!?
JUST CUZ YOU'RE HOT, DOESN'T MEAN YOU CAN'T BE SMART.
MAMADOU!!
AYA! HEY...
WHAT DO YOU WANT?

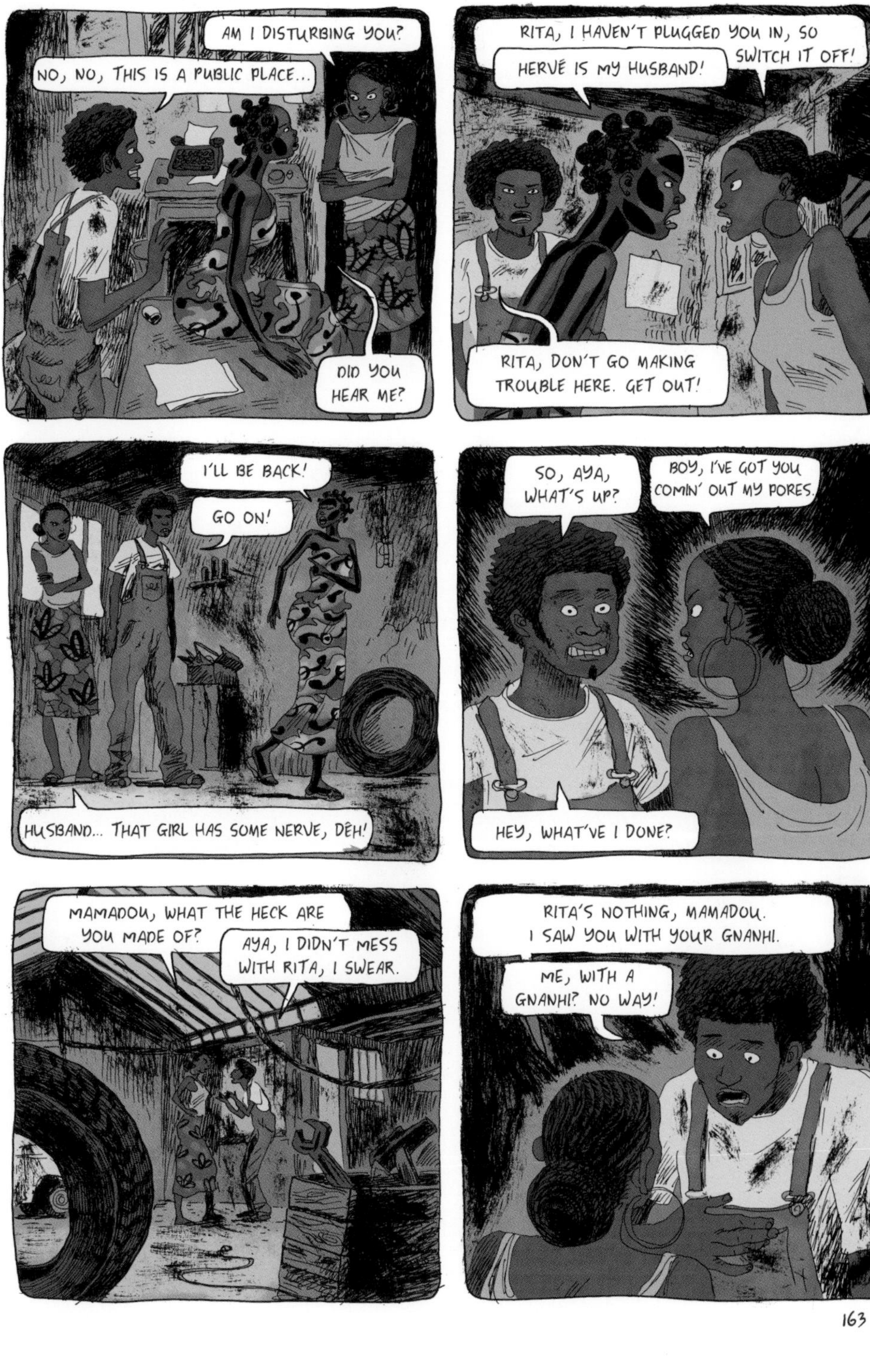
AM I DISTURBING YOU?
NO, NO, THIS IS A PUBLIC PLACE...
DID YOU HEAR ME?
RITA, I HAVEN'T PLUGGED YOU IN, SO SWITCH IT OFF!
HERVÉ IS MY HUSBAND!
RITA, DON'T GO MAKING TROUBLE HERE. GET OUT!
I'LL BE BACK!
GO ON!
HUSBAND... THAT GIRL HAS SOME NERVE, DÊH!
SO, AYA, WHAT'S UP?
BOY, I'VE GOT YOU COMIN' OUT MY PORES.
HEY, WHAT'VE I DONE?
MAMADOU, WHAT THE HECK ARE YOU MADE OF?
AYA, I DIDN'T MESS WITH RITA, I SWEAR.
RITA'S NOTHING, MAMADOU. I SAW YOU WITH YOUR GNANHI.
ME, WITH A GNANHI? NO WAY!

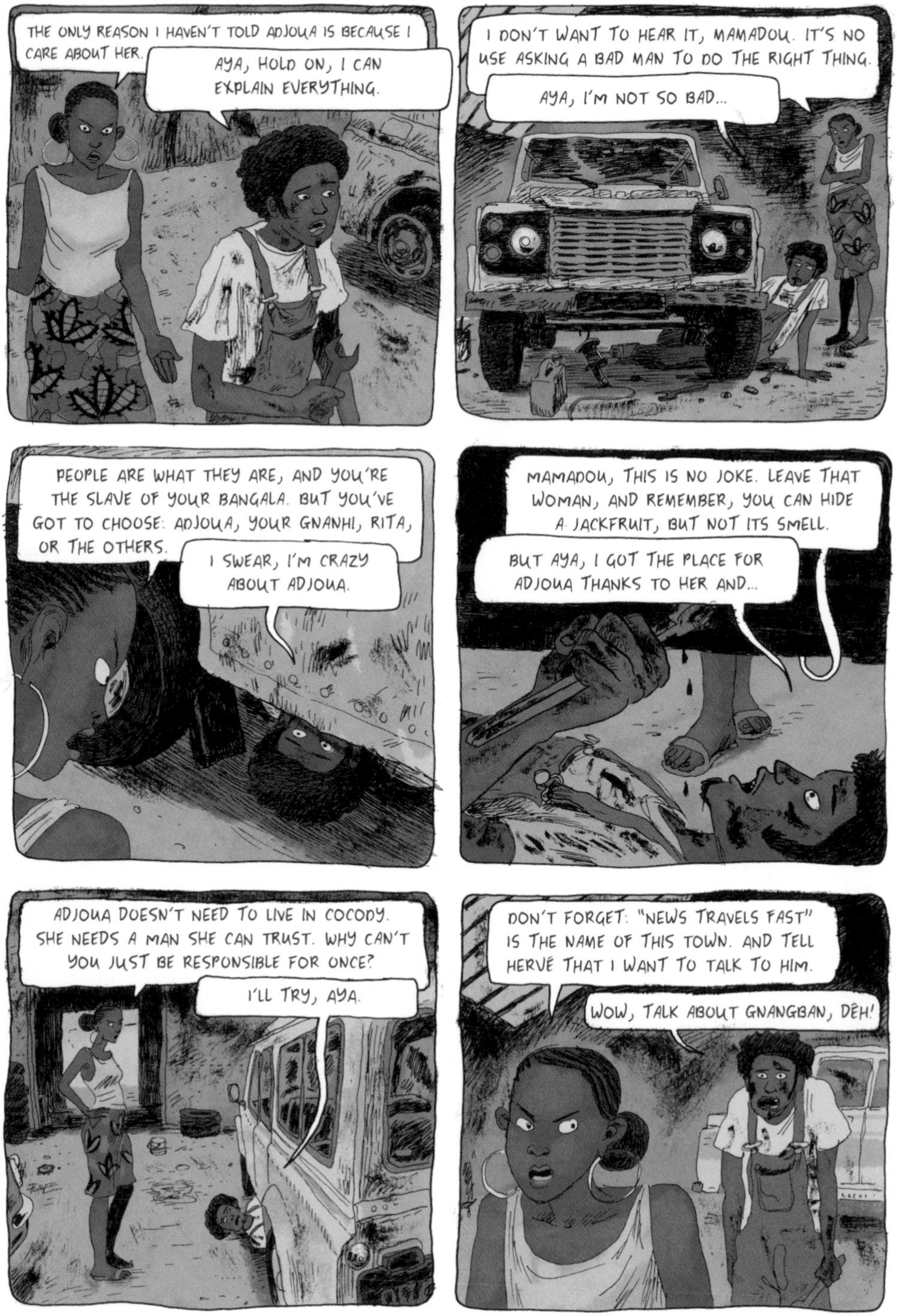
THE ONLY REASON I HAVEN'T TOLD ADJOUA IS BECAUSE I CARE ABOUT HER.
AYA, HOLD ON, I CAN EXPLAIN EVERYTHING.
I DON'T WANT TO HEAR IT, MAMADOU. IT'S NO USE ASKING A BAD MAN TO DO THE RIGHT THING.
AYA, I'M NOT SO BAD...
PEOPLE ARE WHAT THEY ARE, AND YOU'RE THE SLAVE OF YOUR BANGALA. BUT YOU'VE GOT TO CHOOSE: ADJOUA, YOUR GNANHI, RITA, OR THE OTHERS.
I SWEAR, I'M CRAZY ABOUT ADJOUA.
MAMADOU, THIS IS NO JOKE. LEAVE THAT WOMAN, AND REMEMBER, YOU CAN HIDE A JACKFRUIT, BUT NOT ITS SMELL.
BUT AYA, I GOT THE PLACE FOR ADJOUA THANKS TO HER AND...
ADJOUA DOESN'T NEED TO LIVE IN COCODY. SHE NEEDS A MAN SHE CAN TRUST. WHY CAN'T YOU JUST BE RESPONSIBLE FOR ONCE?
I'LL TRY, AYA.
DON'T FORGET: "NEWS TRAVELS FAST" IS THE NAME OF THIS TOWN. AND TELL HERVÉ THAT I WANT TO TALK TO HIM.
WOW, TALK ABOUT GNANGBAN, DÊH!

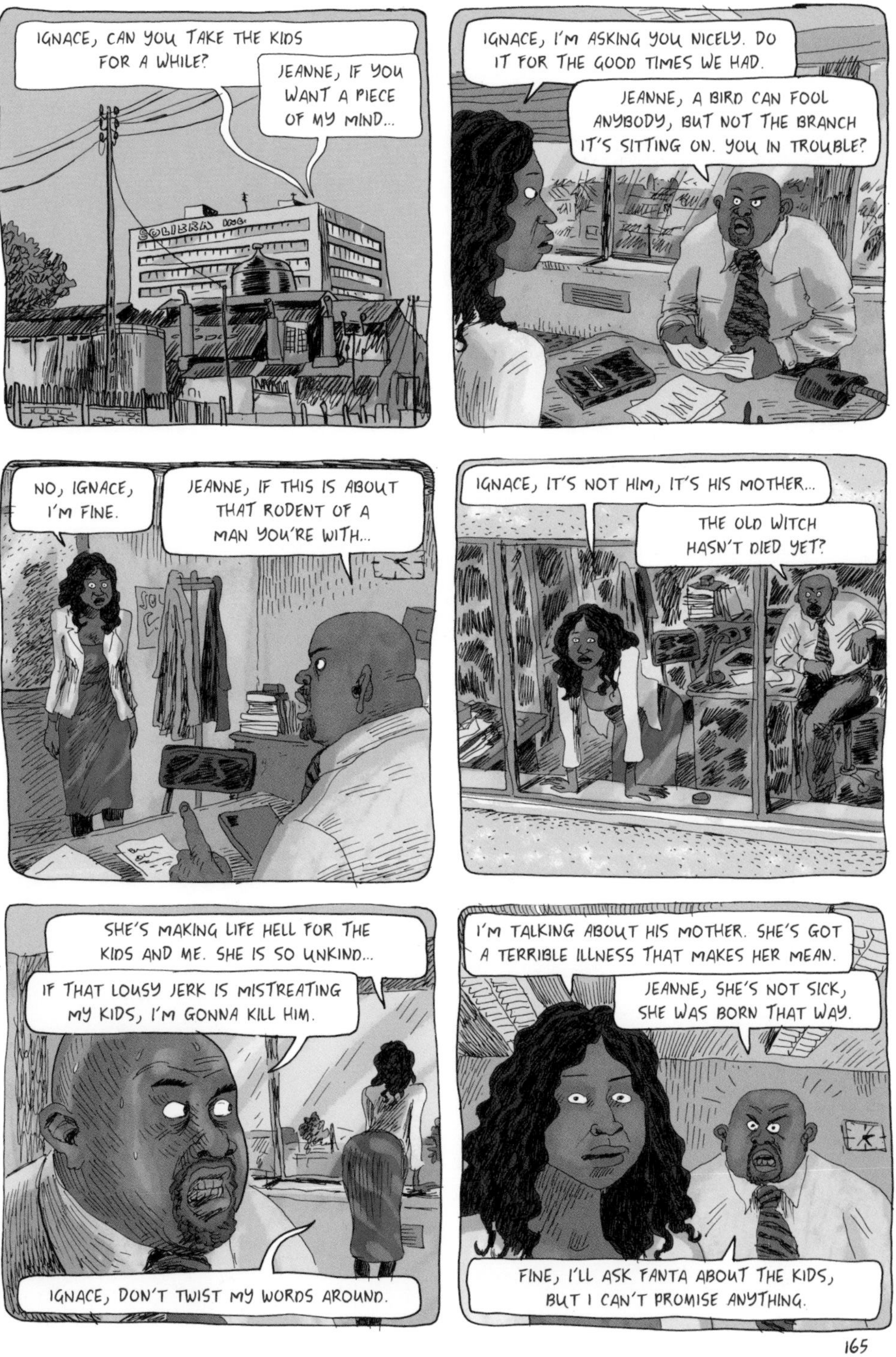
IGNACE, CAN YOU TAKE THE KIDS FOR A WHILE?
JEANNE, IF YOU WANT A PIECE OF MY MIND...
SOLIBRA INC.
IGNACE, I'M ASKING YOU NICELY. DO IT FOR THE GOOD TIMES WE HAD.
JEANNE, A BIRD CAN FOOL ANYBODY, BUT NOT THE BRANCH IT'S SITTING ON. YOU IN TROUBLE?
NO, IGNACE, I'M FINE.
JEANNE, IF THIS IS ABOUT THAT RODENT OF A MAN YOU'RE WITH...
IGNACE, IT'S NOT HIM, IT'S HIS MOTHER...
THE OLD WITCH HASN'T DIED YET?
SHE'S MAKING LIFE HELL FOR THE KIDS AND ME. SHE IS SO UNKIND...
IF THAT LOUSY JERK IS MISTREATING MY KIDS, I'M GONNA KILL HIM.
IGNACE, DON'T TWIST MY WORDS AROUND.
I'M TALKING ABOUT HIS MOTHER. SHE'S GOT A TERRIBLE ILLNESS THAT MAKES HER MEAN.
JEANNE, SHE'S NOT SICK, SHE WAS BORN THAT WAY.
FINE, I'LL ASK FANTA ABOUT THE KIDS, BUT I CAN'T PROMISE ANYTHING.

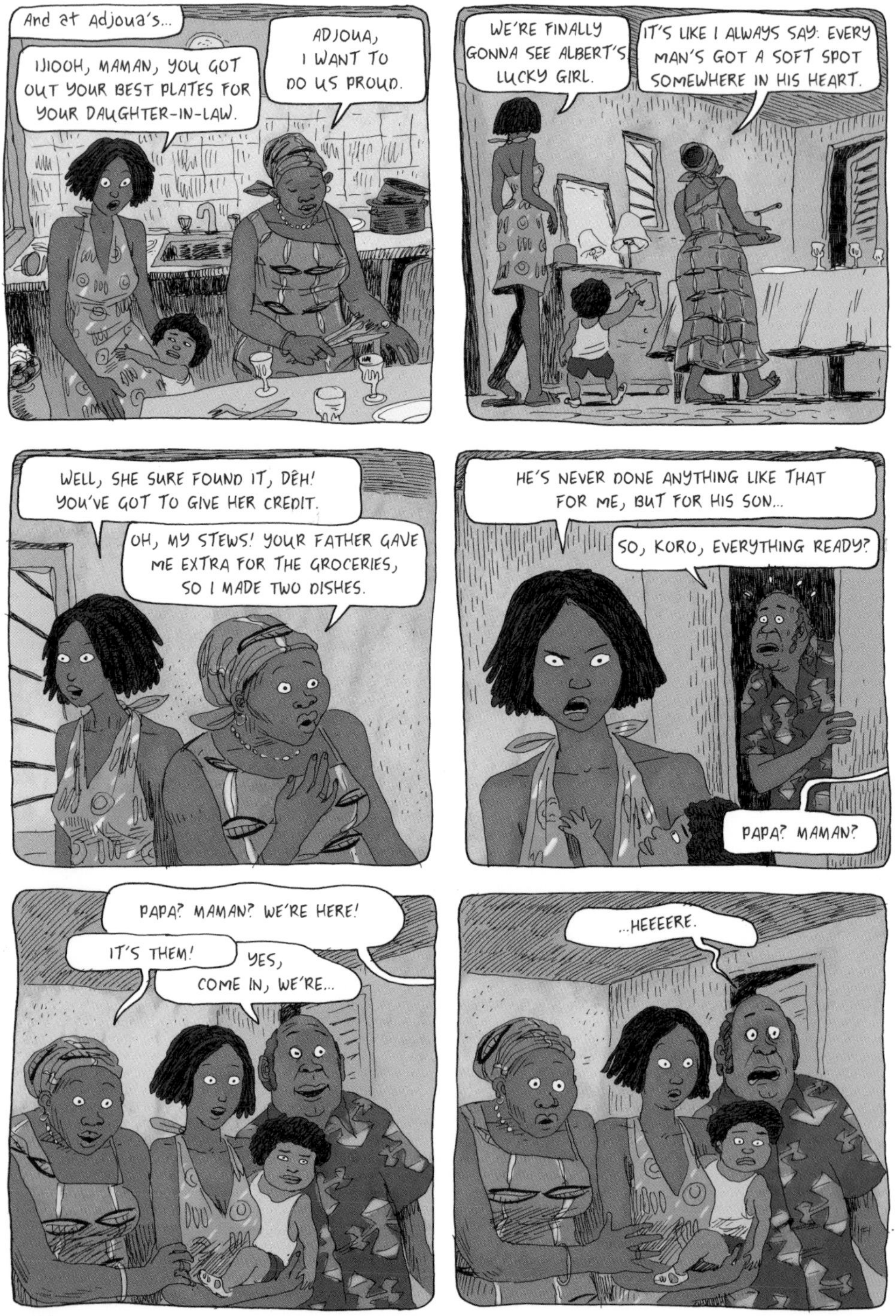
And at Adjoua's...
WOOH, MAMAN, YOU GOT OUT YOUR BEST PLATES FOR YOUR DAUGHTER-IN-LAW.
ADJOUA, I WANT TO DO US PROUD.
WE'RE FINALLY GONNA SEE ALBERT'S LUCKY GIRL.
IT'S LIKE I ALWAYS SAY: EVERY MAN'S GOT A SOFT SPOT SOMEWHERE IN HIS HEART.
WELL, SHE SURE FOUND IT, DÊH! YOU'VE GOT TO GIVE HER CREDIT.
OH, MY STEWS! YOUR FATHER GAVE ME EXTRA FOR THE GROCERIES, SO I MADE TWO DISHES.
HE'S NEVER DONE ANYTHING LIKE THAT FOR ME, BUT FOR HIS SON...
SO, KORO, EVERYTHING READY?
PAPA? MAMAN?
PAPA? MAMAN? WE'RE HERE!
IT'S THEM!
YES, COME IN, WE'RE...
...HEEEERE.

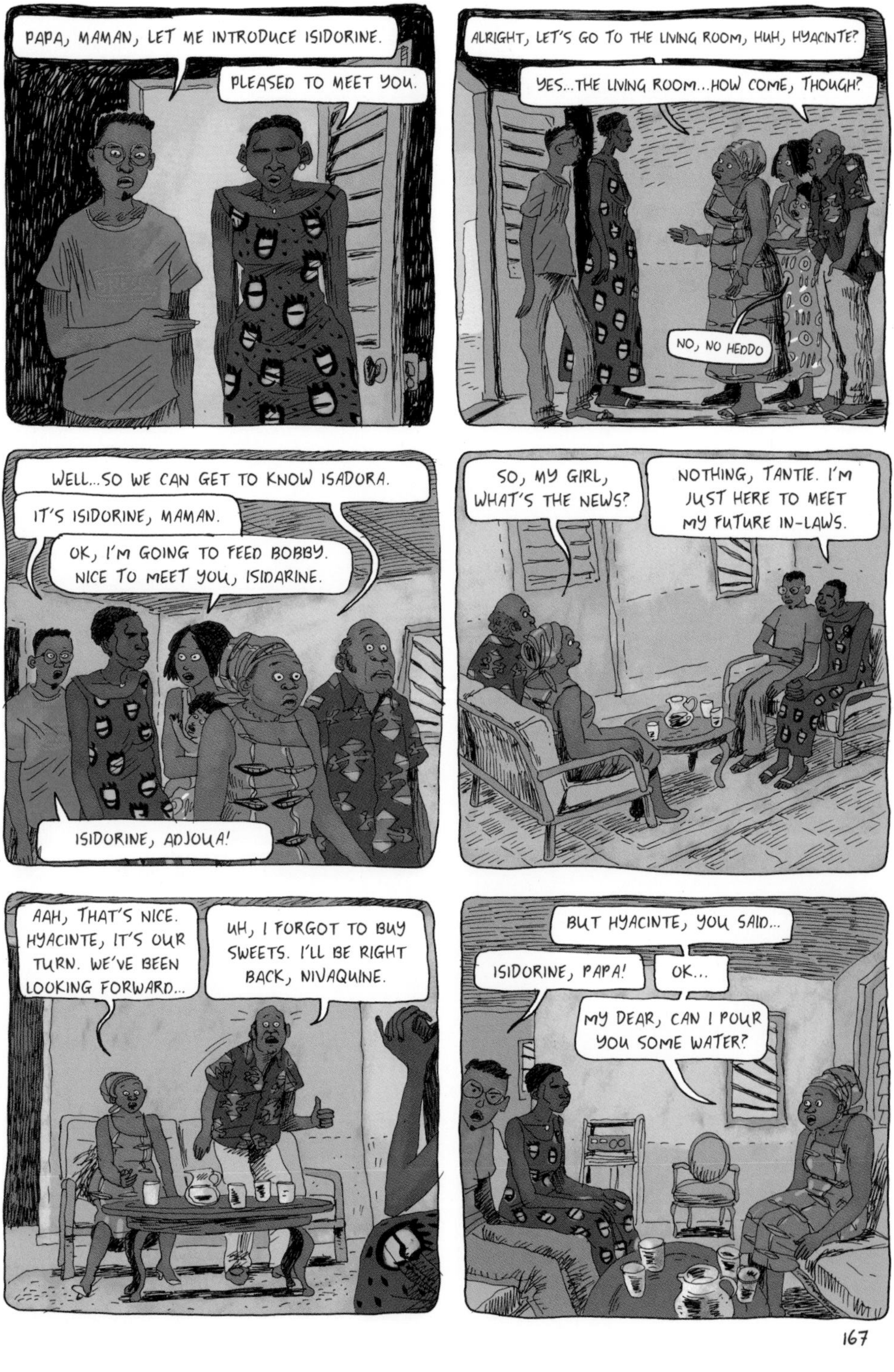
PAPA, MAMAN, LET ME INTRODUCE ISIDORINE.
PLEASED TO MEET YOU.
ALRIGHT, LET'S GO TO THE LIVING ROOM, HUH, HYACINTE?
YES... THE LIVING ROOM... HOW COME, THOUGH?
NO, NO HEDDO
WELL... SO WE CAN GET TO KNOW ISADORA.
IT'S ISIDORINE, MAMAN.
OK, I'M GOING TO FEED BOBBY. NICE TO MEET YOU, ISIDARINE.
ISIDORINE, ADJOUA!
SO, MY GIRL, WHAT'S THE NEWS?
NOTHING, TANTIE. I'M JUST HERE TO MEET MY FUTURE IN-LAWS.
AAH, THAT'S NICE. HYACINTE, IT'S OUR TURN. WE'VE BEEN LOOKING FORWARD...
UH, I FORGOT TO BUY SWEETS. I'LL BE RIGHT BACK, NIVAQUINE.
BUT HYACINTE, YOU SAID...
ISIDORINE, PAPA!
OK...
MY DEAR, CAN I POUR YOU SOME WATER?

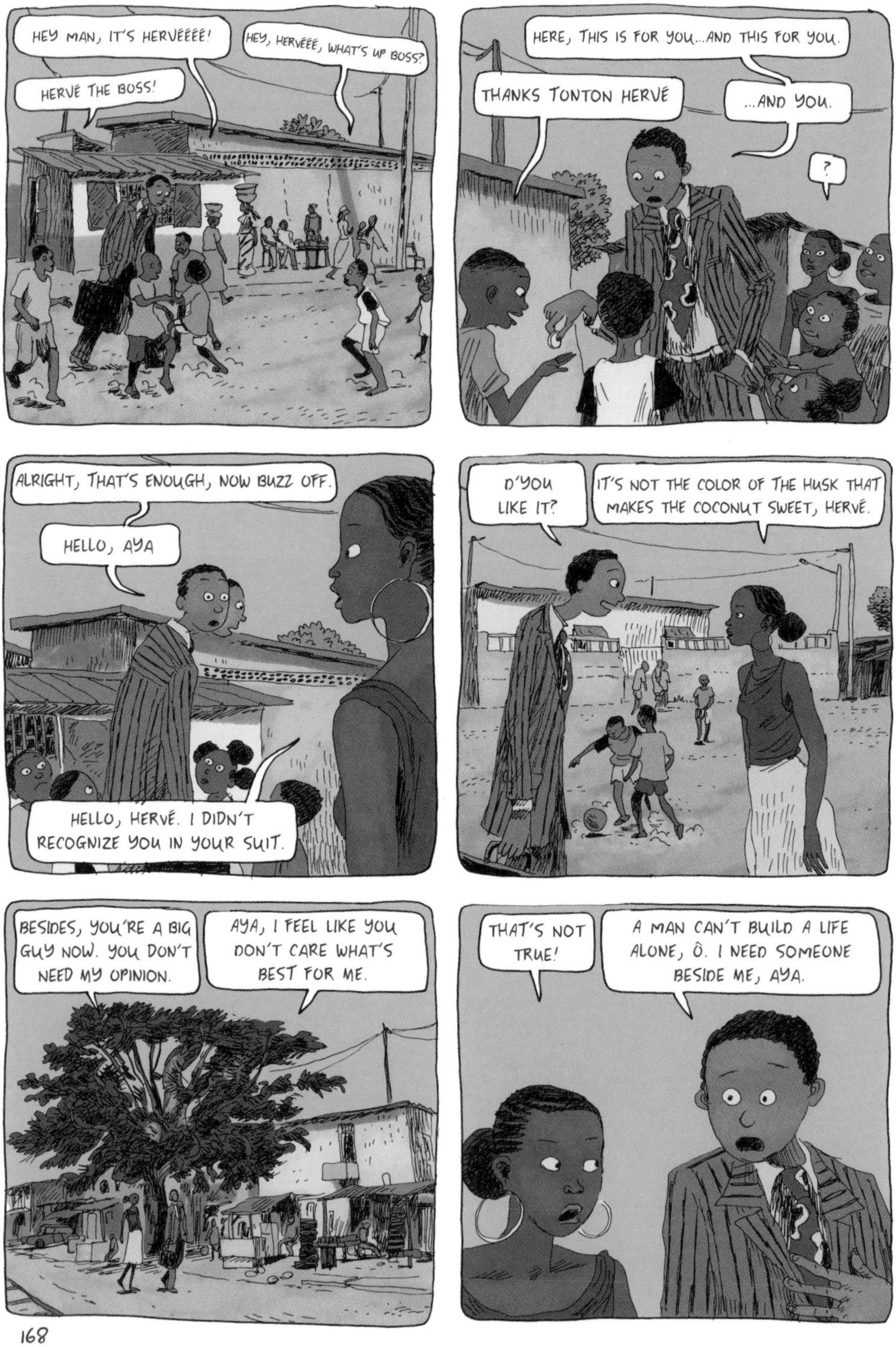
HEY MAN, IT'S HERVÉÉÉÉ!
HEY, HERVÉÉÉ, WHAT'S UP BOSS?
HERVÉ THE BOSS!
HERE, THIS IS FOR YOU...AND THIS FOR YOU.
THANKS TONTON HERVÉ
...AND YOU.
?
ALRIGHT, THAT'S ENOUGH, NOW BUZZ OFF.
HELLO, AYA
HELLO, HERVÉ. I DIDN'T RECOGNIZE YOU IN YOUR SUIT.
D'YOU LIKE IT?
IT'S NOT THE COLOR OF THE HUSK THAT MAKES THE COCONUT SWEET, HERVÉ.
BESIDES, YOU'RE A BIG GUY NOW. YOU DON'T NEED MY OPINION.
AYA, I FEEL LIKE YOU DON'T CARE WHAT'S BEST FOR ME.
THAT'S NOT TRUE!
A MAN CAN'T BUILD A LIFE ALONE, Ô. I NEED SOMEONE BESIDE ME, AYA.

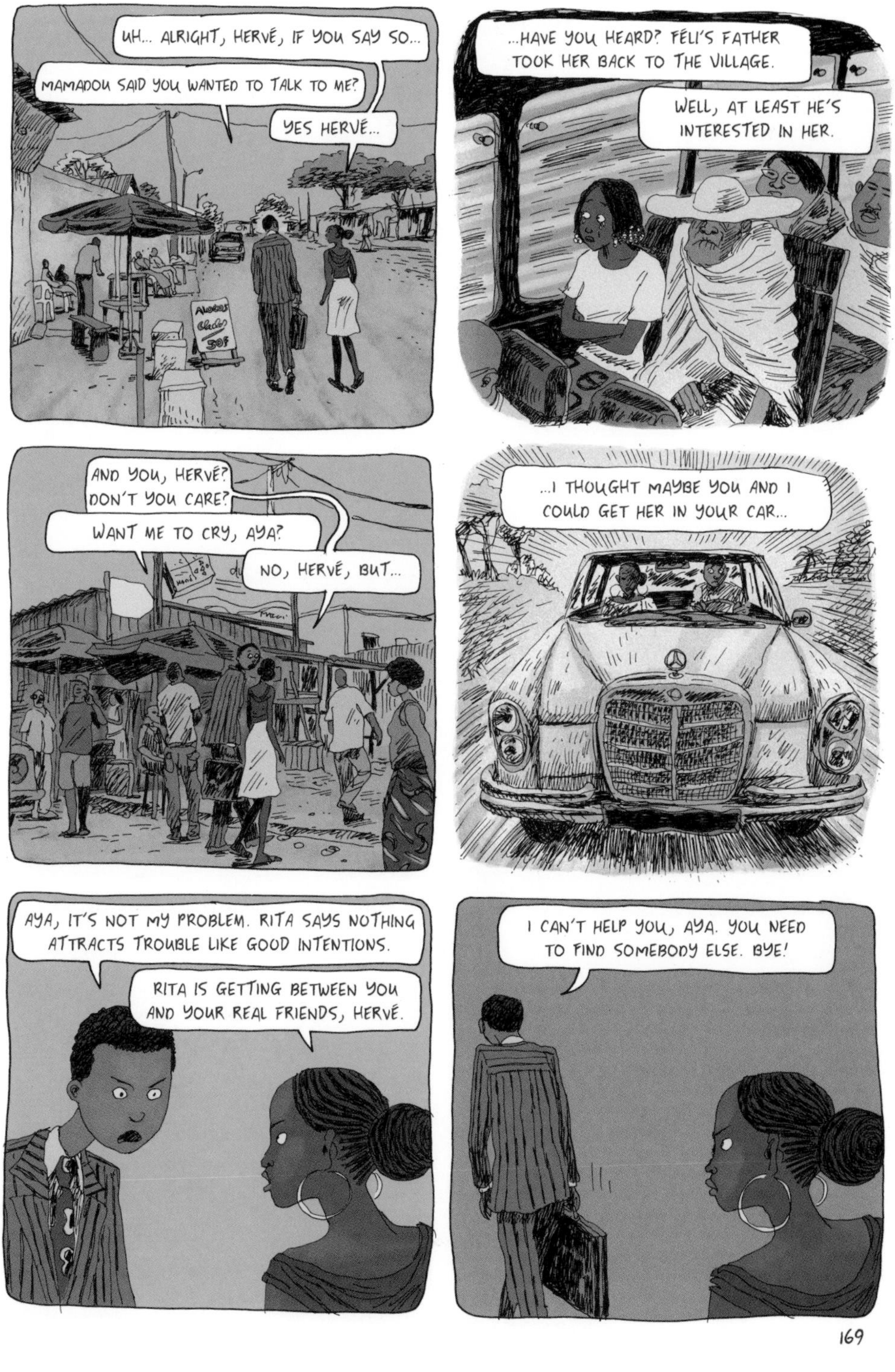
MAMADOU SAID YOU WANTED TO TALK TO ME?
UH... ALRIGHT, HERVÉ, IF YOU SAY SO...
YES HERVÉ...
...HAVE YOU HEARD? FÉLI'S FATHER TOOK HER BACK TO THE VILLAGE.
WELL, AT LEAST HE'S INTERESTED IN HER.
AND YOU, HERVÉ? DON'T YOU CARE?
WANT ME TO CRY, AYA?
NO, HERVÉ, BUT...
...I THOUGHT MAYBE YOU AND I COULD GET HER IN YOUR CAR...
AYA, IT'S NOT MY PROBLEM. RITA SAYS NOTHING ATTRACTS TROUBLE LIKE GOOD INTENTIONS.
RITA IS GETTING BETWEEN YOU AND YOUR REAL FRIENDS, HERVÉ.
I CAN'T HELP YOU, AYA. YOU NEED TO FIND SOMEBODY ELSE. BYE!

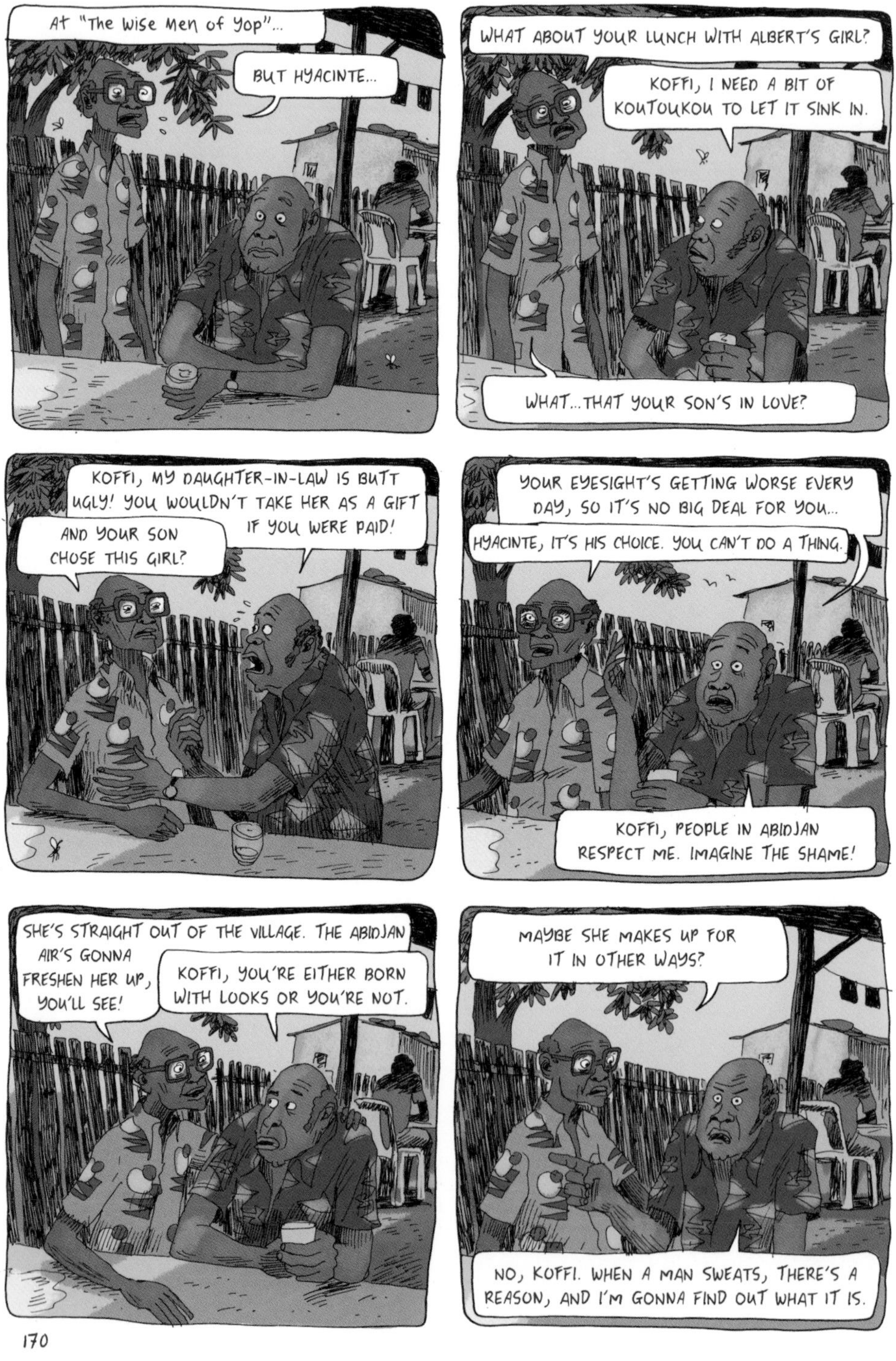
At "The Wise Men of Yop"...
BUT HYACINTE...
WHAT ABOUT YOUR LUNCH WITH ALBERT'S GIRL?
KOFFI, I NEED A BIT OF KOUTOUKOU TO LET IT SINK IN.
WHAT...THAT YOUR SON'S IN LOVE?
KOFFI, MY DAUGHTER-IN-LAW IS BUTT UGLY! YOU WOULDN'T TAKE HER AS A GIFT IF YOU WERE PAID!
AND YOUR SON CHOSE THIS GIRL?
YOUR EYESIGHT'S GETTING WORSE EVERY DAY, SO IT'S NO BIG DEAL FOR YOU...
HYACINTE, IT'S HIS CHOICE. YOU CAN'T DO A THING.
KOFFI, PEOPLE IN ABIDJAN RESPECT ME. IMAGINE THE SHAME!
SHE'S STRAIGHT OUT OF THE VILLAGE. THE ABIDJAN AIR'S GONNA FRESHEN HER UP, YOU'LL SEE!
KOFFI, YOU'RE EITHER BORN WITH LOOKS OR YOU'RE NOT.
MAYBE SHE MAKES UP FOR IT IN OTHER WAYS?
NO, KOFFI. WHEN A MAN SWEATS, THERE'S A REASON, AND I'M GONNA FIND OUT WHAT IT IS.

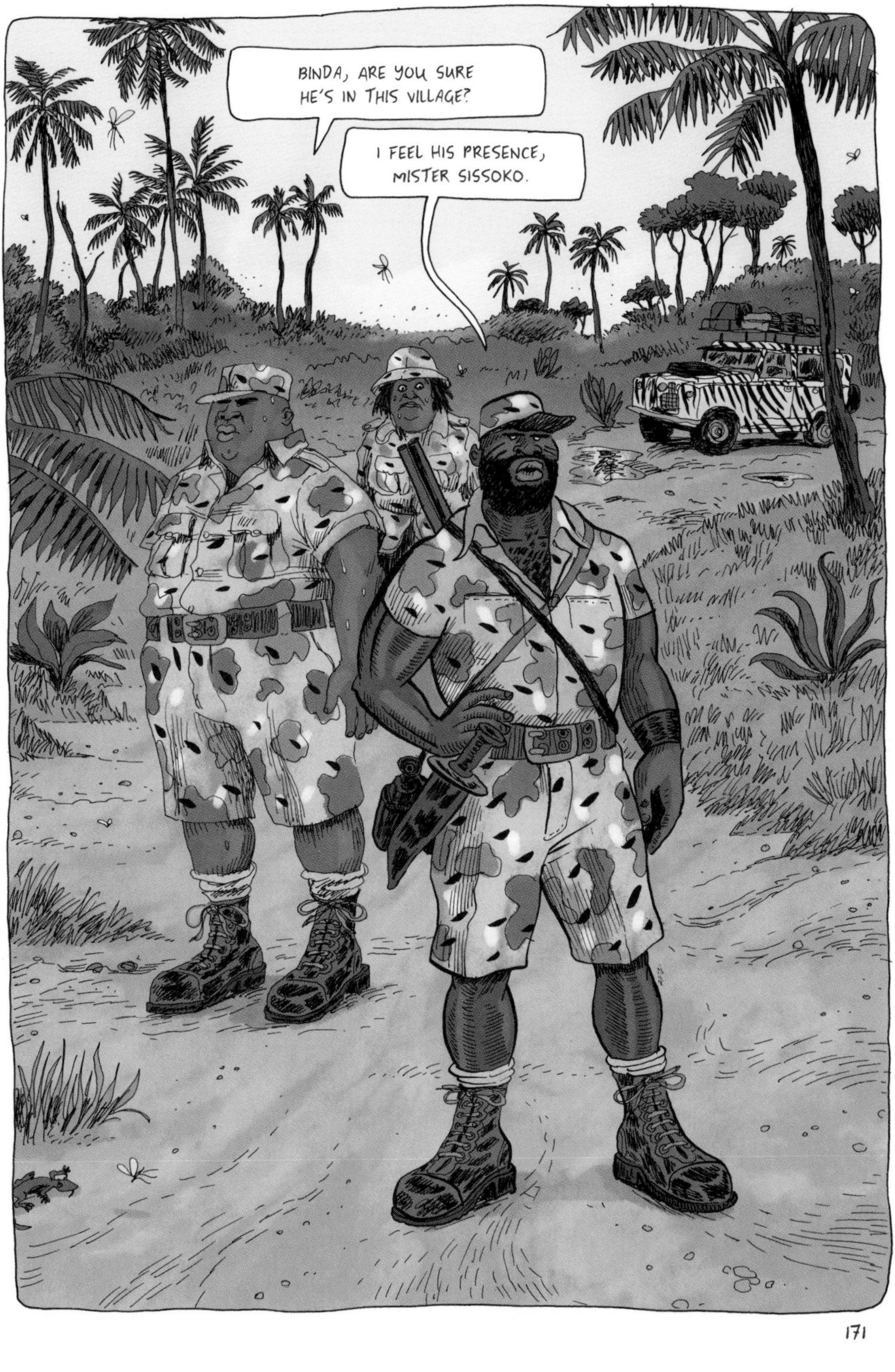
BINDA, ARE YOU SURE HE'S IN THIS VILLAGE?
I FEEL HIS PRESENCE, MISTER SISSOKO.

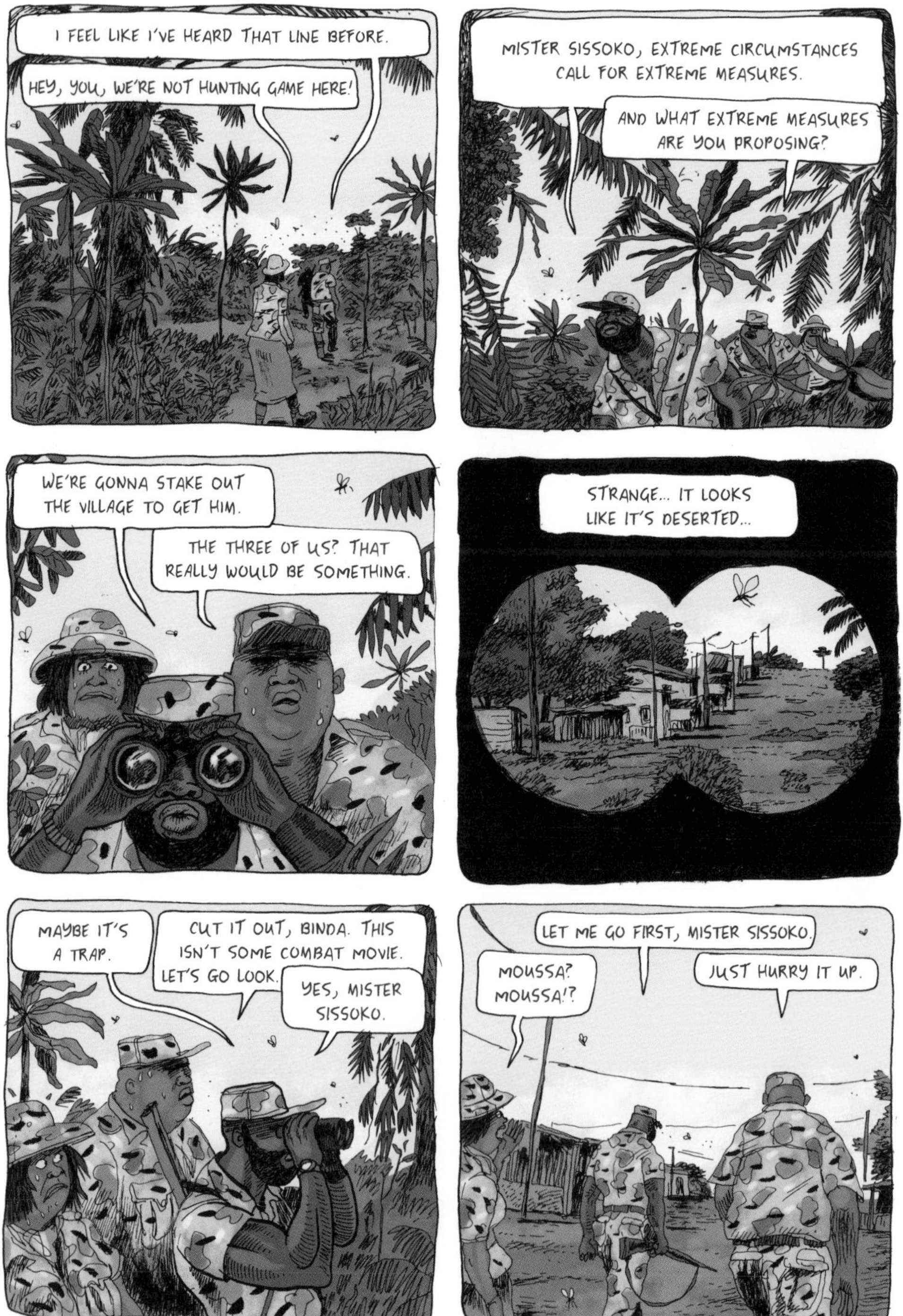
I FEEL LIKE I'VE HEARD THAT LINE BEFORE.
HEY, YOU, WE'RE NOT HUNTING GAME HERE!
MISTER SISSOKO, EXTREME CIRCUMSTANCES CALL FOR EXTREME MEASURES.
AND WHAT EXTREME MEASURES ARE YOU PROPOSING?
WE'RE GONNA STAKE OUT THE VILLAGE TO GET HIM.
THE THREE OF US? THAT REALLY WOULD BE SOMETHING.
STRANGE... IT LOOKS LIKE IT'S DESERTED...
MAYBE IT'S A TRAP.
CUT IT OUT, BINDA. THIS ISN'T SOME COMBAT MOVIE. LET'S GO LOOK.
YES, MISTER SISSOKO.
LET ME GO FIRST, MISTER SISSOKO.
MOUSSA? MOUSSA!?
JUST HURRY IT UP.

MAYBE THEY'VE GONE TO MASS? BUT IT'S NOT SUNDAY, IS IT?
OR OUT TO THE FIELDS?
HEY, THAT'S MOUSSA'S FACE!
SIGN: MOUSSA - THE AMERICAN BIRTH CENTER
I'M CONFIRMING, MISTER SISSOKO. IT'S HIS FACE.
THANKS, BINDA, I NOTICED IT TOO.
MOUSSA!
WE'VE FOUND HIM...
WHAT'D I TELL YOU?... INTUITION.
PRAISE THE LORD!
ALRIGHT, LET'S GET THIS OVER WITH.
THAT'S WHAT I WAS GOING TO SUGGEST, SIR.
WHAT'S MOUSSA DOING IN THE BIRTH CENTER?
DON'T TELL ME HE GOT SOME GIRL PREGNANT!
MATERNITÉ
MOUSSA
l'américain
THERE, I SEE A LADY.
HELLO, MA'AM. WE'VE COME TO SEE MOUSSA.
WHICH ONE?

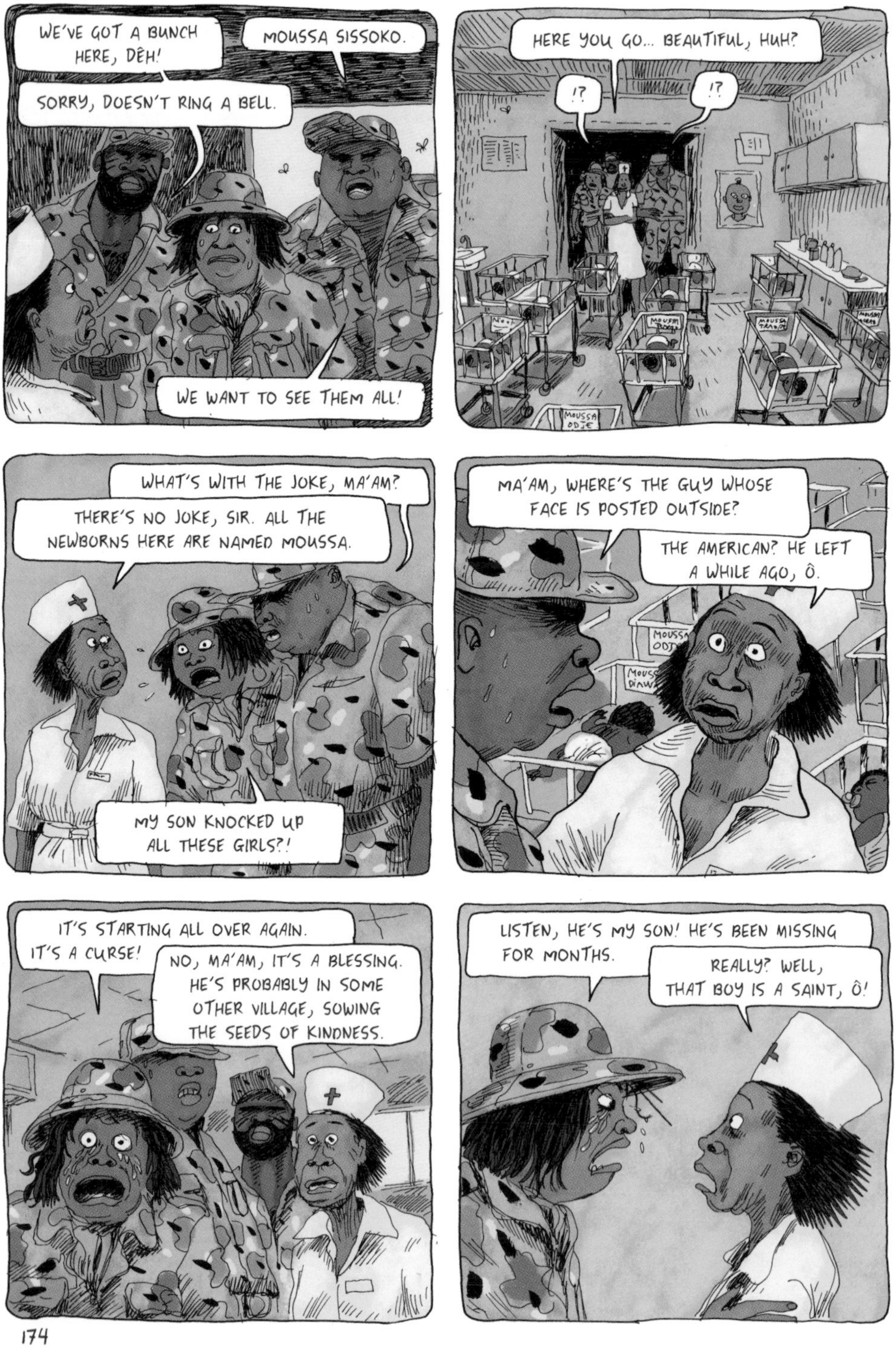
WE'VE GOT A BUNCH HERE, DÊH!
MOUSSA SISSOKO.
SORRY, DOESN'T RING A BELL.
WE WANT TO SEE THEM ALL!
HERE YOU GO... BEAUTIFUL, HUH?
!?
!?
WHAT'S WITH THE JOKE, MA'AM?
THERE'S NO JOKE, SIR. ALL THE NEWBORNS HERE ARE NAMED MOUSSA.
MY SON KNOCKED UP ALL THESE GIRLS?!
MA'AM, WHERE'S THE GUY WHOSE FACE IS POSTED OUTSIDE?
THE AMERICAN? HE LEFT A WHILE AGO, Ô.
IT'S STARTING ALL OVER AGAIN. IT'S A CURSE!
NO, MA'AM, IT'S A BLESSING. HE'S PROBABLY IN SOME OTHER VILLAGE, SOWING THE SEEDS OF KINDNESS.
LISTEN, HE'S MY SON! HE'S BEEN MISSING FOR MONTHS.
REALLY? WELL, THAT BOY IS A SAINT, Ô!

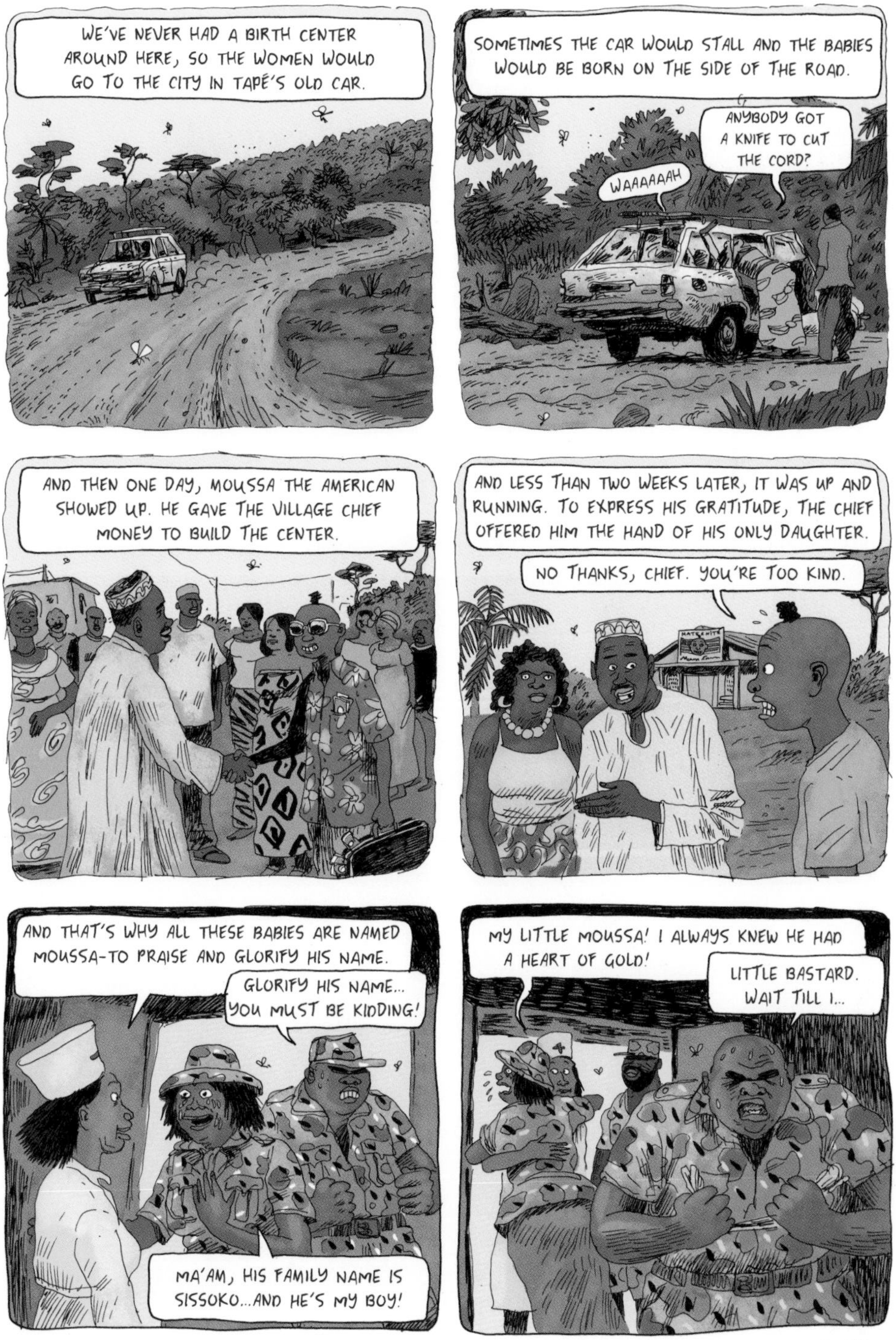
WE'VE NEVER HAD A BIRTH CENTER AROUND HERE, SO THE WOMEN WOULD GO TO THE CITY IN TAPÉ'S OLD CAR.
SOMETIMES THE CAR WOULD STALL AND THE BABIES WOULD BE BORN ON THE SIDE OF THE ROAD.
WAAAAAAH
ANYBODY GOT A KNIFE TO CUT THE CORD?
AND THEN ONE DAY, MOUSSA THE AMERICAN SHOWED UP. HE GAVE THE VILLAGE CHIEF MONEY TO BUILD THE CENTER.
AND LESS THAN TWO WEEKS LATER, IT WAS UP AND RUNNING. TO EXPRESS HIS GRATITUDE, THE CHIEF OFFERED HIM THE HAND OF HIS ONLY DAUGHTER.
NO THANKS, CHIEF. YOU'RE TOO KIND.
AND THAT'S WHY ALL THESE BABIES ARE NAMED MOUSSA-TO PRAISE AND GLORIFY HIS NAME.
GLORIFY HIS NAME... YOU MUST BE KIDDING!
MA'AM, HIS FAMILY NAME IS SISSOKO...AND HE'S MY BOY!
MY LITTLE MOUSSA! I ALWAYS KNEW HE HAD A HEART OF GOLD!
LITTLE BASTARD. WAIT TILL I...

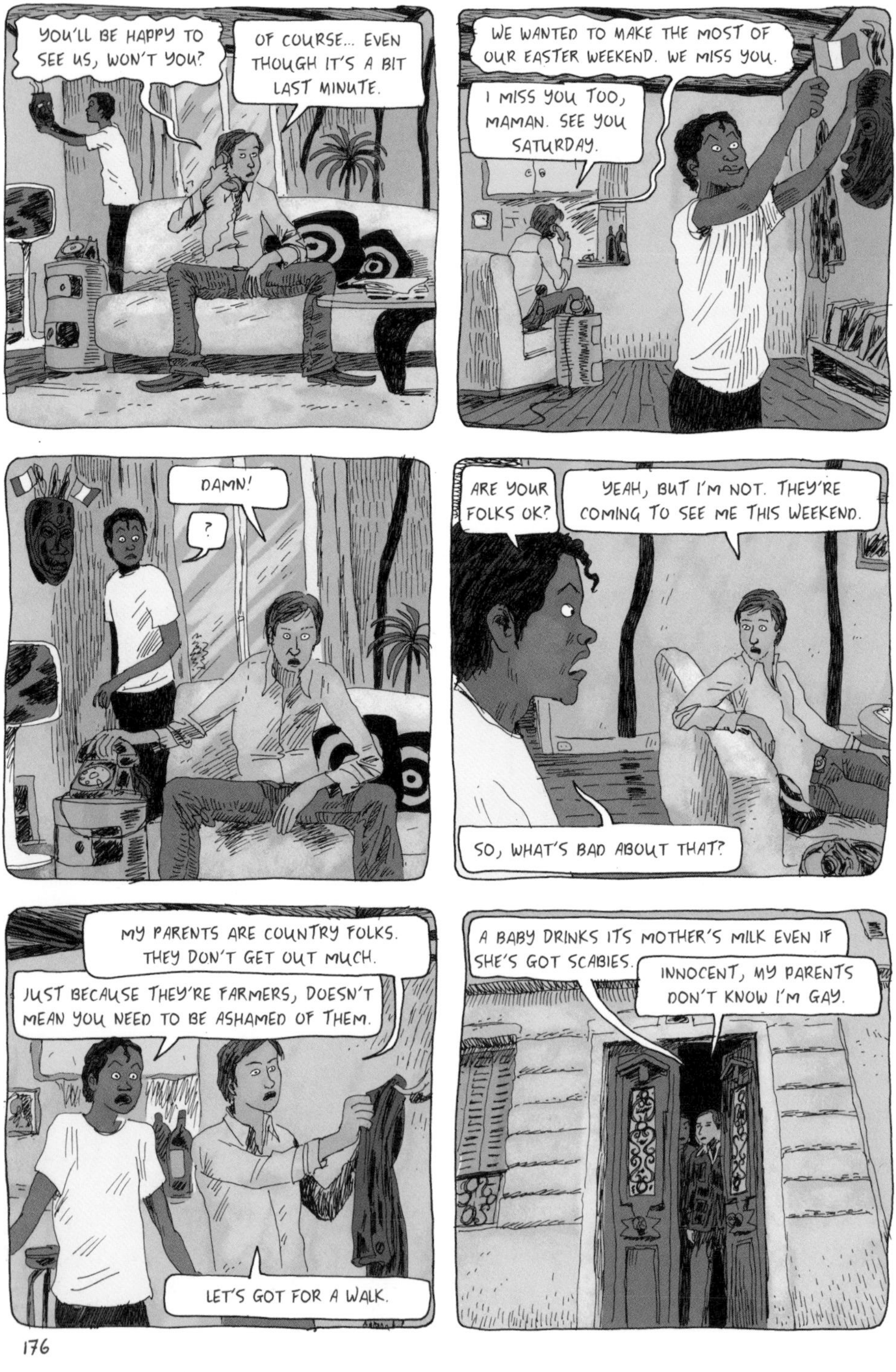
YOU'LL BE HAPPY TO SEE US, WON'T YOU?
OF COURSE... EVEN THOUGH IT'S A BIT LAST MINUTE.
WE WANTED TO MAKE THE MOST OF OUR EASTER WEEKEND. WE MISS YOU.
I MISS YOU TOO, MAMAN. SEE YOU SATURDAY.
DAMN!
?
ARE YOUR FOLKS OK?
YEAH, BUT I'M NOT. THEY'RE COMING TO SEE ME THIS WEEKEND.
SO, WHAT'S BAD ABOUT THAT?
MY PARENTS ARE COUNTRY FOLKS. THEY DON'T GET OUT MUCH.
JUST BECAUSE THEY'RE FARMERS, DOESN'T MEAN YOU NEED TO BE ASHAMED OF THEM.
LET'S GOT FOR A WALK.
A BABY DRINKS ITS MOTHER'S MILK EVEN IF SHE'S GOT SCABIES.
INNOCENT, MY PARENTS DON'T KNOW I'M GAY.

BUT I THOUGHT BEING GAY IS NOT A PROBLEM HERE.

INNO, IF MY PARENTS FIND OUT, THEY'LL NEVER TALK TO ME AGAIN.

YACÔ, SEB.

IT'S NOT THE END OF THE WORLD. I'M JUST TIRED OF LYING TO THEM.

SEB, PEOPLE NEED SUPPORT, OR ELSE THEY CAN GET MISTREATED.

THANKS. YOU NEED SOME HELP, TOO, WITH YOUR PAPERS. YOUR BOSS HAS GOT TO STOP PAYING YOU ILLEGALLY. BOTH OF YOU COULD GET INTO TROUBLE.

YEAH, IT'S BAD ENOUGH BEING BLACK, BUT BEING ON THE BLACK MARKET IS WORSE.

INNO, HE NEEDS TO GIVE YOU A WRITTEN JOB OFFER SO YOU CAN GO TO THE PREFECTURE AND APPLY FOR A RESIDENCE PERMIT.

IF I GO TO THE PREFECTURE, THEY'LL SEND ME HOME, Ô.

SAME IF YOU DON'T HAVE YOUR PAPERS! YOUR VISA EXPIRED AGES AGO, INNOCENT.

IT'S TOUGH FOR FOREIGNERS, DÊH.

YES, BUT THEY HAVE RIGHTS. IF YOUR BOSS LIKES YOU, HE'LL GIVE YOU A JOB OFFER.

SEB, HE'S GOT ME TO THANK FOR HIS PROFITS! I'LL GO SEE HIM RIGHT AWAY.

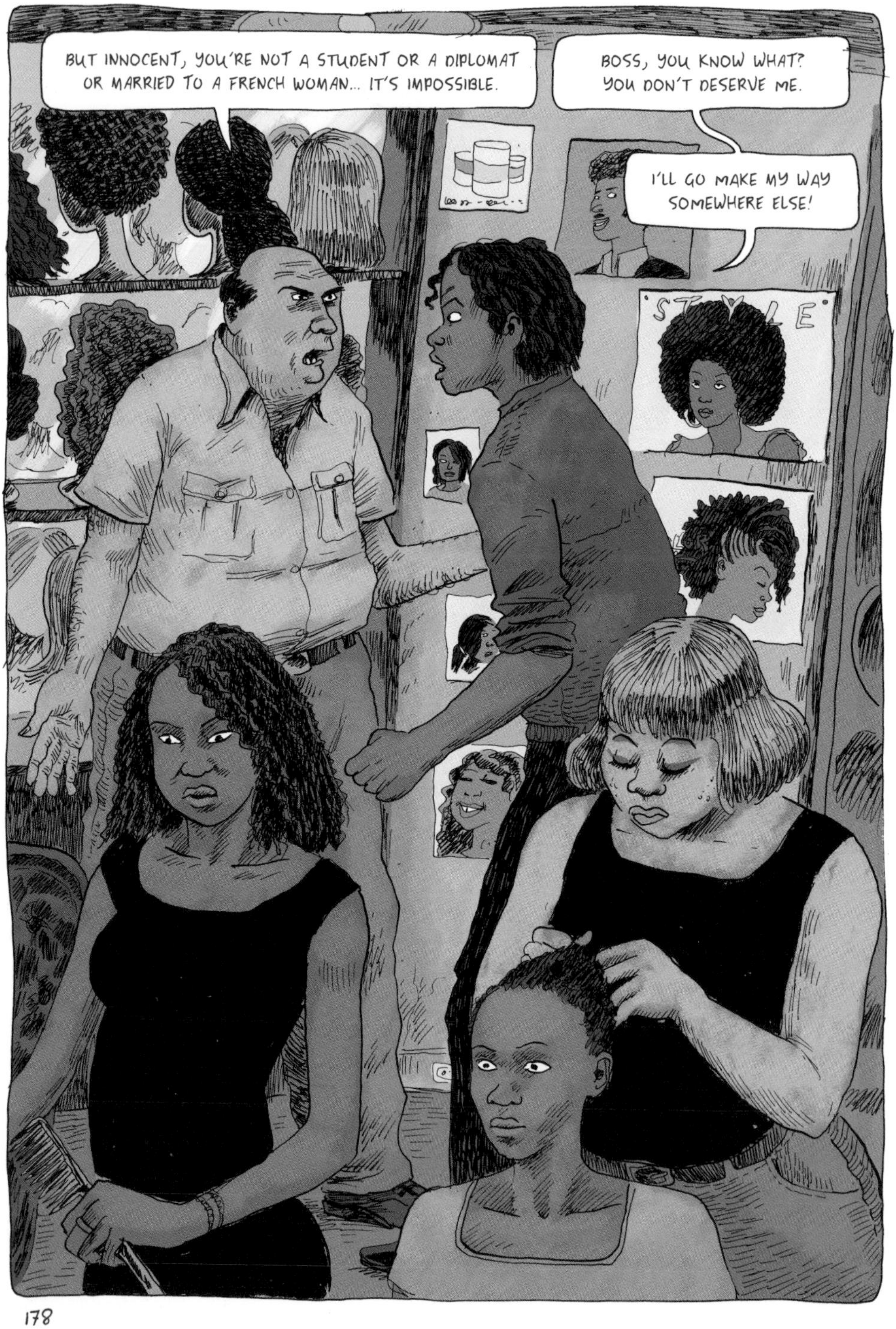
BUT INNOCENT, YOU'RE NOT A STUDENT OR A DIPLOMAT OR MARRIED TO A FRENCH WOMAN... IT'S IMPOSSIBLE.
BOSS, YOU KNOW WHAT? YOU DON'T DESERVE ME.
I'LL GO MAKE MY WAY SOMEWHERE ELSE!
STYLE

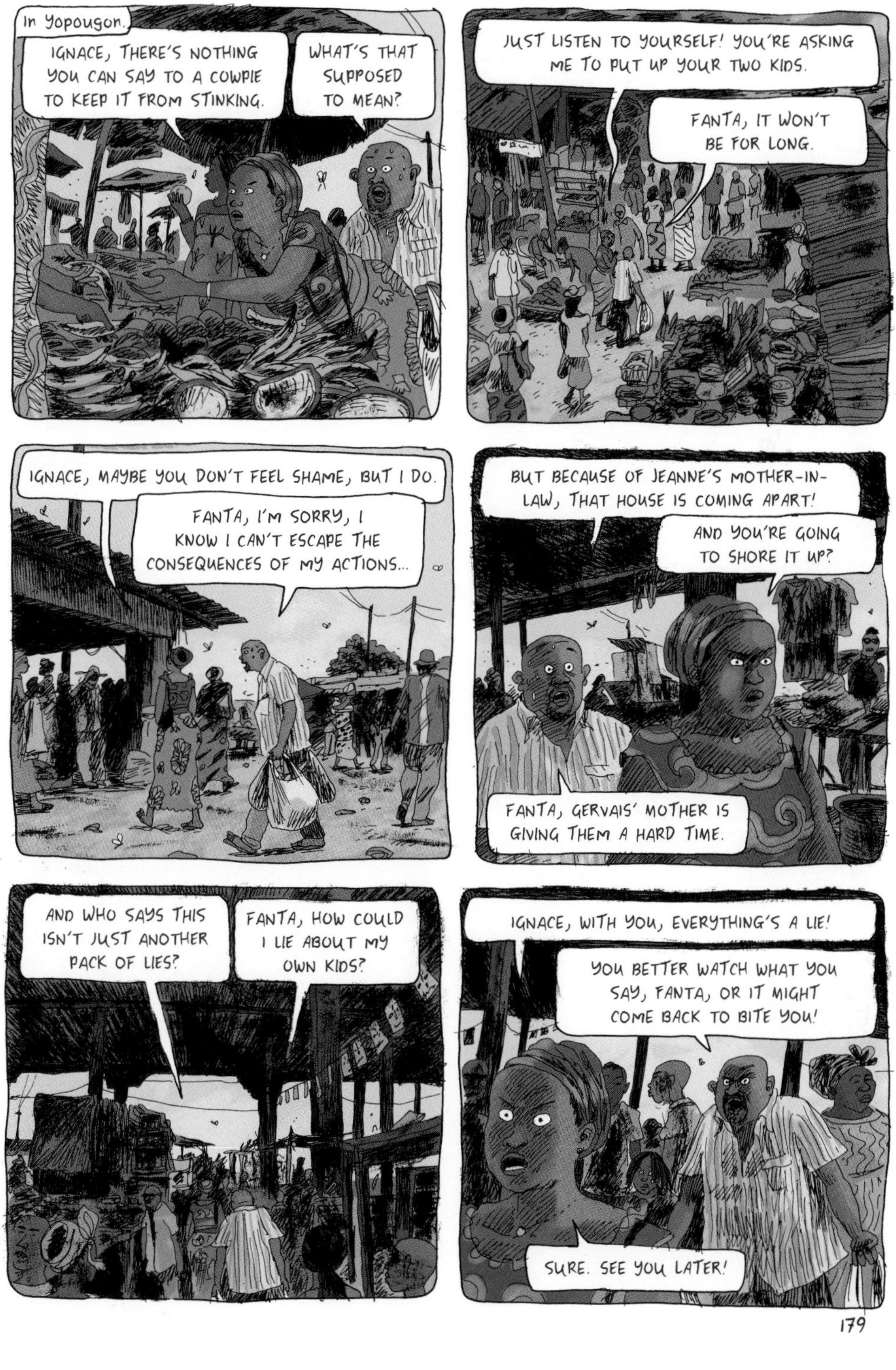
In Yopougon.
IGNACE, THERE'S NOTHING YOU CAN SAY TO A COWPIE TO KEEP IT FROM STINKING.
WHAT'S THAT SUPPOSED TO MEAN?
JUST LISTEN TO YOURSELF! YOU'RE ASKING ME TO PUT UP YOUR TWO KIDS.
FANTA, IT WON'T BE FOR LONG.
IGNACE, MAYBE YOU DON'T FEEL SHAME, BUT I DO.
FANTA, I'M SORRY, I KNOW I CAN'T ESCAPE THE CONSEQUENCES OF MY ACTIONS...
BUT BECAUSE OF JEANNE'S MOTHER-IN-LAW, THAT HOUSE IS COMING APART!
AND YOU'RE GOING TO SHORE IT UP?
FANTA, GERVAIS' MOTHER IS GIVING THEM A HARD TIME.
AND WHO SAYS THIS ISN'T JUST ANOTHER PACK OF LIES?
FANTA, HOW COULD I LIE ABOUT MY OWN KIDS?
IGNACE, WITH YOU, EVERYTHING'S A LIE!
YOU BETTER WATCH WHAT YOU SAY, FANTA, OR IT MIGHT COME BACK TO BITE YOU!
SURE. SEE YOU LATER!

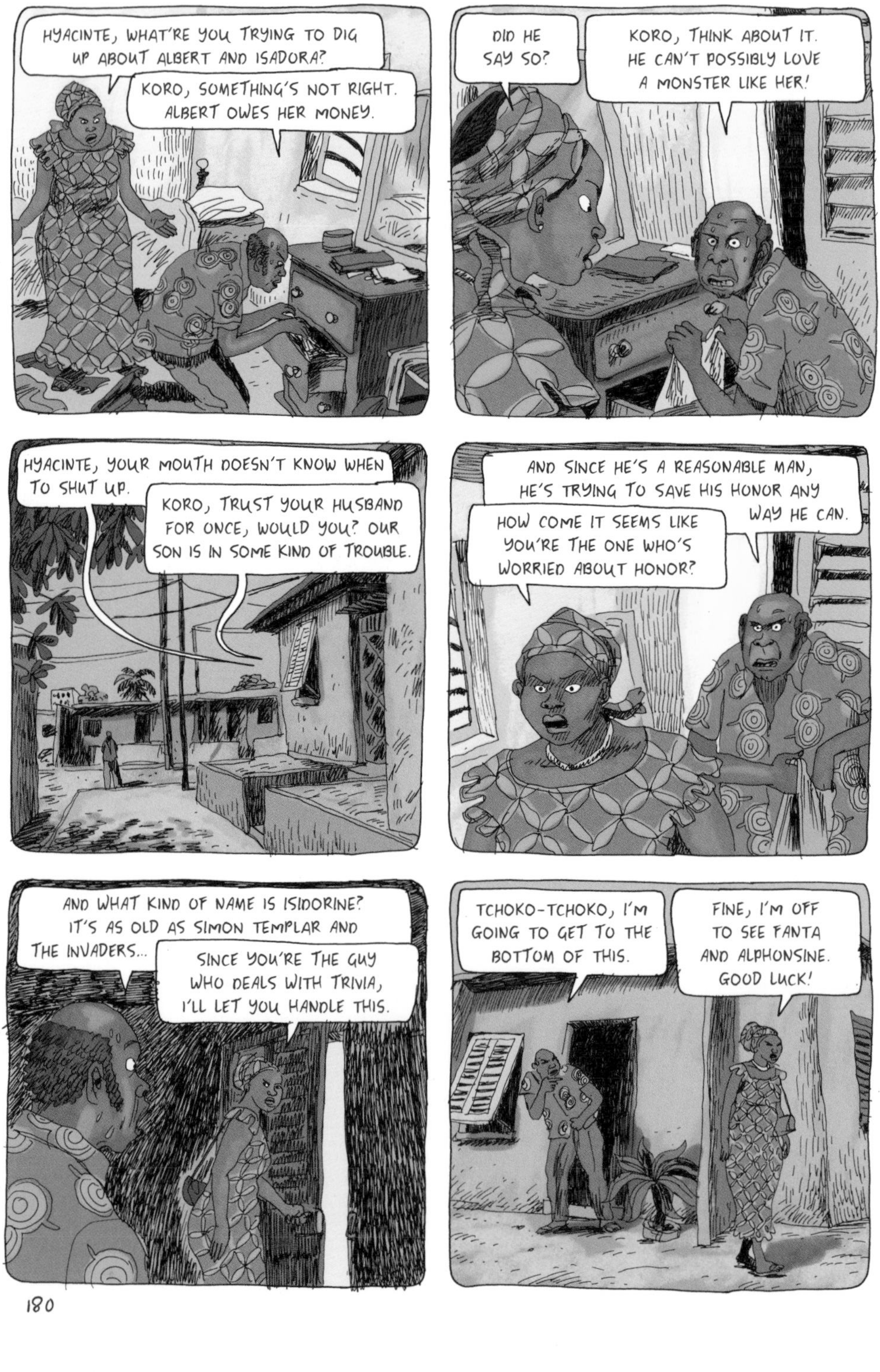
HYACINTE, WHAT'RE YOU TRYING TO DIG UP ABOUT ALBERT AND ISADORA?
KORO, SOMETHING'S NOT RIGHT. ALBERT OWES HER MONEY.
DID HE SAY SO?
KORO, THINK ABOUT IT. HE CAN'T POSSIBLY LOVE A MONSTER LIKE HER!
HYACINTE, YOUR MOUTH DOESN'T KNOW WHEN TO SHUT UP.
KORO, TRUST YOUR HUSBAND FOR ONCE, WOULD YOU? OUR SON IS IN SOME KIND OF TROUBLE.
AND SINCE HE'S A REASONABLE MAN, HE'S TRYING TO SAVE HIS HONOR ANY WAY HE CAN.
HOW COME IT SEEMS LIKE YOU'RE THE ONE WHO'S WORRIED ABOUT HONOR?
AND WHAT KIND OF NAME IS ISIDORINE? IT'S AS OLD AS SIMON TEMPLAR AND THE INVADERS...
SINCE YOU'RE THE GUY WHO DEALS WITH TRIVIA, I'LL LET YOU HANDLE THIS.
TCHOKO-TCHOKO, I'M GOING TO GET TO THE BOTTOM OF THIS.
FINE, I'M OFF TO SEE FANTA AND ALPHONSINE. GOOD LUCK!

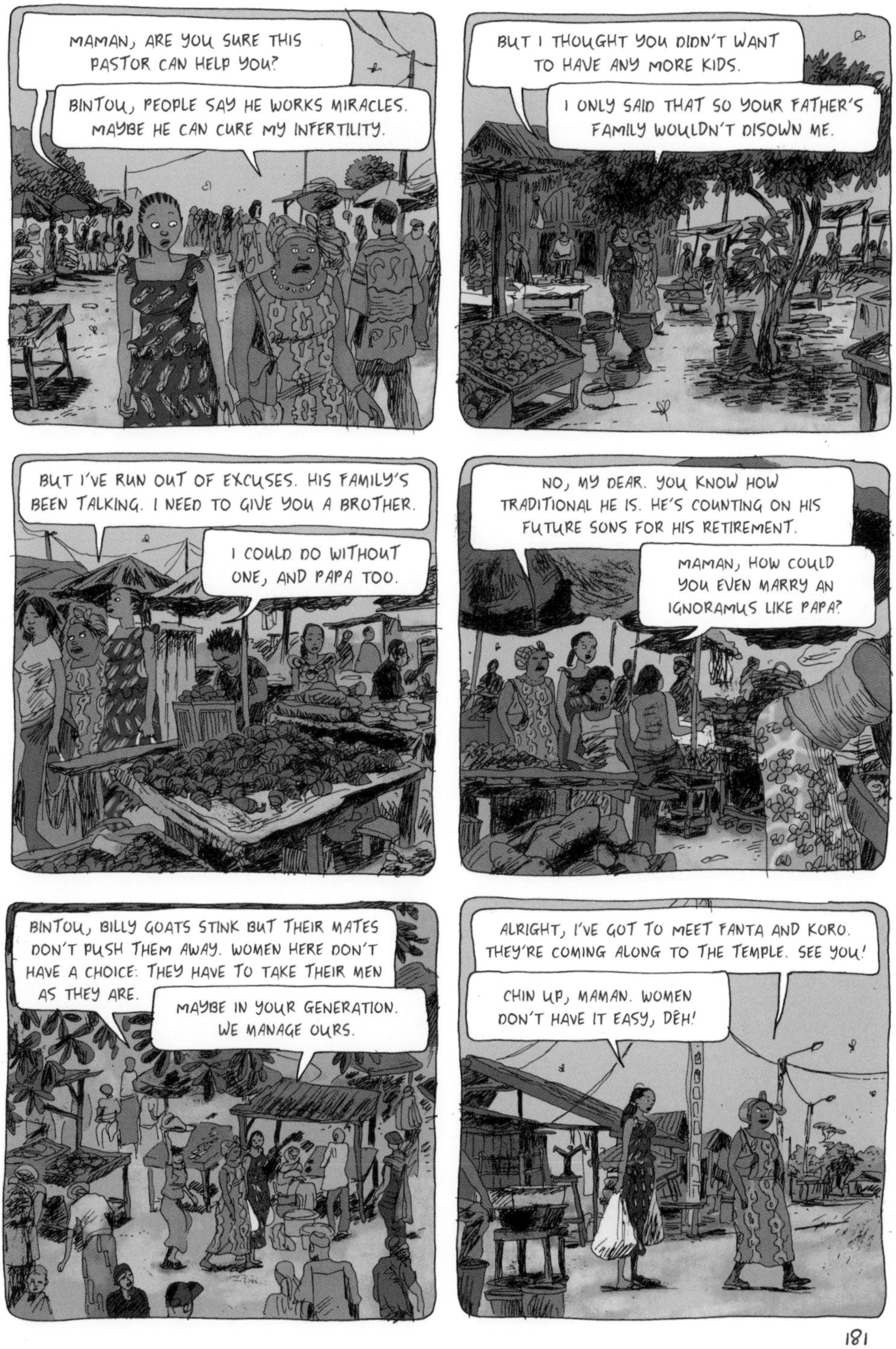
MAMAN, ARE YOU SURE THIS PASTOR CAN HELP YOU?
BINTOU, PEOPLE SAY HE WORKS MIRACLES. MAYBE HE CAN CURE MY INFERTILITY.
BUT I THOUGHT YOU DIDN'T WANT TO HAVE ANY MORE KIDS.
I ONLY SAID THAT SO YOUR FATHER'S FAMILY WOULDN'T DISOWN ME.
BUT I'VE RUN OUT OF EXCUSES. HIS FAMILY'S BEEN TALKING. I NEED TO GIVE YOU A BROTHER.
I COULD DO WITHOUT ONE, AND PAPA TOO.
NO, MY DEAR. YOU KNOW HOW TRADITIONAL HE IS. HE'S COUNTING ON HIS FUTURE SONS FOR HIS RETIREMENT.
MAMAN, HOW COULD YOU EVEN MARRY AN IGNORAMUS LIKE PAPA?
BINTOU, BILLY GOATS STINK BUT THEIR MATES DON'T PUSH THEM AWAY. WOMEN HERE DON'T HAVE A CHOICE: THEY HAVE TO TAKE THEIR MEN AS THEY ARE.
MAYBE IN YOUR GENERATION. WE MANAGE OURS.
ALRIGHT, I'VE GOT TO MEET FANTA AND KORO. THEY'RE COMING ALONG TO THE TEMPLE. SEE YOU!
CHIN UP, MAMAN. WOMEN DON'T HAVE IT EASY, DÊH!

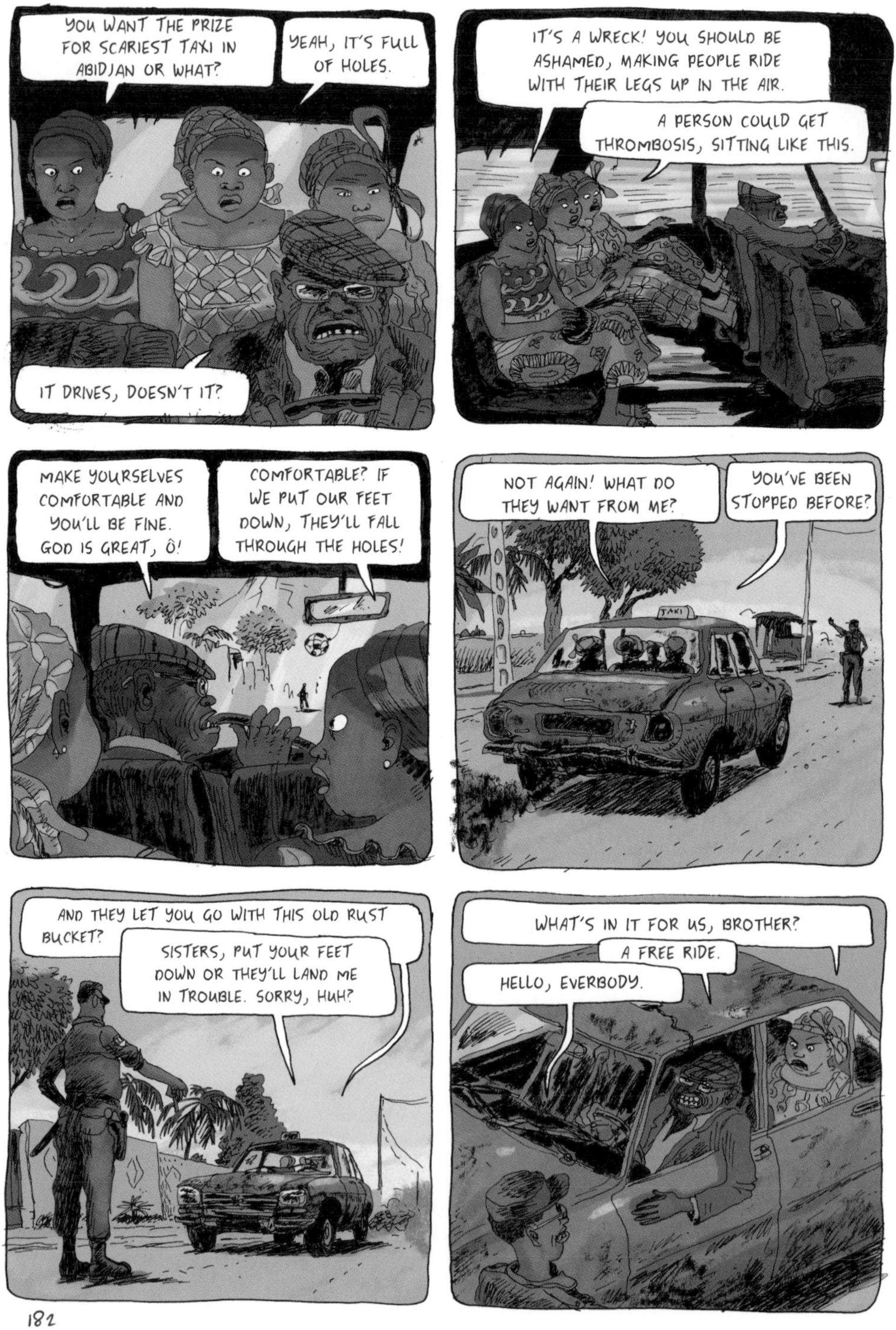
YOU WANT THE PRIZE FOR SCARIEST TAXI IN ABIDJAN OR WHAT?
YEAH, IT'S FULL OF HOLES.
IT DRIVES, DOESN'T IT?
IT'S A WRECK! YOU SHOULD BE ASHAMED, MAKING PEOPLE RIDE WITH THEIR LEGS UP IN THE AIR.
A PERSON COULD GET THROMBOSIS, SITTING LIKE THIS.
MAKE YOURSELVES COMFORTABLE AND YOU'LL BE FINE. GOD IS GREAT, Ô!
COMFORTABLE? IF WE PUT OUR FEET DOWN, THEY'LL FALL THROUGH THE HOLES!
NOT AGAIN! WHAT DO THEY WANT FROM ME?
YOU'VE BEEN STOPPED BEFORE?
TAXI
AND THEY LET YOU GO WITH THIS OLD RUST BUCKET?
SISTERS, PUT YOUR FEET DOWN OR THEY'LL LAND ME IN TROUBLE. SORRY, HUH?
WHAT'S IN IT FOR US, BROTHER?
A FREE RIDE.
HELLO, EVERBODY.

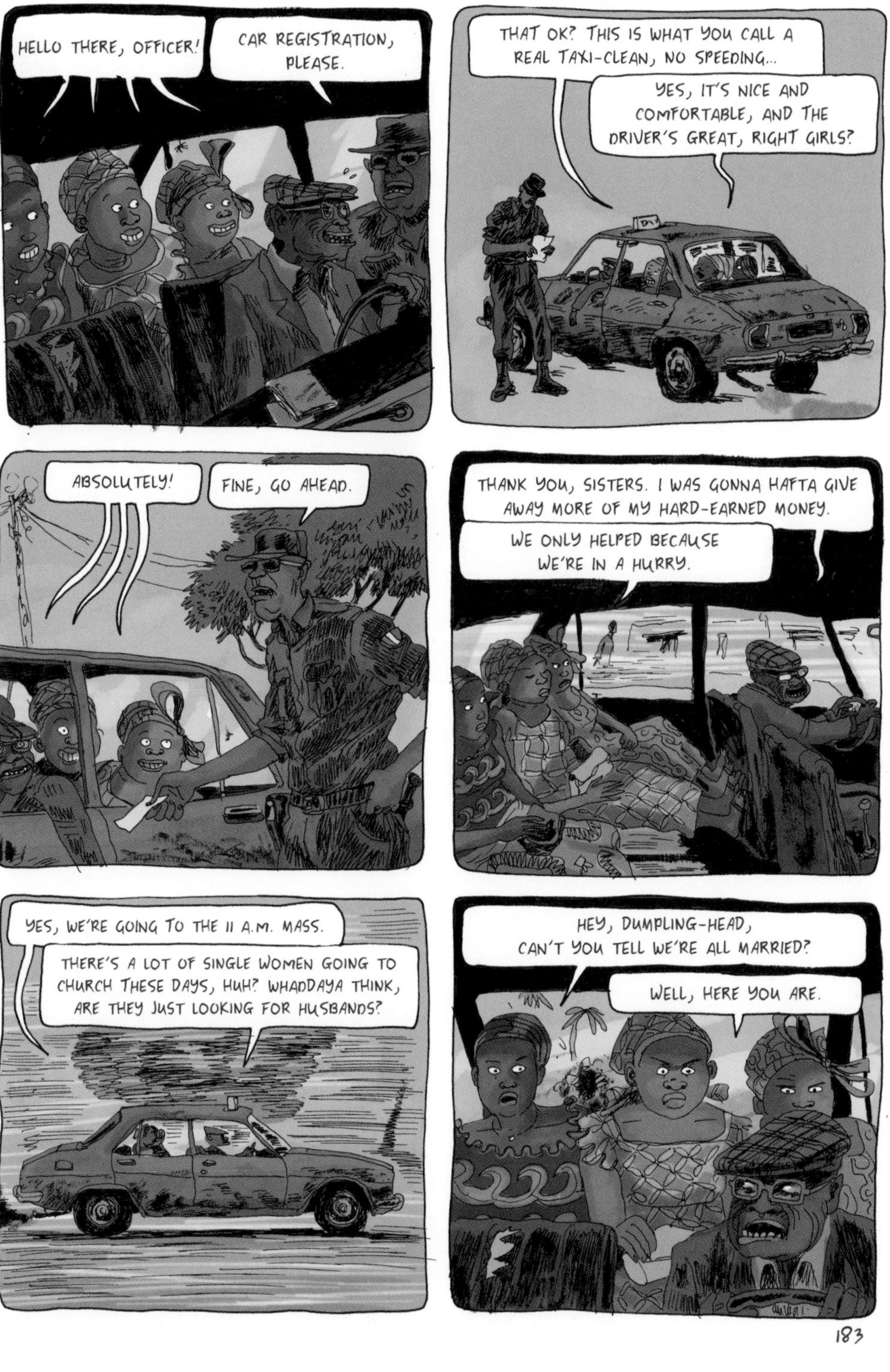
HELLO THERE, OFFICER!
CAR REGISTRATION, PLEASE.
THAT OK? THIS IS WHAT YOU CALL A REAL TAXI-CLEAN, NO SPEEDING...
YES, IT'S NICE AND COMFORTABLE, AND THE DRIVER'S GREAT, RIGHT GIRLS?
ABSOLUTELY!
FINE, GO AHEAD.
THANK YOU, SISTERS. I WAS GONNA HAFTA GIVE AWAY MORE OF MY HARD-EARNED MONEY.
WE ONLY HELPED BECAUSE WE'RE IN A HURRY.
YES, WE'RE GOING TO THE 11 A.M. MASS.
THERE'S A LOT OF SINGLE WOMEN GOING TO CHURCH THESE DAYS, HUH? WHADDAYA THINK, ARE THEY JUST LOOKING FOR HUSBANDS?
HEY, DUMPLING-HEAD, CAN'T YOU TELL WE'RE ALL MARRIED?
WELL, HERE YOU ARE.

AS TITINA WALKED THROUGH THE BRUSH ON HER WAY HOME ONE DAY, TWO THUGS SUDDENLY BLOCKED HER WAY.
Eglise réformée
de Dieu
ONE STARTED PULLING HIS PANTS DOWN TO RAPE HER WHEN TITINA LOOKED HIM STRAIGHT IN THE EYE AND SAID:
YOU SHAMELESS FORNICATOR! IN THE NAME OF JESUS, I REBUKE YOU!
INSTANTLY, THE MAN WAS LIFTED FROM THE GROUND AND THROWN INTO THE BUSHES.
AAAAAAH!
AND A STRANGE THING HAPPENED: HE BEGAN TO EAT THE LEAVES LIKE A GOAT.
SEEING THIS, HIS FRIEND GOT SCARED AND FLED. TITINA, THE LITTLE CHRISTIAN, SPOKE ONCE MORE AND SAID: "IN THE NAME OF JESUS, GET UP AND LEAVE!" WHICH HE DID, RUNNING AS FAST AS HE COULD.
BEHOLD THE POWER OF GOD. HALLELUJAH!
AMEN!

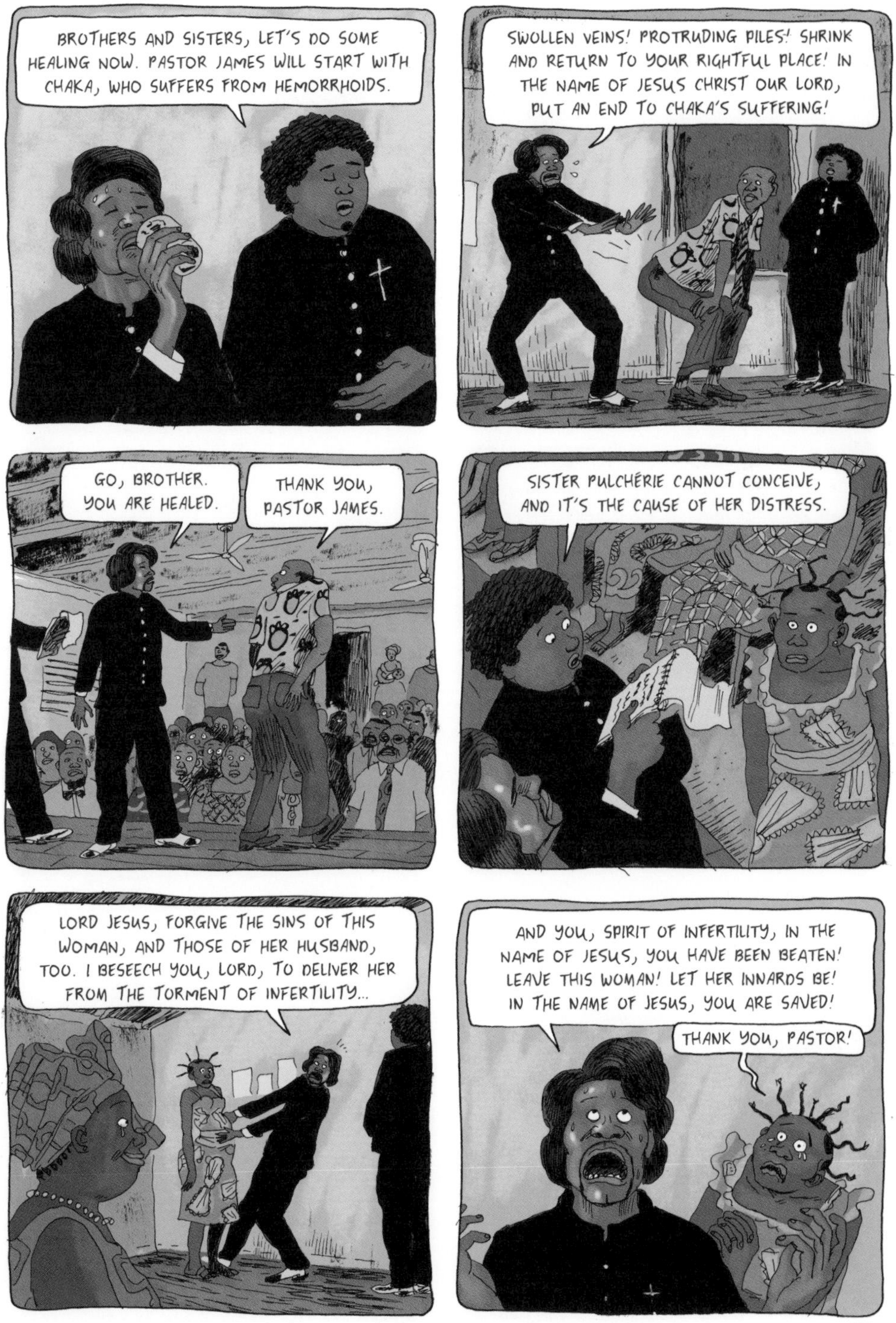
BROTHERS AND SISTERS, LET'S DO SOME HEALING NOW. PASTOR JAMES WILL START WITH CHAKA, WHO SUFFERS FROM HEMORRHOIDS.
SWOLLEN VEINS! PROTRUDING PILES! SHRINK AND RETURN TO YOUR RIGHTFUL PLACE! IN THE NAME OF JESUS CHRIST OUR LORD, PUT AN END TO CHAKA'S SUFFERING!
GO, BROTHER. YOU ARE HEALED.
THANK YOU, PASTOR JAMES.
SISTER PULCHÉRIE CANNOT CONCEIVE, AND IT'S THE CAUSE OF HER DISTRESS.
LORD JESUS, FORGIVE THE SINS OF THIS WOMAN, AND THOSE OF HER HUSBAND, TOO. I BESEECH YOU, LORD, TO DELIVER HER FROM THE TORMENT OF INFERTILITY...
AND YOU, SPIRIT OF INFERTILITY, IN THE NAME OF JESUS, YOU HAVE BEEN BEATEN! LEAVE THIS WOMAN! LET HER INNARDS BE! IN THE NAME OF JESUS, YOU ARE SAVED!
THANK YOU, PASTOR!

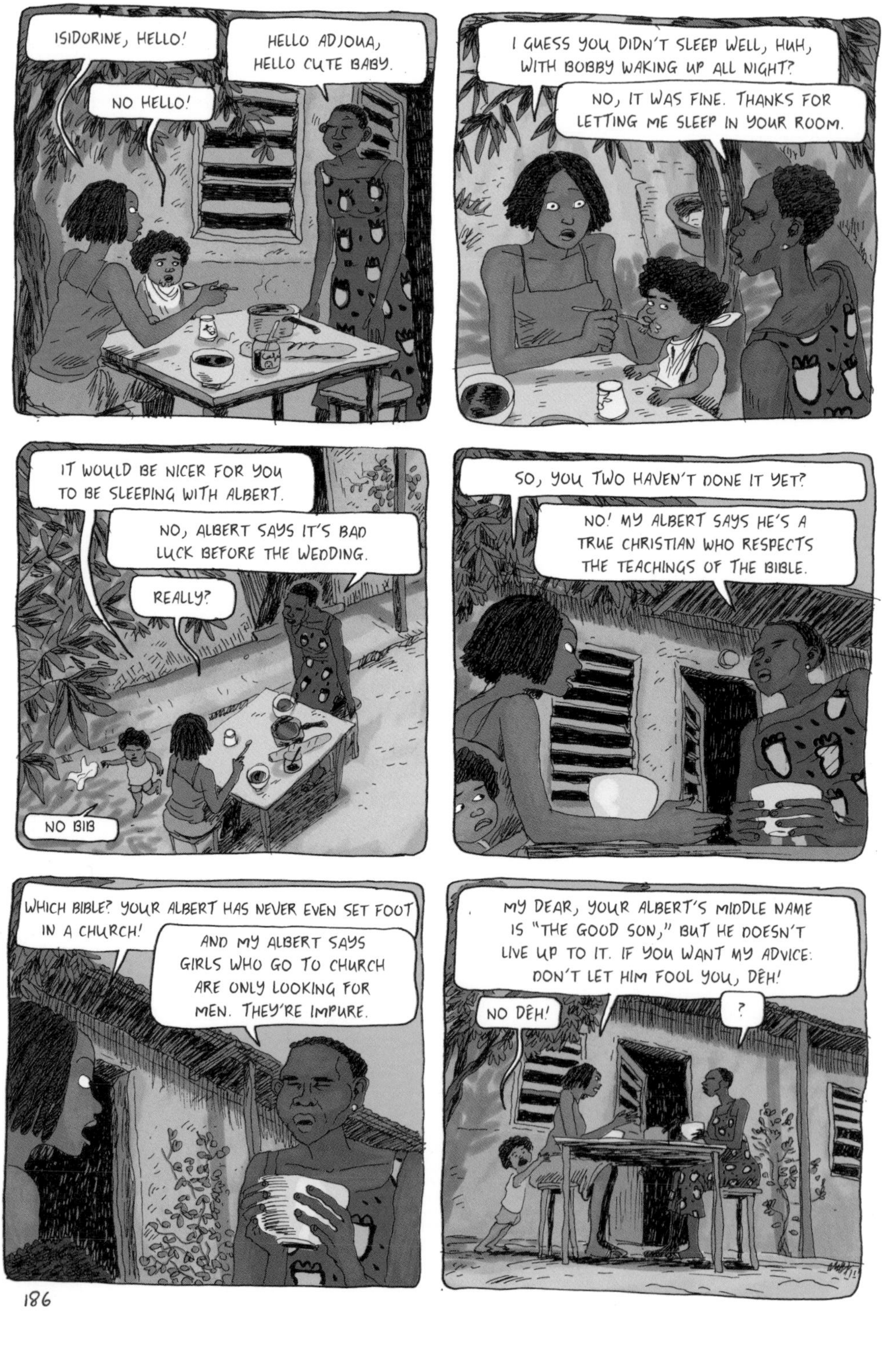

ISIDORINE, HELLO!
NO HELLO!
HELLO ADJOUA, HELLO CUTE BABY.
I GUESS YOU DIDN'T SLEEP WELL, HUH, WITH BOBBY WAKING UP ALL NIGHT?
NO, IT WAS FINE. THANKS FOR LETTING ME SLEEP IN YOUR ROOM.
IT WOULD BE NICER FOR YOU TO BE SLEEPING WITH ALBERT.
NO, ALBERT SAYS IT'S BAD LUCK BEFORE THE WEDDING.
REALLY?
NO BIB
SO, YOU TWO HAVEN'T DONE IT YET?
NO! MY ALBERT SAYS HE'S A TRUE CHRISTIAN WHO RESPECTS THE TEACHINGS OF THE BIBLE.
WHICH BIBLE? YOUR ALBERT HAS NEVER EVEN SET FOOT IN A CHURCH!
AND MY ALBERT SAYS GIRLS WHO GO TO CHURCH ARE ONLY LOOKING FOR MEN. THEY'RE IMPURE.
MY DEAR, YOUR ALBERT'S MIDDLE NAME IS "THE GOOD SON," BUT HE DOESN'T LIVE UP TO IT. IF YOU WANT MY ADVICE: DON'T LET HIM FOOL YOU, DÊH!
NO DÊH!
?

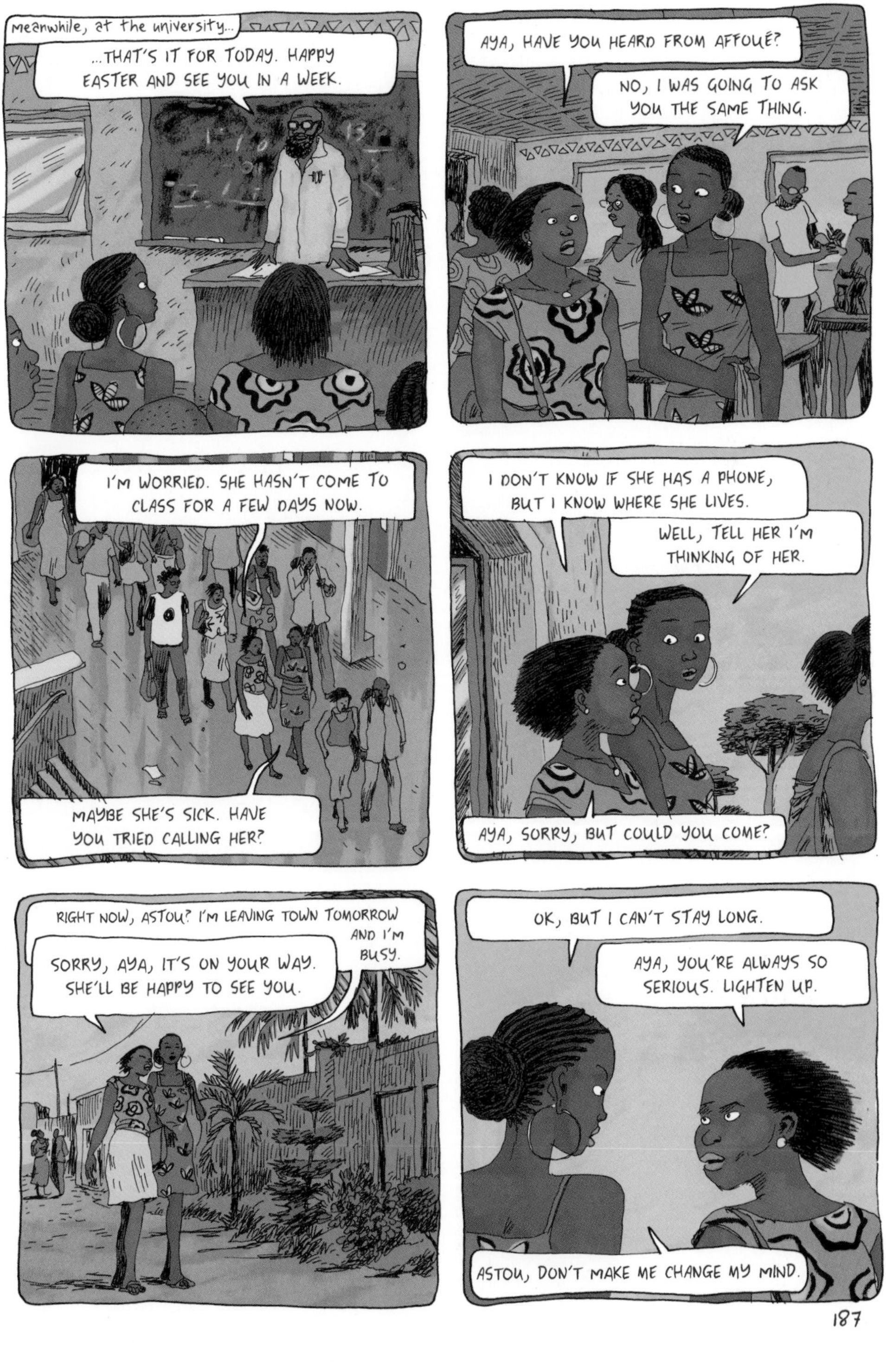

Meanwhile, at the university...
...THAT'S IT FOR TODAY. HAPPY EASTER AND SEE YOU IN A WEEK.
AYA, HAVE YOU HEARD FROM AFFOUÉ?
NO, I WAS GOING TO ASK YOU THE SAME THING.
I'M WORRIED. SHE HASN'T COME TO CLASS FOR A FEW DAYS NOW.
MAYBE SHE'S SICK. HAVE YOU TRIED CALLING HER?
I DON'T KNOW IF SHE HAS A PHONE, BUT I KNOW WHERE SHE LIVES.
WELL, TELL HER I'M THINKING OF HER.
AYA, SORRY, BUT COULD YOU COME?
RIGHT NOW, ASTOU? I'M LEAVING TOWN TOMORROW AND I'M BUSY.
SORRY, AYA, IT'S ON YOUR WAY. SHE'LL BE HAPPY TO SEE YOU.
OK, BUT I CAN'T STAY LONG.
AYA, YOU'RE ALWAYS SO SERIOUS. LIGHTEN UP.
ASTOU, DON'T MAKE ME CHANGE MY MIND.

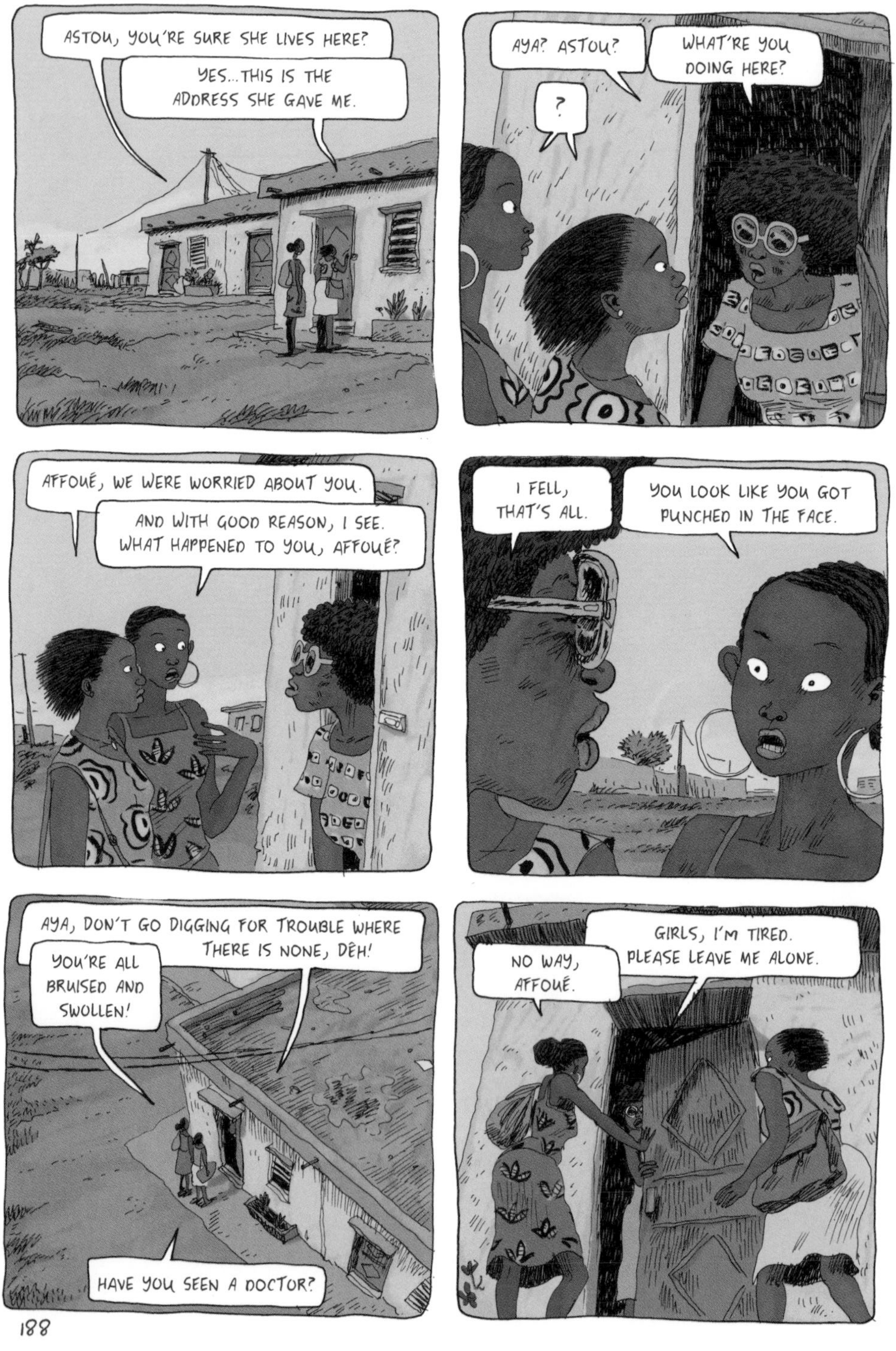
ASTOU, YOU'RE SURE SHE LIVES HERE?
YES... THIS IS THE ADDRESS SHE GAVE ME.
AYA? ASTOU?
WHAT'RE YOU DOING HERE?
?
AFFOUÉ, WE WERE WORRIED ABOUT YOU.
AND WITH GOOD REASON, I SEE. WHAT HAPPENED TO YOU, AFFOUÉ?
I FELL, THAT'S ALL.
YOU LOOK LIKE YOU GOT PUNCHED IN THE FACE.
AYA, DON'T GO DIGGING FOR TROUBLE WHERE THERE IS NONE, DÊH!
YOU'RE ALL BRUISED AND SWOLLEN!
HAVE YOU SEEN A DOCTOR?
NO WAY, AFFOUÉ.
GIRLS, I'M TIRED. PLEASE LEAVE ME ALONE.

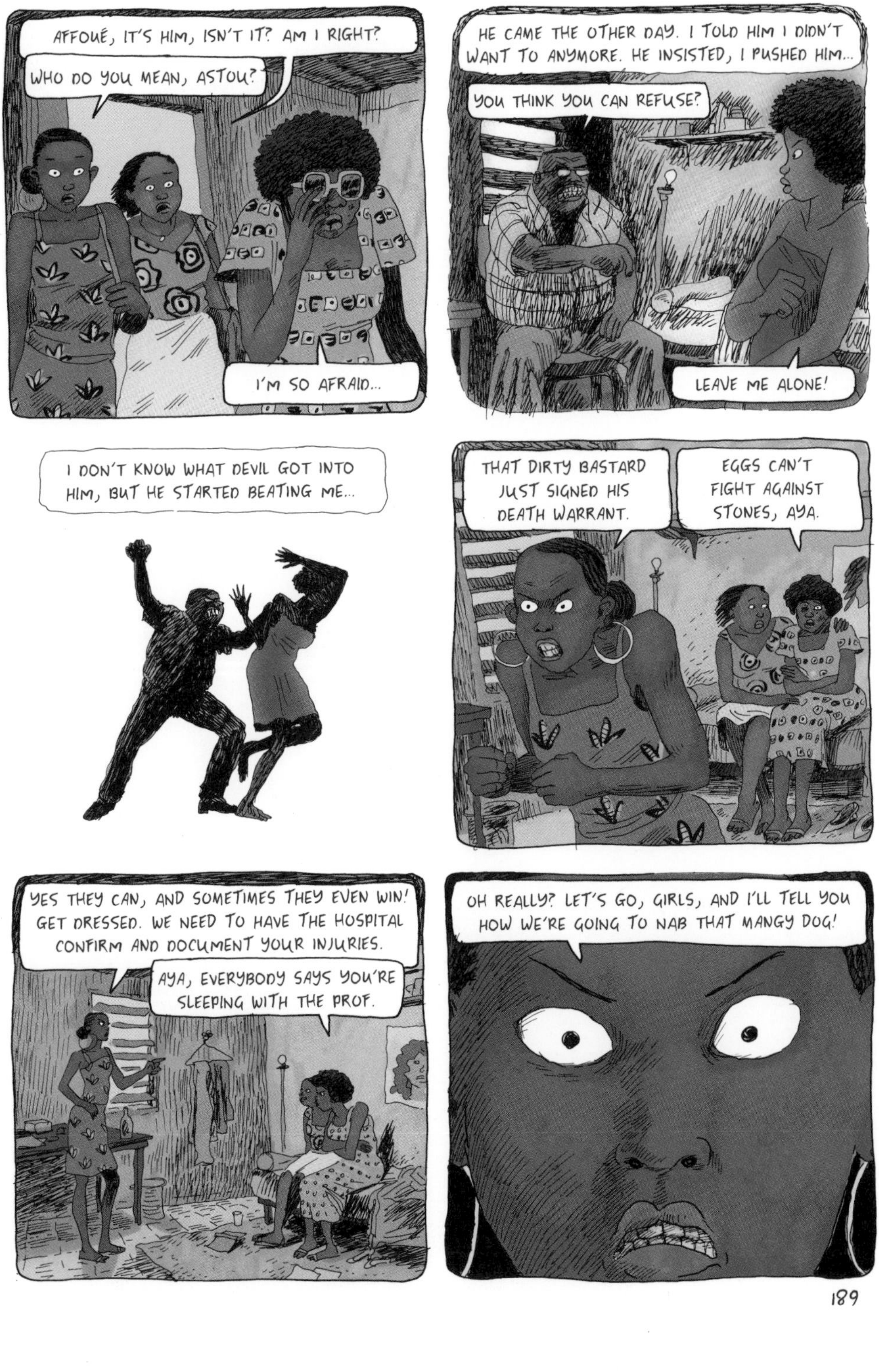
AFFOUÉ, IT'S HIM, ISN'T IT? AM I RIGHT?
WHO DO YOU MEAN, ASTOU?
I'M SO AFRAID...
HE CAME THE OTHER DAY. I TOLD HIM I DIDN'T WANT TO ANYMORE. HE INSISTED, I PUSHED HIM...
YOU THINK YOU CAN REFUSE?
LEAVE ME ALONE!
I DON'T KNOW WHAT DEVIL GOT INTO HIM, BUT HE STARTED BEATING ME...
THAT DIRTY BASTARD JUST SIGNED HIS DEATH WARRANT.
EGGS CAN'T FIGHT AGAINST STONES, AYA.
YES THEY CAN, AND SOMETIMES THEY EVEN WIN! GET DRESSED. WE NEED TO HAVE THE HOSPITAL CONFIRM AND DOCUMENT YOUR INJURIES.
AYA, EVERYBODY SAYS YOU'RE SLEEPING WITH THE PROF.
OH REALLY? LET'S GO, GIRLS, AND I'LL TELL YOU HOW WE'RE GOING TO NAB THAT MANGY DOG!

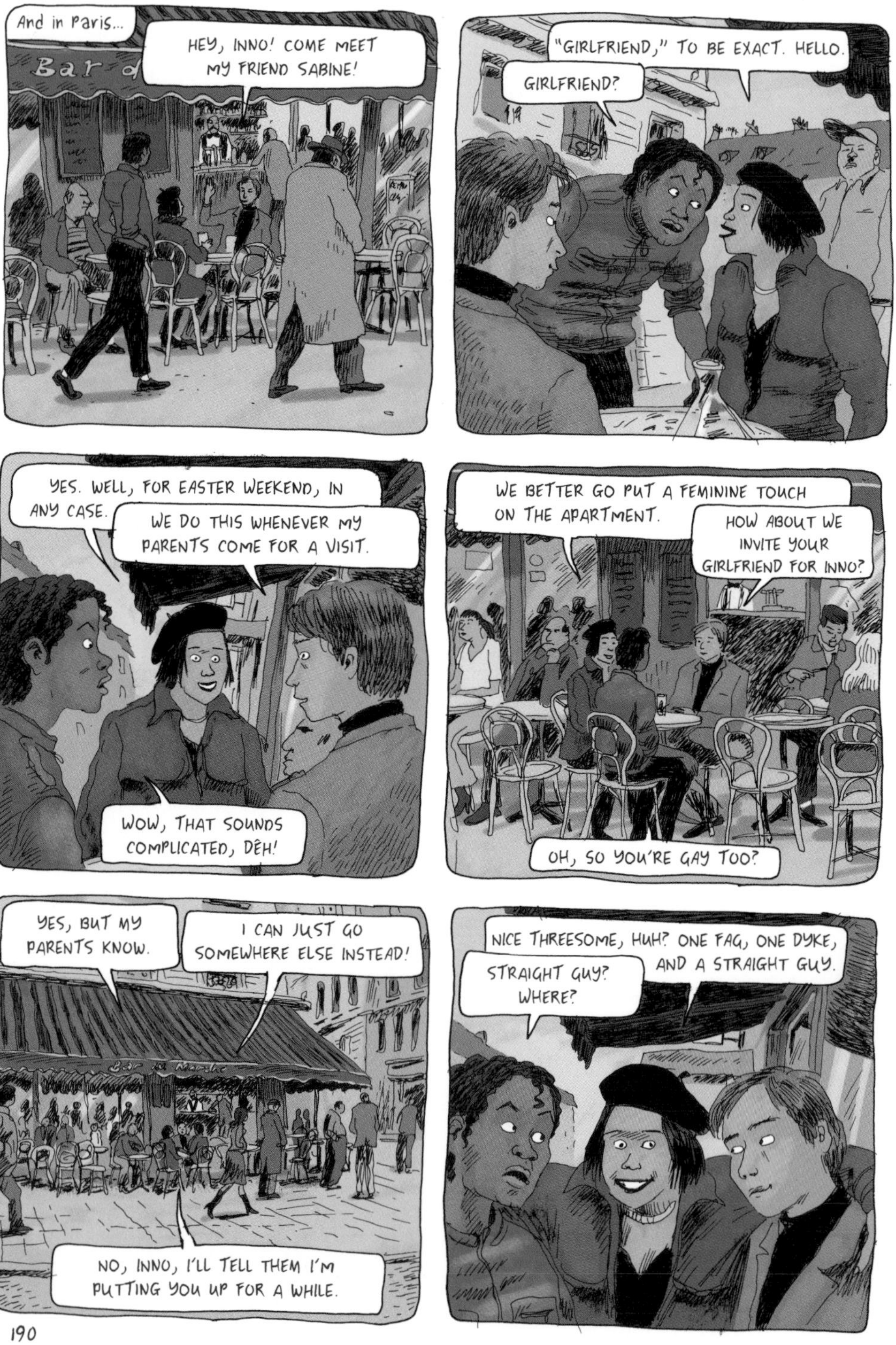
And in Paris...
HEY, INNO! COME MEET MY FRIEND SABINE!
GIRLFRIEND?
"GIRLFRIEND," TO BE EXACT. HELLO.
YES. WELL, FOR EASTER WEEKEND, IN ANY CASE.
WE DO THIS WHENEVER MY PARENTS COME FOR A VISIT.
WOW, THAT SOUNDS COMPLICATED, DÊH!
WE BETTER GO PUT A FEMININE TOUCH ON THE APARTMENT.
HOW ABOUT WE INVITE YOUR GIRLFRIEND FOR INNO?
OH, SO YOU'RE GAY TOO?
YES, BUT MY PARENTS KNOW.
I CAN JUST GO SOMEWHERE ELSE INSTEAD!
NO, INNO, I'LL TELL THEM I'M PUTTING YOU UP FOR A WHILE.
NICE THREESOME, HUH? ONE FAG, ONE DYKE, AND A STRAIGHT GUY.
STRAIGHT GUY? WHERE?

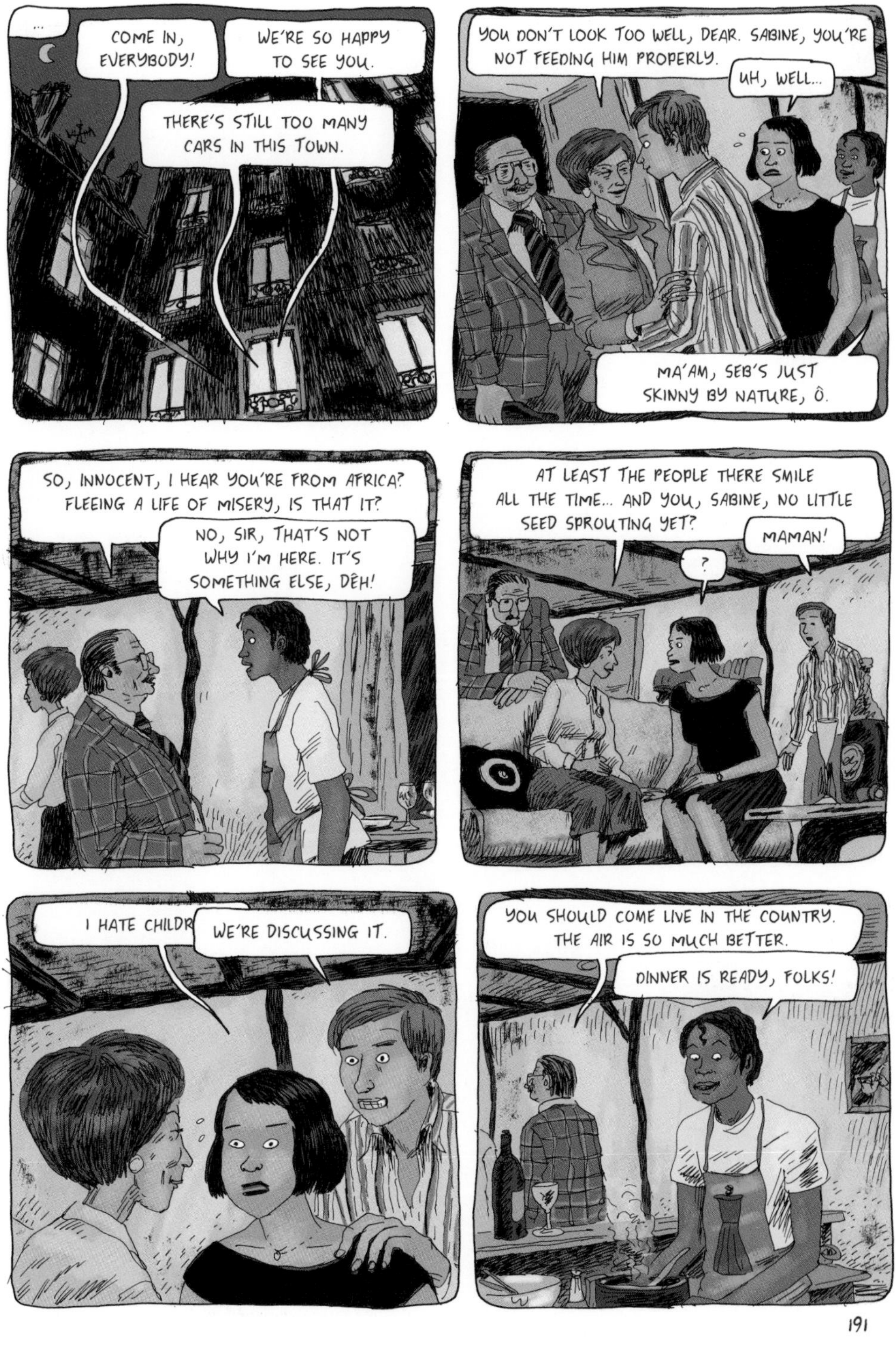
...
COME IN, EVERYBODY!
WE'RE SO HAPPY TO SEE YOU.
THERE'S STILL TOO MANY CARS IN THIS TOWN.
YOU DON'T LOOK TOO WELL, DEAR. SABINE, YOU'RE NOT FEEDING HIM PROPERLY.
UH, WELL...
MA'AM, SEB'S JUST SKINNY BY NATURE, Ô.
SO, INNOCENT, I HEAR YOU'RE FROM AFRICA? FLEEING A LIFE OF MISERY, IS THAT IT?
NO, SIR, THAT'S NOT WHY I'M HERE. IT'S SOMETHING ELSE, DÊH!
AT LEAST THE PEOPLE THERE SMILE ALL THE TIME... AND YOU, SABINE, NO LITTLE SEED SPROUTING YET?
?
MAMAN!
I HATE CHILDR
WE'RE DISCUSSING IT.
YOU SHOULD COME LIVE IN THE COUNTRY. THE AIR IS SO MUCH BETTER.
DINNER IS READY, FOLKS!

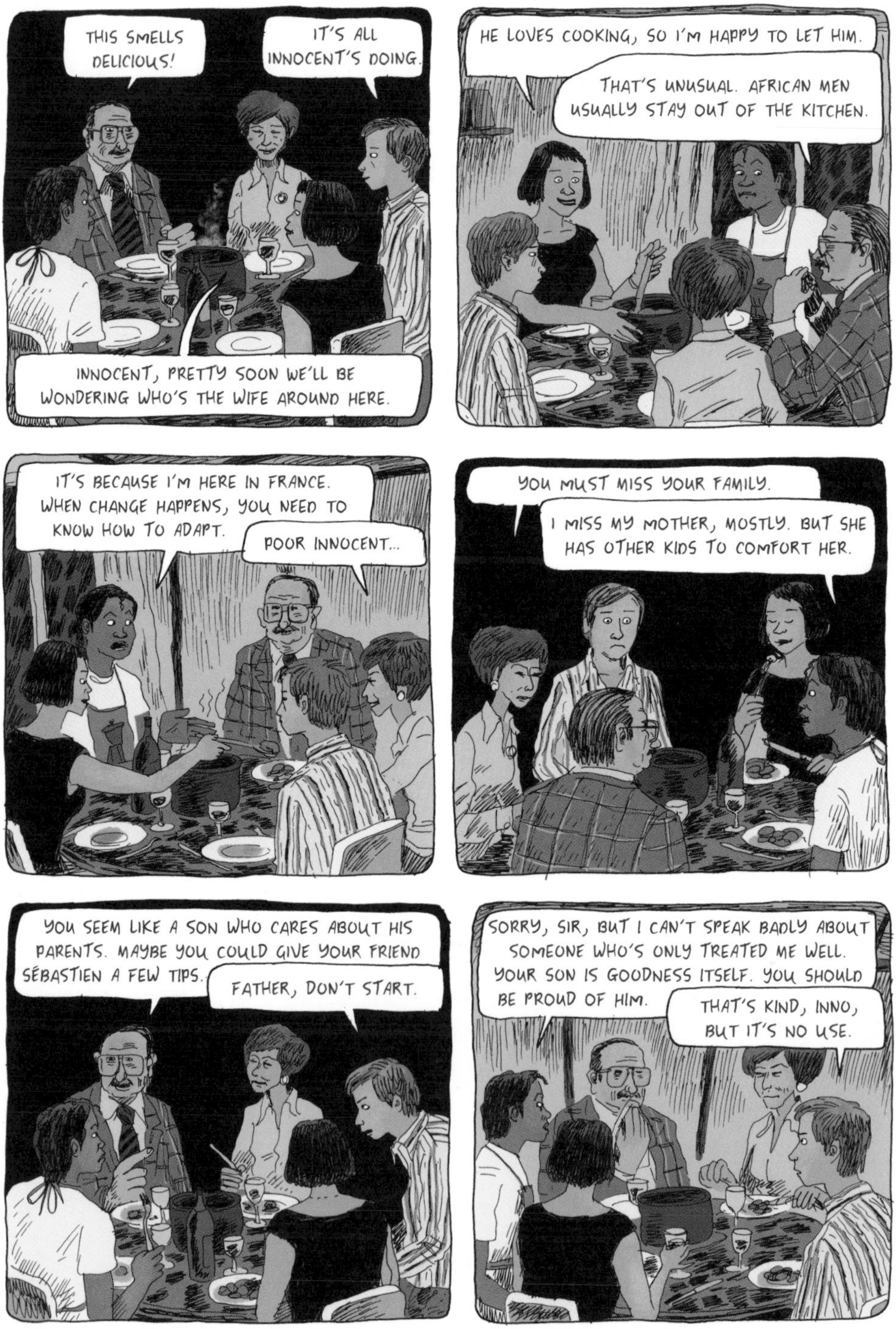
THIS SMELLS DELICIOUS!
IT'S ALL INNOCENT'S DOING.
INNOCENT, PRETTY SOON WE'LL BE WONDERING WHO'S THE WIFE AROUND HERE.
HE LOVES COOKING, SO I'M HAPPY TO LET HIM.
THAT'S UNUSUAL. AFRICAN MEN USUALLY STAY OUT OF THE KITCHEN.
IT'S BECAUSE I'M HERE IN FRANCE. WHEN CHANGE HAPPENS, YOU NEED TO KNOW HOW TO ADAPT.
POOR INNOCENT...
YOU MUST MISS YOUR FAMILY.
I MISS MY MOTHER, MOSTLY. BUT SHE HAS OTHER KIDS TO COMFORT HER.
YOU SEEM LIKE A SON WHO CARES ABOUT HIS PARENTS. MAYBE YOU COULD GIVE YOUR FRIEND SÉBASTIEN A FEW TIPS.
FATHER, DON'T START.
SORRY, SIR, BUT I CAN'T SPEAK BADLY ABOUT SOMEONE WHO'S ONLY TREATED ME WELL. YOUR SON IS GOODNESS ITSELF. YOU SHOULD BE PROUD OF HIM.
THAT'S KIND, INNO, BUT IT'S NO USE.

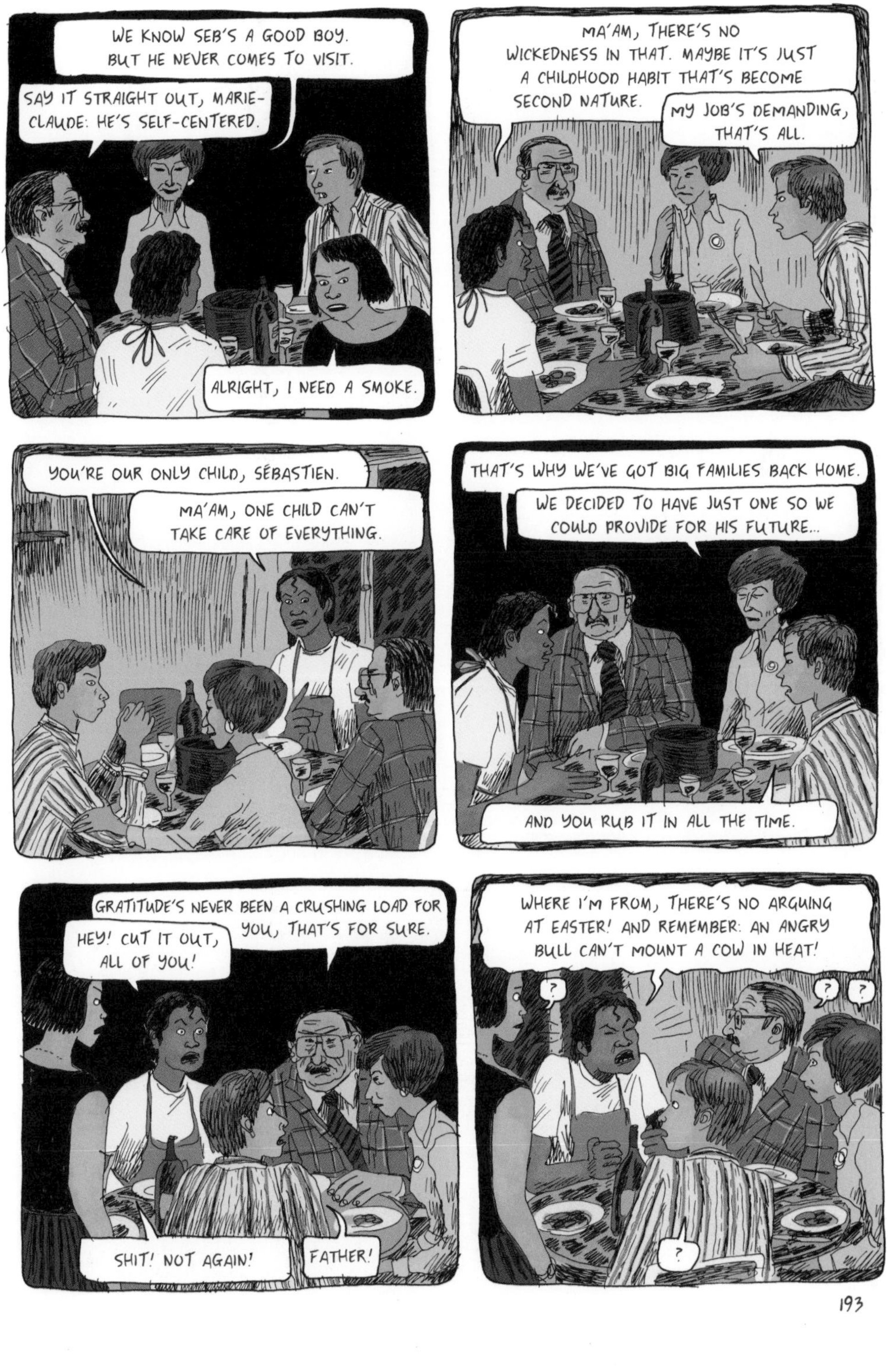
WE KNOW SEB'S A GOOD BOY. BUT HE NEVER COMES TO VISIT.
SAY IT STRAIGHT OUT, MARIE-CLAUDE: HE'S SELF-CENTERED.
ALRIGHT, I NEED A SMOKE.
MA'AM, THERE'S NO WICKEDNESS IN THAT. MAYBE IT'S JUST A CHILDHOOD HABIT THAT'S BECOME SECOND NATURE.
MY JOB'S DEMANDING, THAT'S ALL.
YOU'RE OUR ONLY CHILD, SÉBASTIEN.
MA'AM, ONE CHILD CAN'T TAKE CARE OF EVERYTHING.
THAT'S WHY WE'VE GOT BIG FAMILIES BACK HOME.
WE DECIDED TO HAVE JUST ONE SO WE COULD PROVIDE FOR HIS FUTURE...
AND YOU RUB IT IN ALL THE TIME.
GRATITUDE'S NEVER BEEN A CRUSHING LOAD FOR YOU, THAT'S FOR SURE.
HEY! CUT IT OUT, ALL OF YOU!
SHIT! NOT AGAIN!
FATHER!
WHERE I'M FROM, THERE'S NO ARGUING AT EASTER! AND REMEMBER: AN ANGRY BULL CAN'T MOUNT A COW IN HEAT!
?
? ?
?

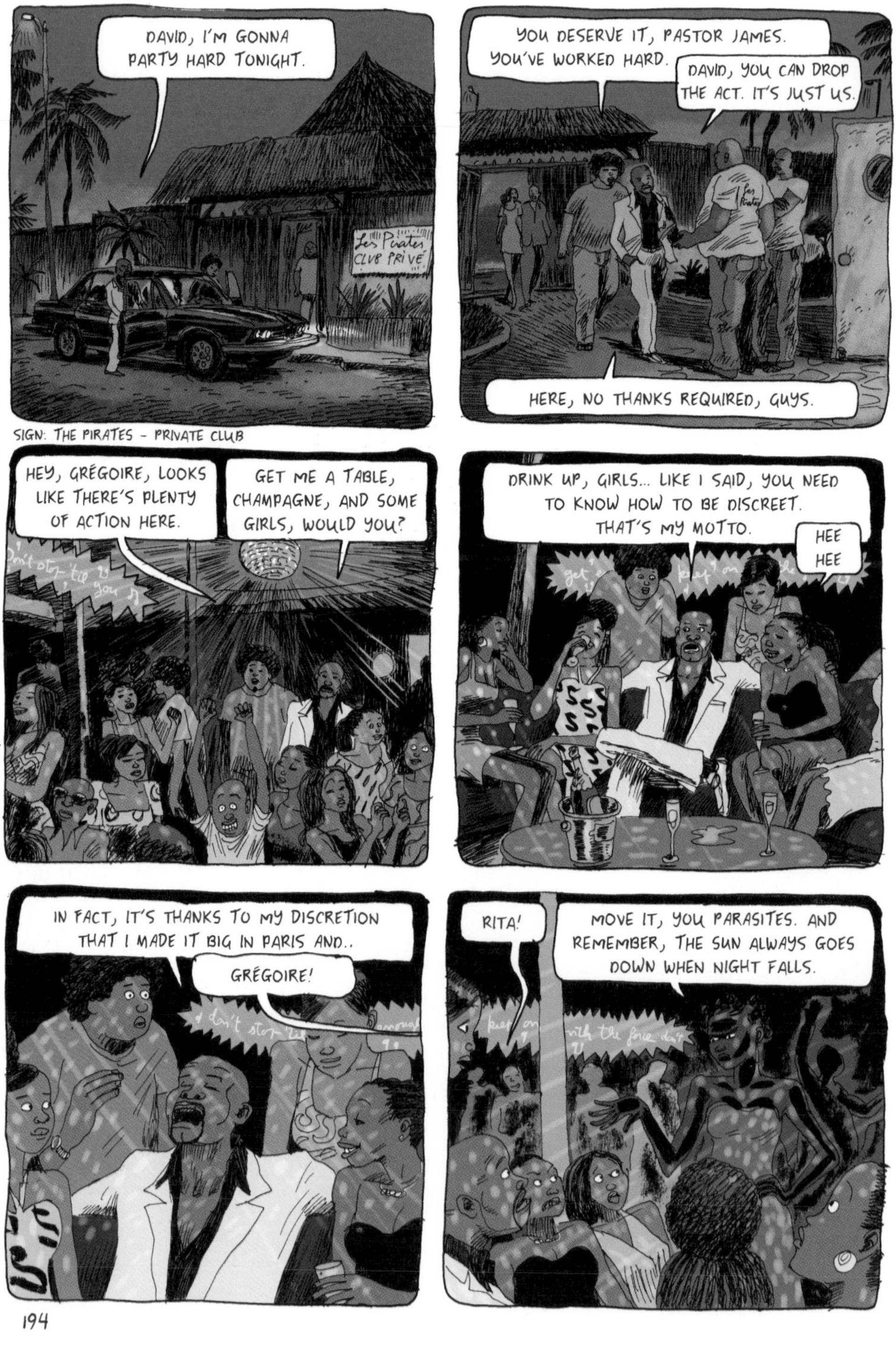
DAVID, I'M GONNA PARTY HARD TONIGHT.
Les Pirates CLUB PRIVÉ
SIGN: THE PIRATES - PRIVATE CLUB
YOU DESERVE IT, PASTOR JAMES. YOU'VE WORKED HARD.
DAVID, YOU CAN DROP THE ACT. IT'S JUST US.
HERE, NO THANKS REQUIRED, GUYS.
HEY, GRÉGOIRE, LOOKS LIKE THERE'S PLENTY OF ACTION HERE.
GET ME A TABLE, CHAMPAGNE, AND SOME GIRLS, WOULD YOU?
DRINK UP, GIRLS... LIKE I SAID, YOU NEED TO KNOW HOW TO BE DISCREET. THAT'S MY MOTTO.
HEE HEE
IN FACT, IT'S THANKS TO MY DISCRETION THAT I MADE IT BIG IN PARIS AND..
GRÉGOIRE!
RITA!
MOVE IT, YOU PARASITES. AND REMEMBER, THE SUN ALWAYS GOES DOWN WHEN NIGHT FALLS.

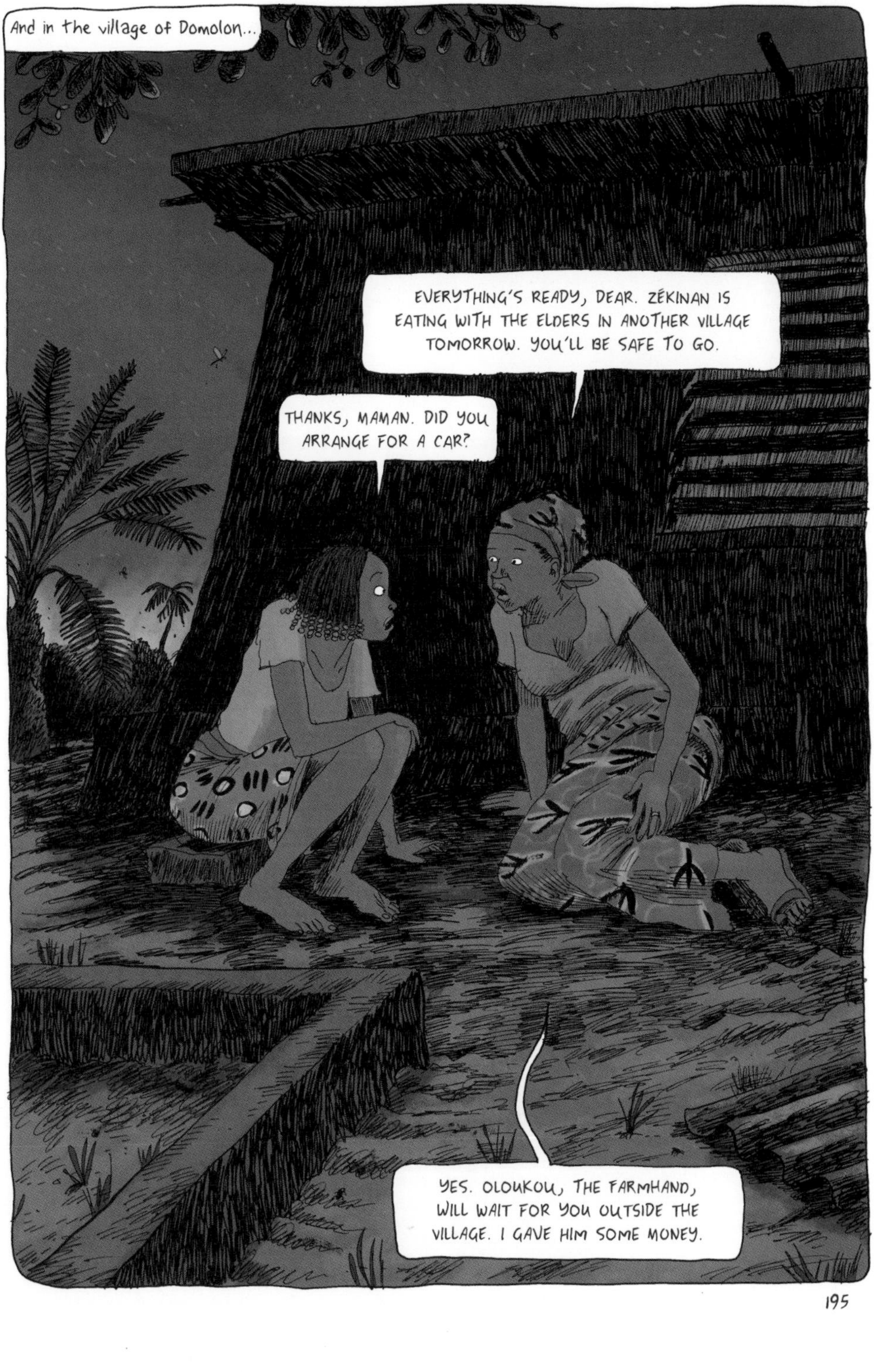

And in the village of Domolon...
EVERYTHING'S READY, DEAR. ZÉKINAN IS EATING WITH THE ELDERS IN ANOTHER VILLAGE TOMORROW. YOU'LL BE SAFE TO GO.
THANKS, MAMAN. DID YOU ARRANGE FOR A CAR?
YES. OLOUKOU, THE FARMHAND, WILL WAIT FOR YOU OUTSIDE THE VILLAGE. I GAVE HIM SOME MONEY.

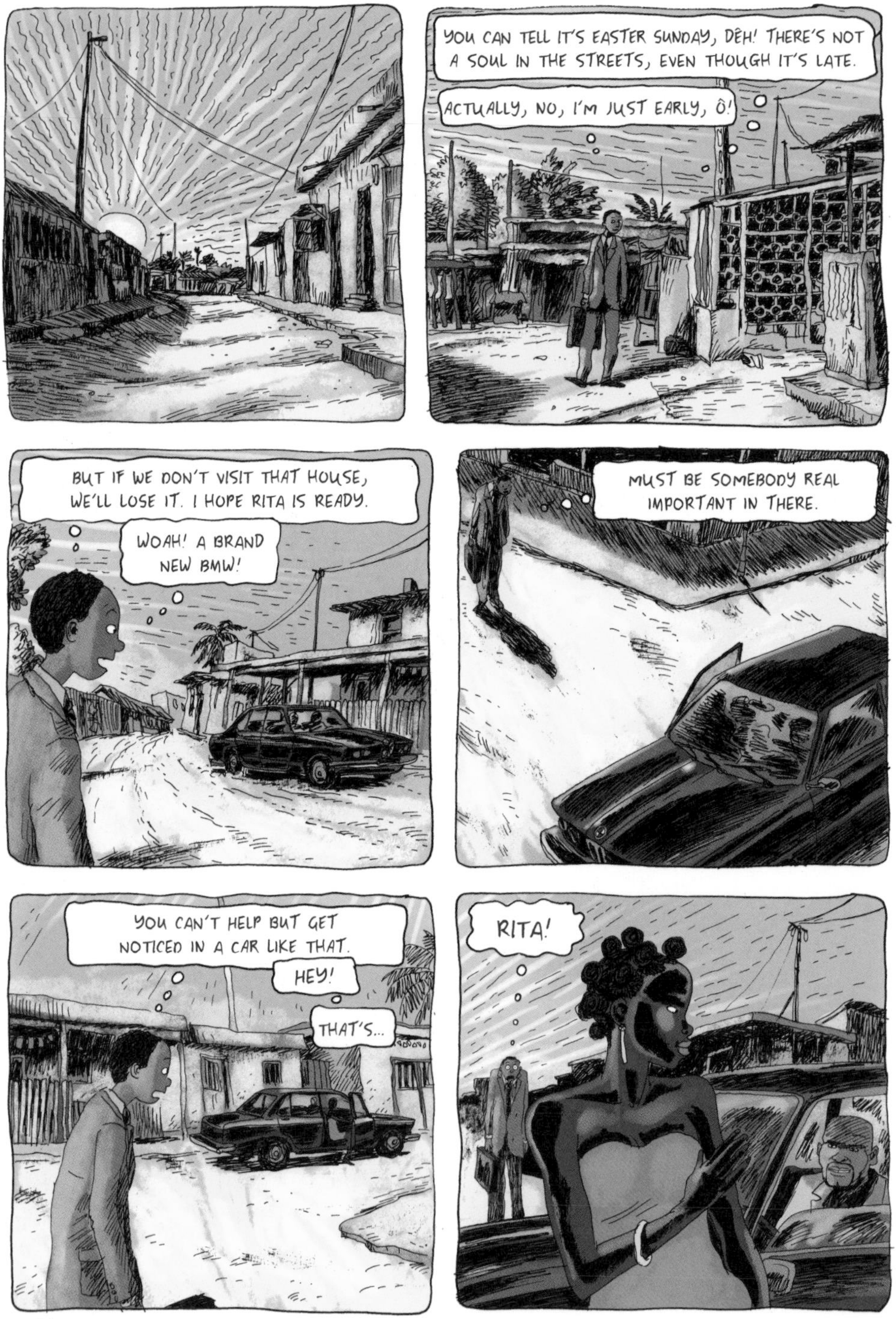
YOU CAN TELL IT'S EASTER SUNDAY, DÊH! THERE'S NOT A SOUL IN THE STREETS, EVEN THOUGH IT'S LATE.
ACTUALLY, NO, I'M JUST EARLY, Ô!
BUT IF WE DON'T VISIT THAT HOUSE, WE'LL LOSE IT. I HOPE RITA IS READY.
WOAH! A BRAND NEW BMW!
MUST BE SOMEBODY REAL IMPORTANT IN THERE.
YOU CAN'T HELP BUT GET NOTICED IN A CAR LIKE THAT.
HEY!
THAT'S...
RITA!

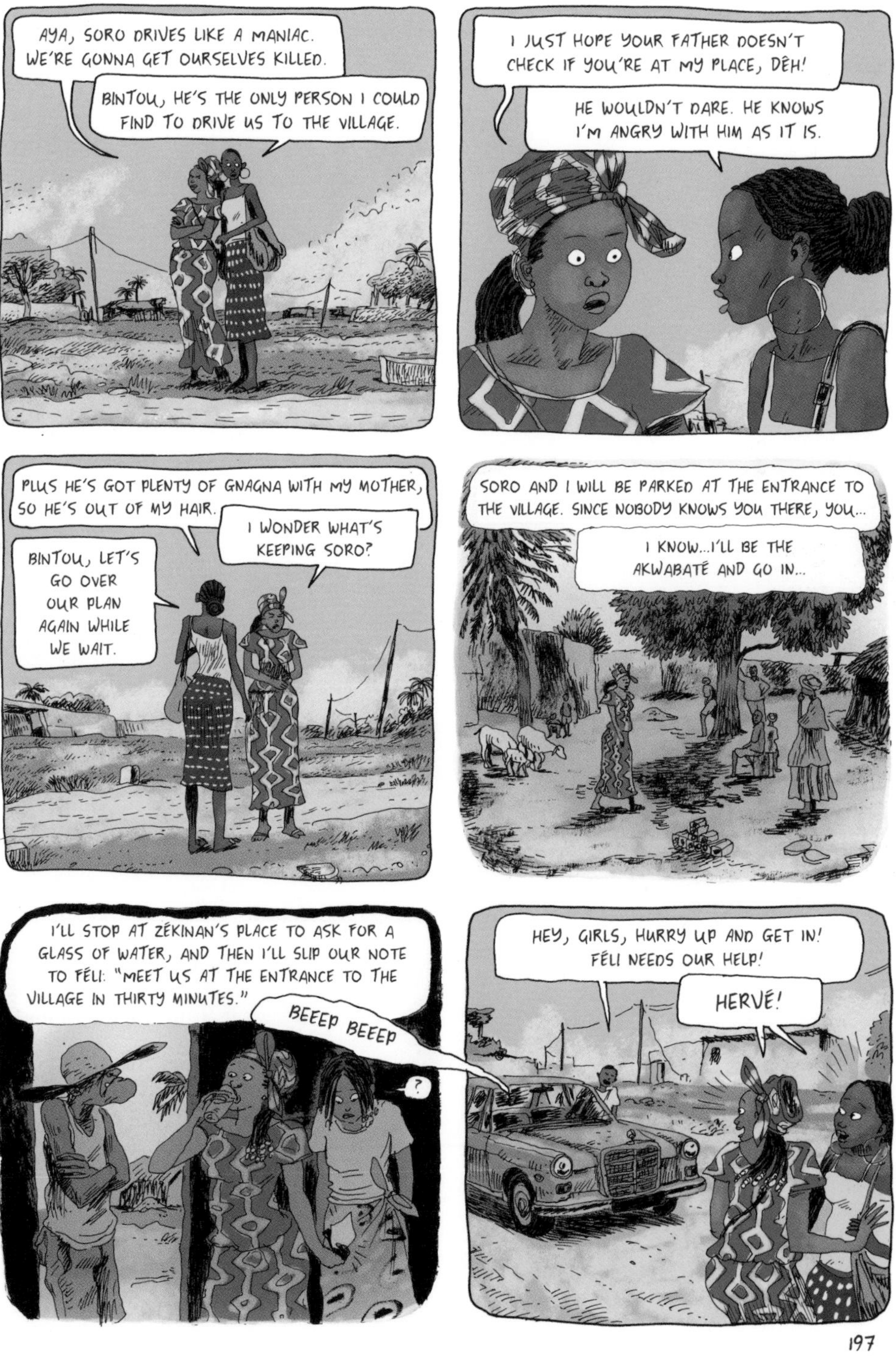
AYA, SORO DRIVES LIKE A MANIAC. WE'RE GONNA GET OURSELVES KILLED.
BINTOU, HE'S THE ONLY PERSON I COULD FIND TO DRIVE US TO THE VILLAGE.
I JUST HOPE YOUR FATHER DOESN'T CHECK IF YOU'RE AT MY PLACE, DÊH!
HE WOULDN'T DARE. HE KNOWS I'M ANGRY WITH HIM AS IT IS.
PLUS HE'S GOT PLENTY OF GNAGNA WITH MY MOTHER, SO HE'S OUT OF MY HAIR.
I WONDER WHAT'S KEEPING SORO?
BINTOU, LET'S GO OVER OUR PLAN AGAIN WHILE WE WAIT.
SORO AND I WILL BE PARKED AT THE ENTRANCE TO THE VILLAGE. SINCE NOBODY KNOWS YOU THERE, YOU...
I KNOW...I'LL BE THE AKWABATÉ AND GO IN...
I'LL STOP AT ZÉKINAN'S PLACE TO ASK FOR A GLASS OF WATER, AND THEN I'LL SLIP OUR NOTE TO FÉLI: "MEET US AT THE ENTRANCE TO THE VILLAGE IN THIRTY MINUTES."
BEEEP BEEEP
?
HEY, GIRLS, HURRY UP AND GET IN! FÉLI NEEDS OUR HELP!
HERVÉ!

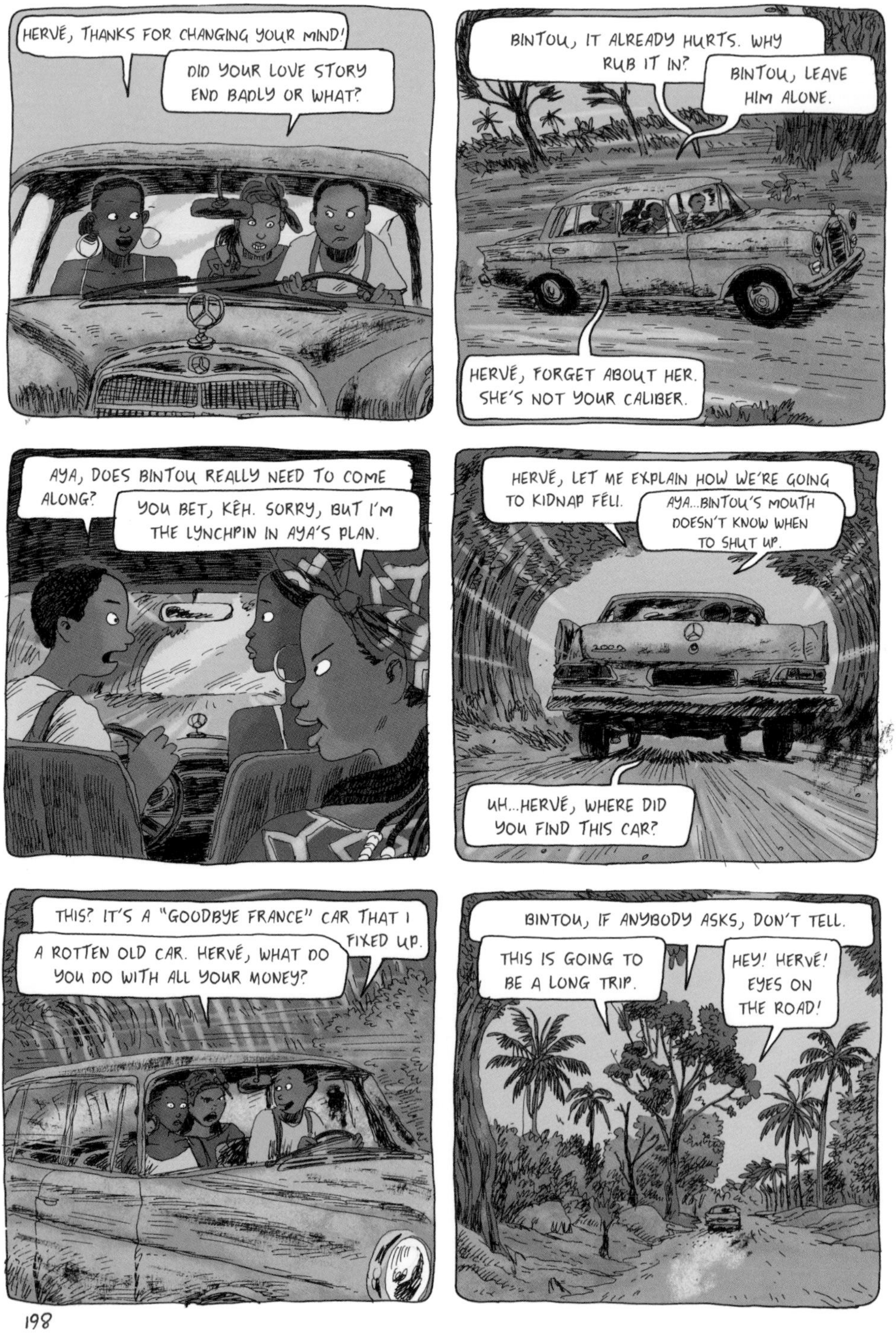
HERVÉ, THANKS FOR CHANGING YOUR MIND!
DID YOUR LOVE STORY END BADLY OR WHAT?
BINTOU, IT ALREADY HURTS. WHY RUB IT IN?
BINTOU, LEAVE HIM ALONE.
HERVÉ, FORGET ABOUT HER. SHE'S NOT YOUR CALIBER.
AYA, DOES BINTOU REALLY NEED TO COME ALONG?
YOU BET, KÊH. SORRY, BUT I'M THE LYNCHPIN IN AYA'S PLAN.
HERVÉ, LET ME EXPLAIN HOW WE'RE GOING TO KIDNAP FÉLI.
AYA...BINTOU'S MOUTH DOESN'T KNOW WHEN TO SHUT UP.
UH...HERVÉ, WHERE DID YOU FIND THIS CAR?
THIS? IT'S A "GOODBYE FRANCE" CAR THAT I FIXED UP.
A ROTTEN OLD CAR. HERVÉ, WHAT DO YOU DO WITH ALL YOUR MONEY?
BINTOU, IF ANYBODY ASKS, DON'T TELL.
THIS IS GOING TO BE A LONG TRIP.
HEY! HERVÉ! EYES ON THE ROAD!

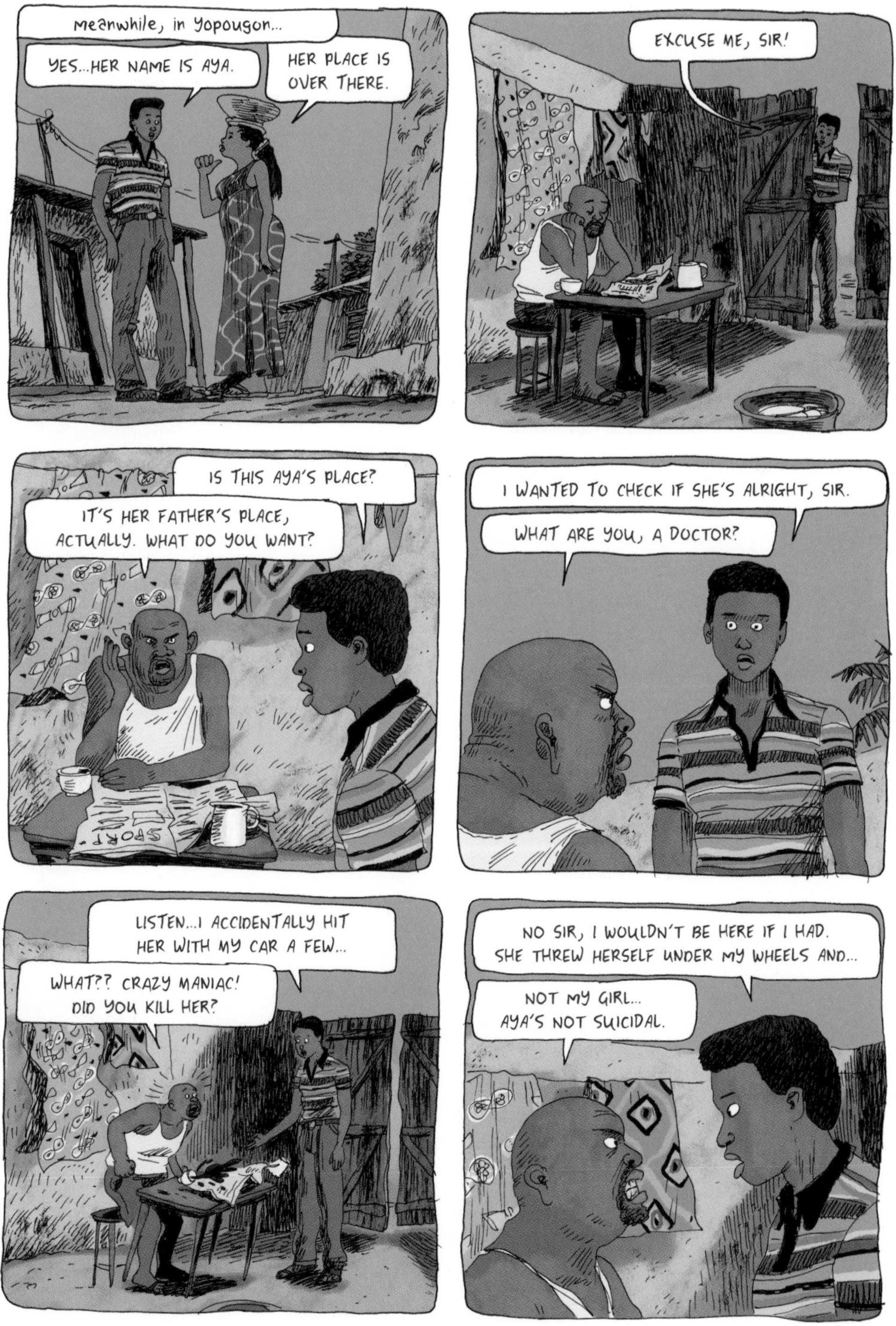
Meanwhile, in Yopougon...
YES...HER NAME IS AYA.
HER PLACE IS OVER THERE.
EXCUSE ME, SIR!
IS THIS AYA'S PLACE?
IT'S HER FATHER'S PLACE, ACTUALLY. WHAT DO YOU WANT?
I WANTED TO CHECK IF SHE'S ALRIGHT, SIR.
WHAT ARE YOU, A DOCTOR?
LISTEN...I ACCIDENTALLY HIT HER WITH MY CAR A FEW...
WHAT?? CRAZY MANIAC! DID YOU KILL HER?
NO SIR, I WOULDN'T BE HERE IF I HAD. SHE THREW HERSELF UNDER MY WHEELS AND...
NOT MY GIRL... AYA'S NOT SUICIDAL.

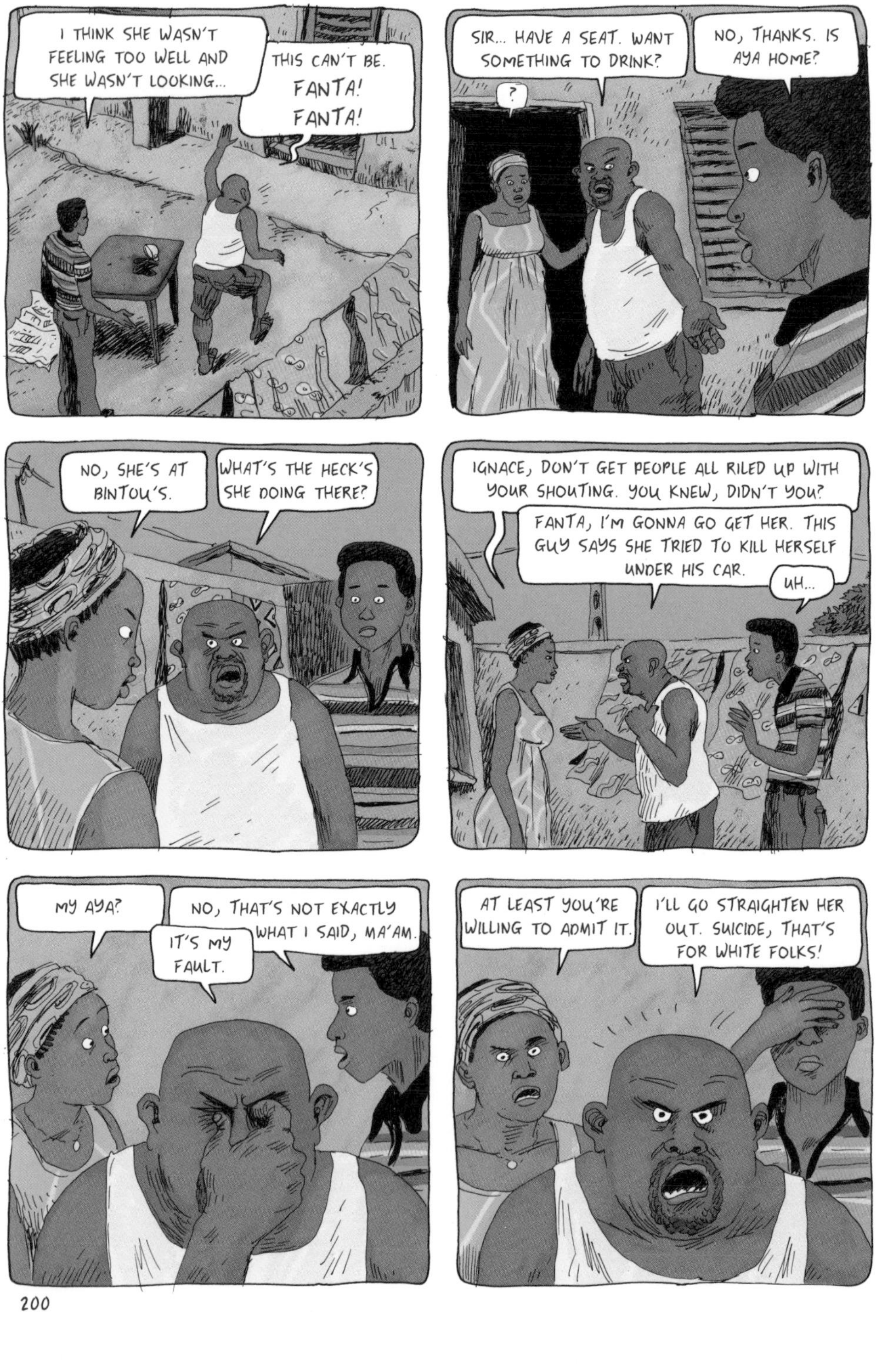

I THINK SHE WASN'T FEELING TOO WELL AND SHE WASN'T LOOKING...
THIS CAN'T BE. FANTA! FANTA!
SIR... HAVE A SEAT. WANT SOMETHING TO DRINK?
?
NO, THANKS. IS AYA HOME?
NO, SHE'S AT BINTOU'S.
WHAT'S THE HECK'S SHE DOING THERE?
IGNACE, DON'T GET PEOPLE ALL RILED UP WITH YOUR SHOUTING. YOU KNEW, DIDN'T YOU?
FANTA, I'M GONNA GO GET HER. THIS GUY SAYS SHE TRIED TO KILL HERSELF UNDER HIS CAR.
UH...
MY AYA?
NO, THAT'S NOT EXACTLY WHAT I SAID, MA'AM.
IT'S MY FAULT.
AT LEAST YOU'RE WILLING TO ADMIT IT.
I'LL GO STRAIGHTEN HER OUT. SUICIDE, THAT'S FOR WHITE FOLKS!

AYA... YOUR OLD MAN WAS WRONG FOR THE FIRST TIME IN HIS LIFE.

AND THERE'S NO DENYING A MISTAKE...

THAT'S WHY WE'RE GONNA SOLVE FÉLI'S PROBLEM.

BINTOU
Conseillère en gars

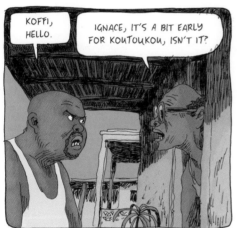

KOFFI, HELLO.

IGNACE, IT'S A BIT EARLY FOR KOUTOUKOU, ISN'T IT?

KOFFI, YOU THINK DRINKING'S A PROFESSION? I'M HERE TO GET AYA.

SHE'S NOT HERE. THE GIRLS WENT TO HYACINTE'S.

HYACINTE? WHAT'S GOING ON? AND HOW COME I DON'T KNOW ABOUT IT?

THAT'S KIDS FOR YOU, MY FRIEND. WAIT WHILE I GET DRESSED. WE'LL GO TO THE "WISE MEN."

NO, KOFFI, I'M NOT JOKING AROUND. THIS IS SERIOUS. SEE YOU LATER.

I'M SERIOUS TOO! WHEN'RE WE GOING TO GET BACK TO THE GOOD OLD DAYS?

201

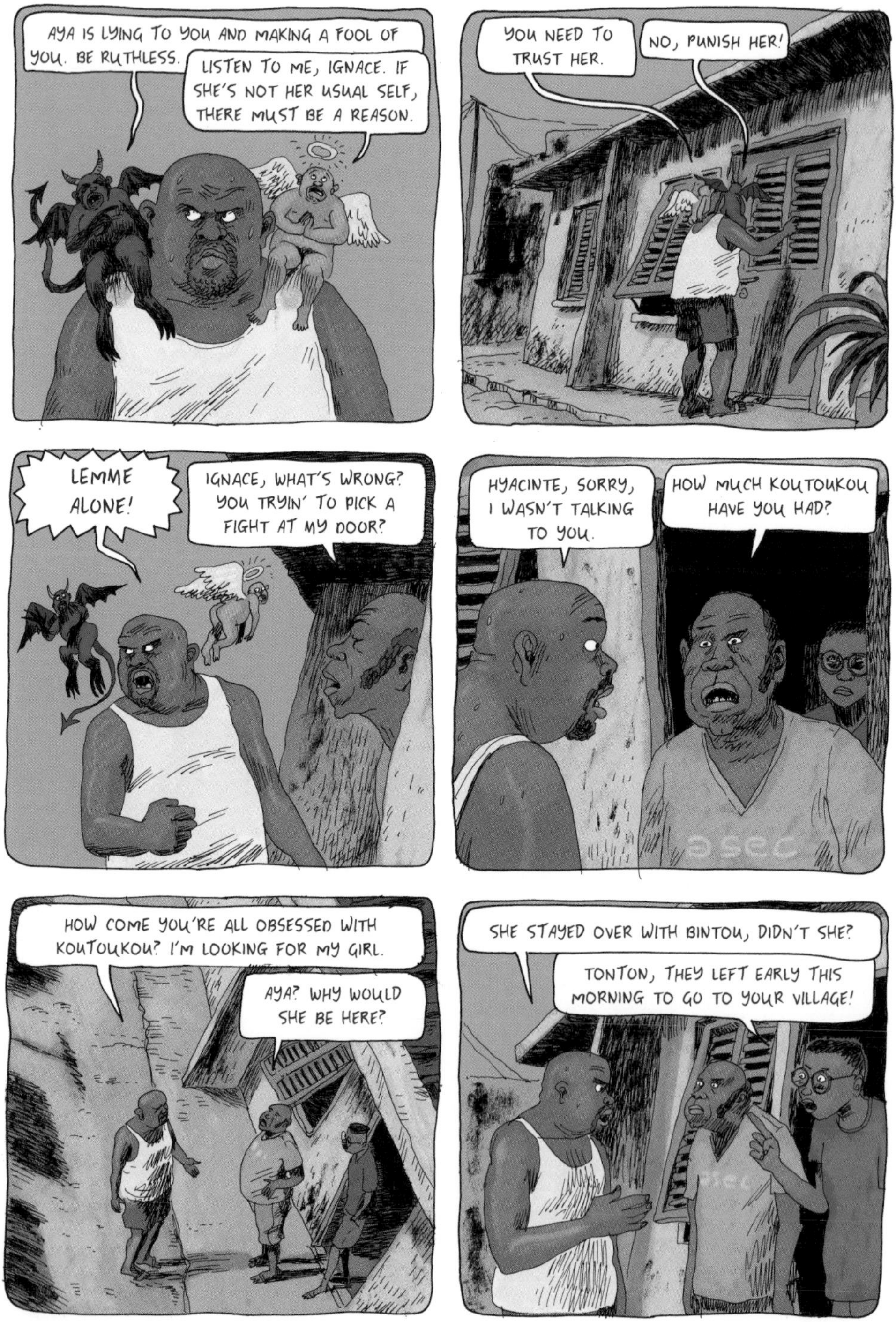
AYA IS LYING TO YOU AND MAKING A FOOL OF YOU. BE RUTHLESS.
LISTEN TO ME, IGNACE. IF SHE'S NOT HER USUAL SELF, THERE MUST BE A REASON.
YOU NEED TO TRUST HER.
NO, PUNISH HER!
LEMME ALONE!
IGNACE, WHAT'S WRONG? YOU TRYIN' TO PICK A FIGHT AT MY DOOR?
HYACINTE, SORRY, I WASN'T TALKING TO YOU.
HOW MUCH KOUTOUKOU HAVE YOU HAD?
asec
HOW COME YOU'RE ALL OBSESSED WITH KOUTOUKOU? I'M LOOKING FOR MY GIRL.
AYA? WHY WOULD SHE BE HERE?
SHE STAYED OVER WITH BINTOU, DIDN'T SHE?
TONTON, THEY LEFT EARLY THIS MORNING TO GO TO YOUR VILLAGE!
asec

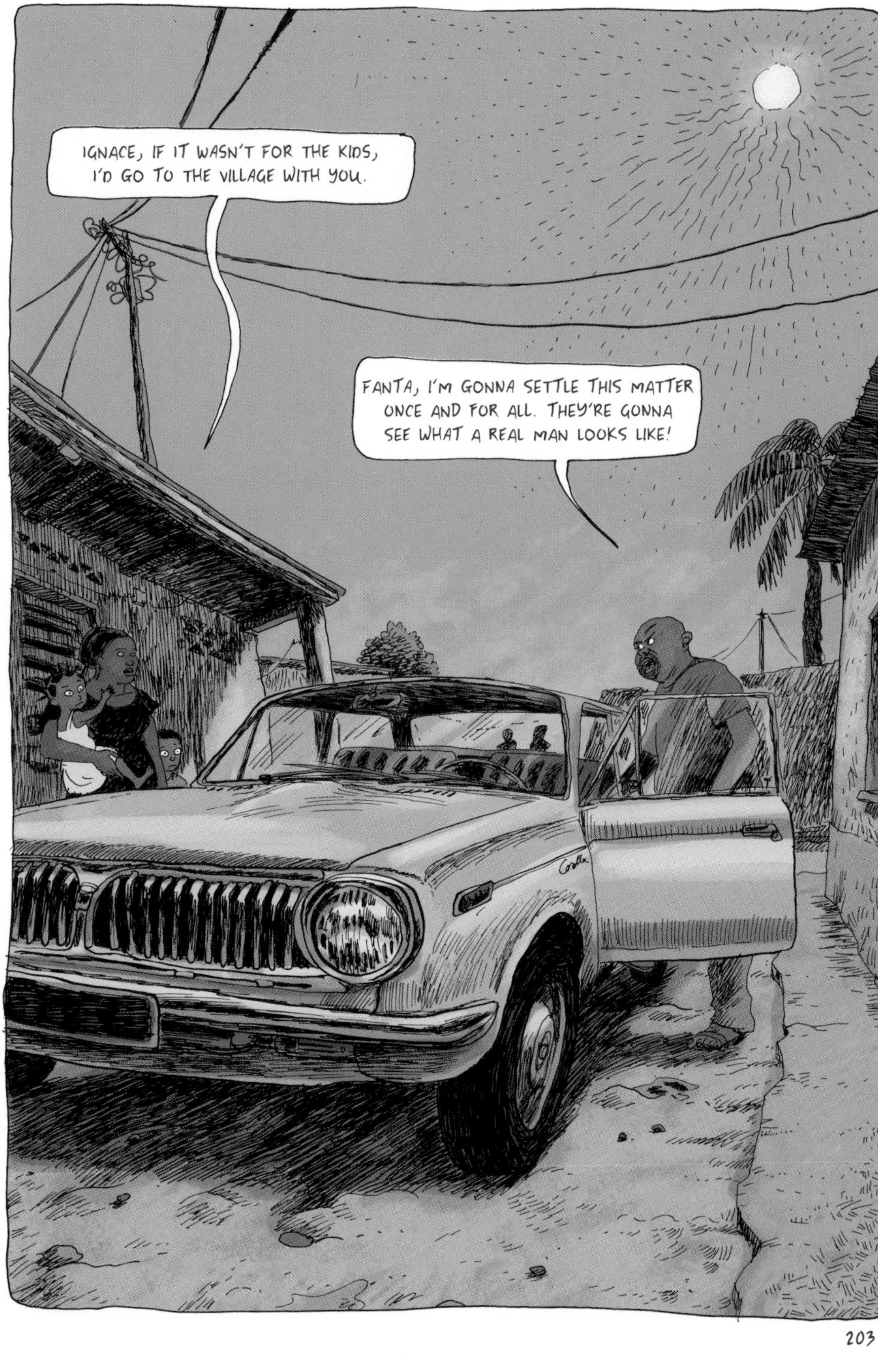
IGNACE, IF IT WASN'T FOR THE KIDS, I'D GO TO THE VILLAGE WITH YOU.
FANTA, I'M GONNA SETTLE THIS MATTER ONCE AND FOR ALL. THEY'RE GONNA SEE WHAT A REAL MAN LOOKS LIKE!

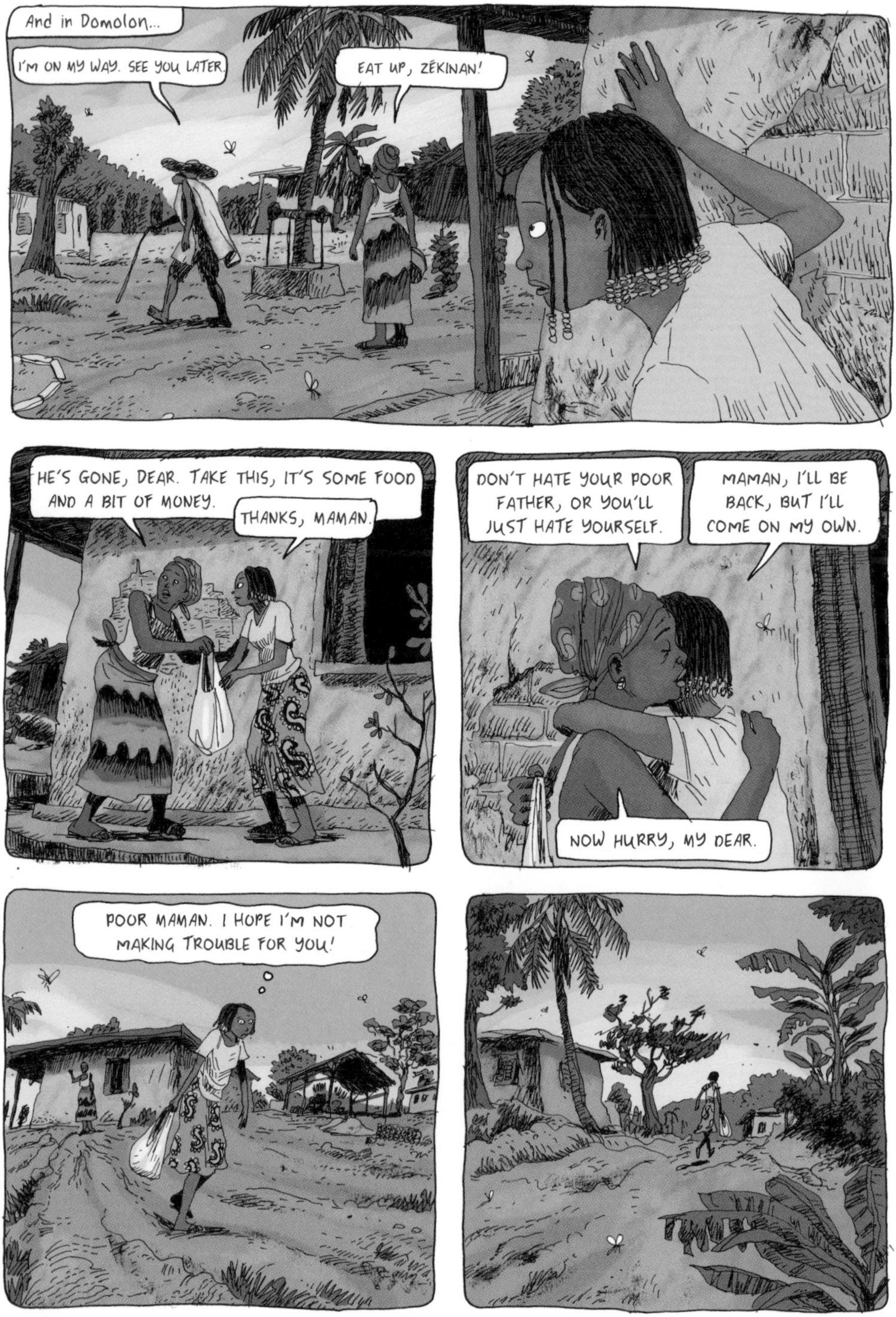
And in Domolon...
I'M ON MY WAY. SEE YOU LATER.
EAT UP, ZÉKINAN!
HE'S GONE, DEAR. TAKE THIS, IT'S SOME FOOD AND A BIT OF MONEY.
THANKS, MAMAN.
DON'T HATE YOUR POOR FATHER, OR YOU'LL JUST HATE YOURSELF.
MAMAN, I'LL BE BACK, BUT I'LL COME ON MY OWN.
NOW HURRY, MY DEAR.
POOR MAMAN. I HOPE I'M NOT MAKING TROUBLE FOR YOU!

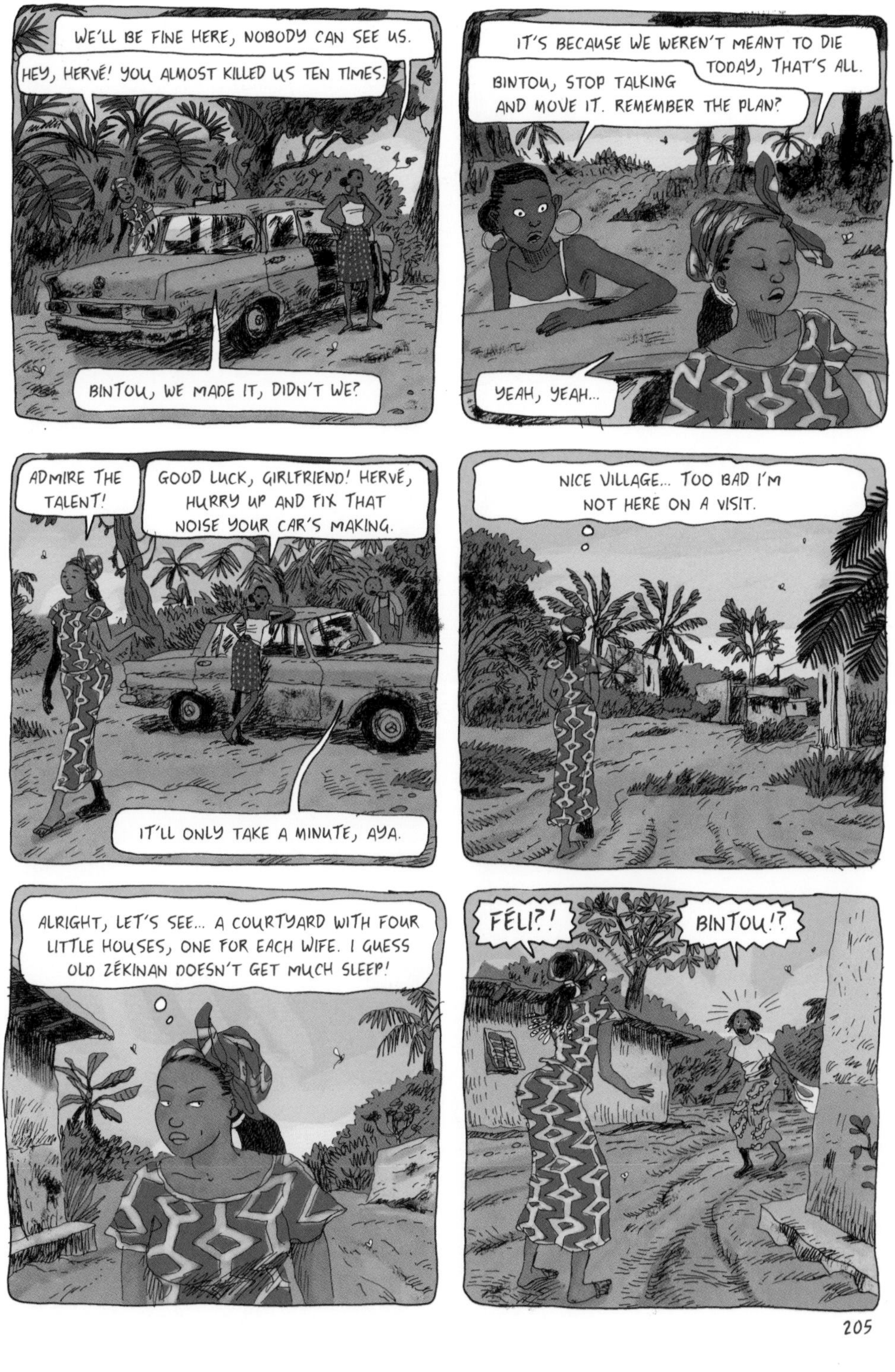
WE'LL BE FINE HERE, NOBODY CAN SEE US.
HEY, HERVÉ! YOU ALMOST KILLED US TEN TIMES.
BINTOU, WE MADE IT, DIDN'T WE?
IT'S BECAUSE WE WEREN'T MEANT TO DIE TODAY, THAT'S ALL.
BINTOU, STOP TALKING AND MOVE IT. REMEMBER THE PLAN?
YEAH, YEAH...
ADMIRE THE TALENT!
GOOD LUCK, GIRLFRIEND! HERVÉ, HURRY UP AND FIX THAT NOISE YOUR CAR'S MAKING.
IT'LL ONLY TAKE A MINUTE, AYA.
NICE VILLAGE... TOO BAD I'M NOT HERE ON A VISIT.
ALRIGHT, LET'S SEE... A COURTYARD WITH FOUR LITTLE HOUSES, ONE FOR EACH WIFE. I GUESS OLD ZÉKINAN DOESN'T GET MUCH SLEEP!
FÉLI?!
BINTOU!?

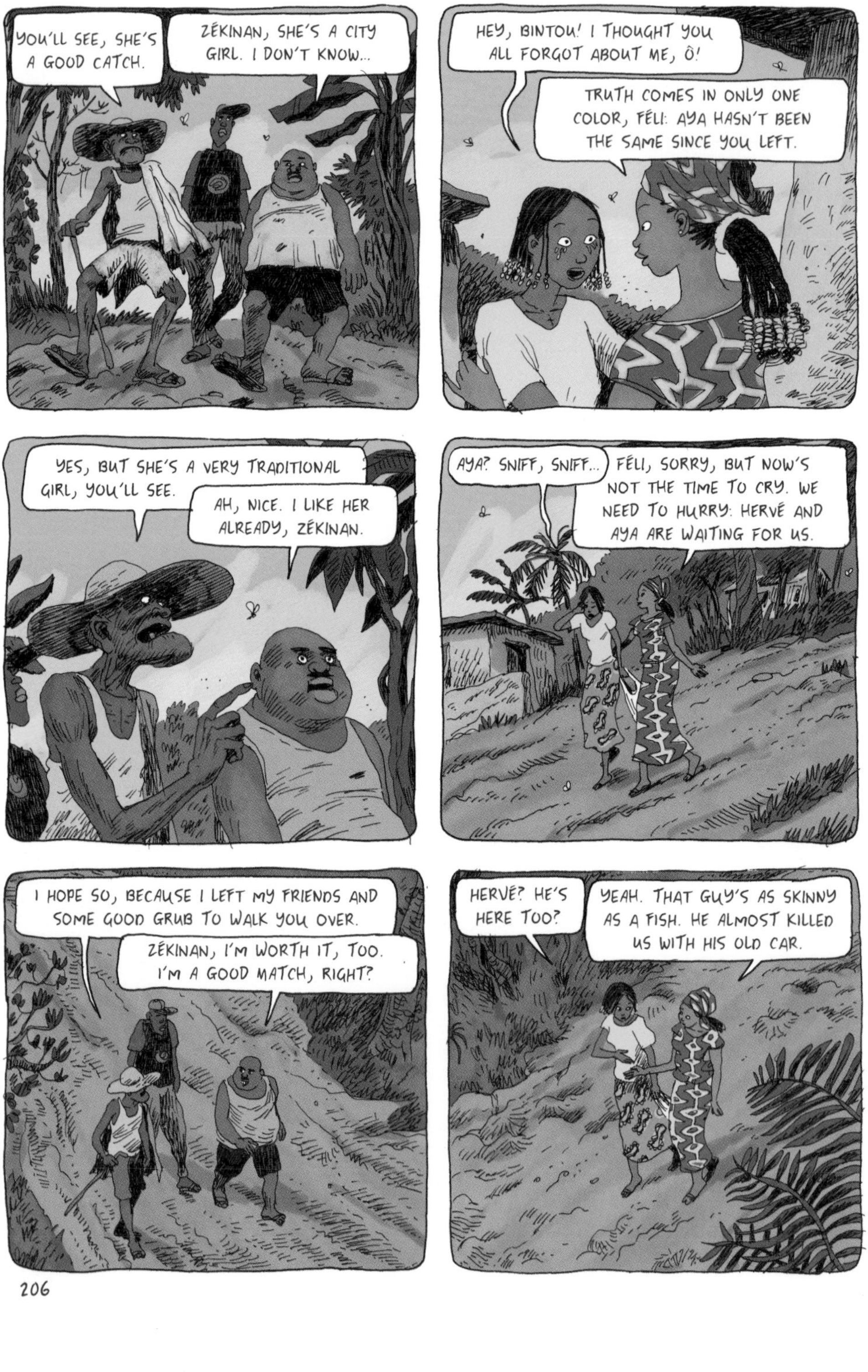
YOU'LL SEE, SHE'S A GOOD CATCH.
ZÉKINAN, SHE'S A CITY GIRL. I DON'T KNOW...
HEY, BINTOU! I THOUGHT YOU ALL FORGOT ABOUT ME, Ô!
TRUTH COMES IN ONLY ONE COLOR, FÉLI: AYA HASN'T BEEN THE SAME SINCE YOU LEFT.
YES, BUT SHE'S A VERY TRADITIONAL GIRL, YOU'LL SEE.
AH, NICE. I LIKE HER ALREADY, ZÉKINAN.
AYA? SNIFF, SNIFF...
FÉLI, SORRY, BUT NOW'S NOT THE TIME TO CRY. WE NEED TO HURRY: HERVÉ AND AYA ARE WAITING FOR US.
I HOPE SO, BECAUSE I LEFT MY FRIENDS AND SOME GOOD GRUB TO WALK YOU OVER.
ZÉKINAN, I'M WORTH IT, TOO. I'M A GOOD MATCH, RIGHT?
HERVÉ? HE'S HERE TOO?
YEAH. THAT GUY'S AS SKINNY AS A FISH. HE ALMOST KILLED US WITH HIS OLD CAR.

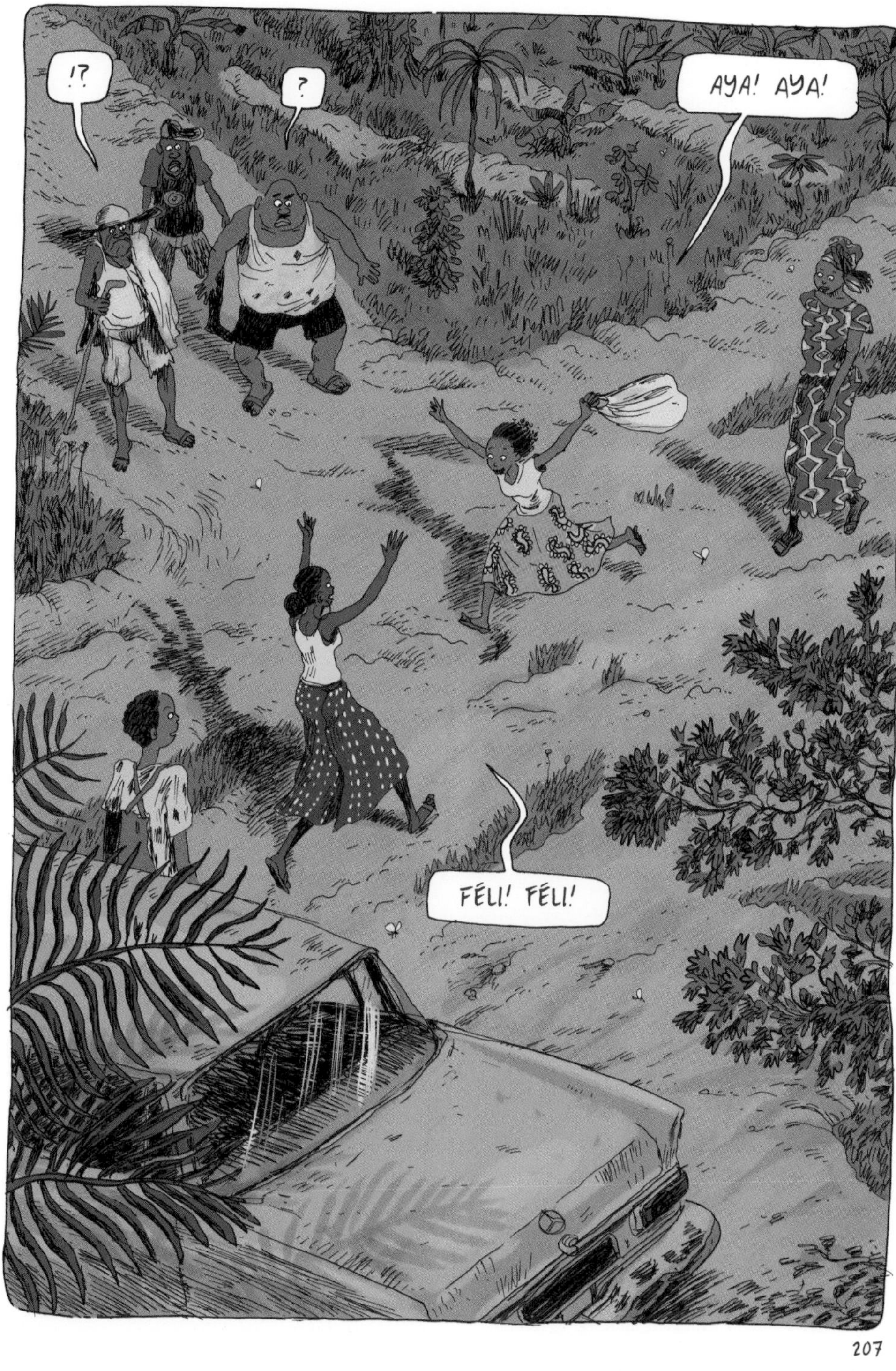
!?
?
AYA! AYA!
FÉLI! FÉLI!

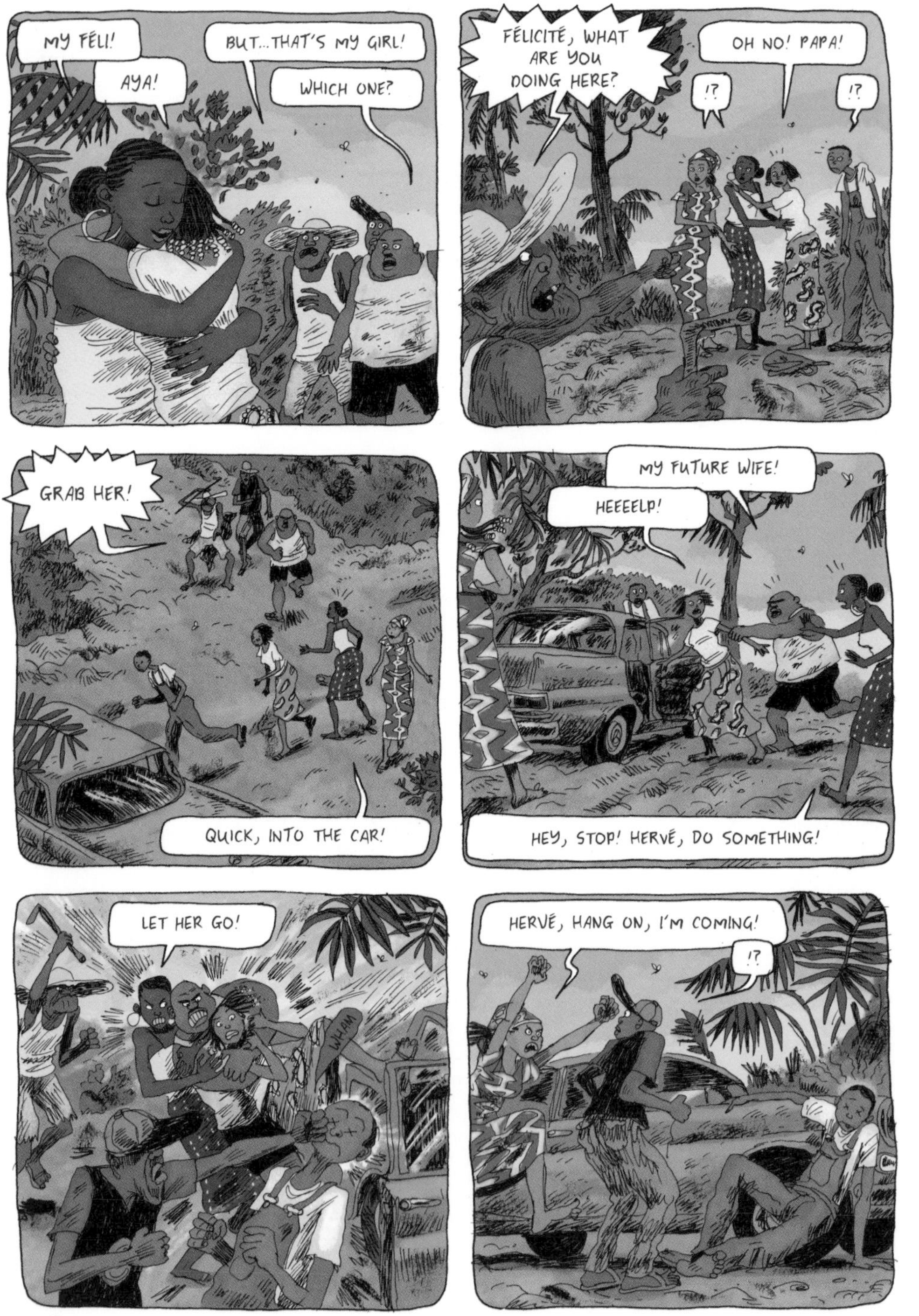
MY FÉLI!
AYA!
BUT... THAT'S MY GIRL!
WHICH ONE?
FÉLICITÉ, WHAT ARE YOU DOING HERE?
!?
OH NO! PAPA!
!?
GRAB HER!
QUICK, INTO THE CAR!
MY FUTURE WIFE!
HEEEELP!
HEY, STOP! HERVÉ, DO SOMETHING!
LET HER GO!
WHAM
HERVÉ, HANG ON, I'M COMING!
!?

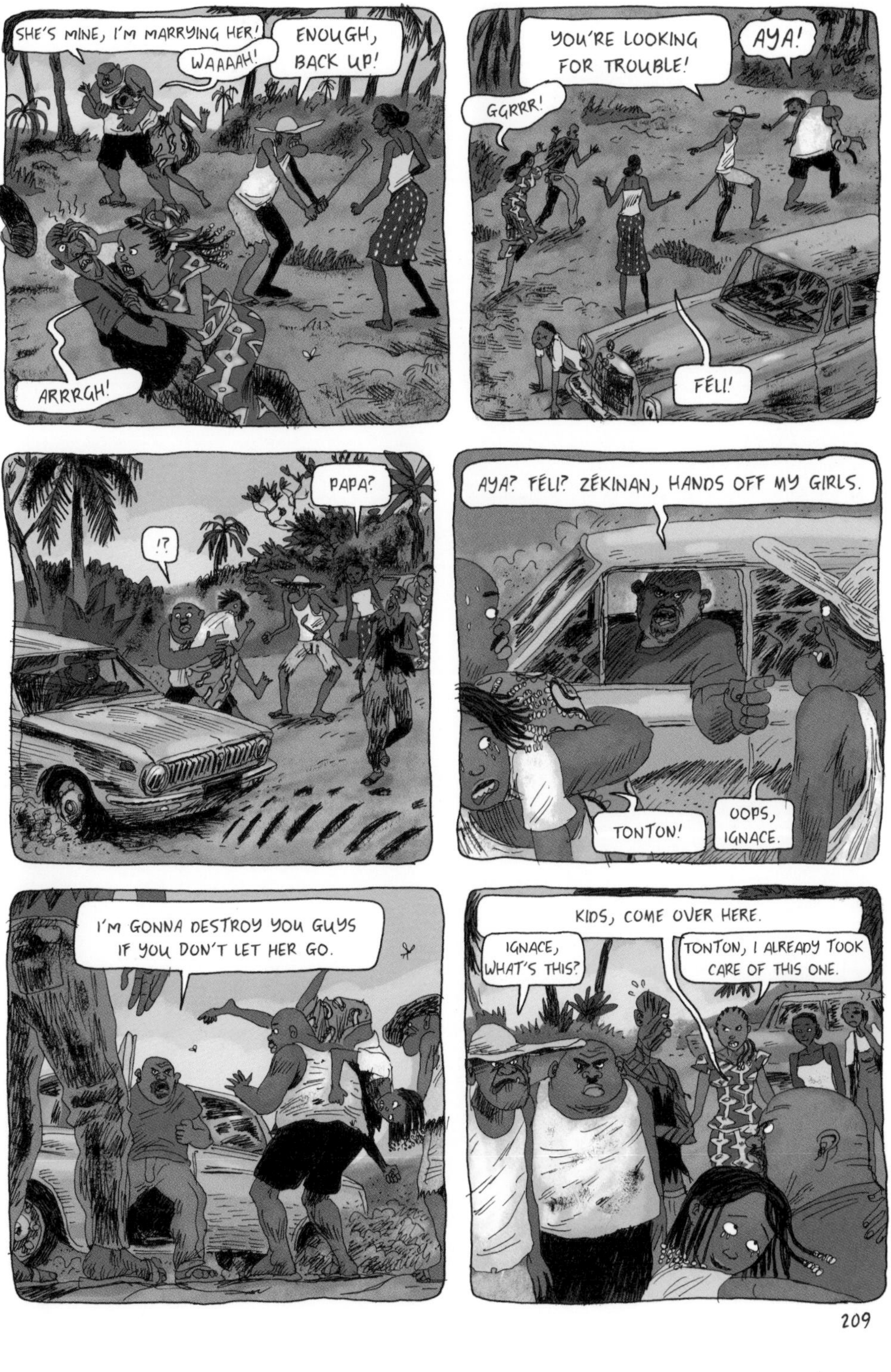
SHE'S MINE, I'M MARRYING HER!
WAAAAH!
ENOUGH, BACK UP!
ARRRGH!
YOU'RE LOOKING FOR TROUBLE!
AYA!
GGRRR!
FÉLI!
PAPA?
!?
AYA? FÉLI? ZÉKINAN, HANDS OFF MY GIRLS.
TONTON!
OOPS, IGNACE.
I'M GONNA DESTROY YOU GUYS IF YOU DON'T LET HER GO.
KIDS, COME OVER HERE.
IGNACE, WHAT'S THIS?
TONTON, I ALREADY TOOK CARE OF THIS ONE.

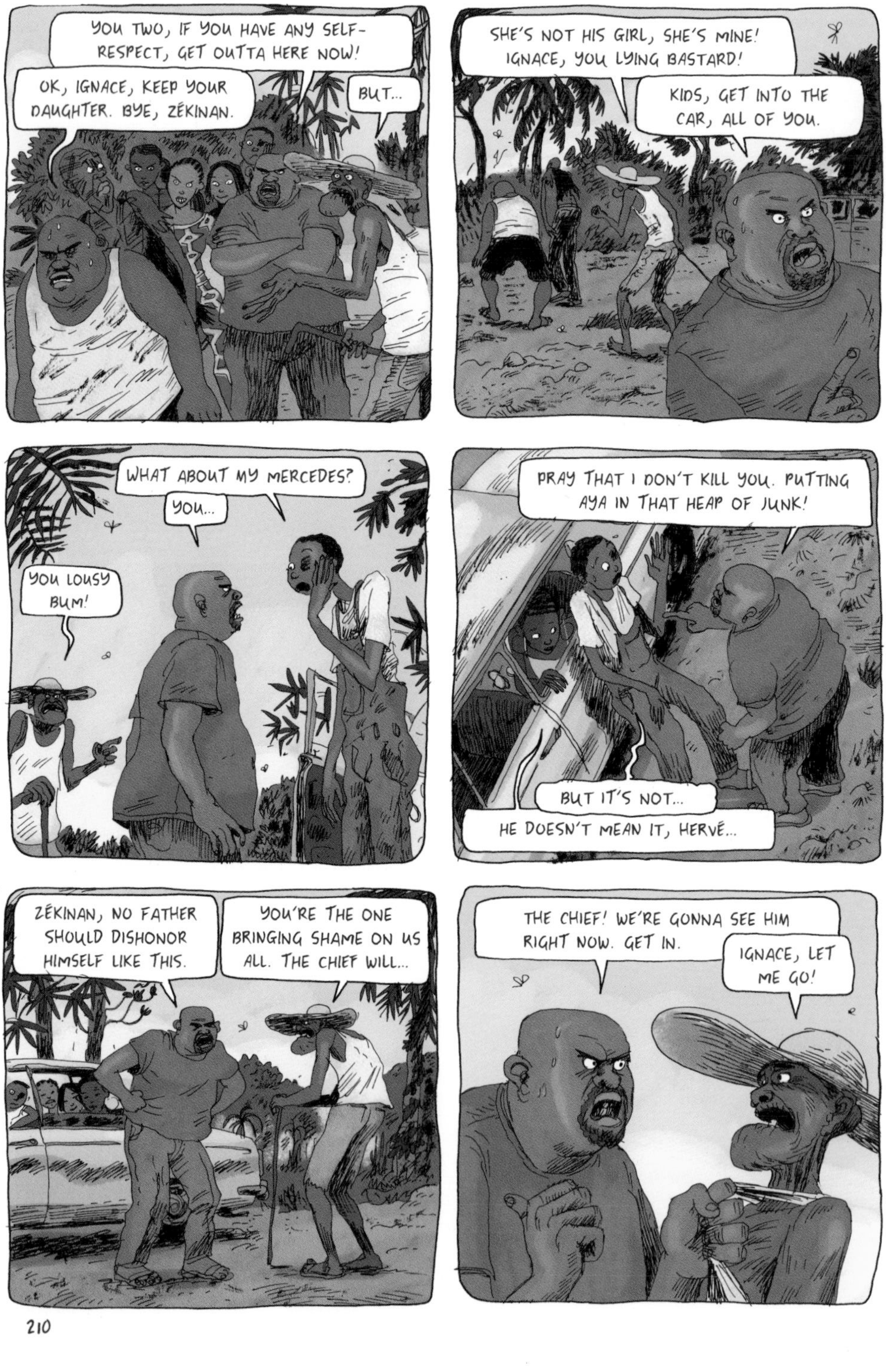
YOU TWO, IF YOU HAVE ANY SELF-RESPECT, GET OUTTA HERE NOW!
OK, IGNACE, KEEP YOUR DAUGHTER. BYE, ZÉKINAN.
BUT...
SHE'S NOT HIS GIRL, SHE'S MINE! IGNACE, YOU LYING BASTARD!
KIDS, GET INTO THE CAR, ALL OF YOU.
WHAT ABOUT MY MERCEDES?
YOU...
YOU LOUSY BUM!
PRAY THAT I DON'T KILL YOU. PUTTING AYA IN THAT HEAP OF JUNK!
BUT IT'S NOT...
HE DOESN'T MEAN IT, HERVÉ...
ZÉKINAN, NO FATHER SHOULD DISHONOR HIMSELF LIKE THIS.
YOU'RE THE ONE BRINGING SHAME ON US ALL. THE CHIEF WILL...
THE CHIEF! WE'RE GONNA SEE HIM RIGHT NOW. GET IN.
IGNACE, LET ME GO!

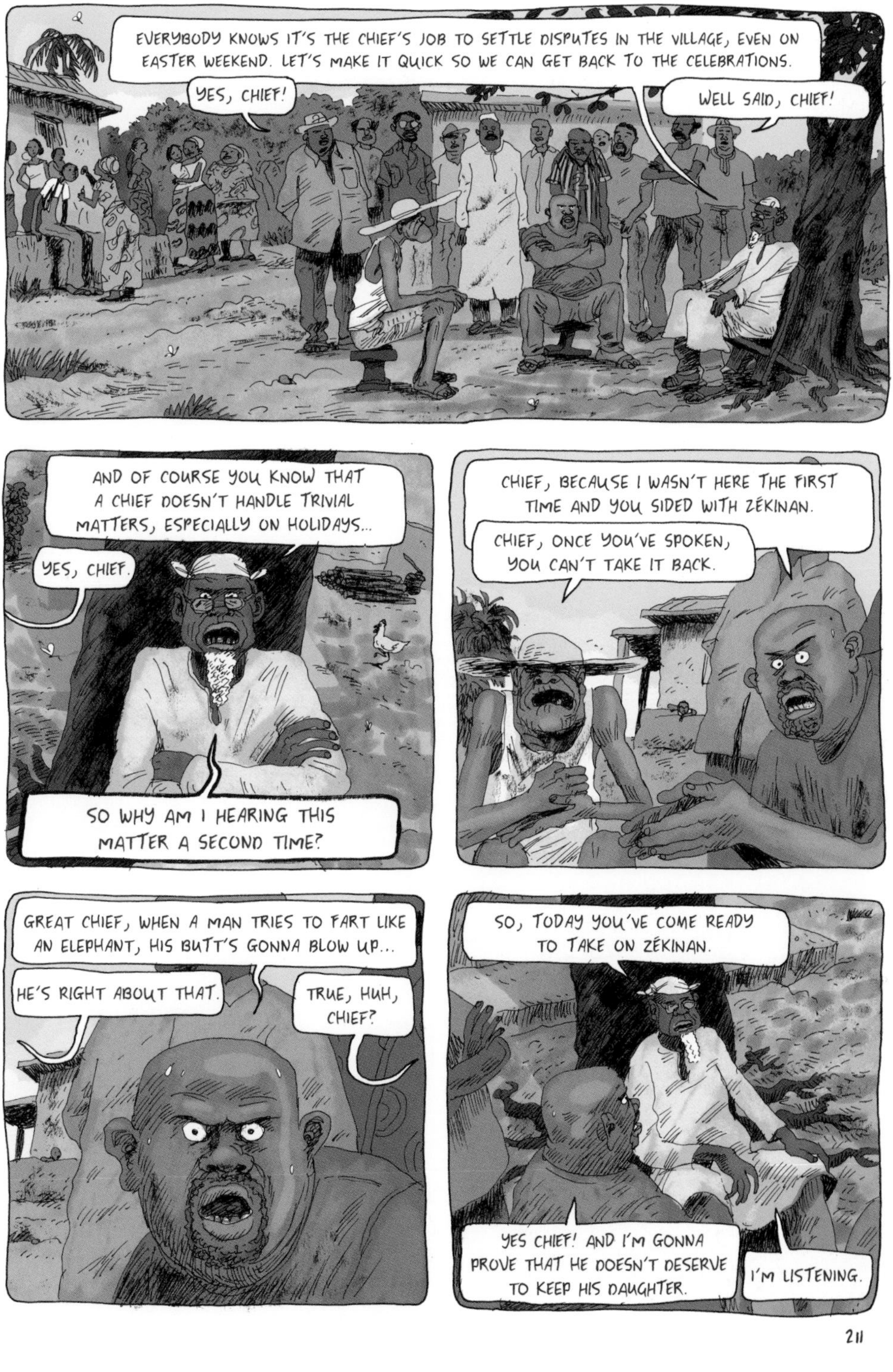
EVERYBODY KNOWS IT'S THE CHIEF'S JOB TO SETTLE DISPUTES IN THE VILLAGE, EVEN ON EASTER WEEKEND. LET'S MAKE IT QUICK SO WE CAN GET BACK TO THE CELEBRATIONS.
YES, CHIEF!
WELL SAID, CHIEF!
AND OF COURSE YOU KNOW THAT A CHIEF DOESN'T HANDLE TRIVIAL MATTERS, ESPECIALLY ON HOLIDAYS...
YES, CHIEF.
SO WHY AM I HEARING THIS MATTER A SECOND TIME?
CHIEF, BECAUSE I WASN'T HERE THE FIRST TIME AND YOU SIDED WITH ZÉKINAN.
CHIEF, ONCE YOU'VE SPOKEN, YOU CAN'T TAKE IT BACK.
GREAT CHIEF, WHEN A MAN TRIES TO FART LIKE AN ELEPHANT, HIS BUTT'S GONNA BLOW UP...
HE'S RIGHT ABOUT THAT.
TRUE, HUH, CHIEF?
SO, TODAY YOU'VE COME READY TO TAKE ON ZÉKINAN.
YES CHIEF! AND I'M GONNA PROVE THAT HE DOESN'T DESERVE TO KEEP HIS DAUGHTER.
I'M LISTENING.

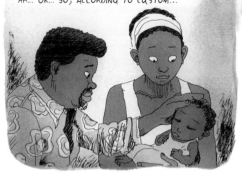

CHIEF, AYA, MY ELDEST, HAD JUST BEEN BORN. YOU'VE SEEN HER—A REAL GEM! THE MOMENT I LAID EYES ON HER... GET TO THE POINT, IGNACE. AH... OK... SO, ACCORDING TO CUSTOM...

WE BROUGHT AYA TO THE VILLAGE TO PRESENT HER, BECAUSE I'M A TRADITIONAL GUY. THAT'S GOOD, IGNACE. HOT WATER NEVER FORGETS THAT IT WAS ONCE COLD.

BUT IT'S NOT A BOY!

THAT'LL BE FOR NEXT TIME, PAPA.

I DON'T KNOW IF IT WAS THOSE WORDS THAT UPSET MY GIRL, BUT SHE STARTED CRYING. NOTHING COULD STOP HER...NOT HER MOTHER'S MILK OR HER FATHER'S VOICE...

SHE'S GOT YOUR BIG HEART, IGNACE.

THAT'S WHEN WE SAW A SHABBY-LOOKING GIRL COME OVER. SHE WAS BARELY FOUR YEARS OLD. THE MOMENT SHE APPROACHED, AYA STOPPED CRYING.

BABY

AND WHEN SHE WALKED AWAY, AYA BEGAN SOBBING AGAIN. SO THEY STAYED TOGETHER DURING OUR VISIT. JUST AS WE WERE LEAVING, ZÉKINAN SHOWED UP.

HEY, IGNACE, IT'S BEEN A WHILE!

ZÉKINAN, HOW ARE THINGS?

NOT GREAT, Ô. TROUBLE'S BEEN HANGING AROUND AND DOESN'T WANT TO GO.

TELL ME, THE GIRL PLAYING WITH YOUR BABY, YOU WANT HER?

212

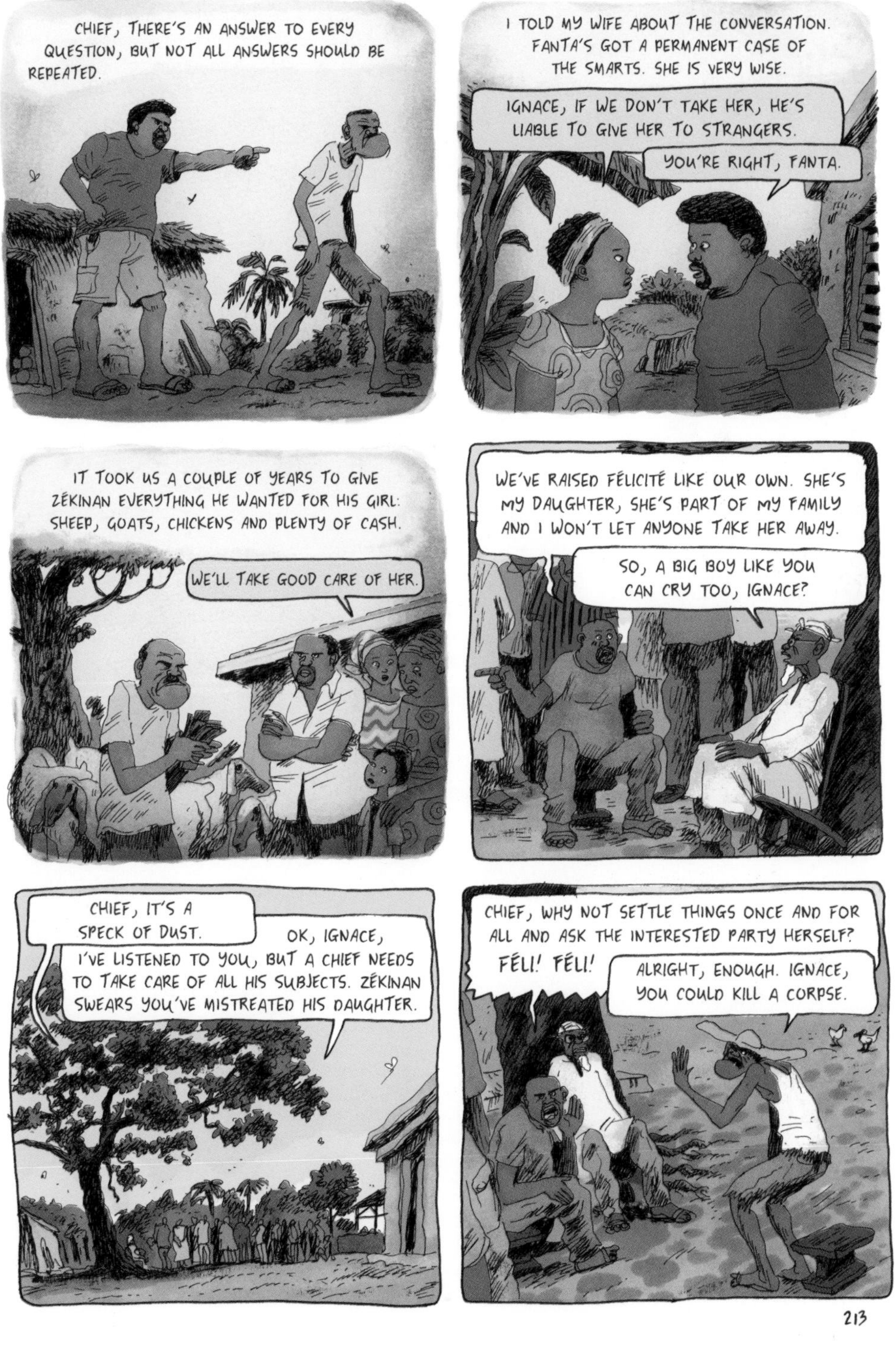
CHIEF, THERE'S AN ANSWER TO EVERY QUESTION, BUT NOT ALL ANSWERS SHOULD BE REPEATED.
I TOLD MY WIFE ABOUT THE CONVERSATION. FANTA'S GOT A PERMANENT CASE OF THE SMARTS. SHE IS VERY WISE.
IGNACE, IF WE DON'T TAKE HER, HE'S LIABLE TO GIVE HER TO STRANGERS.
YOU'RE RIGHT, FANTA.
IT TOOK US A COUPLE OF YEARS TO GIVE ZÉKINAN EVERYTHING HE WANTED FOR HIS GIRL: SHEEP, GOATS, CHICKENS AND PLENTY OF CASH.
WE'LL TAKE GOOD CARE OF HER.
WE'VE RAISED FÉLICITÉ LIKE OUR OWN. SHE'S MY DAUGHTER, SHE'S PART OF MY FAMILY AND I WON'T LET ANYONE TAKE HER AWAY.
SO, A BIG BOY LIKE YOU CAN CRY TOO, IGNACE?
CHIEF, IT'S A SPECK OF DUST.
OK, IGNACE, I'VE LISTENED TO YOU, BUT A CHIEF NEEDS TO TAKE CARE OF ALL HIS SUBJECTS. ZÉKINAN SWEARS YOU'VE MISTREATED HIS DAUGHTER.
CHIEF, WHY NOT SETTLE THINGS ONCE AND FOR ALL AND ASK THE INTERESTED PARTY HERSELF? FÉLI! FÉLI!
ALRIGHT, ENOUGH. IGNACE, YOU COULD KILL A CORPSE.

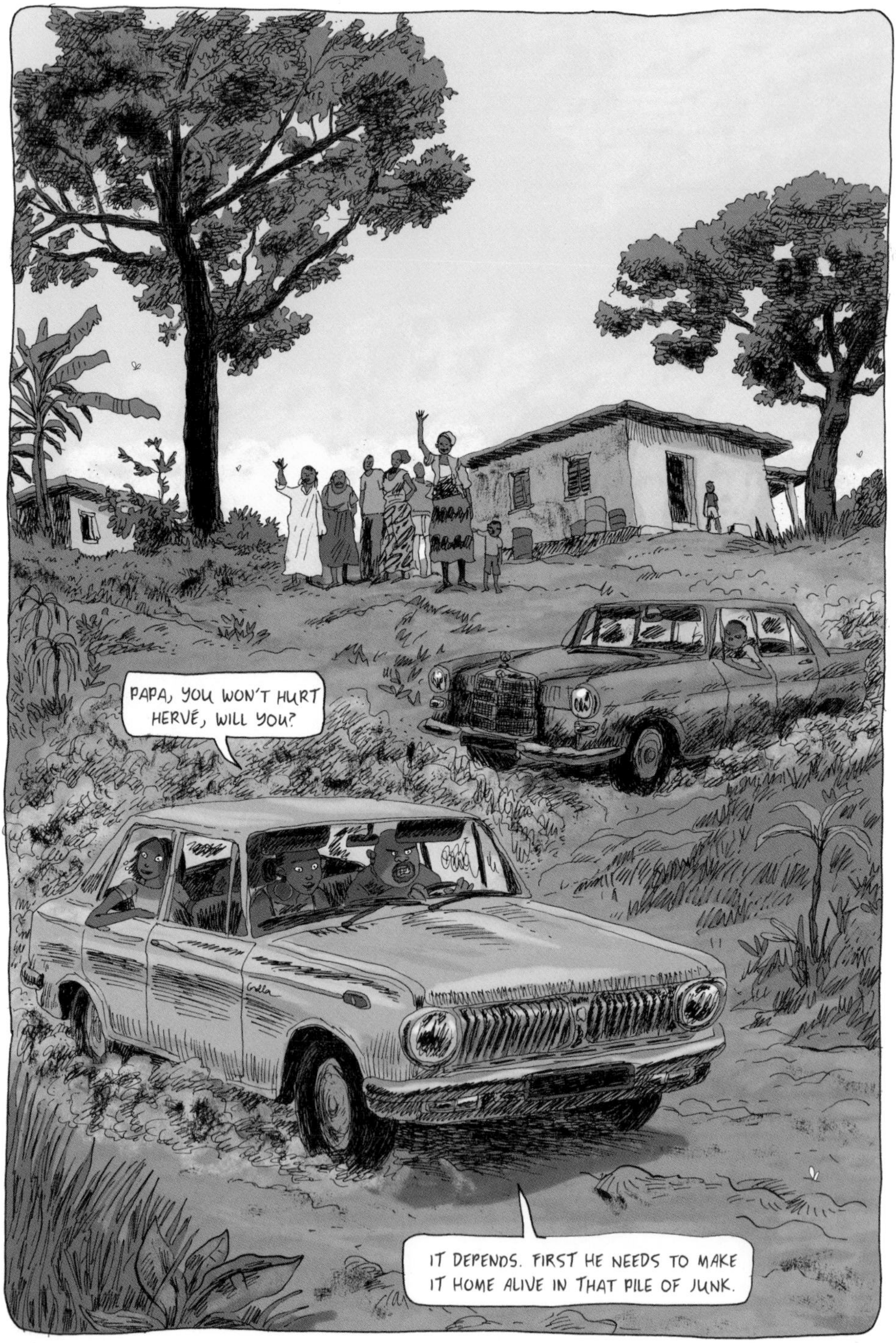
PAPA, YOU WON'T HURT HERVÉ, WILL YOU?
IT DEPENDS. FIRST HE NEEDS TO MAKE IT HOME ALIVE IN THAT PILE OF JUNK.

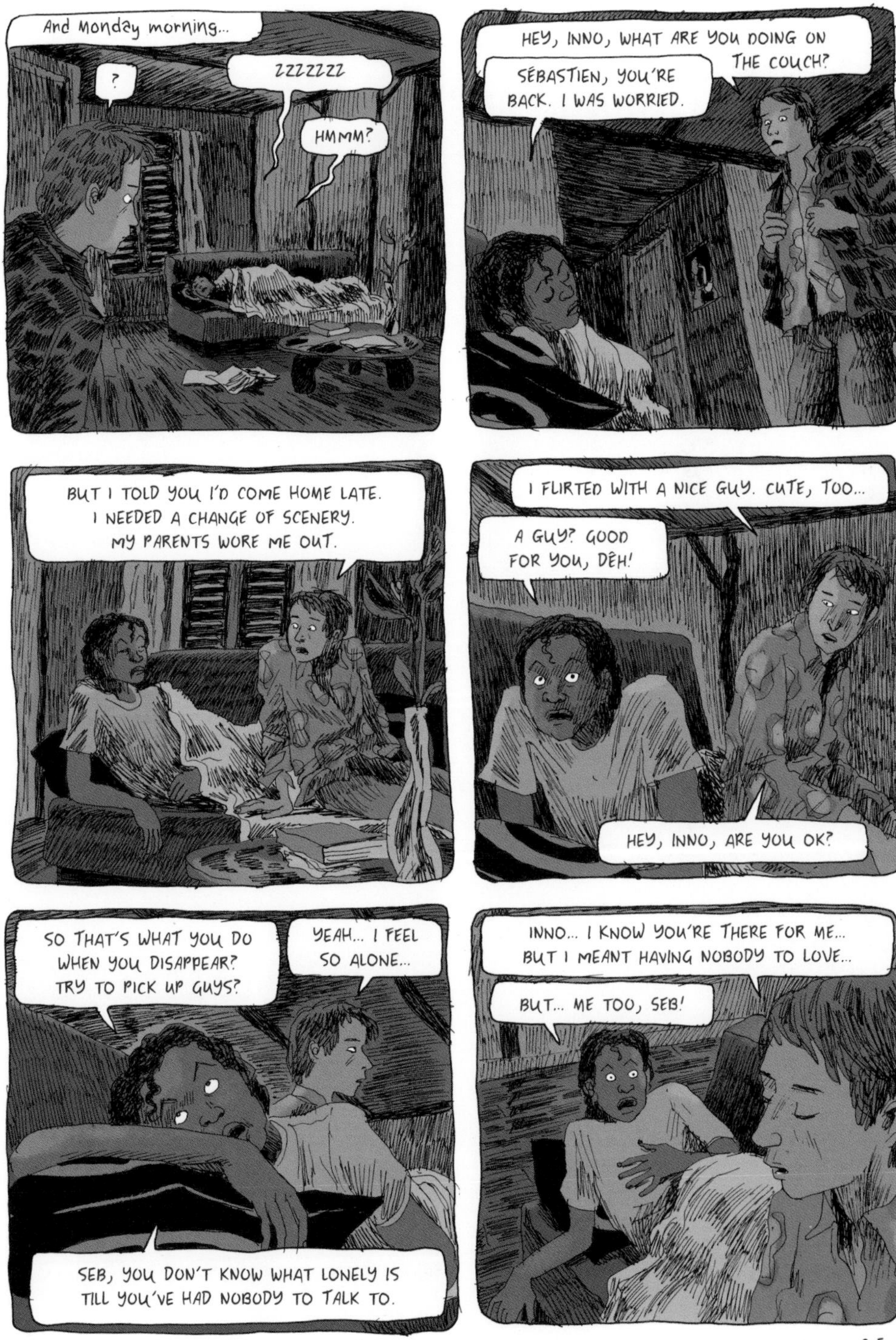
And Monday morning...
?
ZZZZZZZ
HMMM?
HEY, INNO, WHAT ARE YOU DOING ON THE COUCH?
SÉBASTIEN, YOU'RE BACK. I WAS WORRIED.
BUT I TOLD YOU I'D COME HOME LATE. I NEEDED A CHANGE OF SCENERY. MY PARENTS WORE ME OUT.
I FLIRTED WITH A NICE GUY. CUTE, TOO...
A GUY? GOOD FOR YOU, DÊH!
HEY, INNO, ARE YOU OK?
SO THAT'S WHAT YOU DO WHEN YOU DISAPPEAR? TRY TO PICK UP GUYS?
YEAH... I FEEL SO ALONE...
SEB, YOU DON'T KNOW WHAT LONELY IS TILL YOU'VE HAD NOBODY TO TALK TO.
INNO... I KNOW YOU'RE THERE FOR ME... BUT I MEANT HAVING NOBODY TO LOVE...
BUT... ME TOO, SEB!

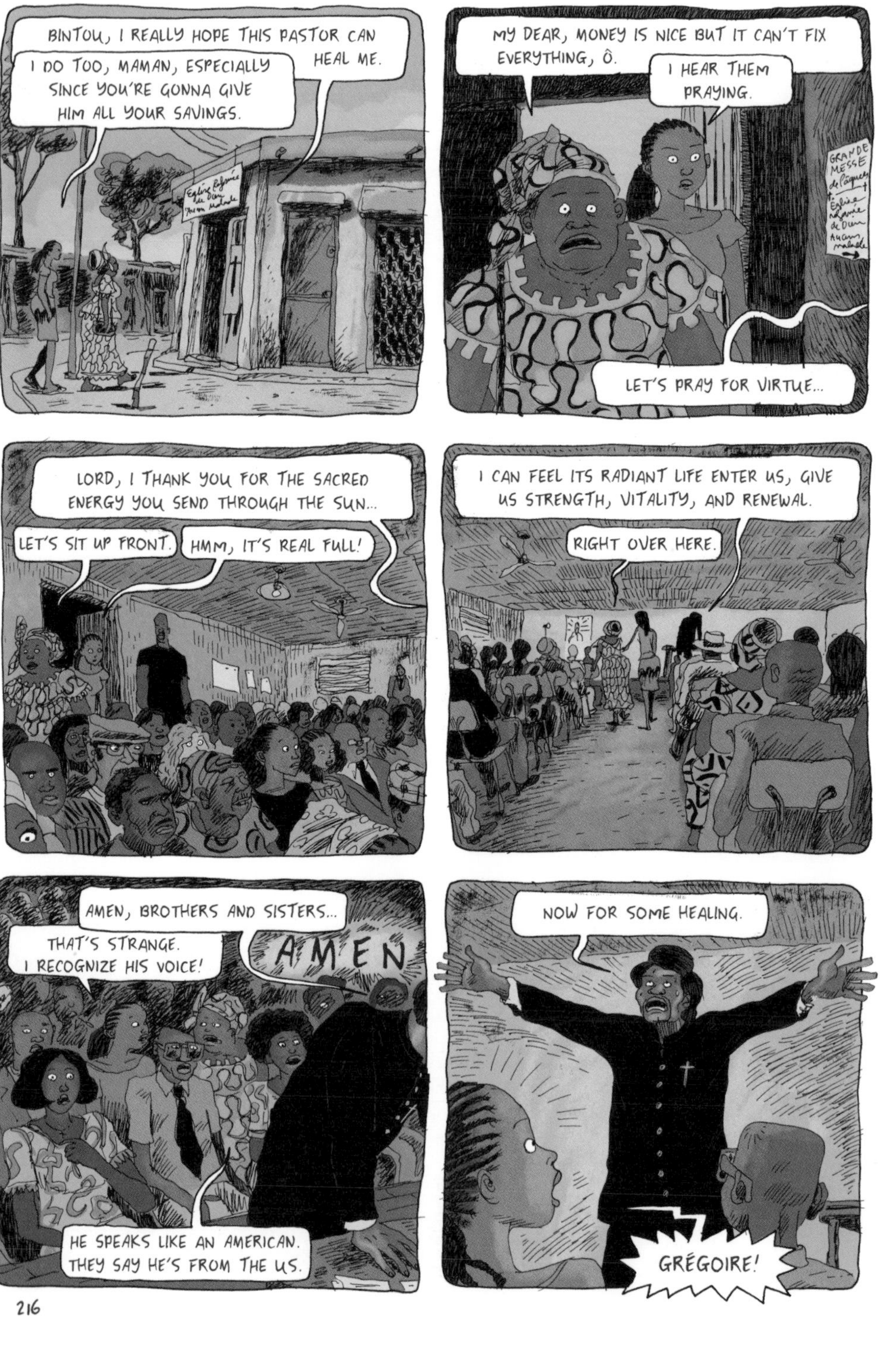
BINTOU, I REALLY HOPE THIS PASTOR CAN HEAL ME.
I DO TOO, MAMAN, ESPECIALLY SINCE YOU'RE GONNA GIVE HIM ALL YOUR SAVINGS.
MY DEAR, MONEY IS NICE BUT IT CAN'T FIX EVERYTHING, Ô.
I HEAR THEM PRAYING.
GRANDE MESSE de Pâques
LET'S PRAY FOR VIRTUE...
LORD, I THANK YOU FOR THE SACRED ENERGY YOU SEND THROUGH THE SUN...
LET'S SIT UP FRONT.
HMM, IT'S REAL FULL!
I CAN FEEL ITS RADIANT LIFE ENTER US, GIVE US STRENGTH, VITALITY, AND RENEWAL.
RIGHT OVER HERE.
AMEN, BROTHERS AND SISTERS...
THAT'S STRANGE. I RECOGNIZE HIS VOICE!
AMEN
HE SPEAKS LIKE AN AMERICAN. THEY SAY HE'S FROM THE US.
NOW FOR SOME HEALING.
GRÉGOIRE!

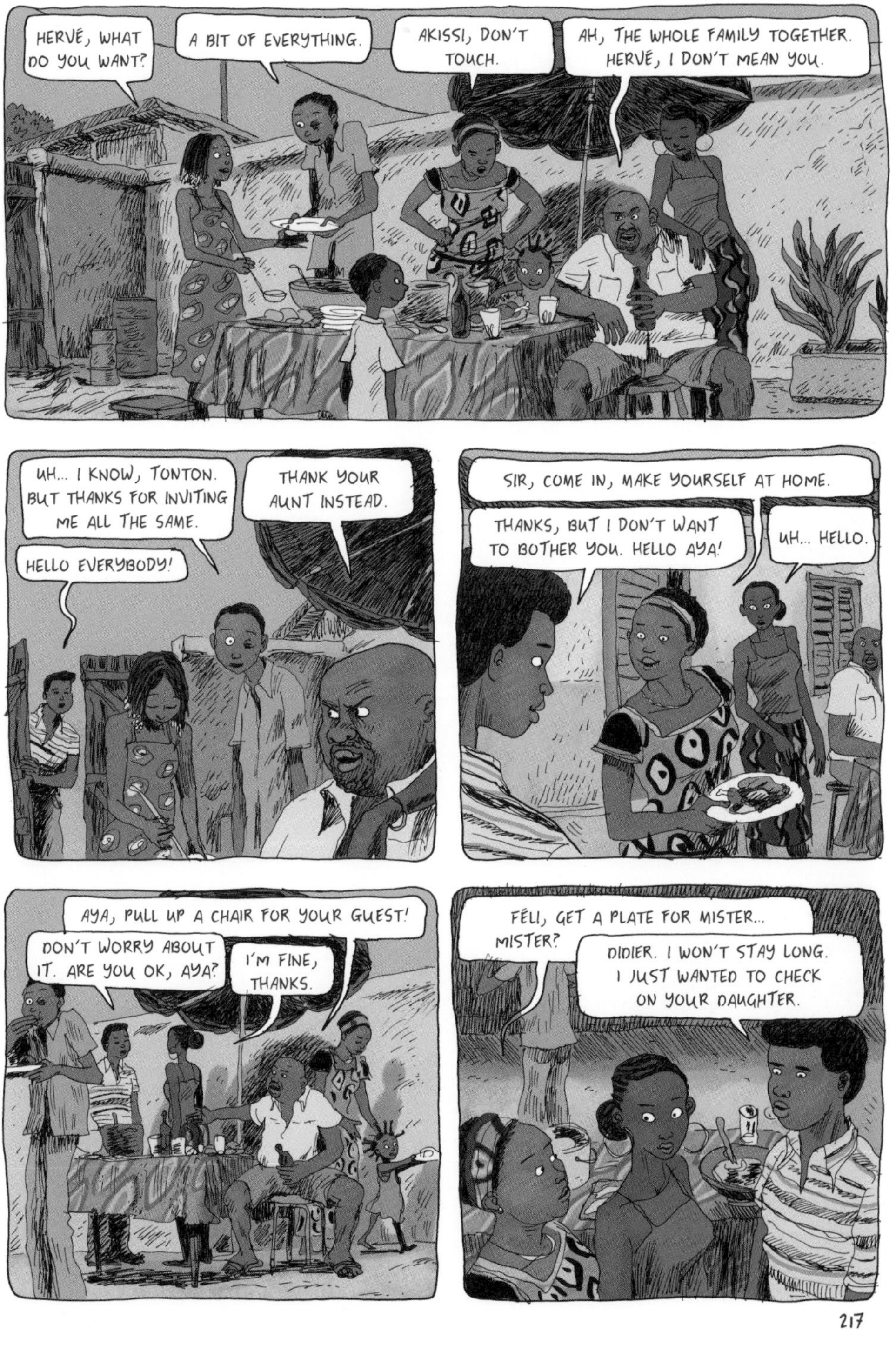
HERVÉ, WHAT DO YOU WANT?
A BIT OF EVERYTHING.
AKISSI, DON'T TOUCH.
AH, THE WHOLE FAMILY TOGETHER. HERVÉ, I DON'T MEAN YOU.
UH... I KNOW, TONTON. BUT THANKS FOR INVITING ME ALL THE SAME.
THANK YOUR AUNT INSTEAD.
HELLO EVERYBODY!
SIR, COME IN, MAKE YOURSELF AT HOME.
THANKS, BUT I DON'T WANT TO BOTHER YOU. HELLO AYA!
UH... HELLO.
AYA, PULL UP A CHAIR FOR YOUR GUEST!
DON'T WORRY ABOUT IT. ARE YOU OK, AYA?
I'M FINE, THANKS.
FÉLI, GET A PLATE FOR MISTER... MISTER?
DIDIER. I WON'T STAY LONG. I JUST WANTED TO CHECK ON YOUR DAUGHTER.

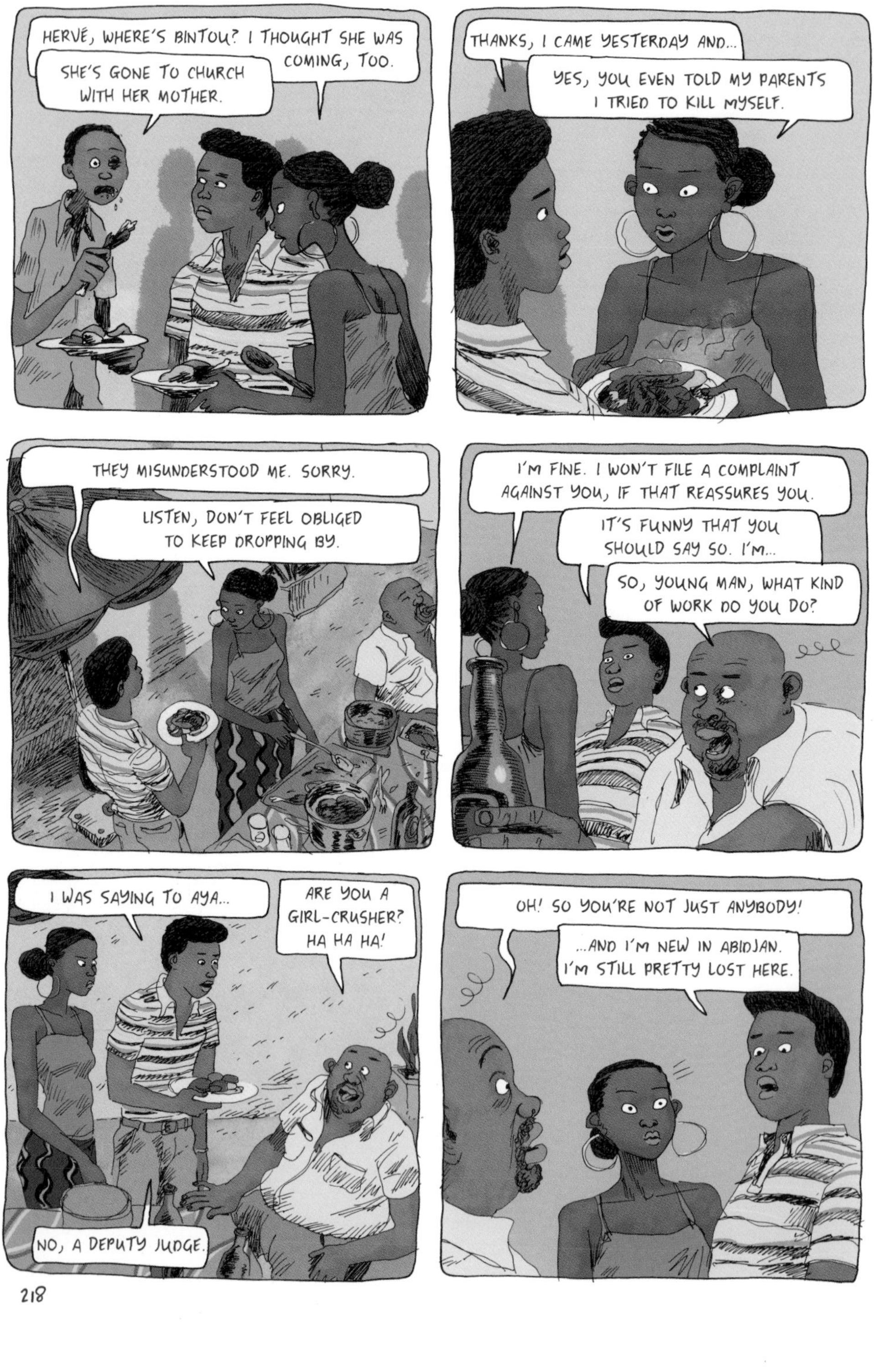
HERVÉ, WHERE'S BINTOU? I THOUGHT SHE WAS COMING, TOO.
SHE'S GONE TO CHURCH WITH HER MOTHER.
THANKS, I CAME YESTERDAY AND...
YES, YOU EVEN TOLD MY PARENTS I TRIED TO KILL MYSELF.
THEY MISUNDERSTOOD ME. SORRY.
LISTEN, DON'T FEEL OBLIGED TO KEEP DROPPING BY.
I'M FINE. I WON'T FILE A COMPLAINT AGAINST YOU, IF THAT REASSURES YOU.
IT'S FUNNY THAT YOU SHOULD SAY SO. I'M...
SO, YOUNG MAN, WHAT KIND OF WORK DO YOU DO?
I WAS SAYING TO AYA...
ARE YOU A GIRL-CRUSHER? HA HA HA!
NO, A DEPUTY JUDGE.
OH! SO YOU'RE NOT JUST ANYBODY!
...AND I'M NEW IN ABIDJAN. I'M STILL PRETTY LOST HERE.

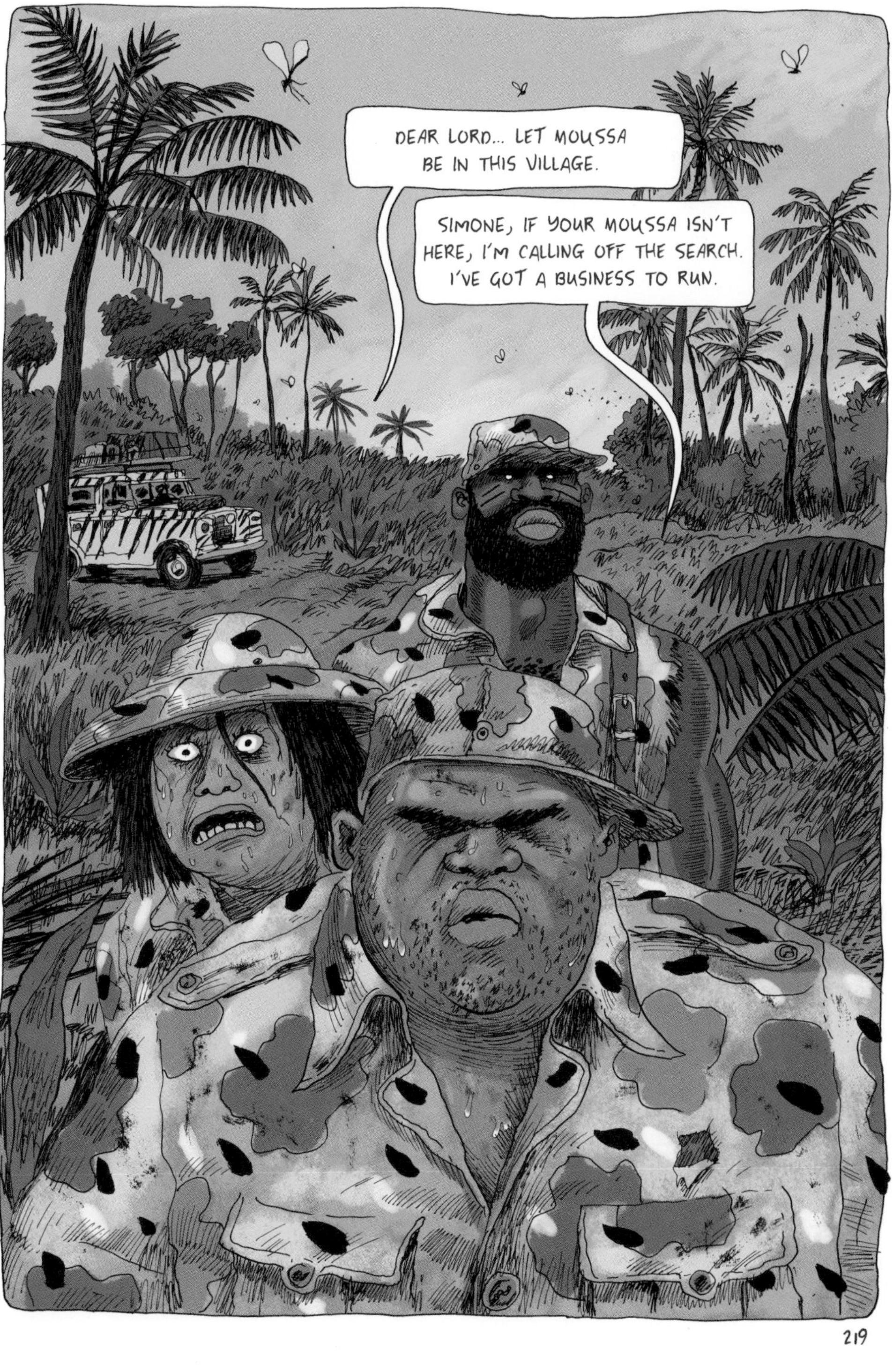
DEAR LORD... LET MOUSSA BE IN THIS VILLAGE.
SIMONE, IF YOUR MOUSSA ISN'T HERE, I'M CALLING OFF THE SEARCH. I'VE GOT A BUSINESS TO RUN.

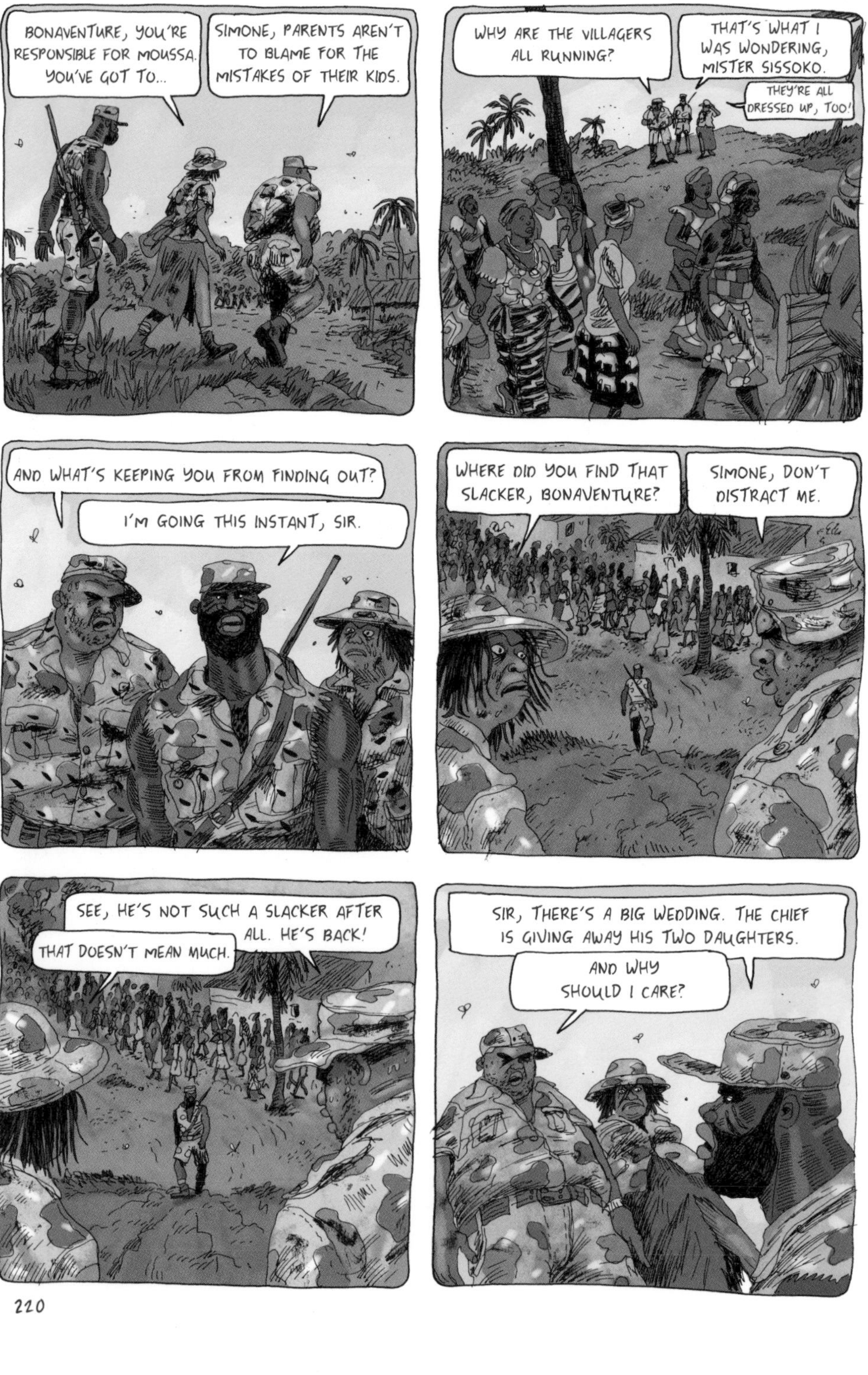
BONAVENTURE, YOU'RE RESPONSIBLE FOR MOUSSA. YOU'VE GOT TO...
SIMONE, PARENTS AREN'T TO BLAME FOR THE MISTAKES OF THEIR KIDS.
WHY ARE THE VILLAGERS ALL RUNNING?
THAT'S WHAT I WAS WONDERING, MISTER SISSOKO.
THEY'RE ALL DRESSED UP, TOO!
AND WHAT'S KEEPING YOU FROM FINDING OUT?
I'M GOING THIS INSTANT, SIR.
WHERE DID YOU FIND THAT SLACKER, BONAVENTURE?
SIMONE, DON'T DISTRACT ME.
SEE, HE'S NOT SUCH A SLACKER AFTER ALL. HE'S BACK!
THAT DOESN'T MEAN MUCH.
SIR, THERE'S A BIG WEDDING. THE CHIEF IS GIVING AWAY HIS TWO DAUGHTERS.
AND WHY SHOULD I CARE?

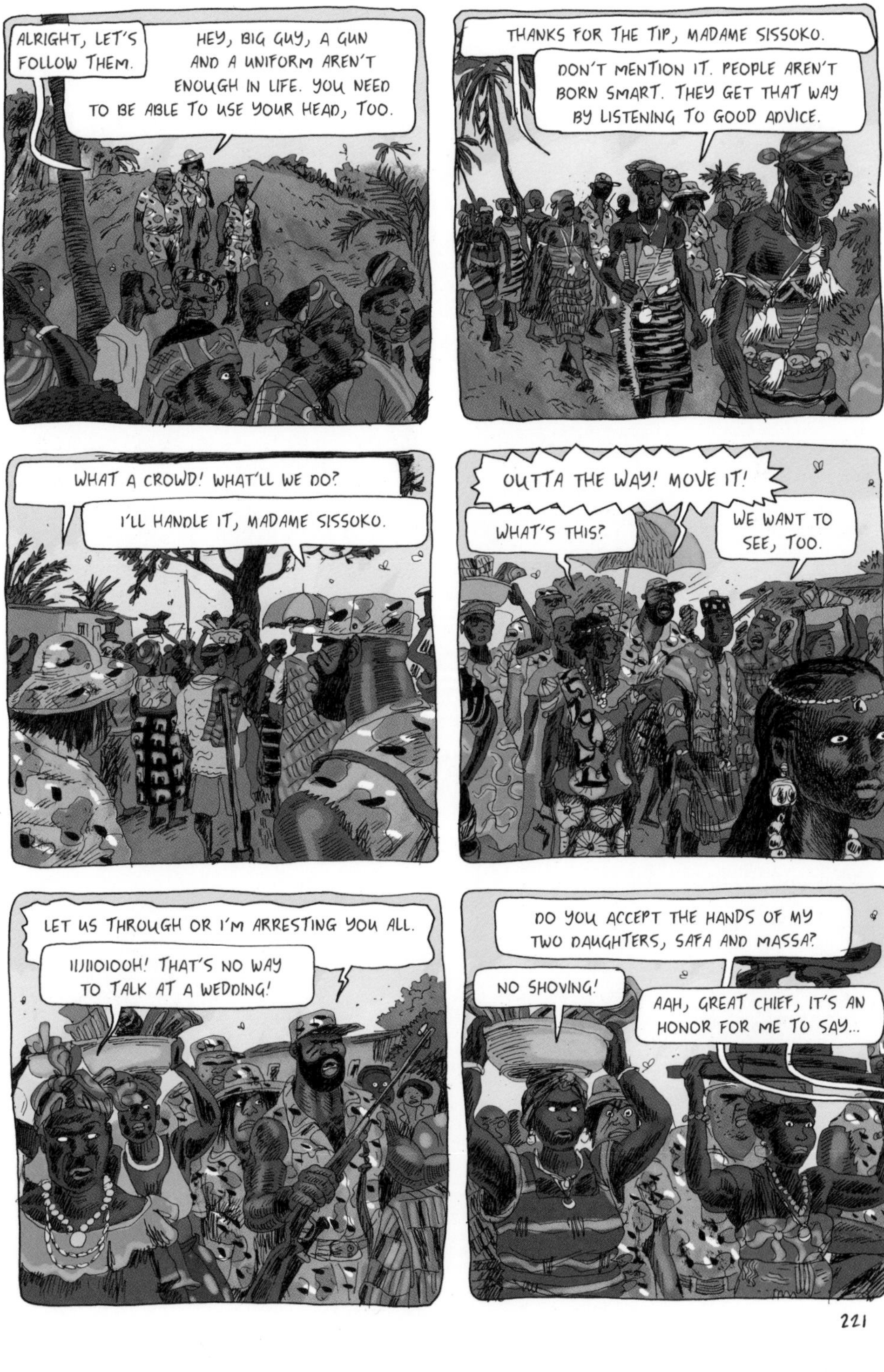
ALRIGHT, LET'S FOLLOW THEM.
HEY, BIG GUY, A GUN AND A UNIFORM AREN'T ENOUGH IN LIFE. YOU NEED TO BE ABLE TO USE YOUR HEAD, TOO.
THANKS FOR THE TIP, MADAME SISSOKO.
DON'T MENTION IT. PEOPLE AREN'T BORN SMART. THEY GET THAT WAY BY LISTENING TO GOOD ADVICE.
WHAT A CROWD! WHAT'LL WE DO?
I'LL HANDLE IT, MADAME SISSOKO.
OUTTA THE WAY! MOVE IT!
WHAT'S THIS?
WE WANT TO SEE, TOO.
LET US THROUGH OR I'M ARRESTING YOU ALL.
IIJIIOIOOH! THAT'S NO WAY TO TALK AT A WEDDING!
DO YOU ACCEPT THE HANDS OF MY TWO DAUGHTERS, SAFA AND MASSA?
NO SHOVING!
AAH, GREAT CHIEF, IT'S AN HONOR FOR ME TO SAY...

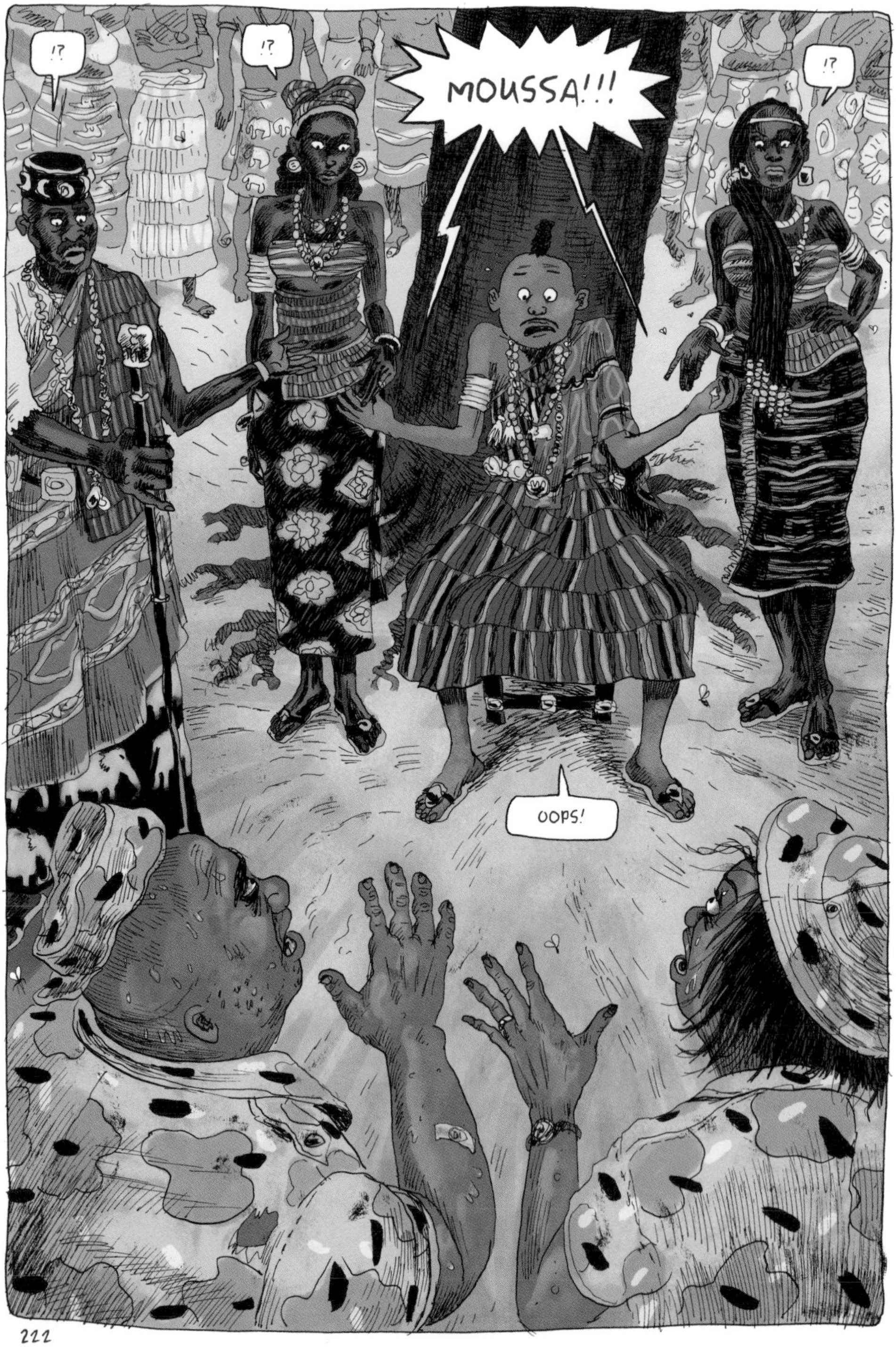
!?
!?
MOUSSA!!!
!?
OOPS!

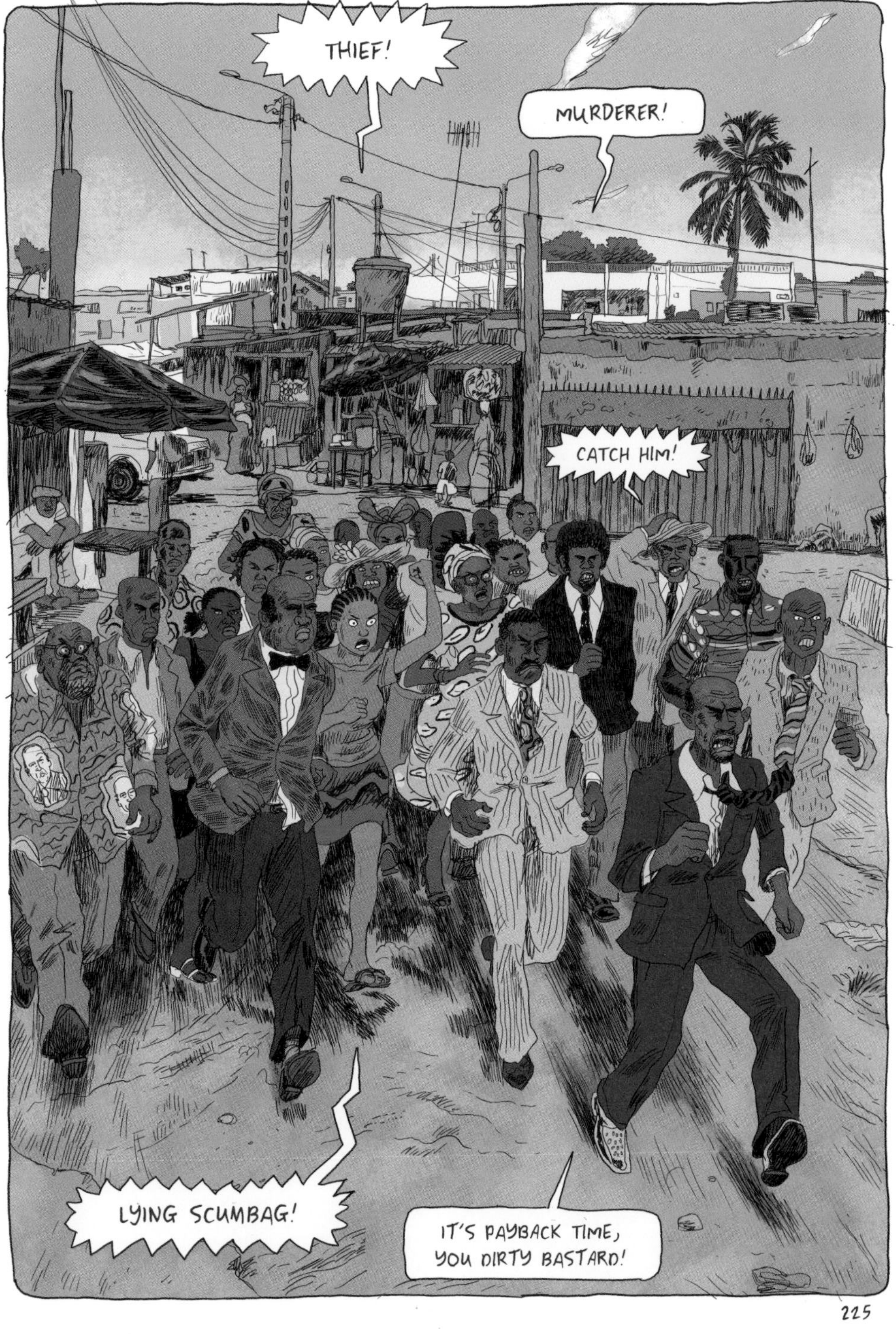
THIEF!
MURDERER!
CATCH HIM!
LYING SCUMBAG!
IT'S PAYBACK TIME,
YOU DIRTY BASTARD!

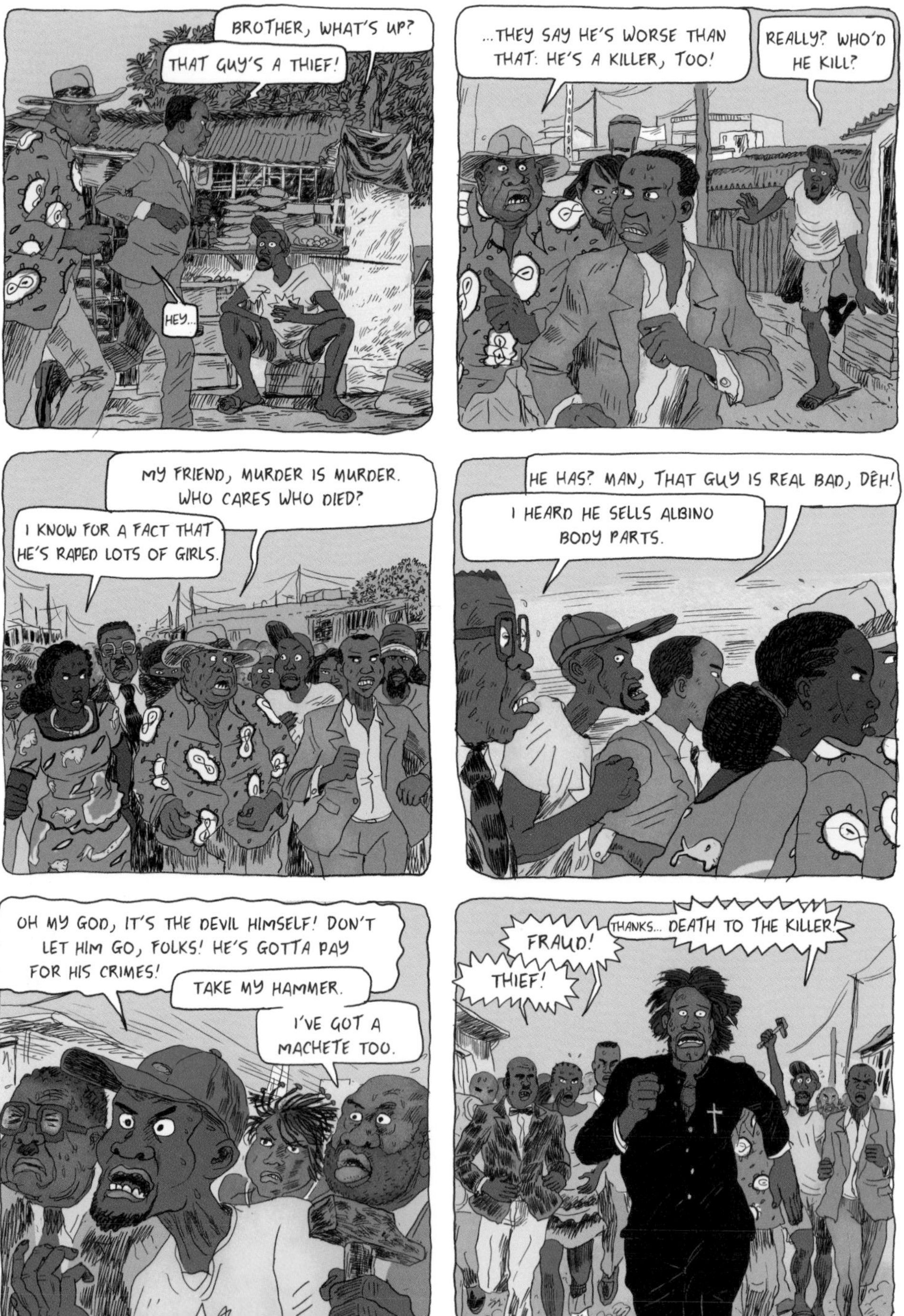
BROTHER, WHAT'S UP?
THAT GUY'S A THIEF!
HEY...
...THEY SAY HE'S WORSE THAN THAT: HE'S A KILLER, TOO!
REALLY? WHO'D HE KILL?
MY FRIEND, MURDER IS MURDER. WHO CARES WHO DIED?
I KNOW FOR A FACT THAT HE'S RAPED LOTS OF GIRLS.
HE HAS? MAN, THAT GUY IS REAL BAD, DÊH!
I HEARD HE SELLS ALBINO BODY PARTS.
OH MY GOD, IT'S THE DEVIL HIMSELF! DON'T LET HIM GO, FOLKS! HE'S GOTTA PAY FOR HIS CRIMES!
TAKE MY HAMMER.
I'VE GOT A MACHETE TOO.
THANKS... DEATH TO THE KILLER!
FRAUD!
THIEF!

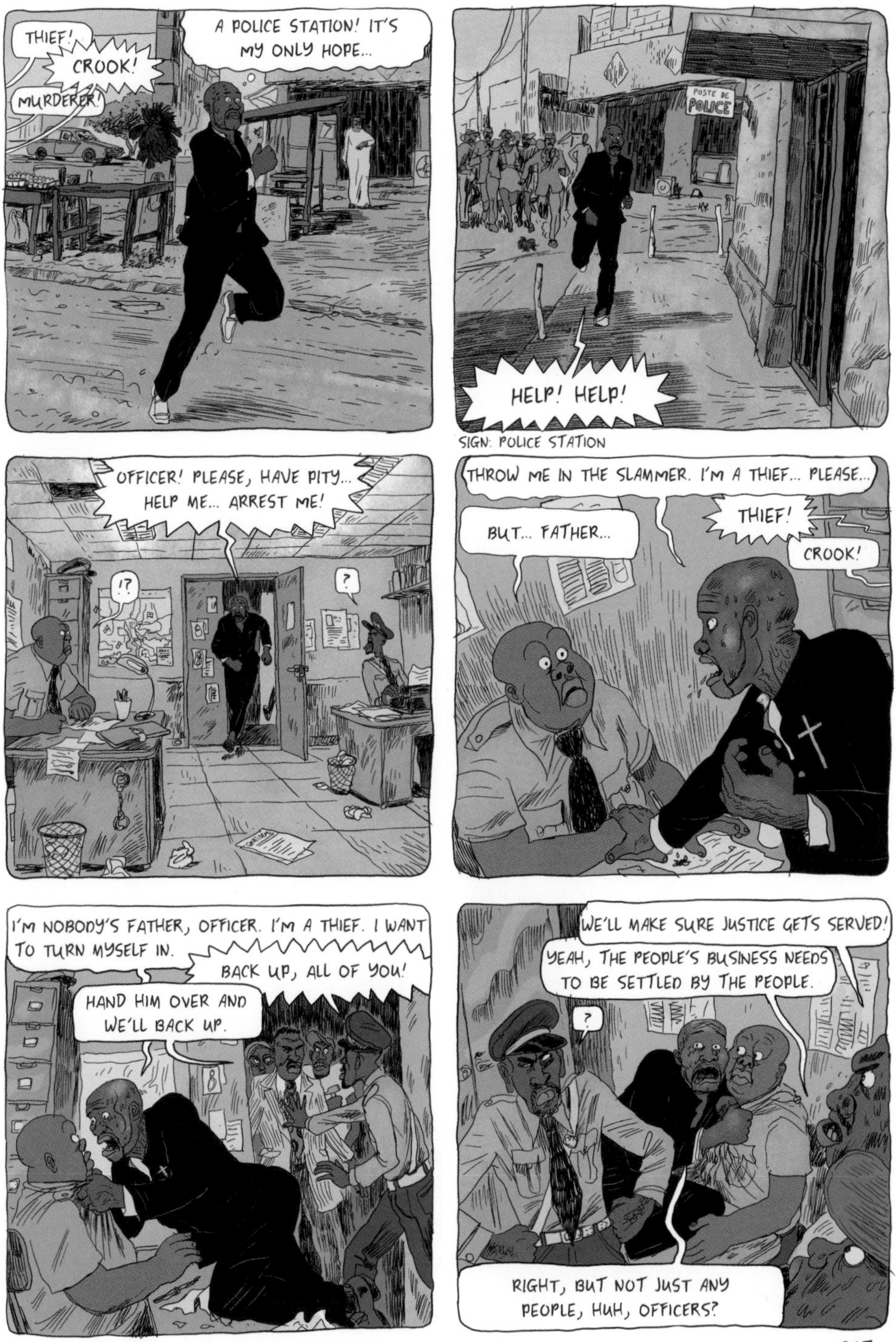
THIEF!
CROOK!
MURDERER!
A POLICE STATION! IT'S MY ONLY HOPE...
POSTE DE POLICE
HELP! HELP!
OFFICER! PLEASE, HAVE PITY... HELP ME... ARREST ME!
!?
?
THROW ME IN THE SLAMMER. I'M A THIEF... PLEASE...
BUT... FATHER...
THIEF!
CROOK!
I'M NOBODY'S FATHER, OFFICER. I'M A THIEF. I WANT TO TURN MYSELF IN.
BACK UP, ALL OF YOU!
HAND HIM OVER AND WE'LL BACK UP.
WE'LL MAKE SURE JUSTICE GETS SERVED!
YEAH, THE PEOPLE'S BUSINESS NEEDS TO BE SETTLED BY THE PEOPLE.
?
RIGHT, BUT NOT JUST ANY PEOPLE, HUH, OFFICERS?

SIGN: POLICE STATION

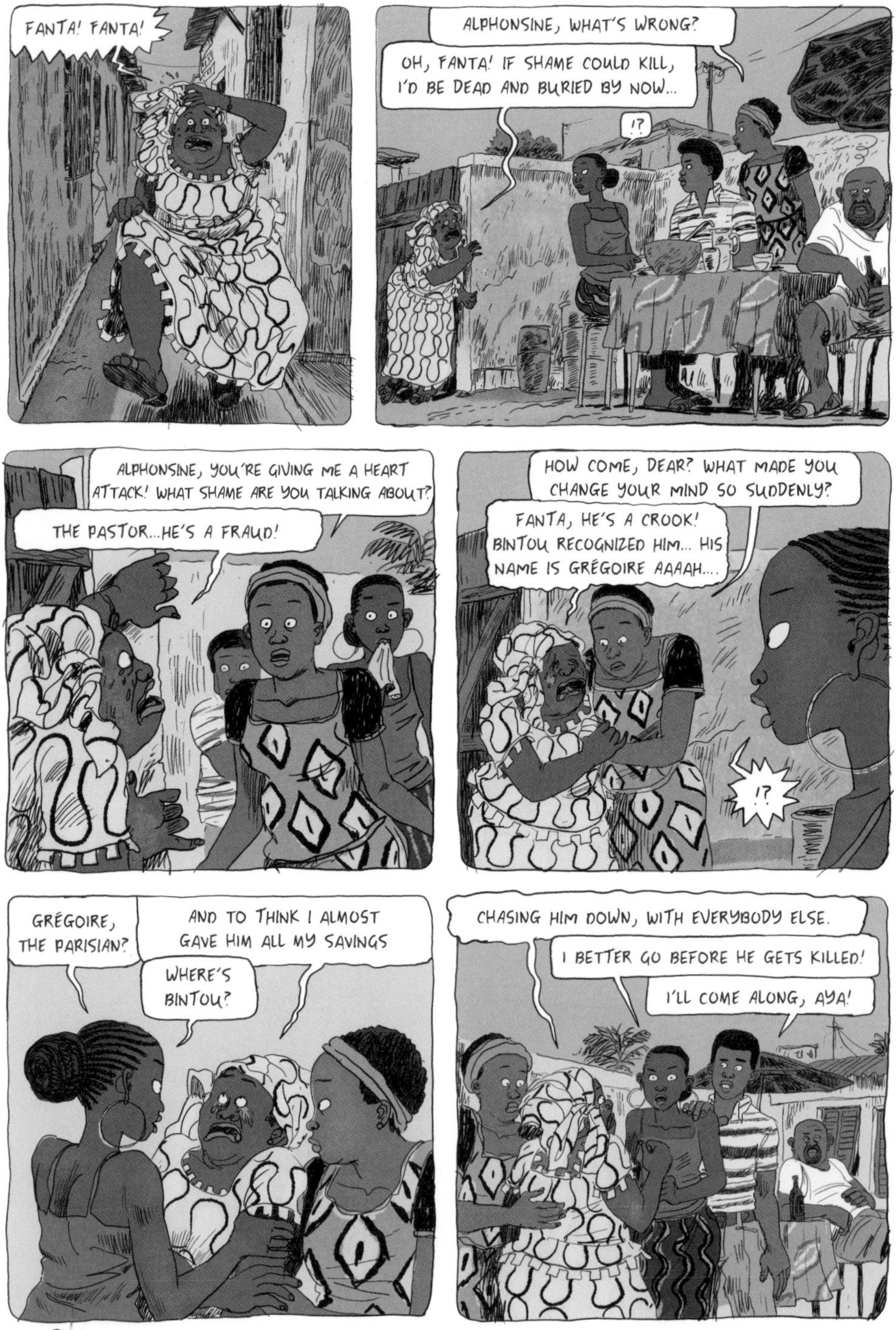
FANTA! FANTA!
ALPHONSINE, WHAT'S WRONG?
OH, FANTA! IF SHAME COULD KILL, I'D BE DEAD AND BURIED BY NOW...
!?
ALPHONSINE, YOU'RE GIVING ME A HEART ATTACK! WHAT SHAME ARE YOU TALKING ABOUT?
THE PASTOR...HE'S A FRAUD!
HOW COME, DEAR? WHAT MADE YOU CHANGE YOUR MIND SO SUDDENLY?
FANTA, HE'S A CROOK! BINTOU RECOGNIZED HIM... HIS NAME IS GRÉGOIRE AAAAH....
!?
GRÉGOIRE, THE PARISIAN?
AND TO THINK I ALMOST GAVE HIM ALL MY SAVINGS
WHERE'S BINTOU?
CHASING HIM DOWN, WITH EVERYBODY ELSE.
I BETTER GO BEFORE HE GETS KILLED!
I'LL COME ALONG, AYA!

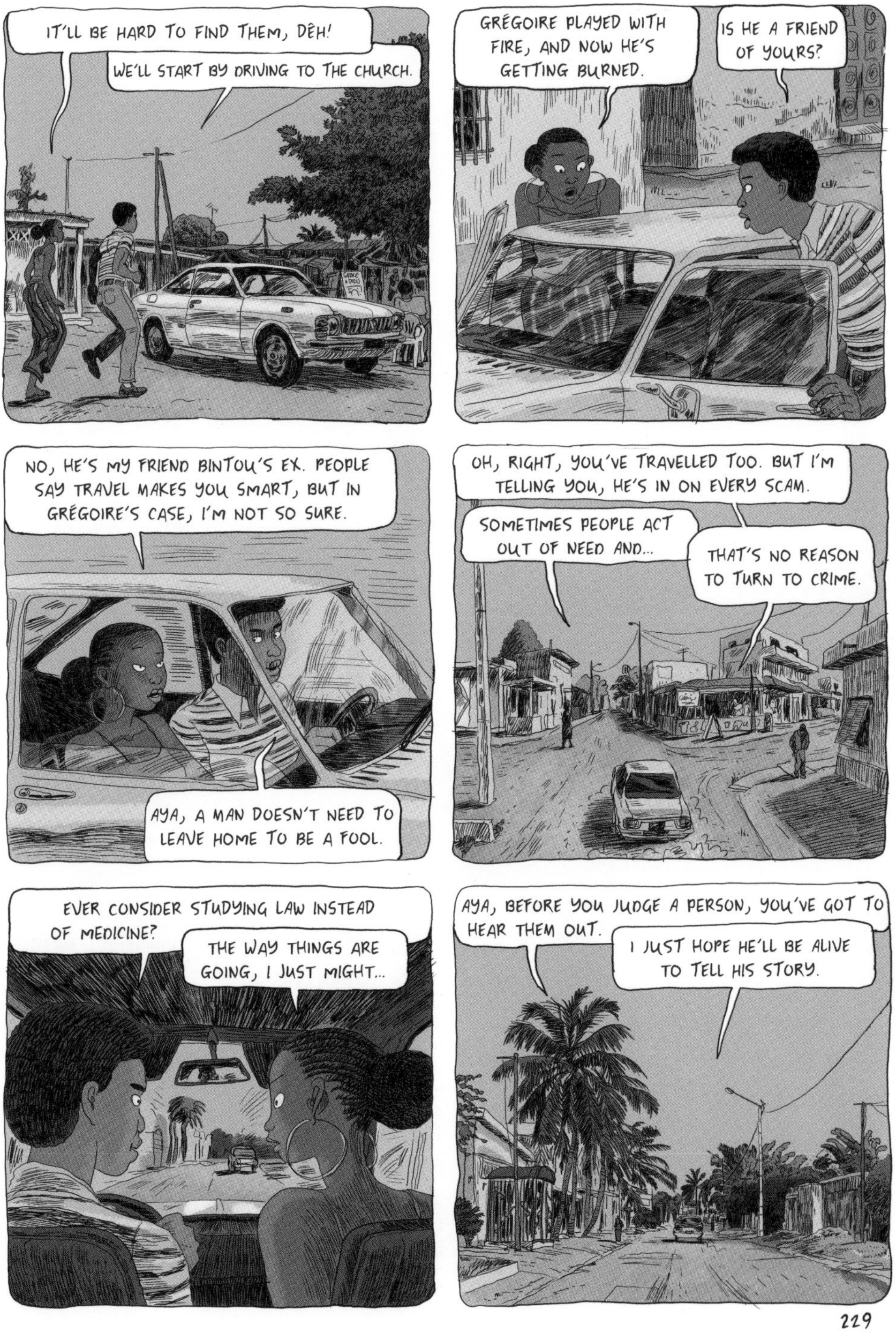
IT'LL BE HARD TO FIND THEM, DÊH!
WE'LL START BY DRIVING TO THE CHURCH.
GRÉGOIRE PLAYED WITH FIRE, AND NOW HE'S GETTING BURNED.
IS HE A FRIEND OF YOURS?
NO, HE'S MY FRIEND BINTOU'S EX. PEOPLE SAY TRAVEL MAKES YOU SMART, BUT IN GRÉGOIRE'S CASE, I'M NOT SO SURE.
AYA, A MAN DOESN'T NEED TO LEAVE HOME TO BE A FOOL.
OH, RIGHT, YOU'VE TRAVELLED TOO. BUT I'M TELLING YOU, HE'S IN ON EVERY SCAM.
SOMETIMES PEOPLE ACT OUT OF NEED AND...
THAT'S NO REASON TO TURN TO CRIME.
EVER CONSIDER STUDYING LAW INSTEAD OF MEDICINE?
THE WAY THINGS ARE GOING, I JUST MIGHT...
AYA, BEFORE YOU JUDGE A PERSON, YOU'VE GOT TO HEAR THEM OUT.
I JUST HOPE HE'LL BE ALIVE TO TELL HIS STORY.

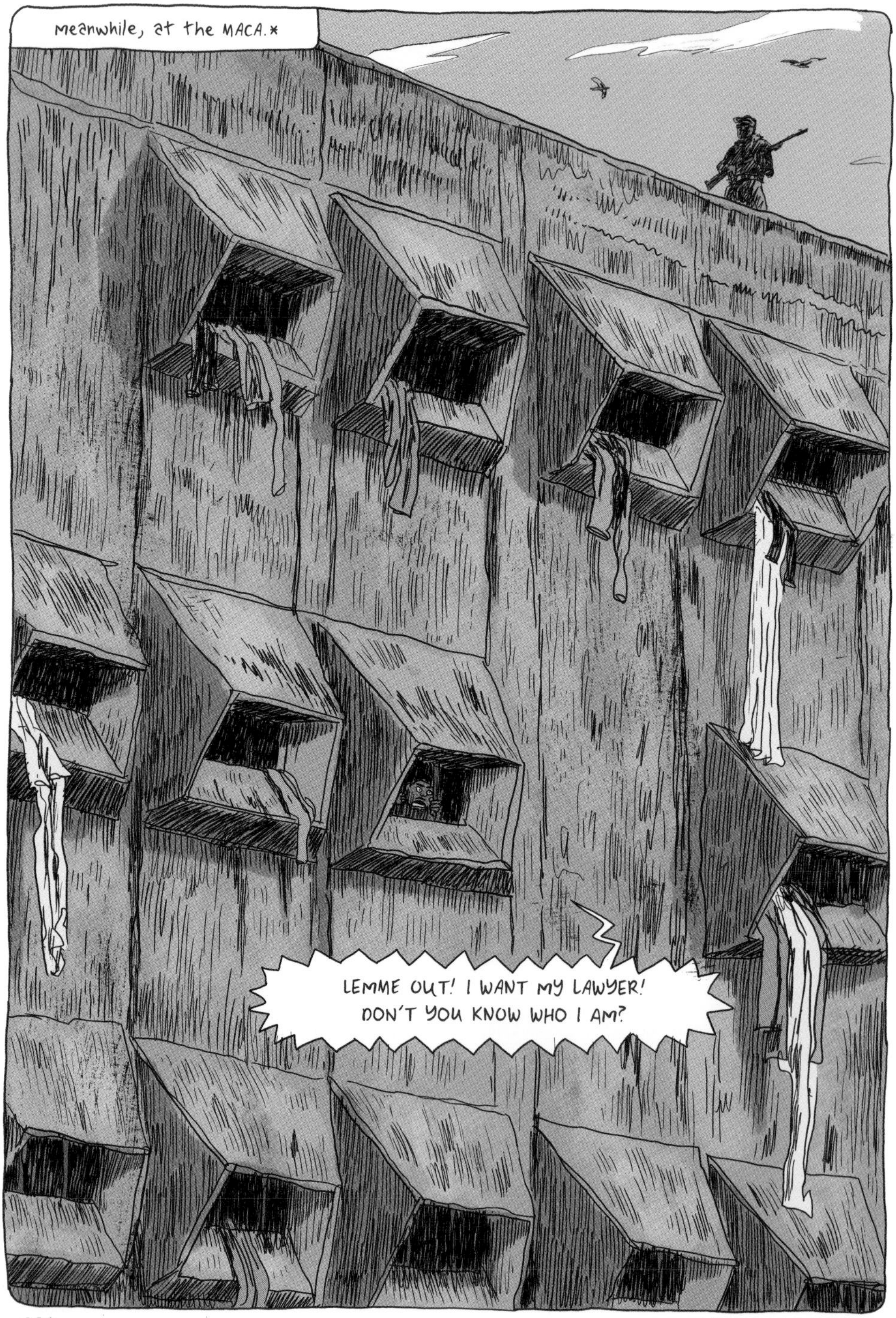
Meanwhile, at the MACA.*
LEMME OUT! I WANT MY LAWYER! DON'T YOU KNOW WHO I AM?



*Abidjan Central Prison

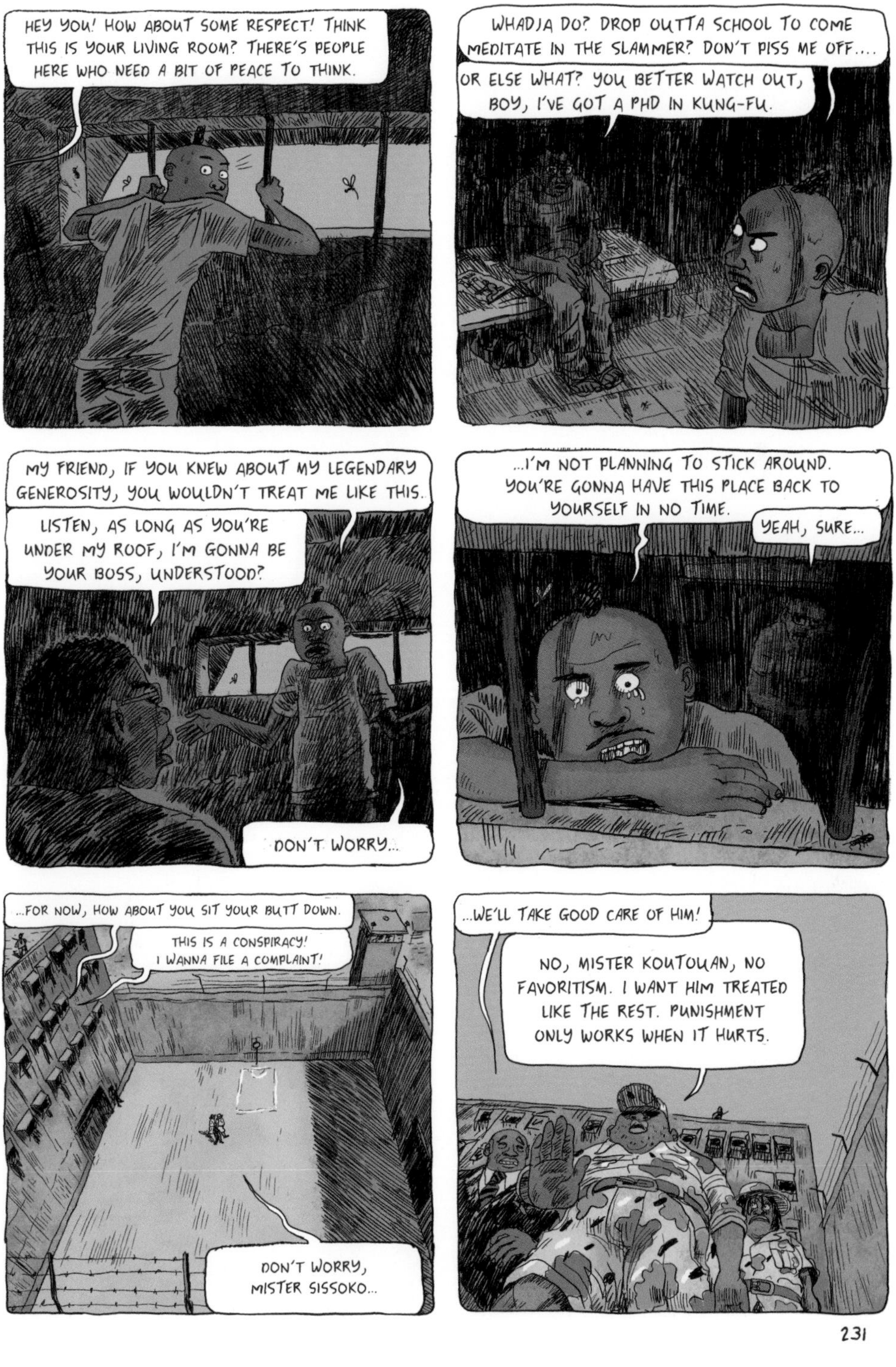
HEY YOU! HOW ABOUT SOME RESPECT! THINK THIS IS YOUR LIVING ROOM? THERE'S PEOPLE HERE WHO NEED A BIT OF PEACE TO THINK.
WHADJA DO? DROP OUTTA SCHOOL TO COME MEDITATE IN THE SLAMMER? DON'T PISS ME OFF....
OR ELSE WHAT? YOU BETTER WATCH OUT, BOY, I'VE GOT A PHD IN KUNG-FU.
MY FRIEND, IF YOU KNEW ABOUT MY LEGENDARY GENEROSITY, YOU WOULDN'T TREAT ME LIKE THIS.
LISTEN, AS LONG AS YOU'RE UNDER MY ROOF, I'M GONNA BE YOUR BOSS, UNDERSTOOD?
DON'T WORRY...
...I'M NOT PLANNING TO STICK AROUND. YOU'RE GONNA HAVE THIS PLACE BACK TO YOURSELF IN NO TIME.
YEAH, SURE...
...FOR NOW, HOW ABOUT YOU SIT YOUR BUTT DOWN.
THIS IS A CONSPIRACY! I WANNA FILE A COMPLAINT!
DON'T WORRY, MISTER SISSOKO...
...WE'LL TAKE GOOD CARE OF HIM!
NO, MISTER KOUTOUAN, NO FAVORITISM. I WANT HIM TREATED LIKE THE REST. PUNISHMENT ONLY WORKS WHEN IT HURTS.

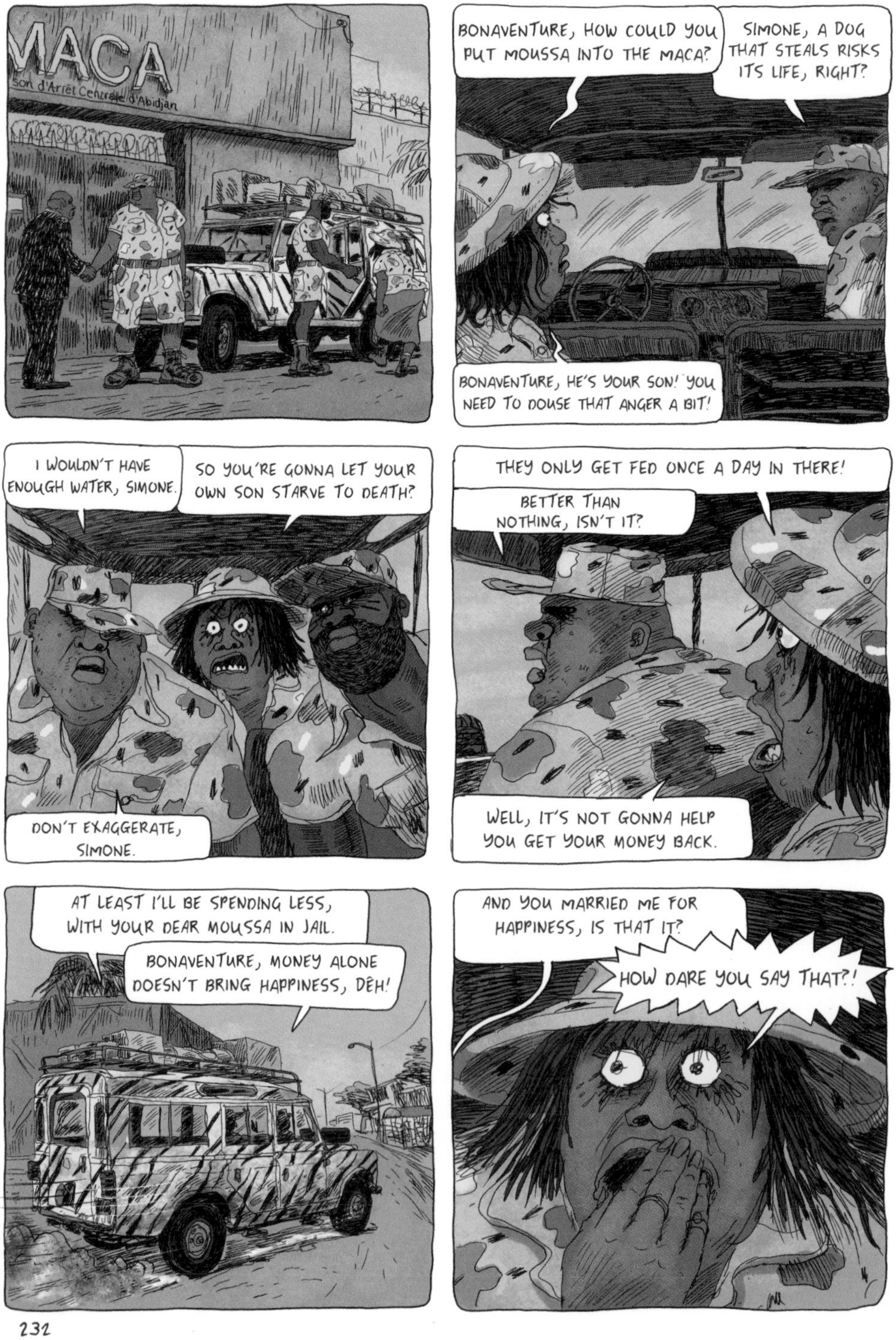
MACA
son d'Arrêt Centrale d'Abidjan
BONAVENTURE, HOW COULD YOU PUT MOUSSA INTO THE MACA?
SIMONE, A DOG THAT STEALS RISKS ITS LIFE, RIGHT?
BONAVENTURE, HE'S YOUR SON! YOU NEED TO DOUSE THAT ANGER A BIT!
I WOULDN'T HAVE ENOUGH WATER, SIMONE.
SO YOU'RE GONNA LET YOUR OWN SON STARVE TO DEATH?
DON'T EXAGGERATE, SIMONE.
THEY ONLY GET FED ONCE A DAY IN THERE!
BETTER THAN NOTHING, ISN'T IT?
WELL, IT'S NOT GONNA HELP YOU GET YOUR MONEY BACK.
AT LEAST I'LL BE SPENDING LESS, WITH YOUR DEAR MOUSSA IN JAIL.
BONAVENTURE, MONEY ALONE DOESN'T BRING HAPPINESS, DÊH!
AND YOU MARRIED ME FOR HAPPINESS, IS THAT IT?
HOW DARE YOU SAY THAT?!

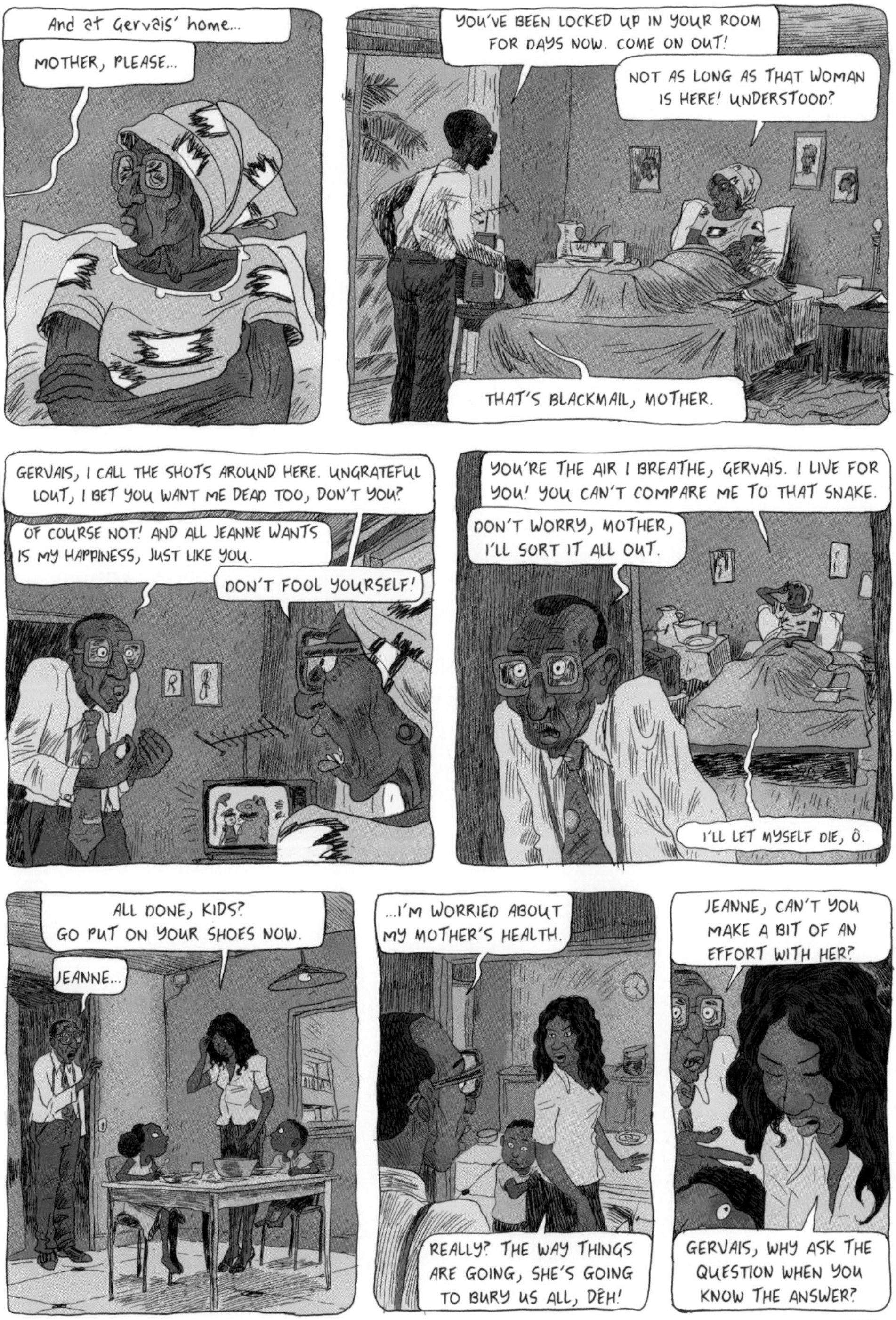
And at Gervais' home...
MOTHER, PLEASE...
YOU'VE BEEN LOCKED UP IN YOUR ROOM FOR DAYS NOW. COME ON OUT!
NOT AS LONG AS THAT WOMAN IS HERE! UNDERSTOOD?
THAT'S BLACKMAIL, MOTHER.
GERVAIS, I CALL THE SHOTS AROUND HERE. UNGRATEFUL LOUT, I BET YOU WANT ME DEAD TOO, DON'T YOU?
OF COURSE NOT! AND ALL JEANNE WANTS IS MY HAPPINESS, JUST LIKE YOU.
DON'T FOOL YOURSELF!
YOU'RE THE AIR I BREATHE, GERVAIS. I LIVE FOR YOU! YOU CAN'T COMPARE ME TO THAT SNAKE.
DON'T WORRY, MOTHER, I'LL SORT IT ALL OUT.
I'LL LET MYSELF DIE, Ô.
ALL DONE, KIDS? GO PUT ON YOUR SHOES NOW.
JEANNE...
...I'M WORRIED ABOUT MY MOTHER'S HEALTH.
REALLY? THE WAY THINGS ARE GOING, SHE'S GOING TO BURY US ALL, DÊH!
JEANNE, CAN'T YOU MAKE A BIT OF AN EFFORT WITH HER?
GERVAIS, WHY ASK THE QUESTION WHEN YOU KNOW THE ANSWER?

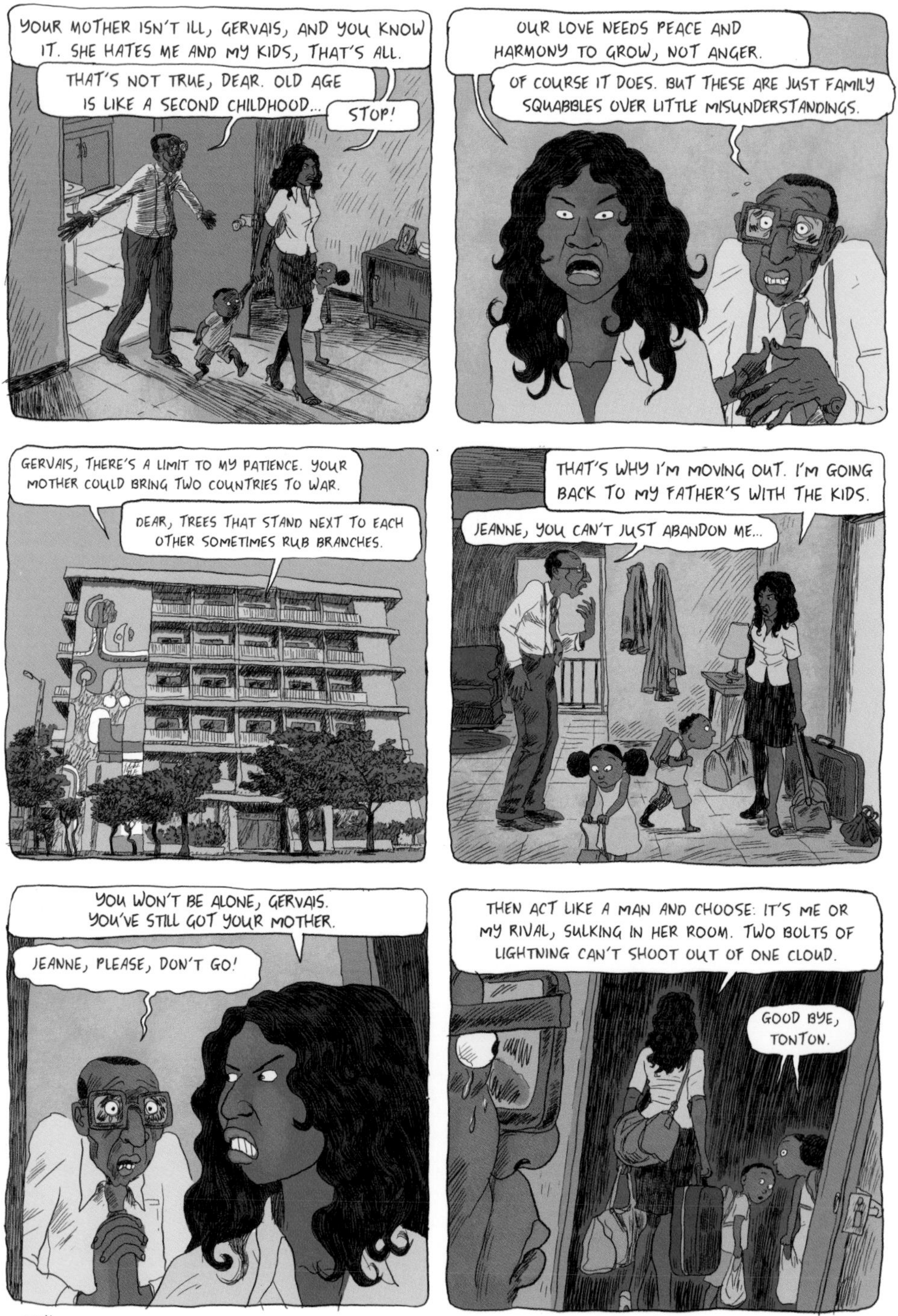
YOUR MOTHER ISN'T ILL, GERVAIS, AND YOU KNOW IT. SHE HATES ME AND MY KIDS, THAT'S ALL.
THAT'S NOT TRUE, DEAR. OLD AGE IS LIKE A SECOND CHILDHOOD...
STOP!
OUR LOVE NEEDS PEACE AND HARMONY TO GROW, NOT ANGER.
OF COURSE IT DOES. BUT THESE ARE JUST FAMILY SQUABBLES OVER LITTLE MISUNDERSTANDINGS.
GERVAIS, THERE'S A LIMIT TO MY PATIENCE. YOUR MOTHER COULD BRING TWO COUNTRIES TO WAR.
DEAR, TREES THAT STAND NEXT TO EACH OTHER SOMETIMES RUB BRANCHES.
THAT'S WHY I'M MOVING OUT. I'M GOING BACK TO MY FATHER'S WITH THE KIDS.
JEANNE, YOU CAN'T JUST ABANDON ME...
YOU WON'T BE ALONE, GERVAIS. YOU'VE STILL GOT YOUR MOTHER.
JEANNE, PLEASE, DON'T GO!
THEN ACT LIKE A MAN AND CHOOSE: IT'S ME OR MY RIVAL, SULKING IN HER ROOM. TWO BOLTS OF LIGHTNING CAN'T SHOOT OUT OF ONE CLOUD.
GOOD BYE, TONTON.

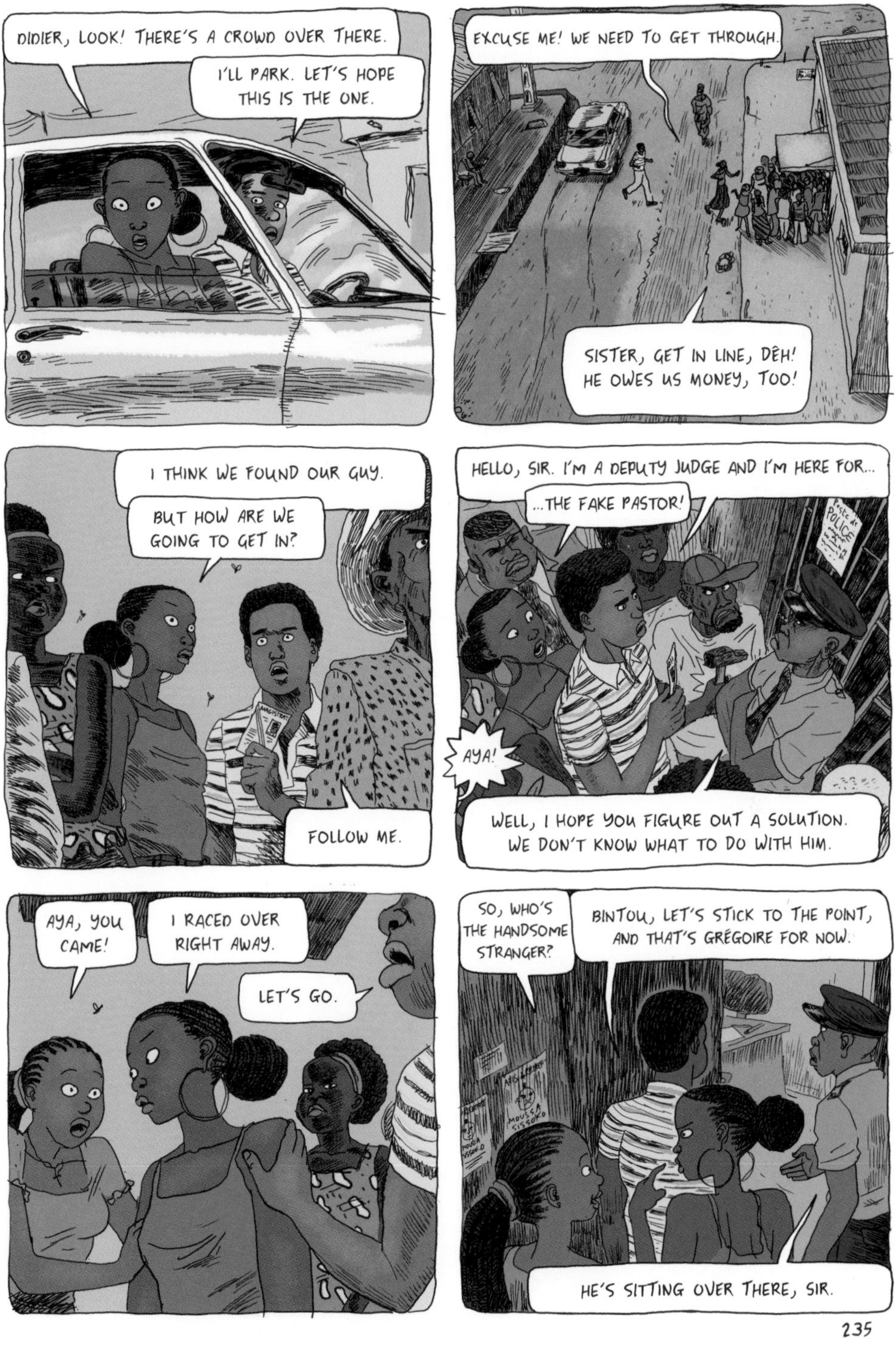
DIDIER, LOOK! THERE'S A CROWD OVER THERE.
I'LL PARK. LET'S HOPE THIS IS THE ONE.
EXCUSE ME! WE NEED TO GET THROUGH.
SISTER, GET IN LINE, DÊH! HE OWES US MONEY, TOO!
I THINK WE FOUND OUR GUY.
BUT HOW ARE WE GOING TO GET IN?
MAGISTRAT
FOLLOW ME.
HELLO, SIR. I'M A DEPUTY JUDGE AND I'M HERE FOR...
...THE FAKE PASTOR!
POLICE
AYA!
WELL, I HOPE YOU FIGURE OUT A SOLUTION. WE DON'T KNOW WHAT TO DO WITH HIM.
AYA, YOU CAME!
I RACED OVER RIGHT AWAY.
LET'S GO.
SO, WHO'S THE HANDSOME STRANGER?
BINTOU, LET'S STICK TO THE POINT, AND THAT'S GRÉGOIRE FOR NOW.
MOUSSA SISSOKO
HE'S SITTING OVER THERE, SIR.

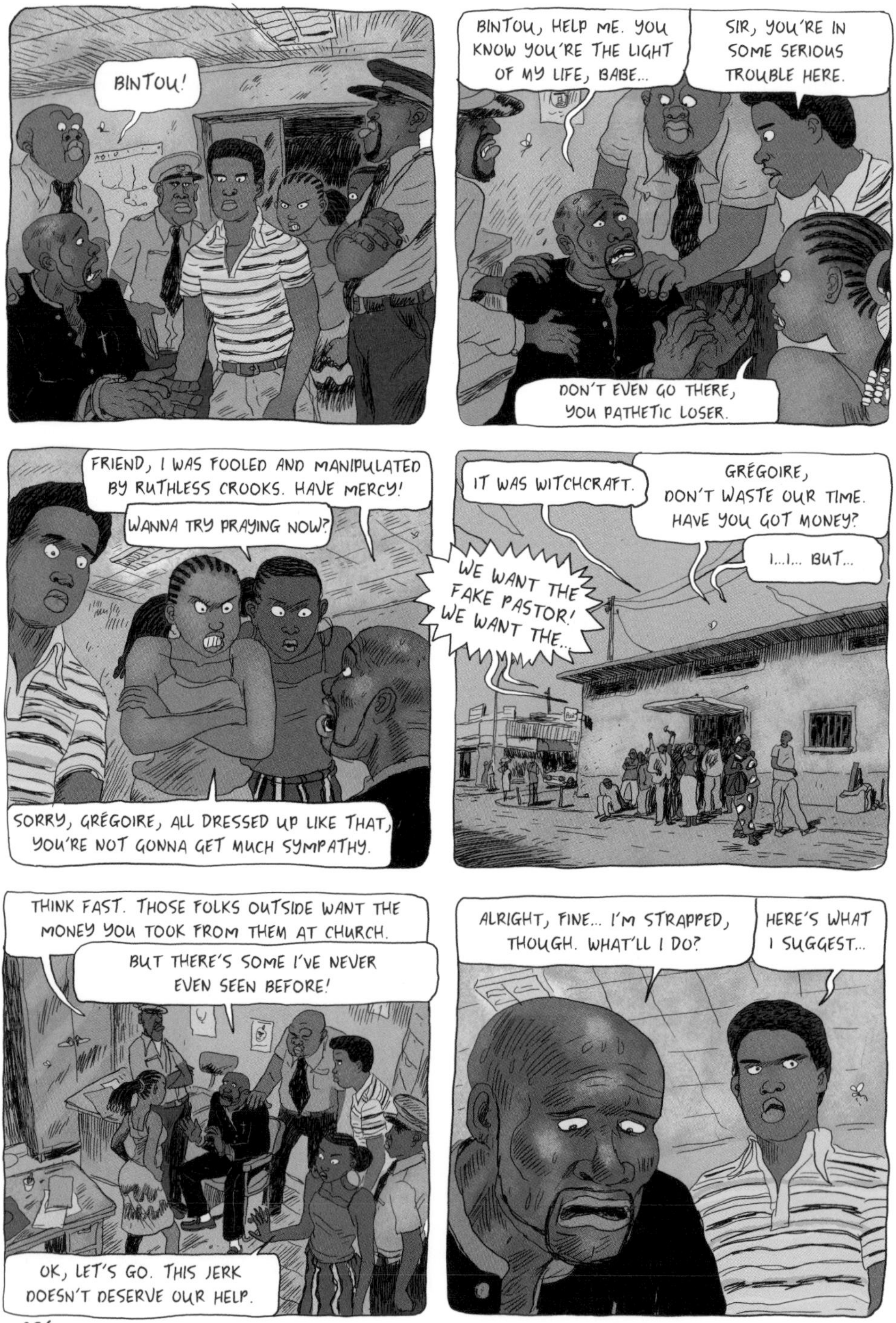
BINTOU!
BINTOU, HELP ME. YOU KNOW YOU'RE THE LIGHT OF MY LIFE, BABE...
SIR, YOU'RE IN SOME SERIOUS TROUBLE HERE.
DON'T EVEN GO THERE, YOU PATHETIC LOSER.
FRIEND, I WAS FOOLED AND MANIPULATED BY RUTHLESS CROOKS. HAVE MERCY!
WANNA TRY PRAYING NOW?
SORRY, GRÉGOIRE, ALL DRESSED UP LIKE THAT, YOU'RE NOT GONNA GET MUCH SYMPATHY.
IT WAS WITCHCRAFT.
GRÉGOIRE, DON'T WASTE OUR TIME. HAVE YOU GOT MONEY?
I...I... BUT...
WE WANT THE FAKE PASTOR! WE WANT THE...
THINK FAST. THOSE FOLKS OUTSIDE WANT THE MONEY YOU TOOK FROM THEM AT CHURCH.
BUT THERE'S SOME I'VE NEVER EVEN SEEN BEFORE!
OK, LET'S GO. THIS JERK DOESN'T DESERVE OUR HELP.
ALRIGHT, FINE... I'M STRAPPED, THOUGH. WHAT'LL I DO?
HERE'S WHAT I SUGGEST...

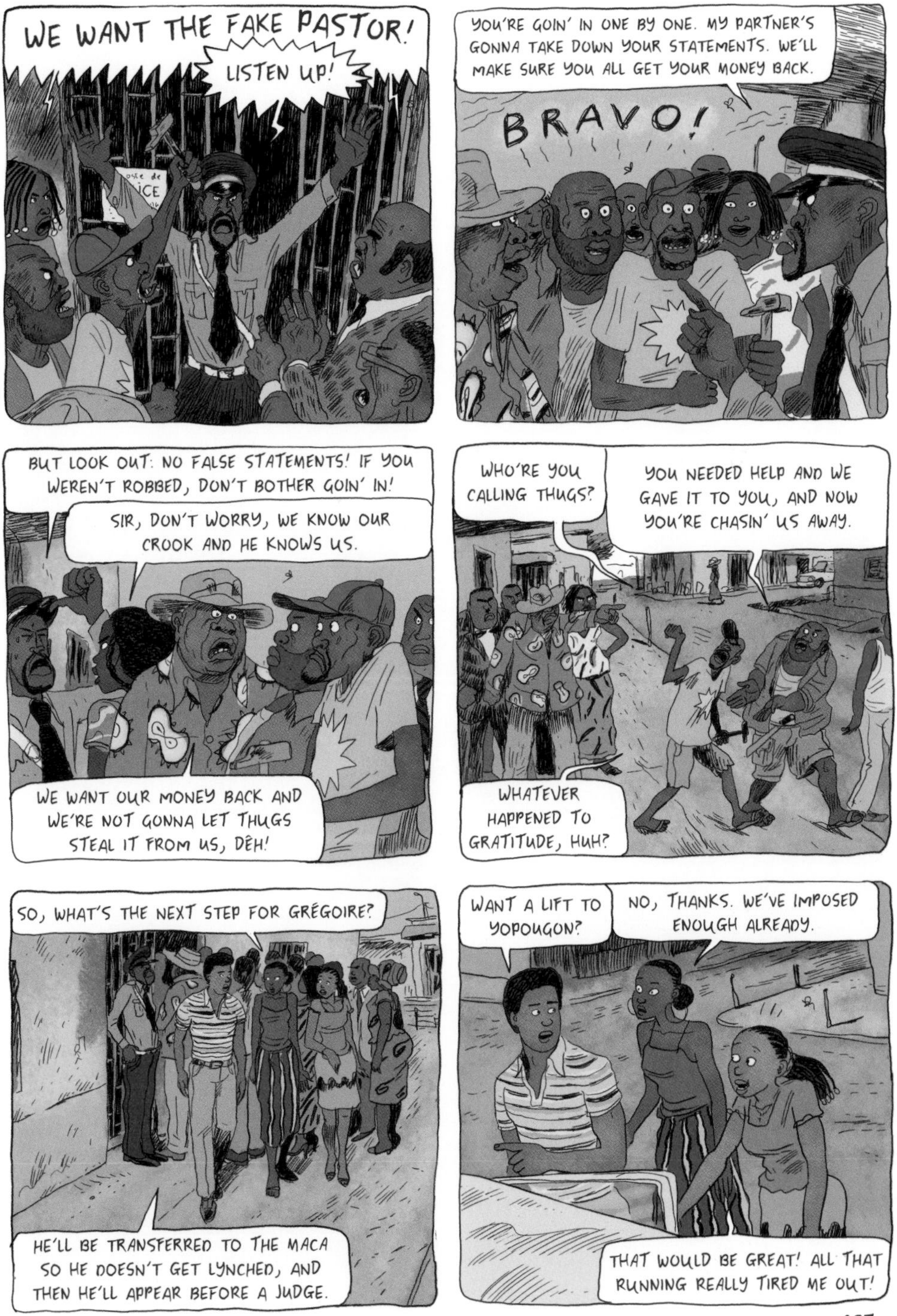
WE WANT THE FAKE PASTOR!
LISTEN UP!
YOU'RE GOIN' IN ONE BY ONE. MY PARTNER'S GONNA TAKE DOWN YOUR STATEMENTS. WE'LL MAKE SURE YOU ALL GET YOUR MONEY BACK.
BRAVO!
BUT LOOK OUT: NO FALSE STATEMENTS! IF YOU WEREN'T ROBBED, DON'T BOTHER GOIN' IN!
SIR, DON'T WORRY, WE KNOW OUR CROOK AND HE KNOWS US.
WE WANT OUR MONEY BACK AND WE'RE NOT GONNA LET THUGS STEAL IT FROM US, DÊH!
WHO'RE YOU CALLING THUGS?
YOU NEEDED HELP AND WE GAVE IT TO YOU, AND NOW YOU'RE CHASIN' US AWAY.
WHATEVER HAPPENED TO GRATITUDE, HUH?
SO, WHAT'S THE NEXT STEP FOR GRÉGOIRE?
HE'LL BE TRANSFERRED TO THE MACA SO HE DOESN'T GET LYNCHED, AND THEN HE'LL APPEAR BEFORE A JUDGE.
WANT A LIFT TO YOPOUGON?
NO, THANKS. WE'VE IMPOSED ENOUGH ALREADY.
THAT WOULD BE GREAT! ALL THAT RUNNING REALLY TIRED ME OUT!

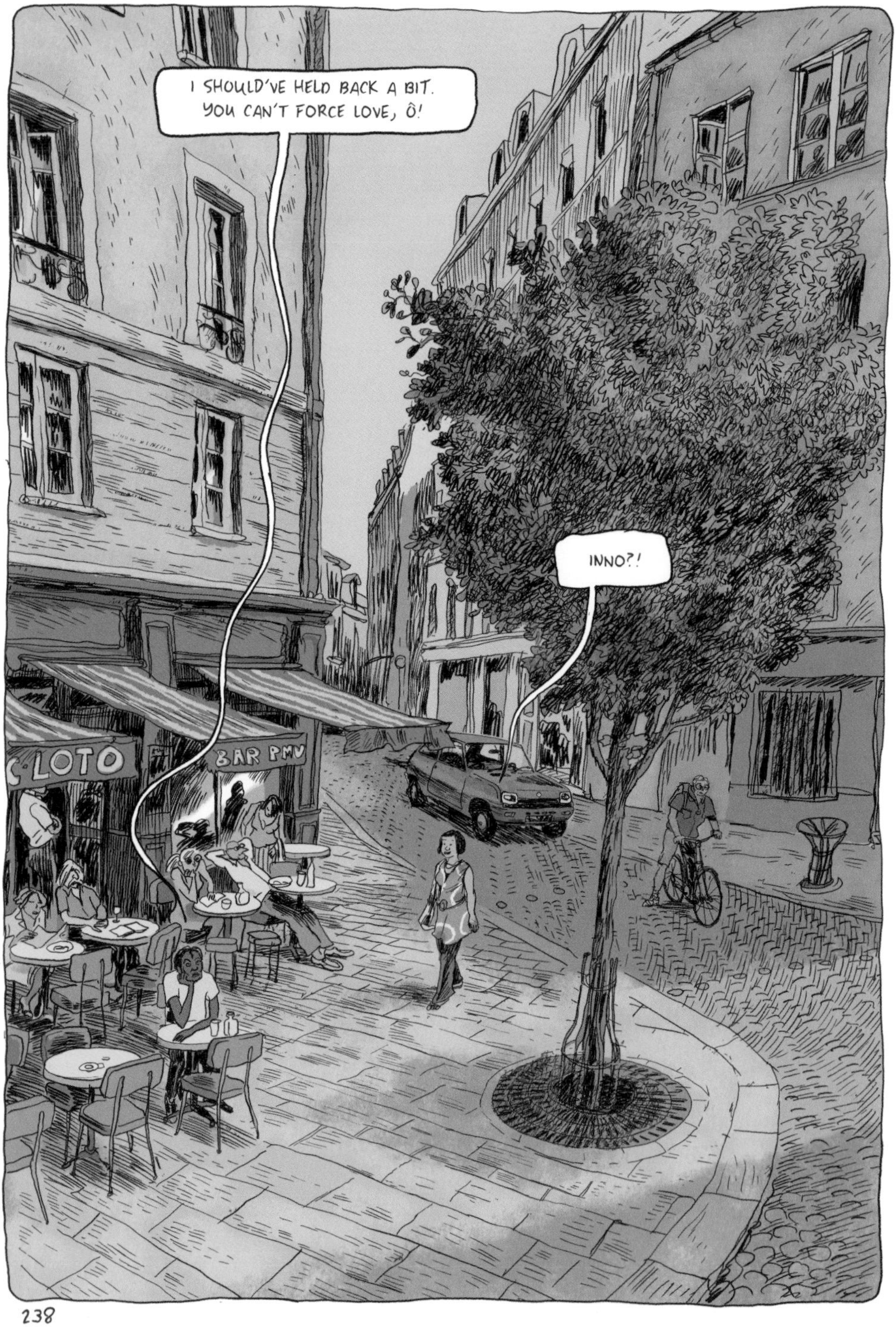
I SHOULD'VE HELD BACK A BIT. YOU CAN'T FORCE LOVE, Ô!
INNO?!
LOTO
BAR PMU

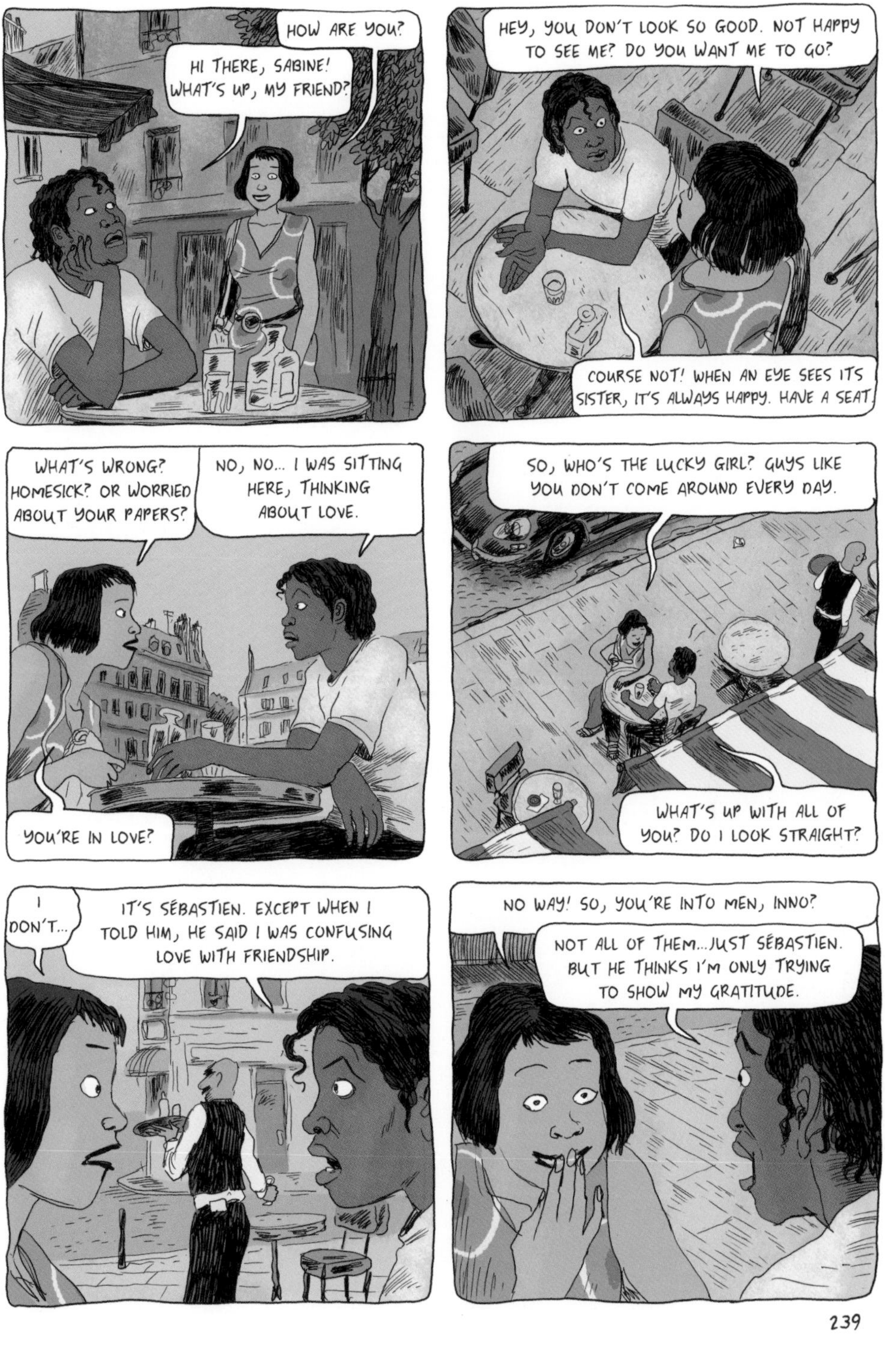
HI THERE, SABINE! WHAT'S UP, MY FRIEND?
HOW ARE YOU?
HEY, YOU DON'T LOOK SO GOOD. NOT HAPPY TO SEE ME? DO YOU WANT ME TO GO?
COURSE NOT! WHEN AN EYE SEES ITS SISTER, IT'S ALWAYS HAPPY. HAVE A SEAT.
WHAT'S WRONG? HOMESICK? OR WORRIED ABOUT YOUR PAPERS?
NO, NO... I WAS SITTING HERE, THINKING ABOUT LOVE.
YOU'RE IN LOVE?
SO, WHO'S THE LUCKY GIRL? GUYS LIKE YOU DON'T COME AROUND EVERY DAY.
WHAT'S UP WITH ALL OF YOU? DO I LOOK STRAIGHT?
I DON'T...
IT'S SÉBASTIEN. EXCEPT WHEN I TOLD HIM, HE SAID I WAS CONFUSING LOVE WITH FRIENDSHIP.
NO WAY! SO, YOU'RE INTO MEN, INNO?
NOT ALL OF THEM...JUST SÉBASTIEN. BUT HE THINKS I'M ONLY TRYING TO SHOW MY GRATITUDE.

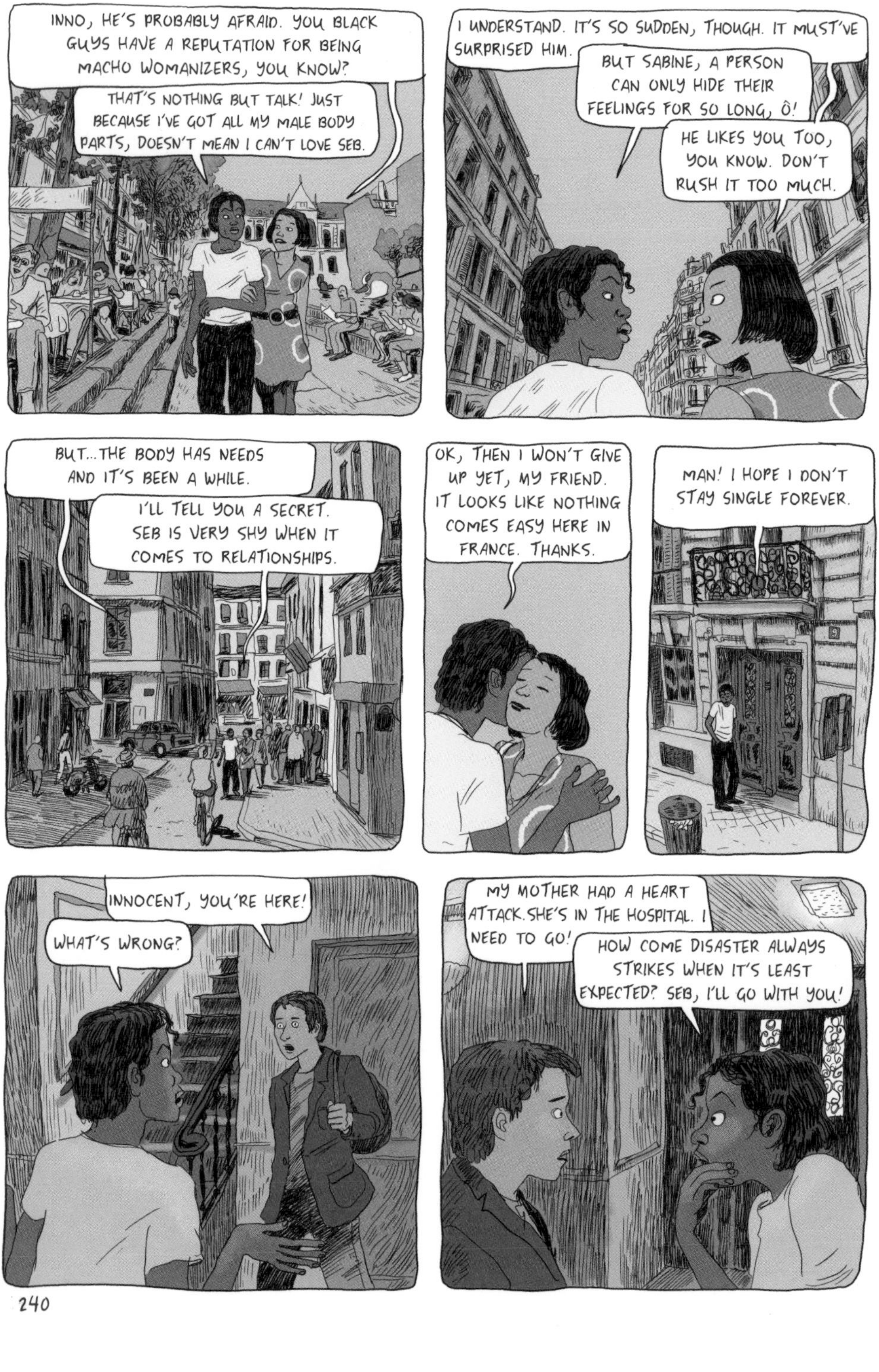
INNO, HE'S PROBABLY AFRAID. YOU BLACK GUYS HAVE A REPUTATION FOR BEING MACHO WOMANIZERS, YOU KNOW?
THAT'S NOTHING BUT TALK! JUST BECAUSE I'VE GOT ALL MY MALE BODY PARTS, DOESN'T MEAN I CAN'T LOVE SEB.
I UNDERSTAND. IT'S SO SUDDEN, THOUGH. IT MUST'VE SURPRISED HIM.
BUT SABINE, A PERSON CAN ONLY HIDE THEIR FEELINGS FOR SO LONG, Ô!
HE LIKES YOU TOO, YOU KNOW. DON'T RUSH IT TOO MUCH.
BUT...THE BODY HAS NEEDS AND IT'S BEEN A WHILE.
I'LL TELL YOU A SECRET. SEB IS VERY SHY WHEN IT COMES TO RELATIONSHIPS.
OK, THEN I WON'T GIVE UP YET, MY FRIEND. IT LOOKS LIKE NOTHING COMES EASY HERE IN FRANCE. THANKS.
MAN! I HOPE I DON'T STAY SINGLE FOREVER.
INNOCENT, YOU'RE HERE!
WHAT'S WRONG?
MY MOTHER HAD A HEART ATTACK. SHE'S IN THE HOSPITAL. I NEED TO GO!
HOW COME DISASTER ALWAYS STRIKES WHEN IT'S LEAST EXPECTED? SEB, I'LL GO WITH YOU!

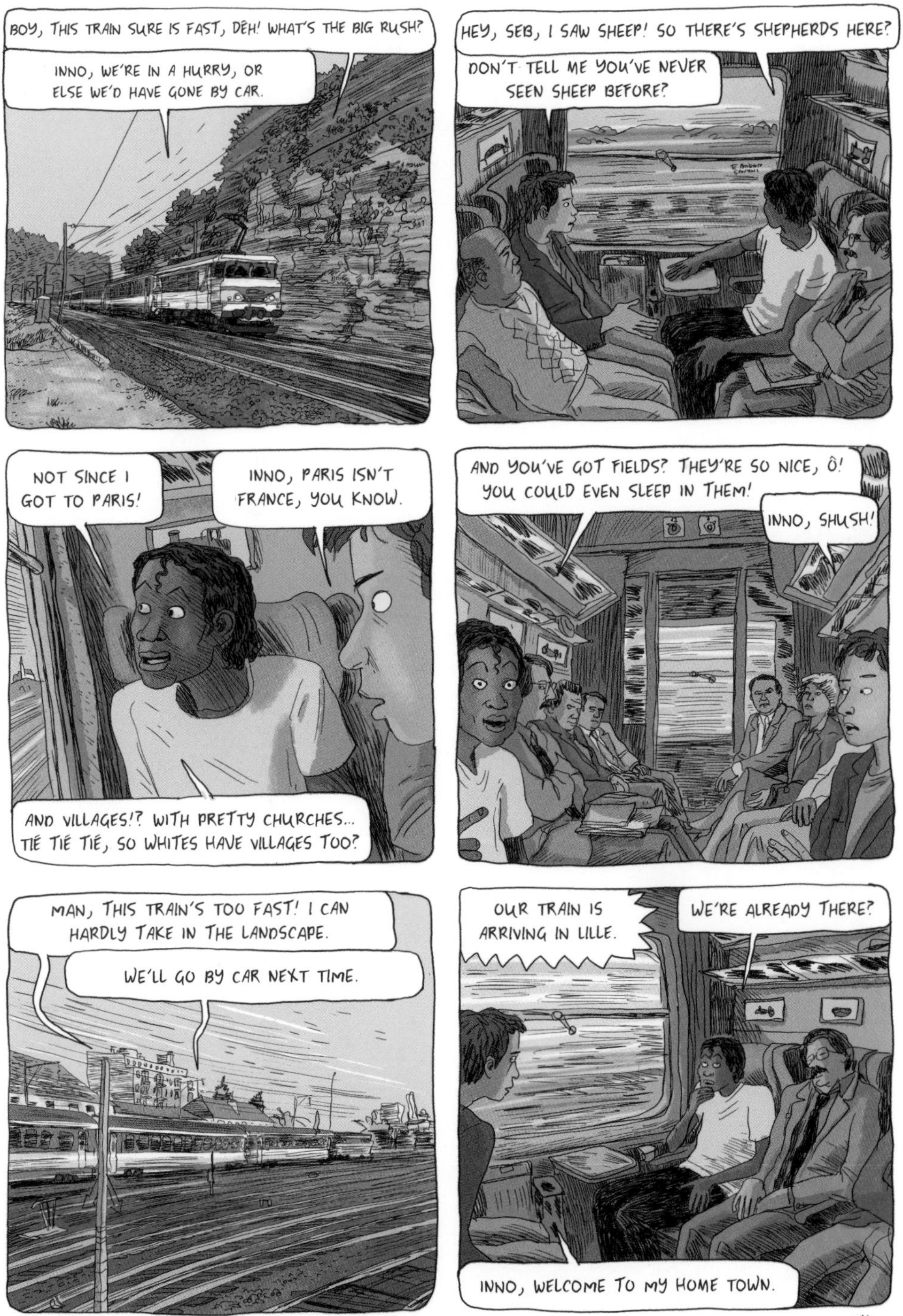
BOY, THIS TRAIN SURE IS FAST, DÊH! WHAT'S THE BIG RUSH?
INNO, WE'RE IN A HURRY, OR ELSE WE'D HAVE GONE BY CAR.
HEY, SEB, I SAW SHEEP! SO THERE'S SHEPHERDS HERE?
DON'T TELL ME YOU'VE NEVER SEEN SHEEP BEFORE?
NOT SINCE I GOT TO PARIS!
INNO, PARIS ISN'T FRANCE, YOU KNOW.
AND VILLAGES!? WITH PRETTY CHURCHES... TIÉ TIÉ TIÉ, SO WHITES HAVE VILLAGES TOO?
AND YOU'VE GOT FIELDS? THEY'RE SO NICE, Ô! YOU COULD EVEN SLEEP IN THEM!
INNO, SHUSH!
MAN, THIS TRAIN'S TOO FAST! I CAN HARDLY TAKE IN THE LANDSCAPE.
WE'LL GO BY CAR NEXT TIME.
OUR TRAIN IS ARRIVING IN LILLE.
WE'RE ALREADY THERE?
INNO, WELCOME TO MY HOME TOWN.

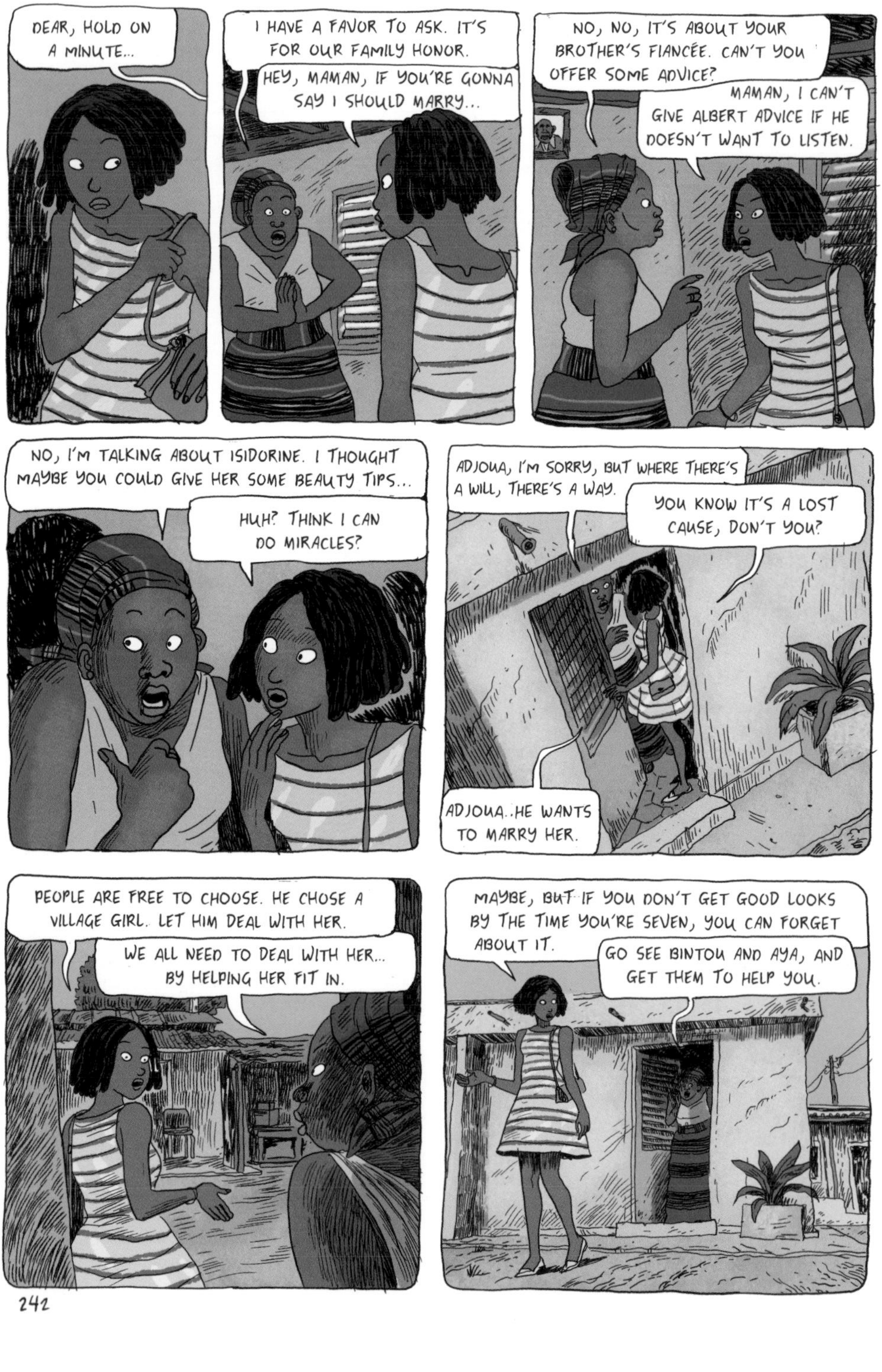
DEAR, HOLD ON A MINUTE...
I HAVE A FAVOR TO ASK. IT'S FOR OUR FAMILY HONOR.
HEY, MAMAN, IF YOU'RE GONNA SAY I SHOULD MARRY...
NO, NO, IT'S ABOUT YOUR BROTHER'S FIANCÉE. CAN'T YOU OFFER SOME ADVICE?
MAMAN, I CAN'T GIVE ALBERT ADVICE IF HE DOESN'T WANT TO LISTEN.
NO, I'M TALKING ABOUT ISIDORINE. I THOUGHT MAYBE YOU COULD GIVE HER SOME BEAUTY TIPS...
HUH? THINK I CAN DO MIRACLES?
ADJOUA, I'M SORRY, BUT WHERE THERE'S A WILL, THERE'S A WAY.
YOU KNOW IT'S A LOST CAUSE, DON'T YOU?
ADJOUA..HE WANTS TO MARRY HER.
PEOPLE ARE FREE TO CHOOSE. HE CHOSE A VILLAGE GIRL. LET HIM DEAL WITH HER.
WE ALL NEED TO DEAL WITH HER... BY HELPING HER FIT IN.
MAYBE, BUT IF YOU DON'T GET GOOD LOOKS BY THE TIME YOU'RE SEVEN, YOU CAN FORGET ABOUT IT.
GO SEE BINTOU AND AYA, AND GET THEM TO HELP YOU.

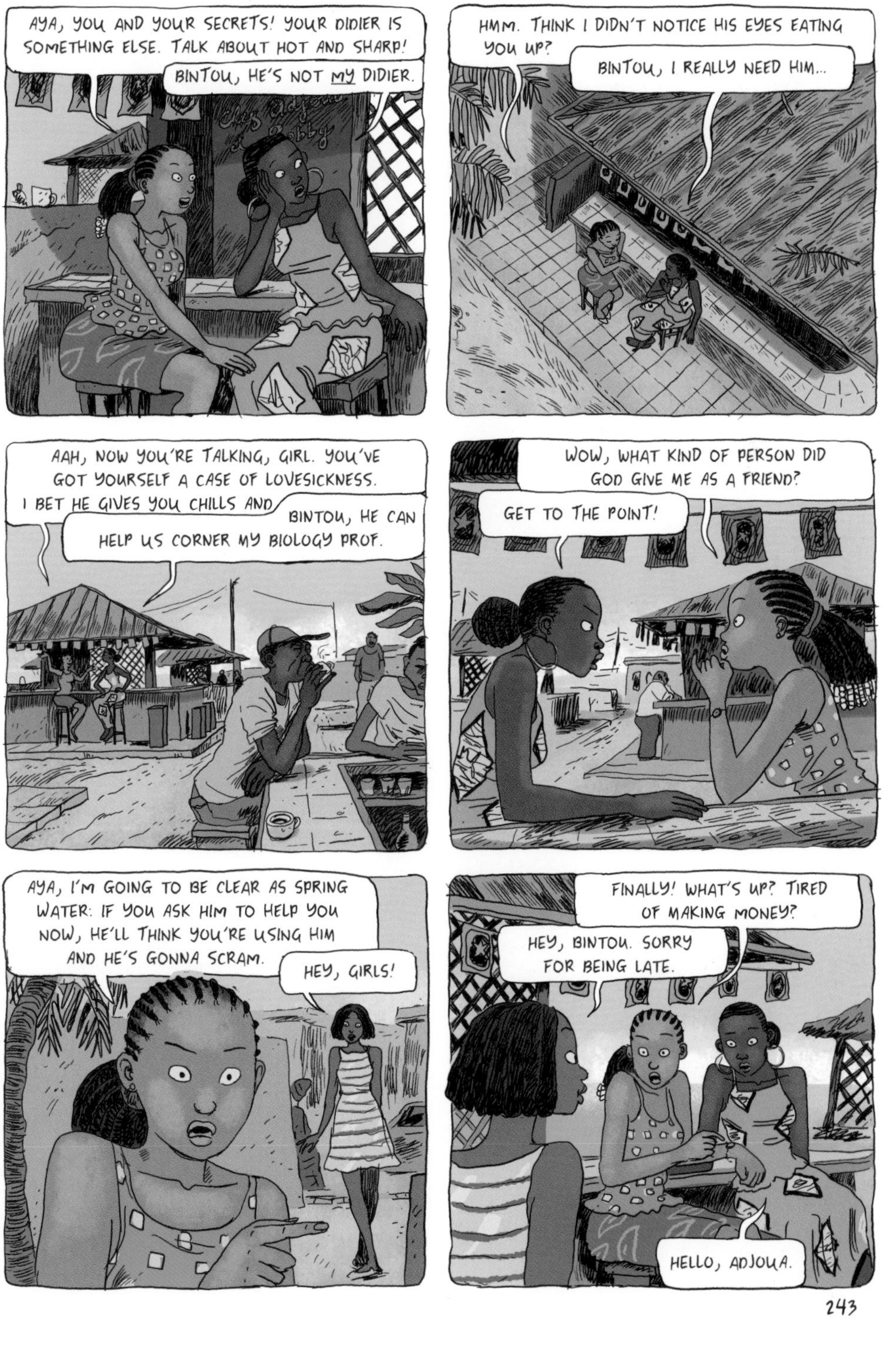
AYA, YOU AND YOUR SECRETS! YOUR DIDIER IS SOMETHING ELSE. TALK ABOUT HOT AND SHARP!
BINTOU, HE'S NOT MY DIDIER.
HMM. THINK I DIDN'T NOTICE HIS EYES EATING YOU UP?
BINTOU, I REALLY NEED HIM...
AAH, NOW YOU'RE TALKING, GIRL. YOU'VE GOT YOURSELF A CASE OF LOVESICKNESS. I BET HE GIVES YOU CHILLS AND
BINTOU, HE CAN HELP US CORNER MY BIOLOGY PROF.
WOW, WHAT KIND OF PERSON DID GOD GIVE ME AS A FRIEND?
GET TO THE POINT!
AYA, I'M GOING TO BE CLEAR AS SPRING WATER: IF YOU ASK HIM TO HELP YOU NOW, HE'LL THINK YOU'RE USING HIM AND HE'S GONNA SCRAM.
HEY, GIRLS!
FINALLY! WHAT'S UP? TIRED OF MAKING MONEY?
HEY, BINTOU. SORRY FOR BEING LATE.
HELLO, ADJOUA.

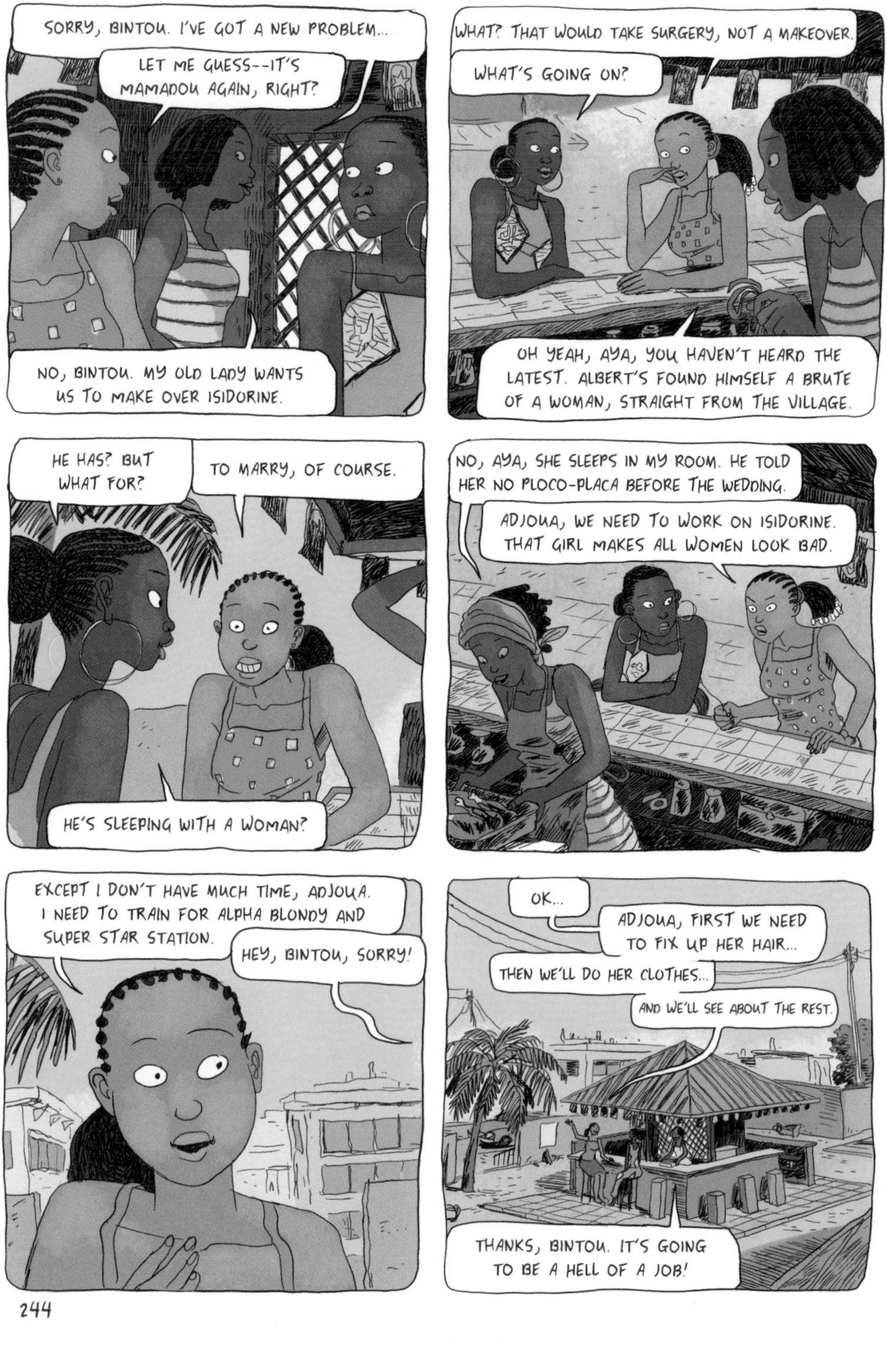
SORRY, BINTOU. I'VE GOT A NEW PROBLEM...
LET ME GUESS--IT'S MAMADOU AGAIN, RIGHT?
NO, BINTOU. MY OLD LADY WANTS US TO MAKE OVER ISIDORINE.
WHAT? THAT WOULD TAKE SURGERY, NOT A MAKEOVER.
WHAT'S GOING ON?
OH YEAH, AYA, YOU HAVEN'T HEARD THE LATEST. ALBERT'S FOUND HIMSELF A BRUTE OF A WOMAN, STRAIGHT FROM THE VILLAGE.
HE HAS? BUT WHAT FOR?
TO MARRY, OF COURSE.
HE'S SLEEPING WITH A WOMAN?
NO, AYA, SHE SLEEPS IN MY ROOM. HE TOLD HER NO PLOCO-PLACA BEFORE THE WEDDING.
ADJOUA, WE NEED TO WORK ON ISIDORINE. THAT GIRL MAKES ALL WOMEN LOOK BAD.
EXCEPT I DON'T HAVE MUCH TIME, ADJOUA. I NEED TO TRAIN FOR ALPHA BLONDY AND SUPER STAR STATION.
HEY, BINTOU, SORRY!
OK...
ADJOUA, FIRST WE NEED TO FIX UP HER HAIR...
THEN WE'LL DO HER CLOTHES...
AND WE'LL SEE ABOUT THE REST.
THANKS, BINTOU. IT'S GOING TO BE A HELL OF A JOB!

BUT JEANNE, WHAT DOES THIS MEAN?

YOU'RE NOT GOING TO KEEP SWITCHING HOUSES LIKE A BIRD HOPPING FROM BRANCH TO BRANCH, ARE YOU?

PAPA, BAD LUCK'S NOT GOING TO STICK TO ME FOREVER.

AND NO MAN EITHER, IT LOOKS LIKE.

WHO'S THE NEXT GUY? ANYBODY I KNOW?

IT'S STILL GERVAIS, PAPA. HIS MOTHER'S THE PROBLEM.

MY GIRL, YOU NEED TO INSPECT THE MOTHER BEFORE PICKING THE SON.

PAPA, THERE'S NO WINNING WITH HER.

JEANNE, YOU DON'T GO TO BATTLE TO LOSE. THAT'S NOT HOW I RAISED MY KIDS.

I HAVEN'T LOST, BUT AS LONG AS SHE'S IN THE HOUSE, IT'LL BE HELL FOR THE KIDS AND ME...

I'VE GOT A WAY OUT OF THIS MESS, THOUGH. I GAVE HIM AN ULTIMATUM...

AN ULTIMATUM? FORGET IT. ESPECIALLY IF SHE'S THE ONE WHO COOKS, CLEANS, AND IRONS FOR HIM.

EITHER WAY, HE HASN'T GIVEN PLEDGE MONEY FOR YOU, SO HE'S NOTHING TO ME. I'M GONNA PUT A BULLET BETWEEN HIS EYES, HE'S GONNA...

SÉRAPHIN, KEEP OUT OF IT. ALL YOU EVER WANT TO DO IS KILL PEOPLE.

245

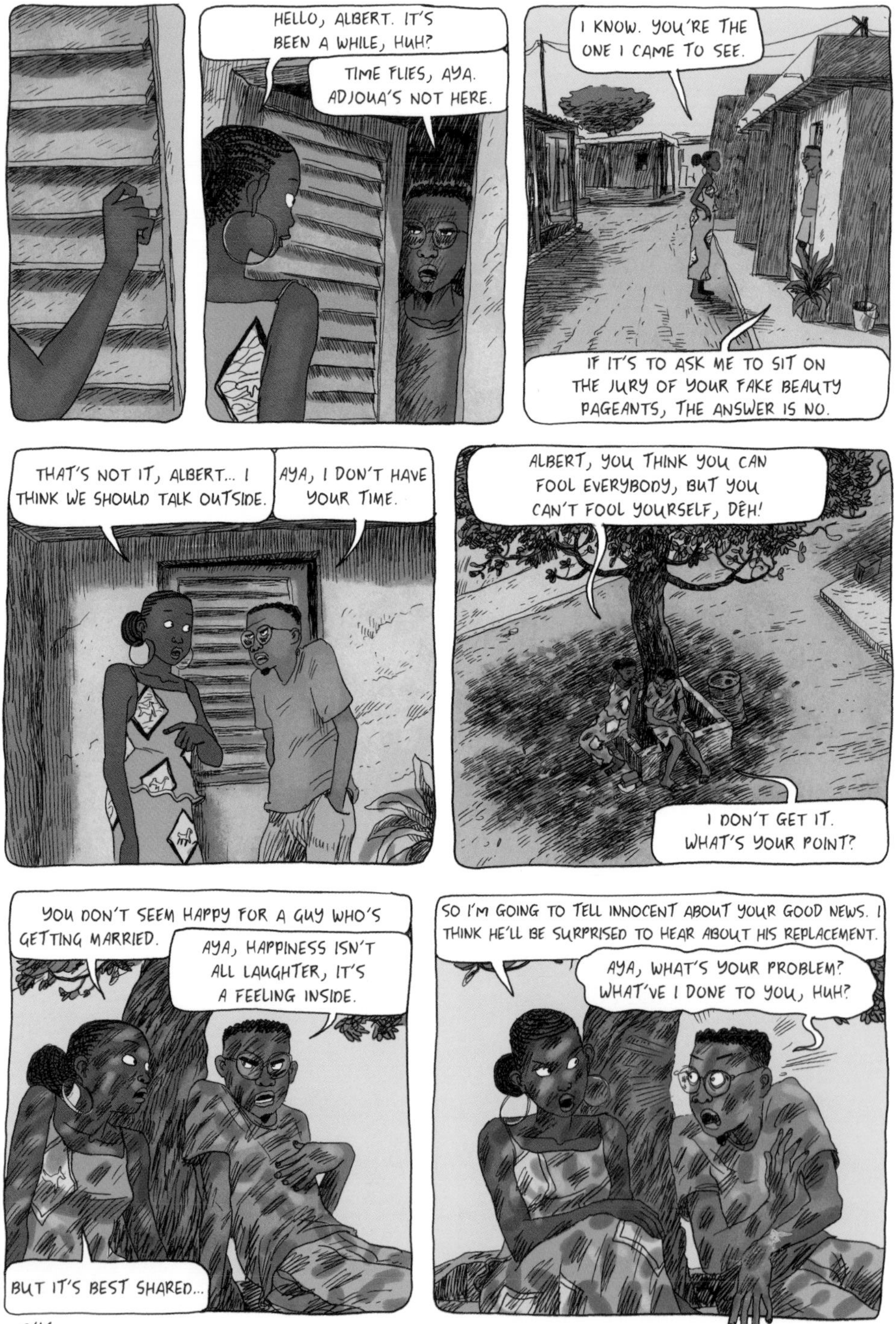
HELLO, ALBERT. IT'S BEEN A WHILE, HUH?
TIME FLIES, AYA. ADJOUA'S NOT HERE.
I KNOW. YOU'RE THE ONE I CAME TO SEE.
IF IT'S TO ASK ME TO SIT ON THE JURY OF YOUR FAKE BEAUTY PAGEANTS, THE ANSWER IS NO.
THAT'S NOT IT, ALBERT... I THINK WE SHOULD TALK OUTSIDE.
AYA, I DON'T HAVE YOUR TIME.
ALBERT, YOU THINK YOU CAN FOOL EVERYBODY, BUT YOU CAN'T FOOL YOURSELF, DÊH!
I DON'T GET IT. WHAT'S YOUR POINT?
YOU DON'T SEEM HAPPY FOR A GUY WHO'S GETTING MARRIED.
AYA, HAPPINESS ISN'T ALL LAUGHTER, IT'S A FEELING INSIDE.
BUT IT'S BEST SHARED...
SO I'M GOING TO TELL INNOCENT ABOUT YOUR GOOD NEWS. I THINK HE'LL BE SURPRISED TO HEAR ABOUT HIS REPLACEMENT.
AYA, WHAT'S YOUR PROBLEM? WHAT'VE I DONE TO YOU, HUH?

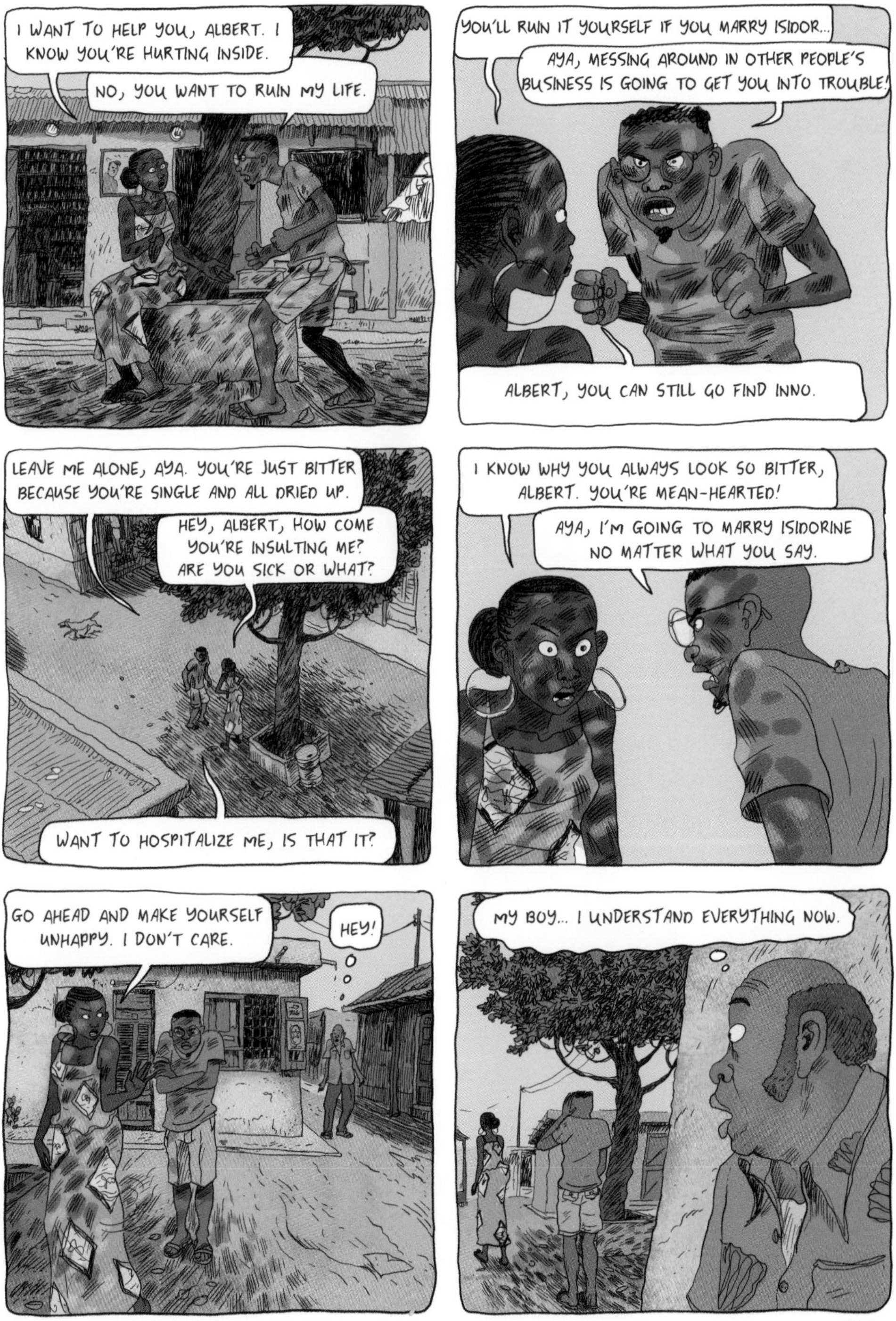
I WANT TO HELP YOU, ALBERT. I KNOW YOU'RE HURTING INSIDE.
NO, YOU WANT TO RUIN MY LIFE.
YOU'LL RUIN IT YOURSELF IF YOU MARRY ISIDOR...
AYA, MESSING AROUND IN OTHER PEOPLE'S BUSINESS IS GOING TO GET YOU INTO TROUBLE!
ALBERT, YOU CAN STILL GO FIND INNO.
LEAVE ME ALONE, AYA. YOU'RE JUST BITTER BECAUSE YOU'RE SINGLE AND ALL DRIED UP.
HEY, ALBERT, HOW COME YOU'RE INSULTING ME? ARE YOU SICK OR WHAT?
WANT TO HOSPITALIZE ME, IS THAT IT?
I KNOW WHY YOU ALWAYS LOOK SO BITTER, ALBERT. YOU'RE MEAN-HEARTED!
AYA, I'M GOING TO MARRY ISIDORINE NO MATTER WHAT YOU SAY.
GO AHEAD AND MAKE YOURSELF UNHAPPY. I DON'T CARE.
HEY!
MY BOY... I UNDERSTAND EVERYTHING NOW.

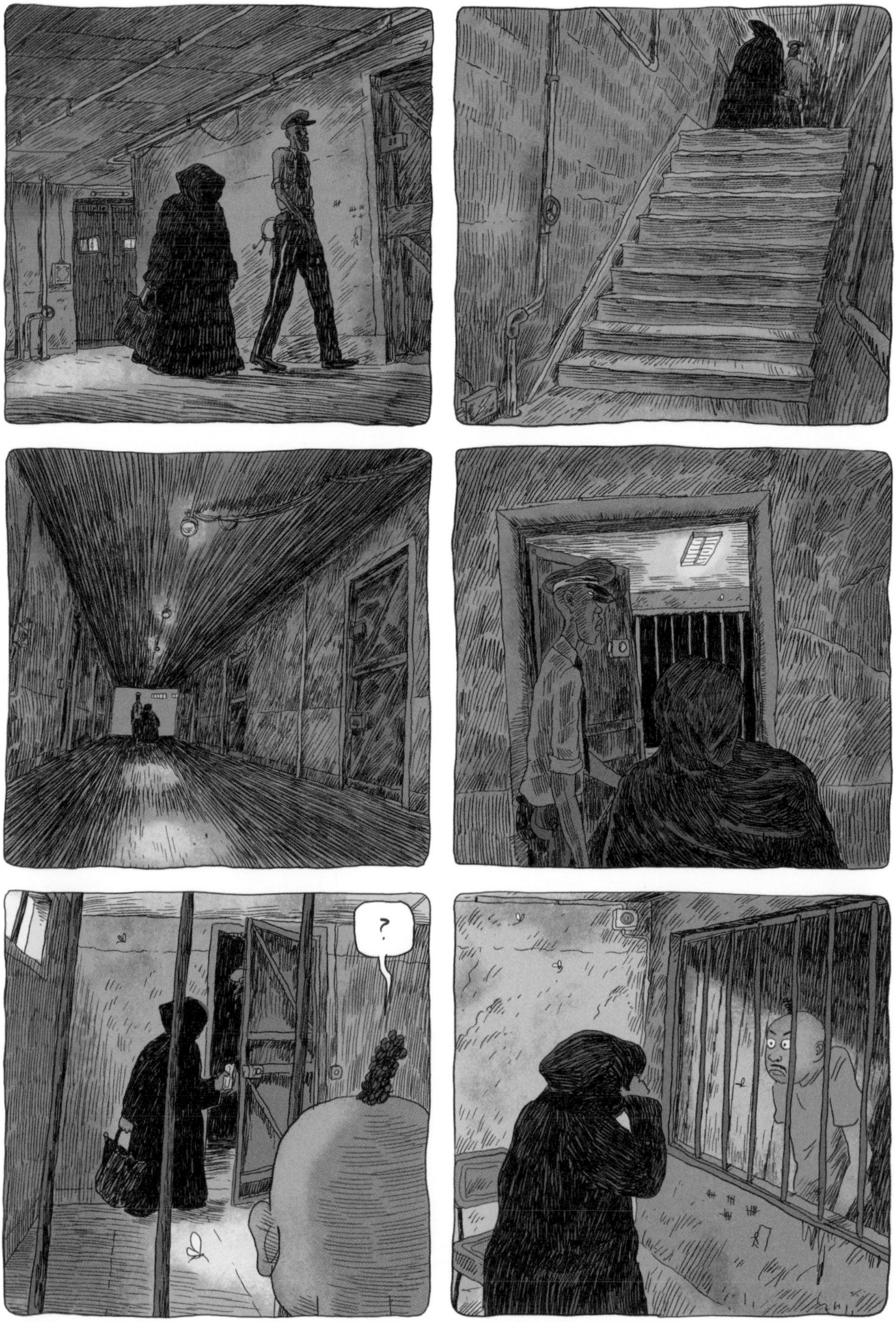
?

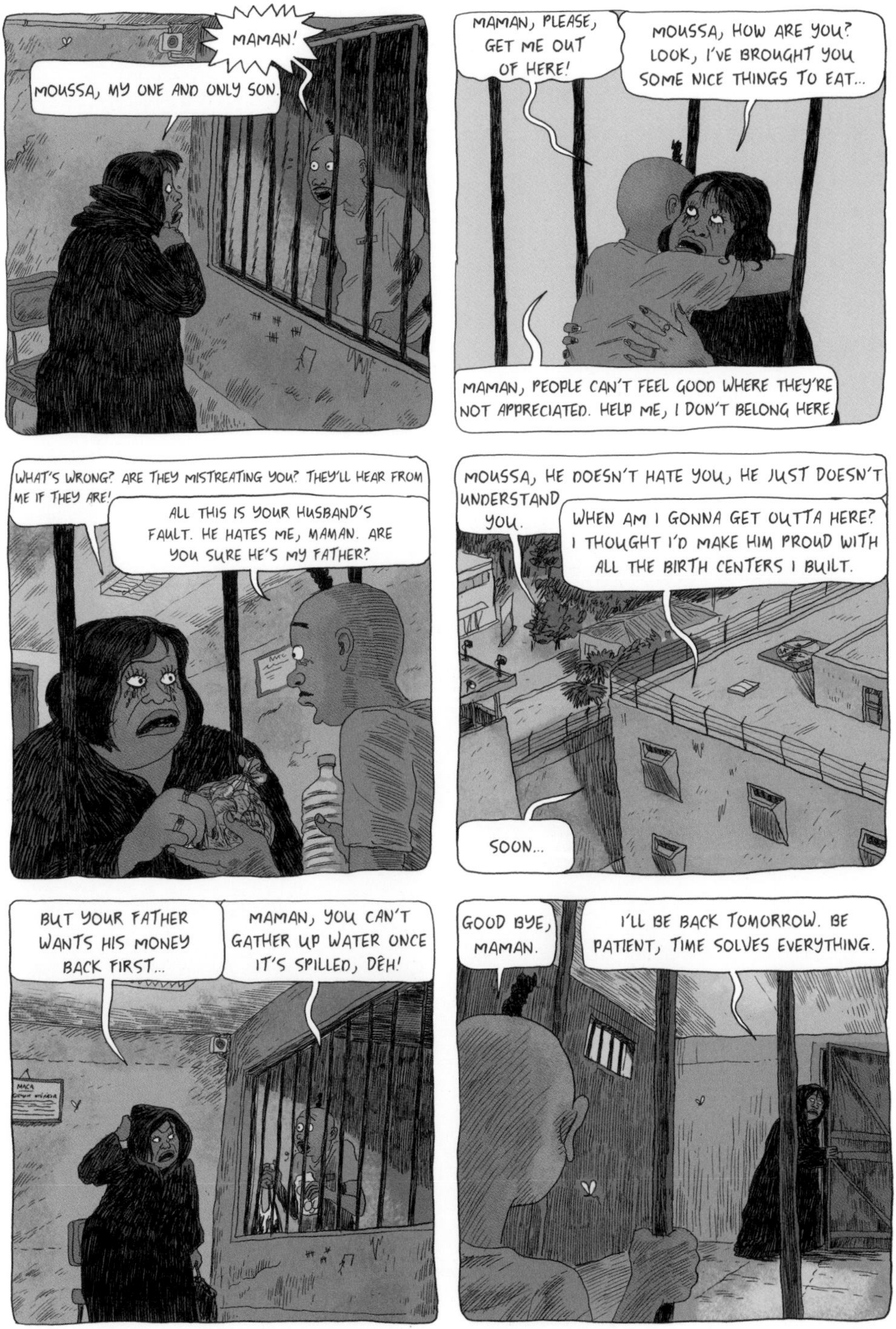
MAMAN!
MOUSSA, MY ONE AND ONLY SON.
MAMAN, PLEASE, GET ME OUT OF HERE!
MOUSSA, HOW ARE YOU? LOOK, I'VE BROUGHT YOU SOME NICE THINGS TO EAT...
MAMAN, PEOPLE CAN'T FEEL GOOD WHERE THEY'RE NOT APPRECIATED. HELP ME, I DON'T BELONG HERE.
WHAT'S WRONG? ARE THEY MISTREATING YOU? THEY'LL HEAR FROM ME IF THEY ARE!
ALL THIS IS YOUR HUSBAND'S FAULT. HE HATES ME, MAMAN. ARE YOU SURE HE'S MY FATHER?
MOUSSA, HE DOESN'T HATE YOU, HE JUST DOESN'T UNDERSTAND YOU.
WHEN AM I GONNA GET OUTTA HERE? I THOUGHT I'D MAKE HIM PROUD WITH ALL THE BIRTH CENTERS I BUILT.
SOON...
BUT YOUR FATHER WANTS HIS MONEY BACK FIRST...
MAMAN, YOU CAN'T GATHER UP WATER ONCE IT'S SPILLED, DÊH!
GOOD BYE, MAMAN.
I'LL BE BACK TOMORROW. BE PATIENT, TIME SOLVES EVERYTHING.

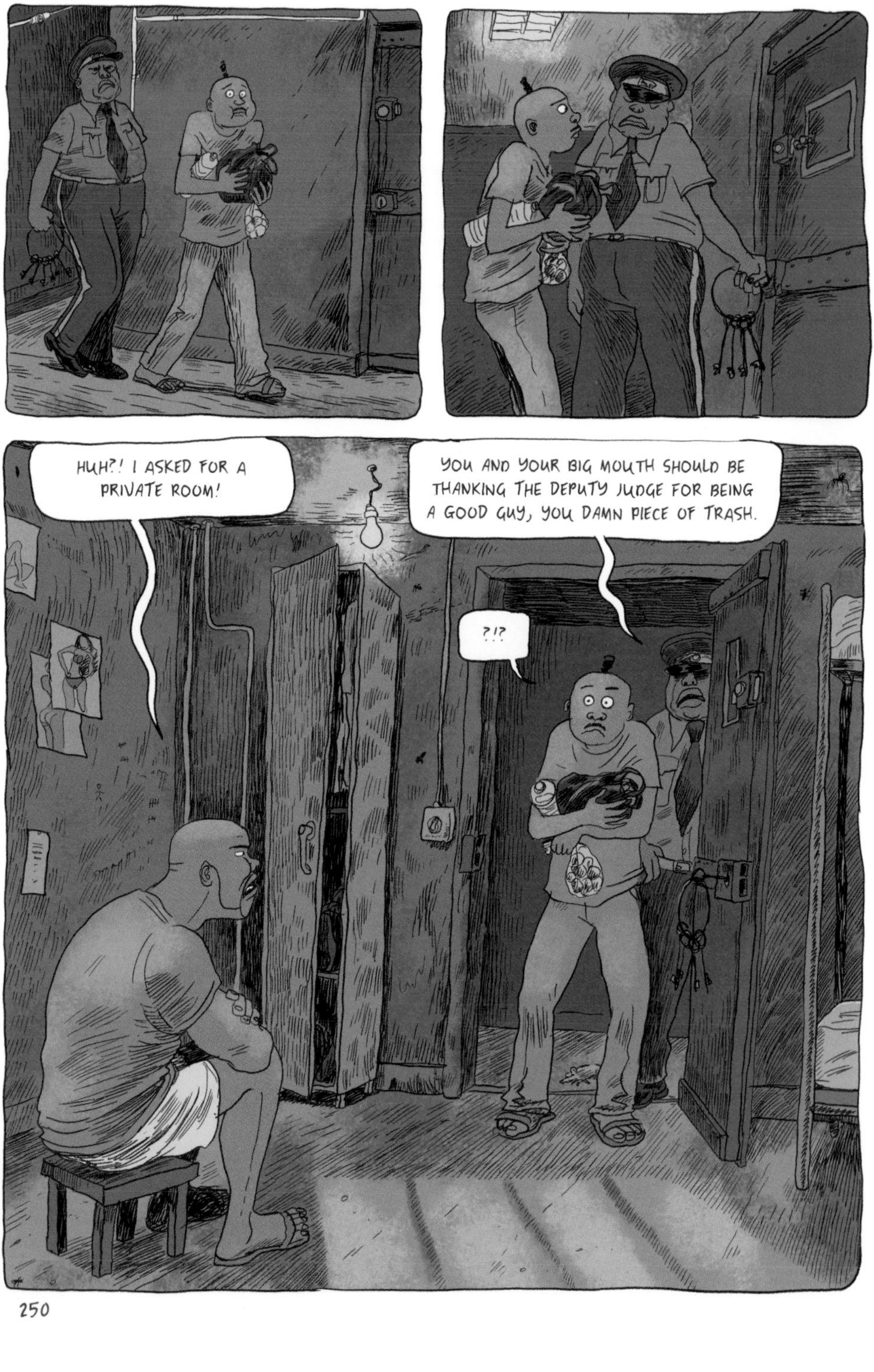
HUH?! I ASKED FOR A PRIVATE ROOM!
YOU AND YOUR BIG MOUTH SHOULD BE THANKING THE DEPUTY JUDGE FOR BEING A GOOD GUY, YOU DAMN PIECE OF TRASH.
?!?

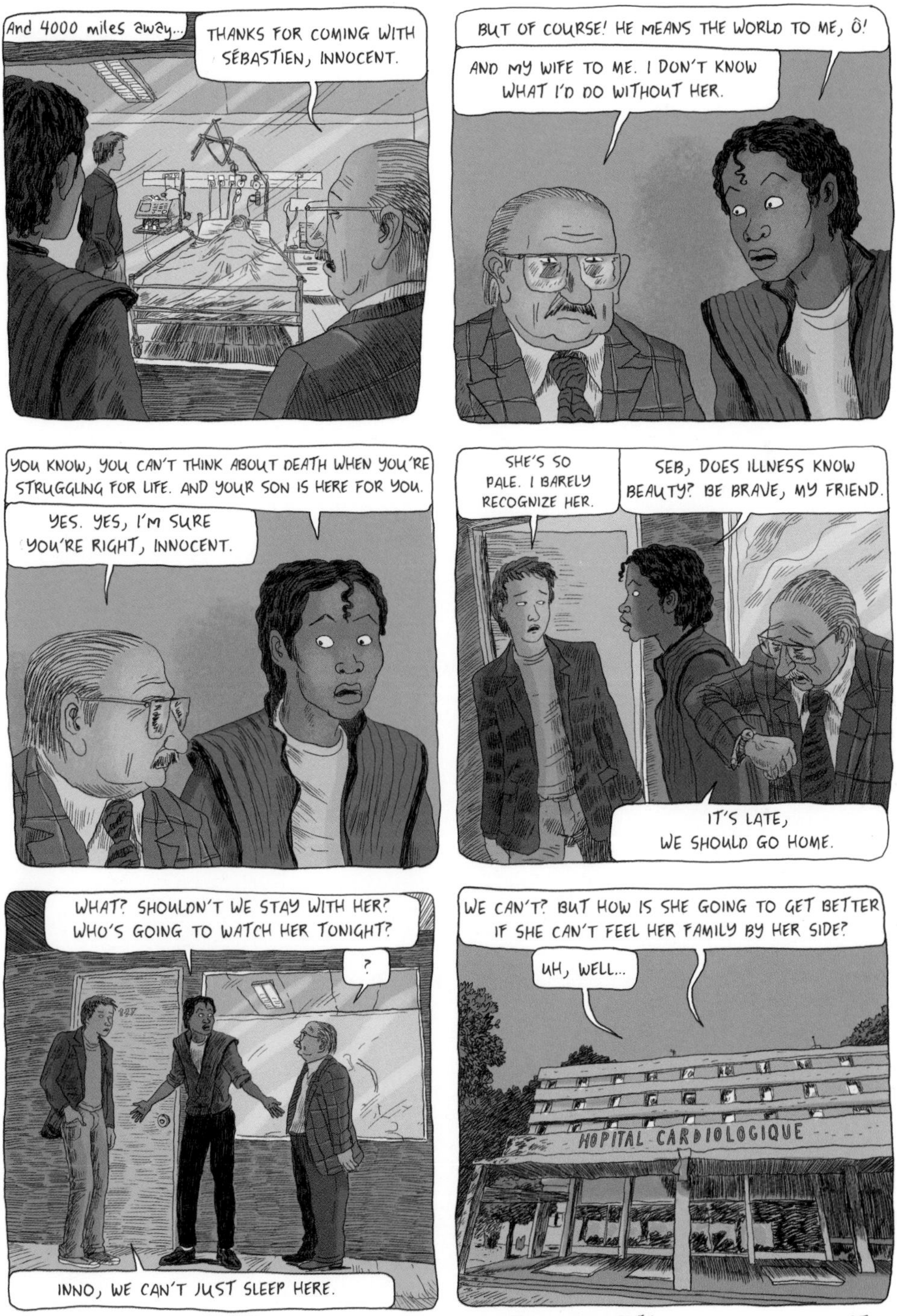
And 4000 miles away...
THANKS FOR COMING WITH SÉBASTIEN, INNOCENT.
BUT OF COURSE! HE MEANS THE WORLD TO ME, Ô!
AND MY WIFE TO ME. I DON'T KNOW WHAT I'D DO WITHOUT HER.
YOU KNOW, YOU CAN'T THINK ABOUT DEATH WHEN YOU'RE STRUGGLING FOR LIFE. AND YOUR SON IS HERE FOR YOU.
YES. YES, I'M SURE YOU'RE RIGHT, INNOCENT.
SHE'S SO PALE. I BARELY RECOGNIZE HER.
SEB, DOES ILLNESS KNOW BEAUTY? BE BRAVE, MY FRIEND.
IT'S LATE, WE SHOULD GO HOME.
WHAT? SHOULDN'T WE STAY WITH HER? WHO'S GOING TO WATCH HER TONIGHT?
?
INNO, WE CAN'T JUST SLEEP HERE.
WE CAN'T? BUT HOW IS SHE GOING TO GET BETTER IF SHE CAN'T FEEL HER FAMILY BY HER SIDE?
UH, WELL...
HOPITAL CARDIOLOGIQUE

SIGN: CARDIAC CARE HOSPITAL

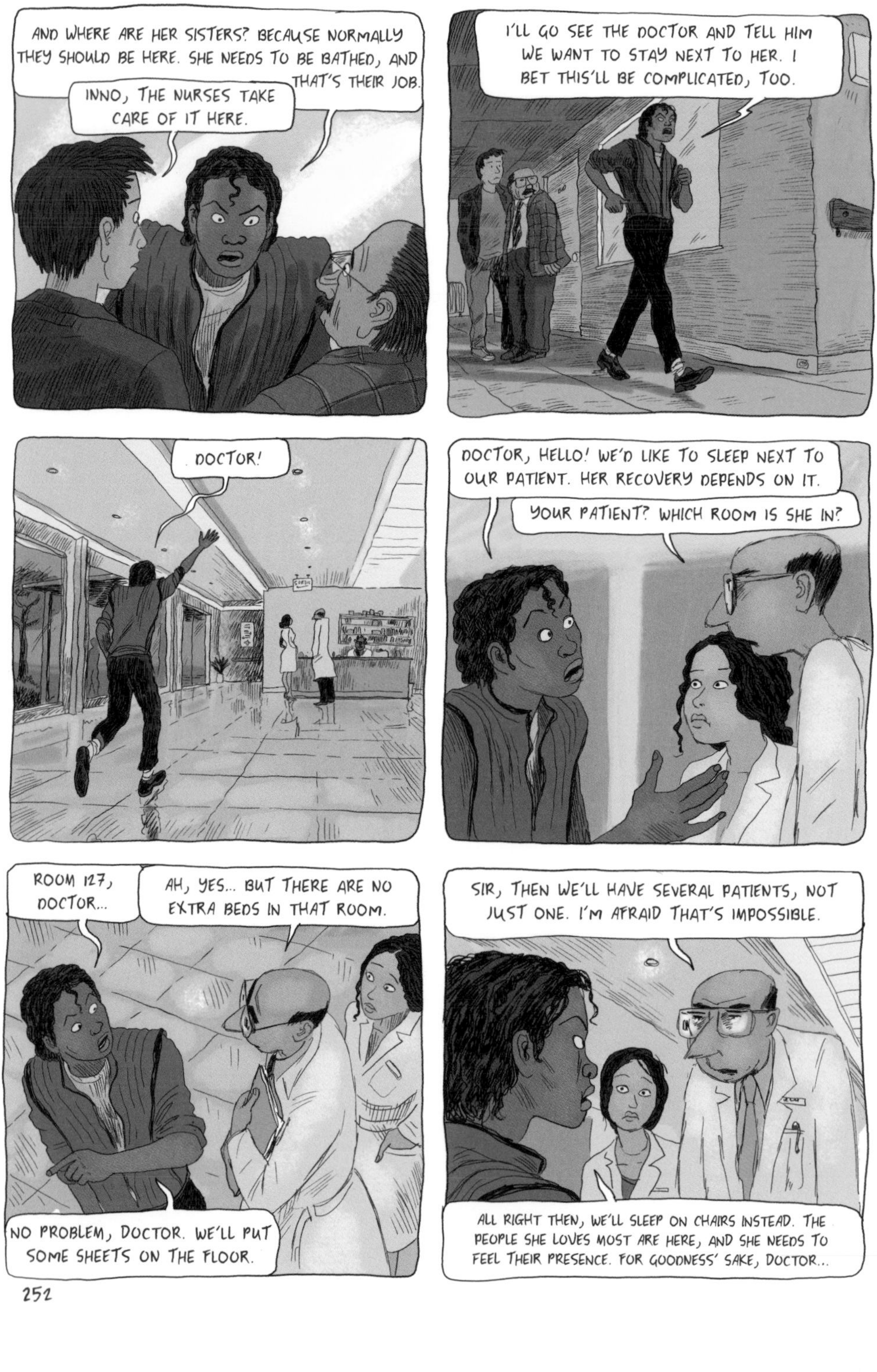
AND WHERE ARE HER SISTERS? BECAUSE NORMALLY THEY SHOULD BE HERE. SHE NEEDS TO BE BATHED, AND THAT'S THEIR JOB.
INNO, THE NURSES TAKE CARE OF IT HERE.
I'LL GO SEE THE DOCTOR AND TELL HIM WE WANT TO STAY NEXT TO HER. I BET THIS'LL BE COMPLICATED, TOO.
DOCTOR!
DOCTOR, HELLO! WE'D LIKE TO SLEEP NEXT TO OUR PATIENT. HER RECOVERY DEPENDS ON IT.
YOUR PATIENT? WHICH ROOM IS SHE IN?
ROOM 127, DOCTOR...
AH, YES... BUT THERE ARE NO EXTRA BEDS IN THAT ROOM.
NO PROBLEM, DOCTOR. WE'LL PUT SOME SHEETS ON THE FLOOR.
SIR, THEN WE'LL HAVE SEVERAL PATIENTS, NOT JUST ONE. I'M AFRAID THAT'S IMPOSSIBLE.
ALL RIGHT THEN, WE'LL SLEEP ON CHAIRS INSTEAD. THE PEOPLE SHE LOVES MOST ARE HERE, AND SHE NEEDS TO FEEL THEIR PRESENCE. FOR GOODNESS' SAKE, DOCTOR...

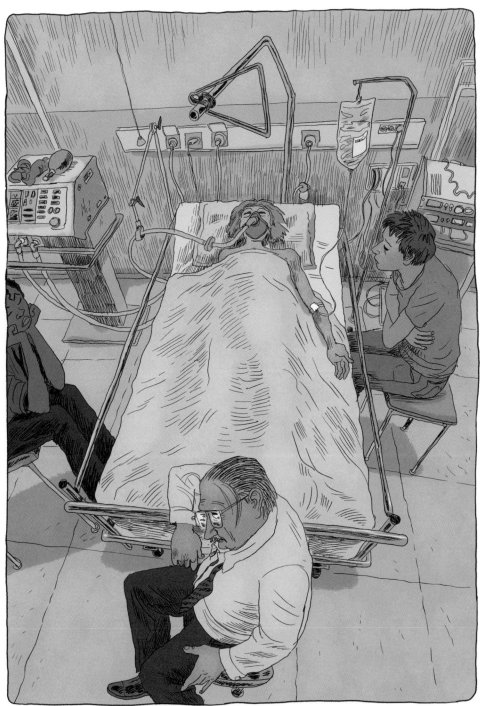

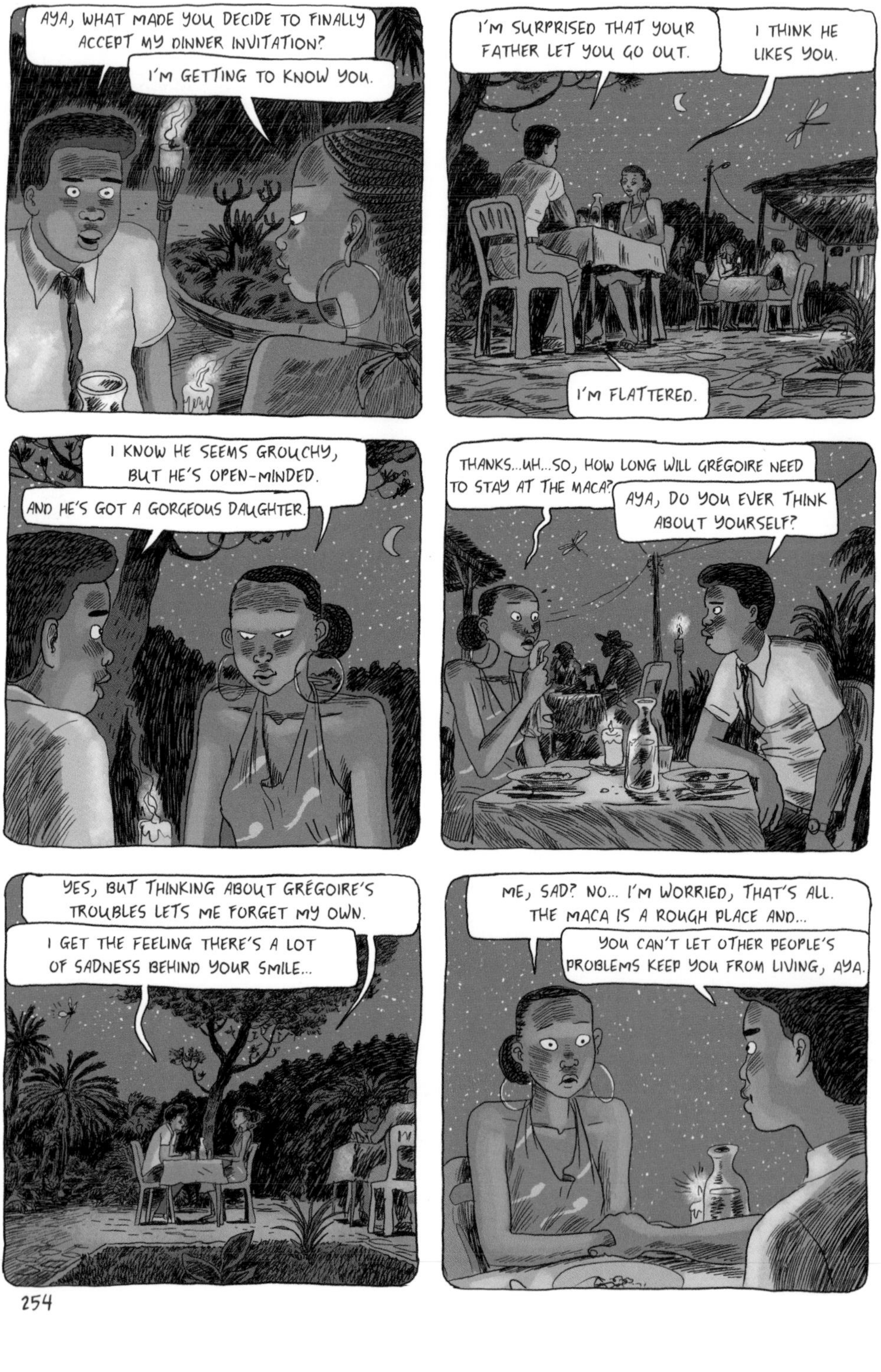
AYA, WHAT MADE YOU DECIDE TO FINALLY ACCEPT MY DINNER INVITATION?
I'M GETTING TO KNOW YOU.
I'M SURPRISED THAT YOUR FATHER LET YOU GO OUT.
I THINK HE LIKES YOU.
I'M FLATTERED.
I KNOW HE SEEMS GROUCHY, BUT HE'S OPEN-MINDED.
AND HE'S GOT A GORGEOUS DAUGHTER.
THANKS...UH...SO, HOW LONG WILL GRÉGOIRE NEED TO STAY AT THE MACA?
AYA, DO YOU EVER THINK ABOUT YOURSELF?
YES, BUT THINKING ABOUT GRÉGOIRE'S TROUBLES LETS ME FORGET MY OWN.
I GET THE FEELING THERE'S A LOT OF SADNESS BEHIND YOUR SMILE...
ME, SAD? NO... I'M WORRIED, THAT'S ALL. THE MACA IS A ROUGH PLACE AND...
YOU CAN'T LET OTHER PEOPLE'S PROBLEMS KEEP YOU FROM LIVING, AYA.

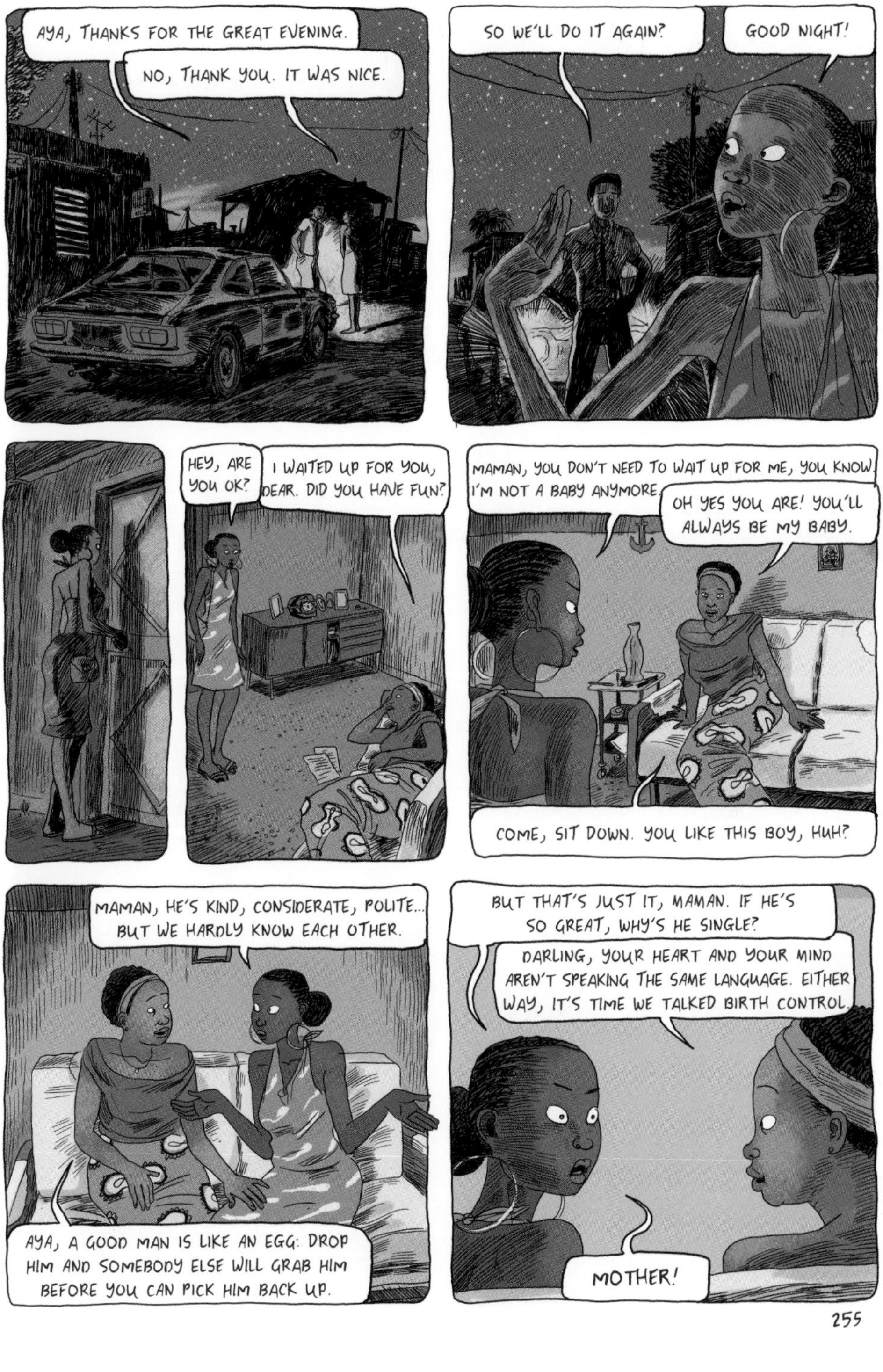
AYA, THANKS FOR THE GREAT EVENING.
NO, THANK YOU. IT WAS NICE.
SO WE'LL DO IT AGAIN?
GOOD NIGHT!
HEY, ARE YOU OK?
I WAITED UP FOR YOU, DEAR. DID YOU HAVE FUN?
MAMAN, YOU DON'T NEED TO WAIT UP FOR ME, YOU KNOW. I'M NOT A BABY ANYMORE.
OH YES YOU ARE! YOU'LL ALWAYS BE MY BABY.
COME, SIT DOWN. YOU LIKE THIS BOY, HUH?
MAMAN, HE'S KIND, CONSIDERATE, POLITE... BUT WE HARDLY KNOW EACH OTHER.
AYA, A GOOD MAN IS LIKE AN EGG: DROP HIM AND SOMEBODY ELSE WILL GRAB HIM BEFORE YOU CAN PICK HIM BACK UP.
BUT THAT'S JUST IT, MAMAN. IF HE'S SO GREAT, WHY'S HE SINGLE?
DARLING, YOUR HEART AND YOUR MIND AREN'T SPEAKING THE SAME LANGUAGE. EITHER WAY, IT'S TIME WE TALKED BIRTH CONTROL.
MOTHER!

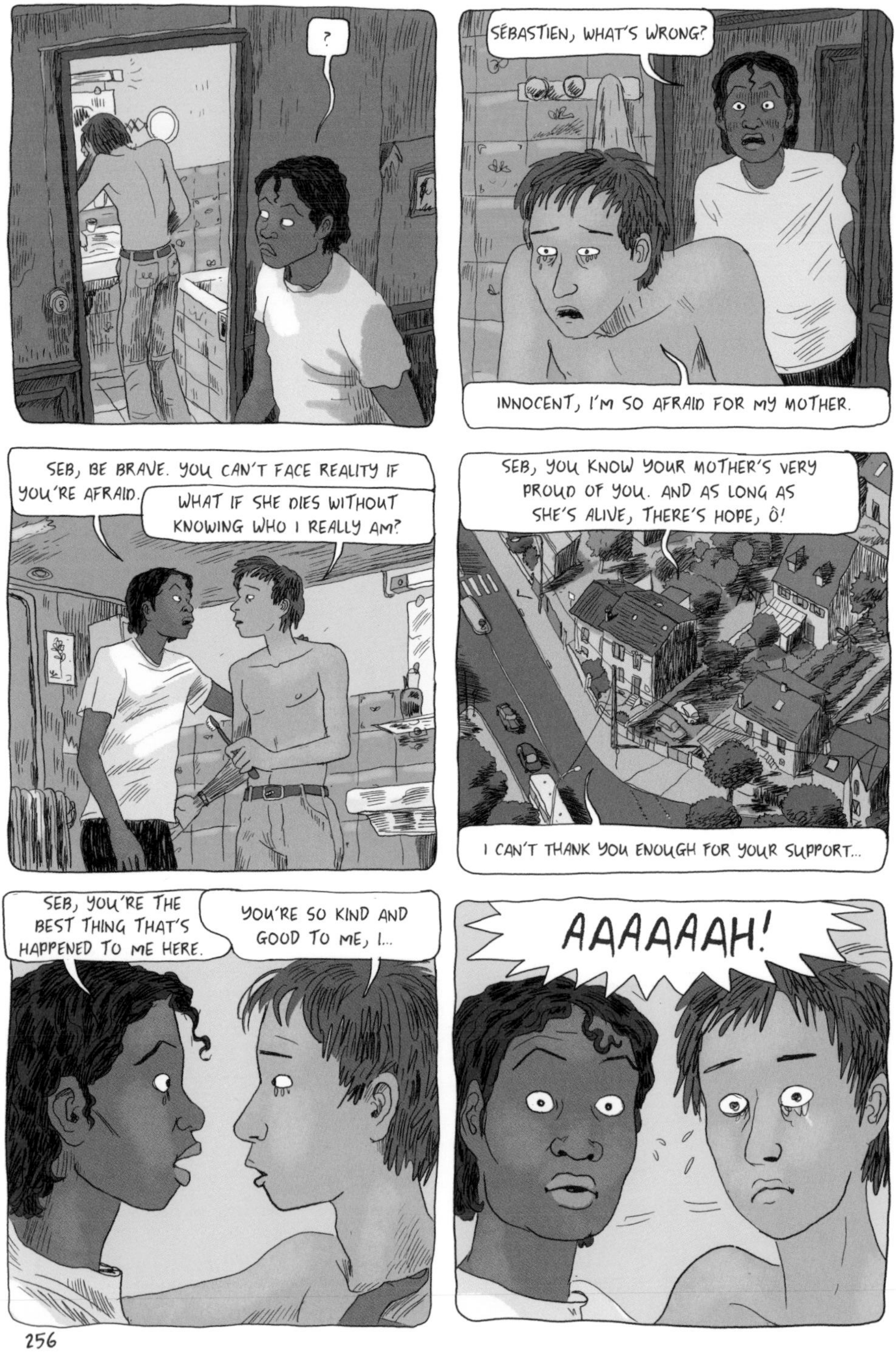
?
SÉBASTIEN, WHAT'S WRONG?
INNOCENT, I'M SO AFRAID FOR MY MOTHER.
SEB, BE BRAVE. YOU CAN'T FACE REALITY IF YOU'RE AFRAID.
WHAT IF SHE DIES WITHOUT KNOWING WHO I REALLY AM?
SEB, YOU KNOW YOUR MOTHER'S VERY PROUD OF YOU. AND AS LONG AS SHE'S ALIVE, THERE'S HOPE, Ô!
I CAN'T THANK YOU ENOUGH FOR YOUR SUPPORT...
SEB, YOU'RE THE BEST THING THAT'S HAPPENED TO ME HERE.
YOU'RE SO KIND AND GOOD TO ME, I...
AAAAAAH!

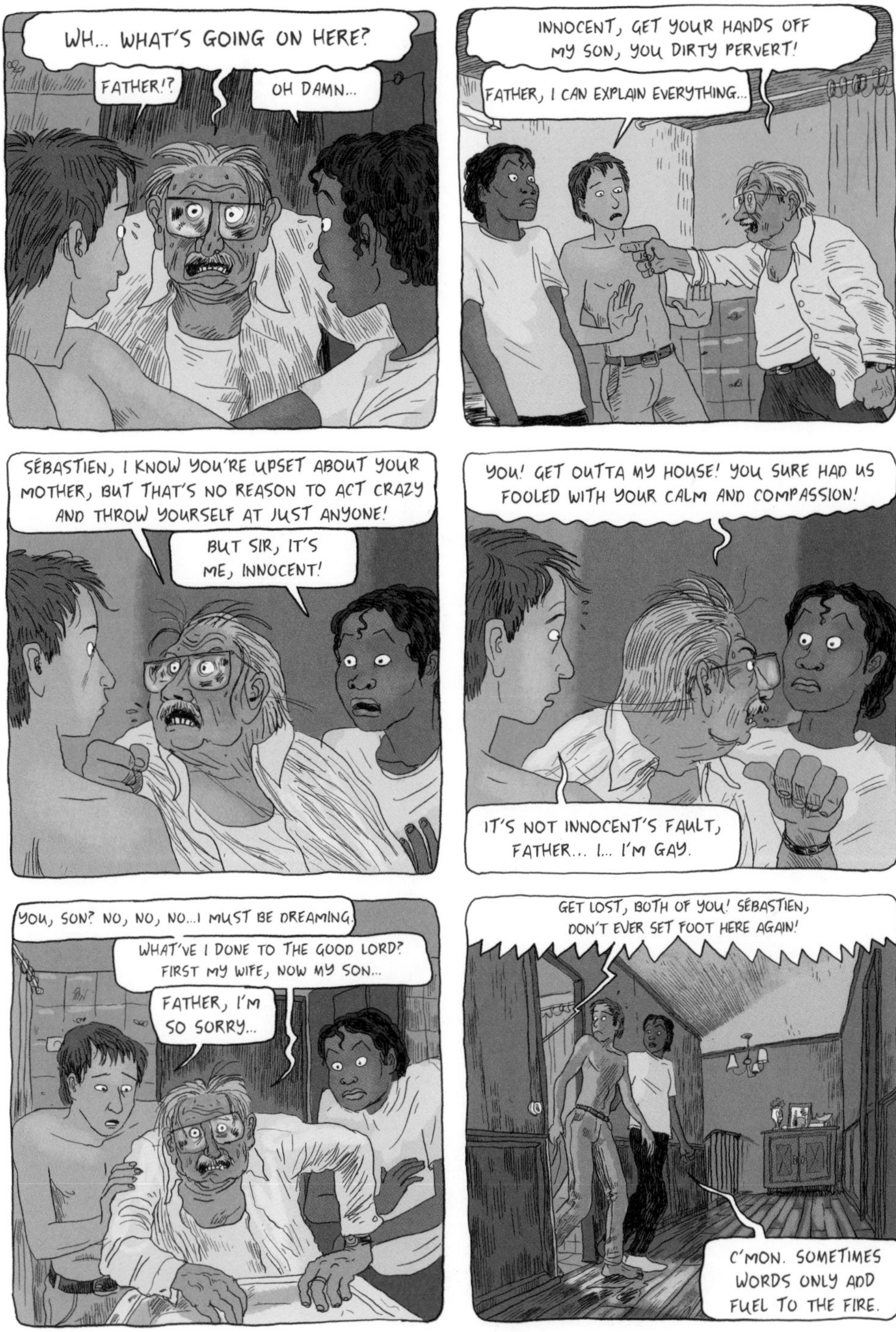
WH... WHAT'S GOING ON HERE?
FATHER!?
OH DAMN...
INNOCENT, GET YOUR HANDS OFF MY SON, YOU DIRTY PERVERT!
FATHER, I CAN EXPLAIN EVERYTHING...
SÉBASTIEN, I KNOW YOU'RE UPSET ABOUT YOUR MOTHER, BUT THAT'S NO REASON TO ACT CRAZY AND THROW YOURSELF AT JUST ANYONE!
BUT SIR, IT'S ME, INNOCENT!
YOU! GET OUTTA MY HOUSE! YOU SURE HAD US FOOLED WITH YOUR CALM AND COMPASSION!
IT'S NOT INNOCENT'S FAULT, FATHER... I... I'M GAY.
YOU, SON? NO, NO, NO...I MUST BE DREAMING.
WHAT'VE I DONE TO THE GOOD LORD? FIRST MY WIFE, NOW MY SON...
FATHER, I'M SO SORRY...
GET LOST, BOTH OF YOU! SÉBASTIEN, DON'T EVER SET FOOT HERE AGAIN!
C'MON. SOMETIMES WORDS ONLY ADD FUEL TO THE FIRE.

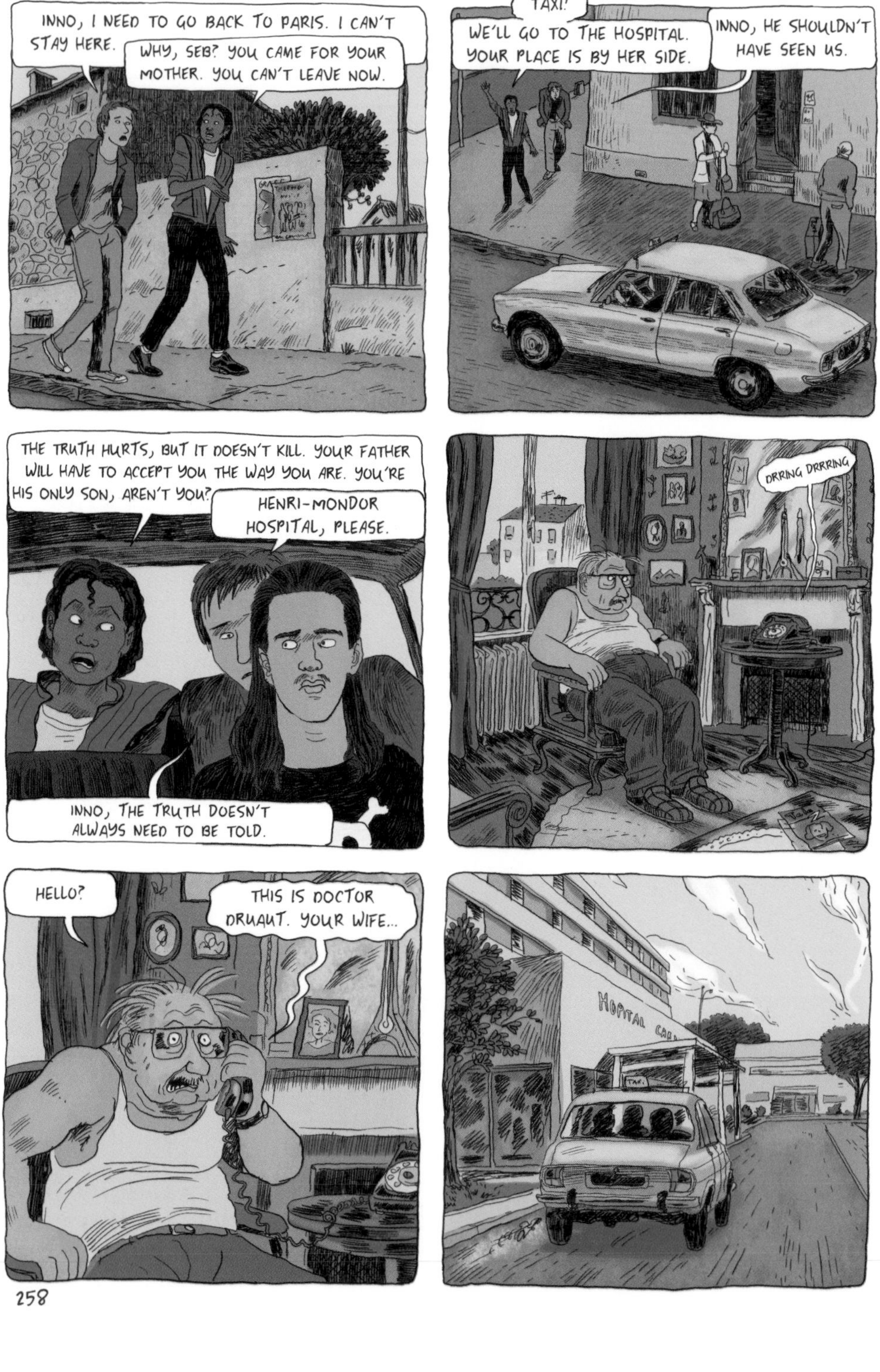
INNO, I NEED TO GO BACK TO PARIS. I CAN'T STAY HERE.
WHY, SEB? YOU CAME FOR YOUR MOTHER. YOU CAN'T LEAVE NOW.
TAXI!
WE'LL GO TO THE HOSPITAL. YOUR PLACE IS BY HER SIDE.
INNO, HE SHOULDN'T HAVE SEEN US.
THE TRUTH HURTS, BUT IT DOESN'T KILL. YOUR FATHER WILL HAVE TO ACCEPT YOU THE WAY YOU ARE. YOU'RE HIS ONLY SON, AREN'T YOU?
HENRI-MONDOR HOSPITAL, PLEASE.
INNO, THE TRUTH DOESN'T ALWAYS NEED TO BE TOLD.
DRRING DRRRING
HELLO?
THIS IS DOCTOR DRUAUT. YOUR WIFE...

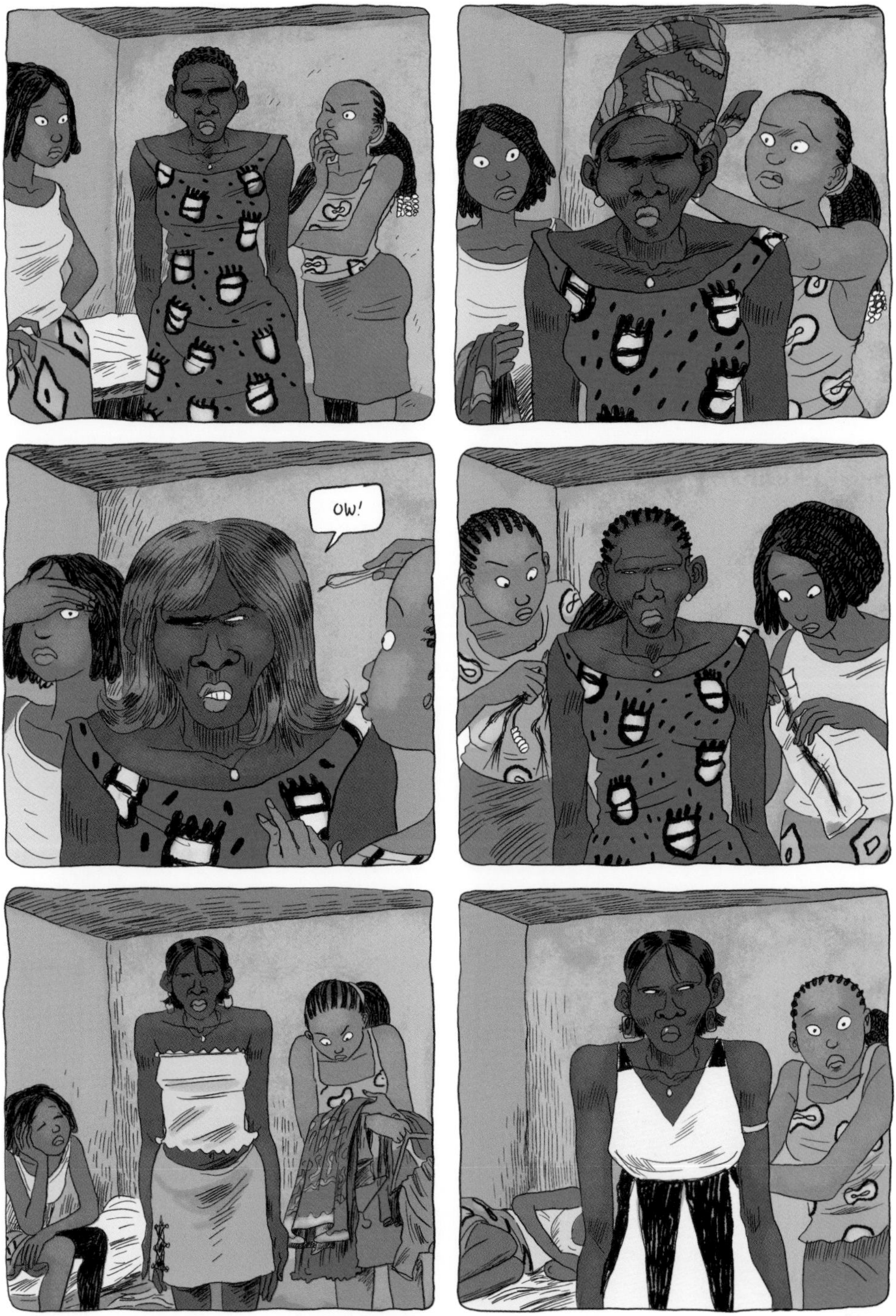
OW!

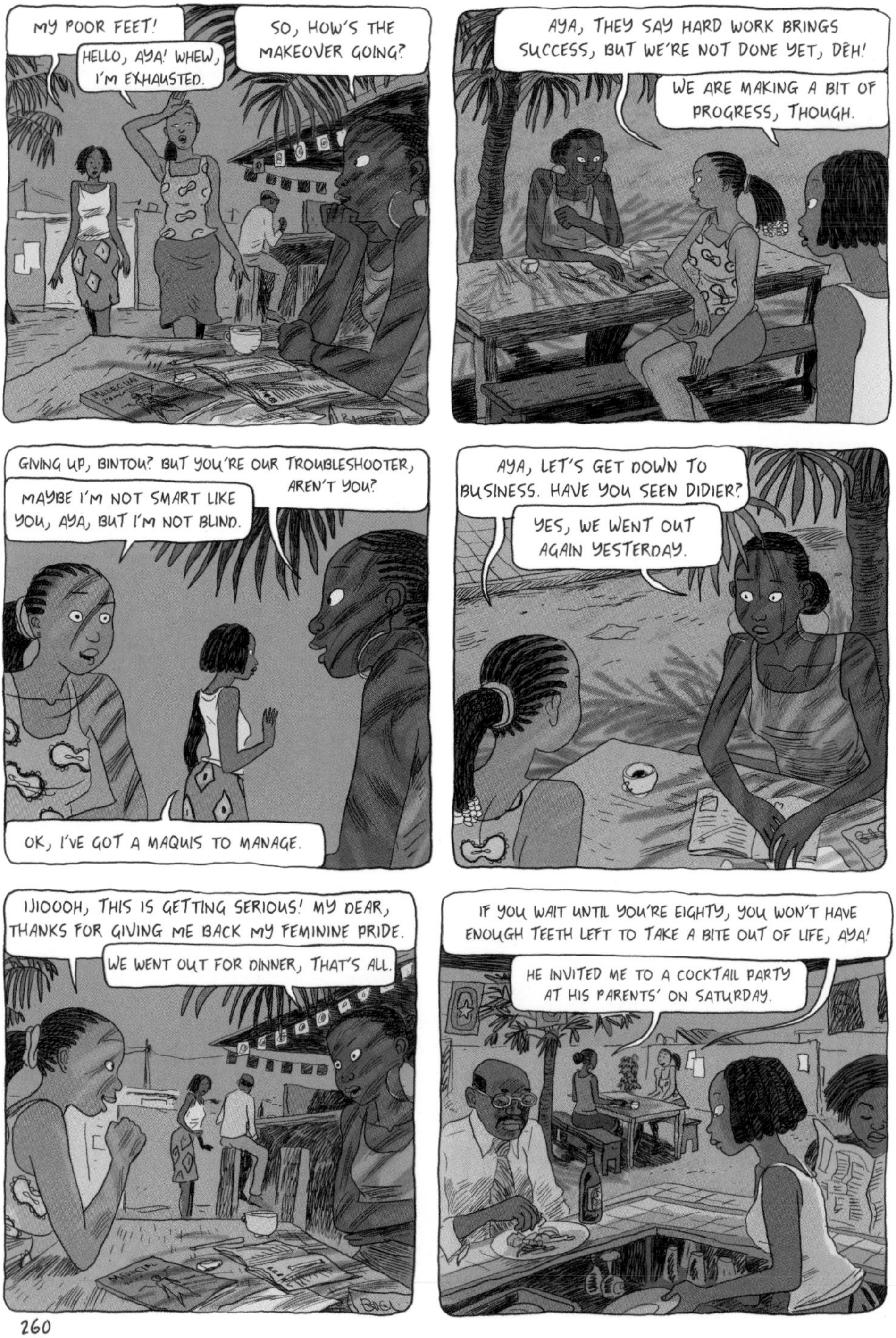
MY POOR FEET!
HELLO, AYA! WHEW, I'M EXHAUSTED.
SO, HOW'S THE MAKEOVER GOING?
AYA, THEY SAY HARD WORK BRINGS SUCCESS, BUT WE'RE NOT DONE YET, DÊH!
WE ARE MAKING A BIT OF PROGRESS, THOUGH.
GIVING UP, BINTOU? BUT YOU'RE OUR TROUBLESHOOTER, AREN'T YOU?
MAYBE I'M NOT SMART LIKE YOU, AYA, BUT I'M NOT BLIND.
OK, I'VE GOT A MAQUIS TO MANAGE.
AYA, LET'S GET DOWN TO BUSINESS. HAVE YOU SEEN DIDIER?
YES, WE WENT OUT AGAIN YESTERDAY.
IJIOOOH, THIS IS GETTING SERIOUS! MY DEAR, THANKS FOR GIVING ME BACK MY FEMININE PRIDE.
WE WENT OUT FOR DINNER, THAT'S ALL.
IF YOU WAIT UNTIL YOU'RE EIGHTY, YOU WON'T HAVE ENOUGH TEETH LEFT TO TAKE A BITE OUT OF LIFE, AYA!
HE INVITED ME TO A COCKTAIL PARTY AT HIS PARENTS' ON SATURDAY.

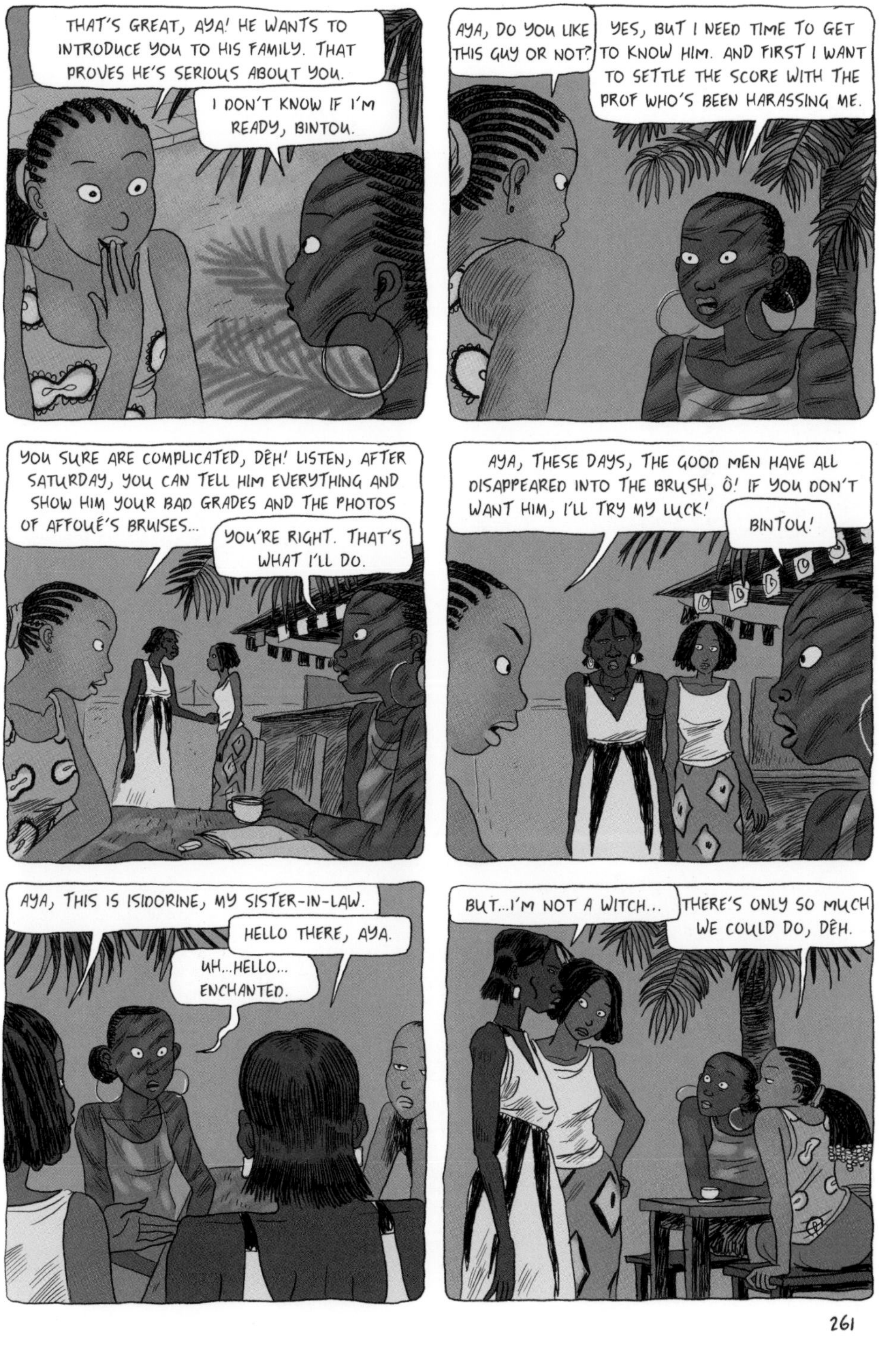
THAT'S GREAT, AYA! HE WANTS TO INTRODUCE YOU TO HIS FAMILY. THAT PROVES HE'S SERIOUS ABOUT YOU.
I DON'T KNOW IF I'M READY, BINTOU.
AYA, DO YOU LIKE THIS GUY OR NOT?
YES, BUT I NEED TIME TO GET TO KNOW HIM. AND FIRST I WANT TO SETTLE THE SCORE WITH THE PROF WHO'S BEEN HARASSING ME.
YOU SURE ARE COMPLICATED, DÊH! LISTEN, AFTER SATURDAY, YOU CAN TELL HIM EVERYTHING AND SHOW HIM YOUR BAD GRADES AND THE PHOTOS OF AFFOUÉ'S BRUISES...
YOU'RE RIGHT. THAT'S WHAT I'LL DO.
AYA, THESE DAYS, THE GOOD MEN HAVE ALL DISAPPEARED INTO THE BRUSH, Ô! IF YOU DON'T WANT HIM, I'LL TRY MY LUCK!
BINTOU!
AYA, THIS IS ISIDORINE, MY SISTER-IN-LAW.
HELLO THERE, AYA.
UH...HELLO... ENCHANTED.
BUT...I'M NOT A WITCH...
THERE'S ONLY SO MUCH WE COULD DO, DÊH.

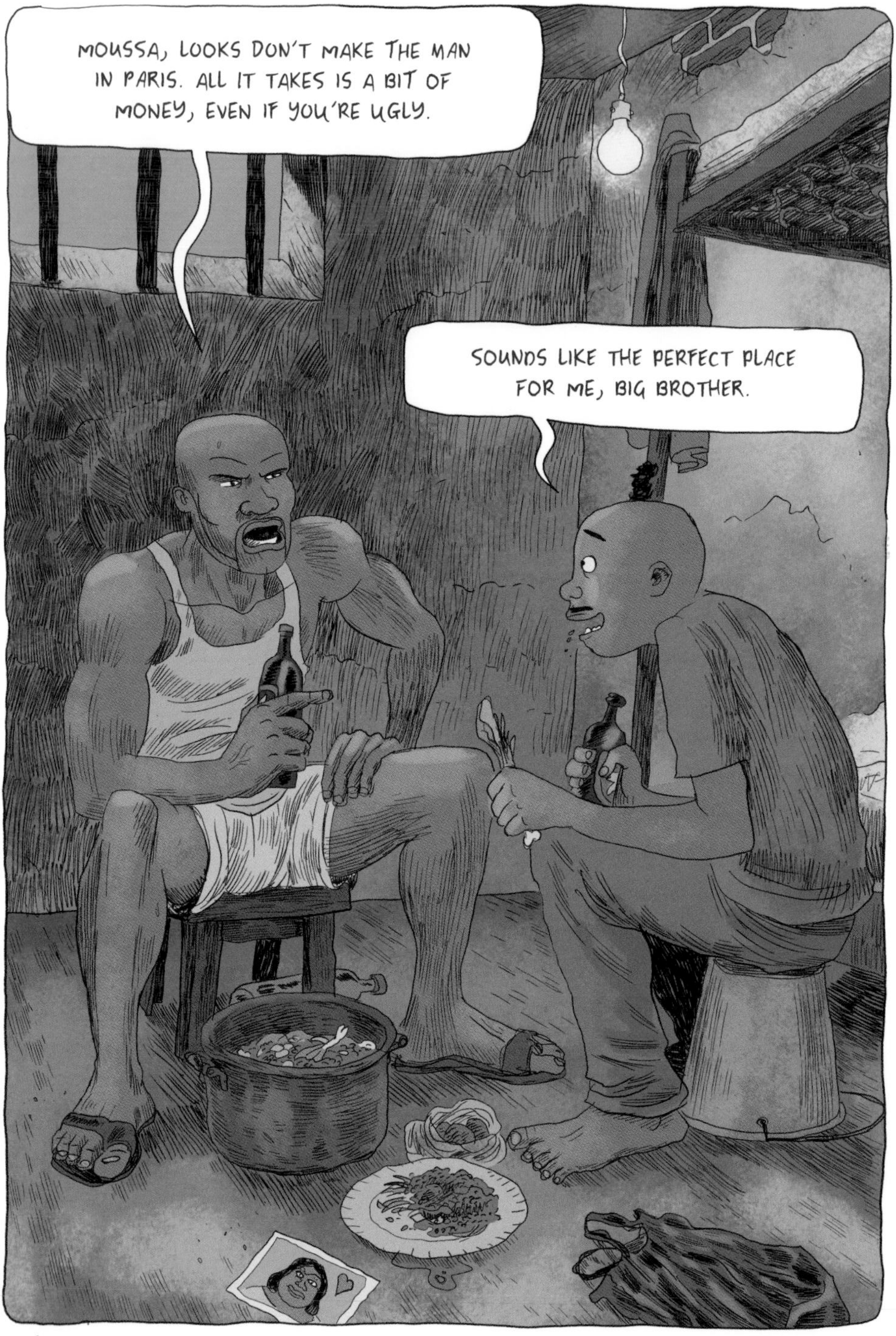
MOUSSA, LOOKS DON'T MAKE THE MAN IN PARIS. ALL IT TAKES IS A BIT OF MONEY, EVEN IF YOU'RE UGLY.
SOUNDS LIKE THE PERFECT PLACE FOR ME, BIG BROTHER.

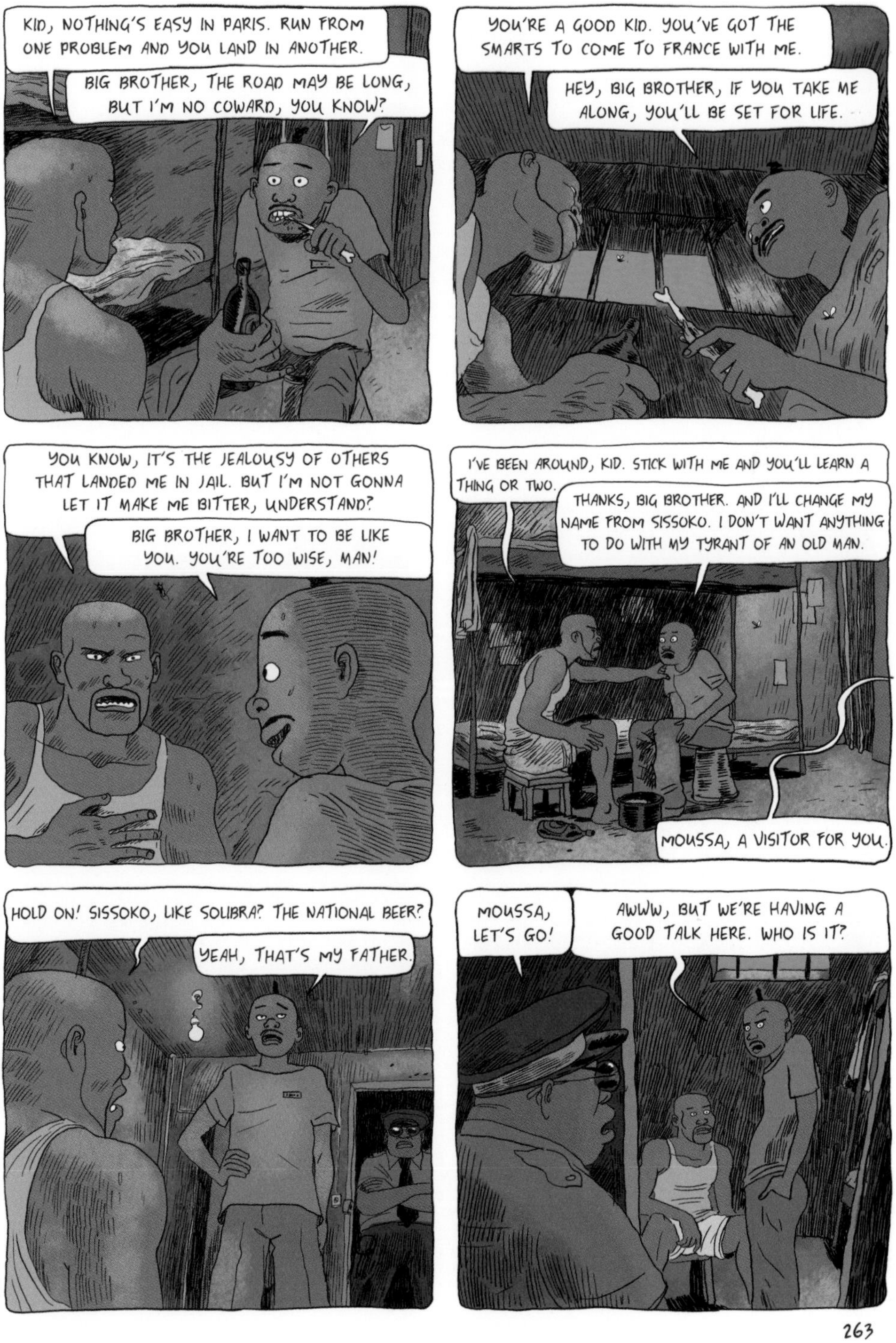
KID, NOTHING'S EASY IN PARIS. RUN FROM ONE PROBLEM AND YOU LAND IN ANOTHER.
BIG BROTHER, THE ROAD MAY BE LONG, BUT I'M NO COWARD, YOU KNOW?
YOU'RE A GOOD KID. YOU'VE GOT THE SMARTS TO COME TO FRANCE WITH ME.
HEY, BIG BROTHER, IF YOU TAKE ME ALONG, YOU'LL BE SET FOR LIFE.
YOU KNOW, IT'S THE JEALOUSY OF OTHERS THAT LANDED ME IN JAIL. BUT I'M NOT GONNA LET IT MAKE ME BITTER, UNDERSTAND?
BIG BROTHER, I WANT TO BE LIKE YOU. YOU'RE TOO WISE, MAN!
I'VE BEEN AROUND, KID. STICK WITH ME AND YOU'LL LEARN A THING OR TWO.
THANKS, BIG BROTHER. AND I'LL CHANGE MY NAME FROM SISSOKO. I DON'T WANT ANYTHING TO DO WITH MY TYRANT OF AN OLD MAN.
MOUSSA, A VISITOR FOR YOU.
HOLD ON! SISSOKO, LIKE SOLIBRA? THE NATIONAL BEER?
YEAH, THAT'S MY FATHER.
MOUSSA, LET'S GO!
AWWW, BUT WE'RE HAVING A GOOD TALK HERE. WHO IS IT?

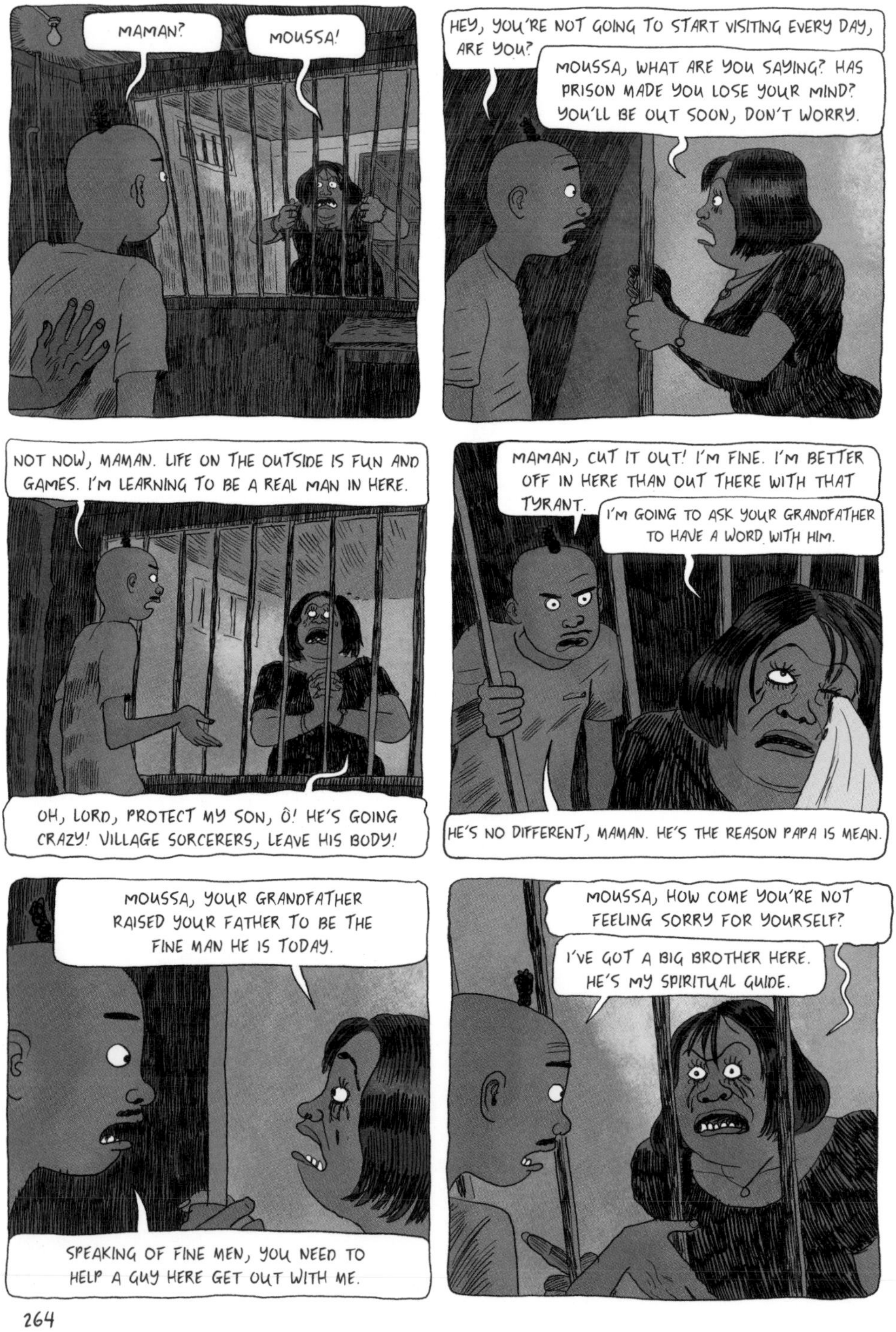
MAMAN?
MOUSSA!
HEY, YOU'RE NOT GOING TO START VISITING EVERY DAY, ARE YOU?
MOUSSA, WHAT ARE YOU SAYING? HAS PRISON MADE YOU LOSE YOUR MIND? YOU'LL BE OUT SOON, DON'T WORRY.
NOT NOW, MAMAN. LIFE ON THE OUTSIDE IS FUN AND GAMES. I'M LEARNING TO BE A REAL MAN IN HERE.
OH, LORD, PROTECT MY SON, Ô! HE'S GOING CRAZY! VILLAGE SORCERERS, LEAVE HIS BODY!
MAMAN, CUT IT OUT! I'M FINE. I'M BETTER OFF IN HERE THAN OUT THERE WITH THAT TYRANT.
I'M GOING TO ASK YOUR GRANDFATHER TO HAVE A WORD WITH HIM.
HE'S NO DIFFERENT, MAMAN. HE'S THE REASON PAPA IS MEAN.
MOUSSA, YOUR GRANDFATHER RAISED YOUR FATHER TO BE THE FINE MAN HE IS TODAY.
SPEAKING OF FINE MEN, YOU NEED TO HELP A GUY HERE GET OUT WITH ME.
MOUSSA, HOW COME YOU'RE NOT FEELING SORRY FOR YOURSELF?
I'VE GOT A BIG BROTHER HERE. HE'S MY SPIRITUAL GUIDE.

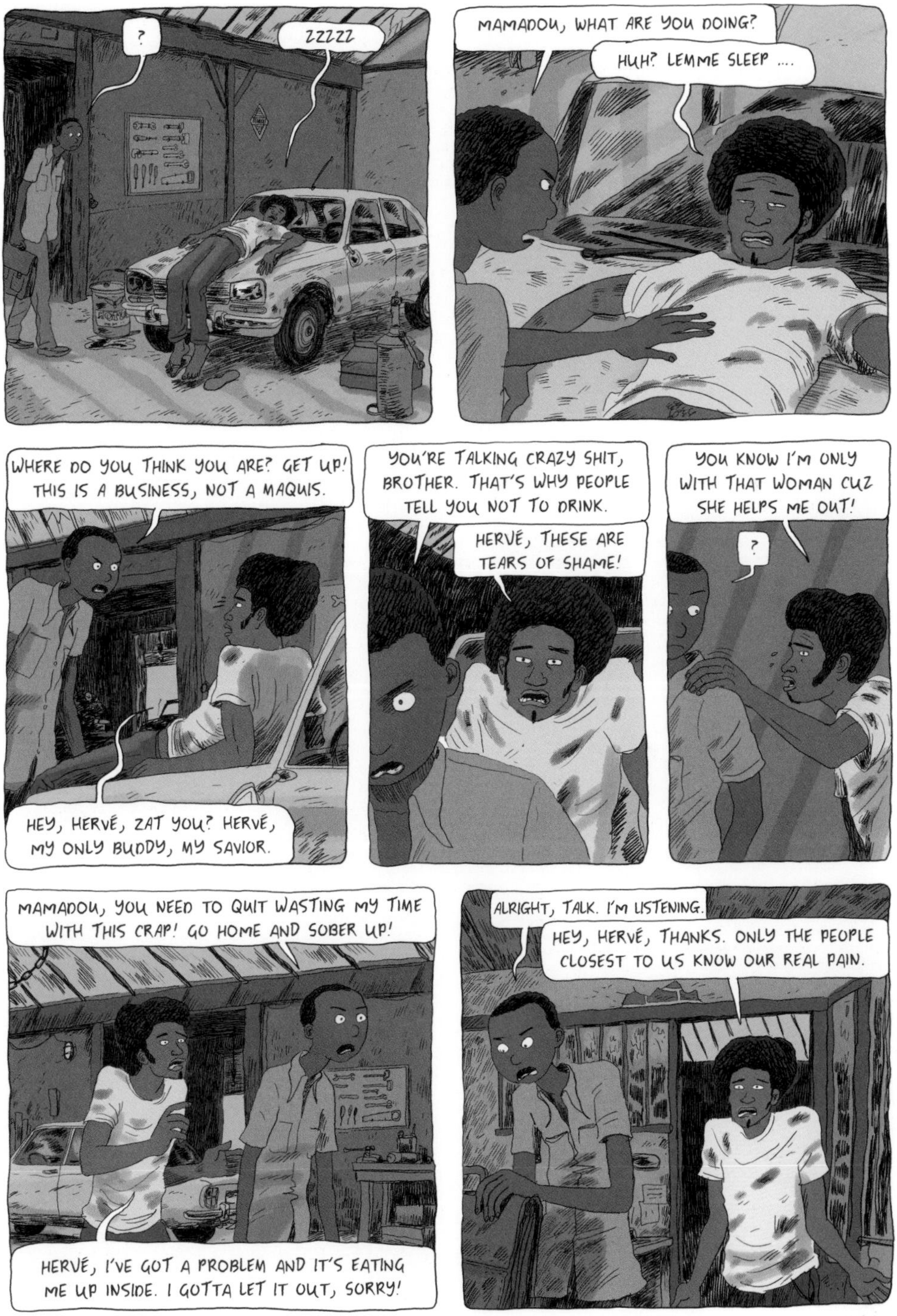
?
ZZZZZ
MAMADOU, WHAT ARE YOU DOING?
HUH? LEMME SLEEP ....
WHERE DO YOU THINK YOU ARE? GET UP! THIS IS A BUSINESS, NOT A MAQUIS.
HEY, HERVÉ, ZAT YOU? HERVÉ, MY ONLY BUDDY, MY SAVIOR.
YOU'RE TALKING CRAZY SHIT, BROTHER. THAT'S WHY PEOPLE TELL YOU NOT TO DRINK.
HERVÉ, THESE ARE TEARS OF SHAME!
YOU KNOW I'M ONLY WITH THAT WOMAN CUZ SHE HELPS ME OUT!
?
MAMADOU, YOU NEED TO QUIT WASTING MY TIME WITH THIS CRAP! GO HOME AND SOBER UP!
HERVÉ, I'VE GOT A PROBLEM AND IT'S EATING ME UP INSIDE. I GOTTA LET IT OUT, SORRY!
ALRIGHT, TALK. I'M LISTENING.
HEY, HERVÉ, THANKS. ONLY THE PEOPLE CLOSEST TO US KNOW OUR REAL PAIN.

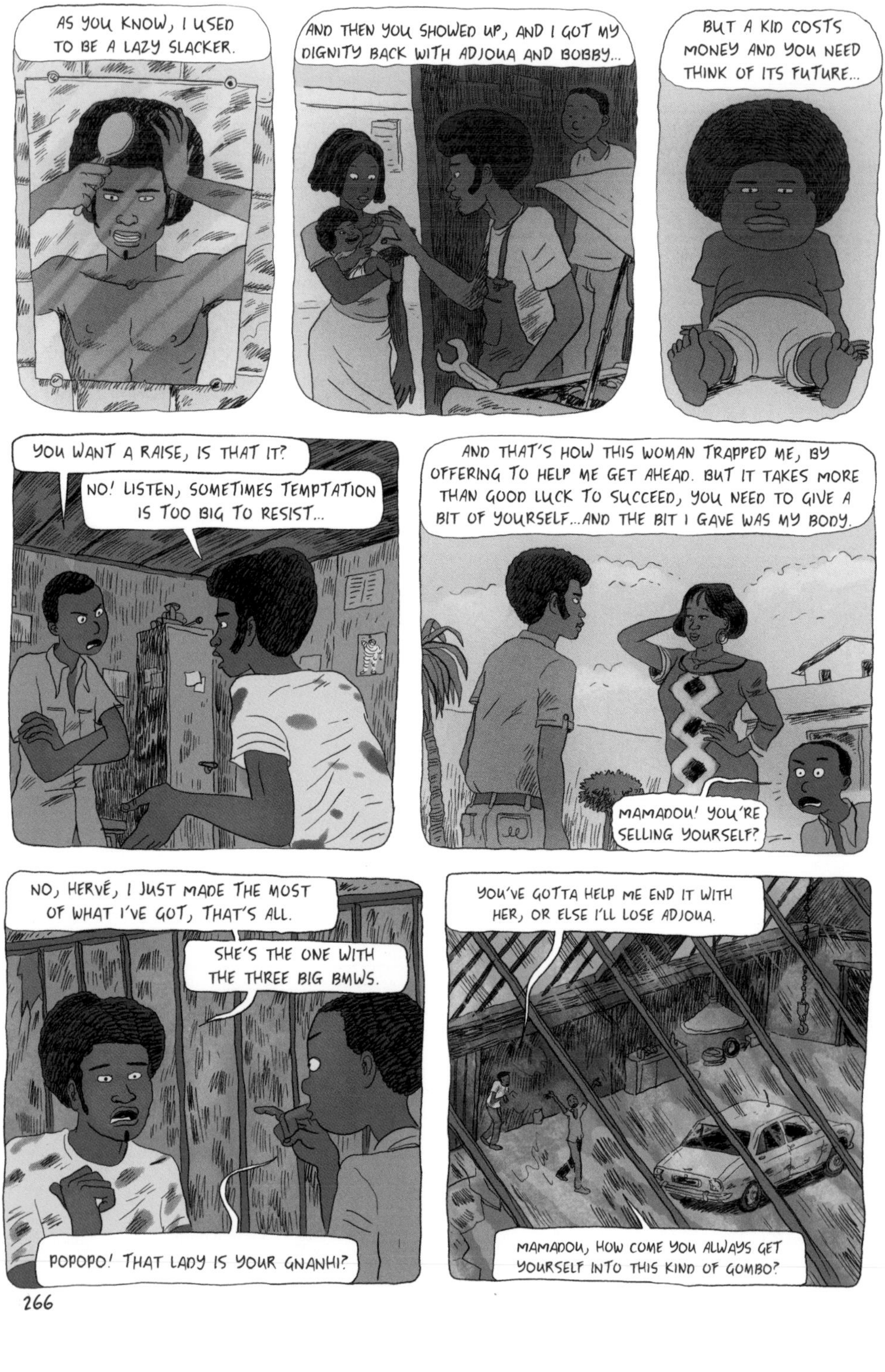

AS YOU KNOW, I USED TO BE A LAZY SLACKER.
AND THEN YOU SHOWED UP, AND I GOT MY DIGNITY BACK WITH ADJOUA AND BOBBY...
BUT A KID COSTS MONEY AND YOU NEED THINK OF ITS FUTURE...
YOU WANT A RAISE, IS THAT IT?
NO! LISTEN, SOMETIMES TEMPTATION IS TOO BIG TO RESIST...
AND THAT'S HOW THIS WOMAN TRAPPED ME, BY OFFERING TO HELP ME GET AHEAD. BUT IT TAKES MORE THAN GOOD LUCK TO SUCCEED, YOU NEED TO GIVE A BIT OF YOURSELF...AND THE BIT I GAVE WAS MY BODY.
MAMADOU! YOU'RE SELLING YOURSELF?
NO, HERVÉ, I JUST MADE THE MOST OF WHAT I'VE GOT, THAT'S ALL.
SHE'S THE ONE WITH THE THREE BIG BMWS.
POPOPO! THAT LADY IS YOUR GNANHI?
YOU'VE GOTTA HELP ME END IT WITH HER, OR ELSE I'LL LOSE ADJOUA.
MAMADOU, HOW COME YOU ALWAYS GET YOURSELF INTO THIS KIND OF GOMBO?

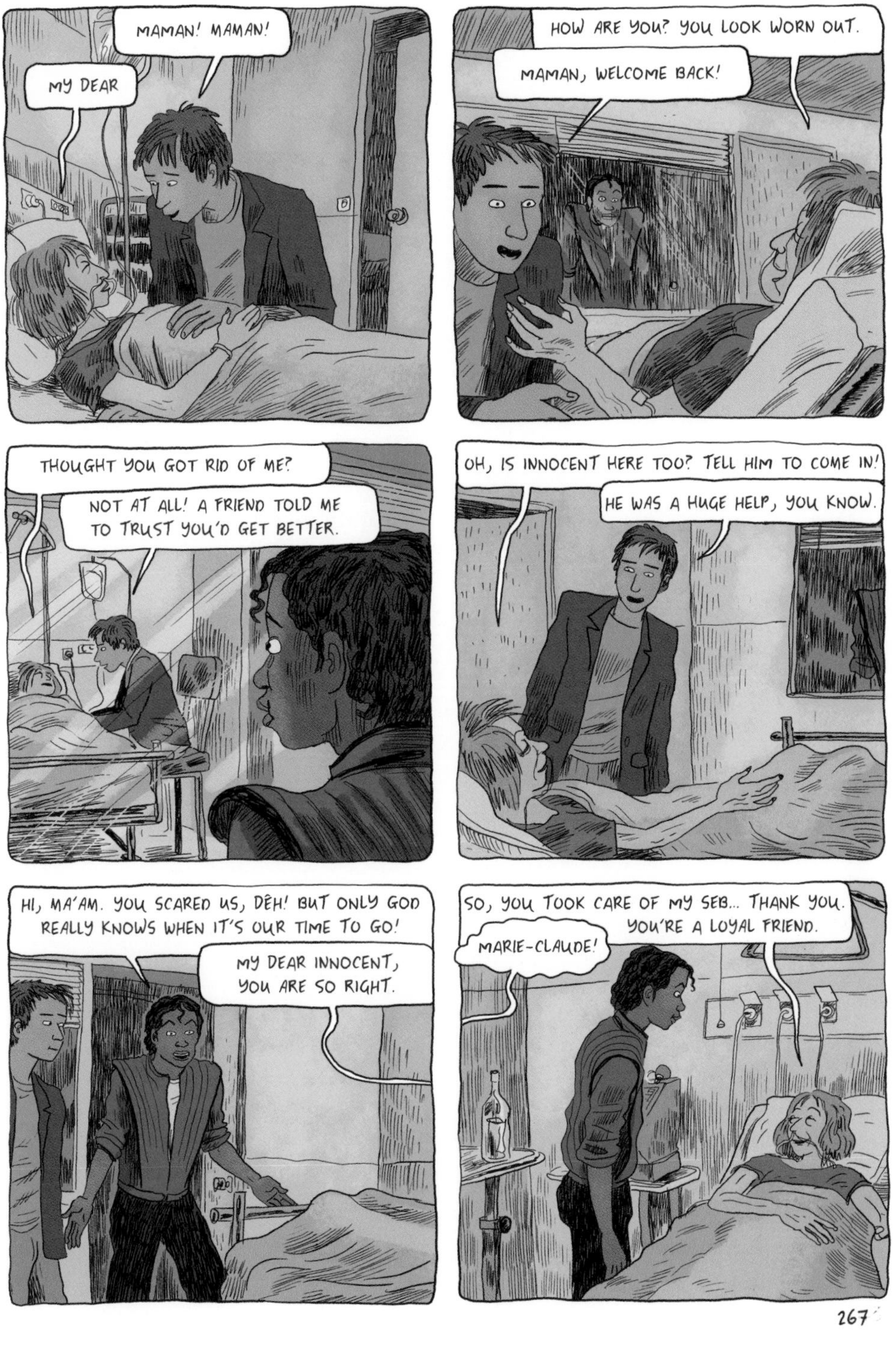
MAMAN! MAMAN!
MY DEAR
HOW ARE YOU? YOU LOOK WORN OUT.
MAMAN, WELCOME BACK!
THOUGHT YOU GOT RID OF ME?
NOT AT ALL! A FRIEND TOLD ME TO TRUST YOU'D GET BETTER.
OH, IS INNOCENT HERE TOO? TELL HIM TO COME IN!
HE WAS A HUGE HELP, YOU KNOW.
HI, MA'AM. YOU SCARED US, DÊH! BUT ONLY GOD REALLY KNOWS WHEN IT'S OUR TIME TO GO!
MY DEAR INNOCENT, YOU ARE SO RIGHT.
SO, YOU TOOK CARE OF MY SEB... THANK YOU. YOU'RE A LOYAL FRIEND.
MARIE-CLAUDE!

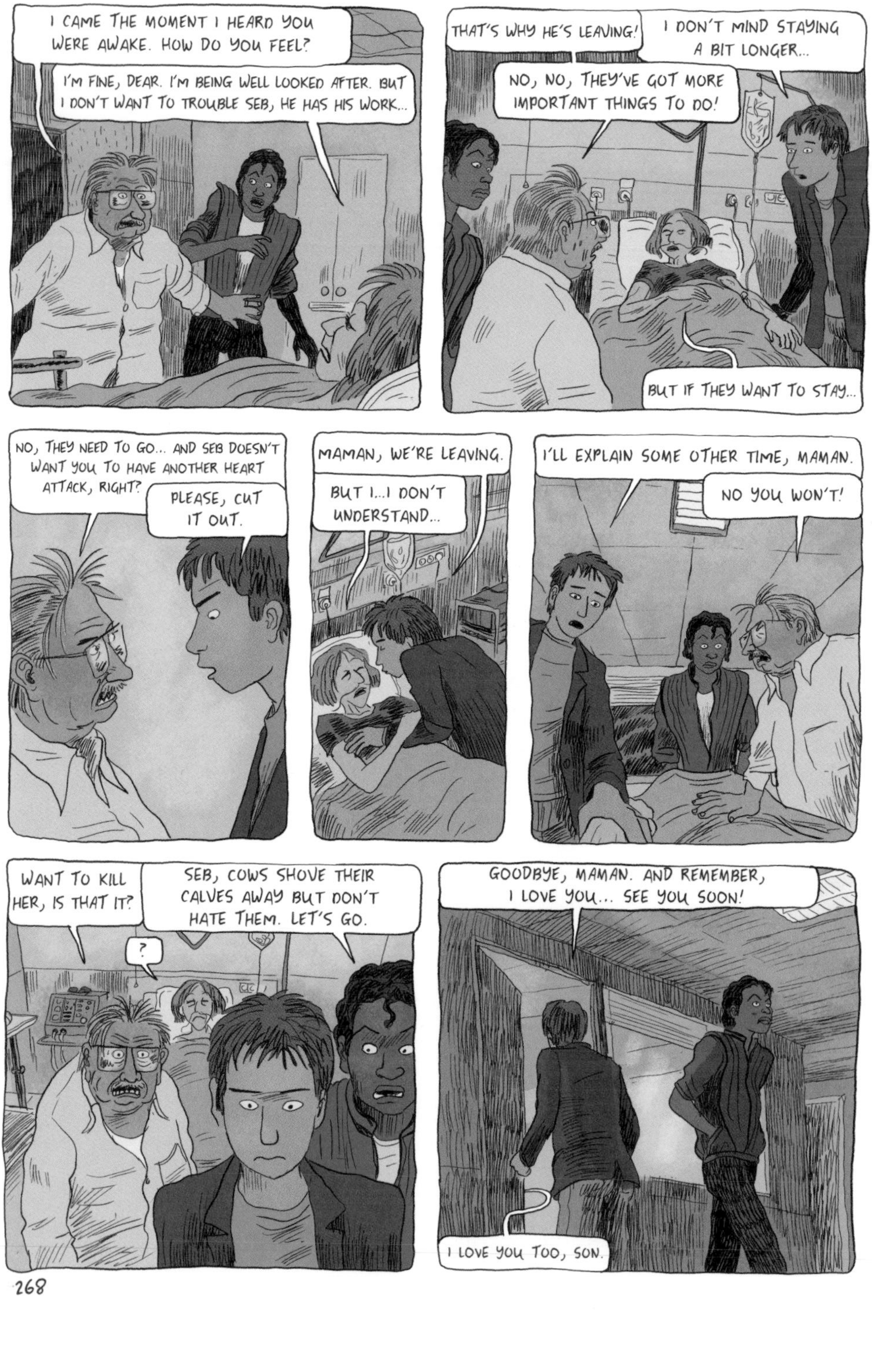
I CAME THE MOMENT I HEARD YOU WERE AWAKE. HOW DO YOU FEEL?
I'M FINE, DEAR. I'M BEING WELL LOOKED AFTER. BUT I DON'T WANT TO TROUBLE SEB, HE HAS HIS WORK...
THAT'S WHY HE'S LEAVING!
I DON'T MIND STAYING A BIT LONGER...
NO, NO, THEY'VE GOT MORE IMPORTANT THINGS TO DO!
BUT IF THEY WANT TO STAY...
NO, THEY NEED TO GO... AND SEB DOESN'T WANT YOU TO HAVE ANOTHER HEART ATTACK, RIGHT?
PLEASE, CUT IT OUT.
MAMAN, WE'RE LEAVING.
BUT I...I DON'T UNDERSTAND...
I'LL EXPLAIN SOME OTHER TIME, MAMAN.
NO YOU WON'T!
WANT TO KILL HER, IS THAT IT?
SEB, COWS SHOVE THEIR CALVES AWAY BUT DON'T HATE THEM. LET'S GO.
?
GOODBYE, MAMAN. AND REMEMBER, I LOVE YOU... SEE YOU SOON!
I LOVE YOU TOO, SON.

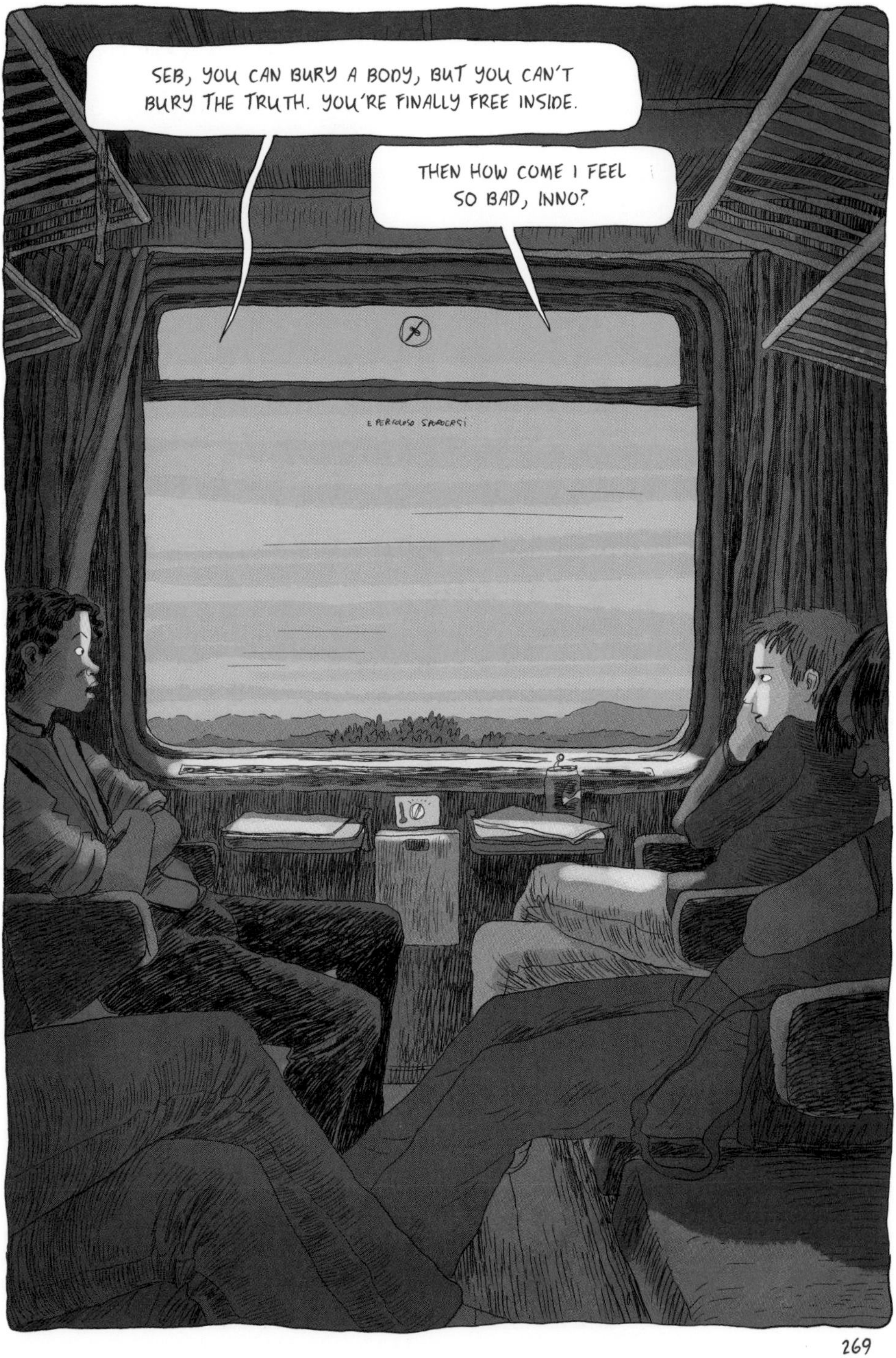
SEB, YOU CAN BURY A BODY, BUT YOU CAN'T BURY THE TRUTH. YOU'RE FINALLY FREE INSIDE.
THEN HOW COME I FEEL SO BAD, INNO?
E PERICOLOSO SPORGERSI

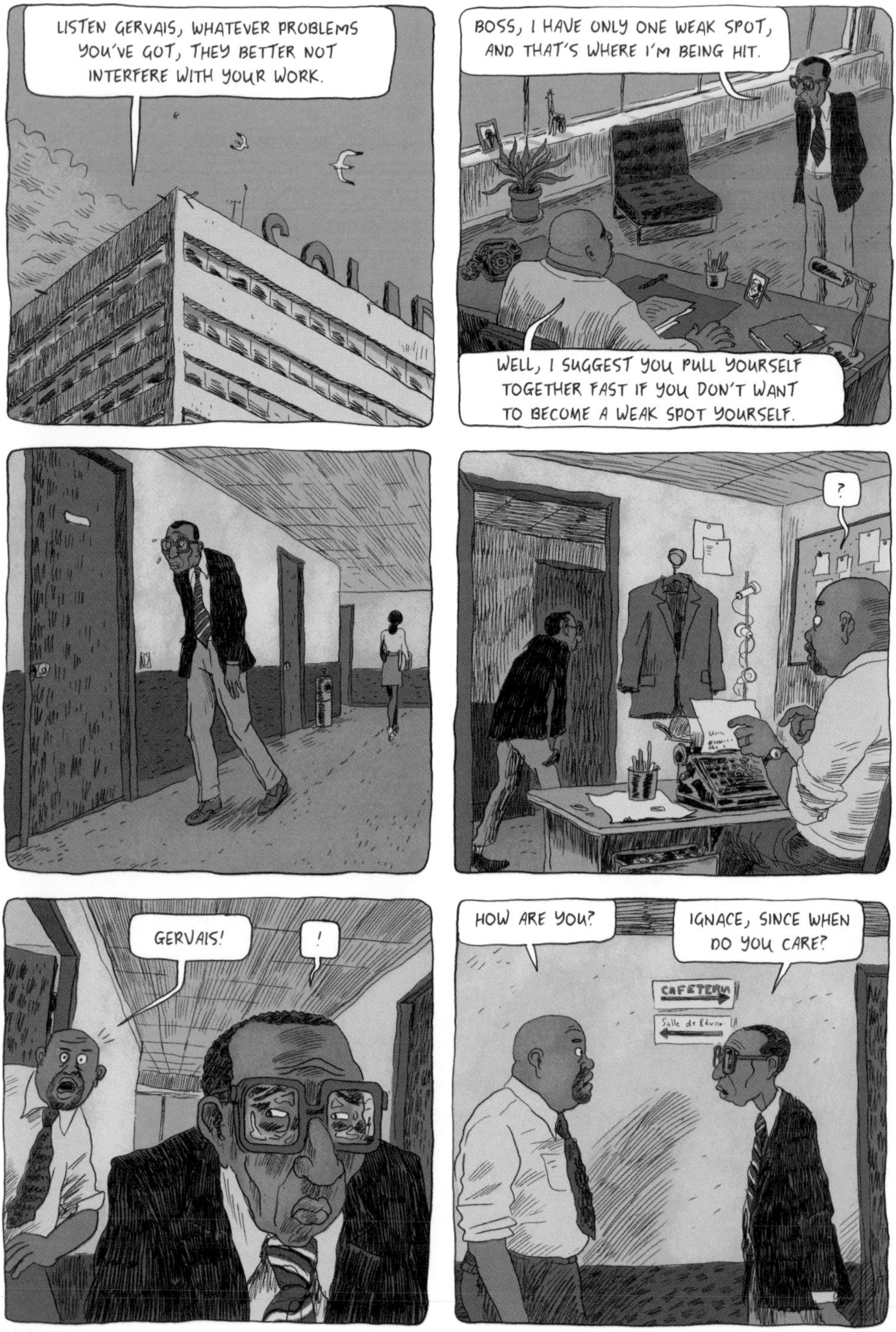
LISTEN GERVAIS, WHATEVER PROBLEMS YOU'VE GOT, THEY BETTER NOT INTERFERE WITH YOUR WORK.
BOSS, I HAVE ONLY ONE WEAK SPOT, AND THAT'S WHERE I'M BEING HIT.
WELL, I SUGGEST YOU PULL YOURSELF TOGETHER FAST IF YOU DON'T WANT TO BECOME A WEAK SPOT YOURSELF.
?
GERVAIS!
!
HOW ARE YOU?
IGNACE, SINCE WHEN DO YOU CARE?
CAFETERIA

MY KIDS ARE IN YOUR HOME, SO IT'S ONLY NORMAL FOR ME TO TAKE AN INTEREST.

IGNACE, I'VE GOT PROBLEMS.

AH! SO THE RAIN'S FALLING ON MORE THAN ONE ROOF, IS THAT IT?

JEANNE TOOK THE KIDS AND WENT TO LIVE WITH HER PARENTS.

ARE YOU KIDDING? SO YOUR MOTHER HAS STRUCK AGAIN! GERVAIS, HOW CAN YOU LET JEANNE LEAVE, WITH HER NICE SHAPE, HER CARAMEL SKIN, THOSE FABULOUS CURVES...

IGNACE, I CAN'T LIVE WITHOUT HER.

YOUR MOTHER OR JEANNE?

JEANNE, OF COURSE... IGNACE, WHAT SHOULD I DO?

OK, LISTEN UP. FIRST YOU BUY HER SOME FLOWERS AND...

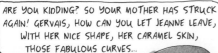

SO, YOU WANT TO SEE MY DAUGHTER?

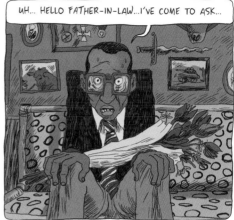

UH... HELLO FATHER-IN-LAW... I'VE COME TO ASK...

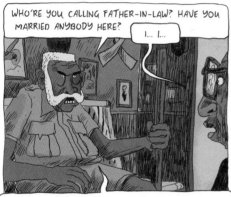

WHO'RE YOU CALLING FATHER-IN-LAW? HAVE YOU MARRIED ANYBODY HERE?

I... I...

SIR, MY APOLOGIES... I'M HERE TO...

"COLONEL, SIR," YOU DAMN CANNIBAL!

YES, COLONEL, SIR...

GERVAIS?

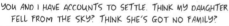

YOU AND I HAVE ACCOUNTS TO SETTLE. THINK MY DAUGHTER FELL FROM THE SKY? THINK SHE'S GOT NO FAMILY?

WHAT'S THIS?

JEANNE! IGNACE SAID I SHOULD...

GET OUTTA HERE!

AND DON'T COME BACK TIL YOU KNOW WHAT YOU WANT!

FATHER, PUT AWAY THE GUN BEFORE YOU HURT SOMEBODY.

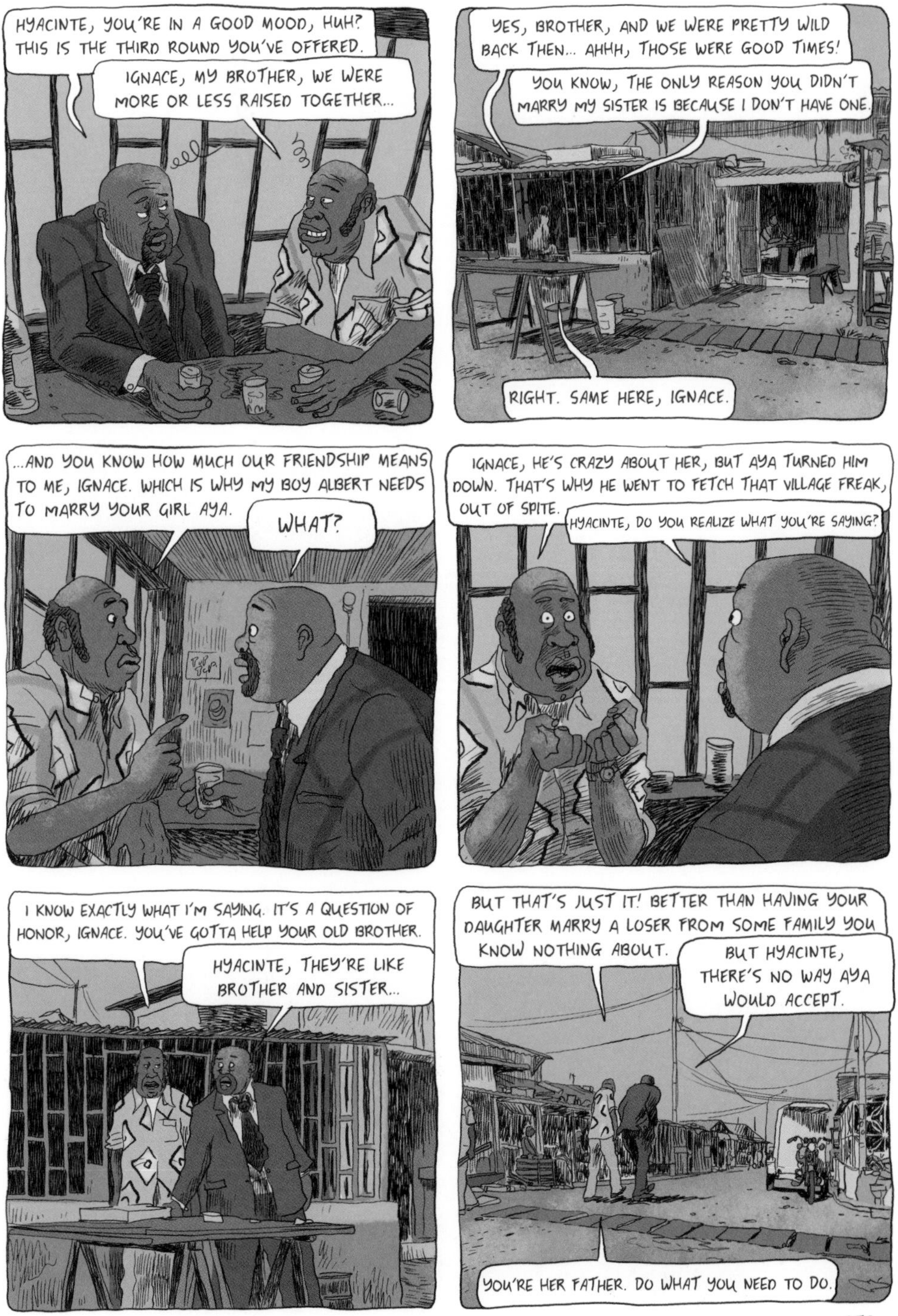
HYACINTE, YOU'RE IN A GOOD MOOD, HUH? THIS IS THE THIRD ROUND YOU'VE OFFERED.
IGNACE, MY BROTHER, WE WERE MORE OR LESS RAISED TOGETHER...
YES, BROTHER, AND WE WERE PRETTY WILD BACK THEN... AHHH, THOSE WERE GOOD TIMES!
YOU KNOW, THE ONLY REASON YOU DIDN'T MARRY MY SISTER IS BECAUSE I DON'T HAVE ONE.
RIGHT. SAME HERE, IGNACE.
...AND YOU KNOW HOW MUCH OUR FRIENDSHIP MEANS TO ME, IGNACE. WHICH IS WHY MY BOY ALBERT NEEDS TO MARRY YOUR GIRL AYA.
WHAT?
IGNACE, HE'S CRAZY ABOUT HER, BUT AYA TURNED HIM DOWN. THAT'S WHY HE WENT TO FETCH THAT VILLAGE FREAK, OUT OF SPITE.
HYACINTE, DO YOU REALIZE WHAT YOU'RE SAYING?
I KNOW EXACTLY WHAT I'M SAYING. IT'S A QUESTION OF HONOR, IGNACE. YOU'VE GOTTA HELP YOUR OLD BROTHER.
HYACINTE, THEY'RE LIKE BROTHER AND SISTER...
BUT THAT'S JUST IT! BETTER THAN HAVING YOUR DAUGHTER MARRY A LOSER FROM SOME FAMILY YOU KNOW NOTHING ABOUT.
BUT HYACINTE, THERE'S NO WAY AYA WOULD ACCEPT.
YOU'RE HER FATHER. DO WHAT YOU NEED TO DO.

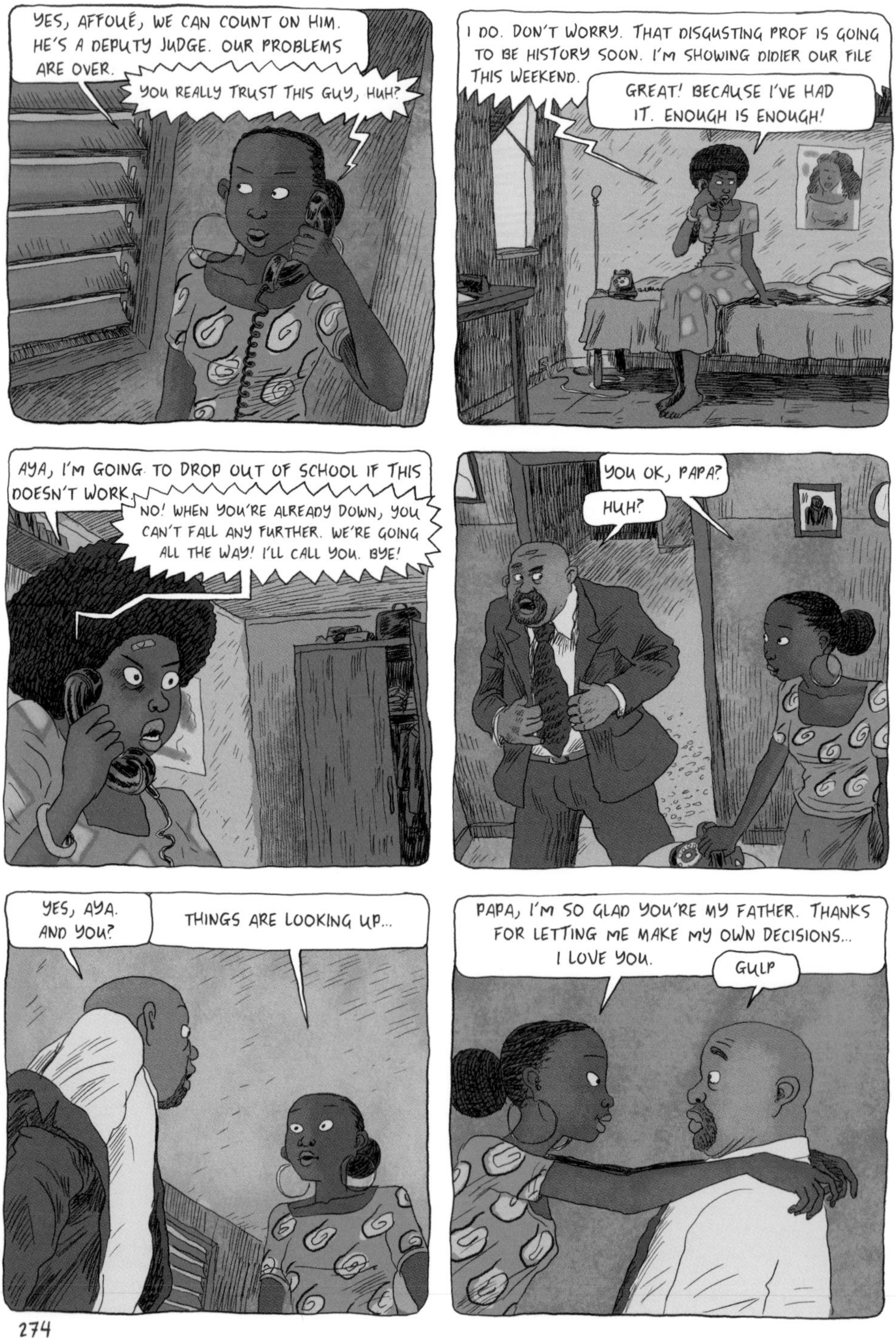
YES, AFFOUÉ, WE CAN COUNT ON HIM. HE'S A DEPUTY JUDGE. OUR PROBLEMS ARE OVER.
YOU REALLY TRUST THIS GUY, HUH?
I DO. DON'T WORRY. THAT DISGUSTING PROF IS GOING TO BE HISTORY SOON. I'M SHOWING DIDIER OUR FILE THIS WEEKEND.
GREAT! BECAUSE I'VE HAD IT. ENOUGH IS ENOUGH!
AYA, I'M GOING TO DROP OUT OF SCHOOL IF THIS DOESN'T WORK.
NO! WHEN YOU'RE ALREADY DOWN, YOU CAN'T FALL ANY FURTHER. WE'RE GOING ALL THE WAY! I'LL CALL YOU. BYE!
YOU OK, PAPA?
HUH?
YES, AYA. AND YOU?
THINGS ARE LOOKING UP...
PAPA, I'M SO GLAD YOU'RE MY FATHER. THANKS FOR LETTING ME MAKE MY OWN DECISIONS... I LOVE YOU.
GULP

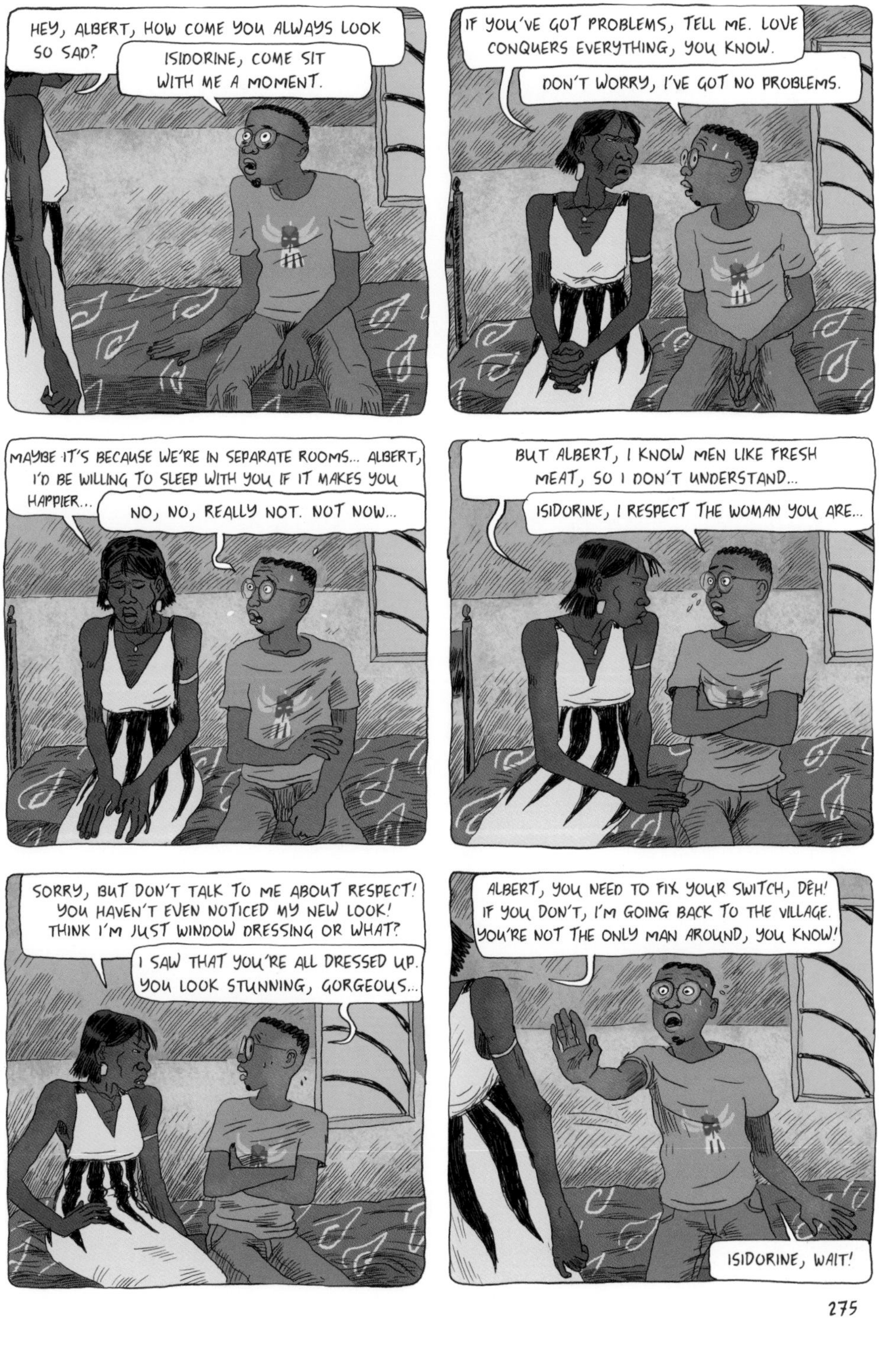
HEY, ALBERT, HOW COME YOU ALWAYS LOOK SO SAD?
ISIDORINE, COME SIT WITH ME A MOMENT.
IF YOU'VE GOT PROBLEMS, TELL ME. LOVE CONQUERS EVERYTHING, YOU KNOW.
DON'T WORRY, I'VE GOT NO PROBLEMS.
MAYBE IT'S BECAUSE WE'RE IN SEPARATE ROOMS... ALBERT, I'D BE WILLING TO SLEEP WITH YOU IF IT MAKES YOU HAPPIER...
NO, NO, REALLY NOT. NOT NOW...
BUT ALBERT, I KNOW MEN LIKE FRESH MEAT, SO I DON'T UNDERSTAND...
ISIDORINE, I RESPECT THE WOMAN YOU ARE...
SORRY, BUT DON'T TALK TO ME ABOUT RESPECT! YOU HAVEN'T EVEN NOTICED MY NEW LOOK! THINK I'M JUST WINDOW DRESSING OR WHAT?
I SAW THAT YOU'RE ALL DRESSED UP. YOU LOOK STUNNING, GORGEOUS...
ALBERT, YOU NEED TO FIX YOUR SWITCH, DÊH! IF YOU DON'T, I'M GOING BACK TO THE VILLAGE. YOU'RE NOT THE ONLY MAN AROUND, YOU KNOW!
ISIDORINE, WAIT!

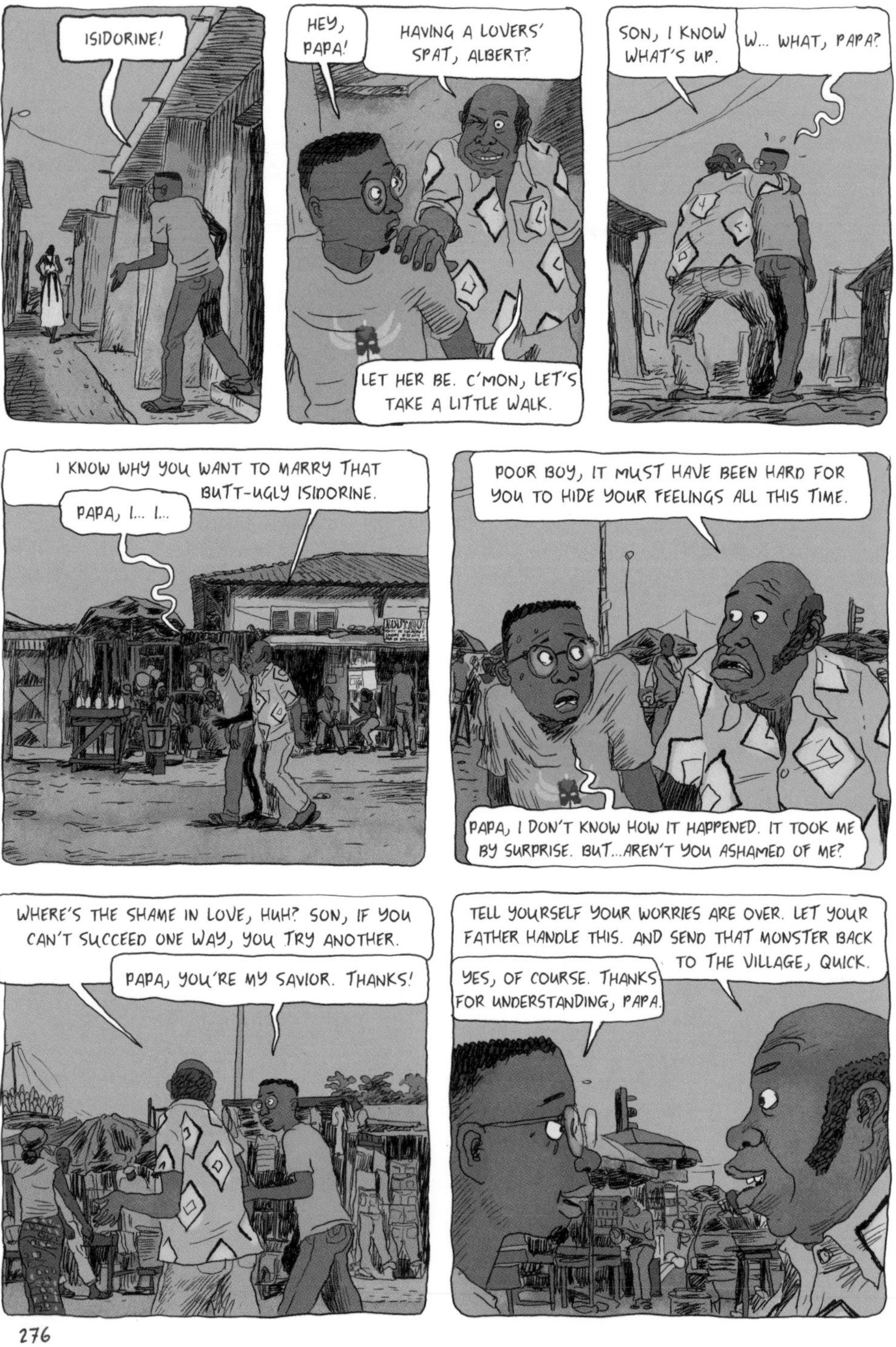
ISIDORINE!
HEY, PAPA!
HAVING A LOVERS' SPAT, ALBERT?
LET HER BE. C'MON, LET'S TAKE A LITTLE WALK.
SON, I KNOW WHAT'S UP.
W... WHAT, PAPA?
I KNOW WHY YOU WANT TO MARRY THAT BUTT-UGLY ISIDORINE.
PAPA, I... I...
POOR BOY, IT MUST HAVE BEEN HARD FOR YOU TO HIDE YOUR FEELINGS ALL THIS TIME.
PAPA, I DON'T KNOW HOW IT HAPPENED. IT TOOK ME BY SURPRISE. BUT...AREN'T YOU ASHAMED OF ME?
WHERE'S THE SHAME IN LOVE, HUH? SON, IF YOU CAN'T SUCCEED ONE WAY, YOU TRY ANOTHER.
PAPA, YOU'RE MY SAVIOR. THANKS!
TELL YOURSELF YOUR WORRIES ARE OVER. LET YOUR FATHER HANDLE THIS. AND SEND THAT MONSTER BACK TO THE VILLAGE, QUICK.
YES, OF COURSE. THANKS FOR UNDERSTANDING, PAPA.

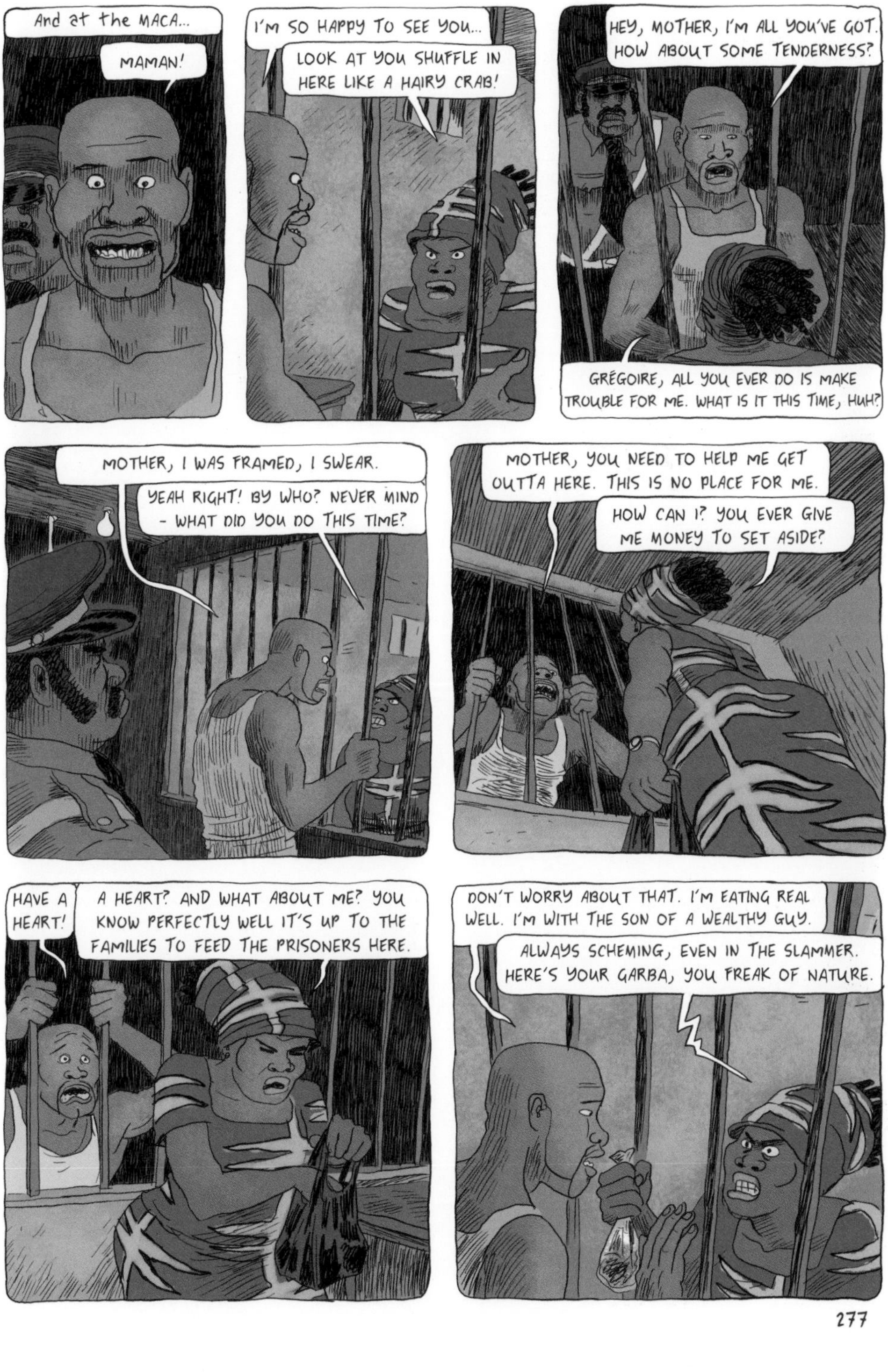
And at the MACA...
MAMAN!
I'M SO HAPPY TO SEE YOU...
LOOK AT YOU SHUFFLE IN HERE LIKE A HAIRY CRAB!
HEY, MOTHER, I'M ALL YOU'VE GOT. HOW ABOUT SOME TENDERNESS?
GRÉGOIRE, ALL YOU EVER DO IS MAKE TROUBLE FOR ME. WHAT IS IT THIS TIME, HUH?
MOTHER, I WAS FRAMED, I SWEAR.
YEAH RIGHT! BY WHO? NEVER MIND - WHAT DID YOU DO THIS TIME?
MOTHER, YOU NEED TO HELP ME GET OUTTA HERE. THIS IS NO PLACE FOR ME.
HOW CAN I? YOU EVER GIVE ME MONEY TO SET ASIDE?
HAVE A HEART!
A HEART? AND WHAT ABOUT ME? YOU KNOW PERFECTLY WELL IT'S UP TO THE FAMILIES TO FEED THE PRISONERS HERE.
DON'T WORRY ABOUT THAT. I'M EATING REAL WELL. I'M WITH THE SON OF A WEALTHY GUY.
ALWAYS SCHEMING, EVEN IN THE SLAMMER. HERE'S YOUR GARBA, YOU FREAK OF NATURE.

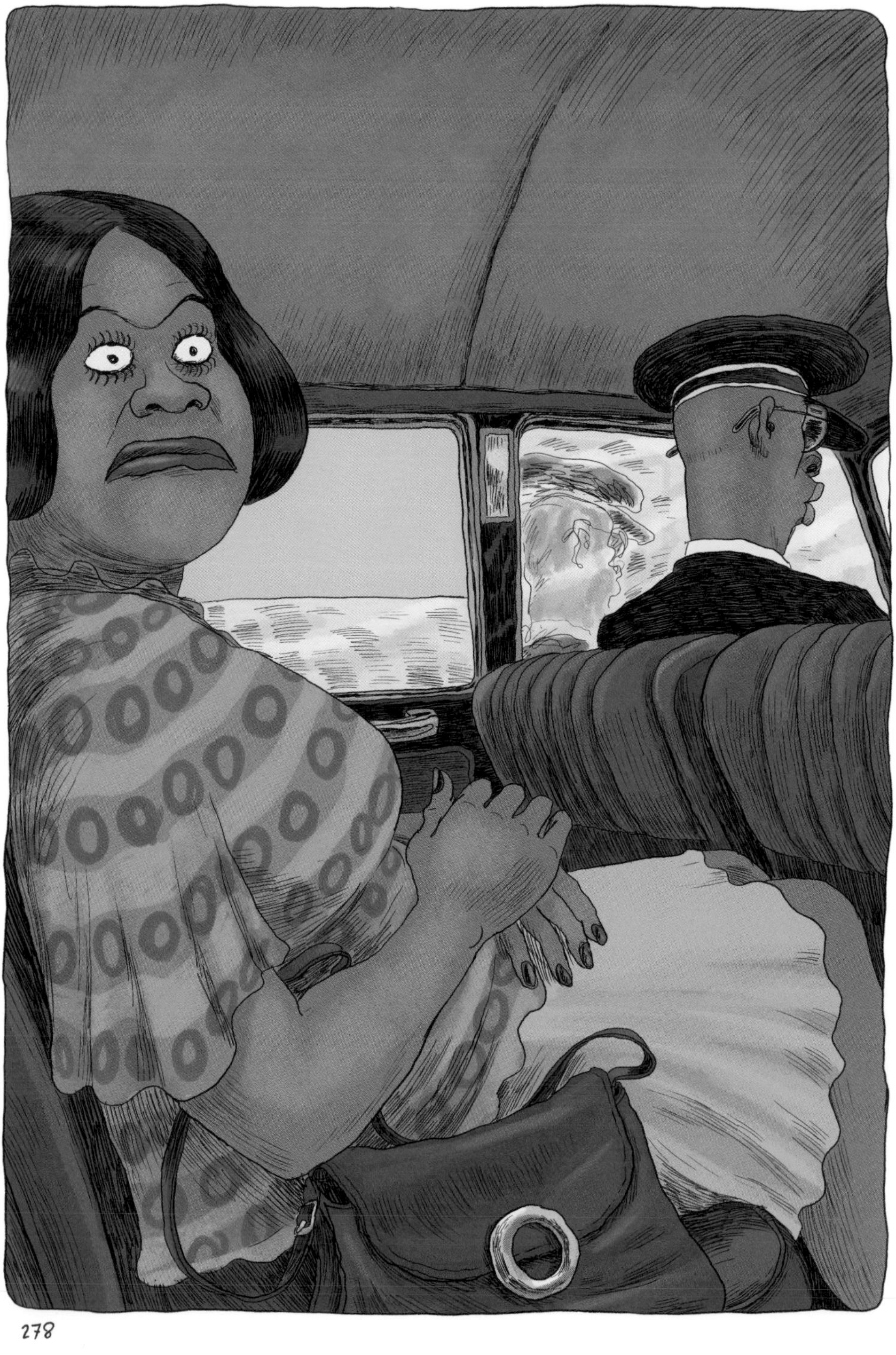

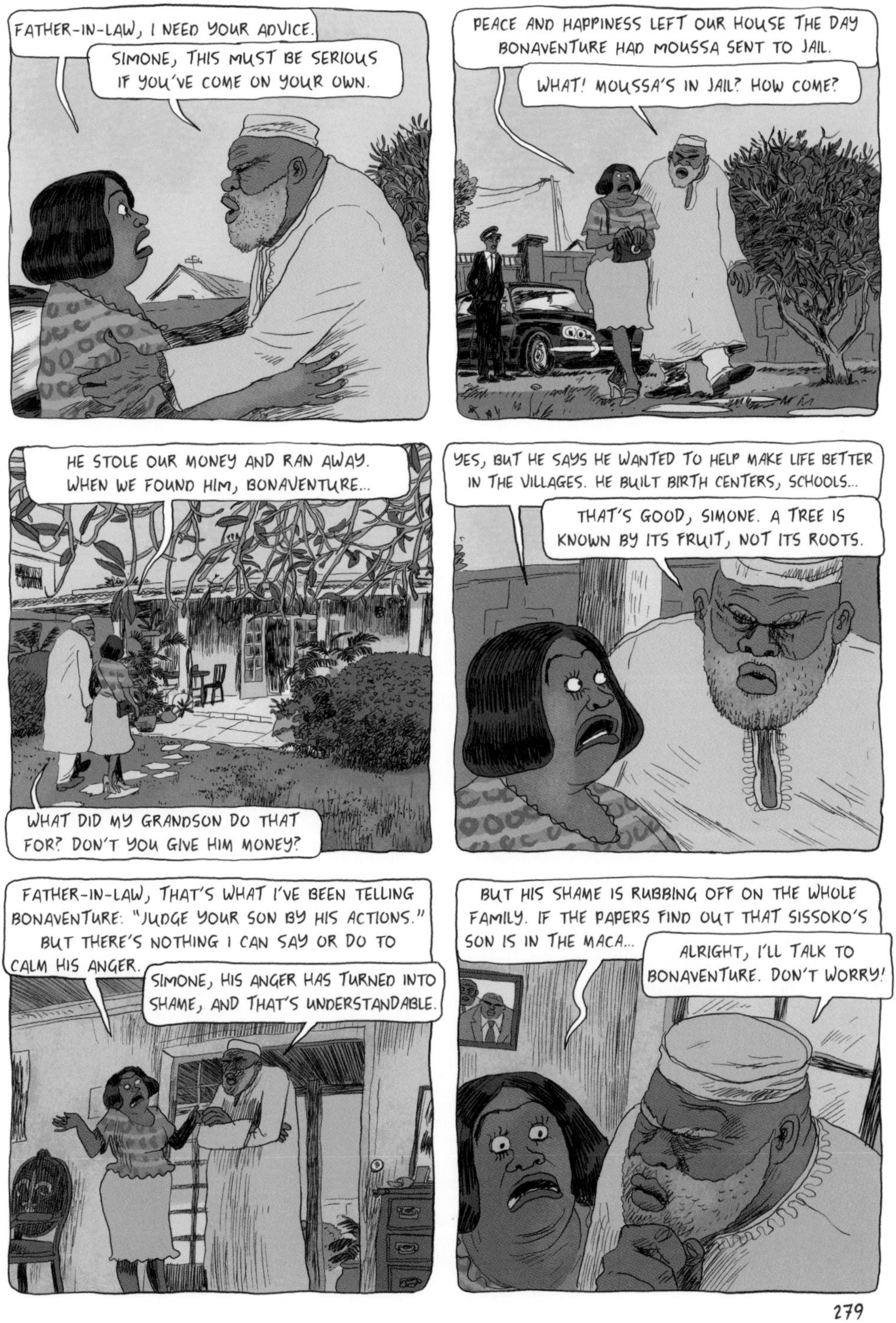
FATHER-IN-LAW, I NEED YOUR ADVICE.
SIMONE, THIS MUST BE SERIOUS IF YOU'VE COME ON YOUR OWN.
PEACE AND HAPPINESS LEFT OUR HOUSE THE DAY BONAVENTURE HAD MOUSSA SENT TO JAIL.
WHAT! MOUSSA'S IN JAIL? HOW COME?
HE STOLE OUR MONEY AND RAN AWAY. WHEN WE FOUND HIM, BONAVENTURE...
WHAT DID MY GRANDSON DO THAT FOR? DON'T YOU GIVE HIM MONEY?
YES, BUT HE SAYS HE WANTED TO HELP MAKE LIFE BETTER IN THE VILLAGES. HE BUILT BIRTH CENTERS, SCHOOLS...
THAT'S GOOD, SIMONE. A TREE IS KNOWN BY ITS FRUIT, NOT ITS ROOTS.
FATHER-IN-LAW, THAT'S WHAT I'VE BEEN TELLING BONAVENTURE: "JUDGE YOUR SON BY HIS ACTIONS." BUT THERE'S NOTHING I CAN SAY OR DO TO CALM HIS ANGER.
SIMONE, HIS ANGER HAS TURNED INTO SHAME, AND THAT'S UNDERSTANDABLE.
BUT HIS SHAME IS RUBBING OFF ON THE WHOLE FAMILY. IF THE PAPERS FIND OUT THAT SISSOKO'S SON IS IN THE MACA...
ALRIGHT, I'LL TALK TO BONAVENTURE. DON'T WORRY!

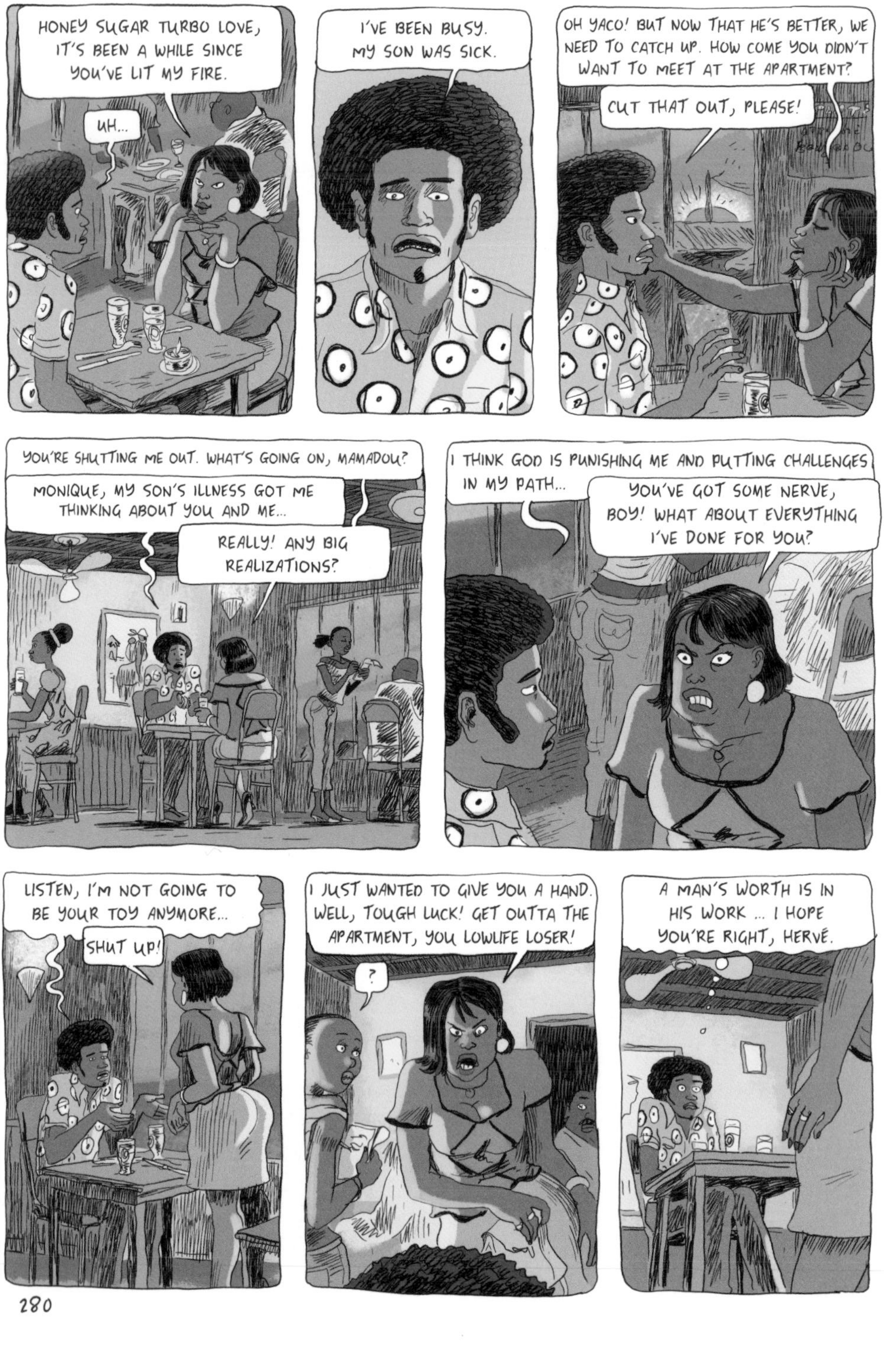
HONEY SUGAR TURBO LOVE, IT'S BEEN A WHILE SINCE YOU'VE LIT MY FIRE.
UH...
I'VE BEEN BUSY. MY SON WAS SICK.
OH YACO! BUT NOW THAT HE'S BETTER, WE NEED TO CATCH UP. HOW COME YOU DIDN'T WANT TO MEET AT THE APARTMENT?
CUT THAT OUT, PLEASE!
YOU'RE SHUTTING ME OUT. WHAT'S GOING ON, MAMADOU?
MONIQUE, MY SON'S ILLNESS GOT ME THINKING ABOUT YOU AND ME...
REALLY! ANY BIG REALIZATIONS?
I THINK GOD IS PUNISHING ME AND PUTTING CHALLENGES IN MY PATH...
YOU'VE GOT SOME NERVE, BOY! WHAT ABOUT EVERYTHING I'VE DONE FOR YOU?
LISTEN, I'M NOT GOING TO BE YOUR TOY ANYMORE...
SHUT UP!
I JUST WANTED TO GIVE YOU A HAND.
WELL, TOUGH LUCK! GET OUTTA THE APARTMENT, YOU LOWLIFE LOSER!
?
A MAN'S WORTH IS IN HIS WORK ... I HOPE YOU'RE RIGHT, HERVÉ.

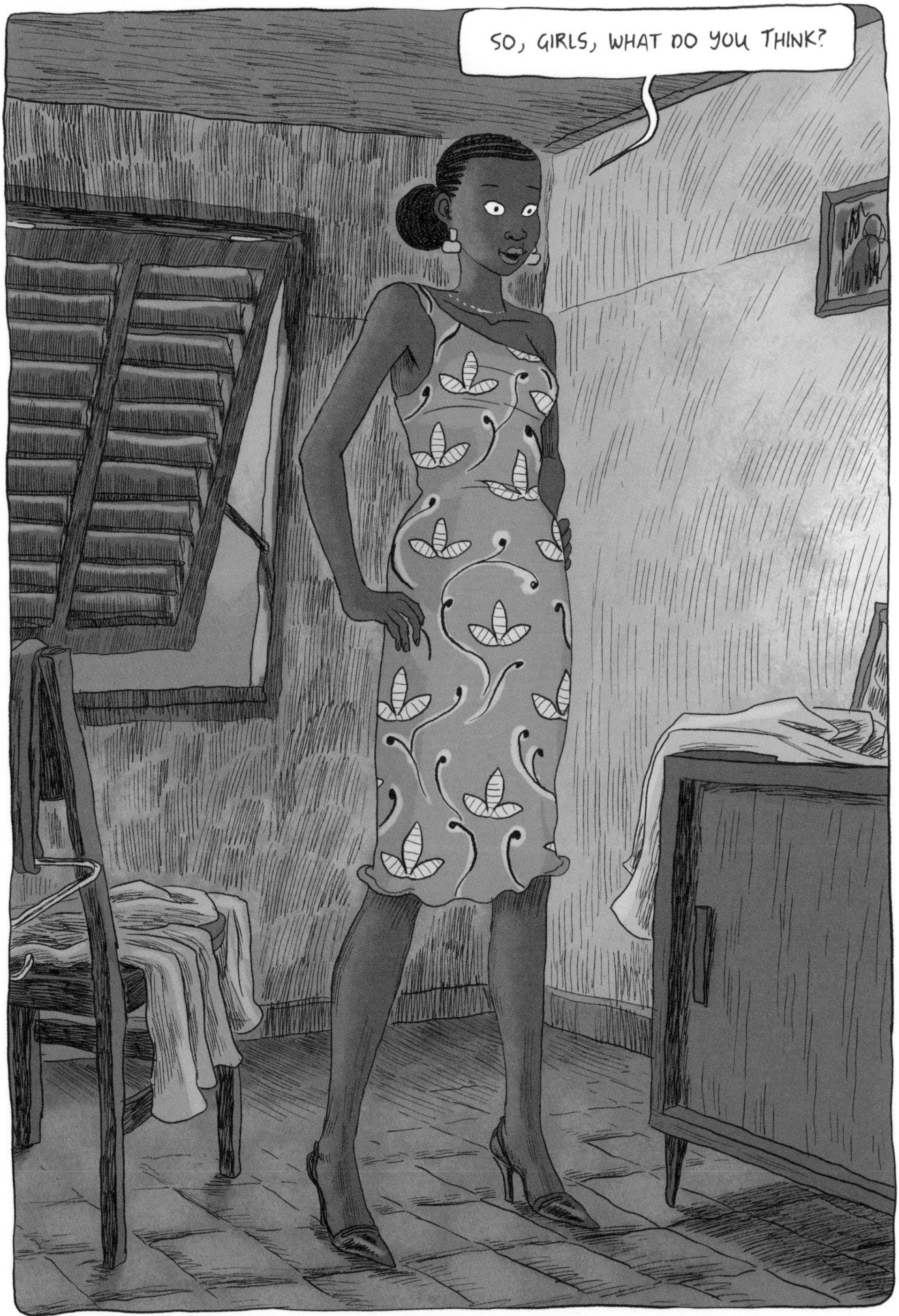
SO, GIRLS, WHAT DO YOU THINK?

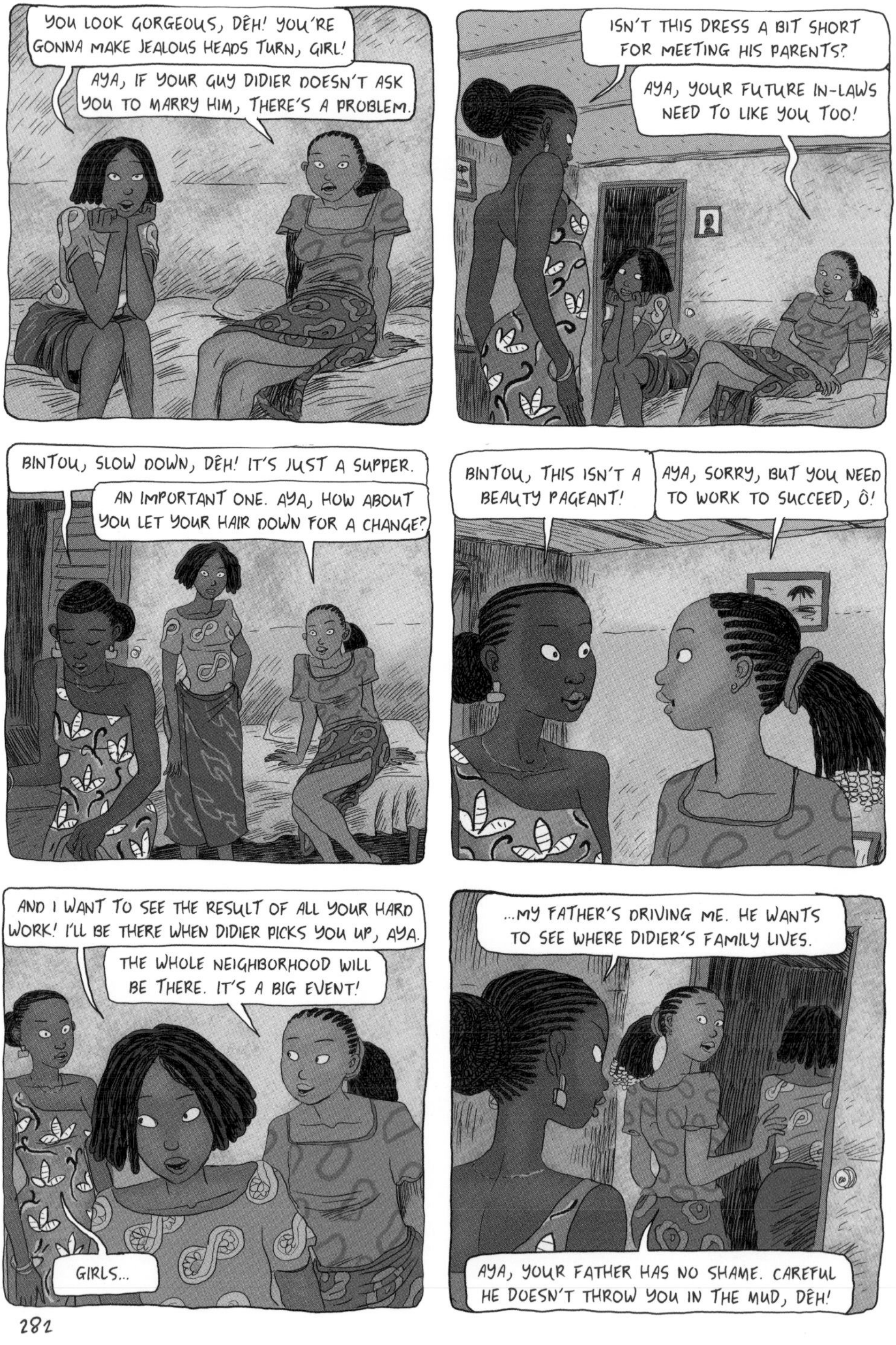
YOU LOOK GORGEOUS, DÊH! YOU'RE GONNA MAKE JEALOUS HEADS TURN, GIRL!
AYA, IF YOUR GUY DIDIER DOESN'T ASK YOU TO MARRY HIM, THERE'S A PROBLEM.
ISN'T THIS DRESS A BIT SHORT FOR MEETING HIS PARENTS?
AYA, YOUR FUTURE IN-LAWS NEED TO LIKE YOU TOO!
BINTOU, SLOW DOWN, DÊH! IT'S JUST A SUPPER.
AN IMPORTANT ONE. AYA, HOW ABOUT YOU LET YOUR HAIR DOWN FOR A CHANGE?
BINTOU, THIS ISN'T A BEAUTY PAGEANT!
AYA, SORRY, BUT YOU NEED TO WORK TO SUCCEED, Ô!
AND I WANT TO SEE THE RESULT OF ALL YOUR HARD WORK! I'LL BE THERE WHEN DIDIER PICKS YOU UP, AYA.
THE WHOLE NEIGHBORHOOD WILL BE THERE. IT'S A BIG EVENT!
GIRLS...
...MY FATHER'S DRIVING ME. HE WANTS TO SEE WHERE DIDIER'S FAMILY LIVES.
AYA, YOUR FATHER HAS NO SHAME. CAREFUL HE DOESN'T THROW YOU IN THE MUD, DÊH!

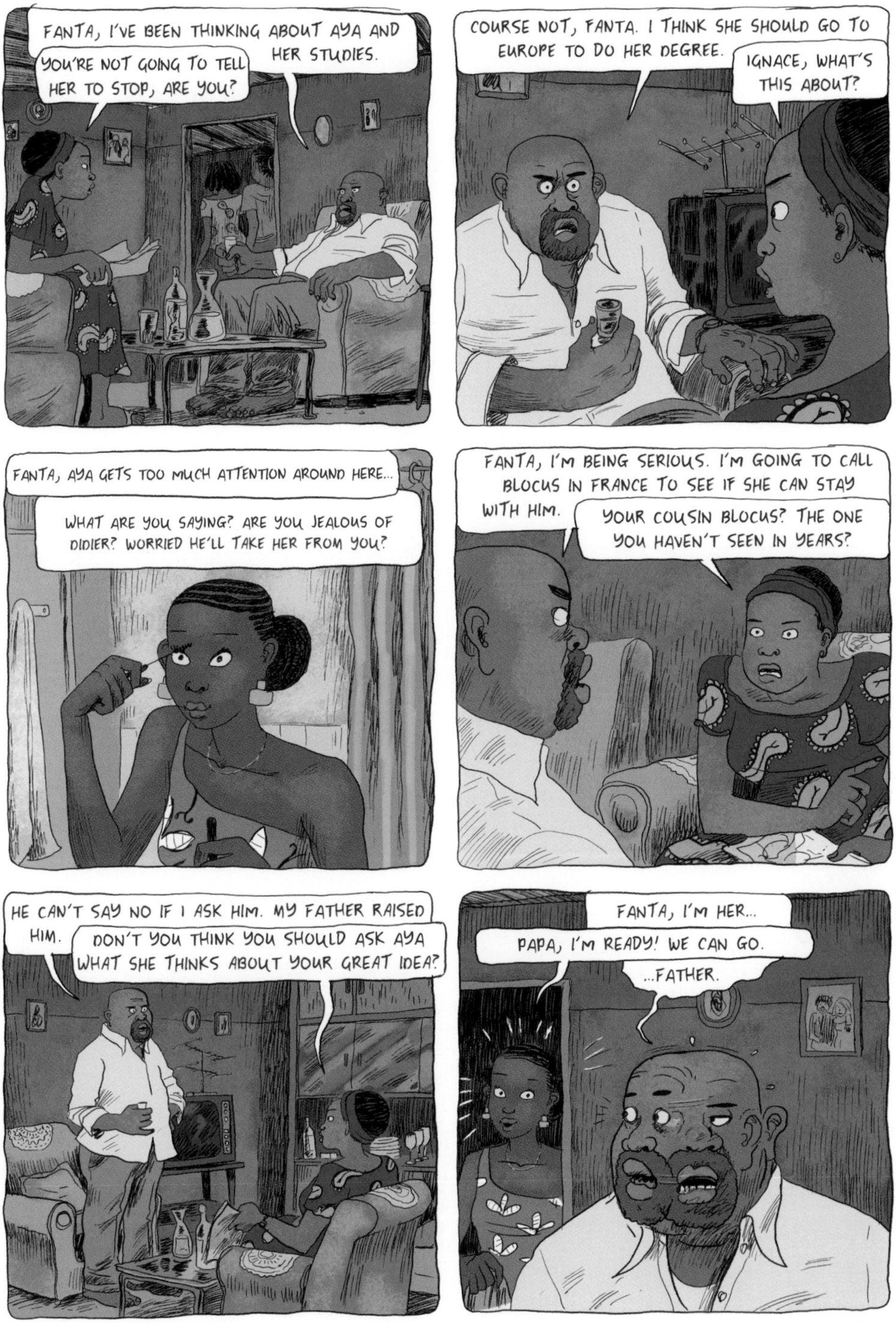
FANTA, I'VE BEEN THINKING ABOUT AYA AND HER STUDIES.
YOU'RE NOT GOING TO TELL HER TO STOP, ARE YOU?
COURSE NOT, FANTA. I THINK SHE SHOULD GO TO EUROPE TO DO HER DEGREE.
IGNACE, WHAT'S THIS ABOUT?
FANTA, AYA GETS TOO MUCH ATTENTION AROUND HERE...
WHAT ARE YOU SAYING? ARE YOU JEALOUS OF DIDIER? WORRIED HE'LL TAKE HER FROM YOU?
FANTA, I'M BEING SERIOUS. I'M GOING TO CALL BLOCUS IN FRANCE TO SEE IF SHE CAN STAY WITH HIM.
YOUR COUSIN BLOCUS? THE ONE YOU HAVEN'T SEEN IN YEARS?
HE CAN'T SAY NO IF I ASK HIM. MY FATHER RAISED HIM.
DON'T YOU THINK YOU SHOULD ASK AYA WHAT SHE THINKS ABOUT YOUR GREAT IDEA?
FANTA, I'M HER...
PAPA, I'M READY! WE CAN GO.
...FATHER.

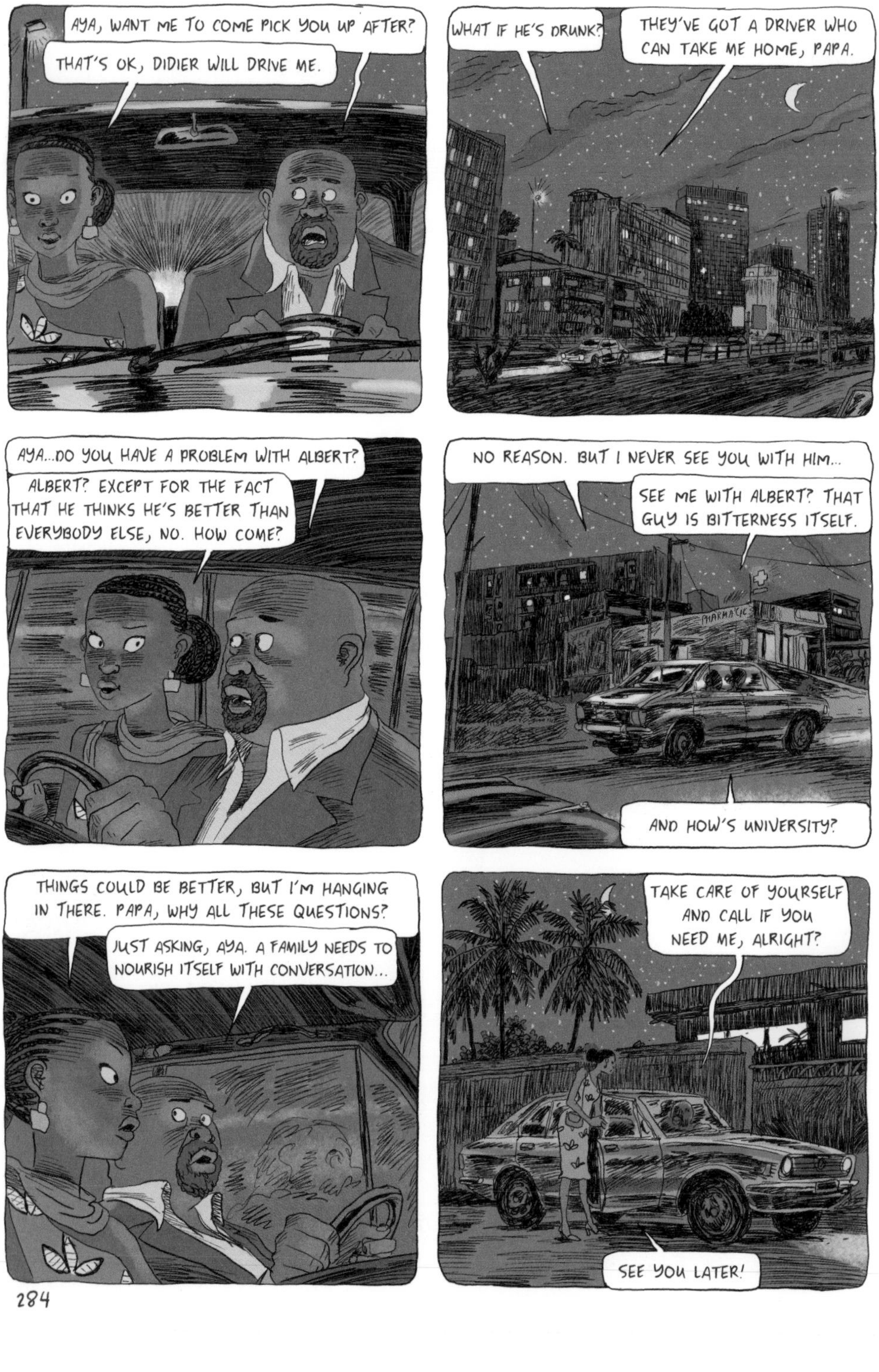
AYA, WANT ME TO COME PICK YOU UP AFTER?
THAT'S OK, DIDIER WILL DRIVE ME.
WHAT IF HE'S DRUNK?
THEY'VE GOT A DRIVER WHO CAN TAKE ME HOME, PAPA.
AYA...DO YOU HAVE A PROBLEM WITH ALBERT?
ALBERT? EXCEPT FOR THE FACT THAT HE THINKS HE'S BETTER THAN EVERYBODY ELSE, NO. HOW COME?
NO REASON. BUT I NEVER SEE YOU WITH HIM...
SEE ME WITH ALBERT? THAT GUY IS BITTERNESS ITSELF.
PHARMACIE
AND HOW'S UNIVERSITY?
THINGS COULD BE BETTER, BUT I'M HANGING IN THERE. PAPA, WHY ALL THESE QUESTIONS?
JUST ASKING, AYA. A FAMILY NEEDS TO NOURISH ITSELF WITH CONVERSATION...
TAKE CARE OF YOURSELF AND CALL IF YOU NEED ME, ALRIGHT?
SEE YOU LATER!

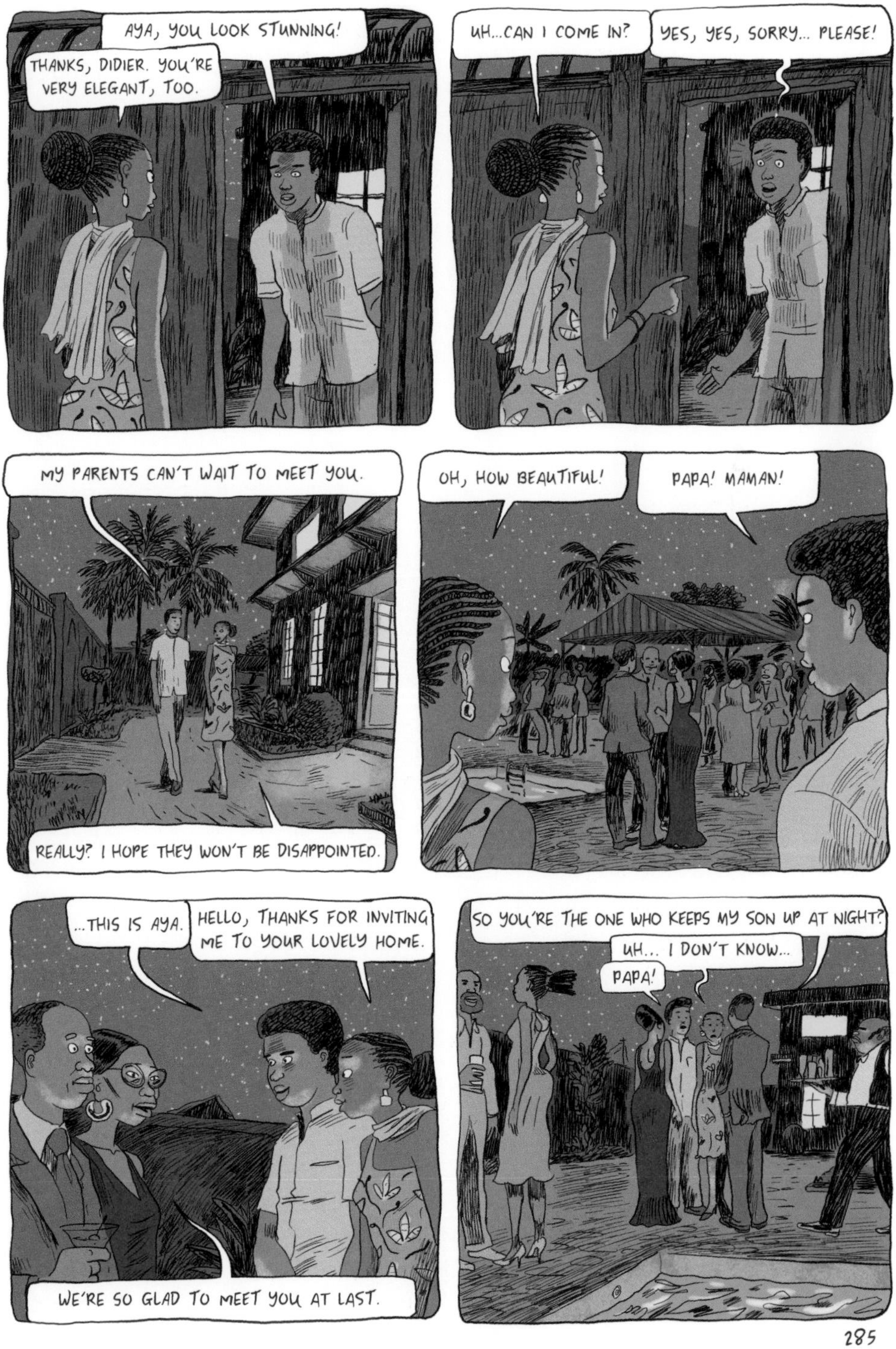
AYA, YOU LOOK STUNNING!
THANKS, DIDIER. YOU'RE VERY ELEGANT, TOO.
UH...CAN I COME IN?
YES, YES, SORRY... PLEASE!
MY PARENTS CAN'T WAIT TO MEET YOU.
REALLY? I HOPE THEY WON'T BE DISAPPOINTED.
OH, HOW BEAUTIFUL!
PAPA! MAMAN!
...THIS IS AYA.
HELLO, THANKS FOR INVITING ME TO YOUR LOVELY HOME.
WE'RE SO GLAD TO MEET YOU AT LAST.
SO YOU'RE THE ONE WHO KEEPS MY SON UP AT NIGHT?
UH... I DON'T KNOW...
PAPA!

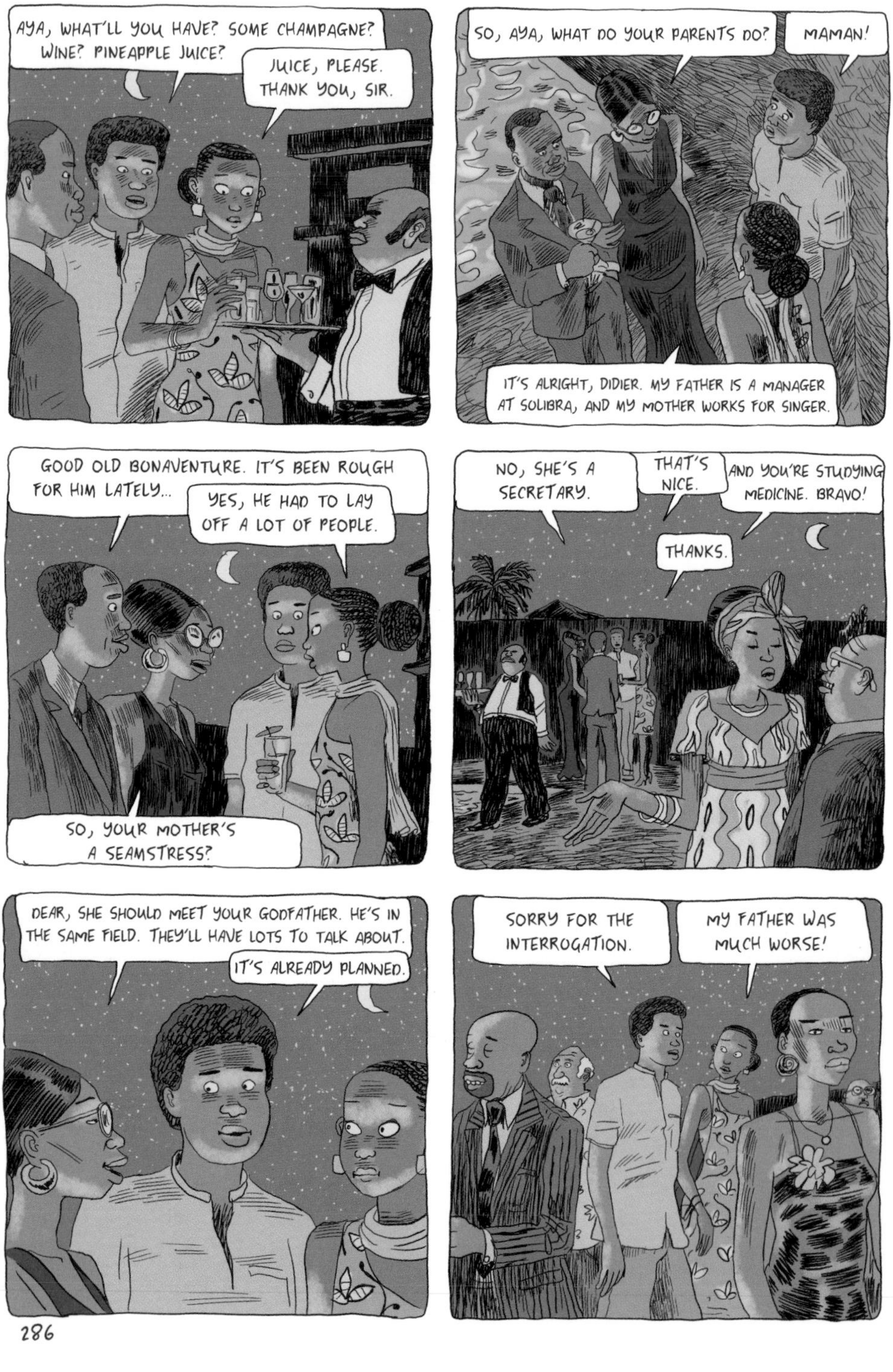
AYA, WHAT'LL YOU HAVE? SOME CHAMPAGNE? WINE? PINEAPPLE JUICE?
JUICE, PLEASE. THANK YOU, SIR.
SO, AYA, WHAT DO YOUR PARENTS DO?
MAMAN!
IT'S ALRIGHT, DIDIER. MY FATHER IS A MANAGER AT SOLIBRA, AND MY MOTHER WORKS FOR SINGER.
GOOD OLD BONAVENTURE. IT'S BEEN ROUGH FOR HIM LATELY...
YES, HE HAD TO LAY OFF A LOT OF PEOPLE.
SO, YOUR MOTHER'S A SEAMSTRESS?
NO, SHE'S A SECRETARY.
THAT'S NICE.
AND YOU'RE STUDYING MEDICINE. BRAVO!
THANKS.
DEAR, SHE SHOULD MEET YOUR GODFATHER. HE'S IN THE SAME FIELD. THEY'LL HAVE LOTS TO TALK ABOUT.
IT'S ALREADY PLANNED.
SORRY FOR THE INTERROGATION.
MY FATHER WAS MUCH WORSE!

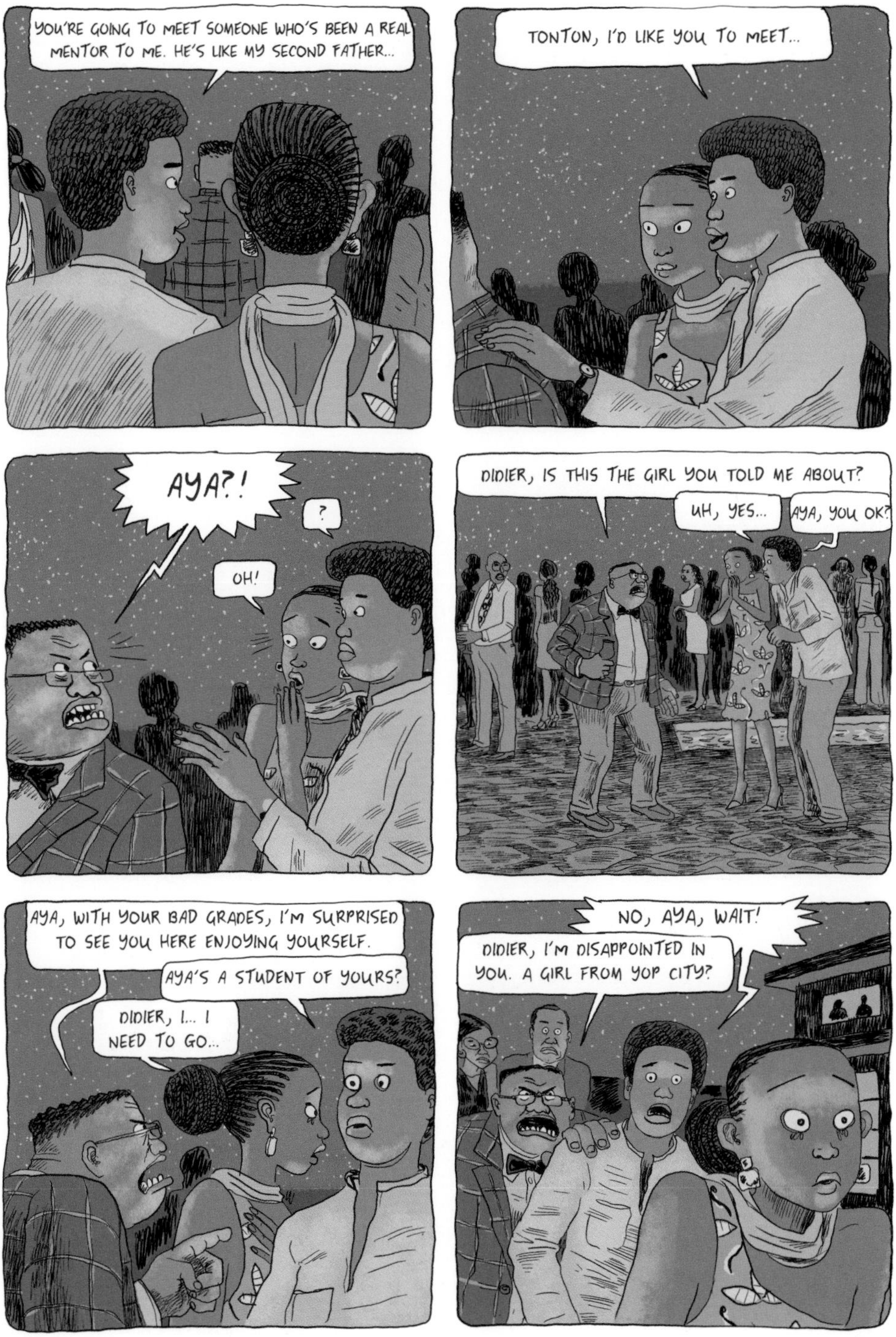
YOU'RE GOING TO MEET SOMEONE WHO'S BEEN A REAL MENTOR TO ME. HE'S LIKE MY SECOND FATHER...
TONTON, I'D LIKE YOU TO MEET...
AYA?!
OH!
?
DIDIER, IS THIS THE GIRL YOU TOLD ME ABOUT?
UH, YES...
AYA, YOU OK?
AYA, WITH YOUR BAD GRADES, I'M SURPRISED TO SEE YOU HERE ENJOYING YOURSELF.
AYA'S A STUDENT OF YOURS?
DIDIER, I... I NEED TO GO...
NO, AYA, WAIT!
DIDIER, I'M DISAPPOINTED IN YOU. A GIRL FROM YOP CITY?

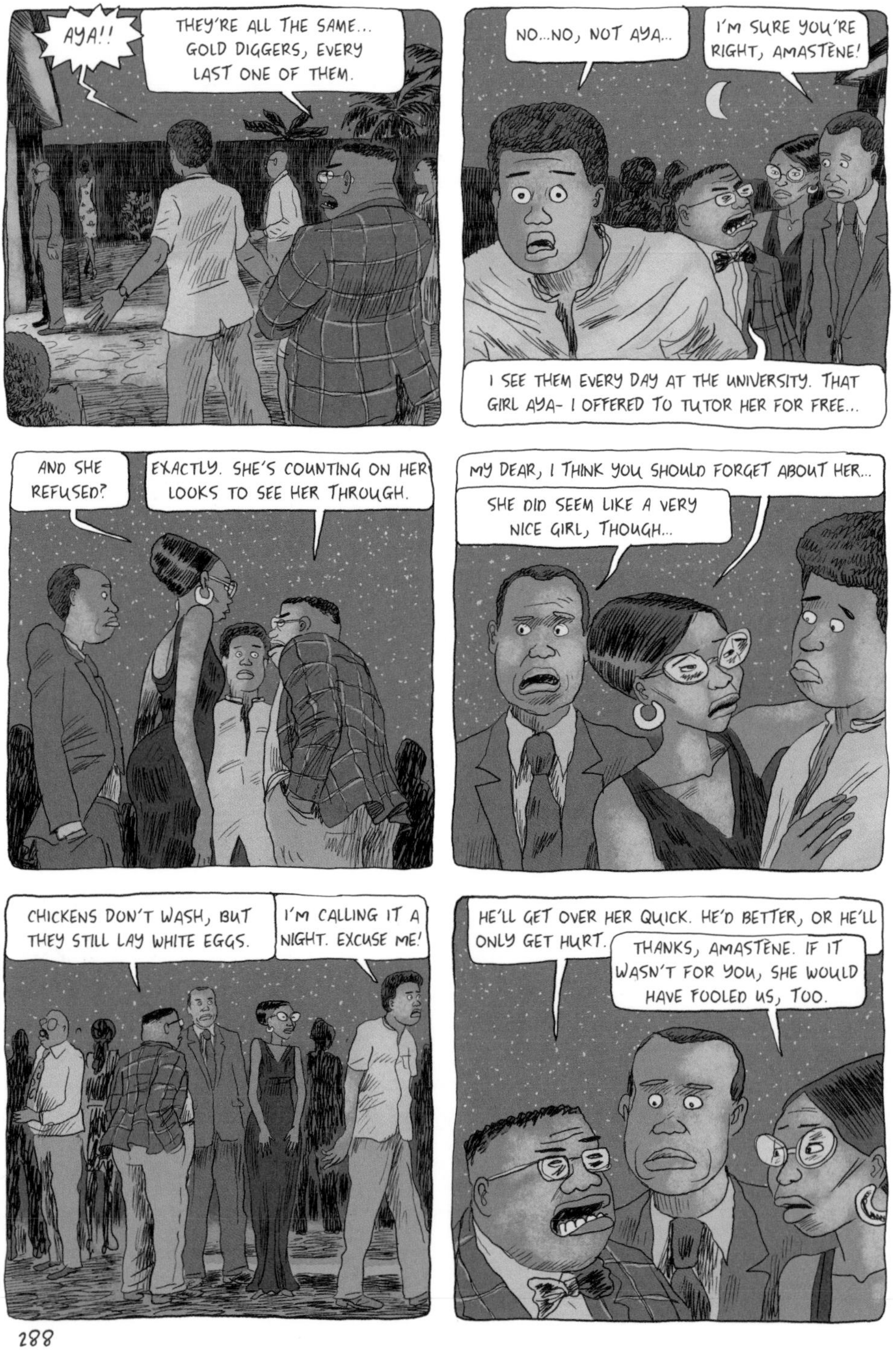
AYA!!
THEY'RE ALL THE SAME... GOLD DIGGERS, EVERY LAST ONE OF THEM.
NO...NO, NOT AYA...
I'M SURE YOU'RE RIGHT, AMASTÈNE!
I SEE THEM EVERY DAY AT THE UNIVERSITY. THAT GIRL AYA- I OFFERED TO TUTOR HER FOR FREE...
AND SHE REFUSED?
EXACTLY. SHE'S COUNTING ON HER LOOKS TO SEE HER THROUGH.
MY DEAR, I THINK YOU SHOULD FORGET ABOUT HER...
SHE DID SEEM LIKE A VERY NICE GIRL, THOUGH...
CHICKENS DON'T WASH, BUT THEY STILL LAY WHITE EGGS.
I'M CALLING IT A NIGHT. EXCUSE ME!
HE'LL GET OVER HER QUICK. HE'D BETTER, OR HE'LL ONLY GET HURT.
THANKS, AMASTÈNE. IF IT WASN'T FOR YOU, SHE WOULD HAVE FOOLED US, TOO.

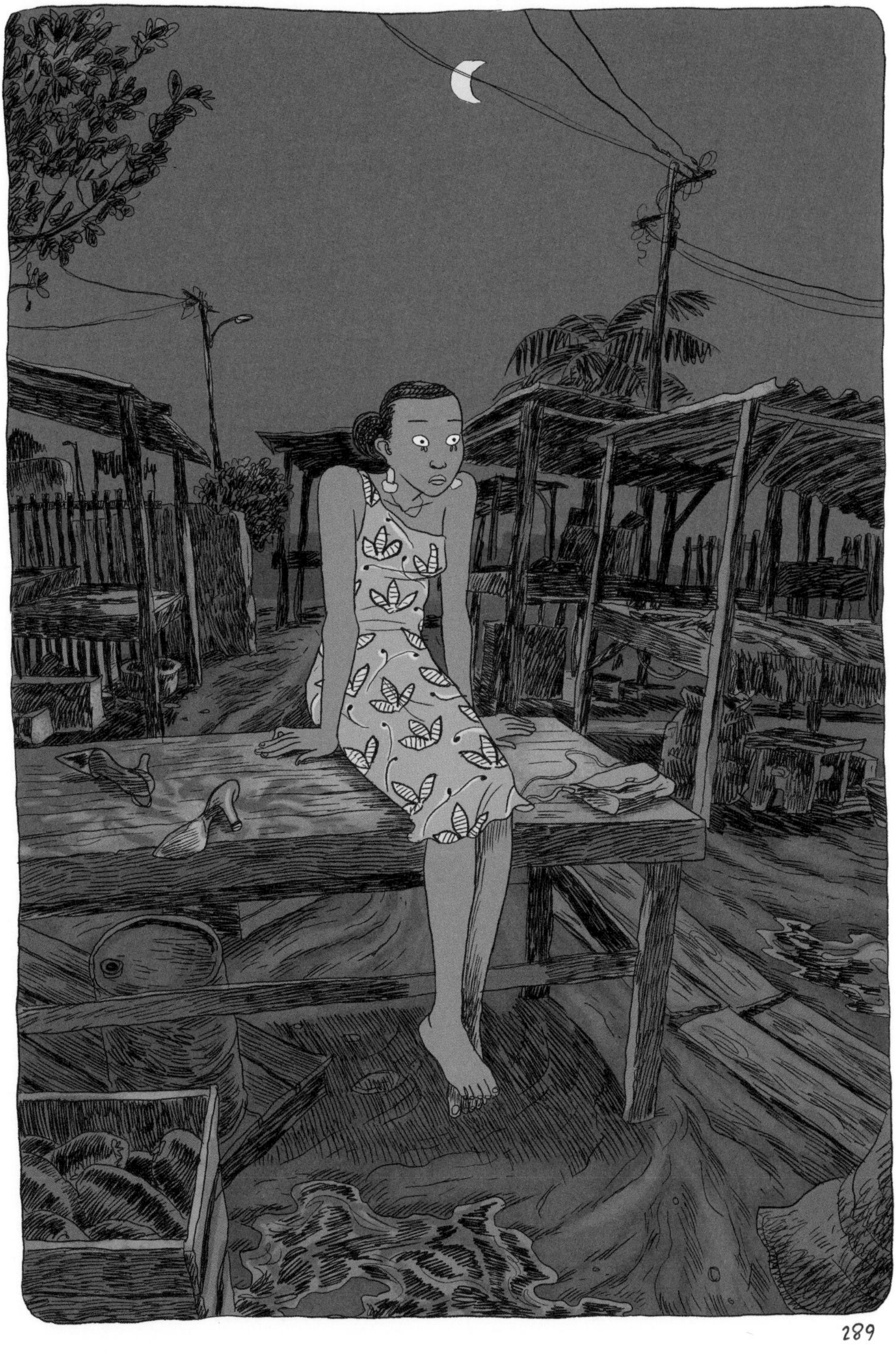

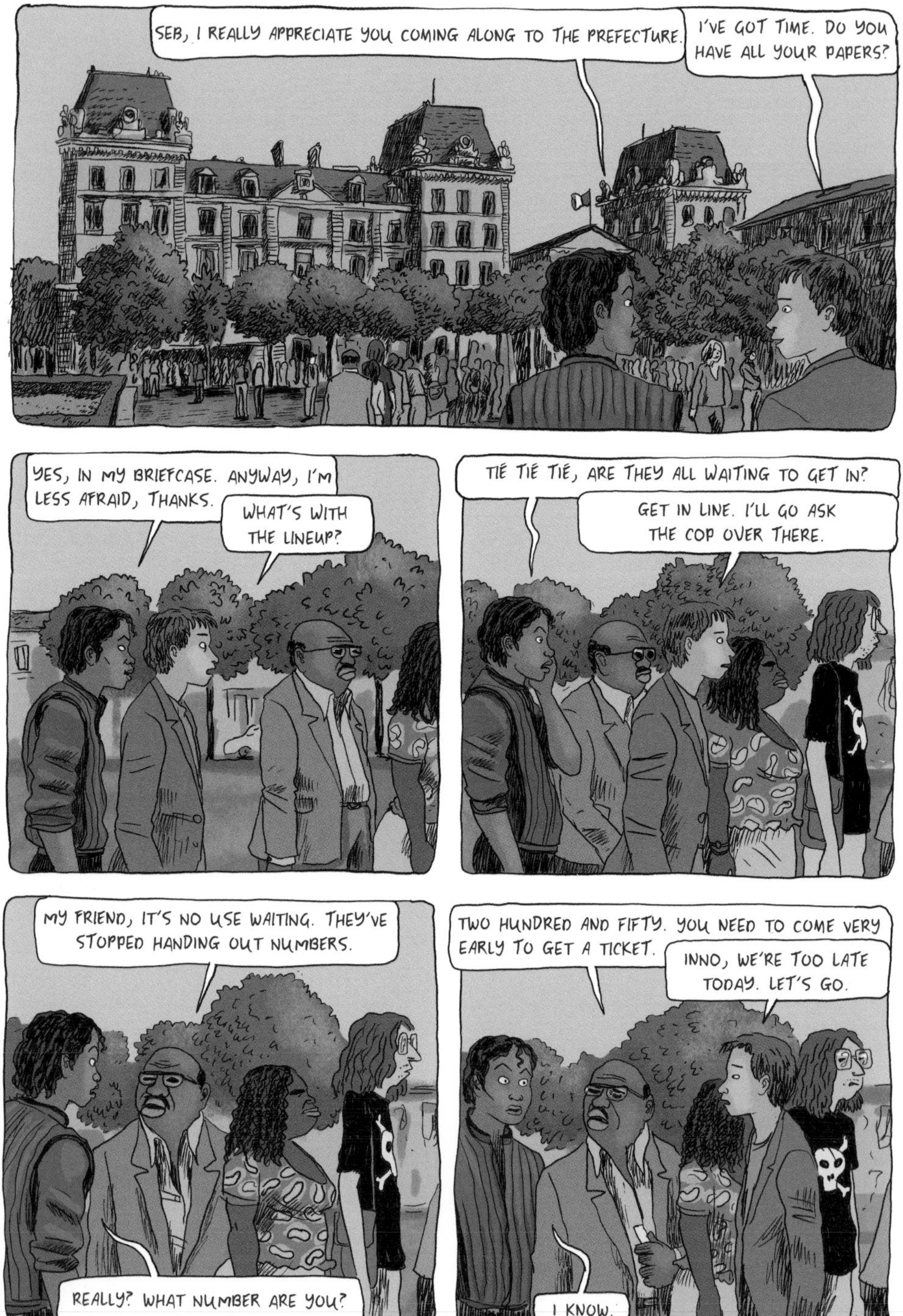
SEB, I REALLY APPRECIATE YOU COMING ALONG TO THE PREFECTURE.
I'VE GOT TIME. DO YOU HAVE ALL YOUR PAPERS?
YES, IN MY BRIEFCASE. ANYWAY, I'M LESS AFRAID, THANKS.
WHAT'S WITH THE LINEUP?
TIÉ TIÉ TIÉ, ARE THEY ALL WAITING TO GET IN?
GET IN LINE. I'LL GO ASK THE COP OVER THERE.
MY FRIEND, IT'S NO USE WAITING. THEY'VE STOPPED HANDING OUT NUMBERS.
REALLY? WHAT NUMBER ARE YOU?
TWO HUNDRED AND FIFTY. YOU NEED TO COME VERY EARLY TO GET A TICKET.
INNO, WE'RE TOO LATE TODAY. LET'S GO.
I KNOW.

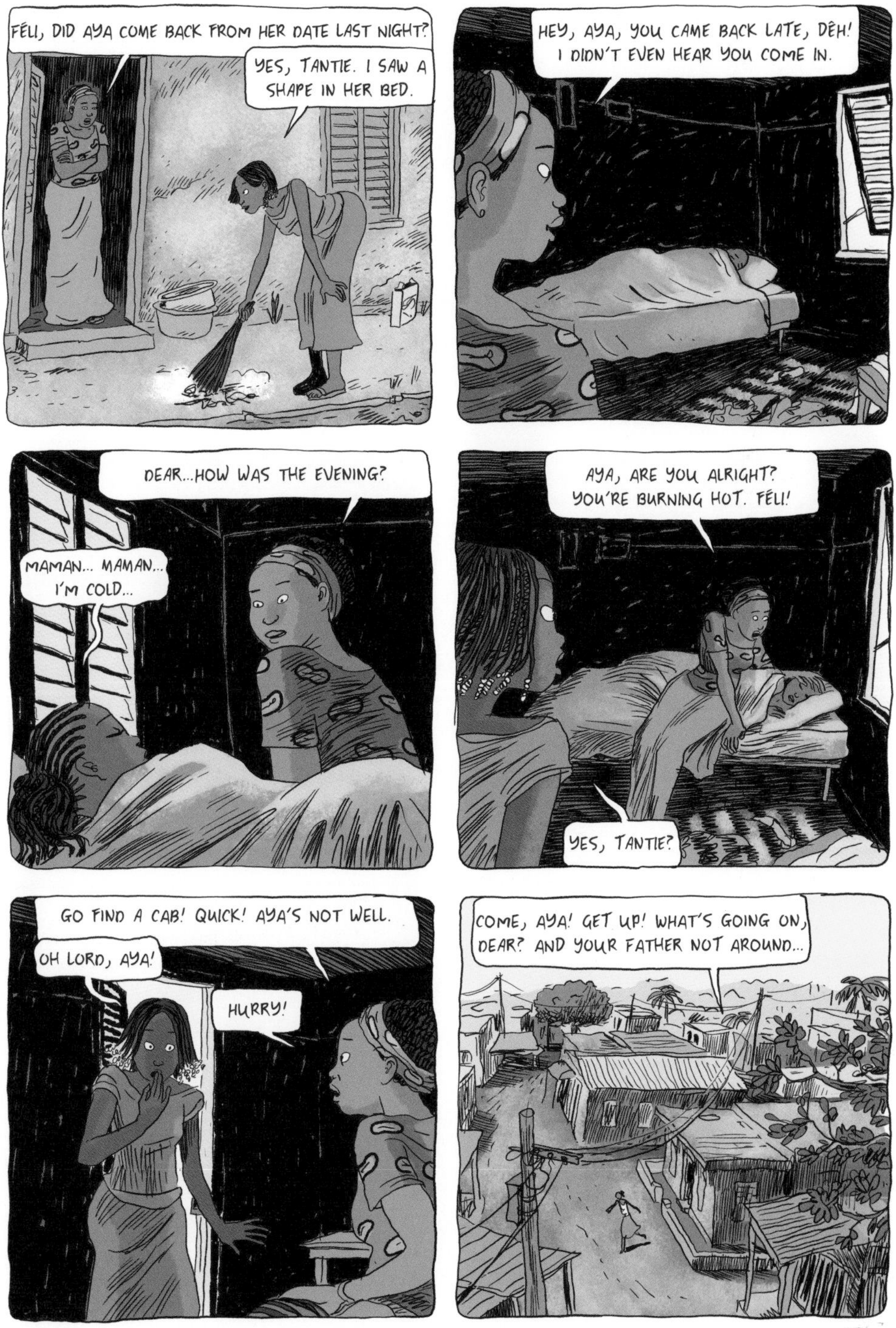
FÉLI, DID AYA COME BACK FROM HER DATE LAST NIGHT?
YES, TANTIE. I SAW A SHAPE IN HER BED.
HEY, AYA, YOU CAME BACK LATE, DÊH! I DIDN'T EVEN HEAR YOU COME IN.
DEAR...HOW WAS THE EVENING?
MAMAN... MAMAN... I'M COLD...
AYA, ARE YOU ALRIGHT? YOU'RE BURNING HOT. FÉLI!
YES, TANTIE?
GO FIND A CAB! QUICK! AYA'S NOT WELL.
OH LORD, AYA!
HURRY!
COME, AYA! GET UP! WHAT'S GOING ON, DEAR? AND YOUR FATHER NOT AROUND...

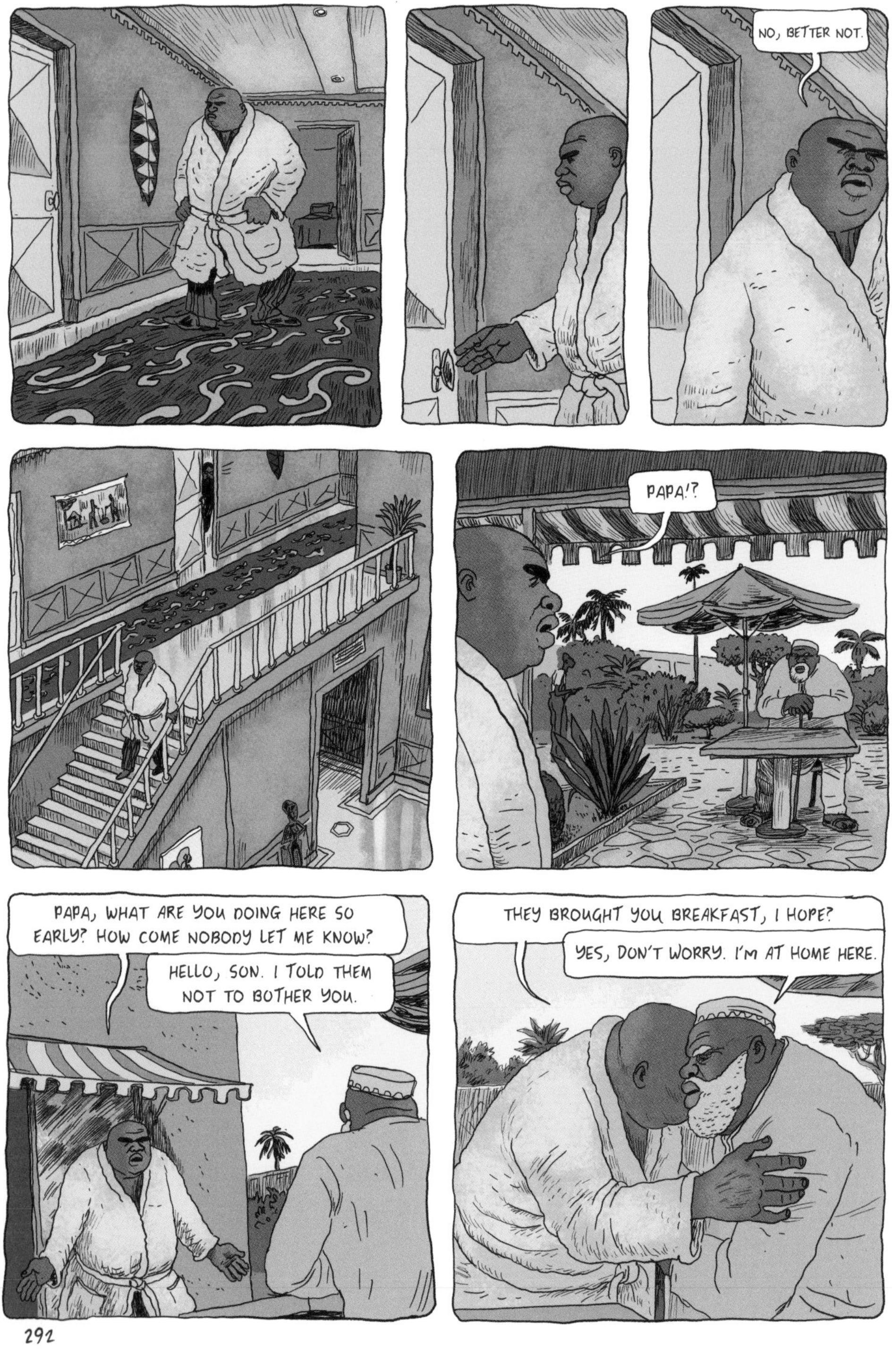
NO, BETTER NOT.
PAPA!?
PAPA, WHAT ARE YOU DOING HERE SO EARLY? HOW COME NOBODY LET ME KNOW?
HELLO, SON. I TOLD THEM NOT TO BOTHER YOU.
THEY BROUGHT YOU BREAKFAST, I HOPE?
YES, DON'T WORRY. I'M AT HOME HERE.

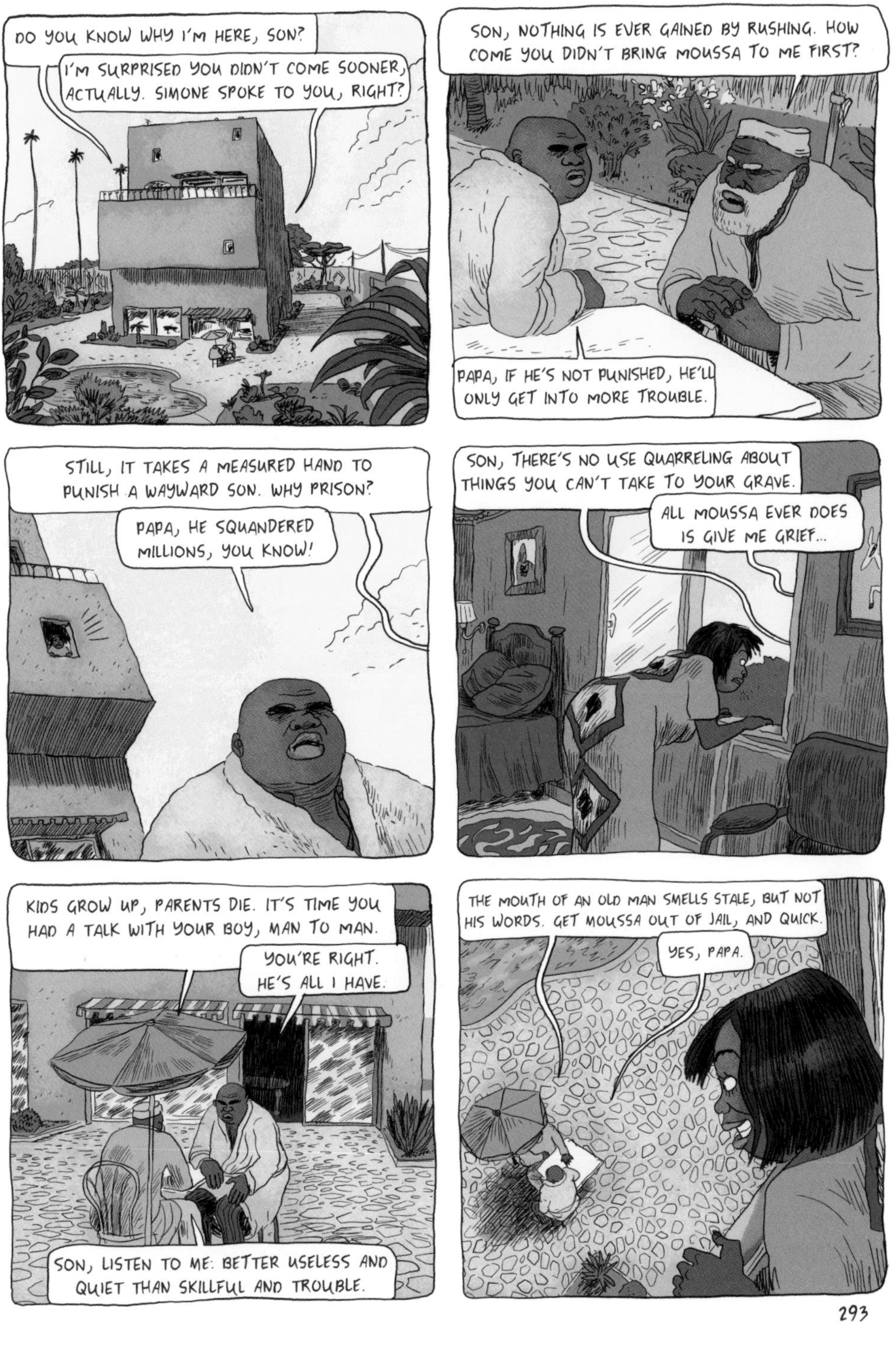

DO YOU KNOW WHY I'M HERE, SON?
I'M SURPRISED YOU DIDN'T COME SOONER, ACTUALLY. SIMONE SPOKE TO YOU, RIGHT?
SON, NOTHING IS EVER GAINED BY RUSHING. HOW COME YOU DIDN'T BRING MOUSSA TO ME FIRST?
PAPA, IF HE'S NOT PUNISHED, HE'LL ONLY GET INTO MORE TROUBLE.
STILL, IT TAKES A MEASURED HAND TO PUNISH A WAYWARD SON. WHY PRISON?
PAPA, HE SQUANDERED MILLIONS, YOU KNOW!
SON, THERE'S NO USE QUARRELING ABOUT THINGS YOU CAN'T TAKE TO YOUR GRAVE.
ALL MOUSSA EVER DOES IS GIVE ME GRIEF...
KIDS GROW UP, PARENTS DIE. IT'S TIME YOU HAD A TALK WITH YOUR BOY, MAN TO MAN.
YOU'RE RIGHT. HE'S ALL I HAVE.
SON, LISTEN TO ME: BETTER USELESS AND QUIET THAN SKILLFUL AND TROUBLE.
THE MOUTH OF AN OLD MAN SMELLS STALE, BUT NOT HIS WORDS. GET MOUSSA OUT OF JAIL, AND QUICK.
YES, PAPA.

DOCTOR, WHAT'S WRONG WITH HER?

SIGN: COCODY UNIVERSITY HOSPITAL

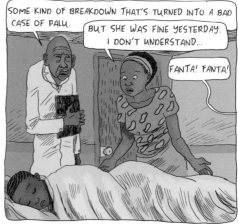

SOME KIND OF BREAKDOWN THAT'S TURNED INTO A BAD CASE OF PALU.

BUT SHE WAS FINE YESTERDAY. I DON'T UNDERSTAND...

FANTA! FANTA!

WHERE'S MY DAUGHTER? WHAT'S SHE GOT?

HELLO DOCTOR!

SIR, CALM DOWN. SHE'S NOT IN ANY DANGER.

THAT'S GOOD NEWS, DOCTOR. IT'S DIDIER, ISN'T IT? WHAT'S HE DONE TO HER?

IGNACE, WHAT ARE YOU TALKING ABOUT? AYA'S WORN OUT AND SICK WITH PALU.

I'LL BE BY AGAIN LATER.

IGNACE, I LEFT THE HOUSE SO FAST THAT I FORGOT ALL MY THINGS. I NEED TO GO BACK.

STAY WITH HER. I'LL BE QUICK.

HOW COME I DIDN'T SEE THIS PALU COMING?

294

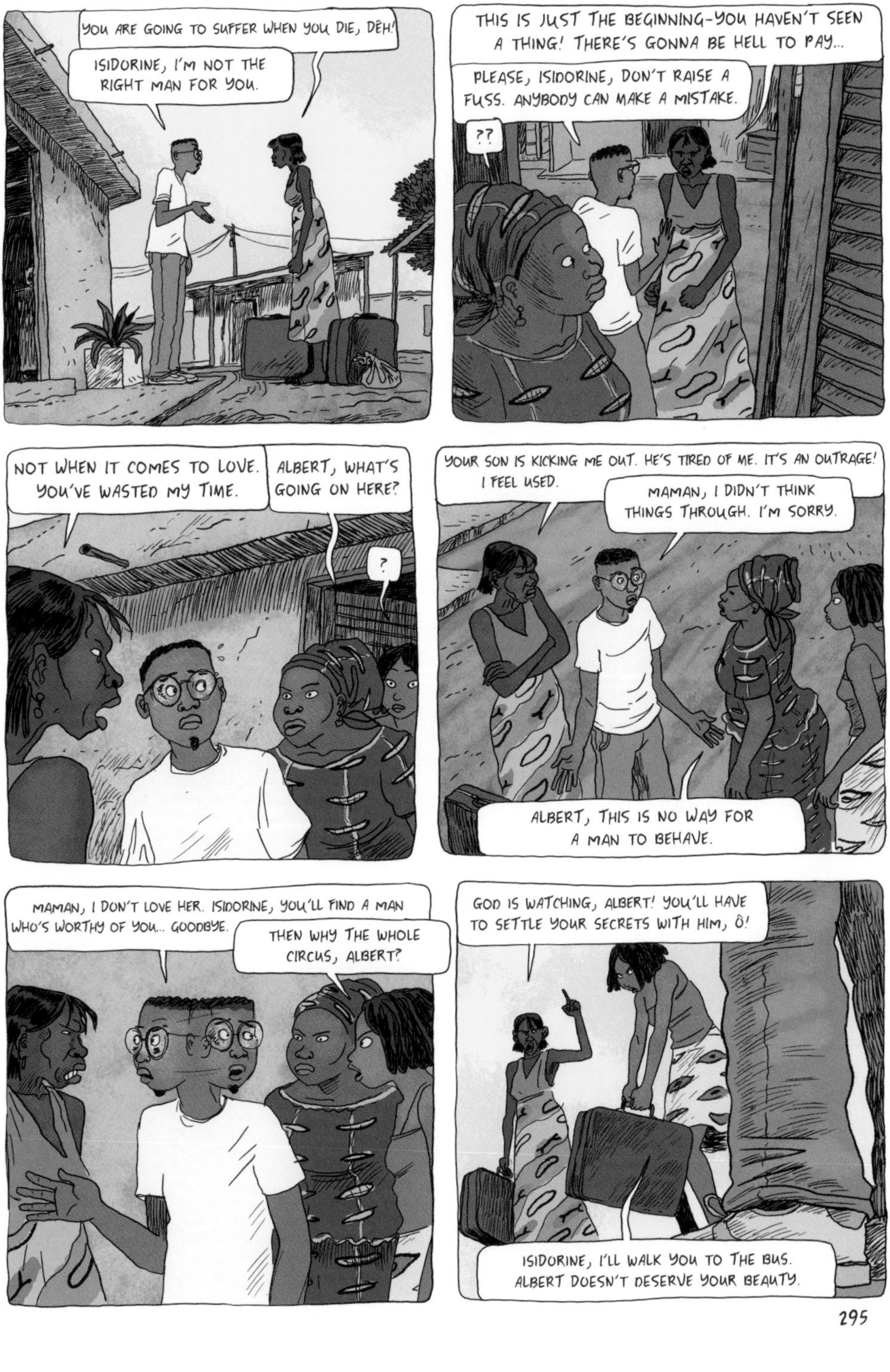
YOU ARE GOING TO SUFFER WHEN YOU DIE, DÊH!
ISIDORINE, I'M NOT THE RIGHT MAN FOR YOU.
THIS IS JUST THE BEGINNING–YOU HAVEN'T SEEN A THING! THERE'S GONNA BE HELL TO PAY...
PLEASE, ISIDORINE, DON'T RAISE A FUSS. ANYBODY CAN MAKE A MISTAKE.
??
NOT WHEN IT COMES TO LOVE. YOU'VE WASTED MY TIME.
ALBERT, WHAT'S GOING ON HERE?
?
YOUR SON IS KICKING ME OUT. HE'S TIRED OF ME. IT'S AN OUTRAGE! I FEEL USED.
MAMAN, I DIDN'T THINK THINGS THROUGH. I'M SORRY.
ALBERT, THIS IS NO WAY FOR A MAN TO BEHAVE.
MAMAN, I DON'T LOVE HER. ISIDORINE, YOU'LL FIND A MAN WHO'S WORTHY OF YOU... GOODBYE.
THEN WHY THE WHOLE CIRCUS, ALBERT?
GOD IS WATCHING, ALBERT! YOU'LL HAVE TO SETTLE YOUR SECRETS WITH HIM, Ô!
ISIDORINE, I'LL WALK YOU TO THE BUS. ALBERT DOESN'T DESERVE YOUR BEAUTY.

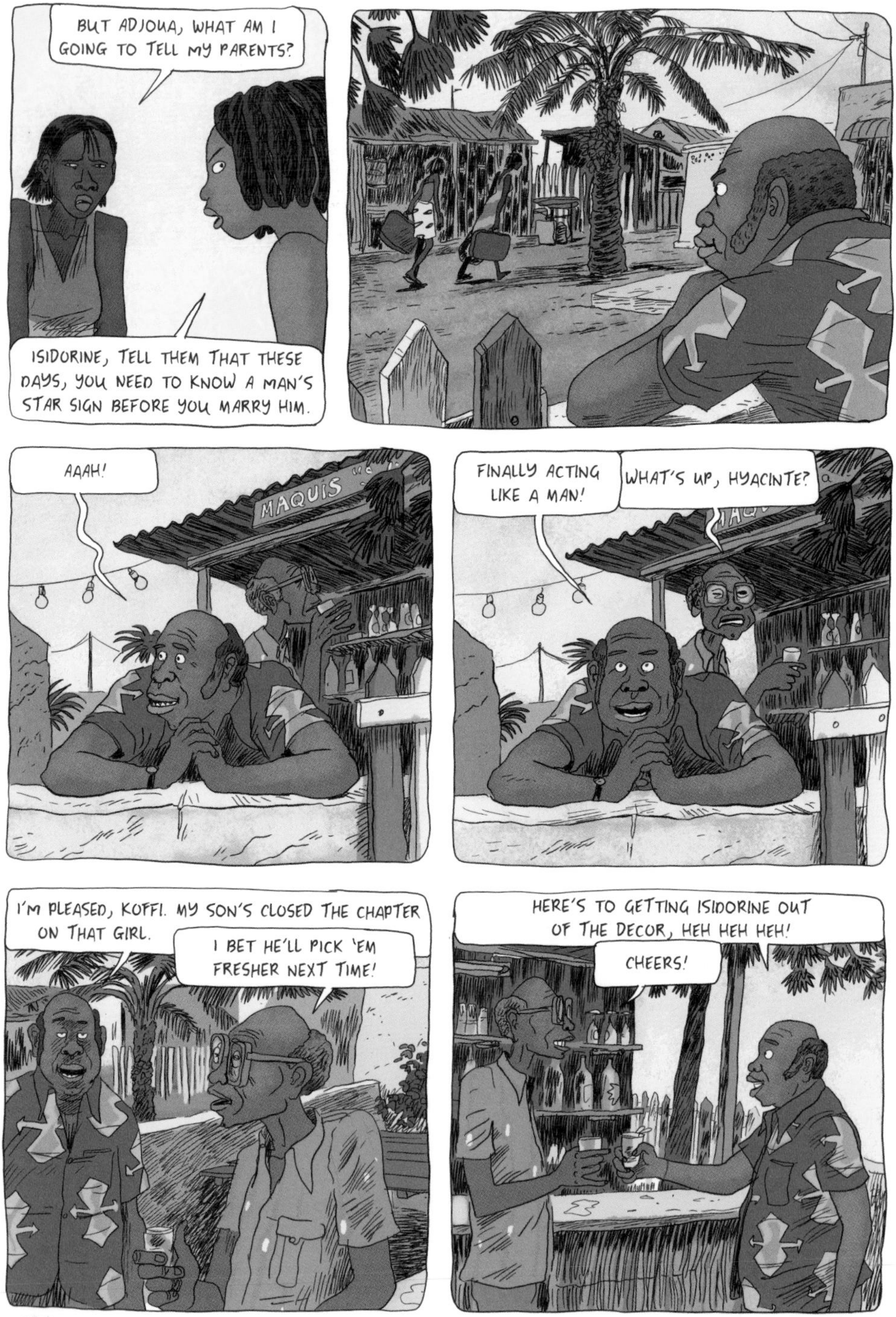
BUT ADJOUA, WHAT AM I GOING TO TELL MY PARENTS?
ISIDORINE, TELL THEM THAT THESE DAYS, YOU NEED TO KNOW A MAN'S STAR SIGN BEFORE YOU MARRY HIM.
MAQUIS
AAAH!
FINALLY ACTING LIKE A MAN!
WHAT'S UP, HYACINTE?
I'M PLEASED, KOFFI. MY SON'S CLOSED THE CHAPTER ON THAT GIRL.
I BET HE'LL PICK 'EM FRESHER NEXT TIME!
HERE'S TO GETTING ISIDORINE OUT OF THE DECOR, HEH HEH HEH!
CHEERS!

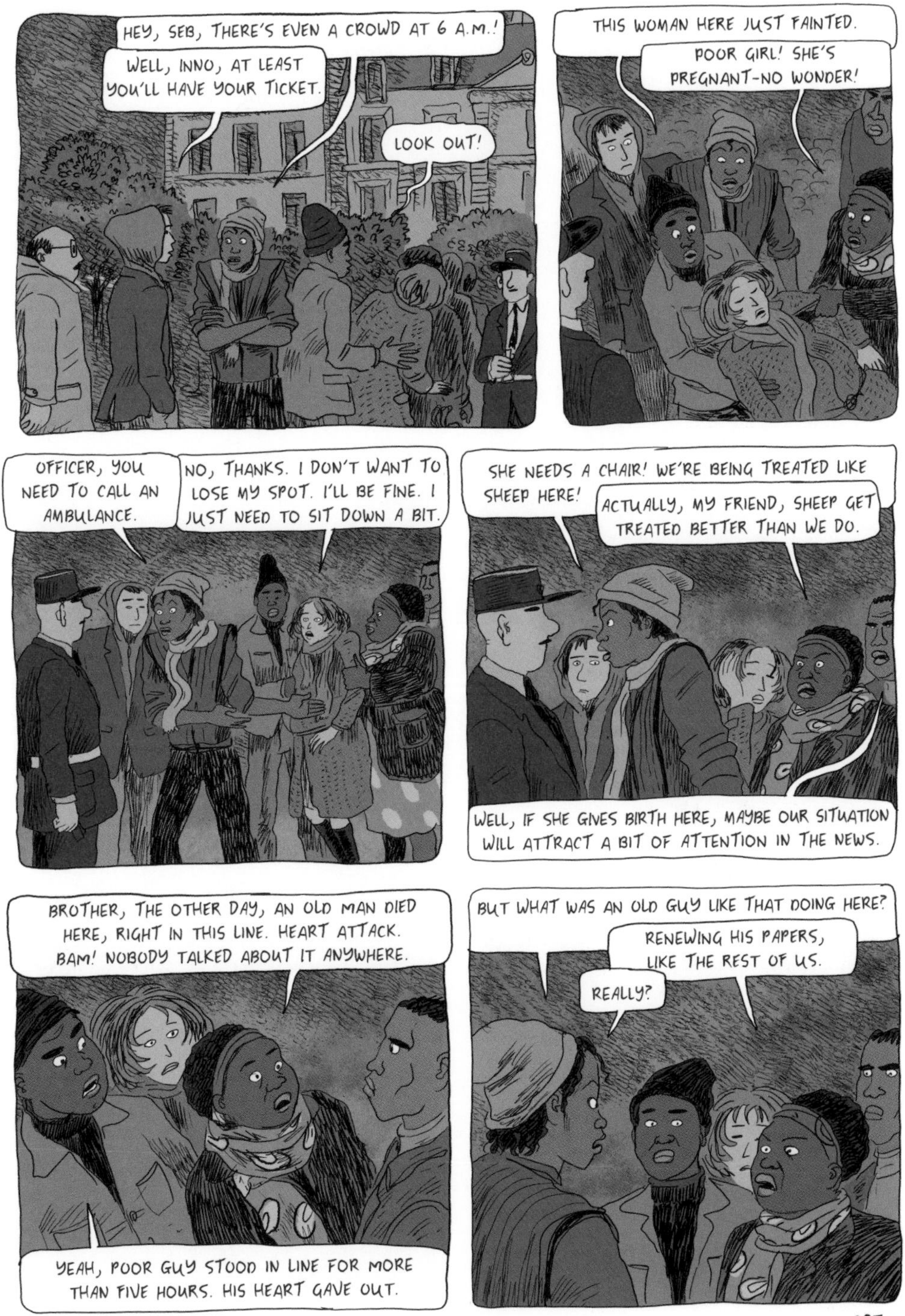
HEY, SEB, THERE'S EVEN A CROWD AT 6 A.M.!
WELL, INNO, AT LEAST YOU'LL HAVE YOUR TICKET.
LOOK OUT!
THIS WOMAN HERE JUST FAINTED.
POOR GIRL! SHE'S PREGNANT—NO WONDER!
OFFICER, YOU NEED TO CALL AN AMBULANCE.
NO, THANKS. I DON'T WANT TO LOSE MY SPOT. I'LL BE FINE. I JUST NEED TO SIT DOWN A BIT.
SHE NEEDS A CHAIR! WE'RE BEING TREATED LIKE SHEEP HERE!
ACTUALLY, MY FRIEND, SHEEP GET TREATED BETTER THAN WE DO.
WELL, IF SHE GIVES BIRTH HERE, MAYBE OUR SITUATION WILL ATTRACT A BIT OF ATTENTION IN THE NEWS.
BROTHER, THE OTHER DAY, AN OLD MAN DIED HERE, RIGHT IN THIS LINE. HEART ATTACK. BAM! NOBODY TALKED ABOUT IT ANYWHERE.
YEAH, POOR GUY STOOD IN LINE FOR MORE THAN FIVE HOURS. HIS HEART GAVE OUT.
BUT WHAT WAS AN OLD GUY LIKE THAT DOING HERE?
RENEWING HIS PAPERS, LIKE THE REST OF US.
REALLY?

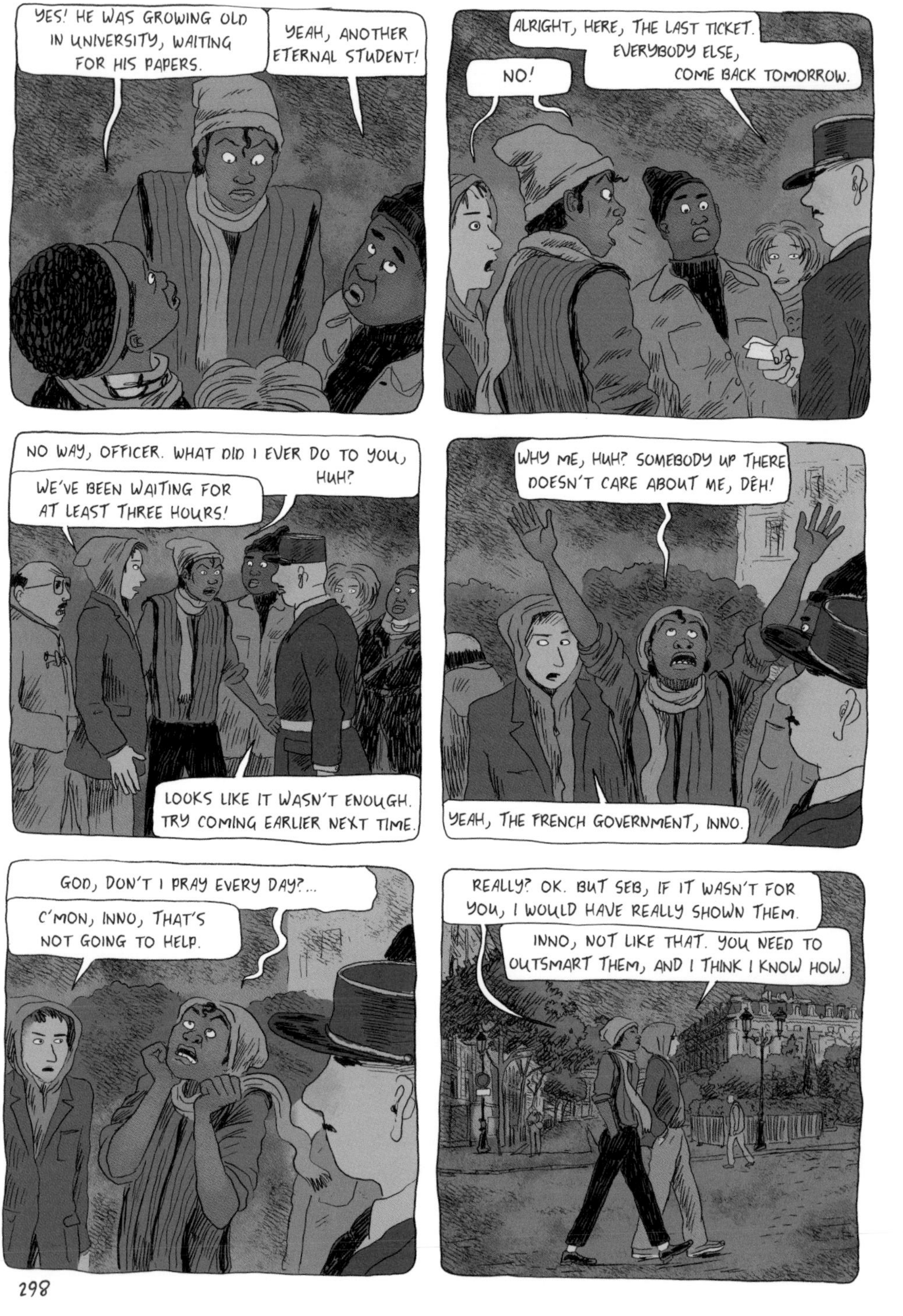
YES! HE WAS GROWING OLD IN UNIVERSITY, WAITING FOR HIS PAPERS.
YEAH, ANOTHER ETERNAL STUDENT!
ALRIGHT, HERE, THE LAST TICKET. EVERYBODY ELSE, COME BACK TOMORROW.
NO!
NO WAY, OFFICER. WHAT DID I EVER DO TO YOU, HUH?
WE'VE BEEN WAITING FOR AT LEAST THREE HOURS!
LOOKS LIKE IT WASN'T ENOUGH. TRY COMING EARLIER NEXT TIME.
WHY ME, HUH? SOMEBODY UP THERE DOESN'T CARE ABOUT ME, DÊH!
YEAH, THE FRENCH GOVERNMENT, INNO.
GOD, DON'T I PRAY EVERY DAY?...
C'MON, INNO, THAT'S NOT GOING TO HELP.
REALLY? OK. BUT SEB, IF IT WASN'T FOR YOU, I WOULD HAVE REALLY SHOWN THEM.
INNO, NOT LIKE THAT. YOU NEED TO OUTSMART THEM, AND I THINK I KNOW HOW.

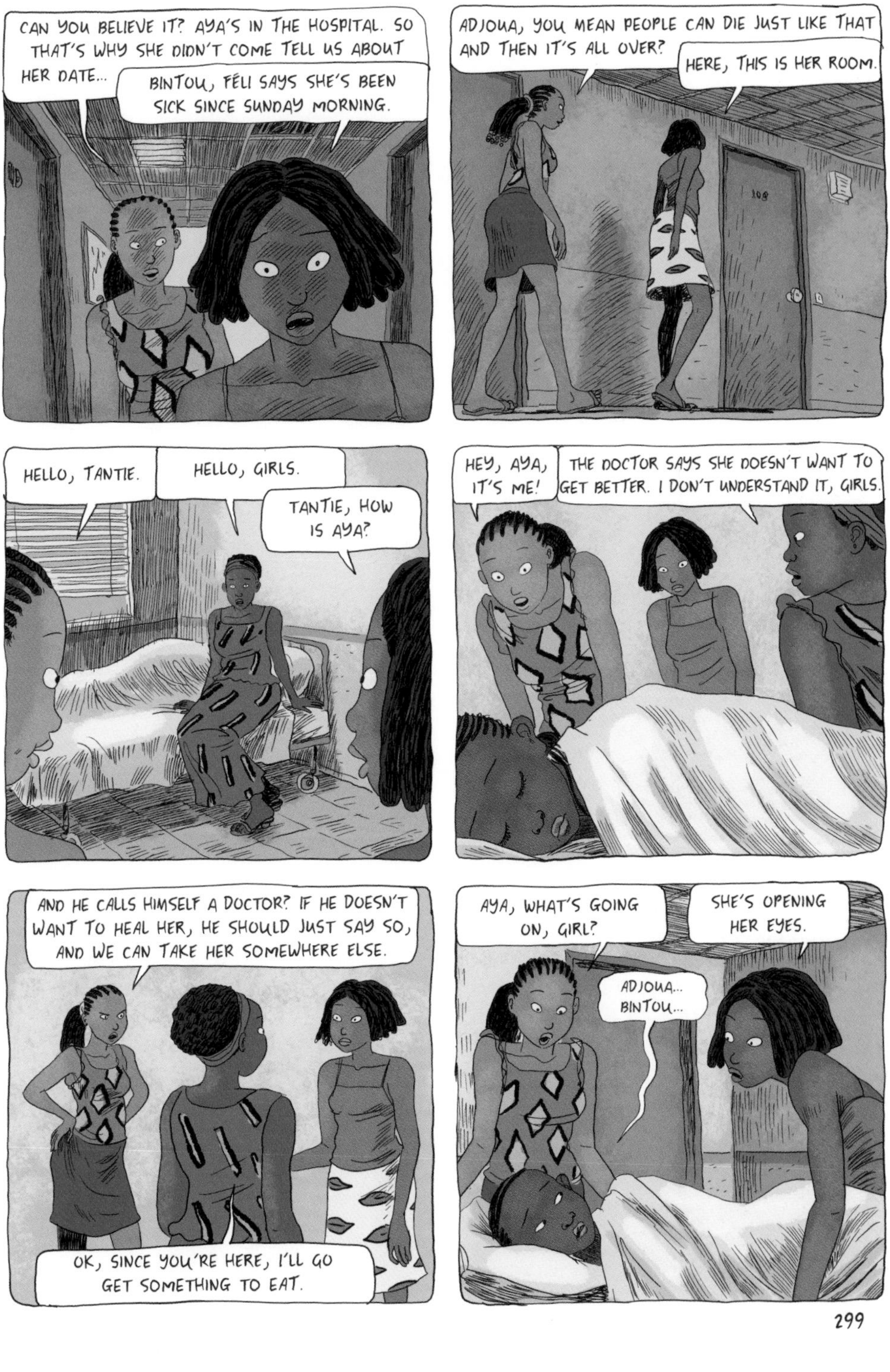
CAN YOU BELIEVE IT? AYA'S IN THE HOSPITAL. SO THAT'S WHY SHE DIDN'T COME TELL US ABOUT HER DATE...
BINTOU, FÉLI SAYS SHE'S BEEN SICK SINCE SUNDAY MORNING.
ADJOUA, YOU MEAN PEOPLE CAN DIE JUST LIKE THAT AND THEN IT'S ALL OVER?
HERE, THIS IS HER ROOM.
HELLO, TANTIE.
HELLO, GIRLS.
TANTIE, HOW IS AYA?
HEY, AYA, IT'S ME!
THE DOCTOR SAYS SHE DOESN'T WANT TO GET BETTER. I DON'T UNDERSTAND IT, GIRLS.
AND HE CALLS HIMSELF A DOCTOR? IF HE DOESN'T WANT TO HEAL HER, HE SHOULD JUST SAY SO, AND WE CAN TAKE HER SOMEWHERE ELSE.
OK, SINCE YOU'RE HERE, I'LL GO GET SOMETHING TO EAT.
AYA, WHAT'S GOING ON, GIRL?
SHE'S OPENING HER EYES.
ADJOUA... BINTOU...

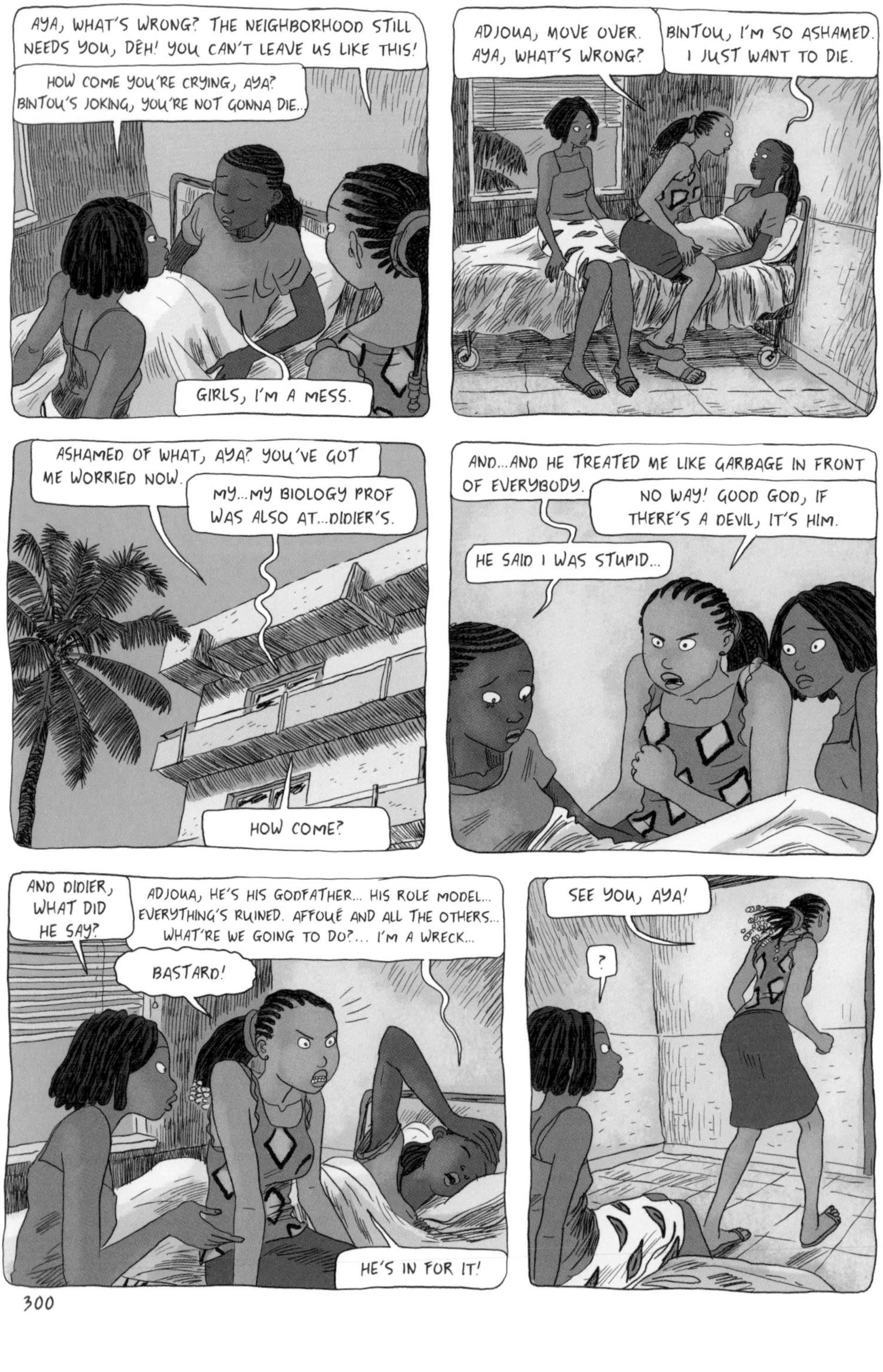
AYA, WHAT'S WRONG? THE NEIGHBORHOOD STILL NEEDS YOU, DÊH! YOU CAN'T LEAVE US LIKE THIS!
HOW COME YOU'RE CRYING, AYA? BINTOU'S JOKING, YOU'RE NOT GONNA DIE...
GIRLS, I'M A MESS.
ADJOUA, MOVE OVER. AYA, WHAT'S WRONG?
BINTOU, I'M SO ASHAMED. I JUST WANT TO DIE.
ASHAMED OF WHAT, AYA? YOU'VE GOT ME WORRIED NOW.
MY...MY BIOLOGY PROF WAS ALSO AT...DIDIER'S.
HOW COME?
AND...AND HE TREATED ME LIKE GARBAGE IN FRONT OF EVERYBODY.
NO WAY! GOOD GOD, IF THERE'S A DEVIL, IT'S HIM.
HE SAID I WAS STUPID...
AND DIDIER, WHAT DID HE SAY?
ADJOUA, HE'S HIS GODFATHER... HIS ROLE MODEL... EVERYTHING'S RUINED. AFFOUÉ AND ALL THE OTHERS... WHAT'RE WE GOING TO DO?... I'M A WRECK...
BASTARD!
HE'S IN FOR IT!
SEE YOU, AYA!
?

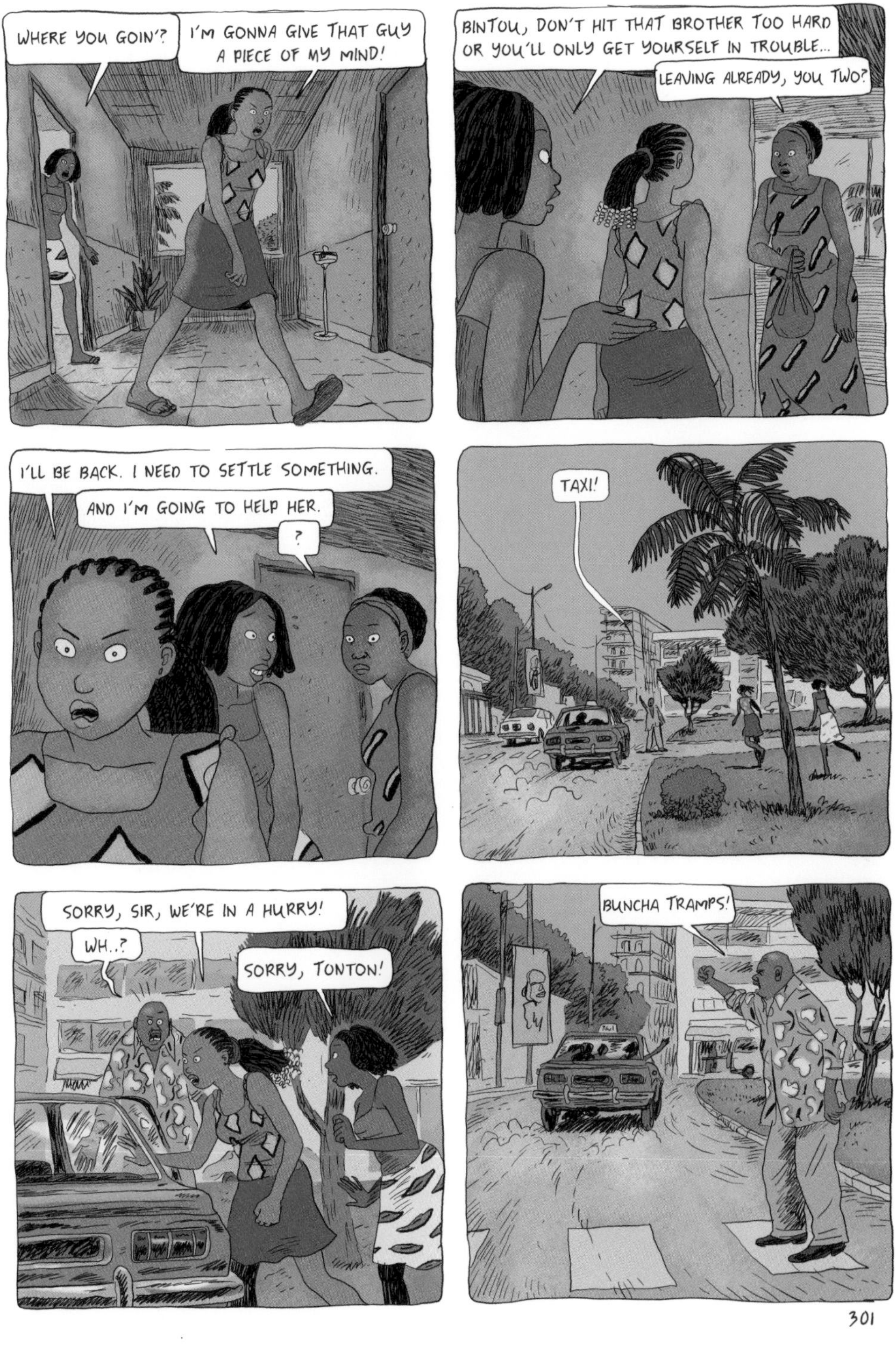
WHERE YOU GOIN'?
I'M GONNA GIVE THAT GUY A PIECE OF MY MIND!
BINTOU, DON'T HIT THAT BROTHER TOO HARD OR YOU'LL ONLY GET YOURSELF IN TROUBLE...
LEAVING ALREADY, YOU TWO?
I'LL BE BACK. I NEED TO SETTLE SOMETHING.
AND I'M GOING TO HELP HER.
?
TAXI!
SORRY, SIR, WE'RE IN A HURRY!
WH..?
SORRY, TONTON!
BUNCHA TRAMPS!

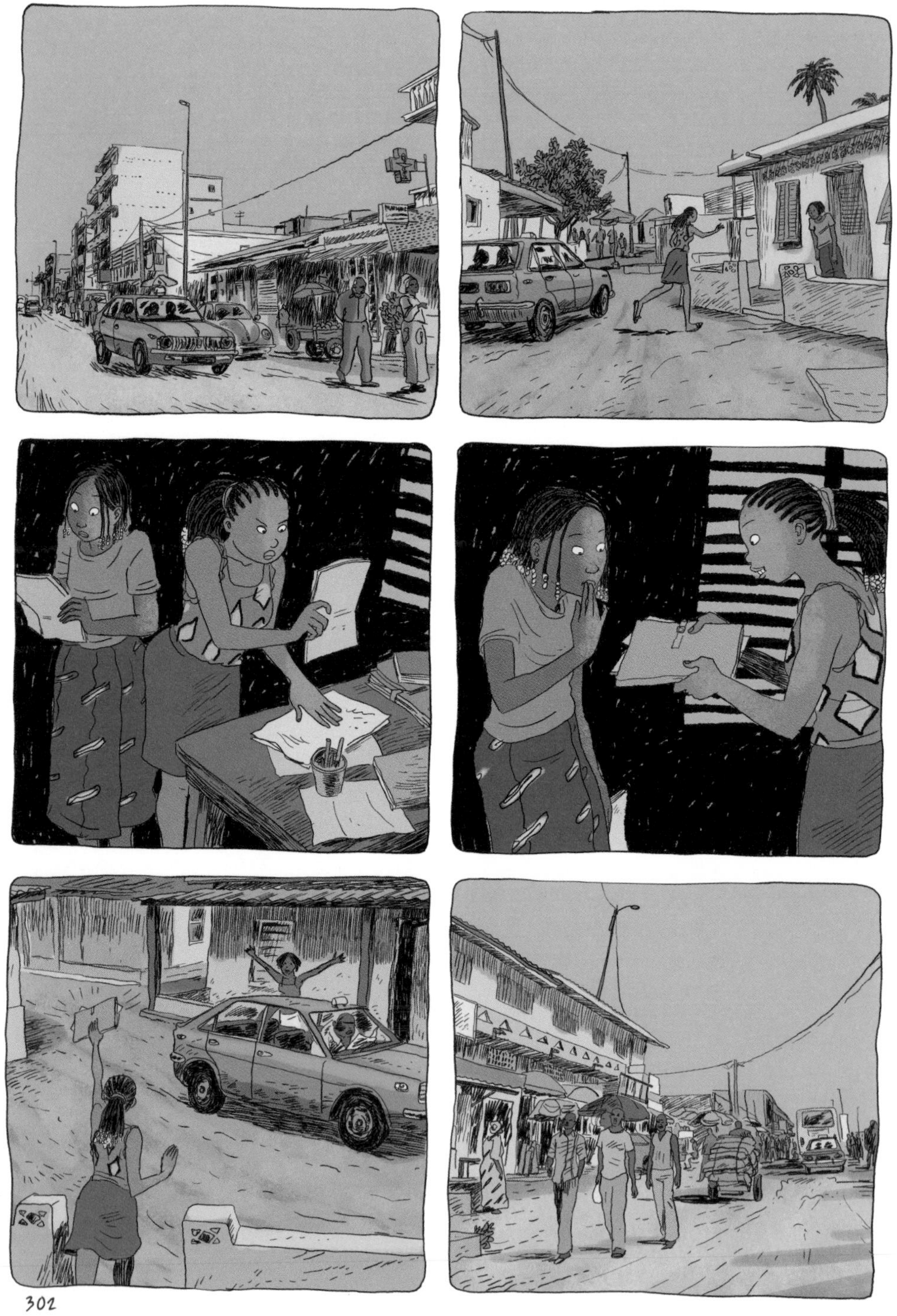

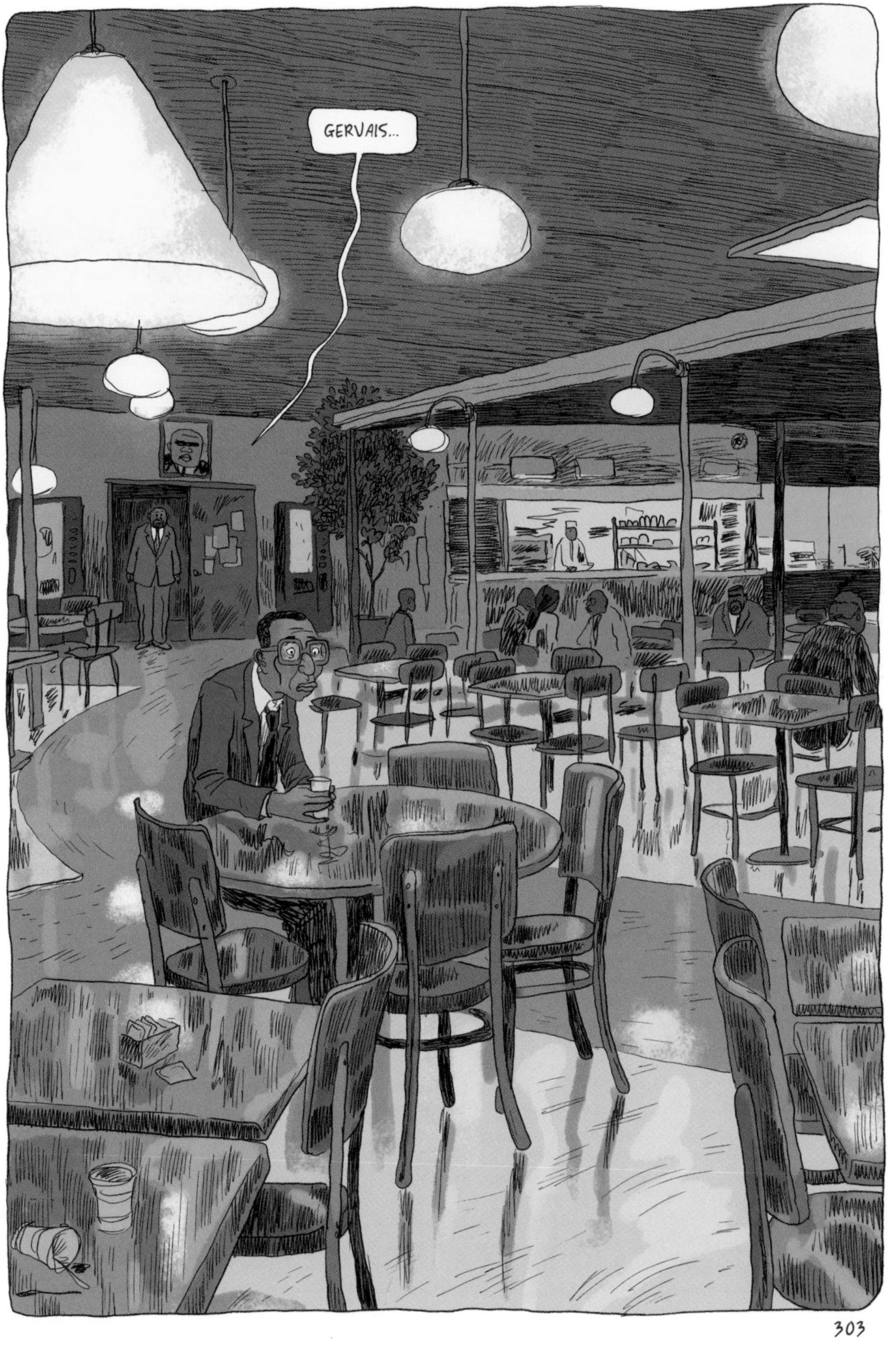
GERVAIS...

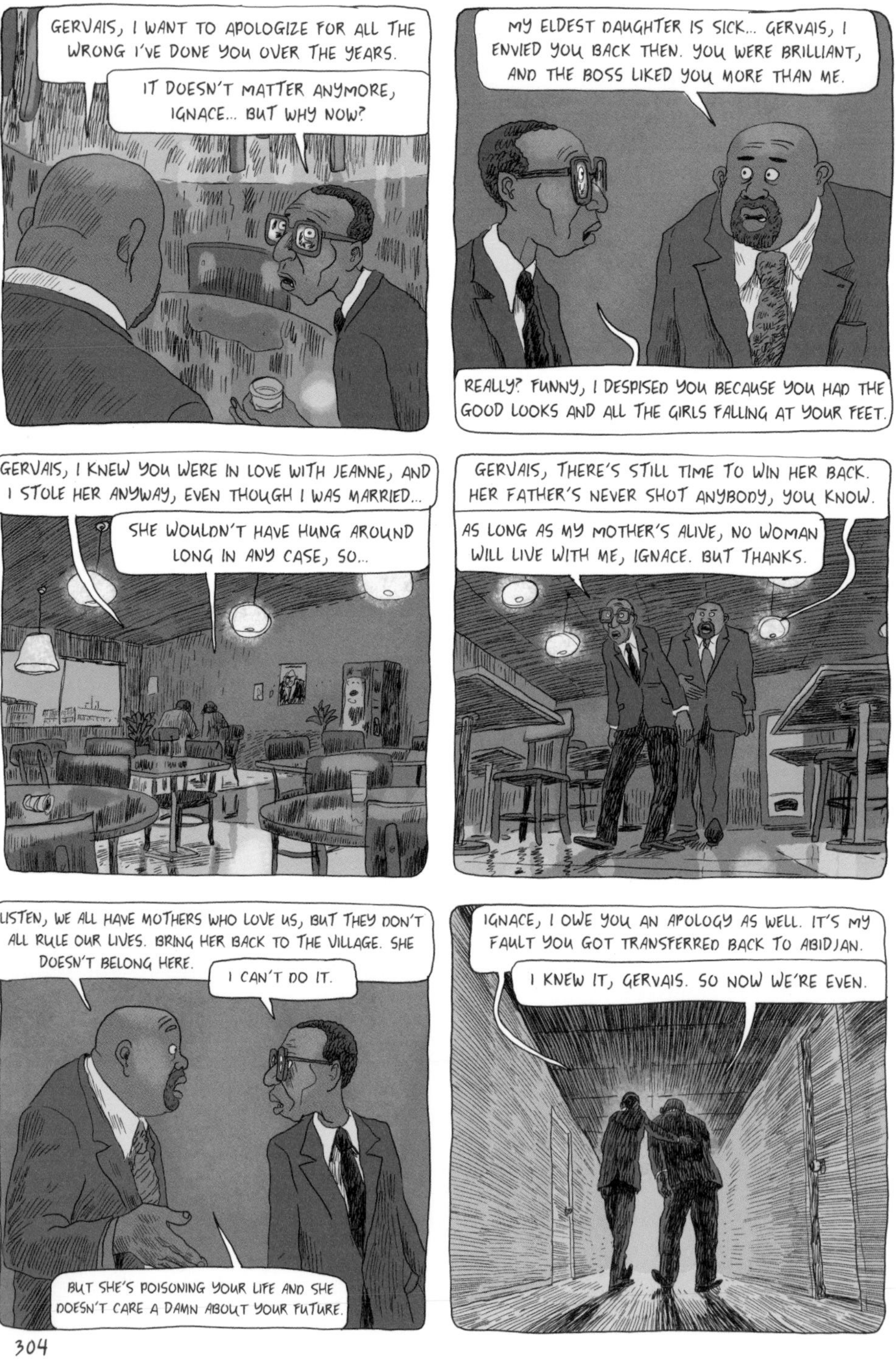
GERVAIS, I WANT TO APOLOGIZE FOR ALL THE WRONG I'VE DONE YOU OVER THE YEARS.
IT DOESN'T MATTER ANYMORE, IGNACE... BUT WHY NOW?
MY ELDEST DAUGHTER IS SICK... GERVAIS, I ENVIED YOU BACK THEN. YOU WERE BRILLIANT, AND THE BOSS LIKED YOU MORE THAN ME.
REALLY? FUNNY, I DESPISED YOU BECAUSE YOU HAD THE GOOD LOOKS AND ALL THE GIRLS FALLING AT YOUR FEET.
GERVAIS, I KNEW YOU WERE IN LOVE WITH JEANNE, AND I STOLE HER ANYWAY, EVEN THOUGH I WAS MARRIED...
SHE WOULDN'T HAVE HUNG AROUND LONG IN ANY CASE, SO...
GERVAIS, THERE'S STILL TIME TO WIN HER BACK. HER FATHER'S NEVER SHOT ANYBODY, YOU KNOW.
AS LONG AS MY MOTHER'S ALIVE, NO WOMAN WILL LIVE WITH ME, IGNACE. BUT THANKS.
LISTEN, WE ALL HAVE MOTHERS WHO LOVE US, BUT THEY DON'T ALL RULE OUR LIVES. BRING HER BACK TO THE VILLAGE. SHE DOESN'T BELONG HERE.
I CAN'T DO IT.
BUT SHE'S POISONING YOUR LIFE AND SHE DOESN'T CARE A DAMN ABOUT YOUR FUTURE.
IGNACE, I OWE YOU AN APOLOGY AS WELL. IT'S MY FAULT YOU GOT TRANSFERRED BACK TO ABIDJAN.
I KNEW IT, GERVAIS. SO NOW WE'RE EVEN.

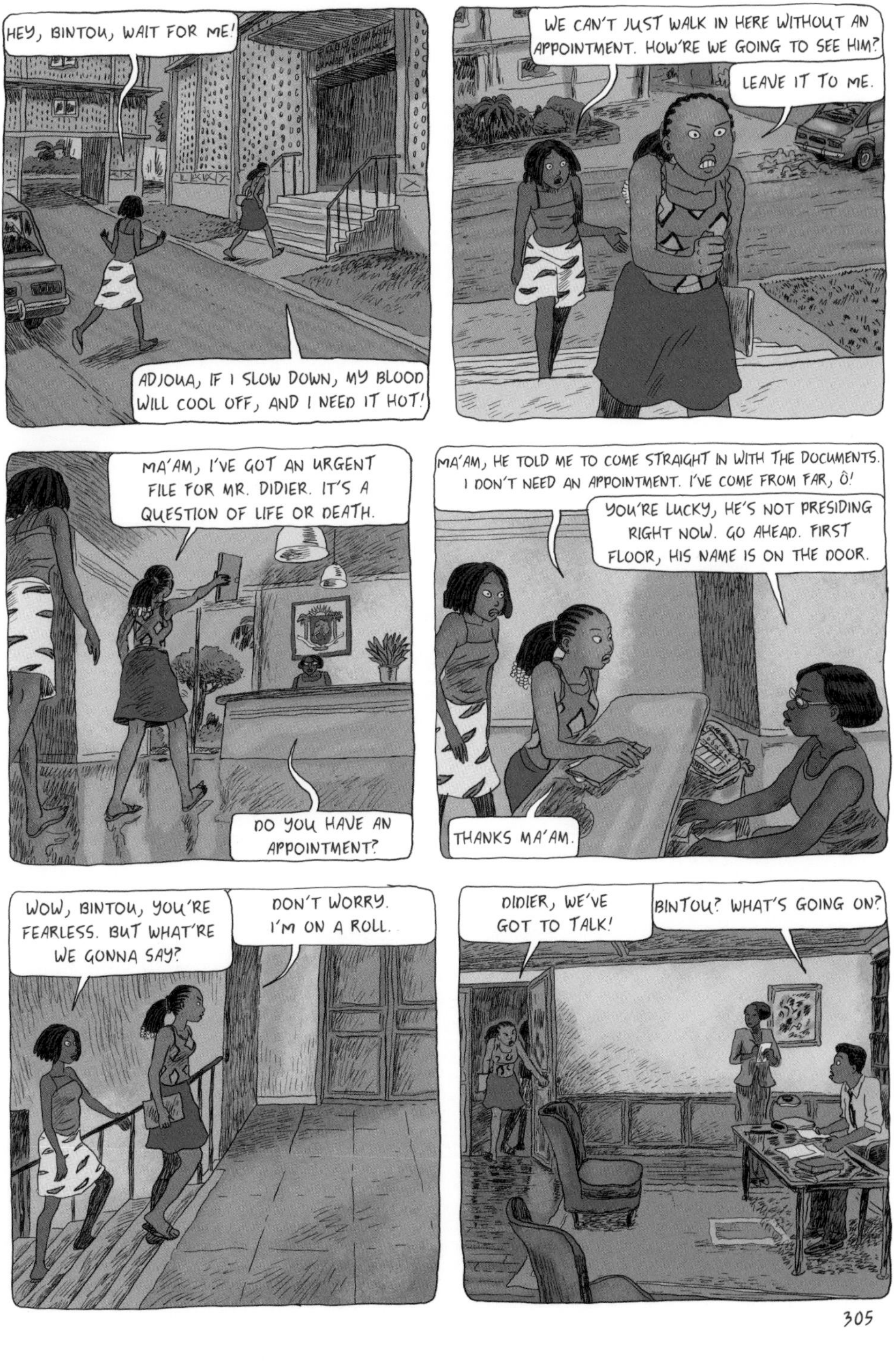
HEY, BINTOU, WAIT FOR ME!
ADJOUA, IF I SLOW DOWN, MY BLOOD WILL COOL OFF, AND I NEED IT HOT!
WE CAN'T JUST WALK IN HERE WITHOUT AN APPOINTMENT. HOW'RE WE GOING TO SEE HIM?
LEAVE IT TO ME.
MA'AM, I'VE GOT AN URGENT FILE FOR MR. DIDIER. IT'S A QUESTION OF LIFE OR DEATH.
DO YOU HAVE AN APPOINTMENT?
MA'AM, HE TOLD ME TO COME STRAIGHT IN WITH THE DOCUMENTS. I DON'T NEED AN APPOINTMENT. I'VE COME FROM FAR, Ô!
YOU'RE LUCKY, HE'S NOT PRESIDING RIGHT NOW. GO AHEAD. FIRST FLOOR, HIS NAME IS ON THE DOOR.
THANKS MA'AM.
WOW, BINTOU, YOU'RE FEARLESS. BUT WHAT'RE WE GONNA SAY?
DON'T WORRY. I'M ON A ROLL.
DIDIER, WE'VE GOT TO TALK!
BINTOU? WHAT'S GOING ON?

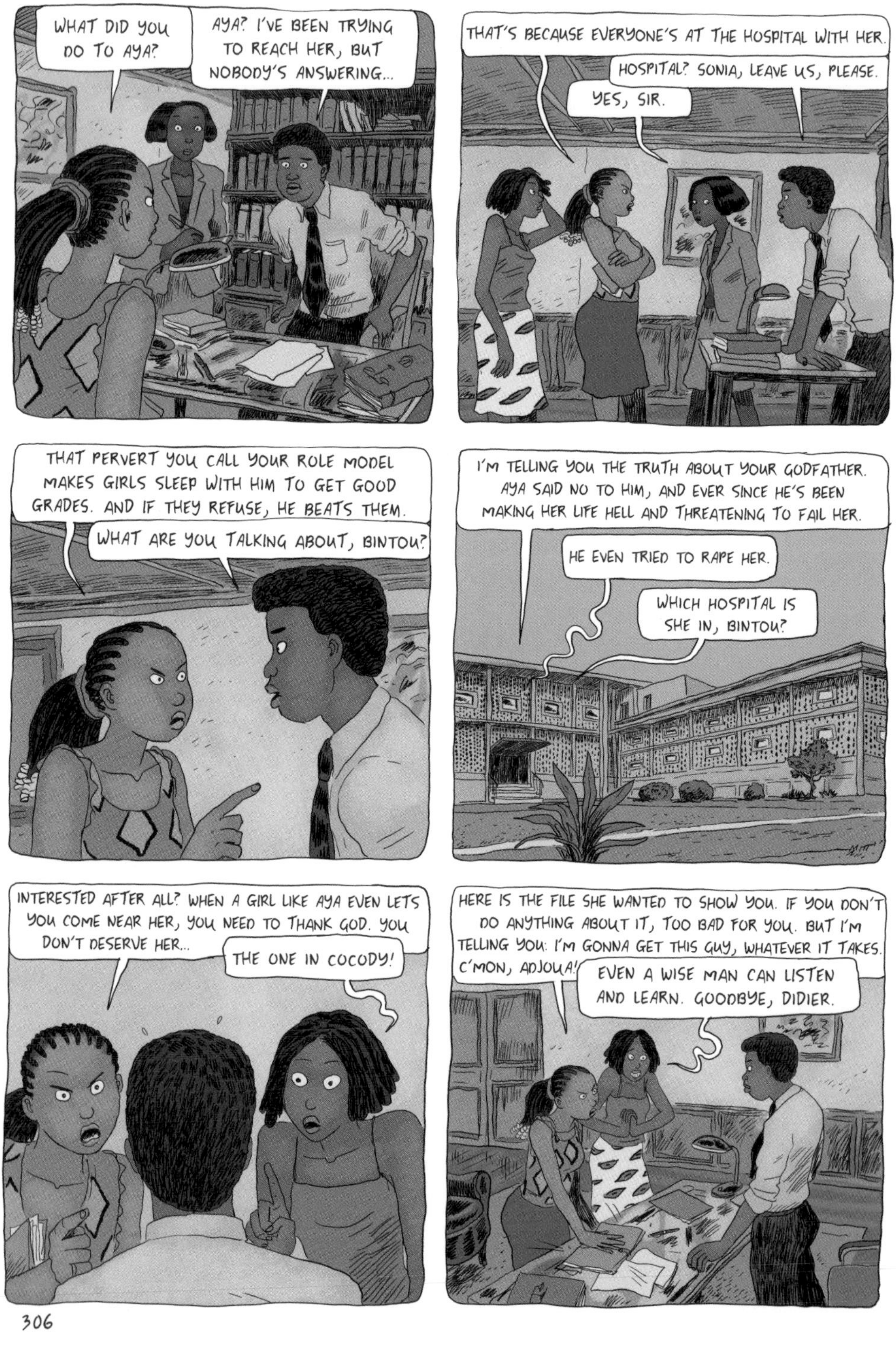
WHAT DID YOU DO TO AYA?
AYA? I'VE BEEN TRYING TO REACH HER, BUT NOBODY'S ANSWERING...
THAT'S BECAUSE EVERYONE'S AT THE HOSPITAL WITH HER.
HOSPITAL? SONIA, LEAVE US, PLEASE.
YES, SIR.
THAT PERVERT YOU CALL YOUR ROLE MODEL MAKES GIRLS SLEEP WITH HIM TO GET GOOD GRADES. AND IF THEY REFUSE, HE BEATS THEM.
WHAT ARE YOU TALKING ABOUT, BINTOU?
I'M TELLING YOU THE TRUTH ABOUT YOUR GODFATHER. AYA SAID NO TO HIM, AND EVER SINCE HE'S BEEN MAKING HER LIFE HELL AND THREATENING TO FAIL HER.
HE EVEN TRIED TO RAPE HER.
WHICH HOSPITAL IS SHE IN, BINTOU?
INTERESTED AFTER ALL? WHEN A GIRL LIKE AYA EVEN LETS YOU COME NEAR HER, YOU NEED TO THANK GOD. YOU DON'T DESERVE HER...
THE ONE IN COCODY!
HERE IS THE FILE SHE WANTED TO SHOW YOU. IF YOU DON'T DO ANYTHING ABOUT IT, TOO BAD FOR YOU. BUT I'M TELLING YOU: I'M GONNA GET THIS GUY, WHATEVER IT TAKES. C'MON, ADJOUA!
EVEN A WISE MAN CAN LISTEN AND LEARN. GOODBYE, DIDIER.

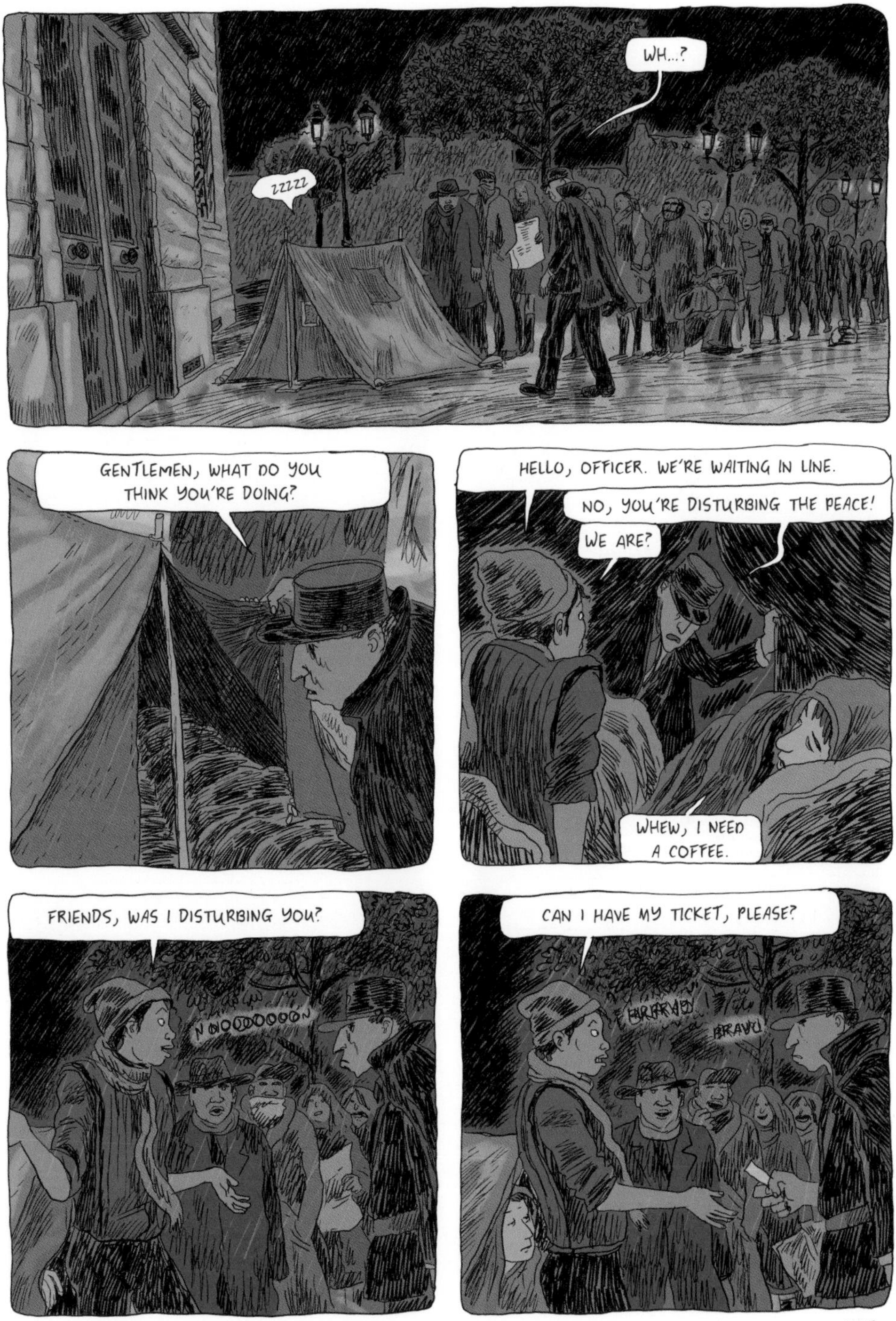
WH...?
ZZZZZ
GENTLEMEN, WHAT DO YOU THINK YOU'RE DOING?
HELLO, OFFICER. WE'RE WAITING IN LINE.
NO, YOU'RE DISTURBING THE PEACE!
WE ARE?
WHEW, I NEED A COFFEE.
FRIENDS, WAS I DISTURBING YOU?
NOOOOOOOON
CAN I HAVE MY TICKET, PLEASE?
BRAVO

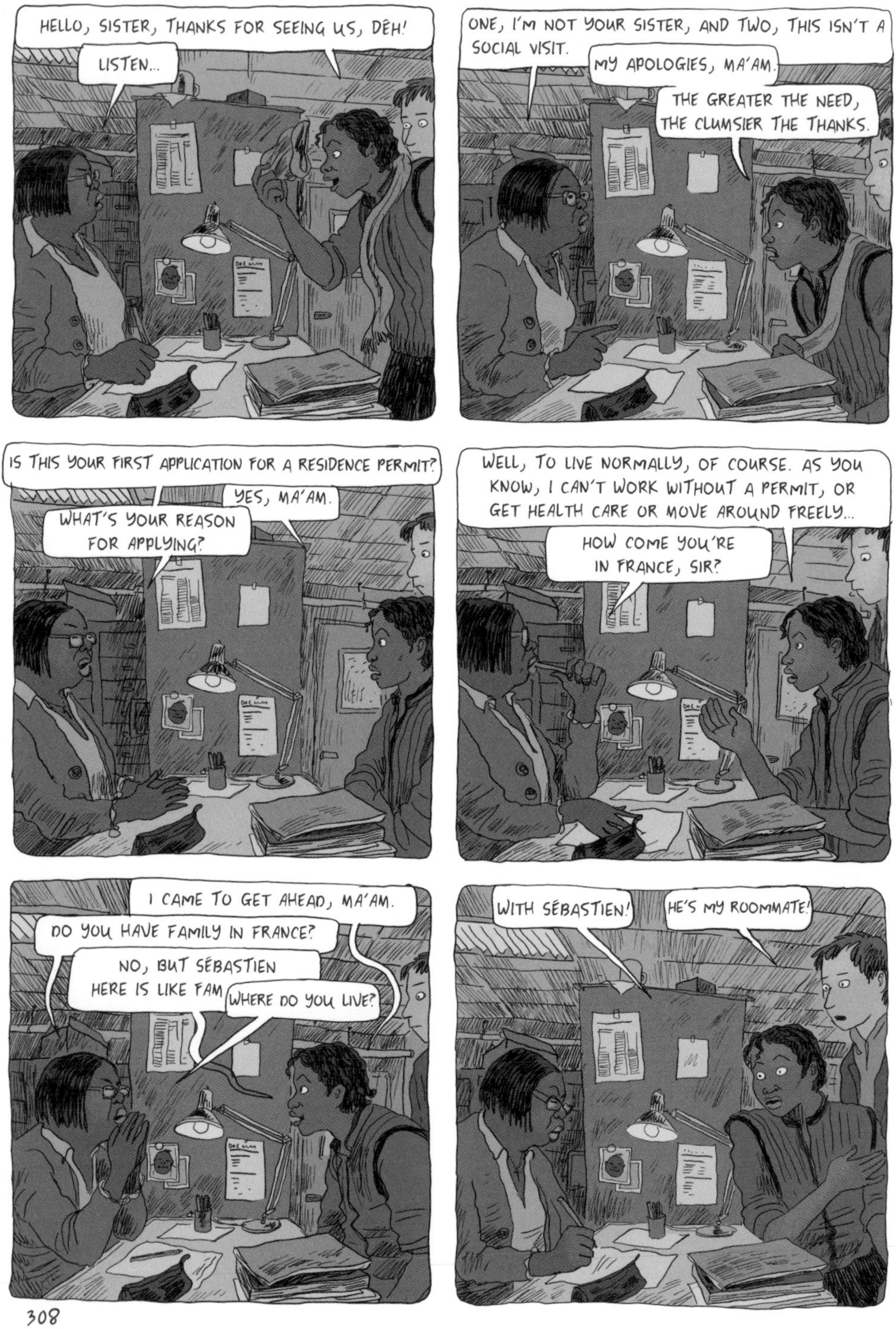
HELLO, SISTER, THANKS FOR SEEING US, DÊH!
LISTEN...
ONE, I'M NOT YOUR SISTER, AND TWO, THIS ISN'T A SOCIAL VISIT.
MY APOLOGIES, MA'AM.
THE GREATER THE NEED, THE CLUMSIER THE THANKS.
IS THIS YOUR FIRST APPLICATION FOR A RESIDENCE PERMIT?
YES, MA'AM.
WHAT'S YOUR REASON FOR APPLYING?
WELL, TO LIVE NORMALLY, OF COURSE. AS YOU KNOW, I CAN'T WORK WITHOUT A PERMIT, OR GET HEALTH CARE OR MOVE AROUND FREELY...
HOW COME YOU'RE IN FRANCE, SIR?
I CAME TO GET AHEAD, MA'AM.
DO YOU HAVE FAMILY IN FRANCE?
NO, BUT SÉBASTIEN HERE IS LIKE FAM
WHERE DO YOU LIVE?
WITH SÉBASTIEN!
HE'S MY ROOMMATE!

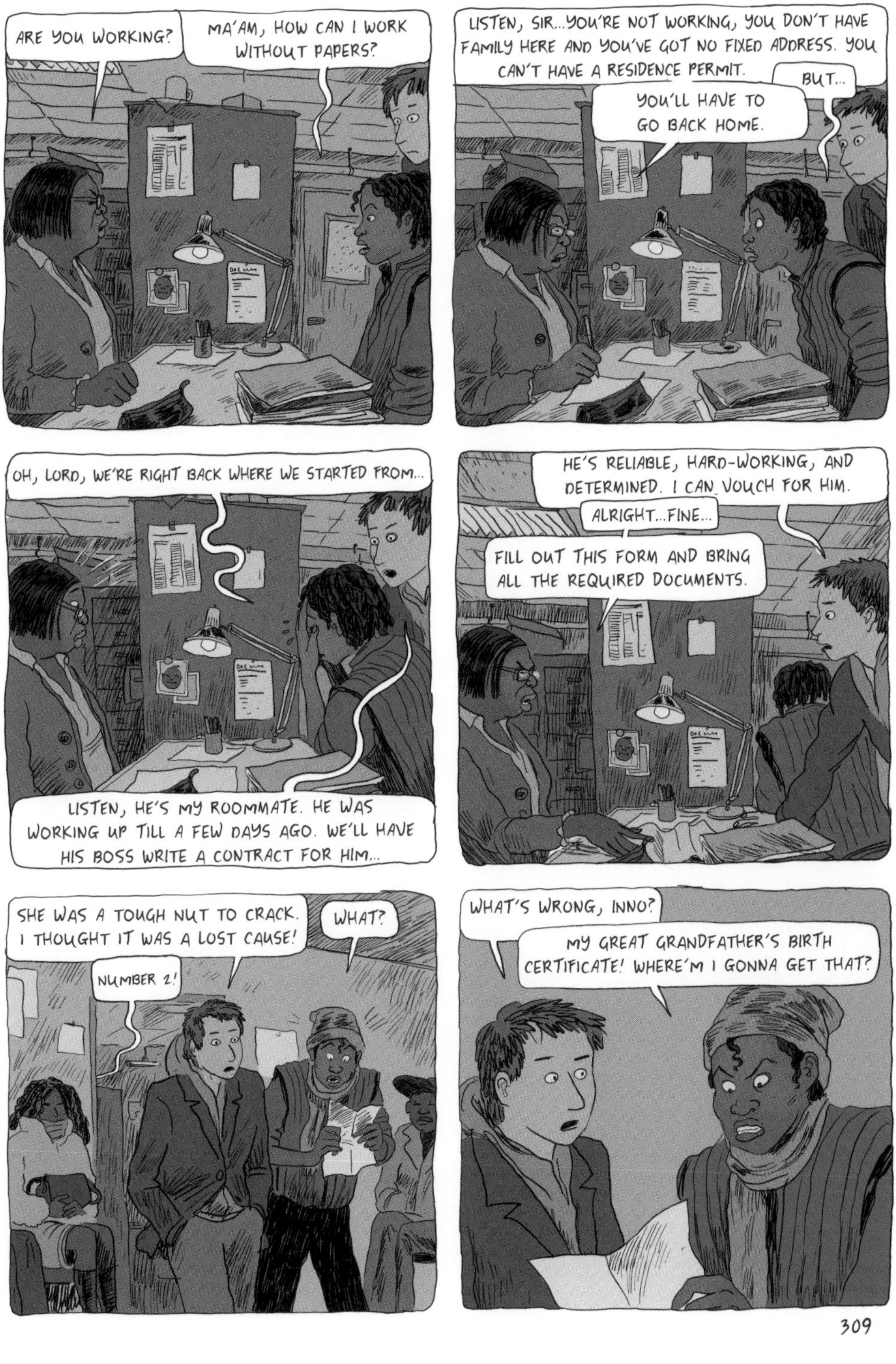
ARE YOU WORKING?
MA'AM, HOW CAN I WORK WITHOUT PAPERS?
LISTEN, SIR...YOU'RE NOT WORKING, YOU DON'T HAVE FAMILY HERE AND YOU'VE GOT NO FIXED ADDRESS. YOU CAN'T HAVE A RESIDENCE PERMIT.
YOU'LL HAVE TO GO BACK HOME.
BUT...
OH, LORD, WE'RE RIGHT BACK WHERE WE STARTED FROM...
LISTEN, HE'S MY ROOMMATE. HE WAS WORKING UP TILL A FEW DAYS AGO. WE'LL HAVE HIS BOSS WRITE A CONTRACT FOR HIM...
HE'S RELIABLE, HARD-WORKING, AND DETERMINED. I CAN VOUCH FOR HIM.
ALRIGHT...FINE...
FILL OUT THIS FORM AND BRING ALL THE REQUIRED DOCUMENTS.
SHE WAS A TOUGH NUT TO CRACK. I THOUGHT IT WAS A LOST CAUSE!
WHAT?
NUMBER 2!
WHAT'S WRONG, INNO?
MY GREAT GRANDFATHER'S BIRTH CERTIFICATE! WHERE'M I GONNA GET THAT?

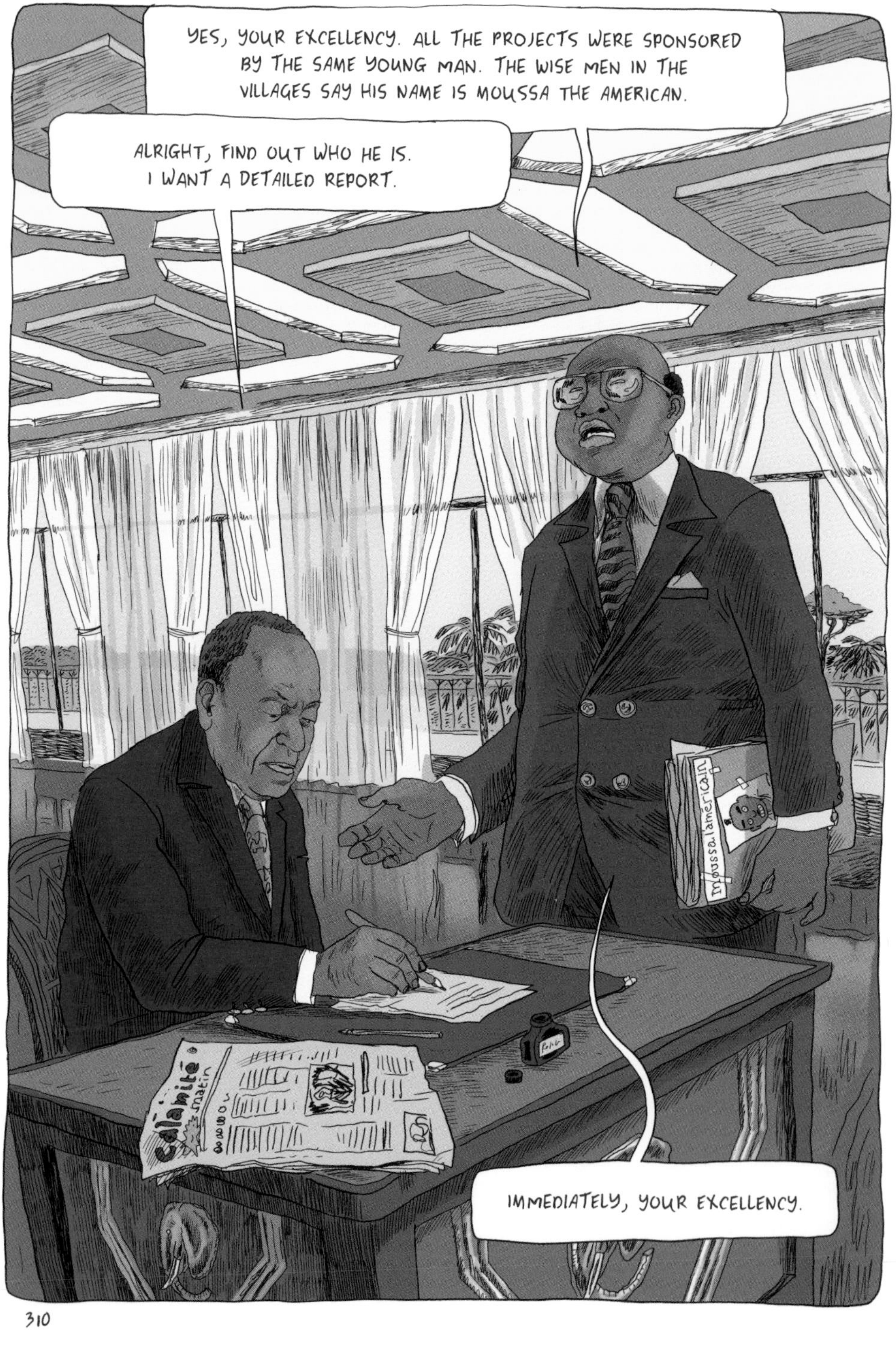
YES, YOUR EXCELLENCY. ALL THE PROJECTS WERE SPONSORED BY THE SAME YOUNG MAN. THE WISE MEN IN THE VILLAGES SAY HIS NAME IS MOUSSA THE AMERICAN.
ALRIGHT, FIND OUT WHO HE IS. I WANT A DETAILED REPORT.
IMMEDIATELY, YOUR EXCELLENCY.
Calamité matin
moussalamericain

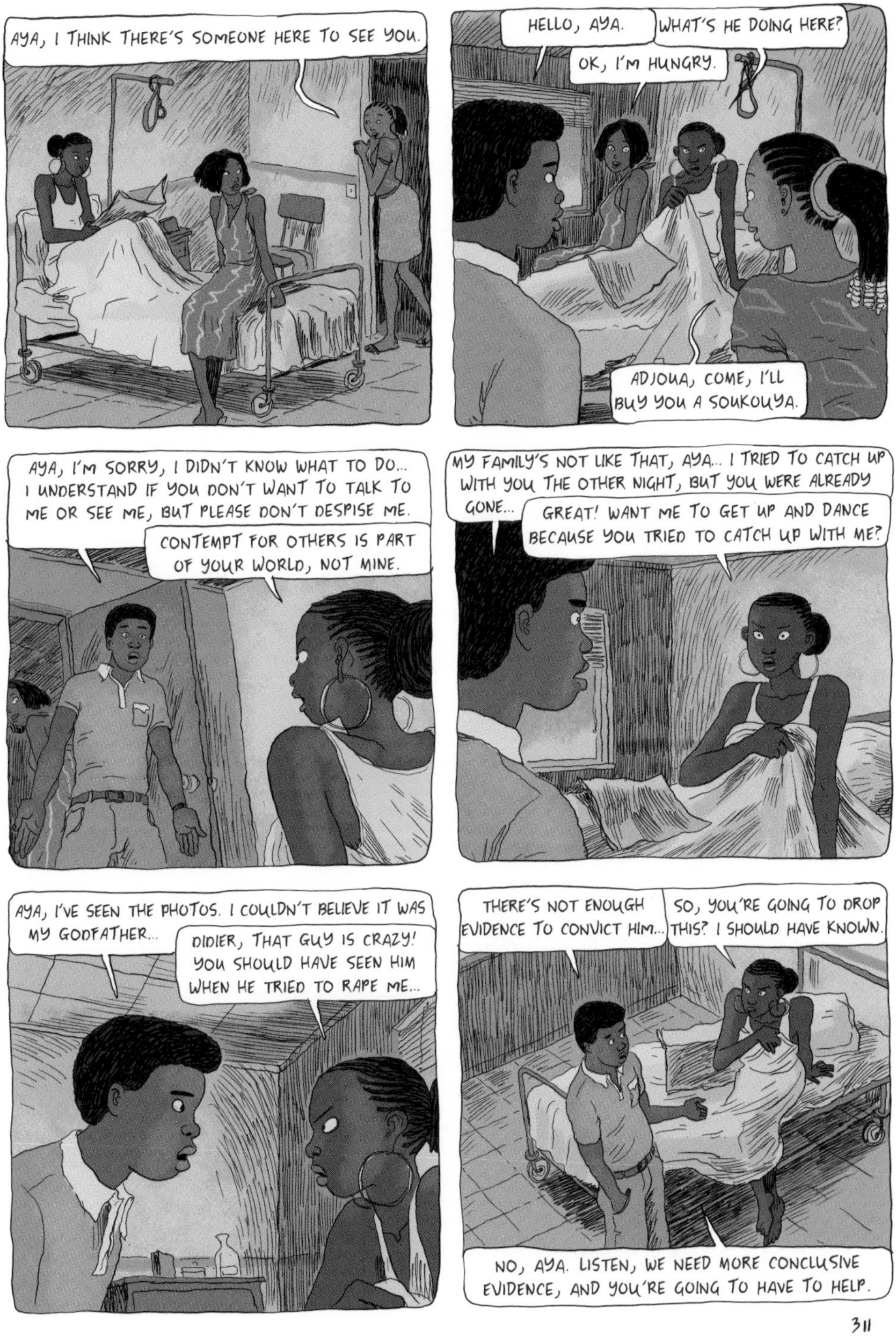
AYA, I THINK THERE'S SOMEONE HERE TO SEE YOU.
HELLO, AYA.
WHAT'S HE DOING HERE?
OK, I'M HUNGRY.
ADJOUA, COME, I'LL BUY YOU A SOUKOUYA.
AYA, I'M SORRY, I DIDN'T KNOW WHAT TO DO... I UNDERSTAND IF YOU DON'T WANT TO TALK TO ME OR SEE ME, BUT PLEASE DON'T DESPISE ME.
CONTEMPT FOR OTHERS IS PART OF YOUR WORLD, NOT MINE.
MY FAMILY'S NOT LIKE THAT, AYA... I TRIED TO CATCH UP WITH YOU THE OTHER NIGHT, BUT YOU WERE ALREADY GONE...
GREAT! WANT ME TO GET UP AND DANCE BECAUSE YOU TRIED TO CATCH UP WITH ME?
AYA, I'VE SEEN THE PHOTOS. I COULDN'T BELIEVE IT WAS MY GODFATHER...
DIDIER, THAT GUY IS CRAZY! YOU SHOULD HAVE SEEN HIM WHEN HE TRIED TO RAPE ME...
THERE'S NOT ENOUGH EVIDENCE TO CONVICT HIM...
SO, YOU'RE GOING TO DROP THIS? I SHOULD HAVE KNOWN.
NO, AYA. LISTEN, WE NEED MORE CONCLUSIVE EVIDENCE, AND YOU'RE GOING TO HAVE TO HELP.

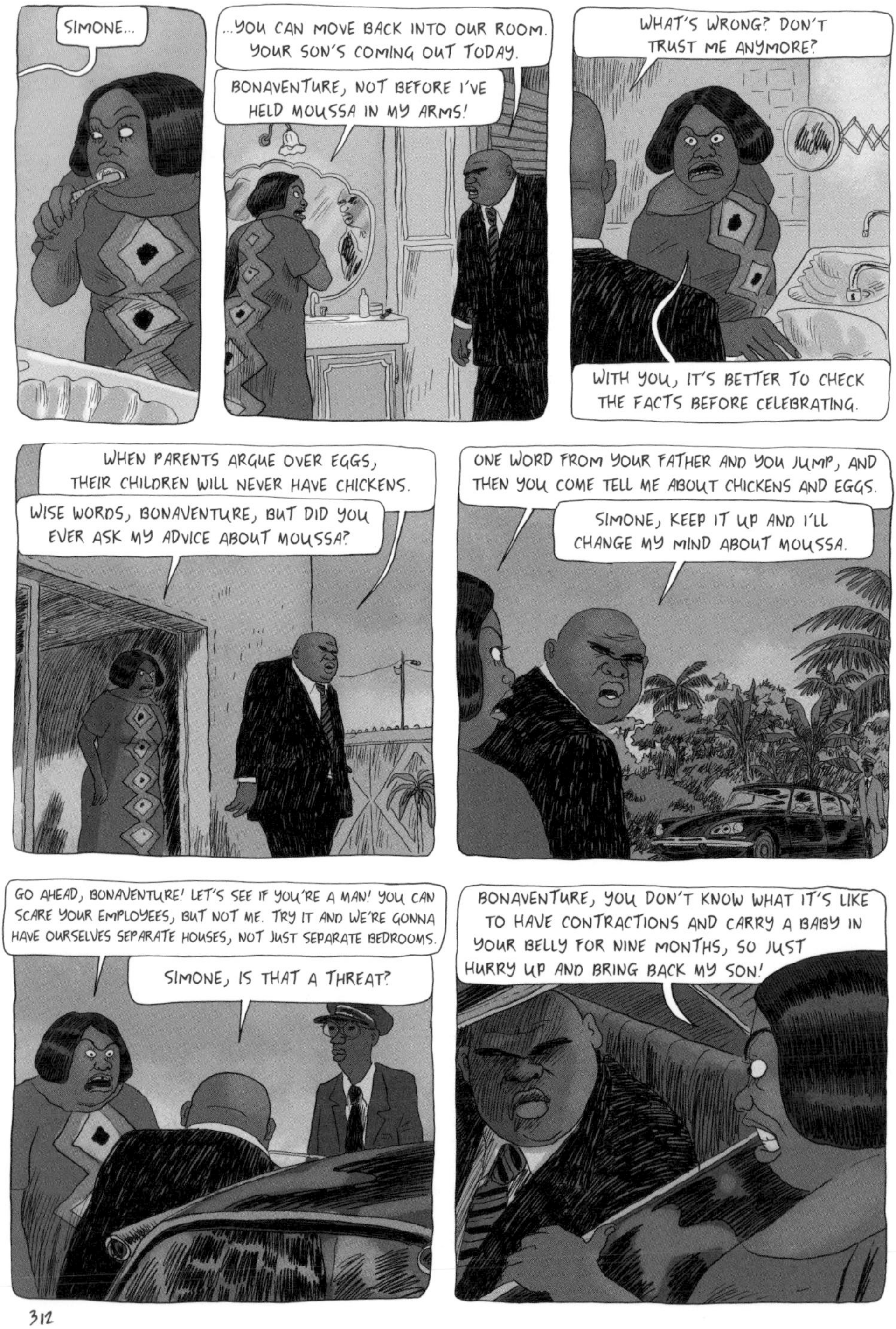

SIMONE...
...YOU CAN MOVE BACK INTO OUR ROOM. YOUR SON'S COMING OUT TODAY.
BONAVENTURE, NOT BEFORE I'VE HELD MOUSSA IN MY ARMS!
WHAT'S WRONG? DON'T TRUST ME ANYMORE?
WITH YOU, IT'S BETTER TO CHECK THE FACTS BEFORE CELEBRATING.
WHEN PARENTS ARGUE OVER EGGS, THEIR CHILDREN WILL NEVER HAVE CHICKENS.
WISE WORDS, BONAVENTURE, BUT DID YOU EVER ASK MY ADVICE ABOUT MOUSSA?
ONE WORD FROM YOUR FATHER AND YOU JUMP, AND THEN YOU COME TELL ME ABOUT CHICKENS AND EGGS.
SIMONE, KEEP IT UP AND I'LL CHANGE MY MIND ABOUT MOUSSA.
GO AHEAD, BONAVENTURE! LET'S SEE IF YOU'RE A MAN! YOU CAN SCARE YOUR EMPLOYEES, BUT NOT ME. TRY IT AND WE'RE GONNA HAVE OURSELVES SEPARATE HOUSES, NOT JUST SEPARATE BEDROOMS.
SIMONE, IS THAT A THREAT?
BONAVENTURE, YOU DON'T KNOW WHAT IT'S LIKE TO HAVE CONTRACTIONS AND CARRY A BABY IN YOUR BELLY FOR NINE MONTHS, SO JUST HURRY UP AND BRING BACK MY SON!

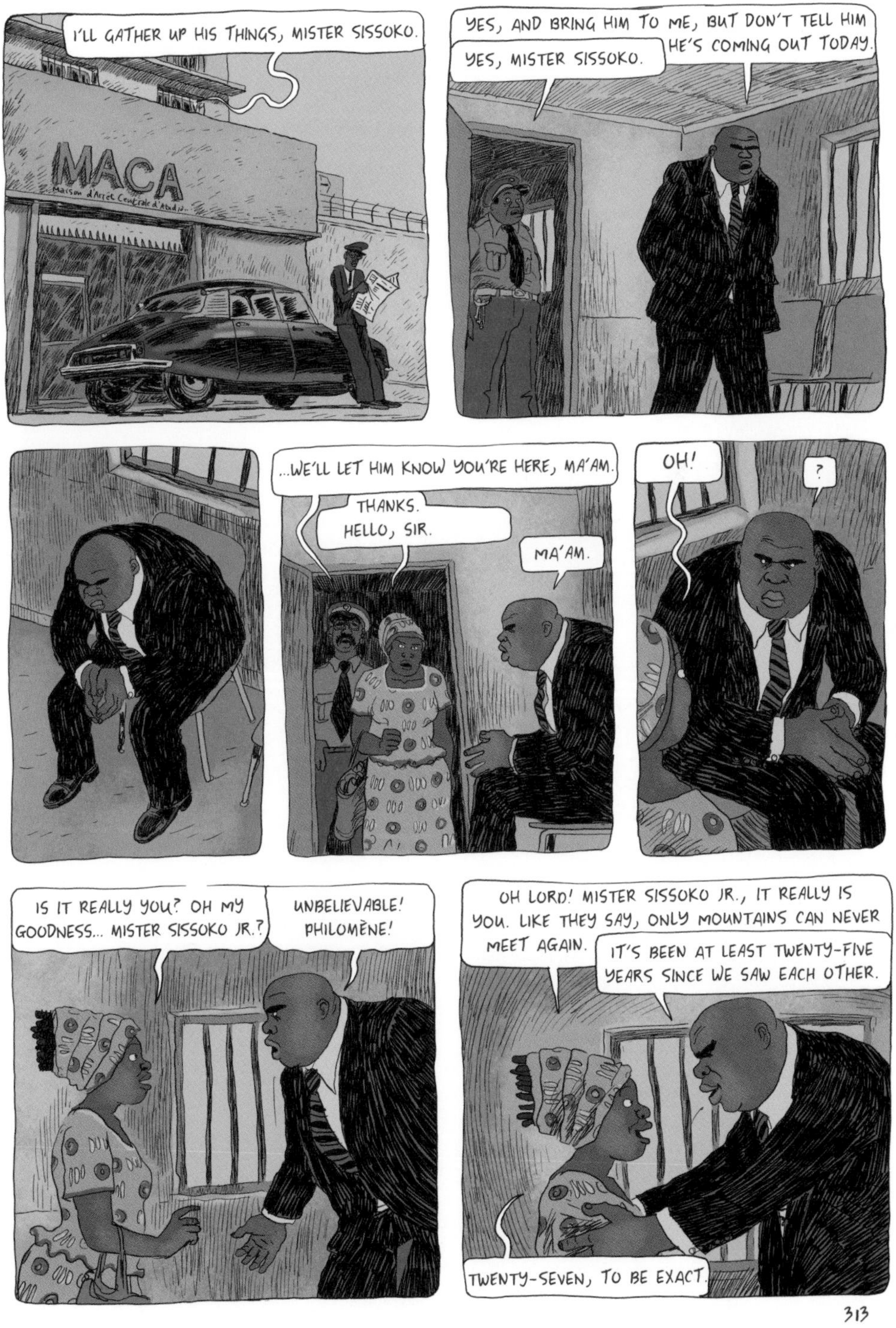
I'LL GATHER UP HIS THINGS, MISTER SISSOKO.
MACA
YES, AND BRING HIM TO ME, BUT DON'T TELL HIM HE'S COMING OUT TODAY.
YES, MISTER SISSOKO.
...WE'LL LET HIM KNOW YOU'RE HERE, MA'AM.
THANKS. HELLO, SIR.
MA'AM.
OH!
?
IS IT REALLY YOU? OH MY GOODNESS... MISTER SISSOKO JR.?
UNBELIEVABLE! PHILOMÈNE!
OH LORD! MISTER SISSOKO JR., IT REALLY IS YOU. LIKE THEY SAY, ONLY MOUNTAINS CAN NEVER MEET AGAIN.
IT'S BEEN AT LEAST TWENTY-FIVE YEARS SINCE WE SAW EACH OTHER.
TWENTY-SEVEN, TO BE EXACT.

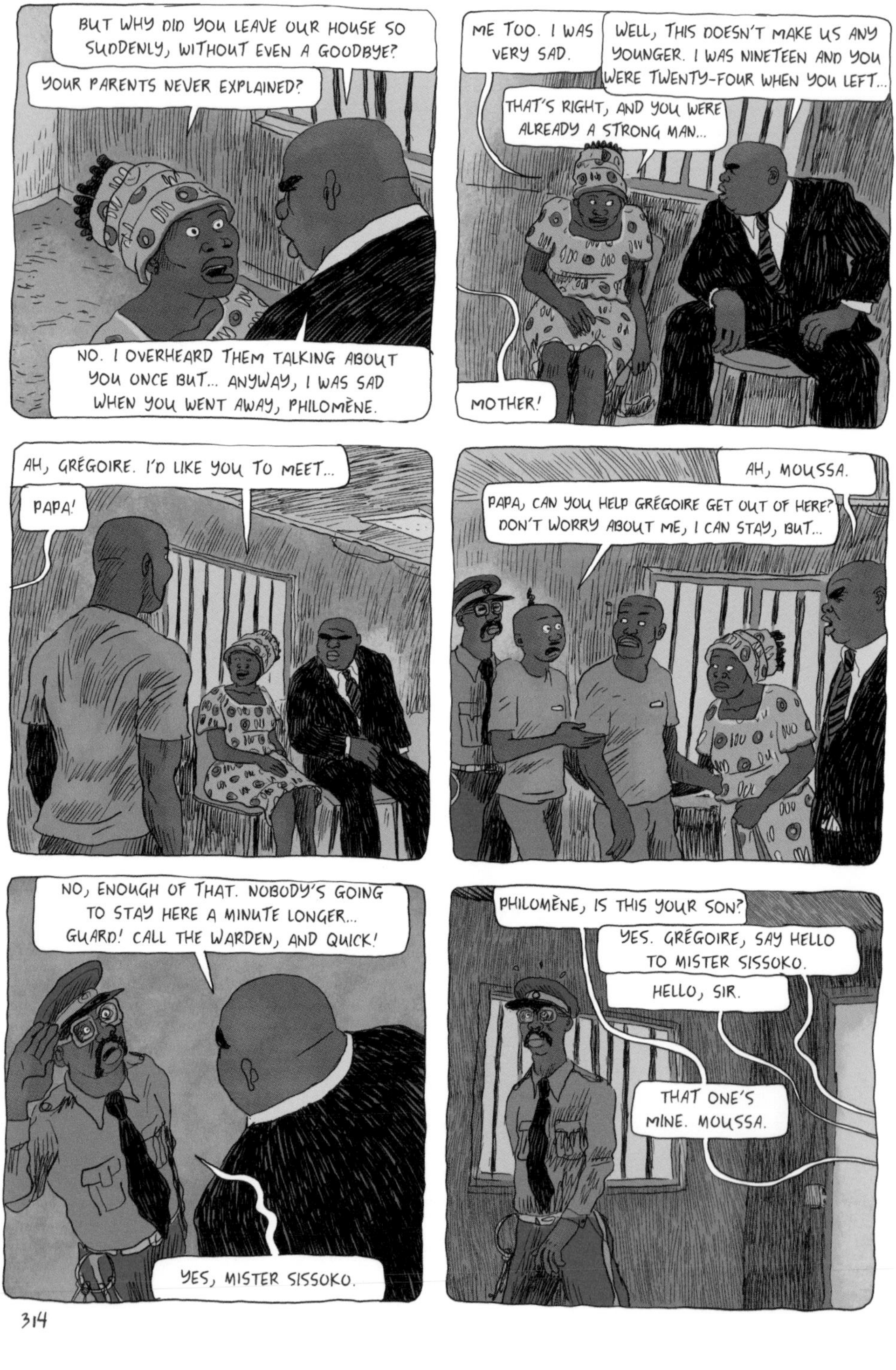
BUT WHY DID YOU LEAVE OUR HOUSE SO SUDDENLY, WITHOUT EVEN A GOODBYE?
YOUR PARENTS NEVER EXPLAINED?
NO. I OVERHEARD THEM TALKING ABOUT YOU ONCE BUT... ANYWAY, I WAS SAD WHEN YOU WENT AWAY, PHILOMÈNE.
ME TOO. I WAS VERY SAD.
WELL, THIS DOESN'T MAKE US ANY YOUNGER. I WAS NINETEEN AND YOU WERE TWENTY-FOUR WHEN YOU LEFT...
THAT'S RIGHT, AND YOU WERE ALREADY A STRONG MAN...
MOTHER!
AH, GRÉGOIRE. I'D LIKE YOU TO MEET...
PAPA!
AH, MOUSSA.
PAPA, CAN YOU HELP GRÉGOIRE GET OUT OF HERE? DON'T WORRY ABOUT ME, I CAN STAY, BUT...
NO, ENOUGH OF THAT. NOBODY'S GOING TO STAY HERE A MINUTE LONGER... GUARD! CALL THE WARDEN, AND QUICK!
YES, MISTER SISSOKO.
PHILOMÈNE, IS THIS YOUR SON?
YES. GRÉGOIRE, SAY HELLO TO MISTER SISSOKO.
HELLO, SIR.
THAT ONE'S MINE. MOUSSA.

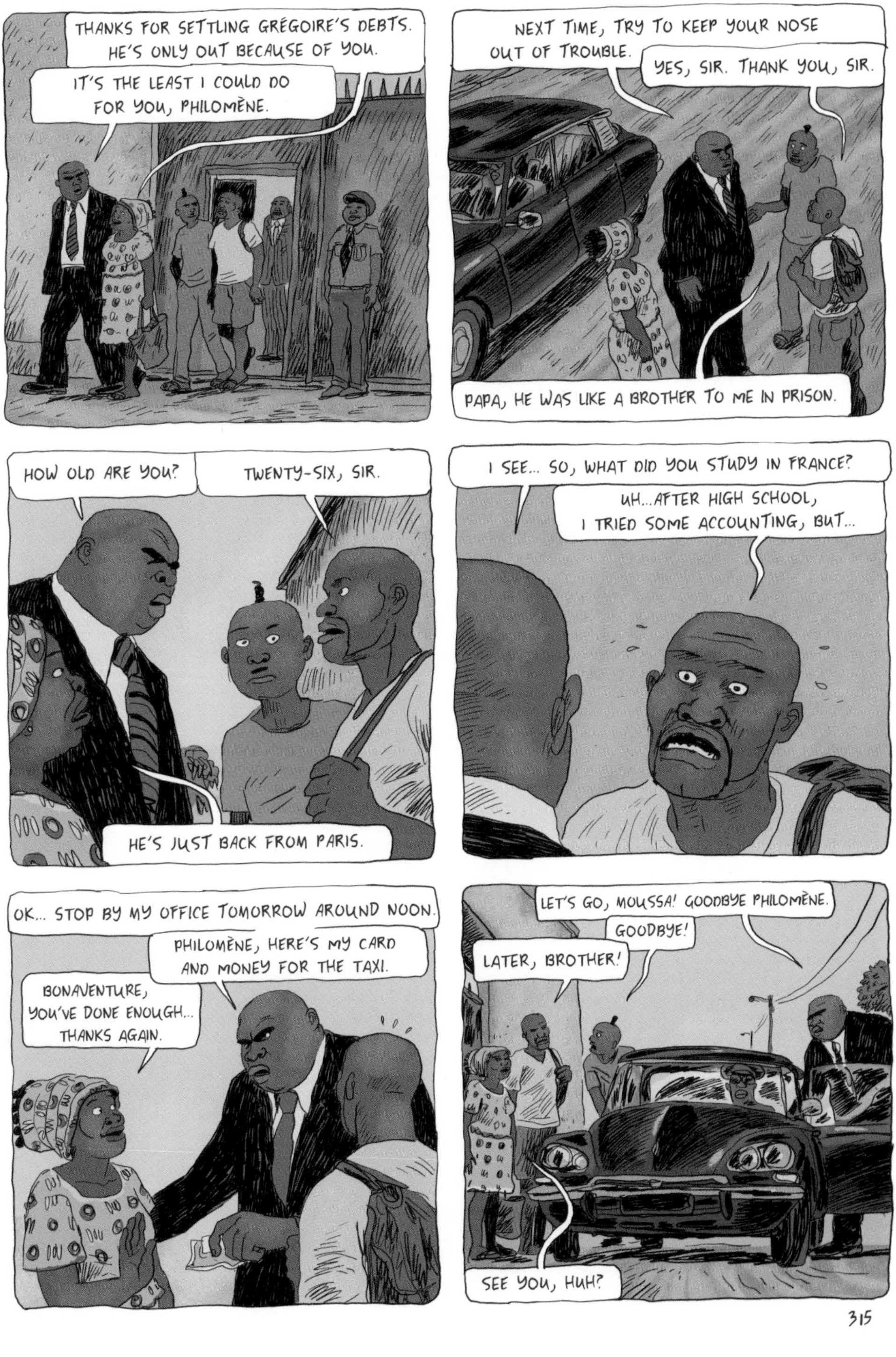
THANKS FOR SETTLING GRÉGOIRE'S DEBTS. HE'S ONLY OUT BECAUSE OF YOU.
IT'S THE LEAST I COULD DO FOR YOU, PHILOMÈNE.
NEXT TIME, TRY TO KEEP YOUR NOSE OUT OF TROUBLE.
YES, SIR. THANK YOU, SIR.
PAPA, HE WAS LIKE A BROTHER TO ME IN PRISON.
HOW OLD ARE YOU?
TWENTY-SIX, SIR.
HE'S JUST BACK FROM PARIS.
I SEE... SO, WHAT DID YOU STUDY IN FRANCE?
UH...AFTER HIGH SCHOOL, I TRIED SOME ACCOUNTING, BUT...
OK... STOP BY MY OFFICE TOMORROW AROUND NOON.
PHILOMÈNE, HERE'S MY CARD AND MONEY FOR THE TAXI.
BONAVENTURE, YOU'VE DONE ENOUGH... THANKS AGAIN.
LET'S GO, MOUSSA! GOODBYE PHILOMÈNE.
GOODBYE!
LATER, BROTHER!
SEE YOU, HUH?

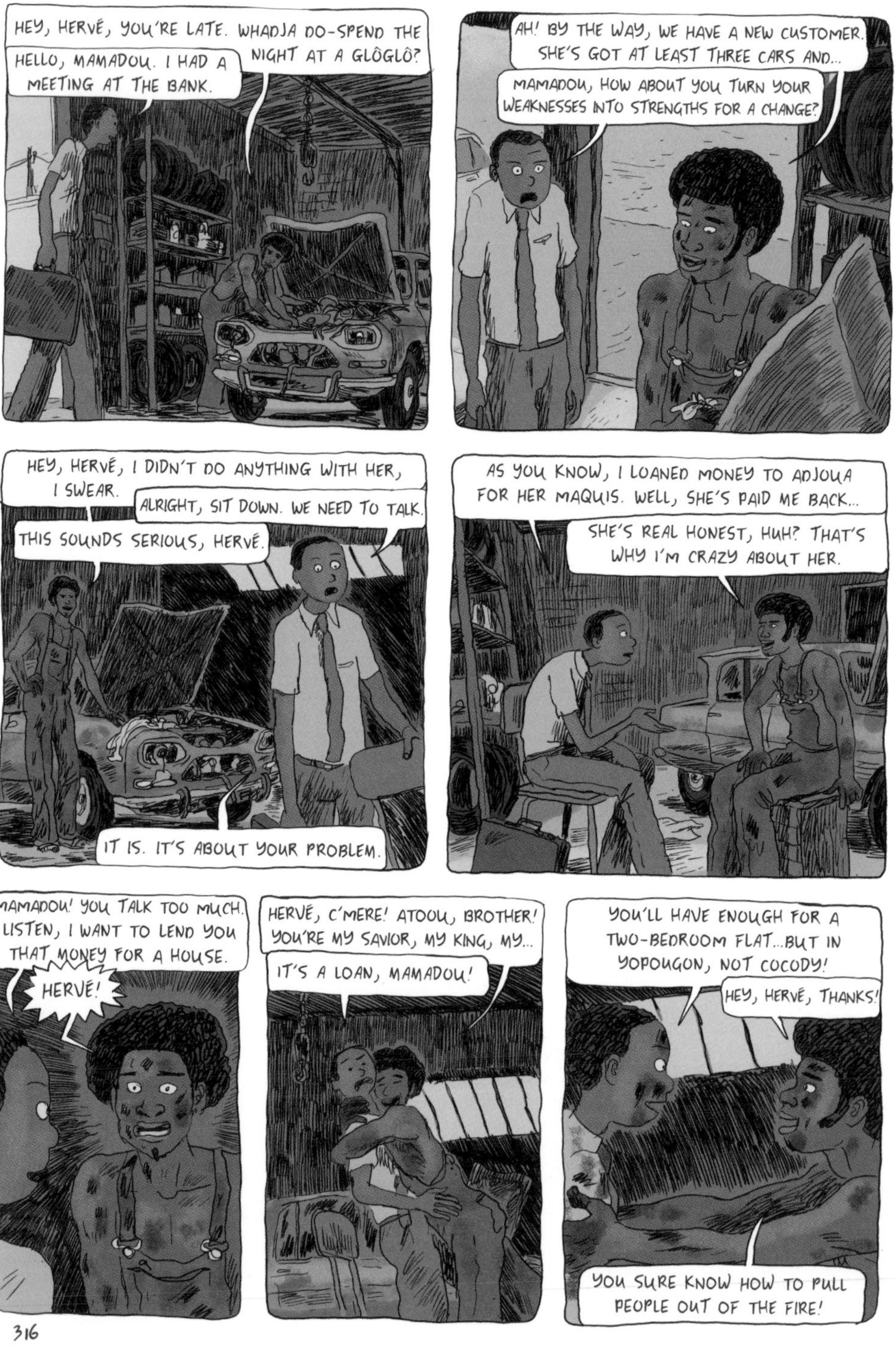
HEY, HERVÉ, YOU'RE LATE. WHADJA DO-SPEND THE NIGHT AT A GLÔGLÔ?
HELLO, MAMADOU. I HAD A MEETING AT THE BANK.
AH! BY THE WAY, WE HAVE A NEW CUSTOMER. SHE'S GOT AT LEAST THREE CARS AND...
MAMADOU, HOW ABOUT YOU TURN YOUR WEAKNESSES INTO STRENGTHS FOR A CHANGE?
HEY, HERVÉ, I DIDN'T DO ANYTHING WITH HER, I SWEAR.
ALRIGHT, SIT DOWN. WE NEED TO TALK.
THIS SOUNDS SERIOUS, HERVÉ.
IT IS. IT'S ABOUT YOUR PROBLEM.
AS YOU KNOW, I LOANED MONEY TO ADJOUA FOR HER MAQUIS. WELL, SHE'S PAID ME BACK...
SHE'S REAL HONEST, HUH? THAT'S WHY I'M CRAZY ABOUT HER.
MAMADOU! YOU TALK TOO MUCH. LISTEN, I WANT TO LEND YOU THAT MONEY FOR A HOUSE.
HERVÉ!
HERVÉ, C'MERE! ATOOU, BROTHER! YOU'RE MY SAVIOR, MY KING, MY...
IT'S A LOAN, MAMADOU!
YOU'LL HAVE ENOUGH FOR A TWO-BEDROOM FLAT...BUT IN YOPOUGON, NOT COCODY!
HEY, HERVÉ, THANKS!
YOU SURE KNOW HOW TO PULL PEOPLE OUT OF THE FIRE!

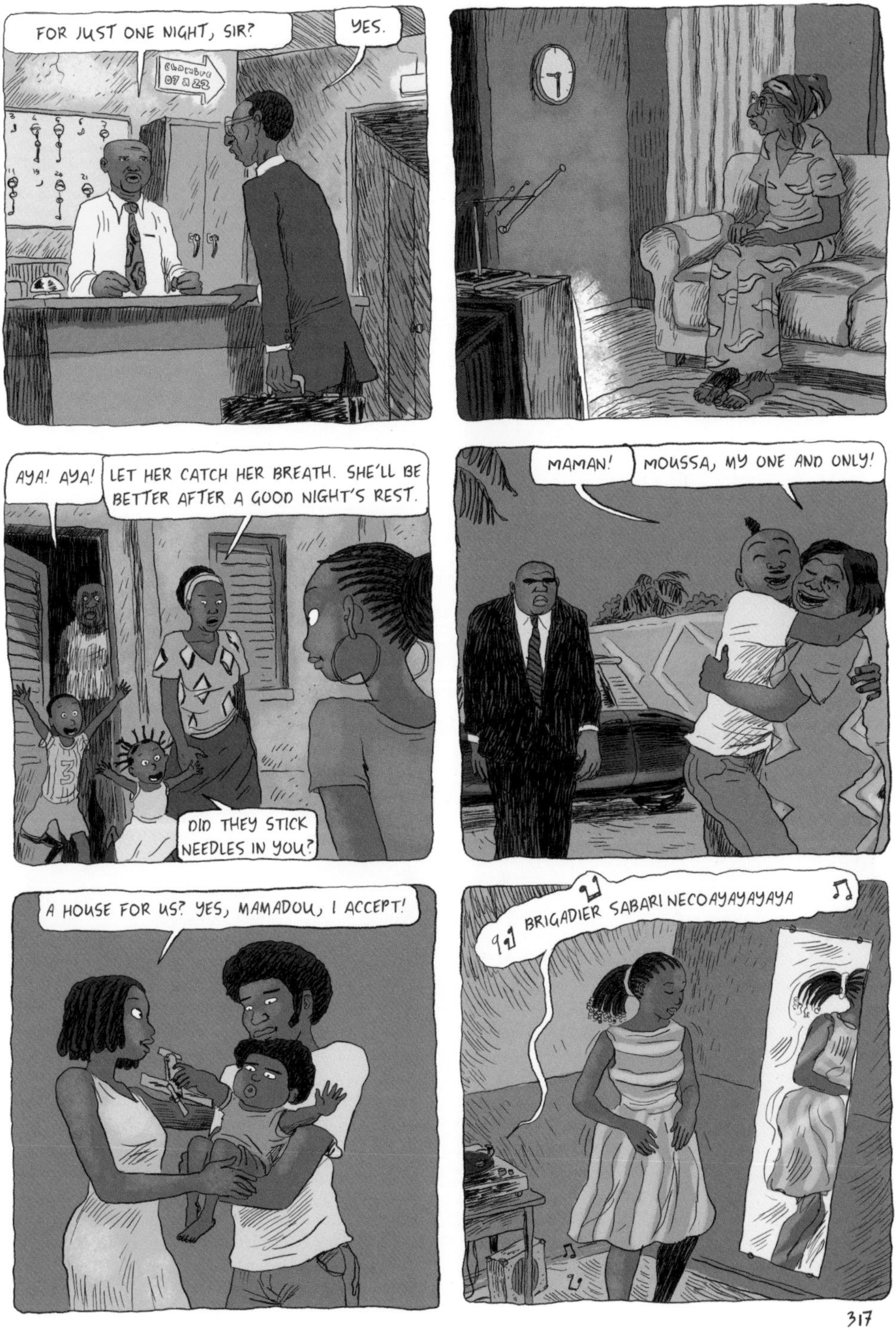
FOR JUST ONE NIGHT, SIR?
YES.
Chambre 07 à 22
AYA! AYA!
LET HER CATCH HER BREATH. SHE'LL BE BETTER AFTER A GOOD NIGHT'S REST.
DID THEY STICK NEEDLES IN YOU?
MAMAN!
MOUSSA, MY ONE AND ONLY!
A HOUSE FOR US? YES, MAMADOU, I ACCEPT!
BRIGADIER SABARI NECOAYAYAYAYA

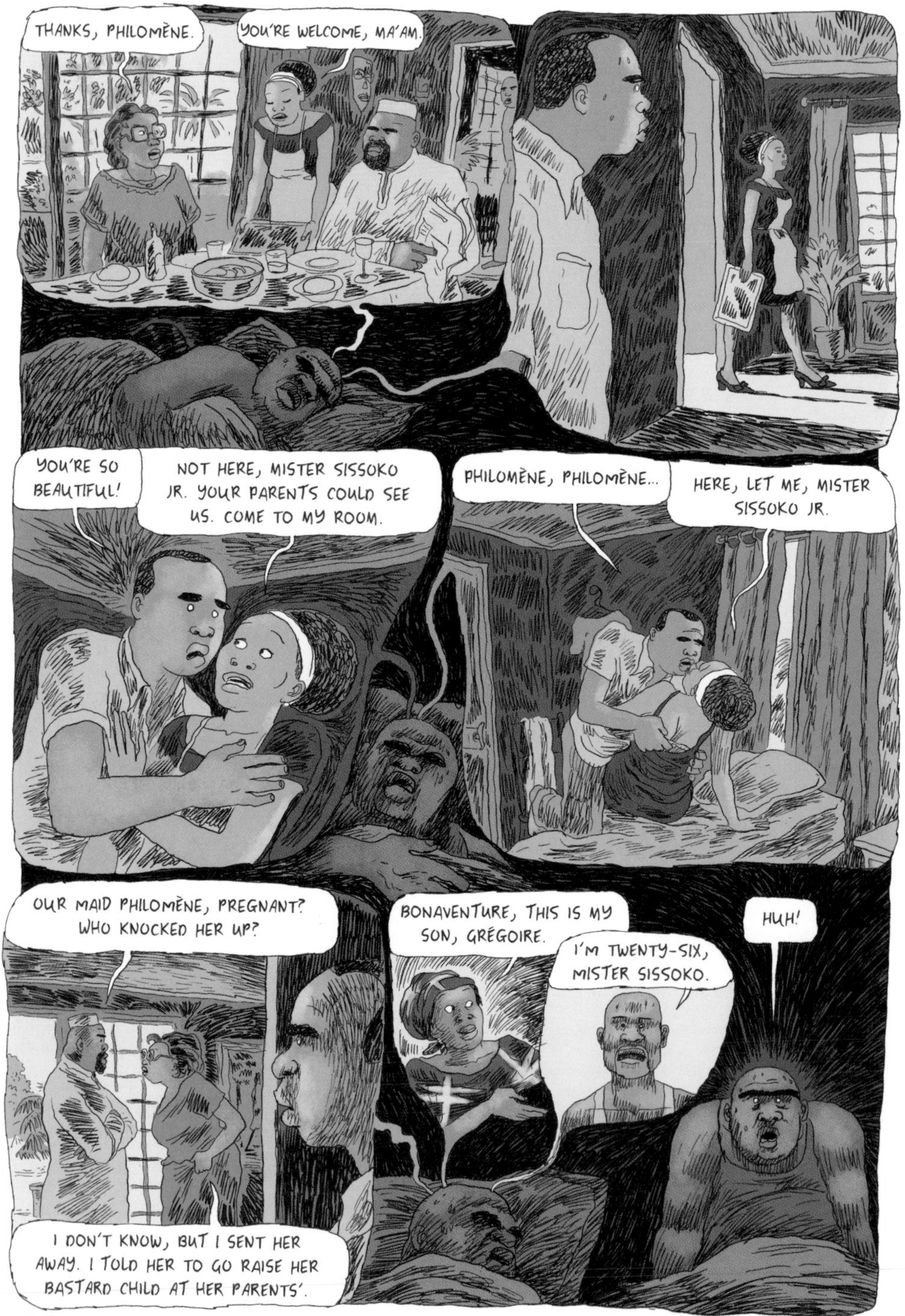
THANKS, PHILOMÈNE.
YOU'RE WELCOME, MA'AM.
YOU'RE SO BEAUTIFUL!
NOT HERE, MISTER SISSOKO JR. YOUR PARENTS COULD SEE US. COME TO MY ROOM.
PHILOMÈNE, PHILOMÈNE...
HERE, LET ME, MISTER SISSOKO JR.
OUR MAID PHILOMÈNE, PREGNANT? WHO KNOCKED HER UP?
I DON'T KNOW, BUT I SENT HER AWAY. I TOLD HER TO GO RAISE HER BASTARD CHILD AT HER PARENTS'.
BONAVENTURE, THIS IS MY SON, GRÉGOIRE.
I'M TWENTY-SIX, MISTER SISSOKO.
HUH!

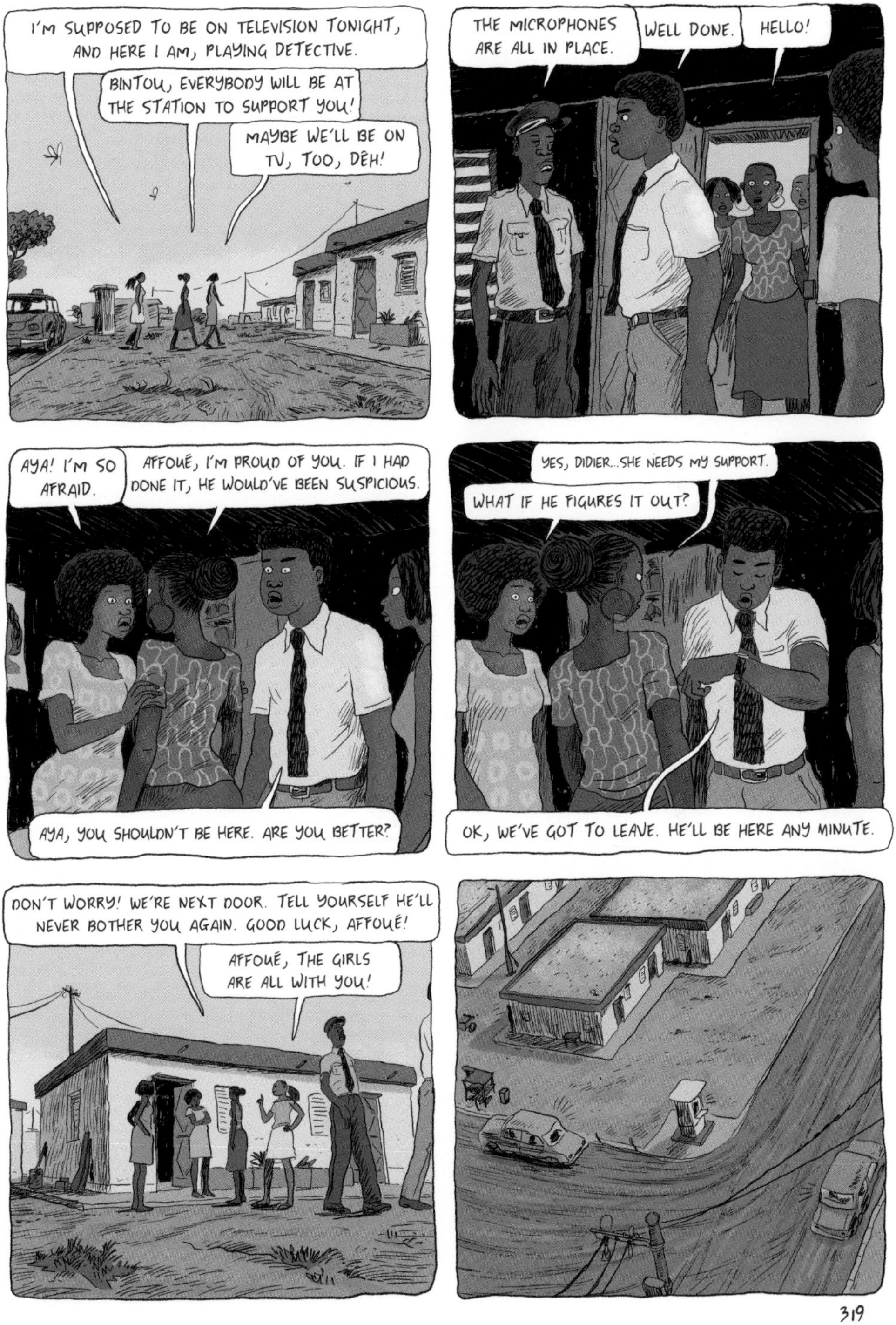
I'M SUPPOSED TO BE ON TELEVISION TONIGHT, AND HERE I AM, PLAYING DETECTIVE.
BINTOU, EVERYBODY WILL BE AT THE STATION TO SUPPORT YOU!
MAYBE WE'LL BE ON TV, TOO, DÊH!
THE MICROPHONES ARE ALL IN PLACE.
WELL DONE.
HELLO!
AYA! I'M SO AFRAID.
AFFOUÉ, I'M PROUD OF YOU. IF I HAD DONE IT, HE WOULD'VE BEEN SUSPICIOUS.
AYA, YOU SHOULDN'T BE HERE. ARE YOU BETTER?
YES, DIDIER...SHE NEEDS MY SUPPORT.
WHAT IF HE FIGURES IT OUT?
OK, WE'VE GOT TO LEAVE. HE'LL BE HERE ANY MINUTE.
DON'T WORRY! WE'RE NEXT DOOR. TELL YOURSELF HE'LL NEVER BOTHER YOU AGAIN. GOOD LUCK, AFFOUÉ!
AFFOUÉ, THE GIRLS ARE ALL WITH YOU!

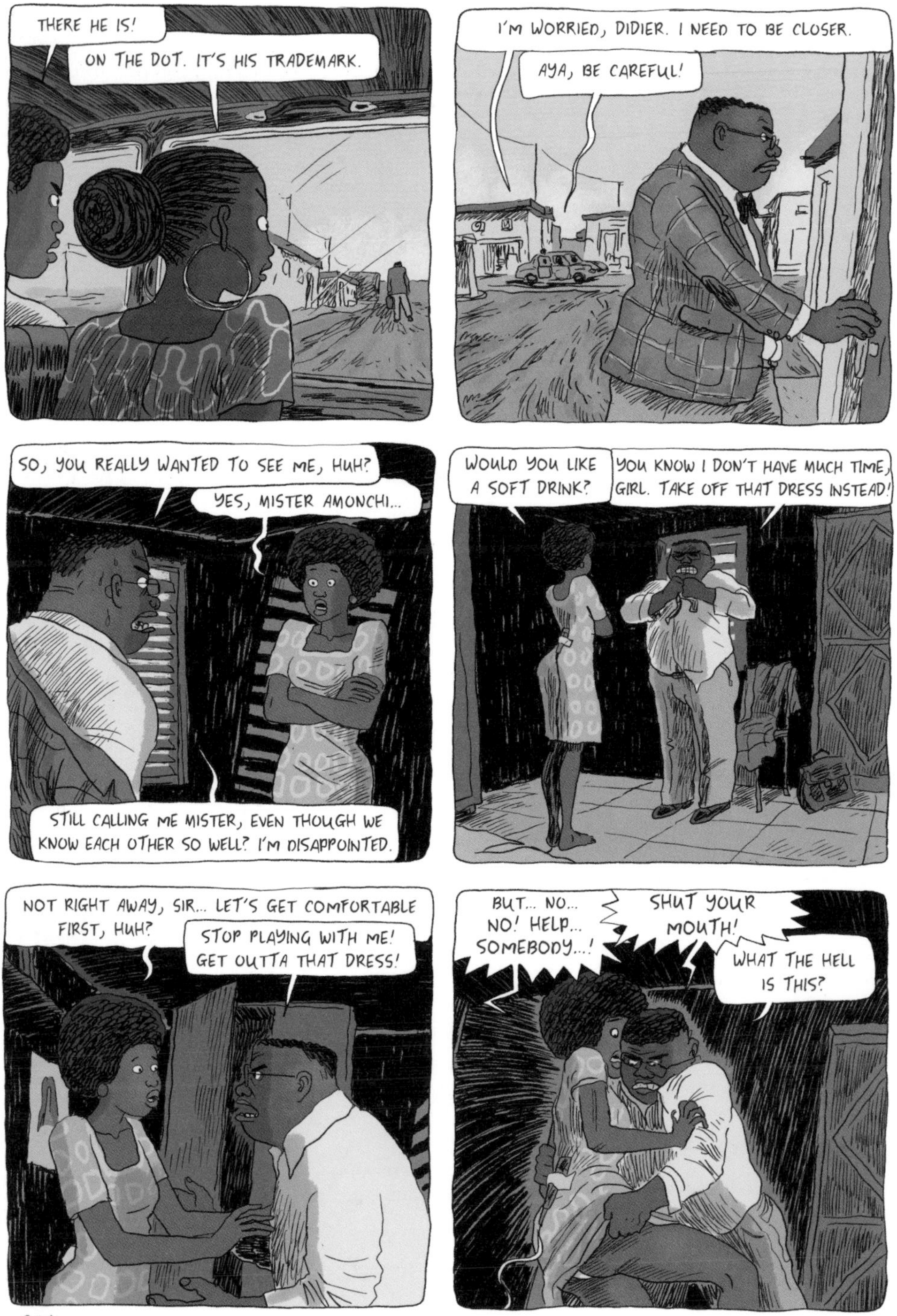
THERE HE IS!
ON THE DOT. IT'S HIS TRADEMARK.
I'M WORRIED, DIDIER. I NEED TO BE CLOSER.
AYA, BE CAREFUL!
SO, YOU REALLY WANTED TO SEE ME, HUH?
YES, MISTER AMONCHI...
STILL CALLING ME MISTER, EVEN THOUGH WE KNOW EACH OTHER SO WELL? I'M DISAPPOINTED.
WOULD YOU LIKE A SOFT DRINK?
YOU KNOW I DON'T HAVE MUCH TIME, GIRL. TAKE OFF THAT DRESS INSTEAD!
NOT RIGHT AWAY, SIR... LET'S GET COMFORTABLE FIRST, HUH?
STOP PLAYING WITH ME! GET OUTTA THAT DRESS!
BUT... NO... NO! HELP... SOMEBODY...!
SHUT YOUR MOUTH!
WHAT THE HELL IS THIS?

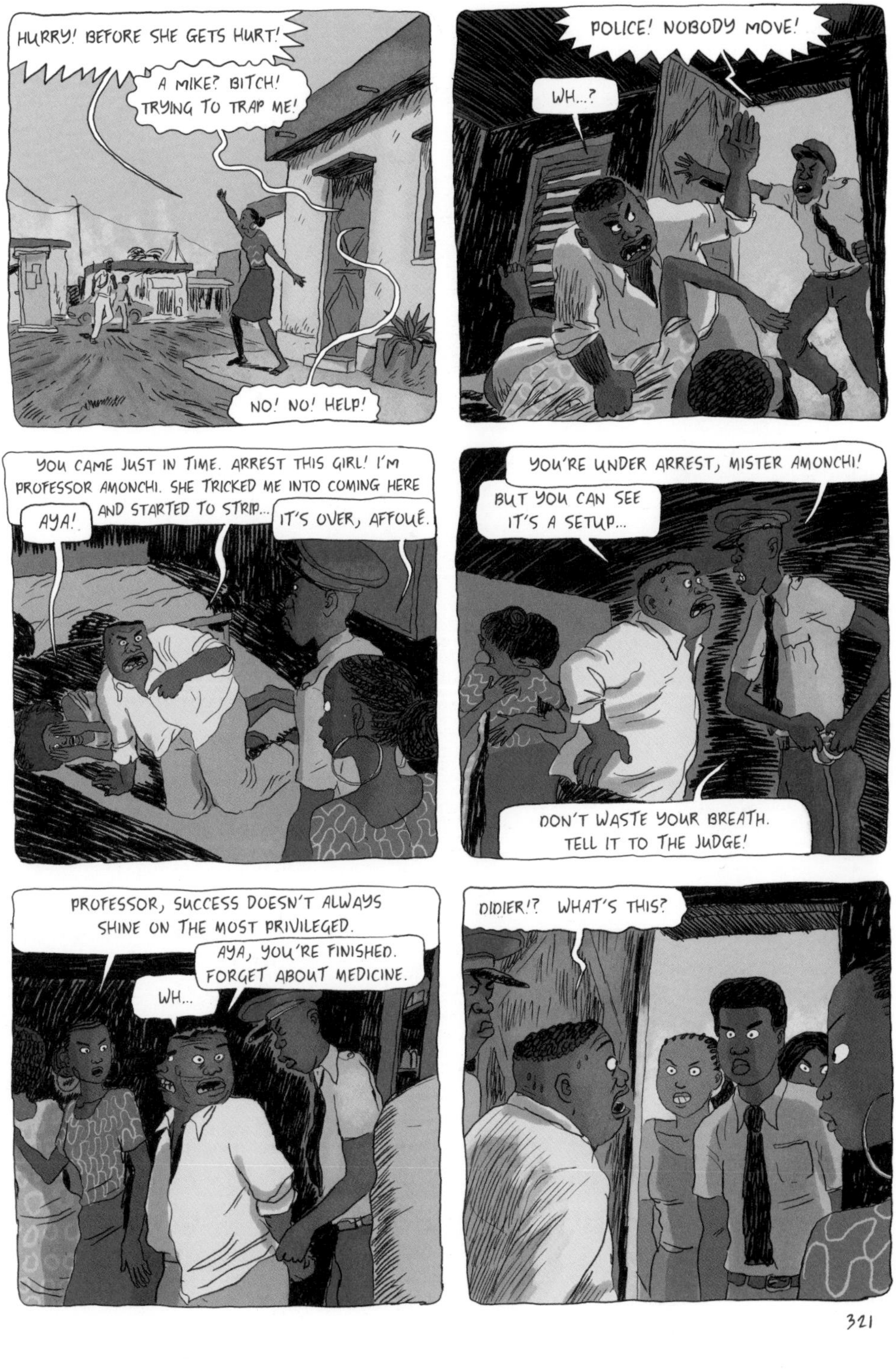
HURRY! BEFORE SHE GETS HURT!
A MIKE? BITCH! TRYING TO TRAP ME!
NO! NO! HELP!
POLICE! NOBODY MOVE!
WH...?
YOU CAME JUST IN TIME. ARREST THIS GIRL! I'M PROFESSOR AMONCHI. SHE TRICKED ME INTO COMING HERE AND STARTED TO STRIP...
AYA!
IT'S OVER, AFFOUÉ.
YOU'RE UNDER ARREST, MISTER AMONCHI!
BUT YOU CAN SEE IT'S A SETUP...
DON'T WASTE YOUR BREATH. TELL IT TO THE JUDGE!
PROFESSOR, SUCCESS DOESN'T ALWAYS SHINE ON THE MOST PRIVILEGED.
AYA, YOU'RE FINISHED. FORGET ABOUT MEDICINE.
WH...
DIDIER!? WHAT'S THIS?

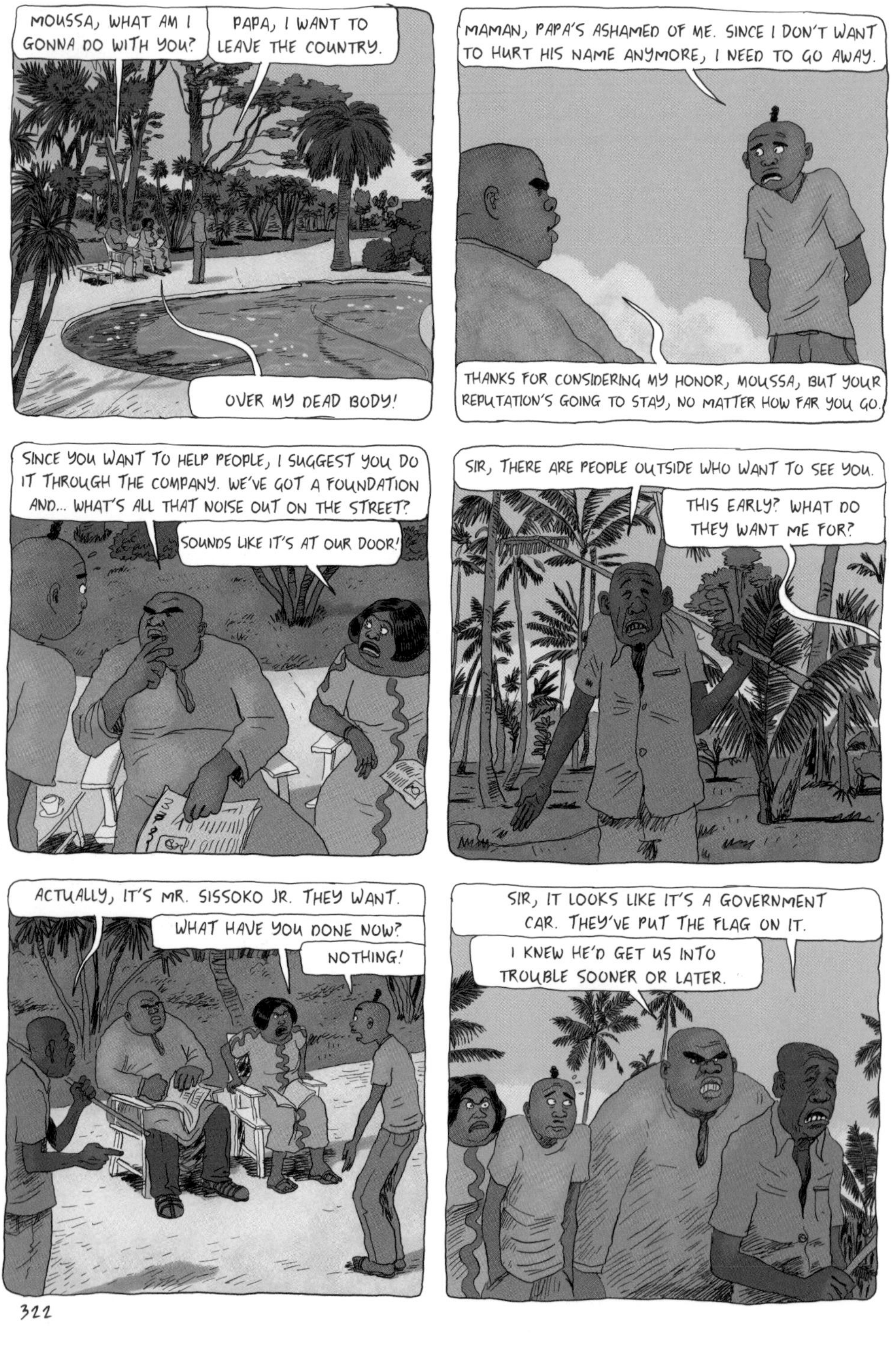
MOUSSA, WHAT AM I GONNA DO WITH YOU?
PAPA, I WANT TO LEAVE THE COUNTRY.
OVER MY DEAD BODY!
MAMAN, PAPA'S ASHAMED OF ME. SINCE I DON'T WANT TO HURT HIS NAME ANYMORE, I NEED TO GO AWAY.
THANKS FOR CONSIDERING MY HONOR, MOUSSA, BUT YOUR REPUTATION'S GOING TO STAY, NO MATTER HOW FAR YOU GO.
SINCE YOU WANT TO HELP PEOPLE, I SUGGEST YOU DO IT THROUGH THE COMPANY. WE'VE GOT A FOUNDATION AND... WHAT'S ALL THAT NOISE OUT ON THE STREET?
SOUNDS LIKE IT'S AT OUR DOOR!
SIR, THERE ARE PEOPLE OUTSIDE WHO WANT TO SEE YOU.
THIS EARLY? WHAT DO THEY WANT ME FOR?
ACTUALLY, IT'S MR. SISSOKO JR. THEY WANT.
WHAT HAVE YOU DONE NOW?
NOTHING!
SIR, IT LOOKS LIKE IT'S A GOVERNMENT CAR. THEY'VE PUT THE FLAG ON IT.
I KNEW HE'D GET US INTO TROUBLE SOONER OR LATER.

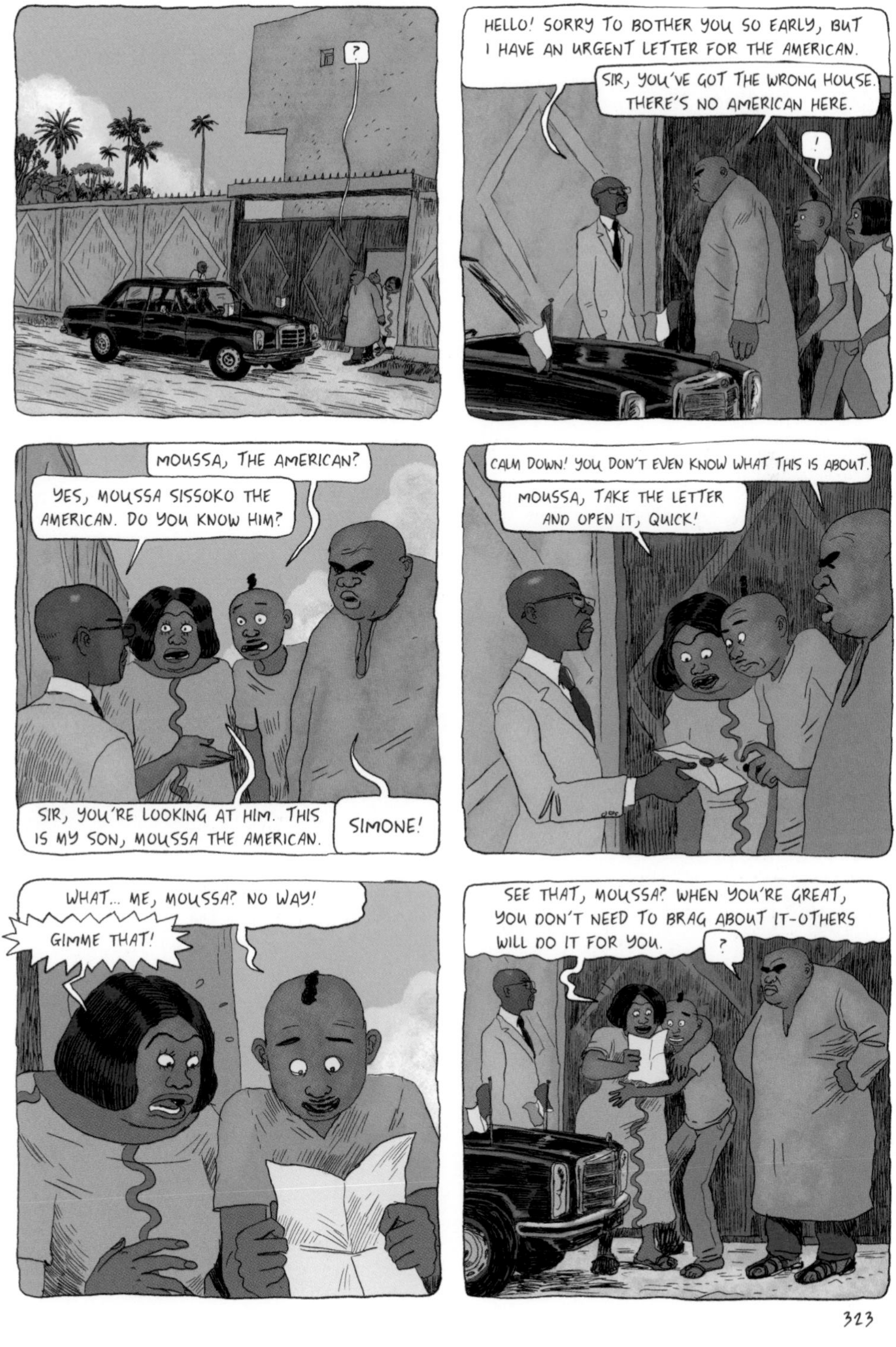
?
HELLO! SORRY TO BOTHER YOU SO EARLY, BUT I HAVE AN URGENT LETTER FOR THE AMERICAN.
SIR, YOU'VE GOT THE WRONG HOUSE. THERE'S NO AMERICAN HERE.
!
MOUSSA, THE AMERICAN?
YES, MOUSSA SISSOKO THE AMERICAN. DO YOU KNOW HIM?
SIR, YOU'RE LOOKING AT HIM. THIS IS MY SON, MOUSSA THE AMERICAN.
SIMONE!
CALM DOWN! YOU DON'T EVEN KNOW WHAT THIS IS ABOUT.
MOUSSA, TAKE THE LETTER AND OPEN IT, QUICK!
WHAT... ME, MOUSSA? NO WAY!
GIMME THAT!
SEE THAT, MOUSSA? WHEN YOU'RE GREAT, YOU DON'T NEED TO BRAG ABOUT IT-OTHERS WILL DO IT FOR YOU.
?

MOTHER-IN-LAW? IT'S ME, JEANNE!
I'M HERE SO WE CAN TALK WOMAN TO WOMAN.
MOTHER-IN-LAW, TODAY'S THE DAY. YOU NEED TO LISTEN TO ME... IF YOU LOVE GERVAIS, YOU HAVE TO LET...
AAARRRRRHHHHH...
MOTHER-IN-LAW!?
AAARRRRRGGGGG
H...HELP...I...I'M DYIIIIING
AAAAAAAAAAAH

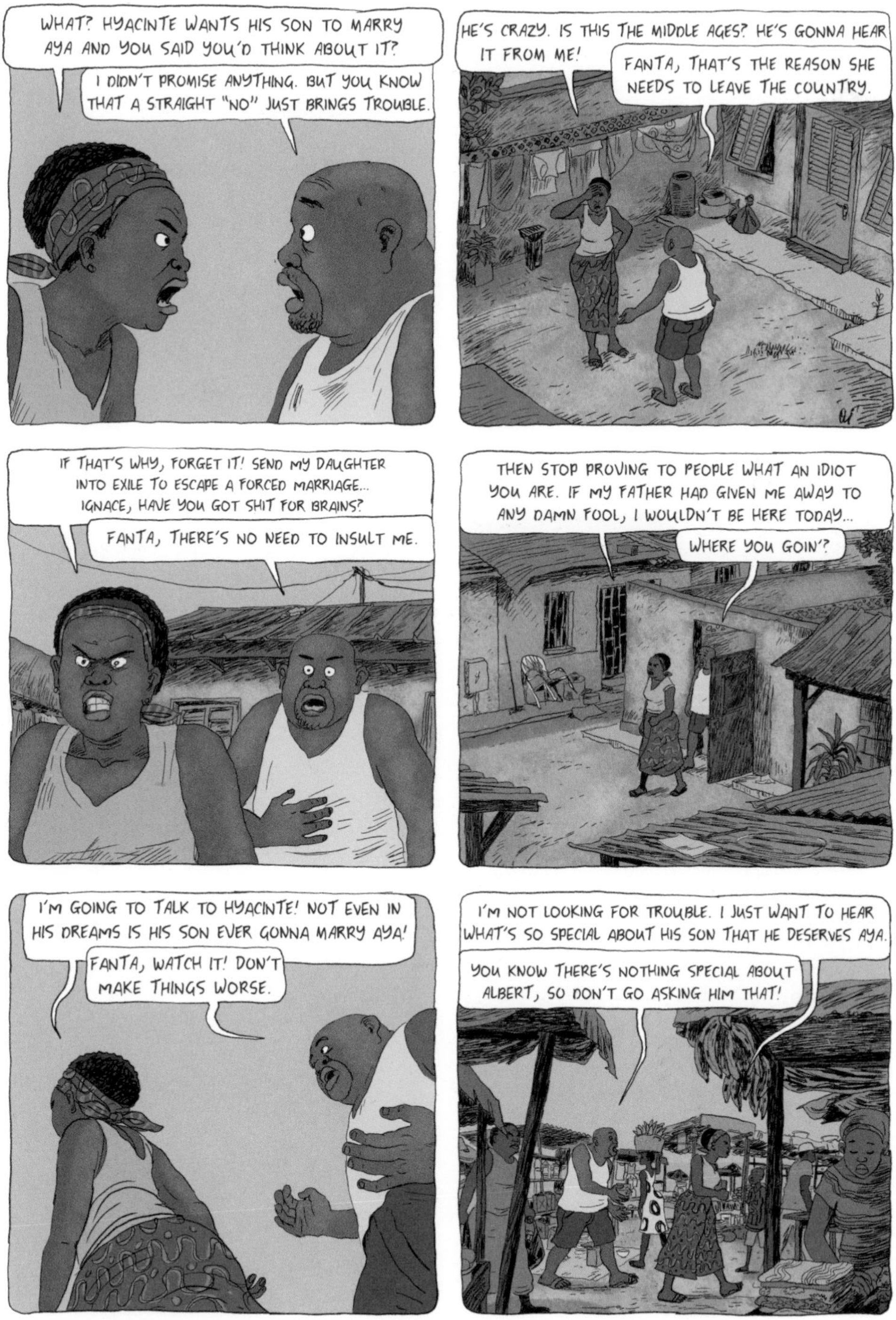
WHAT? HYACINTE WANTS HIS SON TO MARRY AYA AND YOU SAID YOU'D THINK ABOUT IT?
I DIDN'T PROMISE ANYTHING. BUT YOU KNOW THAT A STRAIGHT "NO" JUST BRINGS TROUBLE.
HE'S CRAZY. IS THIS THE MIDDLE AGES? HE'S GONNA HEAR IT FROM ME!
FANTA, THAT'S THE REASON SHE NEEDS TO LEAVE THE COUNTRY.
IF THAT'S WHY, FORGET IT! SEND MY DAUGHTER INTO EXILE TO ESCAPE A FORCED MARRIAGE... IGNACE, HAVE YOU GOT SHIT FOR BRAINS?
FANTA, THERE'S NO NEED TO INSULT ME.
THEN STOP PROVING TO PEOPLE WHAT AN IDIOT YOU ARE. IF MY FATHER HAD GIVEN ME AWAY TO ANY DAMN FOOL, I WOULDN'T BE HERE TODAY...
WHERE YOU GOIN'?
I'M GOING TO TALK TO HYACINTE! NOT EVEN IN HIS DREAMS IS HIS SON EVER GONNA MARRY AYA!
FANTA, WATCH IT! DON'T MAKE THINGS WORSE.
I'M NOT LOOKING FOR TROUBLE. I JUST WANT TO HEAR WHAT'S SO SPECIAL ABOUT HIS SON THAT HE DESERVES AYA.
YOU KNOW THERE'S NOTHING SPECIAL ABOUT ALBERT, SO DON'T GO ASKING HIM THAT!

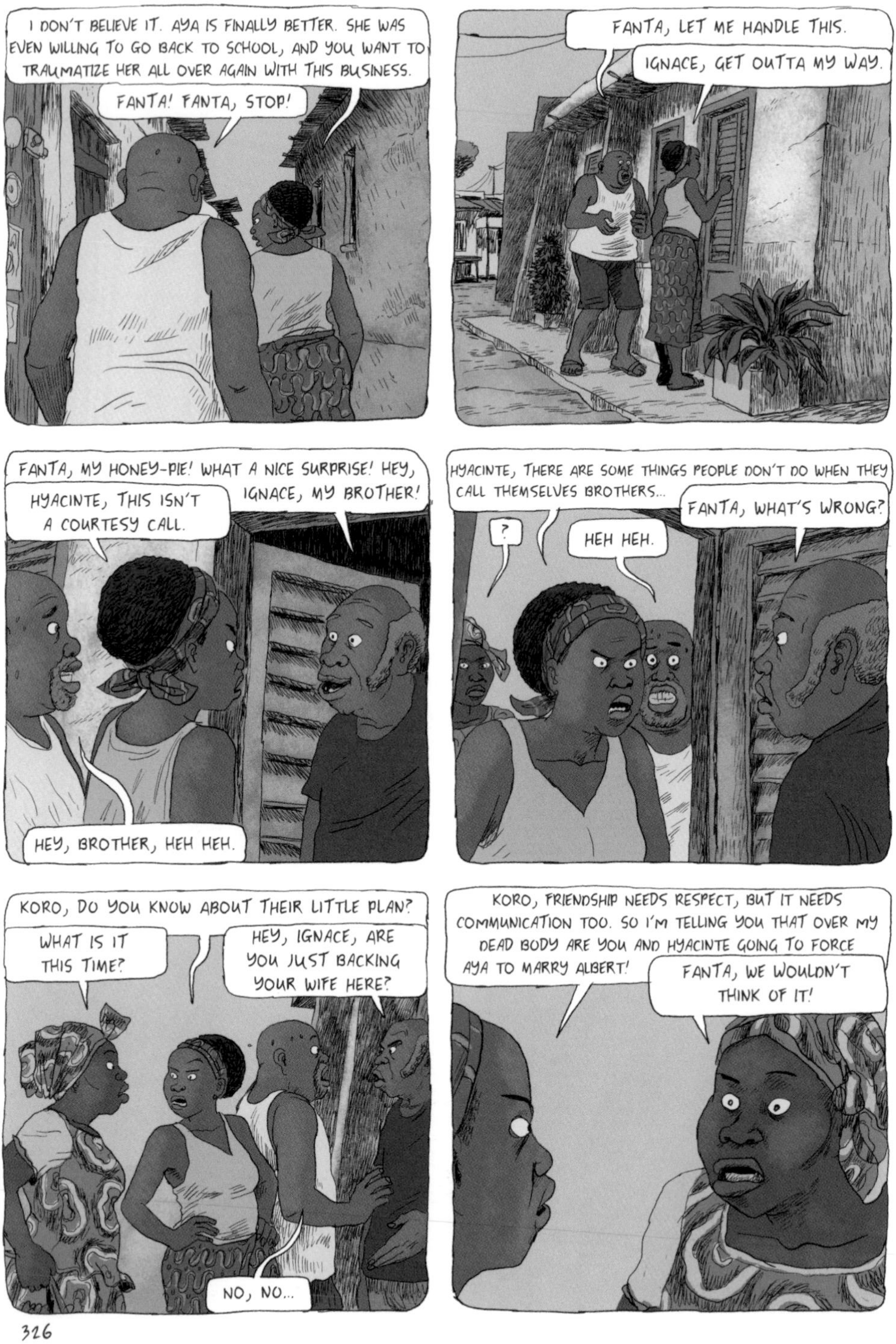
I DON'T BELIEVE IT. AYA IS FINALLY BETTER. SHE WAS EVEN WILLING TO GO BACK TO SCHOOL, AND YOU WANT TO TRAUMATIZE HER ALL OVER AGAIN WITH THIS BUSINESS.
FANTA! FANTA, STOP!
FANTA, LET ME HANDLE THIS.
IGNACE, GET OUTTA MY WAY.
FANTA, MY HONEY-PIE! WHAT A NICE SURPRISE! HEY, IGNACE, MY BROTHER!
HYACINTE, THIS ISN'T A COURTESY CALL.
HEY, BROTHER, HEH HEH.
HYACINTE, THERE ARE SOME THINGS PEOPLE DON'T DO WHEN THEY CALL THEMSELVES BROTHERS...
FANTA, WHAT'S WRONG?
?
HEH HEH.
KORO, DO YOU KNOW ABOUT THEIR LITTLE PLAN?
WHAT IS IT THIS TIME?
HEY, IGNACE, ARE YOU JUST BACKING YOUR WIFE HERE?
NO, NO...
KORO, FRIENDSHIP NEEDS RESPECT, BUT IT NEEDS COMMUNICATION TOO. SO I'M TELLING YOU THAT OVER MY DEAD BODY ARE YOU AND HYACINTE GOING TO FORCE AYA TO MARRY ALBERT!
FANTA, WE WOULDN'T THINK OF IT!

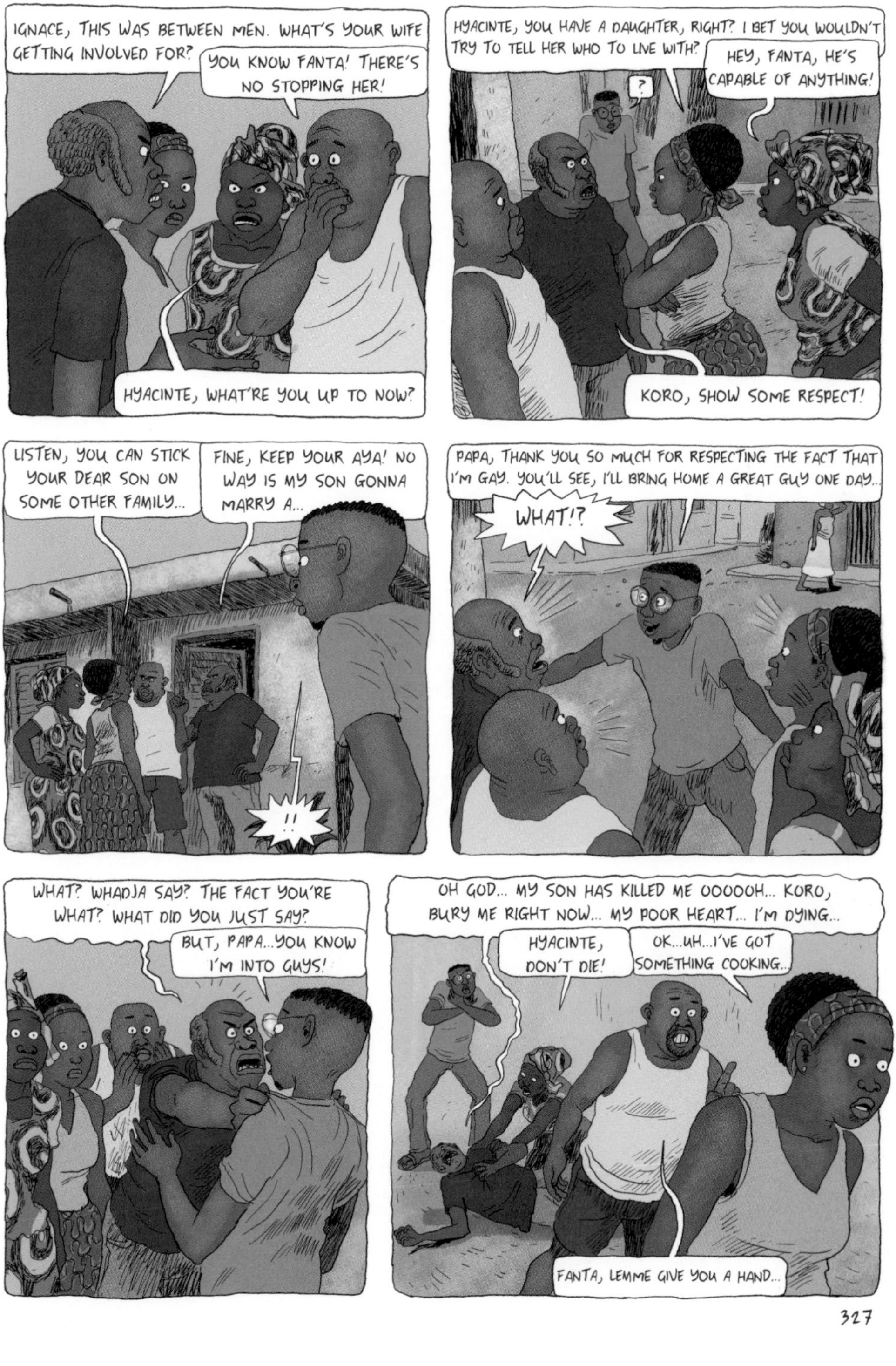
IGNACE, THIS WAS BETWEEN MEN. WHAT'S YOUR WIFE GETTING INVOLVED FOR?
YOU KNOW FANTA! THERE'S NO STOPPING HER!
HYACINTE, WHAT'RE YOU UP TO NOW?
HYACINTE, YOU HAVE A DAUGHTER, RIGHT? I BET YOU WOULDN'T TRY TO TELL HER WHO TO LIVE WITH?
?
HEY, FANTA, HE'S CAPABLE OF ANYTHING!
KORO, SHOW SOME RESPECT!
LISTEN, YOU CAN STICK YOUR DEAR SON ON SOME OTHER FAMILY...
FINE, KEEP YOUR AYA! NO WAY IS MY SON GONNA MARRY A...
!!
PAPA, THANK YOU SO MUCH FOR RESPECTING THE FACT THAT I'M GAY. YOU'LL SEE, I'LL BRING HOME A GREAT GUY ONE DAY...
WHAT!?
WHAT? WHADJA SAY? THE FACT YOU'RE WHAT? WHAT DID YOU JUST SAY?
BUT, PAPA...YOU KNOW I'M INTO GUYS!
OH GOD... MY SON HAS KILLED ME OOOOOH... KORO, BURY ME RIGHT NOW... MY POOR HEART... I'M DYING...
HYACINTE, DON'T DIE!
OK...UH...I'VE GOT SOMETHING COOKING...
FANTA, LEMME GIVE YOU A HAND...

THANKS, MY DEAR, YOU SAVED HER LIFE!
EVERYTHING WILL BE FINE NOW, HONEY.
WHO'S THAT, COMING HERE SO LATE?
MOTHER!?
BOYS, I'M NOT BOTHERING YOU, AM I?
BRIGADIER SABARI NÉCOAYAYAYAYA

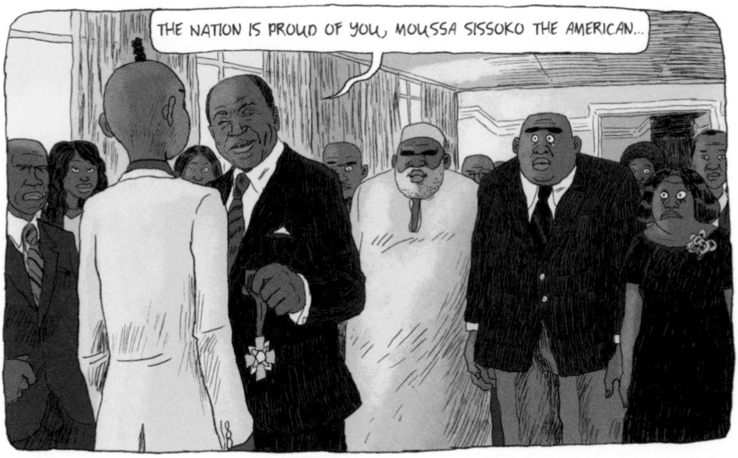
THE NATION IS PROUD OF YOU, MOUSSA SISSOKO THE AMERICAN...

# IVORIAN BONUS

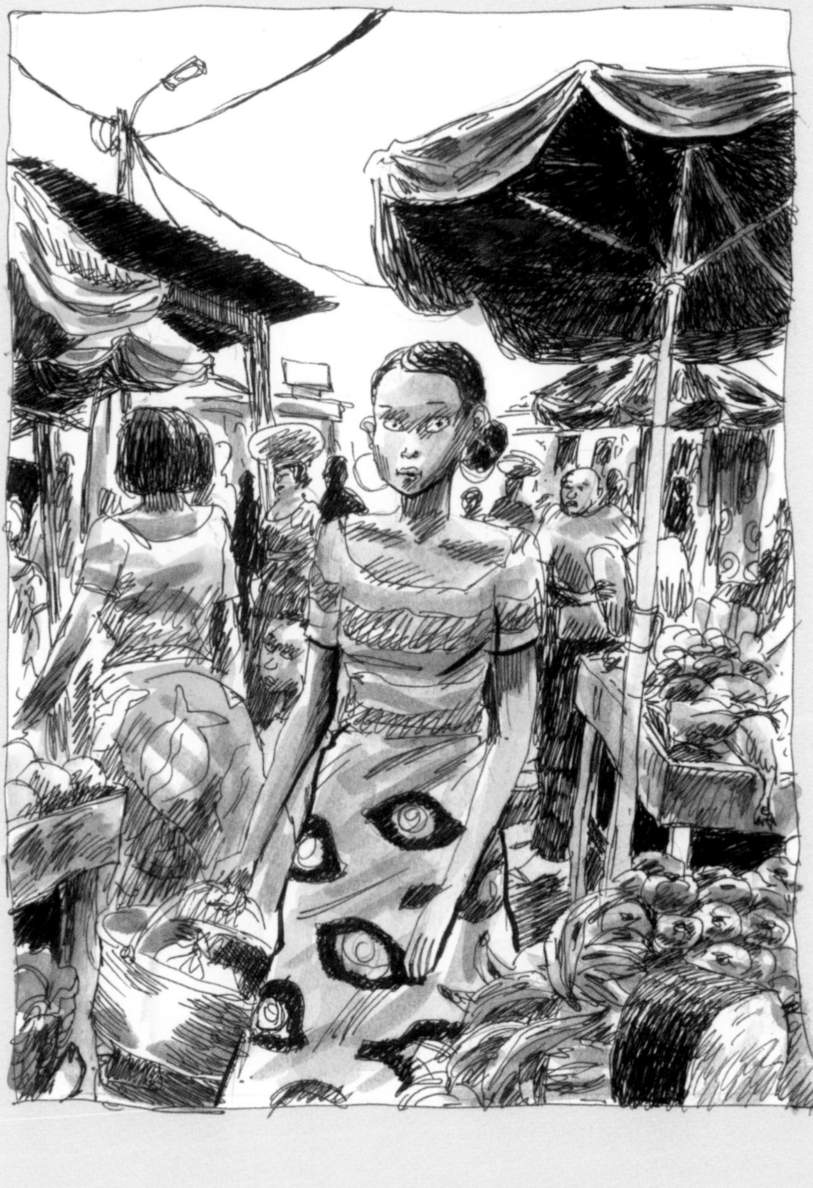

# HERE'S A LITTLE GLOSSARY TO HELP YOU UNDERSTAND THE STORY

**AGOUTI:** RODENT HUNTED FOR ITS SUCCULENT MEAT.

**ALOCO:** TRADITIONAL DISH OF FRIED PLANTAINS SERVED WITH A SPICY TOMATO SAUCE, SOLD AT ROADSIDE RESTAURANTS.

**ATOOUU:** "GIVE ME A HUG."

**ATTIÉKÉ:** CASSAVA COUSCOUS.

**BANGALA:** SLANG FOR THE MALE REPRODUCTIVE ORGAN.

**BENGUISTES:** YOUNG IVORIAN IMMIGRANTS LIVING IN PARIS.

**BOBARABA:** BIG BEHIND.

**CHOCO:** ELEGANT, STYLISH.

**DÊH!:** AN EXCLAMATION THAT INTENSIFIES MEANING. "SHE'S BEAUTIFUL, DÊH!" ("SHE IS SOOO BEAUTIFUL!")

**DJA:** TO KILL.

**DJANDJOU:** PROSTITUTE.

**FLÉKÉ FLÉKÉ:** SCRAWNY WEAKLING.

**FOYER:** IN FRANCE, PUBLICLY FUNDED DORMITORY-STYLE HOUSING INTENDED TO PROVIDE TEMPORARY ACCOMMODATIONS FOR MALE IMMIGRANT WORKERS. IN FACT, RESIDENTS OFTEN LIVE IN FOYERS FOR MANY YEARS, AND IN SOME INSTANCES, WOMEN MAY LIVE IN THEM ILLEGALLY AS WELL.

**GAOU:** IDIOT.

**GARBA:** DISH OF CASSAVA COUSCOUS SERVED WITH FRIED TUNA AND PEPPERS, SOLD BY STREET VENDORS.

**GLÔGLÔ:** PARTY.

**GNANHI:** OLDER WOMAN WHO PREYS ON YOUNG MEN.

**GO:** GIRL OR GIRLFRIEND.

**IJIOH!:** "OOH LA LA!"

**KOUTOUKOU:** ALCOHOLIC BEVERAGE DISTILLED FROM PALM WINE.

**KPAKPATO:** CURIOUS, NOSY.

**KPATA:** BEAUTIFUL.

**MAGGI CUBE:** BRAND OF BOUILLON CUBE COMMONLY USED IN IVORIAN COOKING.

**MAMAN:** MOM.

**MAMIE**: GRANDMA.

**MAQUIS**: OPEN-AIR RESTAURANT WHERE LOCALS GET TOGETHER TO EAT, DRINK, AND RELAX WITH FRIENDS.

**PALU**: MALARIA. ALSO USED TO DESCRIBE A GENERAL FEELING OF FATIGUE OR UNWELLNESS.

**PLOCO-PLACA**: SEX.

**POPOPO**: INTERJECTION EXPRESSING SHOCK OR INDIGNATION. "I CAN'T BELIEVE IT!" "INCREDIBLE!"

**SAFROULAÏ**: "YOU'RE KIDDING!" "NO WAY!"

**SHAWARMADROME**: SHOP WHERE SHAWARMAS ARE SOLD. A SHAWARMA IS A SANDWICH MADE OF THIN SLICES OF GRILLED MEAT AND VEGETABLES, SERVED IN A PITA WRAP.

**SOUKOUYA**: POPULAR SNACK OF SPICY GRILLED MEAT.

**TANTIE**: AUNTIE, ALSO USED AS AN EXPRESSION OF FRIENDLY RESPECT TOWARD AN OLDER WOMAN.

**TCHOKO-TCHOKO**: "...WHETHER YOU LIKE IT OR NOT."

**TIÉ TIÉ TIÉ**: INTERJECTION USED TO EXPRESS SURPRISE.

**TONTON**: UNCLE, ALSO USED AS AN EXPRESSION OF FRIENDLY RESPECT TOWARD AN OLDER MAN.

**TOUBAB**: WHITE PERSON.

**WALAÏ**: "GOOD LORD!"

**WALO**: SLAP.

**WOMEN OF SAND**: POPULAR LATIN AMERICAN SOAP OPERA BROADCAST ON IVORIAN TELEVISION.

**YACÒ**: INTERJECTION USED TO CONVEY HEARTFELT SYMPATHY. "I'M SO SORRY."

# VISA

## AFTERWORD BY MARGUERITE ABOUET

I THINK A LITTLE EXPLANATION IS IN ORDER FOR YOU LOYAL AND FABULOUS READERS WHO ARE WONDERING: "BUT HOW WAS INNOCENT ABLE TO GET A VISA FOR FRANCE SO QUICKLY?" IT WAS EASY. BACK IN THOSE DAYS, IVORIANS DIDN'T NEED A VISA TO ENTER FRANCE. VISAS ONLY BECAME MANDATORY IN 1984. AND THEN, IN 1986, FRANCE INTRODUCED THE PASQUA LAWS, WHICH MADE IT ALMOST IMPOSSIBLE FOR FOREIGNERS TO OBTAIN TEMPORARY RESIDENCY PAPERS AND WORK PERMITS.

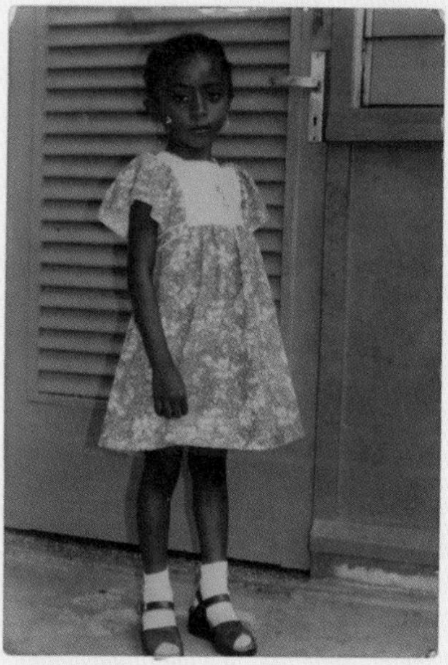

SO, AS YOU CAN SEE, IT WAS "TRUE LOVE" FOR FRANCE AND IVORY COAST AT FIRST.

WHAT HAPPENED? WHY THE DIVORCE? FRIENDS, DON'T GO ASKING ME QUESTIONS THAT I DON'T HAVE ANSWERS TO.

THE STRANGE THING IS, DESPITE THE OPEN DOOR POLICY, IVORIANS WEREN'T FALLING OVER EACH OTHER TO COME TO FRANCE.

WHY NOT, YOU ASK?

FIRST OF ALL, THINGS WERE EASIER IN IVORY COAST BACK THEN. IVORIANS DIDN'T NEED TO GO TO FRANCE OR ELSEWHERE TO MAKE A BETTER LIFE FOR THEMSELVES.

SECOND, EMIGRATION TO FRANCE WAS GENERALLY ONLY AN OPTION FOR THE SONS AND DAUGHTERS OF PRESIDENTS, MINISTERS, DIPLOMATS, THE WEALTHY, AND SO ON. OTHER IVORIANS COULD GO TO FRANCE AS WELL, BUT THEY HAD TO KNOW AT LEAST ONE PERSON ALREADY LIVING THERE WITH WHOM THEY COULD STAY, AND THAT WASN'T ALWAYS EASY.

THIRD, AND THIS IS THE REASON THAT MAKES THE MOST SENSE TO ME: THEY WERE SIMPLY AFRAID OF THE COLD. THEY DIDN'T WANT TO RISK GOING BECAUSE THEY WERE SCARED THEY MIGHT END UP FREEZING IN THE STREETS.

I KNOW I'M REPEATING MYSELF, DEAR READERS, BUT IT'S AN IMPORTANT POINT, BECAUSE THE WORST THING THAT CAN HAPPEN TO AN IVORIAN (AND A NON-IVORIAN, TOO) IS TO HAVE TO SLEEP OUTSIDE IN THE BITTER COLD IN PARIS.

WHICH IS WHAT ALMOST HAPPENED TO INNOCENT.

TODAY, I'M PROUD TO SAY THAT I'M ONE OF THE VERY FEW IVORIANS WHO WENT TO FRANCE WITHOUT A VISA (I'VE GOT THE PASSPORT TO PROVE IT). BUT I'M ALSO ONE OF

THOSE WHO NEVER ASKED TO GO TO FRANCE.

WHEN I FOUND OUT I WAS BEING SENT TO PARIS, I CRIED UNTIL MY TEARS RAN DRY.
AND WITH GOOD REASON. PEOPLE SAID IT WAS SO COLD IN FRANCE THAT YOUR PEE WOULD
FREEZE BEFORE IT HIT THE TOILET, AND YOU WOULD HAVE TO SNAP IT OFF. THEY SAID
THE COLD COULD FREEZE YOUR EARS AND BREAK THEM, AND YOUR FINGERS AND TOES,
TOO. YOU HAD TO BE CRAZY TO GO LIVE THERE. IN FACT, RICH IVORIANS WERE SUSPECTED
OF SENDING THEIR KIDS TO FRANCE TO GET RID OF THEM FOR GOOD.

I FINALLY GOT USED TO THE IDEA (I DIDN'T REALLY HAVE A CHOICE) AND CHEERED MYSELF
UP WITH THE THOUGHT THAT I MIGHT AT LEAST MEET THE MAN OF MY DREAMS: RAHAN,
THE BEAUTIFUL, INTELLIGENT CAVEMAN HERO OF MY FAVORITE COMIC. I THOUGHT ALL MEN
IN FRANCE HAD LONG BLOND HAIR, WORE LITTLE FUR SKIRTS, AND CARRIED A CUTLASS.
AS YOU CAN IMAGINE, I WAS PRETTY DISAPPOINTED WHEN I ARRIVED IN FRANCE (WITHOUT
A VISA, LIKE I'VE EXPLAINED). THE WHITE MEN ALL WORE CLOTHES AND NONE OF THEM
LOOKED LIKE RAHAN.

IT WASN'T COLD, THOUGH. I ARRIVED ON THE THIRTIETH OF AUGUST, IN 1983.

WHEN I WAS A KID, I LOVED GOING TO CHURCH.

I'M NOT SAYING I LIKED THE TERRIBLE SUNDAY PREPARATIONS. I HAD TO WAKE UP EARLY, GET MY HAIR BRAIDED SO TIGHT IT HURT MY SCALP, PUT ON MY PRETTY LONG WHITE "NELLIE OLESON" DRESS THAT BETTER NOT GET DIRTY, AND SQUEEZE MY POOR LITTLE FEET INTO SHINY NEW SHOES I COULDN'T RUN IN. I KNOW WHAT YOU'RE THINKING: SO HOW COULD I LOVE CHURCH WITH ALL THAT? IT'S BECAUSE OUR CHURCH—THE ONLY ONE IN THE NEIGHBORHOOD BACK THEN—WAS NOTHING LIKE THE REST. THE TEMPLE (WE WERE PROTESTANT, AND THAT'S WHAT WE CALLED OUR CHURCHES) WAS TOO SMALL TO FIT ALL THE FAITHFUL, LET ALONE THEIR KIDS. WE COULDN'T SIT THROUGH TWO HOURS OF PREACHING ANYWAY. HAPPY AND EXCITED, I'D MEET UP WITH ALL MY FRIENDS, MOST OF WHOM HAD SUFFERED THE SAME BRAIDING TORTURE AS ME. WE'D STAY IN THE CHURCHYARD, BECAUSE THERE'S A VERSE IN THE BIBLE WHERE GOD SAYS: "LET THE CHILDREN COME TO ME AND DO NOT FORBID THEM." AND PLAYING IS HOW WE PRAISED GOD.

LUCKILY THE SOUND OF OUR VOICES WAS DROWNED OUT BY ALL THE SINGING OUR BEAUTIFUL CHURCH WAS KNOWN FOR.

FROM TIME TO TIME, LIKE THE LITTLE CHERUBS WE WERE, WE'D SLIP INTO THE CHURCH TO BEG OUR PARENTS FOR CHANGE TO BUY ICE CREAM AND CANDY. THE ANSWER ALWAYS CAME QUICKLY SO OUR CRYING WOULDN'T DISRUPT THE MASS. BECAUSE THERE'S ANOTHER BIBLICAL VERSE THAT SAYS: "THOSE WHO LET THE CHILDREN CRY WON'T GET INTO THE KINGDOM OF HEAVEN"...YES, THAT'S RIGHT...WE'D GOBBLE UP OUR SWEETS, AND AFTER THE SERVICE OUR PARENTS WOULD HAVE US SHAKE THE PASTOR'S HAND WITH OUR STICKY FINGERS SO WE COULD BENEFIT FROM HIS WISE WORDS AND BLESSINGS UNTIL THE FOLLOWING SUNDAY.

FOR A FEW MINUTES, WE'D LISTEN WITH BOWED HEADS AS OUR MOTHERS COMPLAINED ABOUT OUR BEHAVIOR, WHICH HAD USUALLY BEEN BAD, AND ABOUT THEIR MARITAL, MONEY, AND HEALTH PROBLEMS.

OUR PASTOR WOULD LISTEN PATIENTLY AND COMFORT, REASSURE, AND ENCOURAGE THEM. HE ALWAYS HAD A KIND WORD FOR EACH OF US KIDS, AND WHEN THE MOTHERS NEEDED A SHOULDER TO CRY ON, HE WAS THERE FOR THEM. BUT HE NEVER, NOT UNDER ANY CIRCUMSTANCES, PRETENDED THAT HE COULD HEAL THEIR MEDICAL PROBLEMS.

BY WAY OF THANKS, THE MOTHERS BROUGHT HIM DELICIOUS HOME-COOKED MEALS OR SPECIAL TREATS LIKE ATTIÉKÉ, PLANTAINS, AGOUTIS, AND SNAILS.

THIS WONDERFUL EXPRESSION OF CHURCH LIFE IS BECOMING INCREASINGLY RARE IN IVORY COAST AND THE REST OF AFRICA. THAT'S BECAUSE JESUS, MARY, GOD, AND THE

SAINTS HAVE BEEN TURNED INTO COMMODITIES, AND THEY SELL VERY WELL.

NEW CHURCHES AND BIBLE SCHOOLS POP UP LIKE MUSHROOMS EVERY DAY, AND EXPENSIVE BUT "ESSENTIAL" SEMINARS ARE ORGANIZED TO PROVIDE TRAINING FOR HUNDREDS OF SWINDLERS—SORRY, I MEAN "FUTURE MEN OF THE CLOTH."

WHETHER THEY'RE YOUNG OR OLD, RICH OR POOR, ILLITERATE OR EDUCATED, THEY HAVE THE HABIT, WHEN TALKING, OF THROWING IN A "GOD WILLING," "BY THE GRACE OF GOD," OR "IN THE NAME OF GOD." AND MANY CAN'T WALK PAST A NEW CHURCH WITHOUT STEPPING THROUGH ITS DOORS. ONCE THEY DO, THESE CHURCHES, MOST OF WHICH START OUT AS SIMPLE MONEY-MAKING SCAMS, BECOME ACTUAL PLACES OF REFUGE FOR PEOPLE SUFFERING REAL HARDSHIP AND HOPING FOR A BETTER LIFE.

PLENTY OF CROOKS SEE THE POTENTIAL AND MAKE SMALL FORTUNES IN THIS BURGEONING MARKET. YOU CAN RECOGNIZE THEM BY THEIR FLASHY SUITS AND TIES. OF COURSE, THEY'VE ALL HAD VISIONS AND RECEIVED A SPECIAL MISSION FROM GOD. FROM ONE DAY TO THE NEXT, THEY CALL THEMSELVES PASTORS, PROPHETS, PREACHERS, REVERENDS, APOSTLES, SHEPHERDS, OR WHATEVER. THEY OFTEN PREACH THE GOSPEL OF PROSPERITY. THEY PROMISE EASY MONEY AND MIRACULOUS CURES. BUT SINCE NOTHING COMES FROM NOTHING, BELIEVERS NEED TO SOW IN ORDER TO REAP. IN OTHER WORDS, THEY NEED TO GIVE UP THEIR LIFE SAVINGS IF THEY ARE TO HAVE ANY HOPE OF SALVATION. CASH GIFTS AND DONATIONS IN KIND ARE COMPULSORY. EVERYBODY OFFERS MONEY TO THE PREACHER AND EVERYTHING IS A PRETEXT FOR PRAYER: PRAYERS IN MEMORY OF THE DEAD, PRAYERS FOR THE ILL, PRAYERS FOR A VISA, PRAYERS TO GET EVEN WITH THE WOMAN NEXT DOOR. THE PREACHERS DRIVE AROUND IN FANCY CARS, TO THE DELIGHT OF THE FOLLOWERS WHO PAY FOR SUCH LUXURIES.

THIS MAFIA IS SOMETIMES SUPPORTED BY LOCAL AUTHORITIES, ESPECIALLY WHEN THE PREACHERS ALSO OPERATE RADIO OR TELEVISION STATIONS THAT PACIFY THE PUBLIC BY BROADCASTING RELIGIOUS PROPAGANDA ALL DAY LONG. ALL THIS RELIGIOUS FERVOR WOULD MAKE FOR A GOOD LAUGH—AND IVORIANS ARE GREAT AT SEEING THE

FUNNY SIDE OF THINGS—EXCEPT THAT THESE CON ARTISTS PROMOTE THEMSELVES AS "HEALERS," DRAWING PEOPLE AWAY FROM REAL PHYSICIANS BY CLAIMING TO HEAL INCURABLE ILLNESSES. AND YOU BETTER LOOK OUT, BECAUSE THE CHURCH VIRUS ISN'T LIMITED TO AFRICA. IT TRAVELS BY PLANE AND BOAT TO SEEK OUT AFRICAN COMMUNITIES ABROAD, NO MATTER WHERE THEY ARE. THE PREACHERS ARE THE SAME GLITZY SHOWMEN WHEREVER THEY GO, BUT THEIR PREACHING IS ADAPTED TO LOCAL REALITIES LIKE THE STRUGGLE TO OBTAIN IMMIGRATION DOCUMENTS AND WORK PERMITS, THE HOPE FOR PROSPERITY, AND THE NEED FOR MORAL SUPPORT. THEY'RE SKILLED AT USING ALL-OUT PR CAMPAIGNS, POSTERS, SEMINARS, AND CONVENTIONS, AS WELL AS VIGILS AND NIGHTS OF FASTING AND PRAYER, TO RECRUIT NEW MEMBERS. NEEDLESS TO SAY, THEY OFFER DIVINE HEALING, TOO.

HEY, MARGUERITE! YOU SURE AREN'T AFRAID OF TROUBLE, DÊH! THE CHURCHES ARE A TABOO SUBJECT HERE BECAUSE EVERYBODY'S IN ON THE ACTION, AND YOU GO AND WRITE A THESIS ABOUT THEM.

WELL, SINCE YOU'RE AT IT, HERE'S A STORY FOR YOU:

LAST WEEK, OUR NEIGHBOR SERI WENT LOOKING FOR HIS PIECE OF THE PIE, Ô! SERI WAS WORKING FOR A BIG COMPANY IN DOWNTOWN ABIDJAN WHEN HE GOT SACKED ONE DAY, JUST LIKE THAT. POOR SERI! HOW WAS HE GOING TO FEED HIS TWO WIVES, TWO MISTRESSES, AND ALL HIS KIDS? I DON'T KNOW IF HE HAD A VISION OF JESUS IN HIS SLEEP OR WHAT, BUT ONE MORNING, SERI EMPTIED OUT HIS LIVING ROOM AND TURNED IT INTO A CHURCH, WITH HIS WIVES AND MISTRESSES AS PROMOTERS OF THE GOSPEL AND HIS MANY KIDS MAKING UP THE CHOIR, BECAUSE SERI HAD DECIDED TO BRING GLORY TO GOD AND BECOME A PREACHER.

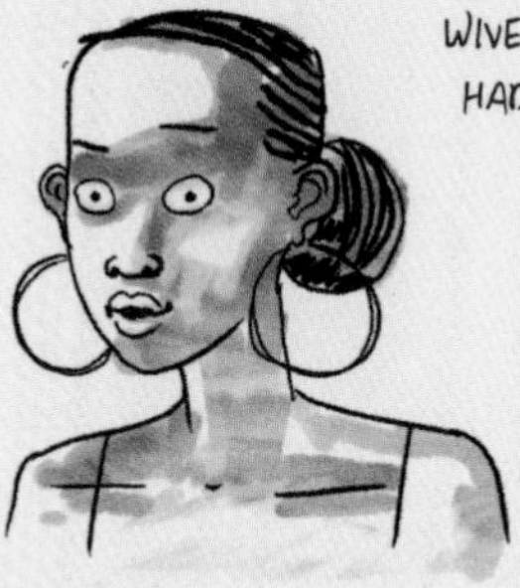

I JUST HOPE THE GOOD LORD HAS PITY ON THOSE OF US WHO LIVE NEXT DOOR TO SERI, BECAUSE WE HAVEN'T BEEN ABLE TO SLEEP PROPERLY EVER SINCE.

DAY AND NIGHT, SERI PREACHES ALL KINDS OF FOOLISHNESS, ALWAYS AT THE TOP OF HIS LUNGS. THE REAL MIRACLE IS THAT HE'S GOT PLENTY OF FOLLOWERS WHO COME TO SING, SHOUT, AND PRAISE THE LORD.

YOU SHOULD SEE HIM STRUT AROUND THE NEIGHBORHOOD, SHAMELESS AS ANYTHING, PREACHING THE WORD OF GOD, LOOKING FOR NEW YOUNG MISTRESSES, AND SWINDLING THE POOR WITH PROMISES OF A BETTER LIFE.

FRIENDS, THAT'S NOTHING. THERE'S THIS BEAUTIFUL GIRL WHO CAME TO ME FOR ADVICE. SHE'S GOT A MASTER'S DEGREE IN SOMETHING OR OTHER. ONE DAY, DURING A JOB INTERVIEW, THE CEO OF A BIG FRENCH COMPANY GETS CHARMED BY HER LOOKS AND HER STYLE. HE'S A WHITE GUY, Ô, AND SHE FIGURES SHE'S FOUND THE MAN OF HER LIFE. THEY EXCHANGE PHONE NUMBERS AND A FEW DAYS LATER HE INVITES HER OUT TO A

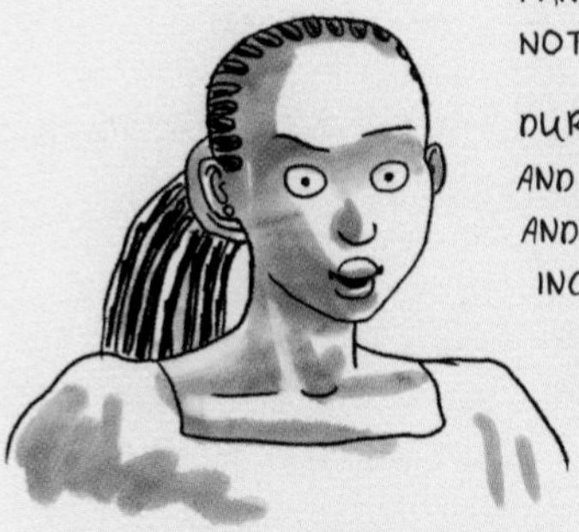

FANCY RESTAURANT—AND I'M TALKING A REAL RESTAURANT, NOT A MAQUIS. THAT'S HOW CLASSY THIS GUY IS.

DURING SUPPER, THEY CHAT, GET TO KNOW EACH OTHER, AND ENJOY THE FINE FOOD. THEY'RE TALKING ABOUT THIS AND THAT WHEN, UNLUCKILY FOR HER, THE SUBJECT OF INCURABLE ILLNESSES COMES UP.

OF COURSE THE GIRL WANTS TO SHOW OFF, SO SHE TELLS THE GUY SHE KNOWS A TRADITIONAL PREACHER-HEALER WHO HAS A CHURCH AND CAN CURE THE TERMINALLY ILL THROUGH PRAYER AND TOUCH ALONE.

THE WHITE GUY, WHO'S CRAZY ABOUT THIS SMART AND BEAUTIFUL GIRL, ASSUMES SHE'S JOKING, BUT THEN SHE STARTS GIVING HIM EXAMPLES TO PROVE IT AND OFFERS TO TAKE HIM TO MEET THE PREACHER.

WELL, TO THIS DAY, THE WHITE GUY HASN'T CALLED HER BACK. SHE'S BROKEN-HEARTED. SHE DOESN'T UNDERSTAND HOW COME HE DOESN'T WANT TO TALK TO HER OR TAKE HER OUT IN PUBLIC ANYMORE.

SHE'S DESPERATE TO WIN HIM BACK AND WANTS ME TO HELP HER.

IT JUST GOES TO SHOW THAT THE CHURCHES HAVE A HOLD ON EVERYBODY, EVEN INTELLECTUALS. SO CAN YOU IMAGINE WHAT IT'S LIKE FOR PEOPLE WHO DROPPED OUT OF SCHOOL YOUNG OR NEVER HAD ANY KIND OF EDUCATION AT ALL?

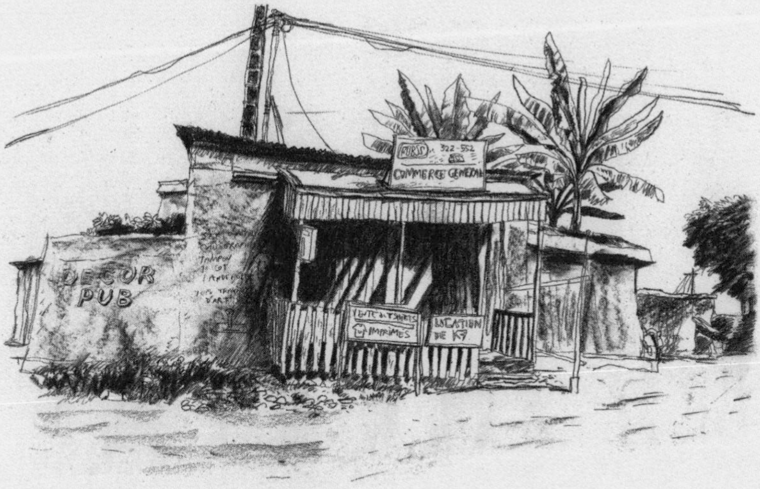
DECOR
PUB
COMMERCE GENERAL
LOCATION

# SUPER STAR STATION WITH ROGER FULGENCE KASSY

## BY MARGUERITE ABOUET, 2010

"HEY, CLARISSA, WHAT'S GOING ON? WE'RE SUPPOSED TO GET TOGETHER, REMEMBER?"

"DJIBRIL, ARE YOU FOR REAL? HOW CAN YOU EXPECT ME TO COME MEET YOU AT 8:30 PM, WHEN SUPER STAR STATION IS ON TV? LISTEN, YOU CAN EAT ON YOUR OWN OR FIND YOURSELF SOME OTHER GO, DÊH!"

"SUPER STAR STATION? OH YEAH, IT'S SATURDAY. I FORGOT. ALL RIGHT, BABE, WE'LL WATCH IT TOGETHER AND THEN WE'LL GO OUT, OKAY?"

POOR DJIBRIL, HE ALMOST LOST HIS CLACLA BECAUSE OF SUPER STAR STATION. BUT WHAT WAS HE THINKING? BACK IN THE DAY, EVERYBODY KNEW THAT SUPER STAR STATION (OR SSS) AIRED AT 8:30 PM ON SATURDAYS, AND THERE WAS NO WAY ANYBODY WOULD MISS AN EPISODE.

WHENEVER THE INCREDIBLY POPULAR VARIETY SHOW SUPER STAR STATION CAME ON, IVORIAN TEENS DROPPED EVERYTHING, PULLED UP IN FRONT OF A TV SOMEWHERE, AND GOT READY TO BE CAPTIVATED, THEIR EYES GLUED TO THE SCREEN. THERE'S NO QUESTION ITS CELEBRITY MC, THE HANDSOME, ELEGANT, AND TALENTED ROGER FLUGENCE KASSY, AKA RFK, HAD A SPECIAL WAY OF CONNECTING WITH HIS VIEWERS. FOR TWO HOURS, HE HAD THEIR UNDIVIDED ATTENTION THANKS TO HIS CANDOR, HIS AMERICAN-STYLE TALK, AND HIS UNRIVALLED KNOWLEDGE OF THE INTERNATIONAL POP MUSIC SCENE.

WHAT WAS IT ABOUT HIS SHOW THAT YOUNG PEOPLE LIKED SO MUCH, YOU ASK? SUPER STAR STATION LET IVORIAN YOUTH BE TOTALLY IN SYNC WITH OTHER TEENS AROUND THE WORLD, ESPECIALLY IN EUROPE AND THE U.S., BECAUSE IT WAS THE ONLY INTERNATIONAL VARIETY SHOW BROADCAST IN IVORY COAST. SSS INTRODUCED YOUNG IVORIANS TO JAMES BROWN AND HIS FAMOUS TUNE "A PILON WÊE HÉ BA HAN HAN" (THEIR PHONETIC VERSION OF "I FEEL ALL RIGHT"), MICHAEL JACKSON'S "WOW, THAT HAIRY THING IS HUGE" (THE MISHEARD LYRIC TO "DON'T STOP 'TIL YOU GET ENOUGH"), FRENCH SINGER MICHEL POLNAREFF AND HIS SONG "JE SUIS UN HOMME, JE SUIS UN HOMME" ("I'M A MAN, I'M A MAN"—WELL, OF COURSE HE WAS), AND MANY OTHERS AS WELL.

SSS WAS ALSO THE PLACE WHERE IVORIAN TEENS PICKED UP ON THE STYLES OF AN ECLECTIC MIX OF AMERICAN AND EUROPEAN STARS, INCLUDING CYNDI LAUPER, FRANCE GALL, DANIEL BALAVOINE, THE BEE GEES, PLASTIC BERTRAND (WHO HAD A HUGE POGO DANCE HIT), BONEY M, DONNA SUMMER, BONNIE TYLER, AND PLENTY OF OTHERS. AND IT WAS THANKS TO SSS THAT YOUNG IVORIANS LEARNED ALL THE LATEST DANCES. IN NIGHTCLUBS, THEY'D IMITATE THE MOVES THEY HAD JUST SEEN ON THE SHOW: THE SMURF, THE BROKEN ROBOT, THE ONE-LEG, THE BEAVER, THE BUMP, THE ELECTRIC BOOGALOO...

SSS ALSO HAD CONTESTS IN WHICH VIEWERS HAD TO CHOOSE THE BEST SINGERS IN THREE CATEGORIES: LOCAL, AFRICAN, AND INTERNATIONAL. YOU SENT YOUR BALLOT TO RTI (THE IVORIAN RADIO AND TELEVISION NETWORK) AND VIEWERS WHO HAD CAST THEIR BALLOTS FOR THE WINNING ARTIST WON PRIZES. EVERY WEEK, GIRLS WOULD HURRY TO DROP THEIR

BALLOTS IN THE MAIL, HOPING TO BE IN THE AUDIENCE OR, BETTER YET, MEET THE SEXY ROGER FULGENCE KASSY. WHEN THEY DIDN'T WIN, THEIR DISAPPOINTMENT WAS TREMENDOUS. IN MY FAMILY, SOME OF US GIRLS WERE KNOWN TO BREAK DOWN IN TEARS AND REFUSE TO EAT. I REMEMBER THE TEASING WE'D GET FROM MY FATHER: "IF THAT ROGER FULGENCE KASSY DID A SHOW ABOUT GRAMMAR, SPELLING, OR MATH," HE'D SAY, "I BET HE WOULDN'T BE HALF AS POPULAR."

FOR YOUNG IVORIANS, SSS WAS A WINDOW TO THE OUTSIDE WORLD. AND IF IVORIANS STILL MOURN THE CHARISMATIC ROGER FULGENCE KASSY TODAY, TWENTY-ONE YEARS AFTER HIS DEATH, IT'S BECAUSE HE GAVE MILLIONS OF THEM A CHANCE TO DREAM.

THANKS, RFK.

FRIENDS, A CLASSY GUY LIKE ME EATS ONLY THE BEST. BUT WHEN YOU'RE IN PARIS AND THERE ARE NO MAQUIS NEARBY, AND NO SISTERS, COUSINS, MOTHERS, OR AUNTS TO MAKE YOUR FAVORITE TREATS, YOU NEED TO BECOME YOUR OWN CHEF, Ô!

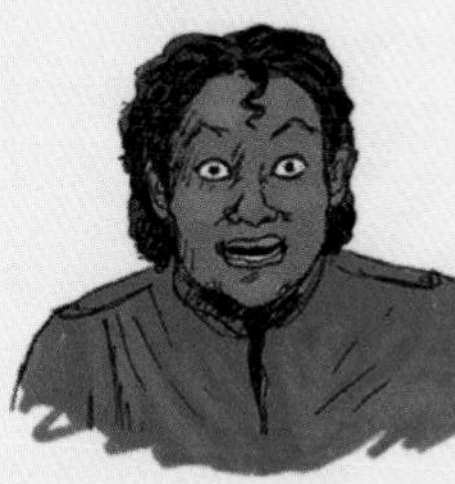

HERE'S MY INNO SPECIAL. IT'S QUICK, EASY, AND DELICIOUS.

## FLAKED FISH AND YAM WITH THE INNO TOUCH

SERVES FOUR (PERFECT WHEN YOU'RE SHARING A ROOM WITH A BUNCH OF GUYS)

2 SMOKED MACKEREL (FRIED OR OVEN-BAKED IS FINE TOO)
1 BIG YAM (IF YOU CAN'T FIND YAMS, USE POTATOES INSTEAD)
3 TABLESPOONS OIL
2 FRESH TOMATOES, CHOPPED
2 ONIONS, CHOPPED
1 BUNCH OF PARSLEY, CHOPPED
1 GARLIC CLOVE, MINCED
2 BAY LEAVES
1 MAGGI CUBE
SALT

SKIN AND FLAKE THE FISH.

COMBINE THE ONIONS, TOMATOES, GARLIC, AND PARSLEY, AND SEASON WITH A PINCH OF SALT.

HEAT THE OIL IN A SAUCEPAN. ADD THE VEGETABLES AND COOK FOR FIVE MINUTES.

ADD THE BAY LEAVES, THE FLAKED FISH, A LITTLE BIT OF WATER, AND THE MAGGI CUBE.

SIMMER FOR FIFTEEN MINUTES.

IN THE MEANTIME, PEEL AND CUT THE YAM INTO BIG CUBES. COOK THE YAM CUBES IN A LARGE POT OF BOILING SALTED WATER UNTIL TENDER. TRANSFER THE YAM CUBES TO A PLATE AND SPOON THE FISH MIXTURE OVER THEM.

EAT UP, MY FRIENDS!

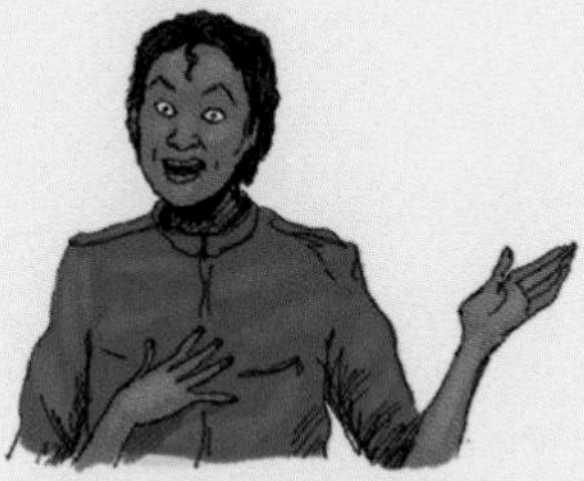

HEY, FRIENDS, IT'S ME AGAIN!

THERE'S ONE THING I REALLY DON'T GET: I'M EVERYWHERE IN THIS BOOK—IT'S INNO THIS AND INNO THAT ALL OVER THE PLACE—BUT THE TITLE IS ONLY ABOUT AYA. MAYBE SOMEBODY SHOULD CHANGE IT? "INNO, THE COOLEST DUDE IN YOP CITY" SOUNDS GOOD TO ME.

ANYWAY, HERE'S ANOTHER RECIPE FOR YOU.

## ALLOCOS WITH THEIR OWN LITTLE SAUCE

YOU CAN SERVE THIS DISH ANYTIME. IT'S EASY TO MAKE, AND IT'S GREAT AS AN APPETIZER, ENTRÉE, SIDE DISH, OR SNACK.

<u>SERVES TWO</u>

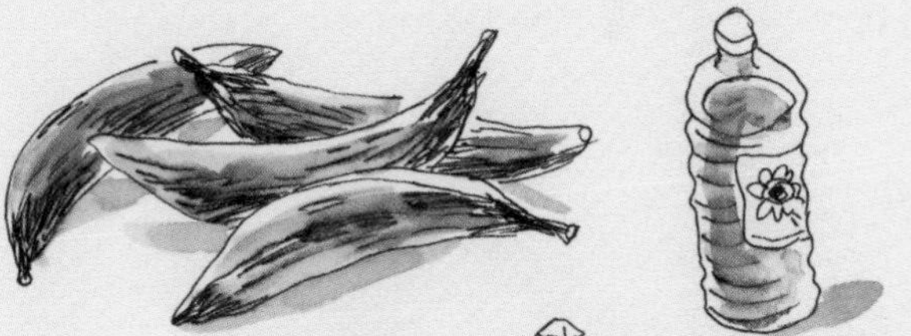

4 LARGE RIPE PLANTAINS
1 CAN OF SARDINES IN OIL
2 TOMATOES
2 ONIONS
OIL
1 MAGGI CUBE
SALT
1 CHILI PEPPER (IF YOU LIKE THINGS SPICY)

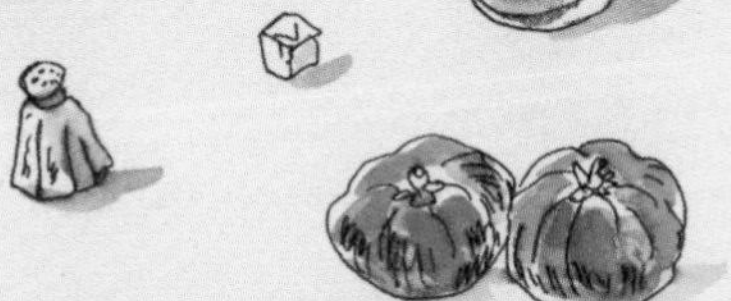

FRY THE ONIONS IN A BIT OF OIL FOR FIVE MINUTES, UNTIL SOFTENED.

ADD THE DICED TOMATOES, SALT, A BIT OF THE MAGGI CUBE, AND THE CHILI PEPPER (IF YOU'RE USING IT).

SIMMER FOR FIFTEEN MINUTES, THEN ADD THE FLAKED SARDINES. SIMMER FOR ANOTHER FIVE MINUTES.

IN THE MEANTIME, PEEL THE PLANTAINS AND CUT THEM CROSSWISE INTO THIN SLICES.

HEAT THE OIL IN A SAUCEPAN OR A DEEP FRYING PAN. WHEN IT'S HOT, FRY THE PLANTAINS FOR ABOUT TEN MINUTES, UNTIL NICE AND GOLDEN.

TRANSFER THE PLANTAIN SLICES TO A SIEVE AND LET THEM DRAIN.

SERVE HOT WITH THE SARDINE AND TOMATO SAUCE.

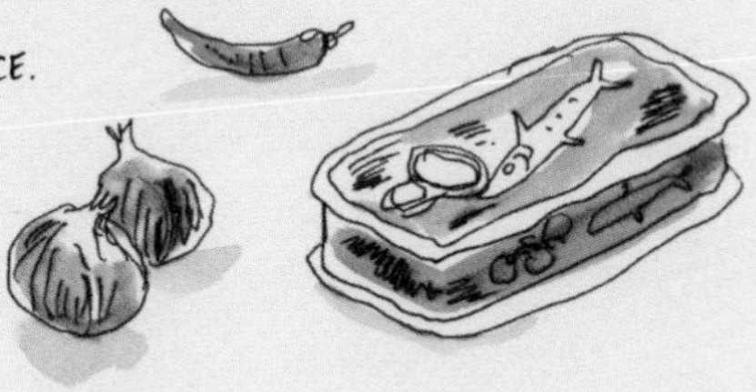

GIVE THESE PLANTAINS A TRY AND YOU'LL BE EATING IN STYLE. NO NEED TO THANK ME, FRIENDS. JUST ENJOY!

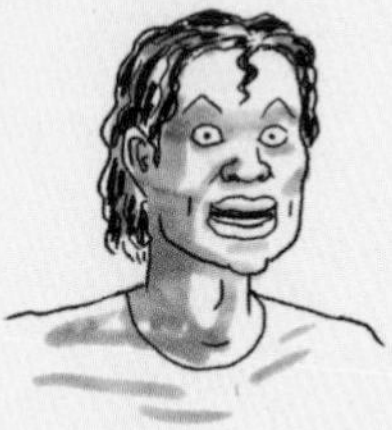

HELLO FRIENDS!

I HOPE YOU'RE ALL DOING GREAT. TODAY, I'D LIKE TO GIVE YOU MY SPECIAL RECIPE FOR BIÉKO...

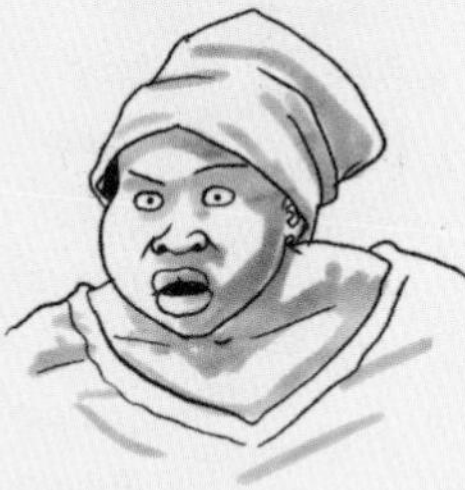

INNOCENT, YOU SHOW UP LOOKING LIKE A WET RAT WITH THAT HAIR, AND YOU THINK YOU KNOW HOW TO COOK A REAL BIÉKOSSEU? EVER SINCE YOUR STORY MADE IT INTO THE AYA BOOKS, YOU'VE BEEN ACTING LIKE SOME KIND OF BIG SHOT. GET OUTTA MY SIGHT, YOU WORTHLESS BUM.

AND THE REST OF YOU, IF YOU LISTEN TO INNOCENT, YOU'RE GONNA GET YOURSELVES POISONED, JUST WAIT AND SEE. YOU BETTER LET ME TEACH YOU THE PROPER WAY TO COOK.

## 100 PERCENT AUTHENTIC BIÉKOSSEU

THIS DISH ISN'T DIFFICULT TO MAKE, BUT IT TAKES A LOT OF PREPARATION. USUALLY IT'S MADE WITH CASSAVA LEAVES, BUT SINCE WE'VE GOT TO THINK INTERNATIONAL HERE, I'M GOING TO KEEP IT SIMPLE.

SERVES FOUR

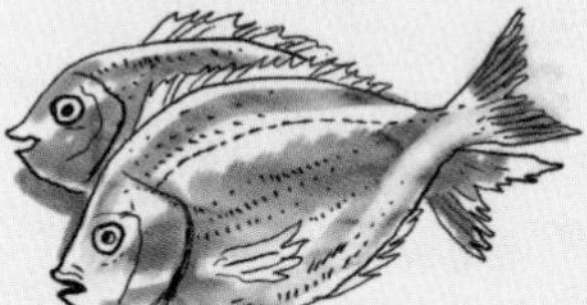

2 FISH (SEA BASS OR SEA BREAM, GET THEM NICE AND FRESH AND HAVE THEM CUT IN TWO)
6 LARGE TOMATOES
8 LITTLE AFRICAN EGGPLANTS (IF YOU CAN'T FIND ANY, USE 2 LARGE ITALIAN ONES)
3 LARGE ONIONS
PEPPER, SALT, OIL, AND, OF COURSE, A FEW MAGGI CUBES

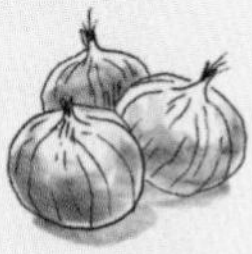

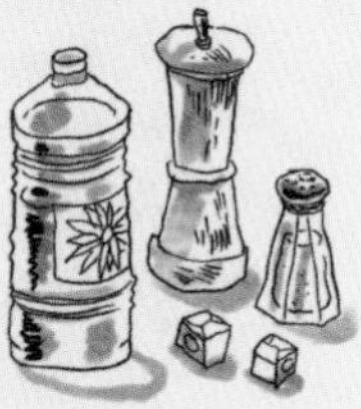

PREPARATION (THIS IS THE COMPLICATED PART, SO I'M GOING TO NUMBER THE STEPS):

1. SEASON THE FISH WITH SALT AND PEPPER, THEN SET IT ASIDE.

2. CUT THREE TOMATOES AND ONE ONION INTO VERY THIN SLICES AND PLACE THEM IN A SALAD BOWL. ADD SALT AND PEPPER, TWO TABLESPOONS OF OLIVE OIL, AND ONE MAGGI CUBE. SET THE MIXTURE ASIDE. DON'T FORGET TO TASTE IT TO SEE IF IT'S GOOD, DÊH!

3. CHOP AND COMBINE THE REMAINING TOMATOES AND ONIONS. ADD A PINCH OF SALT,

SOME PEPPER, A TABLESPOON OF OIL, ONE MAGGI CUBE (TASTE TO CHECK IF IT'S SALTY ENOUGH), THEN PLACE THE PIECES OF FISH ON THIS MIXTURE AND LET THEM MARINATE.

4. IF YOU'RE USING AFRICAN EGGPLANTS, CUT THEM IN HALF. IF YOU'RE USING ITALIAN ONES, REMOVE THE SKIN AND CUBE THEM. BOIL THEM, THEN PURÉE THEM IN A BLENDER UNTIL SMOOTH.

REMOVE THE FISH PIECES FROM THE MARINADE AND PLACE THEM ON A PLATE.

<u>TO COOK</u> (THIS WILL TAKE ABOUT AN HOUR):

YOU'LL NEED A SAUCEPAN WITH A COLANDER SUSPENDED OVER IT, BECAUSE YOU'RE GOING TO BE STEAMING THE FISH.

POUR A GENEROUS LADLE-FULL OF MIXTURE THREE INTO THE SAUCEPAN, THEN PLACE THE COLANDER ON THE PAN AND PUT THE FISH PIECES IN THE COLANDER. POUR THE REST OF MIXTURE THREE OVER THE FISH, THEN COVER IT WITH MIXTURE TWO. PUT A LID ON THE SAUCEPAN AND LEAVE IT TO SIMMER FOR FORTY-FIVE MINUTES. YOU CAN LIFT OUT THE COLANDER FROM TIME TO TIME TO CHECK THAT THE SAUCE ISN'T STICKING TO THE BOTTOM OF THE PAN.

IN THE MEANTIME, POUR THE EGGPLANT PURÉE INTO A SAUCEPAN AND SEASON IT WITH SALT, PEPPER (OR CHILI PEPPER, IF YOU LIKE THINGS SPICY), AND A MAGGI CUBE. SIMMER FOR FIFTEEN MINUTES.

VOILÀ! YOUR BIÉKÒSSEU IS READY, Ô!

YOU CAN SERVE IT WITH RICE, ATTIÉKÉ, COUSCOUS, STEAMED POTATOES, OR BOILED YAMS, AS WELL AS STRING BEANS OR ANY OTHER KIND OF GREEN VEGETABLE.

BUT IF YOU ASK ME, NOTHING GOES BETTER WITH BIÉKÒSSEU THAN RICE AND ATTIÉKÉ!

FOR THOSE WHO GIVE IT A TRY, HERE'S WISHING YOU GOOD LUCK AND A BIG APPETITE, DÊH!

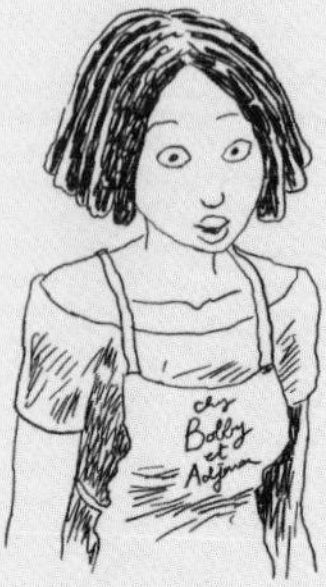
Bobby et Adjoua

FRIENDS,

HERE'S ONE OF THE SPECIALITIES I SERVE AT MY MAQUIS, "CHEZ BOBBY AND ADJOUA." THESE ARE EASY TO MAKE AND DELICIOUS. BUT LOOK OUT...THEY'RE ADDICTIVE!

## FISH PATTIES MY WAY

SERVES TEN

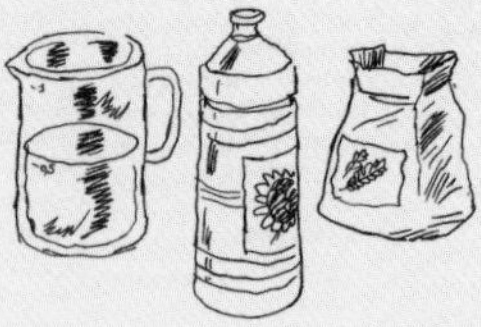

THE DOUGH:
2 CUPS LUKEWARM WATER, WITH SALT TO TASTE
7.5 CUPS FLOUR
2 TABLESPOONS VEGETABLE OIL

PREPARING THE DOUGH:
MIX THE WATER AND FLOUR (PREFERABLY WITH YOUR HANDS) UNTIL YOU GET A FIRM, ROUND DOUGH. THEN COAT THE DOUGH WITH TWO TABLESPOONS OF OIL.

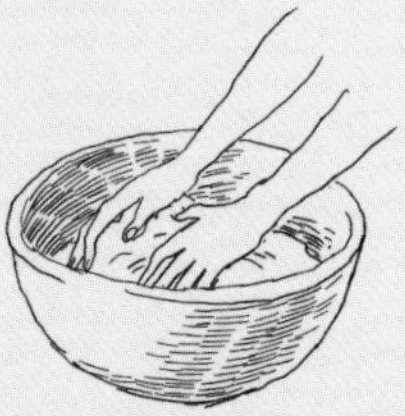

IF YOU LIKE, YOU CAN USE PUFF PASTRY DOUGH INSTEAD.

PREPARING THE FILLING:
2 ONIONS, DICED
2 TOMATOES, CUBED
2 FISH FILLETS (HAKE OR COD), FLAKED
1 TABLESPOON OIL, AND THE REST OF THE OIL IN THE CONTAINER FOR FRYING
SALT, PEPPER, AND 1 MAGGI CUBE

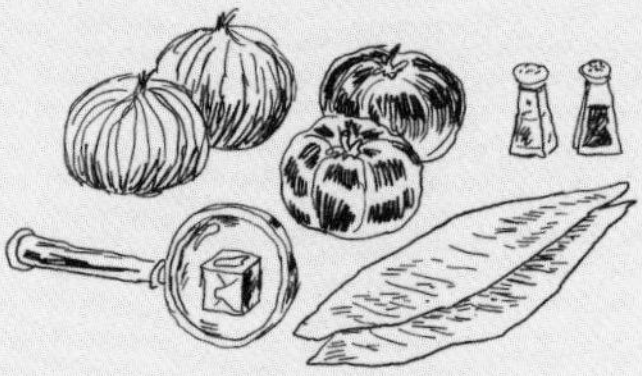

IN A SAUCEPAN, FRY THE ONIONS AND THE TOMATOES IN ONE TABLESPOON OF OIL FOR FIFTEEN MINUTES, THEN ADD THE FLAKED FISH. SIMMER FOR FIFTEEN MINUTES.

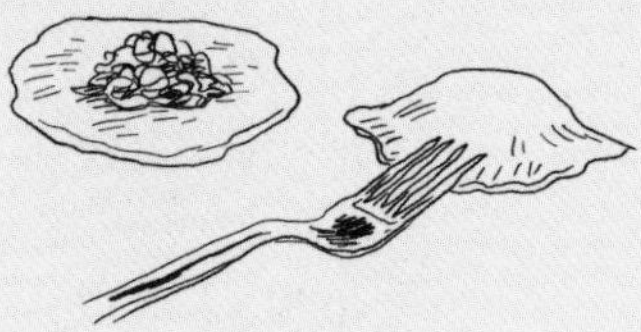

MAKING THE PATTIES:
TAKE A SMALL PIECE OF DOUGH AND FLATTEN IT.

PLACE A SPOONFUL OF FILLING ON THE DOUGH AND FOLD IT OVER. WITH A FORK, PRESS DOWN THE SIDES OF THE PATTIES.

FRY THE PATTIES.(IF YOU USE READY-MADE PASTRY DOUGH, YOU CAN ALSO BAKE THESE IN THE OVEN.)

ENJOY!

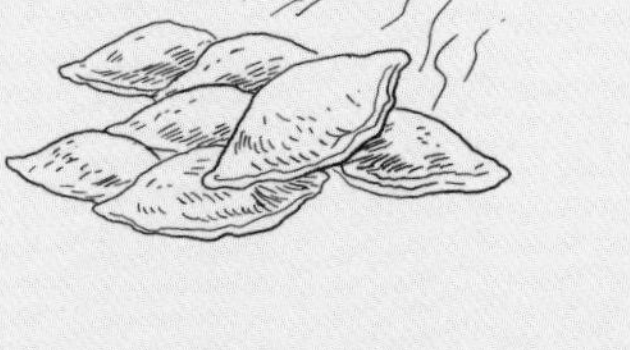

**Marguerite Abouet** was born in Abidjan in 1971. Her mother was a management secretary at Singer and her father was a salesman at Hitachi. She grew up with her family in the working-class neighborhood of Yopougon. When she was twelve, her parents sent her and her older brother to Paris to live with their great-uncle and pursue "extensive studies." Breaking off her studies earlier than expected, she began to write novels that she didn't show to anyone, and was by turns a punk, a super-nanny for triplets, a caregiver for the elderly, a waitress, a data entry clerk, and a legal assistant at a law firm. She now lives in Romainville, a suburb of Paris, and spends all of her time writing. *Aya* and *Aya of Yop City* were her first graphic novels, written in a fresh voice and with a keen sense of humor, and telling the story of an Africa far removed from clichés, war, and famine. In 2006, Marguerite Abouet and Clément Oubrerie received the prize for best first comic book at the prestigious Angoulême International Comics Festival.

**Clément Oubrerie** was born in Paris in 1966. After completing high school, he enrolled at the Penninghen School of Graphic Arts, breaking off his studies after four years to visit the United States. He stayed there for two years, holding down various odd jobs and seeing his work published for the first time before landing in a New Mexico jail for working without papers. Back in France, he went on to a prolific career in illustration as the author of more than forty children's books and as a digital animator. He is the graphic talent behind several television series, including *Moot-Moot*, produced by Eric Judor and Ramzy Bedia. He is also the co-founder of the La Station animation studio and Autochenille Productions, which is working on the screen adaptation of Joann Sfar's *The Rabbi's Cat*. In the Aya books, his first graphic novels, his unique talent brings Marguerite Abouet's stories to life with vibrant spirit and authenticity.

His work can be found online at clementoubrerie.blogspot.com

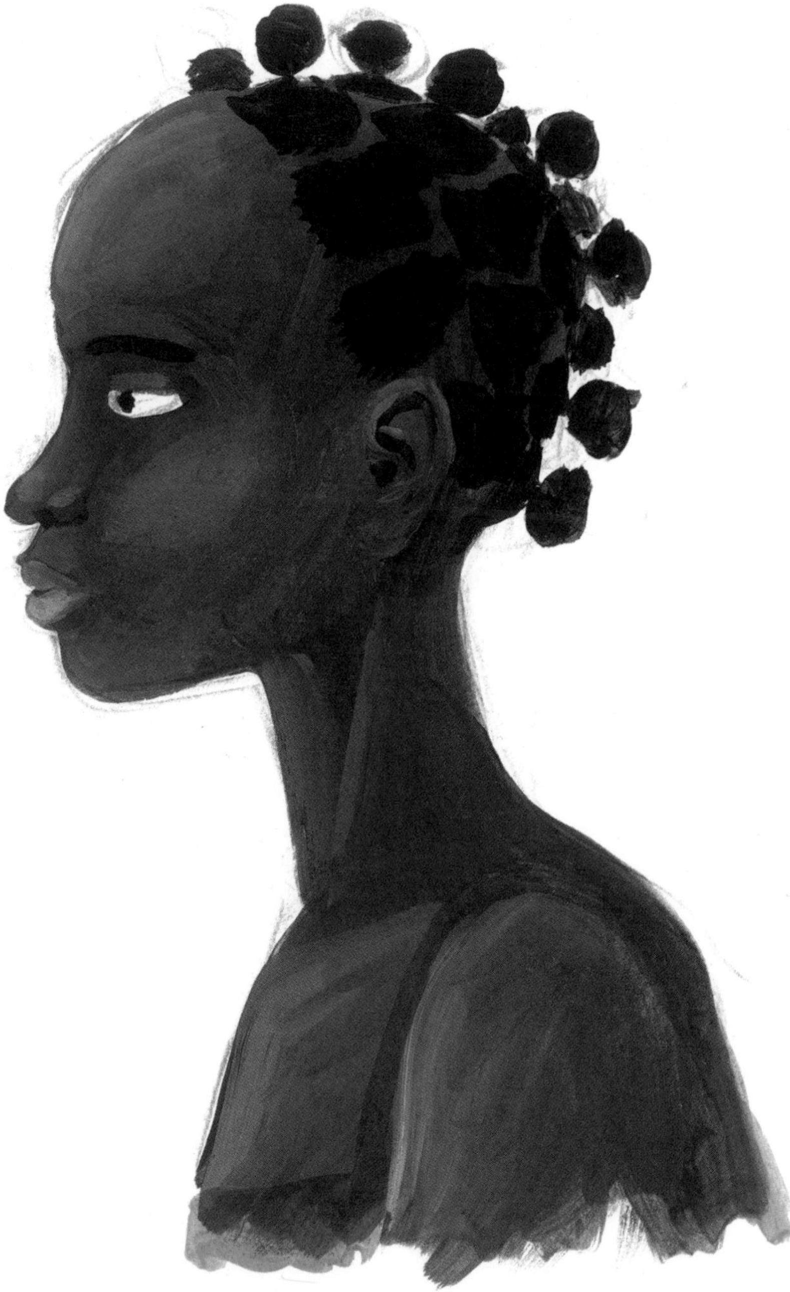

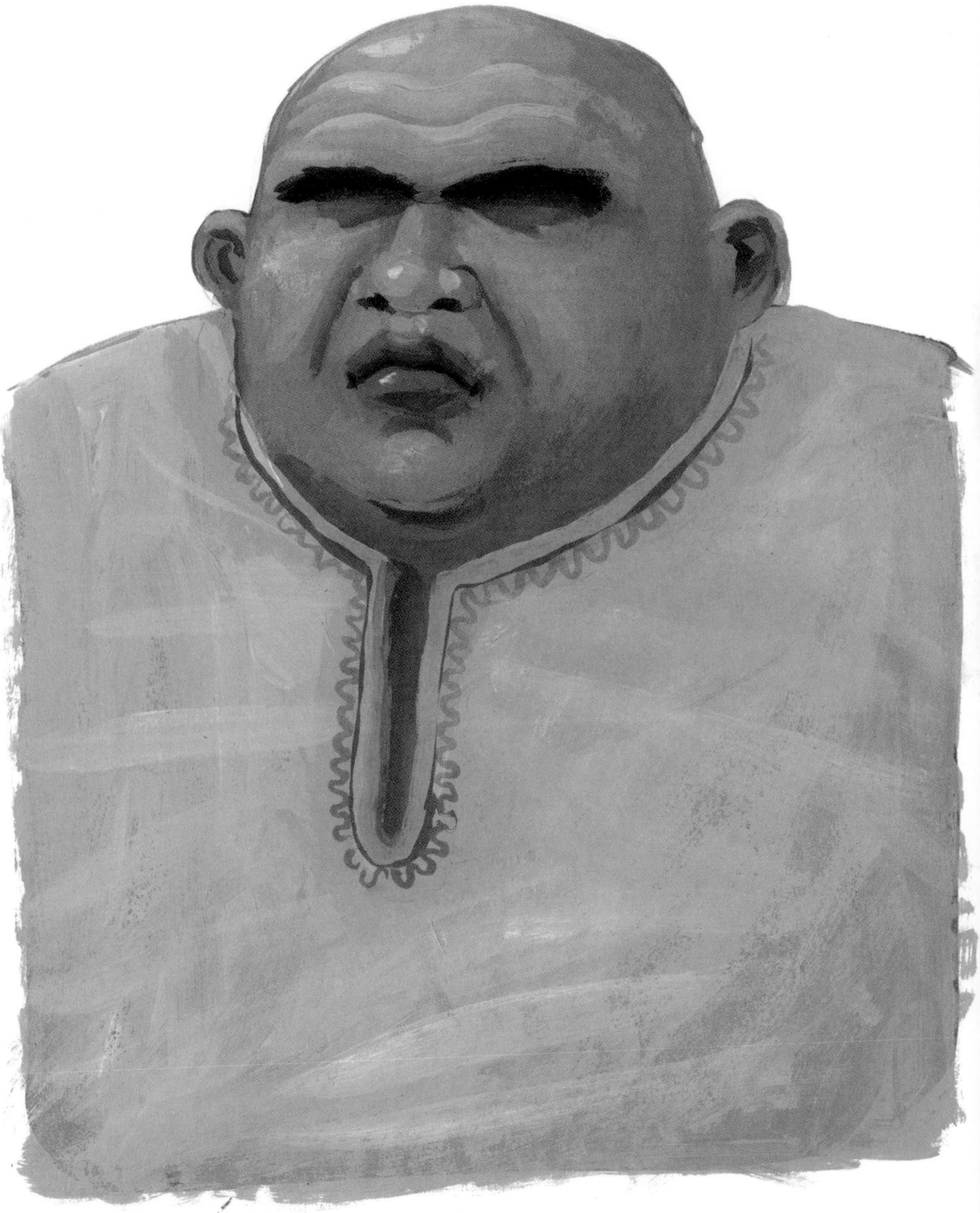

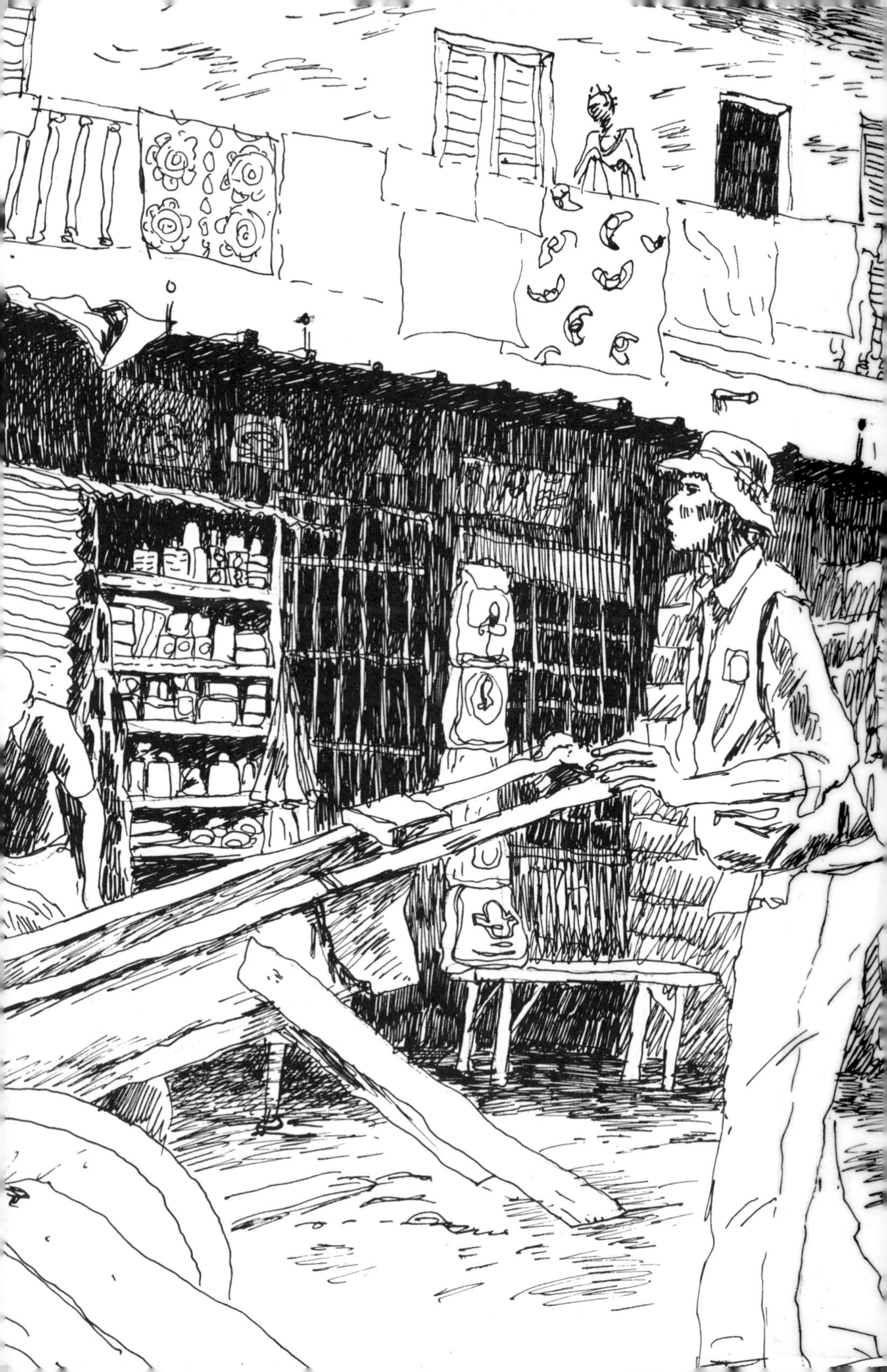

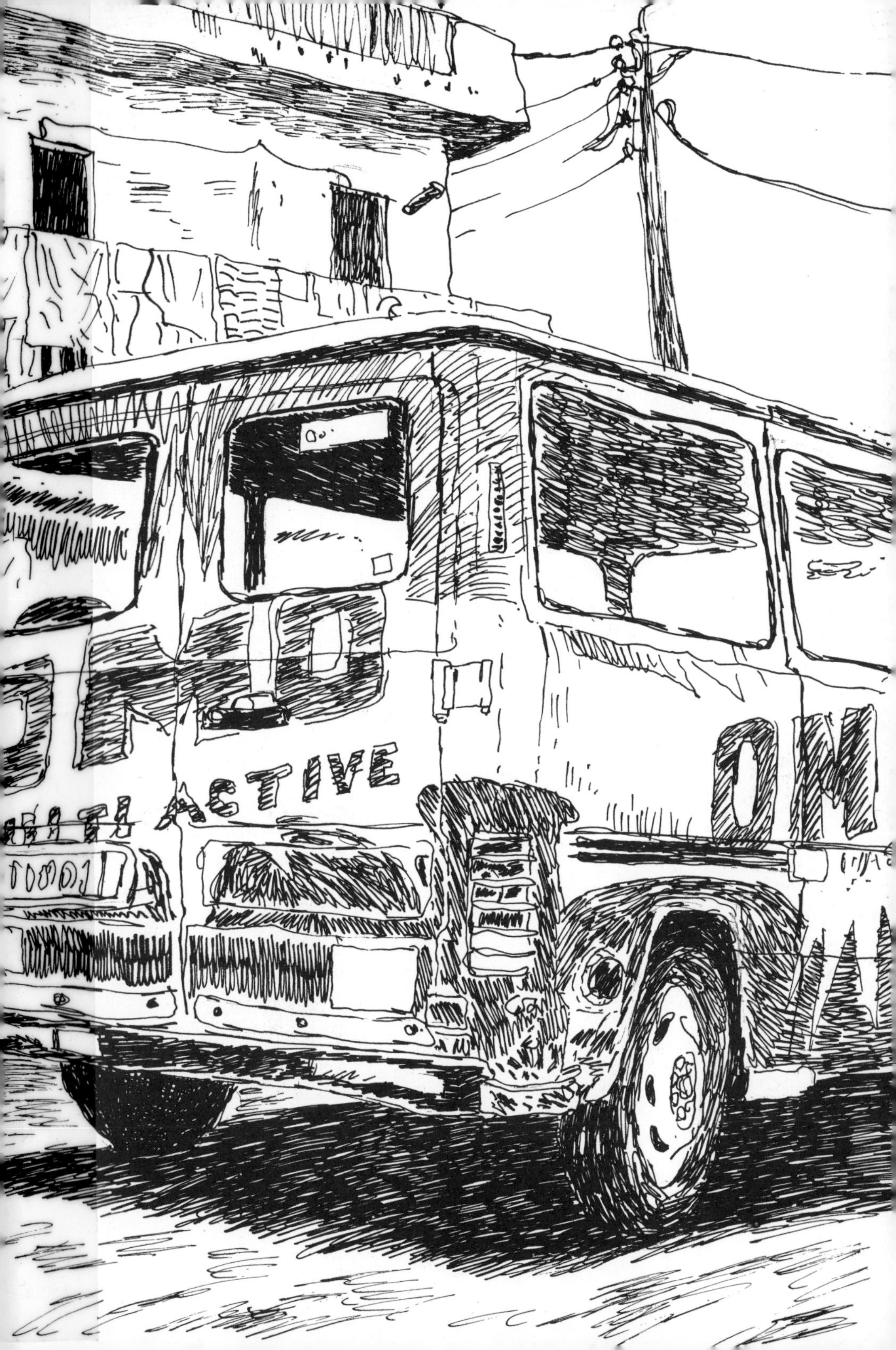
ACTIVE
OM

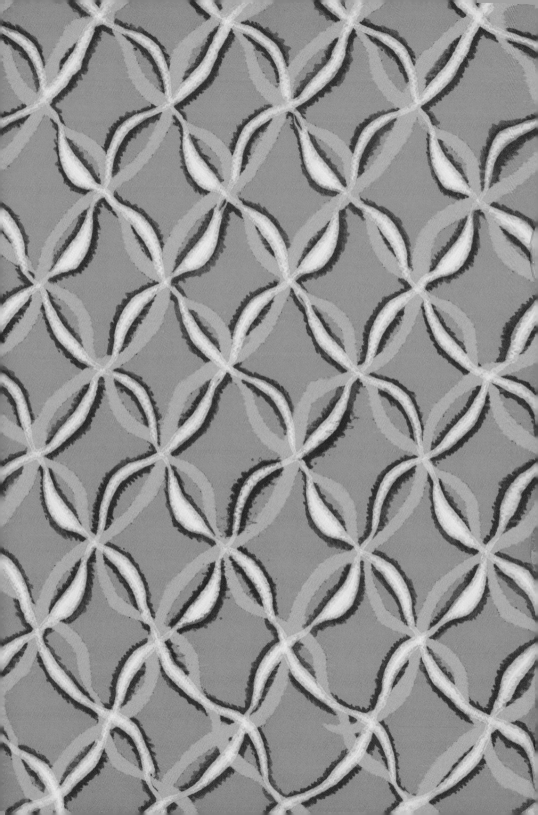